A HISTORY OF BUBONIC PLAGUE
IN THE BRITISH ISLES

A HISTORY OF
BUBONIC PLAGUE
IN THE BRITISH ISLES

J. F. D. SHREWSBURY

Emeritus Professor of Bacteriology
University of Birmingham

CAMBRIDGE

AT THE UNIVERSITY PRESS

1970

Published by the Syndics of the Cambridge University Press
Bentley House: 200 Euston Road, London N.W. I
American Branch: 32 East 57th Street, New York, N.Y. 10022

Library of Congress Catalogue Card Number: 69-10197

Standard Book Number: 521 07083 x

Printed in Great Britain
at the University Printing House, Cambridge
(Brooke Crutchley, University Printer)

TO
MY COUNTRY,
ENGLAND

CONTENTS

PLATES

PREFACE

In the compilation of this history I have received much generous help from many quarters and I tender my sincere thanks to all those literary bodies and individuals who have helped me and are not mentioned here by name. I am particularly indebted to the Librarians of the City of Birmingham Central Reference Library, the Warwickshire County Library, the Borough of Shrewsbury Public Library, and the City of Dublin Public Library. For their help I am grateful; but this study could not have been made without the generous and able help that I have invariably received from the staff of the Library of the University of Birmingham, especially from the late Miss M. P. Russell., one-time Sub-Librarian in charge of the Barnes Library in the Medical School of the University, and from Mr A. Nicholls, the Sub-Librarian responsible for External Readers in the Main Library. I can only place on record my great indebtedness to them because no mere expression of thanks is adequate to repay them for the help they have given to me. I am indebted also to Miss A. P. Barnes, the Librarian in Charge of the Worcestershire County Library, and to Mr D. Newman, Senior Library Assistant, University of Birmingham, for their willing help.

To Dr J. Lunn I owe an especial literary debt for his most generous loan to me some twenty years ago of the typescript copy of his work, *The Black Death in the bishops' registers*, which was the version prepared for publication —but never published—of his thesis, 'The Black Death', which was awarded the Ph.D. degree of the University of Cambridge in 1930. Unfortunately this typescript has since been lost and it has not been possible therefore to paginate my references to it. I hope that the incorporation of some of his work in this history will in some measure discharge my debt to him.

I am much indebted also to my one-time colleague, Professor H. A. Cronne, of the University of Birmingham, who kindly read my draft manuscript and corrected a number of factual errors I had made with respect to British social and economic history. He is in no way responsible, however, for any of the opinions expressed in this work; any criticism of these must fall wholly upon me. I also accept sole responsibility for all errors of omission and commission that may be found in this work.

I hope that Professor G. R. Elton will find in the publication of this history justification for the friendly advice and encouragement that he has given to me in the course of its preparation for publication.

Finally I wish to record my grateful appreciation of the willing and able technical assistance rendered to me by Mr G. J. Barson, who was the Senior Laboratory Technician in the Department of Bacteriology during the latter years of my tenure of the Chair, and who made the photographic copies of the charts, diagrams, maps, and illustrations embodied in this work.

J.F.D.S.

EDITORIAL NOTE

A   Wherever blank columns occur in the tables and histograms in this work they signify that no information is available about the particular detail in the table or histogram. They do not mean that there were no burials or plague-deaths, and so on, in the particular month or year.

B   Throughout this work, irrespective of the particular calendar in use at the time, the seasons of the year have been constituted as follows: Winter—January to March inclusive; Spring—April to June inclusive; Summer—July to September inclusive; and Autumn—October to December inclusive.

C   The sources most frequently referred to in this work are listed with their abbreviations on pp. 542–3. All other sources referred to will be found in the references (pp. 544–621) and in the Bibliography (p. 622).

INTRODUCTION

Our word plague is derived from the Latin word *plaga*, which originally meant a blow or a stroke, but which acquired in late Latin the additional meaning of pestilence, because a pestilence—irrespective of its nature—was regarded by the pagan Romans as a blow from the gods and by the christianized Romans as a stroke expressive of the divine wrath. In its sense of an epidemic of disease or of the sudden appearance of some creature in excessive numbers, the word has been in constant usage in the English language throughout its time, and we still use it in the latter sense when we speak of a plague of field-mice or of flies or of ants. It did not acquire its modern connotation with a specific microbial disease until the seventeenth century and it cannot therefore be accepted in earlier English writings, or in translations of Greek or Latin texts, as indicative of the specific disease of bubonic plague without confirmatory evidence. This fact needs to be emphasized because there is a tendency, especially among medical writers, to affirm that an ancient pestilence was an epidemic of bubonic plague because it was called a 'plague' by ancient recorders or because it happened to occur concurrently with a plague of rodents.

The confirmatory evidence that is required to identify a pestilence in olden times as an epidemic of bubonic plague may be either a contemporary description of the clinical picture of the pestilence that is pathognomonic of plague or a conjunction of certain observations that are exclusive to the epidemiology of plague. Unless one—and preferably both—these conditions are fulfilled the assumption that an ancient pestilence was an epidemic of bubonic plague is not justifiable.

The human disease of plague is caused by the invasion of the body by a bacterium, *Pasteurella pestis*, which is primarily an internal parasite of rodents and particularly of the rat. The transmission of the bacterium from rodents to man is an accidental occurrence that is governed by certain crucial factors. These are the close proximity of plague-infected rodents to human beings and the transference from them to men of *P. pestis* through the intermediacy of an insect vector of that bacterium or, much more rarely, by the injudicious handling of diseased rodents. The essential link in the train of the transmission of the bacterium from rat to rat and from rat to man is a rat-flea, because *P. pestis* can only invade the human and rodent body through certain portals. Of these direct inoculation into the circulation is by far the commonest route in both man and rodents; but in man it can under

certain conditions enter the body by way of the respiratory tract, and in the rat it can enter by way of the alimentary tract as a result of cannibalism. The direct introduction of the bacterium to the blood-stream produces bubonic plague in man and rat; its introduction through the respiratory tract engenders in man pneumonic plague, but this form cannot persist as an independent disease in the absence of the bubonic form.

P. pestis usually multiplies with great rapidity in the blood of an infected rat and quickly produces an overwhelming septicaemia, so that when a flea feeds on a diseased rat it sucks up large numbers of the bacterium in its blood meal. In a proportion of these fleas—which is apparently never more than about 12 per cent—the bacterium manages to establish itself in the flea's stomach, where it multiplies rapidly until that organ is completely filled with a solid mass of it. A rat-flea in this state is technically known as a 'blocked' flea. Such a flea soon becomes ravenously hungry as no blood can now enter its stomach, so hungry in fact that in default of its preferential host, the rat, it will attack any animal within reach, including man. A 'blocked' flea will suck human blood voraciously until its elastic gullet is distended to its utmost limit; but eventually the involuntary recoil of the walls of its gullet forces it to regurgitate some of the blood, which now contains plague bacilli. Of greater significance is the fact that as it feeds a flea automatically synchronously defaecates, so that a 'blocked' flea consequently excretes the bacillus in its faeces. In one or both of these ways *P. pestis* is deposited on the victim's skin and is then inoculated into the circulation through the puncture wound made by the flea as the individual scratches to relieve the irritation caused by the flea-bite. As soon as a plague-rat dies and its cadaver begins to chill, the fleas it has harboured forsake it for fresh, living hosts, and in a rat-infested human dwelling, in which most of the rats are dead or dying of plague, the human occupants will often be the only alternative hosts, although the 'blocked' fleas will attack impartially cats, dogs, and other domestic animals.

A rat can harbour as many as seventeen species of flea and the flea population of a rat may total several score, but only two of its species of flea are constantly capable of acting as vectors of plague. These are the so-called Asiatic rat-flea, *Xenopsylla cheopis*, and the flea known to entomologists as *Nosopsyllus (Ceratophyllus) fasciatus*. Of these the former is much the more dangerous vector and was almost certainly exclusively responsible for the great medieval epidemics of bubonic plague in Europe. Under optimal conditions of temperature and humidity 'blocked' fleas can remain alive and infected for at least 6 weeks; but their effective transmission of plague probably does not exceed 14 days. The seasonal periodicity which was a notable feature of the medieval epidemics in Europe resulted from the effect of the

climatic conditions upon the rat-flea population. Experimentally it has been demonstrated that *X. cheopis* flourishes best in a temperature range of 20° to 25° Centigrade, in conjunction with a certain degree of dryness of the atmosphere. A spell of favourable breeding weather will produce an increase in a *cheopis* population in about a month, and this increase may engender an outbreak of human plague if the disease is already epizootic among the rats. Great heat and drought will often check an epidemic of plague by shortening the life of the 'blocked' fleas, and the advent of frosty weather in temperate latitudes almost invariably arrested an epidemic by causing *X. cheopis* to hibernate. Our modern knowledge of the bionomics of this flea explains why in medieval England epidemics of bubonic plague usually erupted towards the end of the spring, rose rapidly to a peak of intensity in late summer or early autumn, collapsed or declined sharply with the arrival of the autumn frosts, and were extinguished in or remained dormant throughout the winter months. The existence and survival under unnatural conditions of 'blocked' fleas explains why some local outbreaks of the human disease in England were correctly ascribed by contemporary observers to the receipt of bundles of cloth or rags, or consignments of other merchandise from places where the disease was epidemic, because such wares could shelter 'blocked' fleas. In most instances, however, the arrival of such alleged 'plague-goods' merely happened to coincide with the introduction of *P. pestis* by the normal method of rat-contact spread. In the occasional event of the transport of 'blocked' fleas among clothes, rags, or other soft goods, the starving fleas would naturally, immediately they were released, attack the people handling the goods, with the result that cases of bubonic plague would suddenly appear in a village or town, which had previously been free from it, within a few days of the reception of the goods.

Bubonic plague almost never spreads directly from man to man, even when plague-fleas are plentiful, simply because *P. pestis* very rarely causes the degree of septicaemia in man that it does in the rat; consequently the flea does not ingest in its meal of human blood a sufficiently large dose of *P. pestis* to enable that bacterium to colonize the flea's stomach—and in the absence of fleas cases of bubonic plague can be nursed with perfect safety in the wards of any general hospital. The invariable sequence of events in the outbreaks resulting from the transport of 'blocked' fleas in merchandise was the rapid appearance of a few cases of the human disease, with no immediate spread of it; a lag interval—usually of about a fortnight—while the freed 'blocked' fleas infected their natural hosts, the house-haunting rats; the consequent development of an epizootic of rat-plague with a concomitant great increase in the number of 'blocked' fleas, and subsequently the trans-

3

mission of the disease in multiple instances within a short space of time to the local human population, or in other words a local epidemic of bubonic plague.

In every instance of an epidemic of bubonic plague in human history an epizootic of the disease in a domiciliary rat population must have preceded and progressed concurrently with the human disease. As Hirst has emphasized, however, 'evidence of rat mortality is by no means always conspicuous even when the epizootic is severe. Few rats may be found dead or dying in the open, but many if looked for in the right situation. Thus in Ceylon and India numerous carcases may be dug up from complex burrow systems or taken in a mummified condition from the interstices of roof tiles, or in Java from the hollows of bamboos.'[1] The thatch or turves, which were the commonest roofing materials for dwellings below the rank of manor house in medieval Britain, undoubtedly hid the carcases of many plague-rats in epizootic times and so obscured the rat-mortalities that must invariably have preceded the human ones. The nature of the roofing material explains also why bubonic plague was chiefly a disease of the poor, because the poor lived in single-storey hovels in the roofs of which the house-rat lived, bred, and died; while from its nests the starving 'blocked' fleas fell directly among and upon the humans below. When it made its burrows alternatively in the mud-and-wattle walls or under the beaten earth floors of the dwellings of the poor, the 'blocked' fleas still had easy access to the human occupants. The castles and manor houses with their stone or wooden walls and their stone, lead, or shingle roofs gave no such shelter to the house-haunting rat, and all had at least one storey and many had two or three above the ground floor. Consequently their inmates were comparatively exempt from rat-flea attack while they remained within such dwellings.

Plague may manifest itself in man in one of three clinical forms, to wit, bubonic, septicaemic, or pneumonic plague. As far as the historian is concerned, however, only the first and last of these are significant because the septicaemic form is really a fulminant expression of the bubonic form. The pathognomonic sign of this form is the *bubo*, a hard, painful, haemorrhagic swelling of a lymphatic gland. The English word *bubo* is derived from the Greek word for the groin, and the groin group of lymphatic glands is on the whole the commonest site for the plague-bubo. Other sites for this lesion are the armpits and the neck where, as in the groin, groups of lymphatic glands lie just below the skin. The precise site of the bubo in a particular individual is determined by the location of the bite inflicted by a 'blocked' flea on the surface of the body, because the bubo forms in the group of lymphatic glands into which the lymphatic channels drain from the site of the flea-bite.

4

Introduction

The bubo is often palpable on the first day of the disease and is generally conspicuous from the second to the fifth day in the bulk of cases. If the patient survives this period it may suppurate, as a result of secondary infection with pyogenic bacteria, and burst on or after the seventh day, discharging much pus and forming a deep, ragged ulcer that is slow to heal. Other skin lesions that may appear contemporaneously with the bubo are petechiae, purpuric spots, and carbuncles, which constituted the 'blains', 'tokens', 'pushes', 'whelks', and other terms of sixteenth- and seventeenth-century writers. None of these lesions, not even the bubo, is exclusive to plague, however, so that sporadic cases of the disease in inter-epidemic times could reasonably be assigned to other 'fevers' by the ignorant and illiterate 'searchers' of the dead, especially when that diagnosis was prompted with a bribe; but in epidemic times the 'searchers' could not fail to recognize their significance although whether they always reported truthfully what they found is quite another matter. To complete the clinical picture of the bubonic form it must be noted that the disease is usually insidious in its onset but often extremely rapid in its progress. Indeed in its septicaemic form a robust adult may pass from vigorous health to extreme prostration and even death in a few hours. In spite of constant severe prostration, the pain of the rupturing bubo is often so agonizing that many patients in olden days were goaded by it to assault their attendants, throw themselves out of windows, plunge into rivers or pools, or run naked through the streets until they collapsed. No other bacterial disease of man shows with such constancy an equivalent degree of frenzy.

In most of the European epidemics of bubonic plague from the fourteenth to the end of the seventeenth century, the case-mortality rate appears to have approached 90 per cent in the initial weeks of an epidemic, though it commonly fell as low as 30 per cent as the epidemic subsided. In this century, before the discovery of the modern antibiotics, the case-mortality rate was estimated to average from 60 to 70 per cent, and as a notable feature of the disease has been its sustained virulence over the centuries, it is probable that the average case-mortality rate of all its great eruptions in the past never fell below about 60 per cent. In common with every other bacterial disease of man, however, bubonic plague exhibits natural variations in virulence, and a modified form of the disease, known today as *pestis minor*, was undoubtedly sometimes encountered in the past. Although the bubo is present in this form, the virulence of *P. pestis* is so much diminished that the constitutional disturbance may not even be severe enough to confine the patient to bed and the case-mortality rate is comparatively negligible.

Under certain circumstances *P. pestis* may become localized in the lungs

5

of an infected individual to cause the form known as pneumonic plague. One such case may initiate an outbreak of the extremely infectious pneumonic disease, which is probably the deadliest bacterial disease of man as it had in the past a consistent case-mortality rate of practically 100 per cent. Pneumonic plague spreads directly from man to man by 'droplet' infection and its dissemination is therefore independent of the man–rat–flea association which governs the spread of the bubonic disease; but pneumonic plague cannot occur in the absence of the bubonic form and it cannot persist as an independent form of plague. Its characteristic features are a very sudden onset; rapid and extreme prostration; the coughing or spitting of blood or of bloody sputum, and death in from 1 to 4 days in almost every case. As a discharge of blood from the surface or from any of the natural orifices of the body was always a cause of especial alarm to medieval peoples, and an event of mystical significance to ancient peoples, this sign of pneumonic plague would not have passed unnoticed by contemporary recorders of ancient pestilences.

The bubo and the other cutaneous manifestations of the bubonic form, and the bloody expectoration of the pneumonic form, coupled with the experience that recovery from an attack of the disease did not protect the individual from a subsequent attack, comprised all the knowledge about plague in the British Isles up to the end of the seventeenth century, and it comprises all the information that the historian can expect to obtain from contemporary accounts of outbreaks of the disease. There is no evidence that the peoples of these islands had any inkling of the decisive part played by the house-haunting rat in the genesis and maintenance of epidemics of plague. Where contemporary accounts of ancient pestilences do not provide sufficient information for their identification as epidemics of plague, the historian seeking to identify a particular pestilence as an epidemic of plague must produce convincing evidence that the house-haunting rat was established in the afflicted society at the relevant time. It is not sufficient for any historian, however eminent he may be, merely to assert that a particular pestilence in the past was an epidemic of either bubonic or pneumonic plague, although this error is quite frequently encountered among medical historians.

CHAPTER I

THE RAT AND ITS RELATION TO THE HISTORY OF THE PLAGUE

There are two distinct species of rat, namely, *Rattus rattus*, the black, house, or ship-rat, and *Rattus Norvegicus*, the greyish-brown, field, or sewer-rat. Colour distinction can be misleading, however, because the former species shows wide variations in colour from rufous to black, while the latter occurs in many different shades of brown or grey and may also throw off both albino and melanotic sports. A more accurate distinction is that of the house- and the field-rat, because these names indicate their natural relations with man, and their choice of habitation has a decisive bearing upon their importance as sources of human plague. They can be more certainly distinguished by their physical appearance (see plate 1) and by their ecological characteristics than by their coloration.

In 1910 the name *Mus*—which had previously been used as the generic designation for both mice and rats—was officially replaced by *Rattus* as the designation for rats and since that date *Mus* has been retained exclusively for mice. Our word 'rat' is comparatively recent[1]. Its origin is uncertain but it was probably first adopted in the Teutonic languages when the animal came to be known in western Europe, and thence passed into the Romance tongues. The inclusion of the name *raturus* in Ælfric's vocabulary of about A.D. 1000 is the earliest source of our word 'rat'.[2]

Hinton suggests that the house-rat is descended from an ancestral form whose original home was in India and Burma,[3] and Donaldson agrees that it was probably indigenous to India. It is essentially an arboreal or climbing animal, which rarely burrows in the ground and is usually found in human dwellings and other buildings living in the walls, the ceilings, or the roofs. In medieval England it almost certainly entered the dwellings of the commonalty by climbing into them by way of the eaves, whereas after its arrival in England the field-rat—on its forays for food —has usually entered houses and warehouses from below ground level.

From a general knowledge of their bionomics it may be said that as a rule the house-rat is more timid, less muscular, more restricted in its diet, and considerably smaller than the field-rat. Although it can swim it seldom does so voluntarily, whereas the field-rat is essentially a water-loving animal. There does not appear to be any record of the house-rat ever having been seen crossing even a small river, and as it is not normally a migratory animal it does not usually move far from its birthplace of its own accord. On the other hand it may at times be forced to emigrate by the stress of famine or the goad of an epizootic disease such as plague. Although cautious, it does not avoid man and in temperate climates like Britain it can only survive with the aid of the shelter provided by human habitation. As both species are primarily nocturnal or crepuscular, infestation of the dimly-lit medieval dwellings of the common folk by the house-rat could easily have remained unnoticed when the rodents were present only in small numbers. While both species are more or less omnivorous, grain is their chief food and in Europe in the middle ages grain was certainly the staple food of the house-rat. In warm countries, like India, this remains the dominant species, and as its superior climbing powers give it a great advantage over *R. Norvegicus* at sea, it continues to be the principal ship-rat. Today its chief habitats outside its Indian home appear to be the seaports of both tropical and temperate lands.

The original home of the field-rat was in temperate Asia, probably in the territory intervening between the Caspian Sea and Tobolsk—Ælian's description of his *Mures Caspii* fits the creature well. By comparison with the house-rat it is less agile but far more voracious and cunning, and as it is stronger and more fecund it is a much more formidable enemy of mankind; but it is normally shy of man and in temperate climates it will not breed in close contact with him. It is naturally a migratory animal, performing a partial migration at different seasons, sometimes travelling long distances when seized by the migratory impulse and crossing wide rivers, deserts, and mountainous regions in the course of its migrations.

In their relation to human plague the crucial difference between the two species is that the house-rat lives and breeds in close contact with man, either in his dwellings or in adjacent outbuildings, and its fleas can therefore easily attack the human occupants of infested dwellings, whereas the fleas of the field-rat, which normally breeds at a distance from man, have less opportunity to attack man in default of their rodent host. Throughout its long history epidemic bubonic plague has been pre-eminently a disease of the dwelling-house, with a familial incidence that no other *bacterial* disease of man has ever equalled.

Authorities are generally agreed that the field-rat was unknown in Europe

before the eighteenth century, and that it did not arrive in Britain before 1728. It was probably imported into Copenhagen in 1716 by the courtesy visit of a Russian fleet and may well have been imported into England directly from the Russian Baltic ports in 1728 or 1729. Its presence was recorded in France and East Prussia in 1750, in Norway in 1762, Scotland in 1764, the Faeroe Islands in 1768, the United States in 1775, Switzerland in 1809, and Spain in 1880. This dispersal was obviously effected by shipping in several instances, but from the ports the animal rapidly spread inland of its own accord, unlike the house-rat which had to be passively transported inland by human agency along the trade routes from the seaports and river-ports.

Most writers about the field-rat refer to the accounts of its vast migrations given by Pallas, the Russian explorer and scientist. According to Hinton, Pallas reported that in 1727 vast hordes of these rats, moving westwards, swam across the Volga and swarmed into the houses of Astrakhan, whence they spread across Russia and into western Europe. The inference seems to be that Pallas witnessed this migration, but I have been unable to find his eye-witness account of it. In the earlier record of his travels[1] Pallas writes that he was informed by the Cossack inhabitants of Jaitskoi-Gorodok in August 1769 that the brown rat, which had previously been unknown there, arrived in bands during the very dry summer of 1766 from the direction of Samara. In a later record[2] he remarks that 'the large grey house-rat' had not yet appeared in the government of Pensa by the winter of 1793. Later in this work, among some notes about his excursions along the southern Volga,[3] he mentions that in about 1790 'the grey wall-rat' appeared in numbers at Sarepta and swam over the mill-dam on the way towards Tsaritzin.

It is indisputable that the field-rat, which is now the predominant species throughout Europe, could not have been responsible for the epidemics of bubonic plague that ravaged Europe and the British Isles from the middle of the fourteenth to the end of the seventeenth centuries. This distinction belongs exclusively to *R. rattus*, which certainly antedated the field-rat in Europe by some six hundred years. Donaldson states that fossil remains of the house-rat have been reported in the Pliocene in Lombardy, in the Quaternary near Pisa and from the Pleistocene cave deposits of Crete, but also declares that there is no good evidence that the Greeks or Romans before the present era were familiar with the rat as a pest.[4] These statements would seem to be contradictory, unless this prehistoric rat became extinct in Europe before the emergence of those civilizations, or unless the fossils are remains of some other rat-like animal. Certainly, from what is known about the bionomics of the house-rat and of human life in prehistoric Europe, it appears highly improbable that *R. rattus* could have established itself in Europe at

that time, unless the climate was then subtropical over the Continent and it had been passively transported from its Indian home by human agency. As it is wholly dependent upon passive transport by man across terrestrial barriers such as seas, rivers, deserts, and mountains, it is extremely doubtful whether it began to move westwards from its Indian home before Alexander the Great (356–323 B.C.) brought India into contact with Europe. It may have reached Palestine by 175 B.C. because Antiochus IV used elephants, which Wood asserts came from India, in his war against the Maccabees,[1] and it is possible that the house-rat was then unwittingly transported along with those beasts. Hannibal had also used elephants some fifty years earlier during his invasion of Italy, but De Beer states that with one possible exception these were all African elephants, which would certainly seem to have been much more easily obtainable by the Carthaginians.[2] Today the African species seems to be regarded as untameable, but Wood affirms that it has been tamed 'and, in the days of Rome's greatest splendour, was taught to perform a series of tricks that seem almost incredible'.

Among the recipes listed in the Ebers papyrus, which was compiled during the reign of Amen-Hotep I about 1550 B.C., there is one to prevent rodents eating *durra* in the granary, but it is not certain that the rodents referred to were rats as only mice are specifically referred to in the preceding domestic hints.[3]

As inscriptions of the third millennium B.C. seem to reveal a lively maritime trade in the Persian Gulf and Indian Ocean, and show that vessels of considerable size circumnavigated the Arabian peninsula,[4] it is possible that *R. rattus* might have reached Egypt some time during the third millennium. On the other hand the Bible contains no mention of any animal that can be identified with *R. rattus*, and it is inconceivable that the Israelites would have failed to notice it during their captivity in Egypt if it had by then established itself in that country.

In his exhaustive study 'of every creature whose name is given in the Scriptures', Wood has no notice of the house-rat, though he mentions the sand-rat and shows that many small rodents—such as hamsters, field-mice, jerboas, and dormice—were plentiful in Palestine in biblical times and were much feared because of their ravages in standing and stored corn.[5] Moreover, if the rodents mentioned in the Ebers Papyrus were house-rats, it is extremely difficult to understand the apparently complete ignorance of that animal in Greece. I have been authoritatively informed by Professor G. Thomson of Birmingham University that there is no word for 'rat' in classical Greek; but if the house-rat had been known to the Greeks they would certainly have had a name for it.

The rat and bubonic plague

The majority opinion among medical historians is that the first certain notice of bubonic plague is the reference of Rufus of Ephesus, 'who lived during the reign of the Emperor Trajan about A.D. 100', to 'deadly bubonic outbreaks reported by the pupils of Dionysius the Hunchback in the Levant about 300 B.C. and to later epidemics described by Posidonius and Dioscorides in Libya about 50 B.C.'.[1] It seems evident therefore that *R. rattus* had reached the Near East by 300 B.C., and must have been well-established as a household pest throughout the lands of the eastern Mediterranean littoral in the sixth century A.D., because the pandemic of plague which irrupted in the Byzantine Empire in Justinian's reign could not have been generated and maintained in its absence. As far as the colonization of Europe by the house-rat is concerned, however, all that can safely be said is that it probably began shortly before or early in the Christian era and that the animal had spread as far westwards as southern France by the beginning of the sixth century.

There is no evidence that the house-rat was present in the British Isles in the sixth century and there are cogent reasons for postponing its appearance to the ninth century or even later. It has been stated categorically that there were no rats in Britain before the Norman Conquest,[2] and Hinton finds no clear evidence of the presence of *R. rattus* in western Europe before the time of the Crusades.[3] In all probability he is correct as far as the British Isles are concerned, but *R. rattus* must have been well established in Italy and southern France to initiate and sustain the epidemics of bubonic plague which afflicted those countries in the sixth century.

The earliest evidence of its possible presence anywhere in the British Isles would appear to be the ornament at the foot of the 'monogram page' of *The Book of Kells*. Sir E. Sullivan writes of this ornament: 'A strange group of animals will be observed between the bottom of the P and the up line of the X—two rats nibbling the Eucharistic bread under the eyes of a pair of cats.'[4] The precise date of the production of this gospel-book is still a controversial matter and different authorities have dated it as early as the sixth century and as late as the ninth. Sullivan presents strong arguments for dating its production to the latter half of the ninth century. Even if the book had been produced in the sixth century, however, the inclusion of rats in one of its illuminations is no proof that they were present in Ireland at that time, as the artist may have witnessed the scene he depicted or have heard about it while on a pilgrimage outside the British Isles.

In connexion with the destruction of the Host by vermin, Hooper quotes from the Canon of Ælfric and from Myrc's *Duties of a parish priest*.[5] The former, written in the late tenth century, reproves priests who kept the Host

until it putrefied or was eaten by mice. The latter, written about 1420, cautions the priest to preserve the Sacrament from being eaten by mouse or rat under the threat of having to do forty days' penance for such carelessness. It would seem a reasonable presumption that if the house-rat had been known to Ælfric he would have included it in his reproof.

It has been argued that medieval writers before the eleventh century were incapable of distinguishing rats from mice.[1] There are many references to the presence of mice in Europe, among them Reinach's statement that Egyptian cats were imported into Europe after its invasion by the Huns because the barbarians had introduced the rat. Reinach's statement is discredited by modern knowledge of the bionomics of *R. rattus*, which renders its importation by the Huns an impossibility. To begin with the Huns came from a part of the world which was much nearer the homeland of the field-rat than of the house-rat, and they certainly either passed through or close to the homeland of the field-rat without bringing it with them. Furthermore their mode of travel and its speed prohibited any passive transport of the house-rat, even if they had begun their foray from its homeland. The argument that medieval writers could not distinguish between a mouse and a rat is a favourite gambit of medical historians who are obsessed with the notion that almost every ancient pestilence was an epidemic of bubonic plague and does not deserve serious consideration.

The house-rat seems to have reached London some time in the thirteenth century,[2] and it appears to have become a sufficient pest in the fourteenth for Chaucer to mention that apothecaries sold rat poisons.[3] There is convincing evidence, however, that the house-rat had established itself elsewhere in the British Isles before the thirteenth century. This evidence is contained in Gerald de Barry's accounts of Ireland and the Irish, which were written in 1187, and in his later record of a journey through Wales. In the first of his Irish accounts he reports that mice are present in immense numbers in Ireland; that they consume a huge quantity of grain, and that they destroy clothes even when these are kept in locked receptacles.[4] In the second he reports that the 'large mice, popularly called rats', had been expelled from the district of Ferns in Leinster by the curse of Bishop Yvor, whose books they had gnawed.[5] Then in the record of his Welsh journey, which was probably written in 1191, he relates that a man was worried to death by 'large mice, commonly called rats'.[6] His use in both instances of the Latin phrase *mures majores* is such an obvious designation of the rat in the absence of a specific Latin name that it is unlikely that earlier writers, such as the Venerable Bede, would not also have used the phrase if they had been acquainted with *R. rattus*. Moffat emphasizes the importance of this

evidence and of the significance of De Barry's distinction between mice and rats, which he takes to show that the rat was already well known to the British public by 1187.[1]

The British Museum possesses a manuscript roll of the genealogy of the kings of England down to Henry III which is said to have been executed late in the thirteenth century.[2] At the foot of this roll some unknown artist with a sense of humour has drawn a vivid sketch of two black rats hanging a cat (plate 2). There is not the slightest doubt about the identity of the executioners; they are the old English black-rat, the house- or plague-rat, and it is evident from his clever delineation that the artist was well acquainted with them. If this sketch is contemporary with the manuscript and not a later addition, it bridges the gap of nearly two centuries between De Barry's record and Langland's version of the fable of the rats that decided to 'bell the cat'.[3] Langland begins his version with a clear distinction between rats and mice which indicates that both kinds of rodent were known in his time and that the common folk were well aware that they were different animals. He is believed to have written this part of his poem in or soon after 1362, and about thirty years later came Chaucer's reference to the public need for rat poisons.

The house-rat was also known to Chaucer's contemporary, John of Trevisa, and the nature of his comment suggests that it had already earned popular reprobation as a furtive, cunning pest. In his translation of Higden's notice of the Emperor Lucinius[4] the word *sorices*, which literally meant shrew-mice, is rendered as *ratouns*. Whether or not John knew that the squeak of the shrew-mouse was regarded by the Romans as a sound of ill-omen, it seems evident that he knew that his fellow-countrymen regarded the house-rat as a beast of ill omen.

There is conclusive evidence therefore that the house-rat was domiciled in England in time to sustain the great epidemic of bubonic plague which afflicted the country in the fourteenth century; but no pestilence occurring before that date can be identified as plague. Thus the assumption that the pestilence recorded by Bede[5] which ravaged England in 664 and which later writers have called the 'yellow plague' was an epidemic of bubonic plague is untenable. Even a record that an ancient pestilence was accompanied with ulcerating buboes in the inguinal regions does not justify its identification as an epidemic of bubonic plague, because 'bubonous ulcers' may develop in the groins in fatal cases of confluent smallpox.[6] (Though not relevant to this history, the epidemiology of smallpox supplies more reason for the identification of the 'yellow plague' as an epidemic of variola than as an epidemic of any other disease, with the possible exception of malignant influenza.)

If any Englishman, during the centuries from 1348 to 1679 when plague was active in England, had noticed the coincidence of an epizootic of rat-plague with an epidemic of the human disease, surely either Boorde or Pepys would have drawn attention to it. Boorde, who travelled widely on the Continent, had received a good education for his times. He studied and practised medicine at the universities of Montpellier and Glasgow and he was an observant and competent physician in his day. There were numerous outbreaks of plague in England and on the Continent during his lifetime and he probably knew as much as any physician of his day about the clinical nature of the disease. He knew the house-rat also and evidently associated its presence in the dwelling-house with unsatisfactory hygienic conditions, because he wrote: 'Beware that you do not lye in olde chambres whiche be not occupied, specyally such chambres as myse, rattes, and snayles resorteth unto.'[1]

It seems to be a reasonable surmise—from the absence of any reference to the house-rat in his diary—that Pepys was so familiar with the rodent and its depredations that he did not consider it worth a mention. Yet he lived through the great epidemic of bubonic plague that ravaged London in 1665, when dead plague-rats must have been littering the houses and streets in their thousands, and he was an inquisitive man, a keen observer, and a methodical recorder. The timber-built, lath-and-plaster houses of Tudor and Stuart London, with their dark, low rooms, were rat-haunted as a matter of course, so that Pepys and his fellow-citizens were probably so accustomed to seeing dead rats on their premises that an increase in the rat-mortality caused by *pestis* attracted no attention and aroused no apprehension.[2]

Apart from its association with plague the harm wrought by the house-rat was, however, generally recognized. There are churchwardens' accounts of English parish churches dating back to the fifteenth century testifying to damage by rats. For example in 1457 the purchase of 'rattes beyte' is mentioned in the accounts of St Andrew Hubbard, and a little later the wardens of St Michael Cornhill purchased three rat-traps for the church at a cost of sixpence. In 1523–4 the wardens of St Mary-at-Hill expended one penny on the purchase of 'Milke and Rattisbane for the Rattes in the chirch', and in 1537–8 they paid a ratcatcher fourpence for laying his baits.[3] Official recognition of the damage done by the house-rat on a national scale was responsible for its inclusion in the Elizabethan act for the preservation of grain, which authorized churchwardens to levy a tax on all lands and tithes in their parishes in order to provide a fund from which to reward every person bringing the heads of specified vermin to them. The term 'vermin' as used in this act (8 Eliz. c. 15) comprised a variety of wild animals and

birds and the act laid down the payment that was to be made for each beast and bird. For example twopence was to be paid for the head of every otter and hedgehog, and one penny for every three heads of rats and every twelve heads of mice.[1] The scale of these rewards suggests that the house-rat was then reckoned to be much commoner than the hedgehog, which itself was probably much more numerous than it is today.

As this act was expressly renewed in 1572—14 Eliz. c. 11—and again in 1598—39 Eliz. c. 18—the Elizabethan authorities were evidently worried by the depredations of *R. rattus*, and their intention that the act should be obeyed is shown by the record that in 1575 the Shropshire parish of Worfield was 'amased by the commy-soners at bridgenorth for not destroying foules and varmynt according to the Statute in that behalf xxxs. xd.'.[2] The consequence of this penalty was that a general massacre of foxes, otters, badgers, polecats, hedgehogs, rats, and mice took place in the parish the next year. That other parishes paid more respect to the law is shown by the payment for eighty rats' heads by the wardens of St Michael's, Bishops Stortford, in 1569.

The mouse was associated in Greek belief in ancient times with plague in the general sense of pestilence, and in ancient Egypt it was the symbol of destruction on account of its ravages in standing and stored grain.[3] There is no justification whatever, however, for incriminating either the house-mouse or its wild relatives in the genesis and maintenance of epidemics of bubonic plague. The domestic mouse is not a dangerous vector of human plague because it is much less infested with fleas than the rat, and because the flea which it naturally harbours, *Leptopsylla (Ctenopsylla) musculi*, exhibits little tendency to attack man in default of its natural host.[4] Consequently the house-mouse plays only an insignificant part in epidemics of plague, becoming accidentally involved like man in rat-epizootics of the disease and then acting—also like man—merely as a temporary host for the rat-fleas which spread the disease.

It is true that Zabolotny traced the occurrence of endemic plague in the steppes of south-west Russia to spermophiles and field-mice; but the conditions under which these rodents transmitted the disease to man were local and exceptional, and Zabolotny never suggested that they played any part in the genesis of the epidemic disease.[5] He found that when these small rodents hibernate during the winter months they often take refuge in the thatched roofs of the peasants' cottages. If at this time any of the rodents are infected with *P. pestis*, their 'blocked' fleas may attack the occupants of an infested cottage to cause sporadic cases of human plague; but the disease does not spread outside the afflicted household. Sylvatic plague—the name given to the disease when it is enzootic in wild rodents—is widespread in

Russia, Mongolia, Manchuria, the United States, and South Africa; but unless man deliberately interferes with these animals few cases of the human disease are derived from them, and such cases as occur are usually sporadic and self-limiting. Bruce Low, writing about sylvatic plague among ground squirrels (*Citellus beechyi*) in California, states that the destruction of over 20 million of them resulted in only eleven cases of bubonic plague in people who handled the animals.[1] Of course when infected rodents hibernate in intimate contact with people in their homes, as in south-west Russia, transmission of the disease to human beings is more likely to occur; but there is no record that any epidemic of plague has ever originated from a particular association of this kind between wild rodents and man.

CHAPTER 2

THE ENGLISH SETTING FOR
'THE GREAT PESTILENCE'

It must be emphasized that the mere presence of the house-rat in England was not sufficient to engender an epidemic of bubonic plague. For such a thing to happen the rodent must be present in such numbers that the density of the rat population is high enough to enable *P. pestis* to be distributed rapidly over the area of the epidemic by haphazard rat-contacts. The creation of this essential density was a process that undoubtedly occupied many years—possibly the best part of a century in the case of a sparsely populated country of the size of medieval England—but when the necessary density of *R. rattus* had been achieved the fuel was ready for the spark in the guise of the plague bacillus, which obviously had to be transported across the sea in the bodies of infected rats, to ignite an epizootic of rat-plague in this country.

There is no direct evidence that *P. pestis* landed in either England or Ireland before 1348, although the authentic history of plague goes back for possibly another fifteen hundred years in the Near East to its notice by Rufus of Ephesus in the fragment of his writings preserved by Oribasius.[1] 'The buboes that are called pestilential', wrote Rufus, 'are most acute and very often fatal, especially those which one may encounter unexpectedly in Libya, Egypt, and Syria, and which are mentioned by Dionysius the Hunchback as occurring in those parts. Dioscorides and Posidonius give a detailed description of them in their treatise on the plague which, in their time, was prevalent in Libya, and which they say was accompanied by high fever, agonizing pain, severe constitutional disturbance, delirium, and the appearance of large, hard buboes that did not suppurate, not only in the usual regions of the body, but also at the back of the knee and in the bend of the elbow, where, as a rule, similar fevers do not cause their formation'. Dioscorides was a Greek army surgeon in the service of Nero (A.D. 54–68).[2]

This appears to be the earliest extant reference to bubonic plague and it indicates that the certain history of the disease begins somewhere in the lands bordering on the eastern end of the Mediterranean, some time between 300 B.C. and the dawn of the Christian era. Present knowledge does not permit greater precision about the time and place of its historical beginning; but the aetiology of the disease insists that its appearance in those lands was preceded by their intensive colonization by the house-rat and it seems probable that the decisive factor in that colonization was the voluminous trade which the Roman Empire developed with India.[1]

Simpson[2] made the pertinent observation that plague appears to come in cycles with intervening intervals of considerable duration. The global activity of the disease is in fact largely controlled by its behaviour in its birthplace, the region among the foothills of the Himalayas known as Garwhal and Kumaon, and the intervals between its known pandemic outbursts from that region are characteristically measured in centuries. It is not surprising therefore that after its presumptive epidemic activity in Libya some time before the Christian era, plague disappeared—or at any rate no longer advertised its presence as an epidemic disease—until it erupted in the Roman empire in the East in A.D. 540 to produce the major outburst known as the plague of Justinian. The contemporary descriptions supplied independently by Procopius[3] and Evagrius[4] of the pestilence which ravaged the Byzantine empire for many years from 540 onwards identify it as an epidemic of bubonic plague, although it is evident from the latter's account that during this period a number of epidemic diseases in addition to plague afflicted that empire. Smallpox was evidently active then,[5] and in the symptomatology that Evagrius presents there are hints of the coexistence of diphtheria, of either bacillary dysentery or cholera, and of epidemic influenza. There is no reason why each and all of these diseases should not have been epidemic at times in the Byzantine empire in the sixth century, even if it is customary for most medical historians to ignore the existence of any disease other than plague until the eighteenth century. If none of these diseases is as old as the human race, each of them is certainly older than the period of history covered by the Christian era.

When this pandemic of plague erupted in the Byzantine empire, there was a flourishing maritime commerce in the Mediterranean with an active coastal trade from Alexandria and the Levant along the shores of Italy and Provence to Marseilles, which was a great seaport in the sixth century. Pirenne considers that Marseilles must have been very populous at this time on account of the frequency of the epidemics of disease recorded there between 566 and 591.[6] With its free trade with Egypt, where the house-rat must have been

established since before the time of Dioscorides and Posidonius, the rat's transport to Marseilles as the ship-rat was inevitable, to be succeeded as inevitably by the transport to France of *P. pestis*. It is therefore no surprise to find Gregory of Tours recording its epidemic activity in the province of Arles during the lifetime of St Gall.[1] The date of this first appearance of bubonic plague in France was 547, some five years after its eruption in Constantinople, and its presence in France indicates that the house-rat had effectively colonized the south of France by that date.

From that year until the close of the century plague exhibited intermittent epidemic activity in southern Europe, North Africa, and Asia Minor. Agathias records a recurrence in 558 at Constantinople,[2] whence it had apparently never really disappeared since its eruption sixteen years before, and Paul the Deacon records an epidemic of it in Liguria in the time of Narses, probably in 566.[3] Plague broke out again in Italy in 591.[4] Gregory of Tours gives five notices of its epidemic activity in southern France and northern Italy between 566 and the end of the century.[5] He noted that the disease began as a wound like a snake-bite in the groin or the armpit and that death occurred on the second or third day.[6] He also made the significant observation that plague did not spread immediately after its introduction to a town, as a disease that is spread by human contacts would do. Instead there was a certain interval during which (unknown to Gregory) an epizootic was spreading among the house-rats. Then, when a sufficient number of ravenously hungry 'blocked' fleas, deprived by death of their normal rodent hosts, had been produced by this epizootic, 'the whole city blazed with the pest, like a cornfield set aflame'[7]—an acute observation and an effective simile. Procopius made an equally significant observation when he stated that plague always took its start from the coast.[8] This happens in every seaboard country invaded because when ships carrying plague-rats dock in seaports the rats exhibit a strong tendency to leave the ships for the shore.

After the disappearance of plague from southern Europe towards the end of the sixth century, an interval of some 700-odd years elapsed before its authentic reappearance was recorded, although according to Von Kremer repeated epidemics in Asia Minor were reported by Arab chroniclers in the seventh and eighth centuries.[9] Sigerist[10] remarks that we do not know why no authentic epidemic of bubonic plague was recorded in Europe between the sixth and the fourteenth centuries; but Pirenne and other historians have provided a convincing explanation of this period of freedom from the disease in their accounts of the growth and influence of the Saracen empire. It was the interposition of this empire between India and Europe that interrupted what would otherwise have been repeated transmissions of *P. pestis* from

east to west along the 'pipe-line' of *R. rattus*. Genuine epidemics of the disease seem to have occurred in Mesopotamia and Asia Minor during Europe's exemption, but these outbreaks were prevented from extending westwards by the disruption of the commerce that had brought plague into Europe in the sixth century.

No hint of the approach of plague nearer to the British Isles than the south of France occurs in any sixth-century records of the disease; but there was a great outburst of epidemic disease in the islands between the sixth and the fourteenth centuries which appears to have been as deadly and to have exerted as decisive an effect upon their history as the Second Pandemic of plague exerted in the fourteenth century. Under the date of 534 the *Annals of Boyle*[1] record 'a great mortality, i.e. the "Buidhe Chonnaill"', and eleven years later the *Annals of Ulster*[2] record what was in all probability a recurrence under the name of 'blefed'. From that date, 545, until 667 there are numerous notices of this epidemic disease in various Irish Annals. The term *buidhe-conaill* (or *chonaill*), means literally the 'corn-' or 'stubble-coloured yellow-ness'.[3] Other names for its recurrences between 545 and 577 are 'sawthrust',[4] 'samthrosc',[5] 'leaprosie and knobbes',[6] 'scintilla leprae',[7] and 'bolgach',[8] which is the old Irish name for smallpox. Bolgach is recorded again in 675[9] and in 680 there is an entry in the *Annals of Ulster*: 'Lepra gravissima in Hibernia qua vocatur bolgach.'[10]

The next century it was England's turn. There was a total eclipse of the sun in England in 664 and a great pestilence ravaged the country in the same year. Bede,[11] who recorded both events, observed that it first devastated the southern regions of Britain and thence spread north into the kingdom of Northumbria. It raged without intermission over a large part of the country and caused an enormous mortality among the English people. 'Moreover', Bede continues, 'this affliction pressed sore on the island of Ireland with a like destruction',[12] and several of the Irish Annals record its presence in 664.[13] It seems extremely probable that this English pestilence was identical with the disease which the Irish chroniclers originally called *buidhe-conaill*, which had been ravaging Ireland under various names for more than a century before it struck England. About six hundred years later some English chronicler gave the English pestilence the name of the '*yellow plague*', possibly because he knew the literal meaning of the term *buidhe-conaill* and equated the two diseases. Unfortunately Bede omitted to describe the clinical picture of the pestilence which exerted a profound effect upon English history, for its destruction of the people of Northumbria which he describes undoubtedly contributed to the later collapse of the kingdom.

Although there is not the slightest evidence whatever that either the Irish

or the English pestilence was an epidemic of bubonic plague, Simpson[1] asserted that the latter was plague and MacArthur, cited by Bonser,[2] avers that the *blefed* was plague; but in the absence of convincing evidence that Ireland was effectively populated by the house-rat in 534 and England in 664, these identifications of the pestilences as bubonic plague are valueless. This is not the place to discuss their identifications, but elsewhere I have presented an argument[3] identifying them as irruptions of smallpox in 'virgin' societies. Although many subsequent outbreaks of epidemic disease occurred in the British Isles between 664 and 1348, and the various Irish Annals record many during that period, none has been identified as plague by Simpson or any other medical historian of the disease.

As already stated, the distribution and density of the rat population governs the distribution and intensity of the human disease, and the rodent density is decisive because no serious outbreak of bubonic plague can take place in a locality supporting only a small or widely dispersed rat population.[4] But the house-rat's subsistence in the British Isles was dependent upon the satisfaction of three essential requirements, namely, protection from its natural predators, shelter from cold and inclement weather, and the provision of a regular food supply, composed largely of grain, close to its breeding places; and only man could satisfy those needs. As a rule therefore the human disease must have been proportionate in its extent to the density of the human population, and as that density was uneven so the incidence of bubonic plague was uneven.

Unfortunately we have no knowledge of the size, the distribution, and the local densities of the house-rat population of England in 1348. These factors can, however, be inferred from a study of the distribution and local densities of the human population, about which a certain amount of information is available. Moreover, as the house-rat is not normally a migratory animal and its fleas have only a limited range of independent locomotion, the spread of the human disease in the fourteenth century was dependent upon either the passive transport of infected rats or 'blocked' fleas or the slow and haphazard extension of the epizootic disease by rat-contacts. The timid house-rat would only allow itself to be transported in the shelter and obscurity of bulky merchandise, and its passive dispersion must therefore have occurred mainly along recognized trade-channels to and from the seaports, the chief towns, and the national fairs.

Where the rat went some of its fleas would go also, although most of them would remain in the rat's nest. Some could also be transported independently of the rat since a man can carry plague-infected fleas from place to place about his person or belongings, with or without contracting the disease.

These man-carried fleas transfer themselves on arrival to the rats of the visited locality.[1] Gregory of Tours observed the result of such transport.[2] Human transport of 'blocked' fleas may also occur at any time in the absence of the human disease from a place where rat-plague is smouldering as an enzootic disease, a fact which explains some of the apparently spontaneous urban outbreaks of the disease in England in the centuries after 'The Great Pestilence'.

Obviously the amount of human dispersion of 'blocked' fleas will depend upon the amount of human movement from place to place and that—apart from the panic flight of people from plague-stricken towns—must have been governed in the fourteenth century by the needs of war, trade, and labour, and by the conditions of travel. It seems probable that ordinarily there was little opportunity or inducement for the commonalty to move outside their home neighbourhoods; but the demands of war, the lure of the fairs, the grace of pilgrimages, and extraordinary demands for labour, must have been at times responsible for considerable movements of the populace. For instance when Edward III began building operations on his castle at Windsor in 1359 plague killed a large number of his workmen, so in 1362 'writs were issued to the sheriffs of several counties, to impress 302 masons and diggers of stone, to be employed in King's works'.[3] There were undoubtedly other forced movements of labour in connexion with the building and repair of castles, cathedrals, and other ecclesiastical buildings, the construction of defence and harbour works, and the expansion of towns; and in some cases at least the labourer's family may have moved with him. Indeed the adult labouring manpower of England was so small and machines were so few and feeble that such movements would seem to have been inevitable features of any large constructional or land-development work.

Although the common folk may not voluntarily have travelled far from their homes, the *Paston Letters*[4] reveal a surprising amount of travelling about the country on horseback by merchants and landowners, and the womenfolk of the gentry travelled in a similar manner to a lesser extent. Wyke's bill for 'horsemeate'[5] names a number of townships to which some member of the Paston family travelled on horseback. There were therefore opportunities for the passive transport of plague-fleas—which are no re-specters of persons—independently of their rodent hosts and apart from their carriage by panic-stricken fugitives from epidemic areas.

As the total land area of England has not altered appreciably since the fourteenth century, it is possible to obtain a rough idea of the distribution density of the human population at that time by comparing the estimates of the population presented by various authorities with the present area of

50,851 square miles, or 58,324 if Wales is included. Pelham[1] accepts Rogers' estimate of a total population of 2 million in the fourteenth century, with urban populations ranging from nearly 6,000 for Norwich to about 35,000 for London, which was three or four times larger then than any other city in the kingdom. Coulton[2] asserts that at least ninety per cent of the population was composed of villagers and that the villages were very small, with an adult male content of from 40 to 80 men. Bennett[3] believes that the population did not exceed 5 million in 1349. Sellers[4] and Russell[5] are agreed that it was about 2¼ million in 1377, but that was after England had been afflicted by 'The Great Pestilence' and by three more pestilences in 1361, 1369, and 1374. However Russell opines that the population in 1377 was about sixty per cent of that in 1346,[6] which would give a figure of approximately 3½ million just before plague struck the country. As the maximum figure for the population in 1348 is the important one for the present purpose, it would seem reasonable to place it at 4 million.

If this number of people had been uniformly distributed throughout England and Wales the resulting density of the population would have been about 69 persons to the square mile. Allowing an average of five persons to each dwelling and ignoring the aggregation of people in towns, villages, castles, and monasteries, there would not have been more than fourteen dwellings to the square mile in Britain for the house-rat to infest, and even supposing there was an average of 100 rats in each dwelling—which is almost certainly an excessive allowance for the two-room cottages which constituted a majority of the dwellings—the density of the overall house-rat population would have been too low to engender and sustain an epizootic of rat-plague on a national scale. If each lot of fourteen dwellings had been grouped in compact hamlets the local concentrations of house-rats might have been able to support localized epizootics, which might have engendered local epidemics of bubonic plague among the villagers; but the risk of either kind of plague becoming widespread would have been minimized by the long distances separating many of the hamlets. When the urban, baronial, manorial, and monastic aggregations in fourteenth-century England are brought into the picture, it is obvious that there must have been many large areas of land in the country in which there were neither human beings nor house-rats in sufficient numbers to provide subjects for *P. pestis*, and these void spaces must have acted as effective barriers to the spread of the disease.

In fact only the towns in fourteenth-century England provided sufficiently large aggregations of house-rats for dangerous epizootics of rat-plague to develop, and there were few towns with populations exceeding 5,000 persons of all ages. Russell's estimates of the populations of the twenty largest towns

TABLE I

Estimated populations of some English towns*

	1086	1377		1086	1377
Bristol	2,310	9,518	Norwich	4,445	5,928
Canterbury	1,610	3,861	Oxford	1,431	3,536
Colchester	1,452	4,432	Plymouth	—	7,256
Coventry	—	7,226	Salisbury	630	4,829
Exeter	1,438	2,340	Shrewsbury	872	3,123
Gloucester	2,146	3,358	Stamford	1,424	1,827
Leicester	1,278	3,152	Warwick	1,284	—
Lincoln	3,560	5,354	Winchester	6,000	2,160
London	17,850	34,971	Worcester	945	2,336
Northampton	1,032	2,216	York	4,134	10,872

in 1377[1] are presented in table 1, and these would have ranged in 1348 according to his correction from about 3,000 for Stamford to 58,285 for London. Four towns in addition to the capital then had populations of more than 10,000, to wit, Bristol, Coventry, Plymouth, and York, while Norwich came close to that figure with a population of more than 9,800. But most of the fourteenth-century towns were separated from one another by distances in which there were insufficient concentrations of house-rats to enable *P. pestis* to spread from one to another along rat 'pipelines', so that the extension of plague from one town to another could only have occurred as a result of the chance transport of infected rats or 'blocked' fleas.

In the fourteenth century England was a much wilder country than it is now. There were large areas of uninhabited forest, waste, and fenland, and the moorlands of Yorkshire, Somerset, Devon, and Wales were devoid of human and rat life, except for a sprinkling of hamlets on their margins. Everywhere the population was more thinly scattered than it is today, though it is important to remember that 'nearly all the habitations were grouped in villages', there were next to no outlying farms.[2] This fact is essential for a correct understanding of the epidemiology of 'The Great Pestilence' in England. Outlying farms, with their relatively large colonies of house-rats, would have served as links in the train of transmission of rat-plague from one village concentration of house-rats to another. In the absence of such links many—probably very many—villages must have completely escaped the disease. From what is now known about the aetiology of bubonic plague it was therefore a biological impossibility for the whole or even a major part of England to have been ravaged by 'The Great Pestilence' of 1348–50.

* As extracted from the tables given by Russell (1948), p. 142.

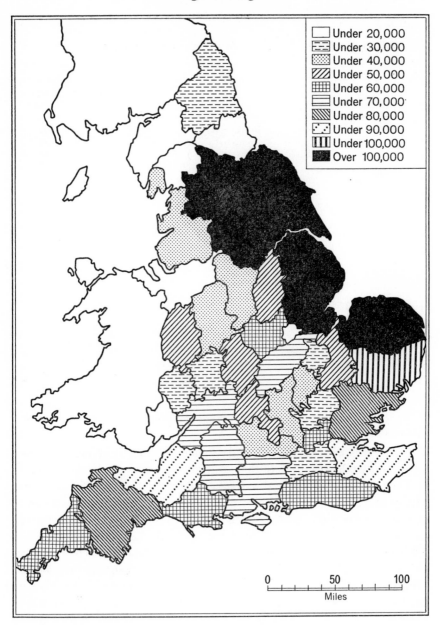

Under 20,000
Under 30,000
Under 40,000
Under 50,000
Under 60,000
Under 70,000
Under 80,000
Under 90,000
Under 100,000
Over 100,000

0   50   100

Miles

1. England in 1377, showing Russell's estimates of county populations.

TABLE 2

Distribution of religious houses in relation to a line drawn from York to Exeter

		North and west	South and east
Monks	Benedictine	47	207
	Cluniac	13	35
	Cistercian	43	50
	Carthusian	0	8
Canons regular	Augustinian	49	181
	Premonstratensian	7	39
	Gilbertine	0	14
	Bonshommes	0	2
Double houses	Gilbertine Nuns and Canons	0	16
	Bridgettine Nuns and Brothers	0	1
Nuns or canonesses	Benedictine	10	69
	Cluniac	2	2
	Cistercian	5	20
	Augustinian	5	15
	Various	0	21
Friars	Austin	8	27
	Carmelite	6	29
	Dominican	12	38
	Franciscan	12	40
	Various	0	24
Male or female	Not included above	380	1057
	TOTAL	599	1891

Certain towns, villages, manors, and religious houses were certainly scourged by it; many others in each of these categories were as surely exempted.

The population of England was not evenly distributed over the country in village aggregates in 1348. A line drawn from York to Exeter (see figure 2) would have divided it into a sparsely populated region in the north and west and a comparatively densely populated region in the south and east.[1] The Ordnance Survey map of Monastic Britain shows the religious houses which existed from 1066 to 1540. There were some 2,500 of them and their location with respect to the York–Exeter line—with the exception of a few that have inadvertently been omitted—is shown in table 2. Practically 76 per cent of them were situated to the south and east of that line. As most of these houses employed some lay workers, utilized some lay services, and depended ultimately upon the laity for their sustenance, their distribution may have to a certain extent reflected that of the populace. And of course except for

26

TABLE 3

*Estimated populations of English counties**

	1086	1377		1086	1377
Bedfordshire	13,982	30,508	Lincolnshire	90,341	142,678
Berkshire	24,640	34,084	Middlesex	25,683	51,835
Buckinghamshire	19,439	37,008	Norfolk	95,438	146,726
Cambridgeshire	20,058	46,461	Northamptonshire	30,040	62,553
Cheshire	6,180	15,503	Northumberland	7,927	25,210
Cornwall	19,033	51,411	Nottinghamshire	20,230	43,328
Cumberland	5,971	18,778	Oxfordshire	25,137	41,008
Derbyshire	10,472	36,433	Rutland	2,992	8,991
Devonshire	62,657	78,707	Shropshire	17,978	40,242
Dorsetshire	29,888	51,361	Somersetshire	50,284	84,111
Durham	4,983	13,091	Staffordshire	11,620	33,734
Essex	56,073	76,375	Suffolk	73,118	93,843
Gloucestershire	33,877	68,016	Surrey	15,925	27,058
Hampshire	42,344	60,849	Sussex	42,623	54,292
Herefordshire	20,534	25,831	Warwickshire	23,915	45,396
Hertfordshire	15,946	29,962	Westmorland	3,098	11,084
Huntingdonshire	10,314	21,243	Wiltshire	40,905	68,742
Kent	48,586	89,551	Worcestershire	16,999	24,148
Lancashire	7,385	35,820	Yorkshire	28,553	196,560
Leicestershire	24,598	50,748			

Plymouth all the fourteenth-century English seaports of any importance lay to the south and east of the line.

The population of England in 1348 was distributed among thirty-nine counties, of which eight lie north and west of the York–Exeter line, seven are traversed by the line, and twenty-four lie to the south and east of it. Russell has estimated the populations of the individual counties[1] at the time of the Domesday Survey and in 1377 (see table 3), and his figures yield aggregates of 211,129, 499,089, and 1,363,041 respectively for the populations of each of these groups in 1377. Allowing for a sixty per cent increase of their populations in 1348, the proportions become respectively 351,881, 831,815, and 2,271,735. Assuming that half of the population of each county traversed by the line lived to the south and east of it, then almost 78 per cent of the national population in 1348 lived in that part of the country. This figure approximates so closely to that obtained for the distribution of the religious houses that it is a reasonable assumption that about three-quarters of the population was living to the south and east of the York–Exeter line when bubonic plague irrupted into England in 1348. As it is also a reasonable assumption that four-fifths of the house-rat population was then located in

* Extracted from J. G. Russell, *British Medieval Population* (Albuquerque, 1948).

that area, it can be categorically stated that for all practical purposes 'The Great Pestilence' was confined to the southern and eastern counties of England.

There is a considerable difference of opinion among authorities about the state of communications in fourteenth-century England. Pelham,[1] Kingsford,[2] and Salzman[3] are in general agreement that land, river and sea communications were better than is generally supposed, and Kingsford supports his opinion by the records of journeyings in the *Stonor* correspondence: barges plied regularly from London to Henley-on-Thames in four days and a messenger covered the distance in a day's ride; there was apparently a regular packhorse service between London and Exeter, and both Thomas Stonor and his son paid frequent visits to their Devonshire estates from their Oxfordshire home.[4] Coulton holds an opposite view. He declares that the difficulties of travel 'were unquestionably very great. Commonly the roads were only tracks,...Moreover, such as they were, these tracks were ill-kept'.[5] And yet the Pastons went about their business in Norfolk, and journeyed to London and Yorkshire, seemingly oblivious to the state of the roads even in winter, when travelling must have been difficult.[6] Coulton's affirmation that an average day's journey was from 20 to 25 miles, is of significance with regard to the speed of spread of plague in fourteenth-century England because, if his statement is correct, it means that twenty-five miles was the maximum distance that an infected rat or a 'blocked' flea could be transported in twenty-four hours, for travel was most probably impossible after dark, except perhaps occasionally on bright moonlight nights. Lunn[7] concluded from his study of the clerical plague-mortalities in English deaneries during 'The Great Pestilence' that navigable rivers and estuaries assisted the spread of the disease, and as his conclusion conforms to the aetiology of bubonic plague it appears probable that there was a considerable volume of marine and river transport of bulky cargoes capable of harbouring *R. rattus* and its fleas in fourteenth-century England.

The truth about English communications in general at that time must lie somewhere between the contrary opinions that have been expressed. England was a civilized country with a central government which required frequent movement by many officials between its centre and its periphery to maintain law and order. It had flourishing industries which necessitated the movement of raw materials and finished products about the country. It had an export and an import trade with Europe and was engaged in a protracted war with France, of which the military needs alone must have entailed considerable movements of men and materials over inland roads and waterways. The rivers could not have carried all the merchandise that was undoubtedly being moved about the country, some of it of necessity all the

year round. It seems certain therefore that there was land transport of goods in bulk, at any rate during the late spring, summer, and early autumn months —that is to say, during the 'plague-season'—and that much merchandise was transported in larger containers than the panniers of pack-horses. Indeed the outstanding feature of the transport of this period according to Pelham[1] 'was the extensive use of carts and wagons for both local and long-distance work'. Undoubtedly given the choice the house-rat would choose to be carried in the dark, warm holds of ships and barges rather than in goods waggons; but it could hide securely in waggon-loads of grain, straw, hay, wool, and hides, and it was probably distributed by both means of transport in England during 'The Great Pestilence'.

Obviously the flea can be securely hidden in much smaller cargoes than the rat and 'blocked' fleas could easily have been transported in goods carried by pack-horses and even by pedlars. Hirst[2] affirms in connexion with the dispersion of plague-fleas that 'in the light of the mass of evidence accumulated in the course of the last forty years, far greater emphasis must be given to the role of merchandise and far less to man as passive porters of the infection'. Modern studies of bubonic plague show that woollen and cotton material, grain, fodder, forage, hides, and furs are the most favourable goods for flea-dissemination. As plague has not changed its epidemiological character during the period of recorded history, the conditions that govern its spread today must have been equally decisive in the England of Edward III. It can therefore be categorically asserted that the spread of bubonic plague in fourteenth-century England was decided by the random spread of the epizootic disease by rat-contacts; by the passive transport of infected rats and 'blocked' fleas in bulky loads of suitable goods; by the passive transport of 'blocked' fleas independently of their rodent hosts in similar cargoes and in smaller packages of fabrics and furs, and by their rarer carriage on the persons of travellers and fugitives. But under no circumstances could bubonic plague ever travel faster than the fastest speed of human transport, so that descriptions of 'The Great Pestilence' sweeping like a pestilential storm over the country merely indicate a regrettable ignorance of the nature of the disease.

The paramount industry of England at the time of 'The Great Pestilence' was the wool trade, although Pelham[3] remarks that its undoubted importance has been rather over-emphasized at the expense of arable farming. The government of England was then 'more consciously interested in wool than in any other product of English agriculture. Wool entered into diplomacy; wool was a leading source of revenue; wool exported brought foreign exchange... There were sheep everywhere, in regions mainly arable and in those specially

suited to grazing. Much of the wool was exported as cloth and there were few villages that had not some interest in the trade'.[1] As wool and its products provide excellent cover for the passive transport of the house-rat and its fleas, the movement of wool and woollen goods about England must have exerted a considerable influence upon the distribution of bubonic plague. Moreover there were certainly many wool stores in the country associated with religious houses like Battle Abbey—which 'possessed the largest flocks'—the Cotswold towns, the residences of landowners and merchants, and possibly numerous villages because even the poorest cottar had a dozen or so sheep, and each of these stores offered a delectable domicile to the house-rat and its fleas.[2] Furthermore around or near each store there would commonly be an aggregation of human dwellings and consequently a concentration of house-rats. The presence of wool and grain stores within their precincts explains why some religious houses were invaded by bubonic plague introduced by chance among their augmented rat populations.

The other commodities which vied with wool in the dispersion of the house-rat and its fleas were grain, hay, and straw. Fitter[3] lists the chief crops grown in medieval England as wheat, barley, oats, rye, vetches, and beans. These crops were grown in small amounts to meet local needs wherever soil and climate permitted; but certain parts of the country were particularly suitable for their cultivation in bulk and from these regions they were exported to other parts of England. Much of the boulder clay which covers a large part of Norfolk and Suffolk 'is well suited for wheat, which requires a stiff soil to support the weight of the ear' and 'the more sandy regions in the north of Norfolk are good for barley'.[4] Tansley affirms that in 1910 East Anglia, Essex, Huntingdonshire, and Lincolnshire comprised the area where most wheat was grown. 'Eight of these eastern counties, including Lincolnshire, provided about 42 per cent of the total area of wheat in Great Britain, while the total of their land area is only 11 or 12 per cent of the whole island'.[5] He adds that the eastern counties also grew considerable quantities of oats.[6]

As much of the midland region of England now under cultivation was apparently dense woodland or wasteland in the fourteenth century, while the north and north-western regions were partially desolate, the region which now produces the major part of the English wheat and barley crops must then have supplied a similar proportion of the home demand for those cereals, even though Pelham's map of the principal low-price wheat areas in the fourteenth century—areas which he equates with abundant supplies—shows areas of the lower Severn basin, the upper Thames basin, and the Bristol region in addition to Tansley's areas. Oats may have been grown in the

south-western counties and rye was possibly cultivated in small amounts wherever there was arable land outside the wheat and barley region.

Unfortunately there appears to be no certain information about the proportions in which these four grains entered into the diet of the average commoner, and nothing is known about the house-rat's preference for them. There appears to be a general impression that the peasant's bread was mainly rye-bread or, at best, a mixture of rye and wheat—Trevelyan[1] says that it was often a mixture of different kinds of grain—but Chaucer's poor widow lived on milk, brown bread, singed bacon, and an occasional egg,[2] and Langland's poor folk subsisted on cheese, curds, haver-cake, bread made from beans and bran, some vegetables, and some fruit.[3] The widow's bread was apparently akin to our 'wholemeal' bread, for it would have been a black bread if it had been made of rye. Trevelyan[4] remarks that 'nothing is more difficult to assess than the real degree of the peasant's poverty or well being, which differed greatly not only from place to place but from year to year'.

Possibly all that can now be safely said about the consumption of cereals in fourteenth-century England is that when wheat was plentiful it was eaten by the common folk in preference to other grains; that rye and oats were used as a substitute for wheat when it was scarce, and that barley was perhaps mainly used for the preparation of ale and beer. There is no doubt, however, that the region which grew the bulk of the edible grains supported a relatively denser population of both humans and house-rats than the rest of the country, which explains why the mortality of 'The Great Pestilence' was both absolutely and relatively greater in East Anglia than in the rest of England and Wales with the exception of London and certain other urban foci.

The movement of goods in bulk must have been made along well-recognized trade-channels which connected the main industrial areas with the chief towns, the principal ports and the great fairs. Although the fairs had lost some of their original importance before the end of the thirteenth century, the trade-routes for which they were the initial foci were undoubtedly still being used in the fourteenth century, and they afforded practically the only routes along which bubonic plague could spread in England. Although Walford describes only Sturbridge and Bartholomew Fairs in detail, he quotes an act of Henry VII (3 Hen. VII, c. 9) which names fairs at Salisbury, Bristol, Oxford, Nottingham, Ely, Coventry, and Cambridge (Barnwell) as important ones, and he states that 'The Great Pestilence' first erupted in London at the time of Bartholomew Fair.[5] This list is not complete because there was an important cattle fair at Abingdon and one at Winchester, 'chiefly for the sale of produce and cloth', a famous fair at Northampton, and important ones at Boston, Stamford, and St Edmunds-

bury.[1] About the fair at Northampton, Professor Cam remarks[2] that a parliamentary petition of 1334 describes it as 'one of the four or five great fairs from which purchases were systematically made for the royal household in the reigns of John and Henry III'. The others were Boston, Stamford, Winchester, St Ives (Huntingdonshire), and Bury St Edmunds. It should be noted that all these fairs are situated south and east of the York–Exeter line.

The great fair at Sturbridge, which opened on 18 September and lasted for three weeks, was the most important of the English fairs and was of sufficient repute to attract merchants from many European trade centres. 'You can be present at the great Sturbridge fair and there see Venetian glass, Bruges linen, Spanish iron, Norwegian tar, Hanse fur, Cornish tin and Cretan wine, all for sale in the half of a square mile which was occupied for three whole weeks'.[3] Walford[4] quotes Thorold Rogers' statement that during Sturbridge Fair, Blakeney, Colchester, King's Lynn, and perhaps Norwich, were filled with foreign vessels. The ships that brought the merchandise of the Levant from Venice, and the other commodities from overseas, would assuredly harbour the ship-rat, which could become the plague-rat whenever the disease was active in Europe, Egypt, or the Near East, and it is no wonder therefore that whenever bubonic plague erupted anywhere in England in the summer months Sturbridge Fair was invariably either postponed or cancelled.

In addition to Canterbury there were many other centres of pilgrimage in medieval England and Wales—among them, Walsingham, Peterborough, St Davids, and Holywell. It seems probable that the pilgrimage to St Davids had become largely restricted to the Welsh and the West Country folk by Chaucer's day because 'for a century at least before he wrote, pilgrimages had been gradually becoming journeys rather of pleasure than of duty',[5] and travelling overland through the broken country of South Wales could have been little more of a pleasure in the fourteenth century than when Gerald de Barry[6] wrote so feelingly about the discomfort and danger of the journey towards the close of the twelfth century. If any English pilgrims did journey to St Davids in 1348 they probably travelled by sea from Bristol or Glastonbury to Milford Haven, in which case the isolated Welsh epidemic of plague that involved Castlemartin, Pembroke, and Tenby, and was almost certainly sea-borne, may have had its origin in that pilgrimage.

One other important centre of pilgrimage, as far as the possible dissemination of 'blocked' fleas by personal carriage is concerned, may have been Hailes Abbey in Gloucestershire, where a phial containing the reputed blood of Christ was the lodestone and where Richard of Cornwall, was buried. Although pilgrimages would seem according to Chaucer[7] to have ceased to have been of a predominantly religious character by the middle of the

2. Sites of important towns, fairs and pilgrimage centres in the fourteenth century.

33

fourteenth century, it seems extremely probable that during the terror excited by 'The Great Pestilence' many fugitives from plague-centres flocked to the famous shrines in the hope of escaping the divine wrath of the pestilence, and some of these fugitives may well have harboured 'blocked' fleas roosting in their clothing.

The most important towns, together with the principal fairs and four of the English centres of pilgrimage (including Canterbury), are marked on figure 2. It is noteworthy that all major towns except Chester, Shrewsbury, and Plymouth; the major fairs, and the major centres of pilgrimage, lie south and east of the York–Exeter line. The significance of this distribution is that the fairs were situated on or near navigable rivers linking them to seaports or in places where there was an easy overland haul from the nearest port, because bubonic plague was an exotic disease which could only invade and be maintained in England by maritime importation. Bristol owes much of its importance as a port to its ease of communication with the Somerset plain, the Severn lowlands, and the relative depression which runs through Wootton Bassett and Swindon to the Vale of the White Horse,[1] which explains why 'The Great Pestilence' spread, according to contemporary records, from Weymouth to London by way of Bristol and Oxford.

The house-rat was largely dependent on man for its food supplies and entirely dependent on him in the British Isles for its accommodation. Bennett[2] shows that few dwellings of the common folk had more than two rooms, one of which was used by the family for all living purposes—including the shelter of domestic animals—while the other was the communal bedroom. Such conditions would be ideal for the propagation of both the human-flea (*Pulex irritans*) and the rat-flea (*X. cheopis*), about which Hirst writes: 'Bubonic plague spreads most actively among man and rat in those places and at those times where, or when, the density of *X. cheopis* is high.'[3]

As was to be expected, the nature of the local supplies of building materials exerted an influence upon the structure of the dwellings, although Bennett[4] asserts that few instances are recorded of the use of stone for walls—even in good stone country—but almost everywhere wattle-and-daub, or cob, or earth and mud were the principal materials in use. Although some cottages were roofed with wooden shingles, most were thatched with straw, either of rye or wheat, or with reeds in the fen country. They were smoky, dark, and humid. The floor was usually earth beaten hard and the beds of straw or flock were either laid on it or rested on rough wooden frames. 'Folk ordinarily slept naked or in their day clothes',[5] according to the prevailing temperature. In London and some of the larger towns the upper classes had somewhat better and more spacious accommodation; but when 'The Great

Pestilence' struck England the average standard of urban dwelling was probably not much better than the rural one. 'It is not generally realized', Coulton remarks about Chaucer's London, 'what draughts our ancestors were obliged to accept as unavoidable, even when they sat partially screened by their high-backed chairs...A man needed his warmest furs still more for sitting indoors than for walking abroad...The important part played by furs of all kinds, and the matter-of-course mention of dirt and vermin, are among the first things that strike us in medieval literature'.[1]

In the north of England, and especially in the Border counties, the dwellings of the commonalty were even more primitive. The Border chiefs lived in strong castles for defence against the Scots and the lesser gentry had their 'peel towers', but the peasants lived in wooden shanties that the raiders burnt as a matter of course. In the more secure parts of England, especially south and east of the York–Exeter line, the gentry were beginning to build moated manor-houses instead of fortresses, fine houses which were built either of stone or of wood and plaster. Brick was very rare in England from the end of the Roman occupation up to the fifteenth century, when it came into general use in East Anglia and other regions where local stone was scarce, and where the timber of the forests was beginning to run short.[2]

The living conditions of the common folk in fourteenth-century England were evidently of such a nature as to provide a favourable environment for the house-rat and its fleas, because bubonic plague is primarily and principally a disease of the poor, although it is not a disease associated with dirt and destitution like typhus fever. *R. rattus* is a splendid climber and a clever burrower in relatively soft material, but it cannot burrow through the hard materials which the field-rat tunnels through with ease. The state of affairs that Trevelyan describes as prevailing in the Border country would certainly be inimical to its colonization of that part of England in sufficient density to sustain an epizootic of rat-plague, for it is a rather timid animal and will not breed where it is frequently disturbed. The stone-built castles with their resistant walls and unfriendly roofs, and the manor-houses with their moats, would also be uncongenial to it. There is nothing surprising therefore about the almost complete exemption of the English nobility and landed class from 'The Great Pestilence'; it just happened that the house-rat could not make itself at home in their castles, 'peel towers', and manor houses. The brick-built house with its slated or tiled roof was also inimical to it, and the national development of this type of dwelling was probably the most important single factor in the eventual disappearance of the house-rat from the bulk of England. It was in the medieval, 'soft-walled' dwelling-house, with its thatched roof, its dark, unventilated, humid interior, and its earthen floor,

that *R. rattus* and *X. cheopis* found mutually congenial conditions for their subsistence and multiplication. Under the floor and in the thickness of the wattle-and-daub or mud walls the house-rat could construct burrows in which it could climb to its resting and breeding nests in the thatch, whence it could emerge at any time between sunset and sunrise safely hidden by the gloom which obscured the interior of the dwelling, whereas it dare venture outside the dwelling only on dry, warm nights.

Where these dwellings crowded together in fourteenth-century towns, and where they clustered around the harbour, the grain-store, the corn-mill, the wool-store, and the general warehouse, the house-rat would especially thrive and its local populations would be large and dense enough to engender and sustain severe *epidemics* of bubonic plague. Where these dwellings were more loosely congregated in villages, with possibly gardens or common land separating one from another, the importation of *epizootic* plague might produce only a few discrete household visitations of the disease, resulting often in the extermination of the unfortunate families but not diffusing through the community. Where these dwellings were more thinly scattered on the ground the density of the house-rat population would be too low for plague to become *epizootic*, and in the absence of epizootic plague in the house-rat man was exempt from epidemic bubonic plague in medieval England.

It is absolutely certain therefore that the great national outburst of bubonic plague in 1348–50 afflicted only a part, and in all probability much the smaller part, of the population of England, and that statements that it destroyed three-quarters or even one half of the nation are flights of fancy boosted by the age-old terror that the name 'plague' still excites. In the comparatively densely populated region of East Anglia, and in the larger towns that were afflicted by it, 'The Great Pestilence' may possibly have destroyed as much as one-third of the population; in the rest of England and Wales it is extremely doubtful if as much as one-twentieth of the population was destroyed by it. These are not random assertions; they are inherent in the aetiology of bubonic plague.

CHAPTER 3

PLAGUE INVADES THE BRITISH ISLES

The invasion of the British Isles by bubonic plague in 1348 was only an incident in a great epidemic outburst of the disease from its Indian home—the second pandemic. Between about 1340 and 1352 this outburst involved most of Asia Minor, much of North Africa, the whole of Europe, and some of the islands lying off that continent such as the Channel Islands, the British Isles, Iceland, and Greenland.

The wave of the second pandemic of plague which reached the British Isles was called by contemporary recorders 'The Great Mortality' or 'The Great Pestilence'. Its modern pseudonym of 'The Black Death' was introduced to English historical writings by Mrs Penrose (Mrs Markham) in 1823—473 years after its extinction in these islands—and to medical literature by Babington's translation of Hecker's *Der Schwarze Tod* in 1833.[1] It is a silly nickname because death from plague is no blacker figuratively than from any other microbial disease of man, and though the cadaver of a plague-victim may exhibit a purplish discoloration the corpse does not turn black. If this distinction belongs to any disease it belongs to smallpox, which has therefore literally a much better claim than plague to be called a 'black death'. In the Milan epidemic of smallpox in 1888 the corpses of some fulminant cases at Salerno exhibited the appearance of having been completely charred.[2] A recent epidemic of cholera in Egypt was also styled a 'black death', although in fatal cases the extremities and the face and neck assume a slate-blue coloration consequent upon the stagnation of the circulation in the cutaneous blood-vessels.[3] For that matter death from any disease, whatever its nature, is a 'black death' to the morbid imagination of the ignorant, and the use of the pseudonym 'The Black Death' for bubonic plague frequently indicates a regrettable ignorance of the nature of the disease. However this pseudonym is so beloved of historical novelists and has such a selling appeal to the public that it is unlikely that it will ever be expunged from the literature of plague—but it has no place in a genuine history of plague.

England was the first part of the British Isles to be attacked by the disease and most of the contemporary English chroniclers of 'The Great Pestilence'

name Melcombe Regis—the modern Weymouth—as its point of entry into this country and the end of July or the beginning of August as the date of entry. Melcombe Regis was certainly a favourable site for its entrance because it was an important town and port in 1348. When Edward III was besieging Calais the town 'furnished him with 20 ships and 264 marines, while Bristol sent only 22 ships and 608 sailors, and even London sent only 25 ships and 662 men'.[1] This plague may have been brought to Melcombe Regis either from Calais, which was then an English possession, or from the Channel Islands which were in constant communication with England and were evidently severely visited by plague prior to its appearance in England. There is a state record, dated 18 February 1350, of an order to the governor of the islands[2] from which it can reasonably be inferred that they were invaded by plague in 1348 and that after the customary winter intermission the disease recrudesced with increased violence in the summer of 1349. A diary of the weather that was kept in England from 1337 to 1344 reports 'a very great prevalence of westerly winds during those years, exceeding their normal frequency in modern times'.[3] As it is a reasonable supposition therefore that the prevailing wind in the English Channel during the summer months of 1348 was a westerly one, *P. pestis* could also have been shipped from the Channel Islands to Southampton, which Knighton took to be the point of entry of 'The Great Pestilence'.[4]

Through whichever port it first entered the country, contemporary chroniclers are agreed that it spread from the south-western coastal area to Bristol and thence by way of Oxford to London, which it reached at the end of October or the beginning of November. Its presence in the capital was not officially recognized, however, until 1 January 1349 (by our calendar), when Parliament was prorogued 'in consequence of a sudden pestilence at Westminster'.[5] As it was prorogued again on 10 March for an indefinite period, it seems evident that plague was active in London during the winter months of that year, as unusual occurrence because in temperate latitudes the rat-fleas hibernate as a rule with the onset of cold, frosty weather, with the result that plague is extinguished or becomes quiescent.

There is evidence which suggests that 'The Great Pestilence' may have been an exception to this rule, because if a half only of the excessive number of vacant benefices in the diocese of Salisbury during the autumn of 1348 and the winter of 1349[6] was caused by the deaths of their incumbents from bubonic plague, the disease must have been continuously active in Dorsetshire, Wiltshire, and Berkshire throughout those seasons. The explanation of this unusual activity appears to be that the autumn of 1348 and the winter of 1349 were exceptionally mild. Knighton's statement[7] that there was such

an abundance of grain of all kinds in the plague-year that people hardly bothered to gather all of the harvest suggests that the weather was unusually mild late into the autumn, and this inference is supported by the report in Adam of Murimuth's chronicle[1] that the weather was exceptionally wet from 24 June to Christmas.

From London the disease spread to East Anglia and especially into Norfolk. No contemporary information is available about its route of spread, but it was probably carried into East Anglian ports by coasting vessels from London. From Norfolk, which appears to have been very severely and extensively afflicted, it travelled discontinuously westwards through the Midlands, reaching the Welsh border counties in some places. It also moved northwards into Lincolnshire, which seems to have suffered severely from its visitation.

Although contemporary writers are in broad agreement about the general course and progress of 'The Great Pestilence', they differ about the intensity and extent of its local prevalences. Robert of Avesbury[2] records that plague erupted in Dorsetshire towards the end of June, 1348, and that it was very deadly, killing many people within half a day. It made no distinction of age or sex among the commonalty but it attacked 'few among the wealthy'. The dead were so numerous that scores of corpses were daily interred in consecrated pits. The disease reached London about the beginning of November and the subsequent epidemic was so malignant that between 2 February and the end of Eastertide, 1349, more than 200 plague-dead 'were buried almost every day in a cemetery then newly made in Smithfield, apart from those which were buried in other cemeteries of the city'. He adds that the epidemic ceased in London at Whitsuntide while the disease was still moving northwards, in which regions—probably the Fenlands, as these would be a barrier to its progress—it subsided about the end of September.

Le Baker[3] records that 'first it almost stripped the seaports of Dorset of their inhabitants' and then spread through Devonshire and Somerset to Bristol. Gloucester tried to escape it by refusing admittance to any persons coming from Bristol and the West Country; but as it was not transmitted by human contacts 'at last Gloucester, Oxford, and London, and at length the whole of England were so violently affected that hardly a tenth of either sex survived'. This is in the best style of 'Black Death' best sellers and is an utter impossibility for bubonic plague to accomplish. Le Baker returns to reality with his statement that few nobles died of the disease, the only notable plague-victim he can name being John de Montgomery, the captain of Calais, who died of it there. It is probable that he saw the human disease for his description of its clinical picture is remarkably accurate. The plague-stricken were he says 'afflicted by swellings which appeared suddenly in

various parts of the body, which were *so hard and dry that when lanced hardly any fluid came from them; many people recovered from these* by lancing or long endurance. Others had small black blisters scattered over the whole body; from which very few, I might almost say hardly any, recovered to life and health.'

The italic is mine to emphasize the homology of Le Baker's buboes with those described by Dioscorides and Posidonius and to emphasize also that statements like his previous assertion that bubonic plague reduced the entire population of England by about ninety per cent are nonsense; as is also his concluding statement that 'many country villages were totally destitute of human beings'. He reports the date of its arrival at Bristol as 15 August and its entry into London as about Michaelmas—29 September.

As has been seen Knighton thought that Southampton was its point of entry and that it then spread through the coastal regions of south-west England to Bristol.[1] This is a significant observation that may well be true because it is indicative of a maritime extension of the disease by coasting vessels, an ideal means of distributing infected ship-rats and their 'blocked' fleas. As he was a canon of Leicester it is tempting to assume that he was recording factual mortality figures in his report that more than 380 plague-deaths occurred in the little parish of St Leonard, more than 400 in the parish of St Cross, and more than 700 in the parish of St Margaret; but people died of other diseases even in plague-time—a fact ignored by many historians—and in the absence of a system of registration of deaths Knighton's figures are hearsay estimates. If Leicester had a population of about 5,000 in 1348, which it most probably had (see table 1 p. 24 above), his mortality figures would represent about thirty per cent of it, a proportion which conforms to modern observations that in ill-developed countries urban communities commonly lose about one-third of their members from a severe epidemic of bubonic plague.

The reputed death-roll of plague in the diocese of Lincoln—which included Leicestershire—induced the bishop to delegate full episcopal authority to both regular and secular clergy to hear confessions and give absolution to the dying except to debtors—for 'business as usual' was apparently the slogan in England during 'The Great Pestilence' as it was during the first world war—and a papal indulgence granted plenary remission to the dying, provided they died of bubonic plague. Knighton records the significant observation[2] that the pestilence was succeeded by a murrain (not plague) among the domestic animals so that 'an incalculable number' of sheep and oxen perished for lack of shelter and attention, 'for there was such dearth[*sic*] of serfs and servingmen that nobody knew what to do'. In other words the wealthy monastic and private owners of the flocks of sheep and herds of

oxen were completely flummoxed when their serfs disappeared, not necessarily because these were all or even in a large proportion killed by bubonic
plague, but because in the breakdown of law and order that invariably
accompanied every great visitation of the disease in the past men seized the
opportunity to escape from bonds that irked them.

Knighton also relates that in the autumn of 1350 'it was impossible to hire
a harvester for less than 8d., plus food; a reaper for 12d., plus food.[1] For
which reason, many crops rotted in the fields for lack of labourers', because
their owners could not break the first strike in English history caused by
bubonic plague. He omits to mention what their wages were before 'The
Great Pestilence' freed them from what was probably agricultural slavery;
but the real significance of his statement is that during the plague-year there
was evidently a sufficient number of workers alive and healthy to harvest the
crops if the owners were willing to pay the wages they demanded.

Similarly formal religion suffered as much as agriculture because 'where
a man could have a Chaplain for 5, 4 or even 2 marks with board, when there
were plenty of priests before the Plague, there was now hardly anyone who
would accept a benefice for up to £20 or 20 marks; but within a short while
there flocked into orders a great multitude whose wives had died of plague,
among whom were many unlettered men, the merest laymen, who could
only read after a fasion, let alone understand'.[2] Only a confirmed celibate
could have written this implied libel on fourteenth-century English wives,
because the natural reaction of most widowers is to seek another partner if
they have been happily married, and as bubonic plague is no respecter of
sex there would have been as many widows looking for husbands after 'The
Great Pestilence' as there were widowers. Indeed Jessopp asserts that the
records of the Norfolk court rolls clearly show that 'hundreds of widows must
have married only a few weeks or days after their husbands' deaths'.[3] As
regards the clergy, the fact seems to be that the pandemic provided them
with a golden opportunity to revalue their services.

One of the most surprising facts about the contemporary literature of
'The Great Pestilence' is the slight notice taken of it by Chaucer and Langland. The former apparently lived through its visitation of London, yet he
ignored both this and the epidemics of 1361 and 1369, assuming that these
were outbreaks of bubonic plague, and 'The Great Pestilence' was undoubtedly the chief medical event in his lifetime. A possible explanation of
his silence about it is that he was too young at the time to appreciate its
impact, and that in adult life he believed in the superstition of the personification of pestilential disease—which was a common aberration of the public
mind up to the end of the eighteenth century—in which case the less he

said about plague the better it would be for his personal safety. Gillies[1] presents an example of the superstition about the personification of communicable disease in his anecdote of the Highland family who would not speak of smallpox by its Gaelic name of *a'bhreac* for fear of offending the disease and accordingly referred to it as the *bean mhaith*, the 'good wife'.

Whatever the reason for his slight notice of it, Chaucer only alludes to plague twice in his *Canterbury Tales* and in neither instance does he use the name, 'The Great Pestilence' or 'The Great Mortality'. The first of his allusions occurs in the Prologue, where the Reeve is said to be 'feared like the plague';[2] the second, which occurs in *The Pardoner's Tale*, may be a timid reference to 'The Great Pestilence' in view of the hearsay exterminating mortality ascribed to the visitation.

Langland's one specific reference to 'The Great Pestilence' occurs in *The Vision of the Field Full of Folk*, where he inveighs against parish priests who alleged its impoverishment of their parishes in order to obtain benefices in London to 'sing masses for souls for silver is sweet'. If he was born around 1330, as is probable, he was of the age at the time of 'The Great Pestilence' when death and the fear of it make least impression on the human mind. Moreover tradition places his birthplace in Shropshire and it is doubtful whether that county was invaded by 'The Great Pestilence'. In the third version of his poem, written in his old age around 1393, he refers to his poverty-stricken life with his wife and daughter in Cornhill, which suggests that he was then living in one of the rat-infested hovels that housed the poor; but the period of his residence in London is not certainly known so that he possibly had no personal experience of plague either in that city or in Shropshire. He does mention plague, however, and he certainly had experience of other epidemic diseases as his reference to fevers and fluxes, running scabs, boils and botches, burning ague, many keen sores, and pocks and pestilence, in *The Vision of Antichrist* clearly shows.[3] 'The Plague' mentioned in *The Vision of Piers Counsel*[4] may not refer to bubonic plague because in his day, as Mullett remarks: '*Plague* was a generic word, no more precise than *Fever* or *Flu*',[5] and any mortal epidemic disease was a 'plague' to the people of his time. The fact that there were numerous plagues other than bubonic plague in fourteenth-century England is commonly ignored; but smallpox, measles, diphtheria, pertussis, influenza, and dysentery undoubtedly occurred in widespread and deadly epidemics, and the 'burning ague' in Langland's list was almost certainly typhus fever. There is little doubt that he had smallpox in mind when he wrote that 'pocks and pestilence slew much people', and it is obvious that he was acquainted with a variety of communicable diseases and other disorders, as anyone would expect who was not obsessed

with the notion that bubonic plague was omnipresent in fourteenth-century England.

Several interesting deductions can be made from these general records of 'The Great Pestilence'. In the initial stages of its invasion of England it was apparently restricted to the south-western ports, from each of which it would radiate for some distance inland and from which it was almost certainly carried farther along the coast by trading and fishing vessels. After Melcombe Regis the next recorded town of importance it afflicted was Bristol. The direct distance between these two places is 69 miles, and if plague spread overland from one to the other it covered the distance—according to the dates given by Roger of Avesbury and Le Baker—in 47 days, an average rate of travel of approximately 1½ miles a day. This is identical with the rate of spread of the second pandemic from Marseilles to Paris* and is only a trifle faster than its pace from Bristol to London. The virtual concurrence of these three rates of travel may be only a coincidence; but, even so, each is too slow to support the supposition that *P. pestis* was transported overland in merchandise harbouring infected rats or 'blocked' fleas, because the clumsiest of fourteenth-century goods waggons would normally cover a distance of from 10 to 12 miles a day during the summer months, and would therefore reach Bristol within ten days of leaving Melcombe Regis and London within a fortnight of leaving Bristol. Plague must have spread from Melcombe Regis to Bristol, therefore, either as a creeping epizootic by rat contacts or much more probably as a maritime extension by coastal shipping. Support for the latter alternative is supplied by the fact that it would not be profitable to discharge bulky cargoes at Melcome Regis and then haul them slowly and expensively by waggon to Bristol when they could be carried there more economically by sea. This argument applies with even more force against the overland haul of such merchandise from Bristol to the nearest point on the Thames from which barges could ply to London, although the fact that Oxford was involved indicates that *P. pestis* made the overland journey there in some way.

The action of the people of Gloucester appears to be the first recorded instance of this kind of municipal action against bubonic plague in England. Although it was unsuccessful it was constantly repeated during subsequent outbreaks of plague, sometimes with apparent success, down to the last great epidemic of the disease in 1665. It is possible that the method had been successfully employed in England prior to 1348 in connexion with epidemics

* There is a general agreement among contemporary chroniclers that plague appeared in Marseilles about Christmas 1347, and Klebs avers that Paris was attacked by it soon after October 1348, 'and not in midsummer as is still frequently asserted in the literature'.[1] If these dates are correct, plague took more than ten months to travel overland the 400-odd miles separating the two cities

of smallpox, St Anthony's Fire, and other diseases that are transmitted by human contacts. In principle it was certainly practised against the various intractable and repulsive skin disorders that were common in medieval England and were regarded as manifestations of leprosy. It is remarkable with what tenacity urban and rural authorities in the British Isles clung to this ineffective method for the public health control of bubonic plague; but they did not know that no *cordon sanitaire* would hold back the nocturnal rat and its inconspicuous flea, and inaction was intolerable in plague-time.

To reach Oxford from Gloucester plague must have travelled either through the wool country of the Cotswolds by way of Northleach, Burford, and Whitney, or along Ermine Street through Circencester to the Thames at Cricklade and then along the Thames valley. From Oxford it may have continued eastwards along that valley either as a creeping epizootic or by river transport. Unfortunately no information seems to be available about the date of its arrival at Oxford, so its rate of spread from Gloucester to Oxford and from Oxford to London cannot be calculated, assuming that it reached London by this route. This assumption may not be justified because even if Le Baker is correct in his sequence of its appearance as Gloucester–Oxford–London, it could have been imported into London by coastal shipping from the south-western ports while it was travelling overland from Gloucester to Oxford. Indeed, in view of the aetiology of the disease, it is far more likely that it reached London as a maritime importation. It is noteworthy that there is no record of its spread northwards from Gloucester to towns on the Severn, although the river is navigable for small modern steamers from Gloucester to Worcester and thence by smaller boats to Shrewsbury.

The common people, as always in epidemics of bubonic plague, bore the main toll of 'The Great Pestilence' and among them it 'fell most heavily on the young and vigorous' according to Le Baker.[1] This is a significant contemporary observation because Hirst affirms that a majority of cases occurs in persons between ten and thirty-five years of age, 'the very young and elderly being comparatively little affected'.[2]

The populace attributed 'The Great Pestilence' to the exceptionally wet summer of 1348, a natural association of calamities in view of its ignorance of the aetiology of plague. It seems probable that the wet summer did exert an influence upon the disease, but in a contrary direction to popular belief because, as both *R. rattus* and *X. cheopis* dislike damp conditions, 'The Great Pestilence' might have spread more extensively and been more deadly if the summer and autumn of 1348 had not been so wet in England. Apparently the weather was not so wet in Scotland; at any rate it was not blamed for the irruption of the pandemic into that country.

'The Scots,' recorded Knighton, 'hearing about the cruel plague in England, believed that this had come about on their behalf through the avenging hand of God' and accordingly assembled an army in the forest of Selkirk for a raid into England; but, he adds with evident relish, the Scottish army was devastated by the pestilence and the survivors, retreating in disorder to their homes, were pursued and cut to pieces by an English army.[1] Barnes[2] states that more than 5,000 of the Scots army died of plague and alleges that the panic-stricken remnants of the English slaughter spread the disease throughout Scotland. The epidemic of bubonic plague in the Scottish army can only have been an incident, however, in an unnoticed epizootic of the disease among Scotland's house-rats, and it was the rodents not the runaways that distributed the disease in that country.

Le Baker's version of this event in that 'while this great disaster was laying England waste, the Scots exultantly imagined that they would gain the height of their ambition against the English, and at this time were in the blasphemous habit of wantonly swearing "By the cheap death of Englishmen!". But their excess of joy was cut off by lamentation; the Sword of the wrath of God turned upon the Scots and slaughtered as many of them with leprosy as of the English with eruptions and pustules.'[3] Le Baker's confused nosology is perhaps excusable in view of the obvious patriotic fervour with which he acclaims the deity's righteous intervention.

It is not to be expected that a Scots chronicler would interpret the divine action in quite the same way, and there is no mention of Scottish exultation over the cheap death of Englishmen provoking God's wrath in Fordun's chronicle. He writes sorrowfully of the awful pestilence which devastated Scotland in 1350 and destroyed, he believed, a third of mankind throughout the known world. It attacked everywhere, he says, 'especially the meaner sort and common people;—seldom the magnates. Men shrank from it so much that, through fear of contagion, sons, fleeing as from the face of leprosy or from an adder, durst not go and see their parents in the throes of death.'[4]

Barbé[5] asserts that the first appearance of the pandemic in Scotland was recorded by the poet Wyntoun under the date of 1349. He notes that Wyntoun also believed that a third of mankind had been destroyed by it and that he recorded that it ravaged Scotland for more than a year, sparing no age and neither sex.

These Scottish records present several points of interest. Each chronicler stresses the malignity of the disease and Fordun emphasizes that the commonalty bore the brunt of its attack. Wyntoun's assertion that it showed no age discrimination is at variance with modern knowledge of the epidemic

disease, and is contradicted by the correct observation of the contemporary French chronicler, William de Nangis, that young people were its chief victims.[1] Each Scots chronicler also emphasizes that the disease excited such a state of terror that the ties of family affection and kinship were disrupted and the plague-stricken were deserted by their nearest and dearest of kin. Guy de Chauliac, cited by Simpson,[2] recorded an identical disruption of family bonds in France and undoubtedly a similar disruption occurred in England.

It is certain, however, that the incidence of bubonic plague in Scotland was uneven because the house-rat would not find congenial conditions for its effective colonization of the bleak and barren Highlands. Even in the more genial and fertile Lowlands its population density undoubtedly varied widely, and it cannot be too often stressed that the density of the house-rat population in a given area governed absolutely the intensity of the disease in that area. No writing that fails to do justice to the fundamental part played by *R. rattus* is of historical value. It can therefore be confidently asserted that the death-roll of 'The Great Pestilence' varied widely in different parts of Scotland and that it was probably insignificant in the Highland districts.

Contemporary Scots chroniclers are silent about the pathway of invasion of their country by the pandemic, but later Scottish writers appear to accept the implication in the English chronicles that the disease spread by contiguity from northern England into Scotland, though there is a noticeable lack of enthusiasm among them to attribute its spread to the deity's righteous intervention. It is very doubtful if this view of its spread is correct. The two countries were virtually at war, and the Border peoples were inflamed and on the alert so that there is unlikely to have been much peaceful transit of bulky merchandise across the Border to carry infected house-rats into Scotland. The Scots army gathering in the forest of Selkirk required supplies of food, fodder, equipment, and munitions which were certainly not supplied from England but may well have been supplied by France, which would have welcomed a conflict between England and Scotland to distract Edward III's designs upon it. In all probability plague invaded Scotland by sea and not by creeping in over the Border, especially as the house-rat would not cross either the Tweed or the Liddell Water of its own accord.

The invasion of Ireland can only have occurred by sea, and the plague was probably shipped from Bristol to ports on the east and south-east coasts of Ireland, where it appeared between 24 June and 1 August 1348. Later in the latter month it was imported almost simultaneously into Dublin and Drogheda, either by coastal shipping from Waterford or Wexford or by vessels from England. The friar, John Clyn, in his contemporary account of Ireland's visitation,[3] records that in 1348 there was a great concourse of the

clergy and the religious orders, 'especially in the months of September and October...for the pilgrimage and the wading in the water of Thaht-Molyng in companies and crowds, so that you might have seen assembling there at the same time for many days many thousands of people; some came for devotional motives; others, and these the more numerous, from fear of the plague, which was then prevalent. This first began near Dalkey and Drogheda, and almost destroyed and denuded of human inhabitants the towns of Dublin and Drogheda themselves, so that in Dublin alone from the beginning of August up to the Nativity of our Lord, 14,000 men died.'

He then relates that of the Friars Minor 25 died of the disease at Drogheda and 23 at Dublin, and that it raged for forty days at Kilkenny, during which time it killed 8 preaching friars there.

In scarcely any house did only one die [he continues] but all together, man and wife with their children and household, traversed the same road, the road of death. Now I, brother John Clyn, of the Order of Minor Friars and the community of Kilkenny, have written in this book these notable events that have occurred in my time, which I have learned from the evidence of my own eyes or upon reliable report. And lest [these] notable events should perish with time and fade from the memory of future generations...while waiting among the dead for the coming of death, I have set them down in writing just as I have truthfully heard and examined them. And lest the writing should perish with the writer and the work with the workman, I leave the parchment for the work to be continued in case in the future any human survivor should remain, or someone of the race of Adam should be able to escape this plague and continue what I have begun.

No more forceful testimony to the feeling of hopelessness inspired by the terror of plague was written in the fourteenth century. The writer died some time in 1349, perhaps of the disease he awaited.

He had a compatriot whose behaviour in the shadow of 'The Great Mortality' also commands respect. On the lower margins of two pages of the *Senchus Mor*, the great collection of ancient Irish laws, there is an inscription which reads:

One thousand three hundred and fifty years from the birth of Christ till this night: and this is the second year since the coming of the plague into Ireland. I have written this in the twentieth year of my age. I am Hugh, son of Conor MacEagen, and whosoever reads it let him offer a prayer of mercy for my soul. This is Christmas night, and I place myself under the protection of the King of heaven and earth, beseeching that He will bring me and my friends safe through this plague. Hugh, son of Conor MacEagan, who wrote this in his father's book in the year of the great plague.[1]

Looking back over six hundred years to that still room where, by rushlight, alone with his faith and his fear, that young Irishman recorded his prayer,

we get a revealing glimpse of the part that medieval Christianity played in the succour of Christendom during the second pandemic of bubonic plague. It is good to know that Hugh survived this ordeal, if the entry of his death in the *Annals of the Four Masters* under the date of 1359[1] is authentic.

His prayer indicates that plague was still prevalent in Ireland at the close of 1350, two years and four months after its arrival, though it was probably not continuously active throughout this period. It was active in Drogheda when the archbishop of Armagh, preaching about the pestilence, censured his congregation for its sins without offering it any consolation for its sufferings, from which castigation Gwynn concludes that his audience in March 1349 was not 'the few broken survivors of an almost annihilated population'.[2]

In the summer of 1349 the archbishop was commissioned by Edward III to go to Avignon to petition the pope for an extension of the 'Jubilee Grace of the Holy Year 1350 in favour of the two kingdoms of England and Ireland, without the obligation of a pilgrimage which it would be impossible for most of the King's subjects to perform'.[3] In the sermon which he preached before the pope, after describing the mutual animosity existing between the English, the Irish, and the Scots, he said that the pestilence was believed to have destroyed two-thirds of the English nation but he had been assured that it had not yet done any notable harm to either the Irish or the Scottish nation. Consequently no large number of English people would be allowed to leave that kingdom for fear that their absence would expose their country to a sudden attack from Scotland or Ireland.

Having made his plea for England, he then asserted that few Irishmen would be able to make the pilgrimage either, because ships were always scarce in Ireland and there was now a shortage of seamen also, 'for the plague has fallen most heavily on those who lived near the sea, and has found more victims among fisherfolk and sailors than among any other class of men'[4]

The various Irish annals add nothing of value to Clyn's account of 'The Great Pestilence'. The *Annals of Ulster* merely records under the date of 1349 that plague was universally active in the country that year and that it caused a great mortality.[5] The *Annals of Clonmacnoise* has the entry under the date of 1348: 'There was a Generall plague in Moylurg and all Ireland in generall, whereof the earle of Ulsters Grandchild Died.'[6] The remaining annals simply repeat with slight variations in wording the entry in the Ulster chronicle.

Barnes,[7] writing more than three centuries later about the impact of 'The Great Pestilence' on Ireland, affirms that it 'made great havoc of the *Englishman* in those Parts; especially about the Sea-Coasts: But as for those who were true *Irishmen* born, and dwelt in the hilly Countries, it scarce

48

just saluted them: So that they suffered but little or no loss thereby.' As this incidence of the disease is exactly what is to be expected from the aetiology of bubonic plague and the distribution of the indigenous population in fourteenth-century Ireland, in all probability Barnes' statement is accurate. As it seems extremely probable that an identical state of affairs occurred in fourteenth-century Scotland, a generous assumption is that 'The Great Pestilence' may have destroyed as much as one-thirtieth of each of their populations. It is not possible to estimate their national death-rolls, however, because no information is available about the sizes of their populations before 1348. Joyce[1] suggests that the multitude of small churches in districts that are now waste and solitary indicates that Ireland was well populated in the early ages of Christianity, and he believes that its population numbered between 2 and 3 million persons before the devastating wars of the sixteenth century. Assuming that it had a population of 3 million when the pandemic irrupted, it is not certain that the inference he has drawn from the derelict churches is correct. In the early ages of Christianity there were few townships in Ireland; the population was diffused like that of Saxon England. The subsequent development of urban settlements induced a movement of people from the remoter and less fertile districts into the growing towns, and the derelict churches therefore possibly represent a shift and not a reduction of the population.

Clyn's figure of 14,000 plague-deaths in Dublin is unacceptable if it refers to adult men only. In most of the urban outbreaks in India resulting from the last pandemic of the disease which erupted in 1898, about one-third of the population was attacked, with a case-mortality rate ranging from 70 to 80 per cent, giving an absolute mortality-rate that did not exceed one-quarter of the population. As the social and domestic conditions relative to house-rat infestation were probably not much different in Dublin in 1348 and in Indian towns in 1898, it is a reasonable supposition that the absolute plague-mortality in Dublin did not exceed one-quarter of its population, especially as there would inevitably have been a panic exodus from the city of all who could flee, which would greatly diminish the number of potential victims. If Clyn's figure were accepted, then at least another 10,000 deaths of women must be added to it, giving a death-roll that would require a population of at least 96,000, whereas with the exception of London no town in the British Isles had a population of 40,000 in 1348. His figure might be nearer the truth if it represents the male mortality in the area controlled from Dublin, known in later times as the 'English Pale'. That there was a heavy plague-mortality in some Irish townships is probable, for they would have the necessary concentration of house-rats to sustain the human disease. The dean and chapter

4   **49**

of Cashel petitioned Edward III in July 1351 to remit their taxes because of the loss of their revenues by the depredations of the king's Irish enemies and the mortality among their tenants from the pestilence;[1] but the effects of the depredations were quite possibly more serious than the mortality.

Detailed information about the progress and behaviour of 'The Great Pestilence' is available to some extent for England, as there are municipal, monastic, and manorial records of it for certain localities, and there are official reports of its local effects in the Close, the Fine, and the Patent Rolls. There is also a large volume of ecclesiastical notices concerning the institution of clergy to benefices falling vacant during the pandemic which has been studied by Thompson[2] and by Lunn,[3] and which Russell[4] considers to be of great value for the assessment of the overall mortality of the pandemic. For full information Russell's exhaustive study must be consulted, but three of his observations must be discussed here because of their bearing upon the evaluation of the English records of the pandemic.

The first is his observation that in the years immediately preceding 'The Great Pestilence' the maximum annual mortality showed two peaks, one of which occupied the months of January and February, the other those of October and November. Between these peaks the annual mortality fell to a minimum in June and July. Plague altered this picture by creating a single maximum peak in the months of August, September, and October; but this peak did not eliminate the other peaks, because the diseases which were killing people in England before plague arrived did not stop their lethal activities after its arrival. This is an incontrovertible fact that many writers about the 'Black Death' have ignored. Bubonic plague could not and did not abolish the other deadly diseases that were then prevalent; it merely reduced the number of their potential victims. The January–February peak represents the mortality from smallpox, typhus fever, and infections of the respiratory tract; the October–November peak represents the mortality from diphtheria, measles, St Anthony's Fire, and infections of the intestinal tract. It is a cardinal mistake therefore to assume that because a person died in 1348 or 1349 he or she necessarily died of bubonic plague. Statements such as: 'From the extant documents of both Church and State it is safe to assert that half the population of England was swept away by plague within a twelve-month',[5] are based on this false assumption and do a great disservice to history, because they mislead the student to believe that bubonic plague then exerted a morbid omnipotence which it has never possessed.

Russell's second observation—based on his study of the four eruptions of epidemic disease in this century, all of which he assumes were epidemics of bubonic plague—is that older men were particularly susceptible and that

children between the ages of 10 and 15 years had a lower rate of mortality than any other age group.[1] This is at variance with Hirst's authoritative statement which has already been quoted, so that if Russell's observation is correct it must mean that diseases other than bubonic plague, with different age incidences, were responsible for a part at least of the mortalities of the four eruptions.

His third observation is that the plague mortality-rate among the beneficed clergy was higher than among the inquisitions group, which he suggests is explicable on the supposition that 'the clergy were probably far older on an average than this group and thus subject to a higher mortality', whereas modern knowledge of the disease indicates that they would have suffered less from plague. They would of course have had naturally a higher mortality-rate from the constitutional breakdowns incidental to old age than the inquisitions group.

Lunn[2] emphasizes that an episcopal register is only of 'statistical value' for mortality studies if the cause of the voidance of a benefice is given when the institution is made. If the cause is given as 'plague' or 'pestilence' it may have been due to bubonic plague or to any one of the other lethal epidemic diseases that were a 'plague' to fourteenth-century recorders. If the incumbent's death can be shown to have occurred during the plague months, coincident with an unusual peak mortality among his parishioners, the possibility that he died from bubonic plague is heightened.

There were seventeen dioceses in fourteenth-century England and for the period of 'The Great Pestilence' thirteen of these provide statistical matter of greater or less value. The remaining four—London, Chichester, Carlisle, and Durham—supply no statistics at all.[3] Of the thirteen registers the most valuable are, in order of importance, Lichfield, Lincoln, and York, with Worcester and Hereford of considerably less value. In fact, however, according to Lunn's findings only the Lichfield register supplies reliable data. The Lincoln register contains 62 unspecified institutions as against 4 in the Lichfield register, while in the diocese of York—by reason of the exempt jurisdictions of the great archdeaconry of Richmond and the chapters of York, Ripon, Beverley, and Southwell—the archbishop only instituted to slightly more than half of the thousand or so parishes in his diocese, and these are the only ones that are recorded in the episcopal register.

As the registers of York and Lincoln had already been examined by Thompson,[4] Lunn confined his studies to the remaining eleven registers. Unfortunately five of these, namely Bath and Wells, Exeter, Winchester, Ely, and Norwich, do not give the causes of the voidance of their benefices. Because of these omissions and of obvious discrepancies in several of the

other registers, he is forced to conclude that 'included in the great number of plague institutions must be many which were not caused by death'.[1] Eventually Russell also is forced to a similar conclusion, as he is obliged to admit 'that the averages for most of the dioceses seem too high to be reconciled with the age-specific rates from the inquisitions post-mortems', and he adds: 'With some reluctance I suggest the possibility that resignations may have been included with deaths or that perhaps second deaths from the benefices may also'.[2]

How many of the beneficed clergy died from bubonic plague during 'The Great Pestilence'; how many died from co-existent communicable diseases or from metabolic disturbances or from other causes, and how many seized the opportunity supplied by 'The Great Pestilence' to desert the church for reasons of their own, will never be known. The man who could no longer abide the life of a parish priest had ample opportunity during that calamitous time to hide his identity in some distant part of England, and the church and plague would then conspire to ensure that his disappearance was credited to the mortality of 'The Great Pestilence', for the medieval church could be relied upon not to admit any desertions from its ordained ranks. The one fact that is certain is that no service is done to history by assuming that every vacant benefice in England during the time of 'The Great Pestilence' signified a clerical plague-death, and then arguing that the plague mortality-rate among the populace must have been commensurate with the suppositious mortality among the beneficed clergy. The aetiology of bubonic plague and the bionomics of the house-rat governed absolutely the incidence of the disease in every class of society, in every occupation, and in every part of the British Isles, and no historian has yet attempted to show how the degree of rat-infestation of the homes of the beneficed clergy compared with that of the cottages of the commonalty in the fourteenth century. And unless and until evidence has been presented that the dwellings of the beneficed clergy were more heavily rat-infested than those of their parishioners, there is no justification whatever for assuming that as a class they suffered any more severely from bubonic plague than the members of equivalent classes in that society.

When the density of population in 1348 is calculated for each English county from Russell's corrected population figures[3] (see table 3 and figure 1) and the area of each in square miles, the five most densely populated counties at that time were—in descending order of density—Norfolk, Bedfordshire, Suffolk, Northamptonshire, and Leicestershire, with densities covering the range from 119 to 101 persons to the square mile. The five least densely populated counties—in ascending order of density—were Cumberland,

Northumberland, Durham, Westmorland, and Cheshire, with densities covering the range from 20 to 25 persons to the square mile. These densities are so low that it would have been biologically impossible for bubonic plague to have spread over any of these counties in the fourteenth century, though it might by chance have been introduced into one or more of their towns and villages. Between these extremes the densities range from 99 persons per square mile in Rutlandshire down to 32 per square mile in Lancashire, with four counties—Devonshire, Worcestershire, Shropshire, and Yorkshire—having densities of between 50 and 60 persons to the square mile, and one, Staffordshire, having a density of 48 persons to the square mile. The epidemiology of bubonic plague renders it improbable that *P. pestis* could have been distributed by rat-contacts as epizootic plague in any English county in 1348–9 having an average density of population of less than 60 persons to the square mile.

CHAPTER 4

'THE GREAT PESTILENCE' IN BRITAIN

The spread of 'The Great Pestilence' is described in this chapter according to the extant records of its incidence in the various English dioceses as it moved, in a general way, from the south to the north of the country.

It will be seen that bubonic plague always struck hardest at seaports and coastal districts, and that stretches of marshland and fen acted as effective barriers against the spread of its epidemic activity. Sparsely populated hilly districts seem to have been usually only slightly affected, though as one would expect villages adjacent to a much-used route of communication were often comparatively severely hit.

It must be emphasized that as there was no national or municipal registration of deaths in fourteenth-century England, statements of percentage mortalities alleged to have occurred during 'The Great Pestilence' are, with rare exceptions, valueless; yet they are still copied from one historical work to another. It must also be borne in mind that people died from many other causes during 'The Great Pestilence' and that the normal expectation of life was low at that time.

Episcopal records of institutions to vacant benefices are frequently used as an indication of the mortality rate among the beneficed clergy, on the erroneous assumption that every vacancy was caused by the death of the previous incumbent from plague.

What was the risk of *P. pestis* infecting a beneficed clergyman in England in 1348–9? If his rectory or vicarage was of similar size and construction and was as heavily rat-infested as the cottages of his parishioners, he stood an equal chance of contracting bubonic plague in his dwelling as they did in theirs, *after* the bacterium had been introduced to his colony of house-rats. If his dwelling was more commodious and had an upper storey with a shingled or tiled instead of a thatched roof, his chance of contracting the disease would be lessened because the plague-fleas in the rats' nests would find it more difficult to attack him. If his dwelling was not rat-infested but the disease was epizootic among the house-rats in his parish, his risk of contracting bubonic plague would depend upon the way in which he discharged his pastoral duties.

It would increase with the frequency of his visits to the plague-sick and with the length of time he spent in the cottages where the rats were dying of plague, although it must be noted that not more than 12 per cent of the rat-fleas in those cottages would be capable of transmitting *P. pestis* from plague-rat to parson. In other words, however conscientious he was in the discharge of his pastoral duties, he ran considerably less risk of contracting the disease than the permanent occupants of the cottages. If he refused to visit the plague-sick, the conscientious discharge of the rest of his priestly duties would not expose him to much risk of contracting bubonic plague as long as his own dwelling was not rat-infested.

The crucial factor in the evaluation of the mortal significance of the vacancies among the beneficed clergy during 'The Great Pestilence', wherever they occurred, is the epidemiology of bubonic plague. When a high vacancy-rate is found in a locality which is unlikely to have sustained an epizootic of rat-plague, because of the presumptive low density of the house-rat population as determined by its geographical, habitable and commercial characters, there must be some other explanation than death from plague to account for the vacancies in the parishes in that locality. Where a high vacancy-rate coincides with conditions that favour the effective colonization of the locality by the house-rat, it can reasonably be presumed that a proportion—in some cases a considerable proportion—of the vacancies was caused by the deaths of the incumbents from plague. Undoubtedly exceptions occurred, in each of these categories during 'The Great Pestilence'; but they were exceptions that did not invalidate the laws governing the genesis, spread, and epidemicity of bubonic plague. Moreover it should be noted that even when the death of a parish priest can be rightly ascribed to plague, it does not necessarily follow that he contracted the infection in his own parish or that he died of it in his own parish.

The true numbers of plague-deaths among the beneficed clergy will never be known. All that can safely be said is that panic fear of the disease will undoubtedly have caused many voidances, through resignation or desertion, and that records of plague-deaths in the episcopal registers may in many cases be due to hearsay, or to exaggeration.

If *P. pestis* in its first incursion invaded England by way of Melcombe Regis, it entered through the county of Dorset, which was a part of the ecclesiastical jurisdiction of the see of Salisbury, a diocese which offers a convenient area from which to begin an examination in detail of this irruption of bubonic plague into England. Figure 3 illustrates some of the possible routes by which the disease spread, the chief places it attacked, and its

3. The incidence of 'The Great Pestilence' of 1348 in England. Maximum percentage mortality rates of the beneficed clergy, by county, are as follows: Beds. 37, Bucks. 37, Cambs. 52, Ches. 33, Cornwall 56, Derbys. 58, Devon 51, Glos. 47, Hants. 49, Herefs. 48, Herts. 35, Hunts. 34, Leics. 36, Lincs. 51, Northants. 37, Notts. 36, Oxon. 34, Salop 43, Som. 47, Staffs. 34, Surrey 56, Warw. 36, Worcs. 48.

supposed mortal effects upon a particular class of the English society—the beneficed clergy.

Le Baker's report of the depopulation of the Dorset ports is a typical plague rumour exaggerated by oral repetition; but like most rumours it had some foundation in fact. In September 1352 an edict stated that no crops, victuals, or men were to be removed from the Isle of Portland during the king's pleasure as the isle had been so depopulated by 'The Great Pestilence' that the surviving men were too few to defend it against enemy attacks.[1] There was an institution to the vacant rectory of Wareham St Michael on 17 July 1348, and Lunn has suggested that this may mark the beginning of clerical mortality from plague in the diocese of Salisbury, though there is no proof that the previous incumbent died of plague. Plague has, however, been held responsible for the voidance in mid-September of the churches of Bridport, Tyneham in Purbeck, Lulworth, and Cerne, due to the deaths of the incumbents.[2] The suggestion that about half the benefices in the county were made void by the deaths of their incumbents from plague is refuted by the epidemiology of the disease, because even though every vicarage in the county was sufficiently rat-infested to engender the human disease, they were so widely separated from one another—with a few urban exceptions—that *P. pestis* could not have been introduced to the house-rats in half of them. One other authentic record of the activity of plague in Dorset survives in the statement that the king had noted in July 1348 that 'the mortality of men' in the prebend of Bere Regis and Charminster in the church of St Mary Salisbury 'in the present pestilence is so great that the lands thereof lie untilled and other profits are lost'.[3]

Although there is no doubt that the neighbouring county of Wiltshire was involved in 'The Great Pestilence' to some extent, the extant records of its involvement seem to be few. In 1334 there were 41 tenants on the manor of Durrington, but 18 holdings were vacant in 1349, presumably because of the deaths of the tenants. No assize rents were paid on the manor of Tidworth as all the tenants had died, and on that of Broughton Gifford only one freeman was alive in August 1349.[4] Rees asserts that all the bond tenants of Westdene and East Grinstead were dead before September 1349,[5] whereas according to Miss Scott[6] three tenants were alive in 1350, though seven free tenants had also died on this manor. The priory of Ivychurch lost its prior and 13 of its 14 canons during 'The Great Pestilence'. Inferentially they died of bubonic plague, but they may simply have scattered as soon as the disease appeared in their priory.

In the Berkshire archdeaconry of the diocese of Salisbury the average annual number of episcopal institutions from 1330 to 1375 was about 50;

but the exact number for the years from 1345 to 1351 respectively was 30, 56, 54, 190, 145, 93, and 66. How many of the benefices were rendered void by the deaths of their incumbents from plague will never certainly be known. The headships of Bromhall nunnery, Newbury hospital, and Poughly priory were made void during 1348–9, the last house twice.[1]

Lodge finds gaps that she believes to be significant in the Court Rolls and Ministers' Accounts during what were probably the worst years of the pandemic.[2] For example the manor roll of Wollstone has a gap from 1348 to 1352, and that of Brightwalton from 1344 to 1350. At Newbury a tanning-mill that was so busy before 'The Great Pestilence' that a half part of it was worth 26s. 8d., was worth nothing after the pestilence. The assize rents, however, remained unchanged. Whatever changes had occurred among the holders during the pandemic no difficulty was experienced in letting this kind of land. There was, however, an enormous increase in defects of work from 16s. 4d. to 55s. 10d., probably on account of deaths. From a comparison of the state of the manor of Woolstone in 1348 and 1352, Lodge concludes that the effects of 'The Great Pestilence' were very marked and that far from being an exception to other manors, 'lying as it does on the edge of the Downs, and having so large a stock of sheep and other animals, it probably suffered less than some of the more purely arable estates'. In fact, however, as *R. rattus* naturally congregated where the foodstuffs and fodder of the domestic animals were stored, if it was the only manor in the county with 'so large a stock of sheep and other animals' it was in all probability the only manor that was seriously attacked by bubonic plague.

The condition of the manors of Crookham and Padworth in 1349 has also been described.[3] On the former, where the value of the rents and services of the customary tenants had previously been worth £10 a year, all the tenants were dead and their holdings in the lord's hands lay useless and uncultivated as no one would take them. On the latter the lord died in May 1349 and his widow a month later, possibly of plague which 'made fearful ravages in the neighbourhood'. At the subsequent *post mortem* inquisition the pleas and profits of the manor were reported as worth nothing because all the tenants were dead.

Rees[4] finds that during 'The Great Pestilence' all the fee tenants at Newbury and all the villeins and cottars of Bokeland died, and that there were several deaths among the bondmen on the manors of Morton and Crookham. By contrast it has been remarked that though the town of Wallingford was involved in 'The Great Pestilence', its effects there 'must not be exaggerated, as no great falling off of business is revealed by the records of the borough courts'.

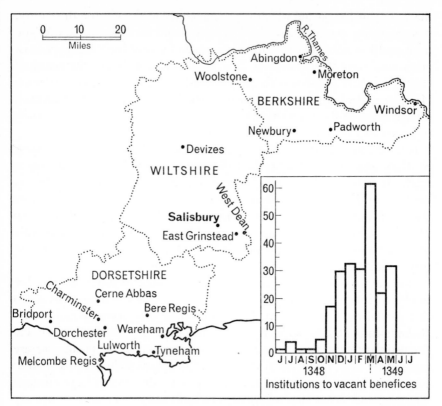

4. Plague in the diocese of Salisbury, 1348-9.

DIOCESE OF SALISBURY

At the time of 'The Great Pestilence' the diocese of Salisbury was co-extensive with the counties of Dorsetshire, Wiltshire, and Berkshire (see figure 4). Lunn was unable to calculate the mortality-rates among the beneficed clergy in the three counties because the episcopal register is defective during the plague period. The institutions to vacant benefices are recorded fully up to 8 March 1349, but thereafter there are two blank periods, to wit, for twenty days after 8 March and for ten days after 20 April. He estimates that the institutions in March averaged two a day, and he suggests that as it was the month with the maximum institutions the pandemic reached its peak in this diocese in February. He may be right; but his suggestion runs counter to the usual epidemiological behaviour of bubonic plague in a temperate climate

Because of the large area of moorland which occupies the central part of

the county of Devon and which was uninhabited in the fourteenth century, it is practically certain that bubonic plague could not have spread overland from south to north Devon and that its inland spread from the south coast ports must have been restricted. It is unlikely therefore that the beneficed clergy in inland parishes such as Holsworthy, Okehampton, and Moreton Hampstead died of plague in their parishes during 'The Great Pestilence', though some of them may have been bitten by 'blocked' fleas during visits to Exeter or the ports and fishing villages of the county.

If the deaths recorded among the canons of the collegiate church of Ottery St Mary were plague-deaths, the pandemic was prevalent there in August 1348.[1] It must also have been active at Honiton, if *P. pestis* killed the 23 brethren of the 26 in the Cistercian house of Newenham.[2] Lunn concludes that 'in Honiton deanery, cloister and parish suffered alike'. At Exeter two priors of St Nicholas died in succession in March and April 1349, supposedly of plague, and the death of the prebendary of Hayes early in November 1348 may indicate the presence of plague in the city then.[1]

If the death of the incumbent of St Perran Uthnoe in July 1348[2] was due to plague, it almost certainly signifies that the disease was brought by sea to that part of the Cornish coast. Plague may have been active in and around Bodmin during the winter of 1349 if it killed the prior and all but two of the Augustinian house there;[1] but typhus fever, smallpox, or pneumonia are more likely causes of death at that time of the year. Bodmin is also said to have been so populous in 1351 that 1,500 persons died there of a pestilence.[3] The pestilence is not said to have been bubonic plague and no contemporary evidence is supplied for what would seem to be a dubious statement.

DIOCESE OF EXETER

In the fourteenth century the diocese of Exeter comprised the counties of Devon and Cornwall. As figure 5 shows, it had the longest coastline relative to its area of any of the English bishoprics, and as the bulk of its population undoubtedly lived in a coastal zone of varying width, the heaviest plague-mortalities among the beneficed clergy must have occurred in the coastal and estuarine parishes. Up to a point Lunn's figures for the diocesan institutions conform to this distribution; but there are several noteworthy exceptions, such as the deaneries of Holsworthy, Chulmleigh, Moreton Hampstead, and Tavistock, where his figures are too high in comparison with the coastal deaneries to be acceptable as plague-mortalities in the absence of conclusive contemporary evidence. It seems probable that either some deadly communicable disease like smallpox was concurrently active during 'The

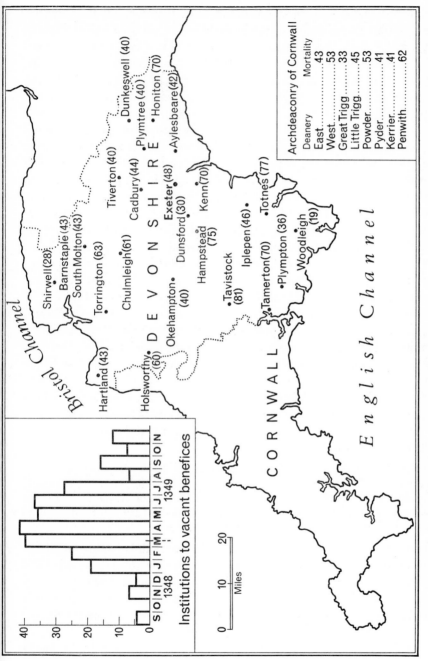

Archdeaconry of Cornwall

Deanery	Mortality
East	43
West	53
Great Trigg	33
Little Trigg	45
Powder	53
Pyder	41
Kerrier	41
Penwith	62

Bristol Channel

English Channel

CORNWALL

DEVONSHIRE

Shirwell (28)
Barnstaple (43)
South Molton (43)
Torrington (63)
Tiverton (40)
Dunkeswell (40)
Plymtree (40)
Honiton (70)
Cadbury (44)
Aylesbeare (42)
Chulmleigh (61)
Exeter (48)
Dunsford (30)
Kenn (70)
Hampstead (75)
Okehampton (40)
Iplepen (46)
Totnes (77)
Hartland (43)
Tavistock (81)
Plympton (36)
Holsworthy (60)
Tamerton (70)
Woodleigh (19)

Institutions to vacant benefices

S O N D J F M A M J J A S O N
1348   1349

Miles
0   10   20

5. Plague in the diocese of Exeter, 1348–9. The figures in brackets attached to each deanery represent the maximum possible percentage mortality among the beneficed clergy.

61

Great Pestilence' in these inland deaneries or that many of the vacancies were not due to the deaths of the incumbents. It has been inferred from a blank in the *Registrum Commune* for 1349 that 'The Great Pestilence' completely paralysed all diocesan business,[1] but Lunn contends that this inference is erroneous and that the record for 1349 has been lost. Bishop Grandisson, like his counterpart of Norwich, feared that the pestilence would deplete the ranks of the clergy much more seriously than it did. Lunn's studies of the registers show that this fear was unfounded, and also that the statement (see above p. 41) about a flood of semi-literate widowers entering the priesthood is untrue. A figure of 320 has been given as the number of benefices to which institutions were made in this diocese in 1349 compared with 26 in 1348.[2] Of the former number 173 or 54 per cent were made during the four months from March to June inclusive. As the plague-fleas would normally be in hibernation for a part of this period, it is uncertain how many of the vacancies were caused by the deaths of the incumbents from bubonic plague.

For Somerset Bradford comments: 'If the mortality was at all commensurate with the rest of England, one third of the inhabitants must have perished';[3] adding: 'An eloquent silence in most of the records during the year of the plague shows the extent of the visitation. Presentations of deaths increase alarmingly, there are notes of heriots due not paid, "because there is nothing living there"; many holdings were in the lords' hands through lack of tenants; everywhere the empty houses of the tenants were fast falling into ruins.'

In his article in the *Victoria County History of Somerset*, Scott Holmes declares that the first notice of plague in the county is Bishop Ralph's issue of prayers for general use in the diocese in August 1348.[4] Scott Holmes also tells us that the disease

raged at Evercreech in November, and devastated Castle Cary and Ansford in December. In Bristol, Clevedon, Weston-super-mare and Bridgwater the mortality amounted to fifty per cent. Grass grew high in the streets of Bristol, for there were not people to trample it down...The monks of Glastonbury, fell from eighty to forty, and at Bath to half their previous number.

The average number of brethren in the priory at Bath before the pestilence was about 40, but in a *Clerical Subsidy* of 1377 only 16 were recorded and this number was never much exceeded up to the dissolution of the priory in 1539. The abbey of Athelney also lost some of its members and Scott Holmes concludes that monasticism in this county never recovered from the ravages of the pandemic. Rees states that by the beginning of August 1348 most of the tenants of Frome Braunch were dead and that there were deaths among those of North and South Cadbury.[5]

It would be of interest to know the authentic contemporary source from which Scott Holmes obtained his plague-mortality figure of 50 per cent in the four places he names, and whether this figure is intended to mean half the population in each town or half the number of the plague-stricken. The latter rate is feasible; the former is nonsense.

The statement that grass grew in the streets of a town in consequence of the slaughter of the townsfolk by bubonic plague is one of the most popular of 'Black Death' *clichés*. If it happened in plague-time it was because all the townsfolk who could do so wisely left the town until the epidemic subsided.

Turning to Bristol it is not possible now to assess its degree of affliction by 'The Great Pestilence', but some idea of its ordeal emerges from the grant of a royal pardon in November 1349

to the good men and parishioners of the church of St Cross of the Temple, in the suburb of Bristol, for acquiring without the king's licence from the prior to the Hospital of St John of Jerusalem in England, parson of that church, half an acre of land contiguous to their churchyard, they having acquired the same for the enlargement of the churchyard which has been filled up by bodies buried in the last pestilence[1]

There is also an authentic reference to the activity of the pandemic in the county in a petition from the Carthusian priory of Wytham, dated 16 January 1354, affirming that all its servants and household died 'in the last pestilence'.[2]

DIOCESE OF WELLS

The diocese of Bath and Wells, which was contained within the county of Somerset in the fourteenth century (see figure 6), comprised the arch-deaconries of Bath, Taunton, and Wells. Most of the vacant benefices in the deanery of Frome—one of the 6 deaneries constituting the archdeaconry of Wells—were in parishes in the valley of the river Frome, which runs north-wards to join the Avon. The river Cary runs westwards in this archdeaconry to cross Sedgemoor and empty into the Parret, so that: 'in seasons of heavy rain access to many parishes was made impassable and at the best of times it was a watery waste of swamp'.[3] As the summer and autumn of 1348 were exceptionally wet, the valley of the Cary and probably the entire area of Sedgemoor must have been a waste of water, which makes it almost certain that *P. pestis* did not enter either of the monasteries of Glastonbury or Athelney in the body of an infected house-rat. If it entered either it could only have been in the stomach of a 'blocked' flea, in which case the subse-quent development of an outbreak of bubonic plague in either house would depend absolutely upon their respective degree of rat-infestation, and in view

of their isolated situations and their watery surroundings it is probable that the house-rat had not colonized either of them in 1348.

The reduction in the monastic personnel of Glastonbury reported by Scott Holmes could have been effected in the absence from the monastery of bubonic plague. Some two hundred years later the Tudor physician, Boorde, who had been educated as a youth in the Carthusian Order, wrote to the prior of Hinton Charterhouse in Somersetshire: 'I am nott able to byd

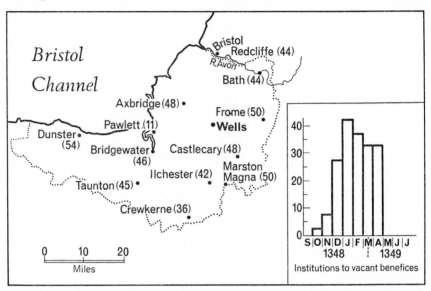

6. Plague in the diocese of Bath and Wells, 1348–9. The figures in brackets attached to each deanery represent the maximum possible percentage mortality among the beneficed clergy.

the rugorosite off your relygyon'.[1] There were in all probability similarly minded inmates of Glastonbury in 1348 who, after being marooned for months in a waste of water and terrified by exaggerated rumours of the omnipotence of the pestilence, seized the opportunity to disappear and start a fresh life elsewhere.

Lunn confesses that he is puzzled by the fact that the most mountainous deanery in this diocese, that of Dunster, had the largest number of vacant benefices: 'In the recesses of Exmoor itself there were few parishes which escaped—Dulverton, Winsford, Exford, Cutcombe, Stoke Pero, Porlock and Culbone form one unbroken chain of parishes which saw a change of parson in the plague.'[2] His siting of these parishes is faulty, however, as a study of the One-Inch Ordnance Survey map of this deanery (National Grid Sheet 164) will show. Of the parishes he names only Stoke Pero and Exford are

within Exmoor; the others all lie on the fringes of the moor, and in the fourteenth century all these hamlets were accessible—at any rate during the summer months—from either Porlock Bay or the ports of Minehead and Watchet, while Exmoor was an important grazing ground for the breed of short-fleeced sheep for which England was then noted. It seems a reasonable presumption that these sheep would be driven down from the moor to the fringe hamlets to be sheared or slaughtered to obviate the haulage of bulky and awkward loads over hill-tracks across wind-swept expanses of moorland. The ports of Minehead and Watchet, which probably handled this wool trade, would very probably be involved in 'The Great Pestilence' by coastal shipping plying to and from Bristol; and from these ports plague would tend to spread inland in its characteristic radiating fashion wherever the house-rat was present in sufficient density to support an epizootic of the disease. The wool trade would encourage and assist it to colonize the five fringe hamlets, but it is questionable whether by 1348 it had penetrated to Exford and Stoke Pero in sufficient numbers to sponsor epidemic plague. Lunn's study of the institutions reveals that diocesan business proceeded normally to the end of September 1348, but was then more or less interrupted until after April 1349. In January of that year the bishop issued a confessional mandate in which he described the extenuating circumstances that made a relaxation of the confessional imperative.

The contagion of pestilence in these days of ours spreading everywhere [he explained] hath left many parish churches and other livings in our diocese with their parishioners desolate and without parson and priest; and since no priests are found, who are willing either in zeal of devotion or for any stipend to accept the pastoral care of the aforesaid places or to visit the sick and minister the church sacraments to them, perchance by reason of the infection and the horror of contagion: therefore many folk, as we have heard, died without the sacraments[1].

This grim picture is challenged, however, by Lunn's assertion that the internal evidence of the episcopal register 'shows little sign of any disturbance of routine in the diocese'. As the bishop apparently isolated himself at Wiveliscombe as soon as plague appeared in Somerset, he was probably one of those contemporary chroniclers who wrote their reports of 'The Great Pestilence' from hearsay and who have thereby left exaggerated and misleading accounts of it to posterity.

Excluding the deanery of the Forest of Dean to the west of the Severn, which was part of the see of Hereford, the county of Gloucestershire together with Worcestershire and the southern half of Warwickshire constituted the fourteenth-century diocese of Worcester (see figure 7).

Graham[2] states that the county was invaded by plague in the early spring

of 1349, cites Seyer for the statement that Bristol suffered severely, and comments that in the rest of the county the mortality was seemingly not nearly so great as in East Anglia. Her note that the survivors among the clergy were discontented with their salaries and tried to supplement them by

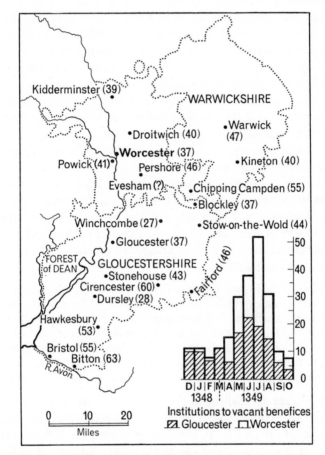

7. Plague in the diocese of Worcester, 1348–9. The figures in brackets attached to each deanery represent the maximum possible percentage mortality among the beneficed clergy.

wandering out of their parishes and charging higher fees for masses for the dead is of significance, even though it is possibly an unacknowledged echo from Langland.

At Ham, near Berkeley, as much land was escheated to the lord in 1349 as required 1,444 days' labour to clear at harvest and this debt is ascribed to the deaths of the tenants from plague. At Horsleigh priory some 80 tenants

66

were reported to be dead.[1] It seems probable that Llanthony priory was involved in the city's visitation because Lunn reports that in this house 19 of the 30 canons died during 'The Great Pestilence', a mortality-rate of 63·3 per cent. But according to Russell[2] 26 of them died, a mortality-rate of 86·6 per cent.

'The Great Pestilence' was apparently at its peak in Worcestershire in the summer of 1349, but it is as usual difficult to form an accurate estimate of the proportion of the population that was destroyed by it.[3] The inference that the numerous institutions to vacant benefices between March 1348 and July 1349—67 presentations to 138 parishes, in some instances more than once—represent a heavy death-roll among the clergy is of dubious validity. The distress in the county generally seems to have been intense and numerous instances have been cited of decayed rents, including the report by the royal escheators after the death of Bishop Wulstan that a rent deficiency of some £84 had accumulated during the three months' vacancy, of which they had found it impossible to collect more than £38 'on account of the dearth of tenants and of customary tenants...who had all died in the deadly pestilence which raged in the lands of the bishopric'.[4] The monastery of Evesham was so ravaged by plague that special provision was made for a mass to be celebrated 'for the souls of the brethren departed in this fearful pestilence'.[5] No mortality statistics are supplied however.

'The potters of Hanleye, who used to pay 13s. yearly for clay', disappeared during 'The Great Pestilence', and at Havercote the rents were reduced from 10s. to 3s. 4d. through the loss of tenants.[6]

Plague reached the county of Warwickshire in the early spring of 1349 and Warwick and the adjacent parishes seem to have suffered most severely, 76 of the 175 benefices in the county changing incumbents during the year.[7] The religious houses also suffered badly. Kenilworth priory lost three superiors in succession between May and August, and 12 of the 15 sisters in Henwood nunnery died. Other reported victims were the abbot of Combe, the prior of Wootton, the abbess of Polesworth, the prioress of Henwood, the archdeacon and the prior of Coventry, and several of the city clergy. In the priory of Nuneaton, where there were 89 nuns in 1328, only 46 were present in 1370, about 40 in 1459, and 23 in 1507.[8] At Lapworth 21 names disappear from the village records after 1349, in many instances possibly representing whole families.[9] Alcester too must have been grievously afflicted by the pestilence because a *post-mortem* inquisition in 1350 records that tenements of the rental value of 100s. were then in the lord's hands owing to the deaths of their tenants[10] Lunn states that Warwick lost three of its priests and that the prior of Coventry died during 'The Great Pestilence', but he remarks

that the episcopal register records no unusual mortality among the inmates of the priory. The only reference that Rees gives to Warwickshire is that at Wappenbury there was a considerable decrease in the rents during 1349.[1]

DIOCESE OF WORCESTER

The episcopal register contains an early record of a sanitary attempt to control bubonic plague. In a letter written in April 1349 to the rural dean of Worcester, the bishop commanded that burial of all plague victims should take place outside the city walls in the cemetery of St Oswald's hospital. Two reasons are advanced for this injunction. The cathedral church was totally insufficient and secondly the manifold dangers which would threaten the citizens, the monks and others gaining access to the cathedral if burial of corpses were permitted during the pestilence. The sacrist of the cemetery of St Oswald was ordered to admit the burial of all dead belonging to the cathedral church, so long as the mortality continued.[2]

Plague appeared first in the Gloucestershire deaneries of the diocese (see figure 7) and apparently spread from them into the deanery of Warwick, which took in the left bank of the Avon and was intersected by its tributaries, the Arrow and the Alne.[3] Lunn finds that most of the vacancies occurred among the benefices in the watersheds of these rivers. It is noteworthy that he apparently found no record of institutions in the deanery of Evesham in the episcopal register in view of the report about the monastery's visitation by plague. A majority of the recorded clerical deaths in the archdeaconry of Worcester occurred in the hilly country in the north of the county. Here, in the deaconry of Kidderminster, the parsons of the four neighbouring parishes of Clent, Belbroughton, Pedmore and Hagley are reported to have died during 'The Great Pestilence'. Anxiety about the rumoured havoc wrought by the pestilence is the main theme of a royal letter to the prior of Worcester in September 1349. 'The keeper of the see', Lunn writes, 'was urged in terms of anxious terror to exhort the people to resort to the efficacy of prayer "so that utter destruction shall not ensue". In one passage the king's hope is that if the people will cast out from their hearts spiritual wickedness, "this scourge of the air...may depart from them".'[4]

It is noteworthy that Edward III subscribed to the general belief in the atmospheric source of 'The Great Pestilence' under divine control; but his anxiety about its havoc in the diocese was perhaps somewhat misplaced in view of Lunn's declaration that 'research where we will in a host of documents, any evidence of a complete paralysis in daily activities is sought in vain. In no other diocese is that calm orderly development of diocesan

business demonstrated so well as in the see of Worcester',[1] in spite of the bishop's death at this time. The royal apprehension is understandable when the news of the bishopric's affliction, magnified and distorted by the panic fear of the reporters, reached the king at Westminster.

In the fourteenth century the Forest of Dean probably had a number of small settlements of charcoal-burners within its confines and a string of hamlets around its outskirts, where it gave employment to iron-smelters and swineherds. It must have been through such trade channels that *P. pestis* was enabled to cross the Severn and invade some of these settlements.

In November 1349 Edward III granted a 'remission to Guy de Briane of 40 *l.* of the farm of 120 *l.* for the keeping of the castle of St Briavels and the forest of Dene...from Michaelmas next for his life, the issues and profits of the castle and forest being so diminished owing to the present pestilence and other causes that the farm cannot be paid.'[2] This concession was repeated with the substitution of 30 for the 40 *l.* to be remitted.[3] Whichever grant was actually made, the sum in either case was so large a proportion of the farm that it must represent a considerable degree of impoverishment of the estate, and a part of this depreciation was apparently caused by the plague-deaths of some of the tenants and bondsmen. The royal grant explicitly states, however, that the pestilence was not the sole cause of the decline in the value of the estate; there were other causes but unfortunately they are not specified. Nevertheless their existence erases the pen-picture of a sable Apollyon, under the sobriquet of the 'Black Death', stalking through the forest and sowing the deadly pestilence wherever human beings were encountered. Yet this is the kind of literary picture of the second pandemic that is frequently presented, and it would still be absurd if Apollyon were depicted as a black rat. In all probability what actually happened in the Forest of Dean was that *P. pestis* sneaked into one or two of the hamlets on the fringe of the forest in the body of an infected house-rat or the stomach of a 'blocked' flea, and that in some of the cottages an epizootic developed among the house-rats. When these had been exterminated the cottagers were attacked and the invaded hamlets may possibly have lost a third of their inhabitants from bubonic plague. Fugitives and rumour then depopulated the De Briane estate.

THE DIOCESE OF HEREFORD

The fourteenth-century diocese of Hereford was much larger than the present one as it included Gloucestershire west of the Severn, Herefordshire, and the southern half of Shropshire. Lunn finds the episcopal register defective in two respects, to wit, it records no cause for the vacancy in a benefice,

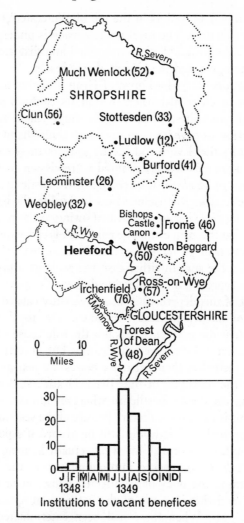

8. Plague in the diocese of Hereford, 1349. The figures in brackets attached to each deanery represent the maximum possible percentage mortality among the beneficed clergy.

and it contains no record of any vacancy caused by plague in any one of the religious houses in the diocese. Apparently it did not occur to him that the absence of any such record signified that no religious house in this relatively isolated diocese was involved in 'The Great Pestilence'. He suggests that the death of the vicar of Westbury-on-Severn in January 1349 was probably due to plague, and that as the maximum of institutions occurred in the following July the pandemic reached its peak in June. He notes that the

parish of Knill in the deanery of Leominster (see figure 8) was one of two benefices which were vacant twice during the pestilence. In the deanery of Frome both the parishes of Great and Little Collington were vacant twice and in 1352 they were consolidated. 'It was then stated, that because of the pestilence the diminished value of both livings was itself hardly sufficient to maintain one priest.'[1] Lunn declares that the deanery of Irchenfield, which embraced the triangle of land lying between the rivers Wye and Monnow, 'was the plague-patch of the diocese', although he found no church in it void of its priest twice during 'The Great Pestilence', whereas there were three institutions to the vicarage of Ross-on-Wye in the contiguous deanery of Ross.[2] As this little town may have been an important river-port in the fourteenth century, it is possible that the deanery of Ross was the real plague-patch of the diocese. Lunn concludes from his study of the episcopal register that 'The Great Pestilence' seemingly did not interfere in any way with the bishop's discharge of his diocesan duties, and that throughout the plague-year Trilleck moved normally about his see.[3] But with due respect to the memory of a man who was fortified by an implicit faith, it is extremely difficult to imagine a fourteenth-century bishop moving normally about a see in which bubonic plague was extensively epidemic. If Bishop Trilleck's episcopal movements were normal, it was because in all probability there were only a few scattered and localized incursions of the disease into his diocese.

As a river is often a barrier to the spread of bubonic plague, it is noteworthy that the Severn flows in a great curve through the county of Shropshire dividing it into two unequal and dissimilar parts—hilly towards the west, while nearly all the county south of the Severn is upland. A large part of the county was covered by great forests, the largest of which, Worf Forest, originally measured at least 8 by 6 miles in area.[4] Auden says that in 1235 a survey of the county's forests indicated that it was densely wooded, and in another context he remarks: 'The jurisdiction of the Long Forest covered a great part of the south-east of Shropshire...It was disafforested by degrees during the thirteenth century, but *boscs*—i.e. tracts of woodland—were retained.'[5]

As the unquiet state of the Welsh Border discouraged habitation outside the immediate protection of the Border castles, it seems a reasonable assumption that apart from the little towns of Oswestry and Ludlow, the bulk of the county's population lived east of the Severn in the area circumscribed by the towns of Shrewsbury, Whitchurch, Market Drayton, and Bridgnorth. If 'The Great Pestilence' struck anywhere in the county, it would therefore be in this area in all probability.

Bubonic plague in the British Isles

Among the many assertions of local historians that 'The Great Pestilence' devastated the particular county, town or parish of their study, it is refreshing to find Bellett[1] affirming that there is no record of its invasion of Bridgnorth. It is a pity that he spoils this declaration somewhat by asserting immediately afterwards that Shropshire suffered very severely from the pestilence without supplying any contemporary confirmative evidence. It is a remarkable fact that most English local historians who mention disease at all appear to take pride in claiming that the localities in which they are interested were devastated by the 'Black Death', as if such a devastation conferred some peculiar honour upon the locality. Owen and Blakeway[2] likewise do not claim that Shrewsbury was devastated by 'The Great Pestilence', and Wright[3] is similarly silent about its involvement of Ludlow; but four other local historians present notices of its alleged activity in the county. Watkins-Pitchford[4] states that 13 of the 26 incumbents in the district around Morville died of plague within four months in 1349. Peake[5] affirms that 'two vicars of Ellesmere and one vicar of Welsh Hampton died in the same year of the Pestilence...and these events show that it must have been very fatal in this neighbourhood'; a fallacious assumption that recurs repeatedly in the literature of plague. Auden[6] alleges that the vicar of Montford died of it in 1349. Walker[7] notes that an inquisition of Lilleshall abbey in 1353 found that the underwood of a certain park was then worth nothing because all the customary buyers had perished in the 'Great Plague'. The inquisition also mentioned 'a certain foreign wood, the underwood of which used to be worth before the pestilence 3s. 4d., and now it is only worth 12d. beyond the sustentation of the house'. It recorded also that the land belonging to the abbey, which was worth £15 in 1330, was worth only £10 after the pestilence because there were no tenants. 'One Abbot died 1350', Walker continues, 'another 1353, and the deaths of the Canons are unrecorded, but in our excavations [in the abbey ruins] we found masses of lime in various places many feet deep of which no explanation can be given why it was there. It may have been used to bury those who died of plague.'[8] In which case, if it had been so used, the bones of the victims would have been found preserved in the lime.

A common type of reference to the 'Black Death' to be found in local histories is the one given by Auchmuty.[9] He asserts that in four unspecified Shropshire parishes 158 tenants were killed by plague in 1349, but he omits to name the contemporary source from which he obtained this report.

Rees[10] supplies several references to the loss of rents in the county after 'The Great Pestilence'. At Yokelton the rents of assize of free tenants fell from £8 to 30s.; at Colmere and Hampton from £4 to 10s.; in the hundred of

Bradefeud from £16 to £8; at Wentemore from £5 to 40s.; at Schelve from 36s. to 26s. 6d.; at Harlegh from £4 to 10s.; at Wylely from 20s. to 12s., and he notes that all these reductions were specifically attributed to the pestilence.

Lunn affirms that the lay records taken in conjunction with the institutions in Staffordshire prove that the county was little affected by 'The Great Pestilence', which is not surprising in view of its low density of population in 1348 and its large area of forest, of which Cannock Chase is now the vestigial remnant. He mentions that the prior of the small Benedictine house of Sandwell died in June 1349, supposedly of plague, and that only one monk was living there in 1361.[1]

Rees[2] reports that at Great Wyrleye the rent was reduced from £5 to £3 in consequence of the pestilence and the poverty of the tenants.

On 1 July 1351 Edward III granted a pardon

to Roger de Elmrugge of 8 *l.* yearly, as well for the past as the future, of the farm of 38 *l.*....for keeping of the lands late of Laurence de Hastynges, earl of Pembroke, in Wyginton and Tomworth, co. Stafford...as it appears by a petition of the said Roger that on account of the deadly pestilence lately in those parts the lands are so much deteriorated in value that he will not be able to answer the whole farm without too great a loss.[3]

Lunn is emphatic that the tragedy at Henwood nunnery (see above p. 67) was an exceptional one and 'can in no wise be taken as a typical example of claustral mortality'. He remarks that there must have been many religious houses which completely escaped 'The Great Pestilence' and he mentions Norwich as an example, while in others such as Canterbury the death-roll was extremely light.[4]

In the deanery of Stoneleigh (see figure 9) the benefices of Kenilworth and Fenny Compton were each vacant twice during the pandemic. Lunn stresses that there is a distinct and sharp contrast between the benefices in the deaneries of Arden and Stoneleigh where vacancies occur and those in the deaneries of Coventry and Marton, the latter having physical features that are considerably more rugged than the former. In the deanery of Marton the vacancies were nearly all confined to the valley of the Itchen, while in that of Coventry most of them were located in the watershed of the Avon. In the deanery of Stoneleigh the voided parishes were all situated in the Avon valley; no parish in the hill country was made vacant. Similarly in the deanery of Arden, which included broad acres in the valley of the Blythe, the vacancies were all in the valley; none occurred among the hill parishes.

'The Great Pestilence' seems to have invaded Derbyshire in May 1349.[5] The total number of benefices subject to episcopal institution was 108 and

the average annual voidance through death or resignation during the four-teenth century was 7, whereas in 1349 there were 63 institutions and 41 in 1350. The abbeys of Beauchief, Dale, and Darley, and the priories of Gresley, St James Derby, and King's Mead, all lost their superiors during the plague-year, and Cox avers that the county was pre-eminent in desolation in so far as the episcopal registers testify and that it lost two-thirds of its beneficed clergy within twelve months. 'In Derbyshire', he declares, 'no class of the community seems to have been spared, and no place was too remote or healthily situated to escape desolation.' As a disciple of the 'Black Death' he seems to be pre-eminent among the writers of his time. Lander[1] on the contrary remarks that there are very few indications of the extent of this county's involvement in 'The Great Pestilence', but she says that Drakelow was very severely afflicted by it and names Derby, Eckington, Darley, Langwith, Mugginton, Barlborough, Bolsover, Horsley, Longford, Sutton-on-the-Hill, Willington, Pentrich, Beauchief, and Dale as places that were attacked by it. She notes that a *post-mortem* inquisition in 1351 concerning a lead-mine at Ashwell, which was usually worth a rent of £20, recorded that it was then worth only 20s. for lack of labour.

Lunn affirms that the average plague-mortality rate of this county's beneficed clergy was almost twice as high as that of Staffordshire.[2] He based this statement upon the assumption that the records of the plague-deaths of incumbents in the Lichfield episcopal register are absolutely reliable; but in the absence of an official system of registration of deaths such an assump-tion is unfortunately not justifiable, especially as there is no knowledge of the criteria employed by the episcopal registrar to check the truth of the hearsay reports he received about supposed and actual clerical deaths.

Lunn remarks that the orographical features of the two deaneries of Repton and Derby

have much in common; both are watered by wide river valleys with undulating land that rises to a level of some two hundred feet above the sea. Of the two, Derby is the more rugged...The northern half in the middle ages was densely forested... each parish priest on the fringe of this wooded area perished in 1349 (i.e. those of Crich, Pentrich, Heanor, Mugginton (both modities) and Horsley). Pentrich was one of those few churches void thrice in succession and each time by death. Where tracts of countryside stood afforested, the plague made little headway. But the southern half was rich pasture drained by numerous rivulets.[3]

Evidently a countryside supporting herds of cattle and giving lush hay crops in good seasons, conditions favourable for the establishment and multiplica-tion of *R. rattus* and its fleas.

Goostrey, in the deanery of Middlewich (see figure 9) was

74

a chapelry of Sandbach, and six miles distant from the mother church. Encumbered by the necessity of burying their dead at Sandbach, the parishioners of Goostrey experienced serious inconvenience during the excessive mortality of 1349. Corpses of plague-victims were left to rot at the roadside...so great were the perils and hazards of the way...

But elsewhere the great woodlands, for which Cheshire in the middle ages was so famous, impeded the progress of the plague.[1] There was a decrease of rents from the lord's lands 'in Old Castle, Church Schocklach, and Peckforton' amounting in 1354 to a total of £9 16s. 6d., and several more instances of reduced rents and of lands lying idle through lack of tenants occur at Middlewich, Russheton, Chelmondeston, and Kingsley in 1350, all attributed to 'The Great Pestilence' in the manorial records. Numerous deaths and payments of relief are recorded at these places.[2] On the manor of Bucklow in 1350 there were 215 acres of land lying vacant for want of tenants because of the pestilence.[3]

In the fourteenth century the duchy of Lancashire was divided ecclesiastically between the sees of Lichfield and York, the former ruling south and the latter north of the river Ribble. As episcopal divisions have no significance where bubonic plague is concerned, however, the county is here presented as an entity.

Vacancies caused by deaths among the beneficed clergy in South Lancashire in 1349–50 seem to have been less than a third of the total benefices,[4] so that the clerical mortality in this part of the diocese of Lichfield was less than in either Derbyshire or Yorkshire, where more than 50 per cent of the beneficed clergy are said to have died. The mortality among the clergy in the deanery of Amounderness—the part of the county north of the Ribble—was greater than in south Lancashire, and between 8 September 1349 and January 1350 'the churches of Lytham, Poulton, Lancaster, Kirkham, and Garstang, half the benefices of the deanery, were all vacated by death, the last two twice'.[5]

Law[6] remarks that the archdeacon of Richmond gave the plague-mortality figure of 13,180 for this deanery in his claim for probate dues, alleging that the parochial death-rolls ranged from 3,000 in each of the parishes of Preston, Lancaster, and Kirkham, down to 60 in the parish of Chipping; but she warns that his figures are certainly exaggerated and that the contemporary manuscript which records these figures must be read with caution as it contains several glaring errors.[7] As the jurors allowed the archdeacon only £30 3s. 4d. of his claim for £113 10s.,[8] it seems evident that they knew that his figures were exaggerated.

Manchester apparently experienced an outbreak of epidemic disease with a high mortality-rate some time in 1350 which may have been bubonic

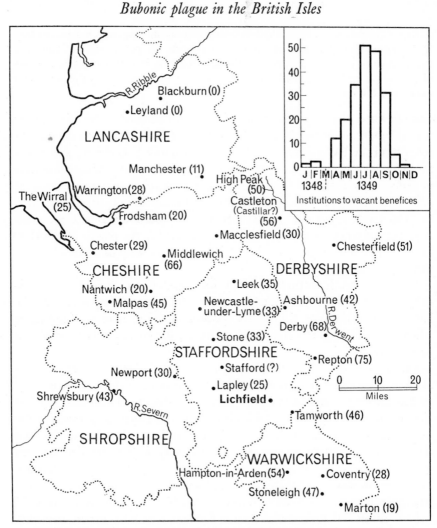

9. Plague in the diocese of Lichfield, 1349. The figures in brackets attached to each deanery represent the maximum possible percentage mortality among the beneficed clergy.

plague. The evidence for this visitation is the consecration in 1352 of the Didsbury burial ground which was opened during a time of great mortality.[1]

Lunn asserts that in Lancashire south of the Ribble no living was void by death twice in succession. He found that in the deanery of Amounderness Kirkham vicarage and Goosnargh chapel were each vacant twice; that the chapels of Lancaster and Stalmine were each void once; that the church of St Mary Magdalen in Preston was without an incumbent for eight weeks, and that the prior of Lytham died of plague. His conclusion, however, is that

Lancashire suffered little from the ravages of the Black Death...The county in the middle ages was sparsely populated; churches were few and far between; parochial areas were of excessive magnitude. In many parts easy travel met with unsurmountable obstacles and the pestilence made little impress upon those parish folk who were cut off from the main stream of civilized life.[1]

DIOCESE OF LICHFIELD

Lunn considers that the register of the diocese of Lichfield is the most important single source of information about the mortal effect of 'The Great Pestilence' upon the beneficed clergy in England. Bishop Norburg instituted to 459 livings, of which 188 were void once during the pandemic, and the value of the register is that in all but 4 of them the cause of the vacancy is specified as death. If all these deaths are accepted as plague-deaths, the clerical mortality-rate of the disease in this see was a trifle over 40 per cent. Lunn comments that

the united testimony of the three registers of York [see below p. 112], Lincoln [see below p. 104] and Lichfield, show the mortality of the Black Death to have been remarkably uniform, when its effects are spread over large areas. This rate of 40 per cent which the registers of Lichfield, York and Lincoln have produced is surely no mere coincidence. Four out of every ten of the parish clergy in England died in the Black Death...Whether this death-rate of 40 per cent among the clergy exceeds that of the general average can never be determined.[2]

Regrettably I must challenge his conclusion on two grounds. The first is that it conflicts with the epidemiology of bubonic plague, the incidence of which over large areas must inevitably have been most erratic. The second is that it is based on the assumption that all the deaths recorded in the registers were plague-deaths and takes no account of the mortality among the clergy in the absence of that disease. Before his mortality-rates can be assessed with respect to bubonic plague we need to know the rates in these sees in the years before 1348, because obviously these rates must be deducted from those presented by him since bubonic plague was not the sole cause of death among the beneficed clergy during 'The Great Pestilence'. Lunn concludes from his study of the Lichfield episcopal register that 'The Great Pestilence' 'definitely began in April 1349 and to all intents was virtually over by the end of the following October'. He asserts that the erroneous claims made by previous writers for a much longer duration of the pestilence derive from the fact that the institutions continued for several months after the deaths which caused the vacancies had ceased, and he claims that this fact is clearly revealed in Norburg's register. His view of the course of events is that plague traversed the diocese from south to north, so that it was at its peak in the archdeaconry

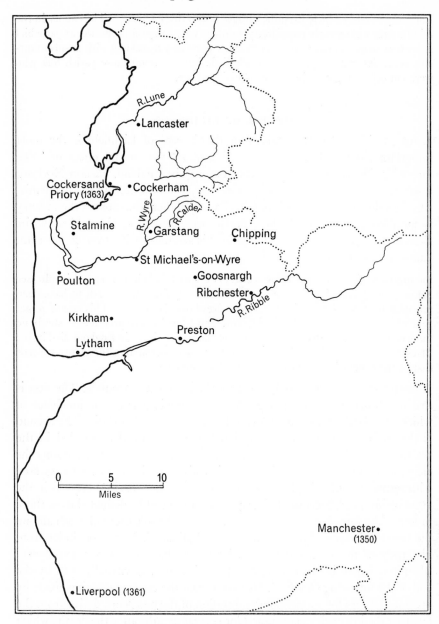

10. Plague in the county palatine of Lancaster, 1349.

of Coventry in May and June; in that of Derby in July and August; in that of Shropshire in August, and in that of Cheshire during September. He finds that the disease was active in some part of the diocese therefore from April to November 1349, during which period 35 of the beneficed clergy resigned their livings. He affirms that the bulk of these resignations occurred, however, after the pestilence had ceased and he opines that in many cases 'impoverishment was the sole factor making for the resignation...They found it impossible to exist, because the parish had been so heavily visited by the plague and prices had been forced up by the economic crises, which the pestilence created.'[1] So at least in these 'heavily visited' parishes the beneficed clergy escaped the disease.

It is difficult to reconcile a death-roll of four out of every ten beneficed clergymen in this diocese, and a supposititious commensurate mortality among the laity, with Lunn's assertion that the pandemic in no way interfered with Norburg's episcopal activities. 'Throughout the worst period of the plague', he says, 'the bishop's own register discovers a varied itinerary containing nothing untoward or unusual...There is no trace of confusion, not one vestige of panic, but simply a crescent mortality that reached its peak in the month of July and then speedily set on its wane.'[1] The two findings are incompatible, and both are at variance with the epidemiology of bubonic plague and with the panic fear that its presence invariably created among people ignorant of its nature.

In 1348 Oxfordshire formed part of the diocese of Lincoln, but it was apparently invaded by 'The Great Pestilence' earlier than the rest of the see. The pandemic has left curiously little trace in the episcopal registers of this county.[2] (See figure 11.) The diocesan business continued as usual and only the increase of institutions to vacant benefices to 103 from the usual 13 or 14 in a year provides evidence of any disturbance. The gaps of seven years—from 1348 to 1355—in the accounts of Bicester priory, and of fourteen years—from 1344 to 1358—in its manorial court rolls have been taken to be significant evidence of the destruction wrought by plague. The Eynsham Chartulary records in 1349 that 'in the time of the mortality of men or pestilence scarce two tenants remained in the manor [of Woodeaton] and they would have departed' if the abbot had not come to an acceptable agreement with them and 'the other tenants who came in afterwards'.[3] Lees seems to have missed the significance of this record, however, which is that in spite of the pestilence there were tenants available, but they refused to accept the conditions of servitude that prevailed before the pandemic.

In 1357 Eynsham abbey petitioned for licence to appropriate the church of Merton on the grounds of poverty resulting from 'The Great Pestilence'.[4]

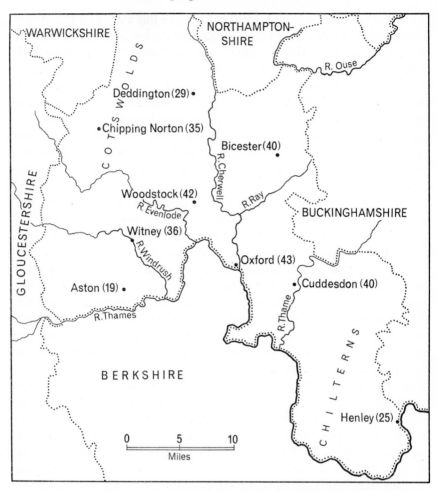

11. Plague in Oxfordshire, 1348. The figures in brackets attached to each deanery represent the maximum possible percentage mortality among the beneficed clergy.

There is no evidence that Merton was involved in the pestilence and, as Lobel says: 'If it can be assumed that the abbey would naturally seek to appropriate prosperous parishes, and not those whose labour force had been decimated, then Merton must have escaped the ravages of plague lightly.' In all probability it escaped them completely. Rees on the other hand declares that the county was very severely scourged by 'The Great Pestilence' and presents several records of heavy mortalities among its peasantry in support of his assertion. At Hethe he says that 21 of 27 villeins died before Michaelmas, 1349; at Staunton Harcourt 7 of 13; at Condelyngton

6 of 14, while deaths were also recorded at Ewelme, Bicester, and March Baldon.[1] To his notes may be added many others about the ravages of the pandemic in this county. The plague is said to have caused a great mortality at Heyford, where in 1350 there were 22 messuages and virgates and one cottage vacant on the manor.[2] At Islip 27 heriots were paid in the manorial year of 1348–9, whereas in 1351 it was recorded that 11 of the 17 villeins owing chevage had died and 9 half-virgates and 7 cottages were still vacant.[3] A jurors' statement survives stating that all the men at Middleton Stoney had died and that the value of the manor had fallen from 24s. in 1328 to 6s. in 1349 on account of the pestilence,[4] and the fact that the village of Tetsworth was allowed in 1354 a tax abatement of 30s.—'a very high figure as compared with neighbouring villages'—has been seen as evidence that the village was ravaged by plague.[5] The plague is also said to have raged at Watlington and seriously afflicted Pyrton, where the manor was valued in 1360 at only one-third of its value in 1340; where only one-half of the demesne of 400 acres could be tilled because the shortage of labour was so great, and where the mill which was normally worth 66s. 8d. was now in ruins and worth only 6s. 8d.[6]

Allyn asserts that the Universities of Oxford and Cambridge lost 'thousands' of their students during 'The Great Pestilence'[7] and he quotes the Archbishop of Armagh, who was chancellor of the former university prior to 1348, for the statement that in his time 'in ye University of Oxenford were thrilty thousand scolers at ones, and now beth unneth six thousand'. In support of this statement Allyn then quotes Gascoigne to the effect that he had seen the figure of 30,000 scholars at Oxford on the rolls 'of the ancient Chancellors' when he was the chancellor of the university. As the modern city of Oxford could not find accommodation for 30,000 students even if the university could absorb them, and its fourteenth-century predecessor could not have housed and taught a tenth of that number, there is obviously something seriously wrong with these statements. It has been remarked that there are few records of mortality at Oxford due to the plague,[8] although this is not so strange in view of later records that at both Oxford and Cambridge the masters and scholars immediately fled into the country at the first hint of plague, because in all probability that is what happened in 1348–9. Whether or not the University of Oxford was afflicted by 'The Great Pestilence', there is evidence that the city suffered from it because in April 1350 the burgesses voluntarily granted their fellow-citizens a stay of toll and other customs on wools, hides, and any kind of animal for ten years on account of their impoverishment by 'the pestilence lately reigning there', an action that won royal approval.[9]

A few records are extant of mortalities in religious houses in the county during the pandemic, including a report of multiple deaths among the monks of Eynsham abbey.[1] Figures for the percentages of vacant benefices are shown in figure 11.

In February 1358 a royal licence was granted to Roger de Cotesford 'to enclose his hamlet of Toresmere, and a way therein leading from Cotesford to Suthorn, which hamlet his bondmen only dwelt in before the time of the pestilence, and which by their death has since remained without inhabitant and is expected so to remain'.[2] Tusmore was probably the smallest village in the hundred of Ploughley and after de Cotesford had obtained licence to enclose it, it was probably never resettled.[3] Langer[4] presents an aerial photograph of its site with the comment: '*Deserted English village*, typical of many medieval communities made ghost towns by the Black Death and succeeding plagues'. Unfortunately for this venerable myth, as far as Tusmore was concerned it was its enclosure and not the 'Black Death' that prevented it from being reoccupied.

According to contemporary accounts 'The Great Pestilence' reached London at the beginning of November 1348, and they imply that the city suffered a very severe visitation of plague, but it is not possible now to give an exact figure for its death-roll. It has been remarked that by the usual reckoning of the poll-tax of 1377 the city's population would then have been 44,770.[5] Russell's corrected figure (see table 1) for the population in 1348 is 58,283, so it would seem to be a reasonable assumption that when 'The Great Pestilence' struck London its population did not exceed 60,000. It probably fluctuated by several hundred temporary residents according to whether the king and his court were there, and it was certainly rapidly diminished by the panic exodus of all who could manage to leave it as soon as plague advertised its presence. If its population did not exceed 60,000, a generous estimate of its plague death-roll—based on late nineteenth-century statistics of urban epidemics of bubonic plague in India—would place it between 15,000 and 20,000. Creighton's estimate is that its mortality ranged between 20,000 and 30,000.[6] The Bishop of London bought the farm known as 'Nomanneslond' for the Londoners, and Master Walter de Magne that which is called 'The Newe Chierche hawe' for the burial of the plague-dead, and no judgements were delivered in the Courts of King's Bench of Common Pleas during the pestilence.[7] This record is confirmed by a royal order, dated 12 May 1349, adjourning the law term until the succeeding Michaelmas as the pestilence was increasing, 'wherefore not a few attorneys suing in the Common Bench at the present Easter have died suddenly, and others will probably do so unless they depart, and several have not dared to

go before the Bench by reason of the said mortality, so that some persons are disinherited for the aforesaid causes'.[1] As a previous proclamation towards the end of January had adjourned the Hilary term to Easter 'on account of the mortality due to the terrible plague chiefly in the city of London and the neighbouring parts',[2] it seems evident that the capital was severely afflicted. A royal pardon, which was granted in August 1350 'in consideration of the mortal pestilence of men which lately prevailed everywhere in England to such an extent that there was no concourse of men at the Bench as usual',[3] suggests also that London was extensively and heavily attacked.

Robert of Avesbury affirms that more than 200 bodies were buried almost every day in a cemetery in which Stow saw standing a memorial cross with a Latin inscription which recorded that more than 50,000 corpses had been interred there.[4] Noorthouck[5] supplies a translation of the inscription and repeats Stow's funeral figure with the addition 'beside many others thenceforeward to the present'. He says that the Charterhouse was afterwards built on this burial ground and that a clergyman named Corey also purchased another burial ground just outside the city wall at the east end of London on which the abbey of St Mary of Grace was afterwards built. Stow also relates that in 1348 John Corey, a clerk, 'procured of Nicholas, prior of the Holy Trinity within Aldgate, one toft of ground near unto East Smithfield, for the burial of them that died, with condition that it might be called the churchyard of the Holy Trinity'. 'The Newe Chierche hawe' had an area of 13 acres and 1 rod, and was situated in a place called Spittle-Croft, because it belonged to St Bartholomew's Spittle or Hospital in Smithfield. This may have been the cemetery with the memorial cross that Stow describes, but Creighton thinks that the inscription on the cross was apocryphal as it was written subsequent to the erection of the Charterhouse, the building of which was not begun until 1371.[6] In that case the inscription was not written until at least 22 years after the cessation of 'The Great Pestilence', by which time terror and rumour had almost certainly much exaggerated the number of the dead.

The date of Easter Sunday in 1349 was 12 April,[7] so that, assuming that Avesbury's record is correct, a maximum number of 13,800 corpses could have been buried in the Smithfield cemetery between 2 February and 12 April. Unfortunately it is not possible to interpret his qualifying phrases 'until after Easter' and 'almost every day'. Supposing that 200 corpses were buried every day excluding Sundays until 19 April, the total interments amount to 13,000. There are contemporary notices of three plague-burial grounds for the London dead and it is probable—in view of the church's apprehension about the interment of plague-corpses in established church-

yards—that the bulk of the metropolitan plague-dead was buried in the three cemeteries that were acquired for this specific purpose. If the Smithfield cemetery had the area that Barnes gives it, it was probably very much larger than either of the others and may well have received therefore the majority of the corpses. If it received as many as the other two cemeteries combined, the total number of corpses interred in them must have been of the order of 30,000. This figure is certainly too high for an epidemic of bubonic plague in a population not exceeding 60,000, especially as some proportion of that population undoubtedly fled from the city as soon as plague appeared in it. If the true plague death-roll in London was of the order of 30,000, then the city's population in 1348 must have approached 100,000.

The plague erupted in Westminster in March 1349 and shortly afterwards invaded the abbey, where it killed the abbot and 27 of the monks early in May.[1] It is said to have left only one inmate alive in the Hospital of St James and possibly the dean of St Martin le Grand and about 100 Grey Friars died of it.[2] The master of the Hospital of St Thomas and many of the brethren also died during the year, inferentially from bubonic plague. In November 1348 a papal indulgence was granted to every citizen to choose his own confessor, who should have powers of plenary remission of sins at his death, to remain effective until the succeeding Whitsuntide.

On 29 December 1349 Edward III ordered the civic officers of London to concert measures to control 'the present great concourse of aliens and denizens to the city and suburbs, *now that the pestilence is stayed*'.[3] (The italics are mine.)

In 1881 a large repository of human bones was uncovered when a number of condemned houses in Cartwright Street, London, were being demolished and it was discovered that this was in fact the burial ground upon which the abbey of St Mary of Grace or East Minster had been built and which was completely demolished after the Dissolution in 1536. It was also found that in Aggas's map of London, drawn in 1562, the East Minster was marked exactly upon the site of this burial ground.[4] It seems evident therefore that the slum-clearance work of 1881 revealed the plague-cemetery that John Corey purchased, and it is much to be regretted that Fowler made no attempt to compute the number of corpses that had been interred in this cemetery.

The terror of bubonic plague has had a long life in England and Riley[5] supplies an instance of the persistence in London in 1856 of a tradition of 'The Great Pestilence'. He states that a plant, known as 'the plague plant', grew then in the grounds of the Charterhouse. He believed that the plant had

a small yellow flower and that it exuded a milky juice from its broken stem. 'This milky juice either had, or was fancied to have, a sickly smell, and it was a current tradition that it only grew on that spot, owing its nutriment to the bodies interred there during the great plague of 1348–52.' Riley's vague description of this plant seems to apply to the coltsfoot, *Tussilago farfara*.

With bubonic plague epidemic in London in 1349, the county of Middlesex could not have escaped some degree of invasion. Fugitives from the city undoubtedly carried into some of its townships 'blocked' fleas roosting in their clothing, and there was probably some spread into it of the epizootic disease by rat contacts from the outskirts of the city. However, owing to the scarcity of early court rolls, little information is available about the impact of 'The Great Pestilence' on this county.[1] The manorial Court Roll of Stepney bears witness to an 'appalling mortality' there, for between February 1349 and the following Michaelmas no less than 105 tenements were void by death. Though the manor of Teddington was not nearly so severely afflicted, it nevertheless lost by death 5 of its 15 customers between Michaelmas 1349 and Michaelmas 1350, and its profits fell from £13 8s. 5d. to £2 2s. 8¼d. The tenants of the St Albans manor of Barnet apparently took advantage of the disorganization caused by 'The Great Pestilence', 'when hardly any reeves or cellarers survived, and certainly could not care for such transitory and mortal things',[2] to tamper with the manor tolls.

DIOCESE OF LONDON

The fourteenth-century see of London embraced the counties of Essex, Hertfordshire—south of Hatfield—and Middlesex (see figure 12), although in the latter there were numerous detached areas and 'peculiar' jurisdictions which belonged either to the see of Canterbury or to that of Lincoln. As the episcopal register and records of this see for the period of 'The Great Pestilence' have been lost or destroyed without trace, information about the behaviour of the pandemic within its boundaries is restricted to the scanty monastic and lay records that are extant.

Colchester was a relatively populous town in fourteenth-century England, with a population in 1348 of upwards of 7,000 people (see table 1, p. 24), of whom 400 were burgesses.[3] It was a river-port and as such likely to be involved in 'The Great Pestilence', either by the carriage of plague by the road traffic between London and Harwich or by its maritime importation through Harwich, which was possibly its point of entry to this county.[4] It is therefore no surprise to find the assertion that Colchester was violently attacked, 'so that no less than 111 wills were entered on the Town-rolls'

during its visitation.[1] Only persons who were worth 100*s*. and upwards were entitled to make a will in 1348, and as many of these well-to-do people in Colchester may have died intestate, this figure of wills represents a heavy death-roll in a population of less than 8,000.

MacMunn claims that there was a very heavy plague-mortality among the peasantry, probably amounting to one-third of the county's population, but she supplies no contemporary evidence to support this assertion.[2] She also

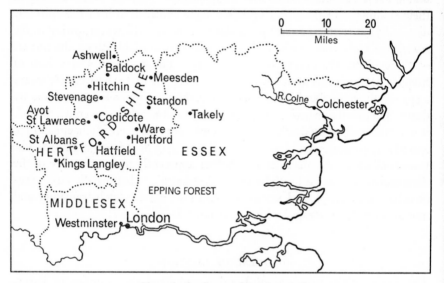

12. Plague in the diocese of London, 1348–9.

declares that its smaller market towns were so blighted by the pestilence that they still showed signs of decay early in the sixteenth century. There does not appear to be any authentic evidence that the blight of 'The Great Pestilence' was so persistent anywhere in England as to be responsible for a state of decay lasting for some two hundred years, and her declaration seems to belong therefore among the many exaggerations that pepper the history of bubonic plague.

A reminder of the invasion of the county of Hertfordshire by 'The Great Pestilence' in 1349 is the well-known Latin inscription carved on the north wall of Ashwell Church inside the tower, which Cussans has transcribed.[3] He notes that Ashwell was an appendage of the abbey of Westminster and he suggests that one of the survivors of the plague-toll there cut the three-line inscription. He affirms that this 'Commemorates the first great pestilence which devastated England in the year 1349' and another pestilence which

86

thirteen years later raged throughout Europe and to which the last two lines of the inscription refer. Johnson, however, believes that Cussans misread the inscription and missed the significance of the subordinate inscriptions above the main one, which are to be regarded as glosses.[1] He supplies this translation of the first two lines: '1000, three times 100, five times 10, pitiable, savage and violent. A wicked populace survives to witness [to the shocking plague].' He suggests that the gloss at the end of the second line should be translated as 'a great wind at the end of Lent', and he declares that the third line, 'as appears from the gloss at the end, related to 1361, and to the great storm on St Maur's Day (15 January), alluded to by the author of the *Eulogium Historiarum*'.

In the abbey of St Albans the prior, the subprior, and 47 of the monks died of plague, 'besides those who died in the cells of the abbey'.[2] The first cases of the disease may have occurred in this county in the autumn of 1348, but it probably did not reach its peak violence until the spring of 1349. 'At Codicote early in November 1348...there is a suspicious mortality of five tenants...In May 1349 at Tyttenhanger 31 tenants died, at Codicote 59 before 19 May and later 25 more.'[3] Plague was at its worst at Stevenage in March and at Standon in April, with a maximal death-roll of 16. There were marked increases in the cost of hired labour after 1349 in the manorial accounts at Pre, Ashwell, and Meesden. Niemayer remarks that 'the immediate result of "The Great Pestilence" was the emptiness of the land and the poverty of the survivors. At Martinmas 1350 at Codicote, 15 tenements were still in the lord's hand. Sixteen tenements were neither given nor leased at Ashwell in 1352...The lords were poor too; unoccupied houses were allowed to decay or were pulled down, dovecotes fell down, underwood was cut and not replaced. As late as 1375 three water-mills were ruinous. They were not repaired ten years later.'[4]

Knight[5] asserts that St Albans abbey never recovered completely from this visitation by plague. She opines that it probably had 60 to 70 monks in 1335; but in 1396 there were only 51; in 1452 but 48, and at its dissolution no more than 39. This progressive decline over a period of more than two hundred years should not rightly be ascribed, however, to the effect of 'The Great Pestilence'. It was surely due chiefly to the failure of the monastic system to compete against the increased freedom of living that was becoming available to the commonalty. Under feudalism monasticism appealed to many men and women as a freedom; in a democracy the monastic life is a discipline few choose. The decay of monasticism in England was a concomitant of the change from a feudal to a free state; it was not caused by bubonic plague, though plague may have hastened the change.

For all practical purposes Hampshire and Surrey constituted the fourteenth-century diocese of Winchester and much of our knowledge about the impact of 'The Great Pestilence' on these counties is derived from its episcopal records.

Lunn declares that the first plague-death among the clergy of the diocese was that of the rector of Niton in the Isle of Wight in November 1348. The first clerical plague-death in the city of Winchester, that of the incumbent of St Elizabeth's chapel, occurred on 1 January 1348/9. He says that Bishop Edyngdon's customary journeys in his diocese were not affected by the pandemic and he concludes that it was a matter of small concern to the bishop, although Edyngdon's issue of his *Mandatum ad Orandum pro Pestilentia* in October 1348 clearly shows that he was distressed over the destruction wrought by plague in his diocese. The plague was epidemic in Southampton county by Christmas 1348, and on 19 January the pope granted plenary indulgence to all people of the true faith, religious and secular, in the county.[1] The original grant expired at Easter, but before that date arrived it was extended to Michaelmas. Plague-deaths in Winchester were so numerous that considerable difficulty was experienced in disposing of the corpses, and the presumptive plague-deaths in two of the religious houses suggest that the city's death-roll may have been a heavy one. In the priory of St Swithun, for example, an annual average of 60 brethren resided up to 1349 compared with an average of about 35 from 1350 to its dissolution.[1] 'At the Sustern Spital (The Sisters' Hospital), now "Commoners", the normal number of brethren and sisters was 21';[2] but in 1352 there were only 6 inmates, no more than 10 a year later, and only 16 in 1387.[2] At the nunnery of Romsey 90 nuns voted at the election of the abbess in 1333, whereas from 1350 until its dissolution never more than 25 voted.[3] The plague-mortality apparently varied in different parts of the county, though in most places it was heavy, and the central area around Winchester and Alresford seems to have been very much distressed.[4] The manor of Manydown in the neighbourhood of Basingstoke suffered very severely and did not recover for many years, and on the small manor of Cheriton the families of 25 tenants were exterminated, leaving their holdings in the lord's hands. The north and north-west parts of the county also seem to have suffered severely. On the manor of Burghclere, for instance, the families of 35 tenants were exterminated and the manorial receipts were 10 per cent less in 1352 than in 1346. Though there were many plague-deaths in Southampton town the country districts to the south of it apparently escaped a severe visitation of the disease, because on the large manor of Farnham only 9 tenants died without leaving successors. The districts in the north-east corner, around Bramshott and Liphook, were also only lightly attacked.

That Southampton experienced a severe visitation of bubonic plague appears to be confirmed by the royal grant in March 1351 of a 'release for eight years to the mayor and burgesses of Southampton on their petition showing that they are so impoverished and oppressed as well by pestilence as by the burning and destruction of their town by the King's enemies lately invading the same'.[1] Although this record explicitly indicates that 'The Great Pestilence' was not the sole cause of Southampton's distress or even certainly the chief cause, it can perhaps be argued that it was the plague-toll of its able-bodied townsmen that rendered it too weak to repel the French raiders. On the other hand Shillington's belief that the rural districts in the south-east of the county escaped lightly is challenged by the plea for the remission of their taxes which the king received in May 1352 from the inhabitants of 'Stoke, Estoke, Northwode, Southwode, Mengham, Weston, and Haillyng, in the island of Haillyng; [in which towns] a very great number of the said men have been destroyed by the said mortal pestilence'.[2]

Rees confirms that the bishop's manors immediately east and south of Winchester—for example those of Cheriton and Twyford—suffered heavier mortalities than those farther south such as Droxford and Bishop's Stoke, which were almost untouched.[3] His conclusion is that the toll of plague on the episcopal estates was insignificant compared with its death-roll in certain parts of England. Branston and Leroy[3] have more justification than many local historians for their claim that Winchester was ravaged by 'The Great Pestilence'; evidence of the destructive effect of the pandemic on the city is supplied by the royal grant which was made in February 1352 because of the 'waste and depression in the city from the time when the deadly pestilence last prevailed'.[5]

Malden[6] states that the number of benefices in the county of Surrey made void during 1349 was about twice the normal number.

Lunn can only supply one record of the involvement of a religious house in this county in the pandemic, but that one is the terrible visitation of the St Mary Magdalen Hospital, Sandon, 'where all the members including the prior perished'.[7] This house was presumably the priory of Sandown, close to Esher,* which was one of the Lesser Hospitals with a net income of less than £50 a year. It seems therefore that it was only a small establishment and it is unfortunate that the exact number of victims was not recorded.

* See the Map of Monastic Britain, South Sheet, s 51/16, H.M.S.O. 1950.

In 1349–50 the institutions to vacant benefices in the see of Winchester were about 'ten times the normal number, probably from death of clergy'.[1]

In Hampshire and the Isle of Wight only 20 institutions to vacant benefices were made during the twelve years preceding 'The Great Pestilence', whereas 228 were made in 1349, and—judging from the distribution of the institutions—plague may have entered the diocese from Wiltshire as well as from the county's seaboard.[2] Cox declares that the deanery of Basing in the north part of the county suffered most severely, particularly during March and April, in which months the bulk of the vacant benefices was recorded, and that on the south coast those in Portsmouth, on Hayling Island, and in the Isle of Wight were synchronously afflicted.

Lunn's corresponding figure for the diocesan institutions is 264,[3] so it would seem that there were only 31 institutions in Surrey during the plague-year. If this is correct that county must have been very little affected by the epidemic.

It is difficult to form an estimate of the losses of the Sussex clergy from plague as the episcopal register of the diocese of Chichester is missing for the period of 'The Great Pestilence'.[4] Salzman seems to imply that it has been lost, but according to Lunn it did not begin until 1396. Nevertheless Salzman sees no reason to believe that the plague-toll among the beneficed clergy in this county was lower than elsewhere in England, and in support of his belief he records that in 1349 the king presented to 26 vacancies in the county, an exceptionally large number. He states that the abbots of Battle and Brox-grove; the prior, sub-prior, and third prior of Lewes, and the heads of the monasteries of Hastings, Michelham, Rusper, Baynham, and Arundel, all died during that year. At Michelham there were only 5 brethren in 1353 instead of the 13 who were in residence there before the pestilence.

At Wartling, at a court held in March 1349, the deaths of 12 freemen and villeins were recorded according to Wragge.[5] At the next court held there in October the number of victims had risen to more than 60, of whom 25 had left no direct heirs. At Apuldram the customary reapers were reduced in 1349–50 from 234 to 168. Prior to 'The Great Pestilence' eight hundreds in the honour of the Eagle paid a sum—realized by a rate of 1*d*. per head—of £27 19*s*. 8*d*., which she calculates implies a population of roughly 6,700 persons. During the pandemic 9 villages on the coast were, she asserts, completely destroyed and desolated and the population of the honour was so reduced that in order to raise the above-mentioned amount some people had to pay 2*s*. 8*d*. or even 5*s*. The result was that many people left the district.

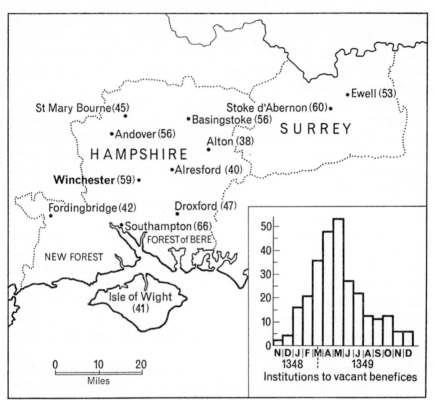

13. Plague in the diocese of Winchester, 1348–9. The figures in brackets attached to each deanery represent the maximum possible percentage mortality among the beneficed clergy.

In 1440 the reintroduction of the 1*d.* rate yielded only £6 5*s.* 3*d.*, from which she deduces that the population of the honour was then about 1,500.

Page and Peckham advance the curious argument that the absence of any record of plague in Chichester must mean that the city was ravaged by 'The Great Pestilence' because cases of plague were recorded at Apuldram.[1]

There is a reference in the royal archives to the damage done by a local visitation of bubonic plague in this county, but I have not been able to identify the locality involved. It is described as the lands of the abbot of Fécamp, which were held of the king, who was constrained in January 1350 to release the tenants of '100 *l.* of the first year's farm of 300 *l.*' because the revenue of the lands had been 'very greatly diminished by reason of the increase of the pestilence'.[2] Then in May 1356 the king granted a remission of taxes to the town of 'Sefford (on the Sea)'—presumably the modern Seaford—because it had been 'so desolated by plague and the chances of war that

91

men living there are so few and poor that they cannot pay their taxes or defend the town'.[1] Obviously bubonic plague was not the sole cause of this town's desolation, a fact that applies in all probability to most of the towns and villages that have been depopulated and desolated by many writers about the 'Black Death'.

In the fourteenth century the county of Kent was divided for ecclesiastical governance between the sees of Canterbury and Rochester, the former exercising jurisdiction east of Maidstone, the latter over the county west of that town. The deanery of Shoreham, the area of which was equal to almost one-quarter of the diocesan area of Rochester, was, however, under the jurisdiction of Canterbury,[2] so that owing to the loss of the Canterbury records, no statistics are available for at least half and possibly for as much as three-quarters of the benefices in this county.

The death of Archbishop Stratford in August 1348 has been ascribed to bubonic plague and in little more than a year three successors had been appointed to his vacant throne.[3] Lunn, on the contrary, believes that Stratford's death was not due to plague because at the time of his death neither of the sees of Canterbury and Rochester had been invaded by 'The Great Pestilence'.[2] There seems to be no doubt though that both his immediate successors died of plague—John de Ufford in May 1349 and Thomas Bradwardine in the ensuing August.[4]

Lunn affirms that owing to the loss of the Canterbury register, and the confusion that undoubtedly resulted from the deaths of three archbishops in rapid succession, it is impossible to produce statistics of clerical mortality from plague in this diocese that are of any value.[5] Simkins agrees with him about the statistics but declares that the numbers of the secular clergy were so reduced by death that the parochial services were only maintained with difficulty.[4]

Two Kentish clerics—Stephen Birchington of Canterbury and William Dene of Rochester—recorded the behaviour of 'The Great Pestilence' in the county. The former stated that the pestilence appeared in Canterbury immediately after Christmas 1348 and prevailed without intermission to the end of May 1349, though in Sandwich it was still raging in June where, as the town cemetery could not hold any more corpses, the earl of Huntingdon gave a piece of land for the interment of the plague-dead. The latter recorded that 'the mortality was so great that none could be found to carry the corpses to the grave. Men and women bore their own offspring on their shoulders to the church and cast them into a common pit.' It is more probable, however, that terror of the disease was responsible for the lack of professional pall-bearers and not their extermination by plague. Dene then describes the

impoverishment and decay of the episcopal manors; the scarcity of food in the monastery of Rochester which forced the monks to grind their own bread, and the dearth of fish throughout the diocese which constrained people to eat meat in Lent and evoked an order that four herrings should be sold for one penny.[1] Slater deduces from this record that the lack of fish signifies that 'the dwellers in the ports and fishing villages died in great numbers' from the pestilence, and his deduction is consistent with the epidemiology of bubonic plague; but it is also possible that stormy weather kept the fishing-fleets port-bound, for gales in the North Sea and the English Channel are

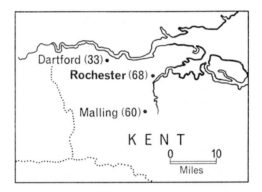

14. Plague in the diocese of Rochester, 1348–9. The figures in brackets attached to each deanery represent the maximum possible percentage mortality among the beneficed clergy.

not uncommon in March. Lunn reports a severe visitation by plague of the abbey of Malling (see figure 14), where the abbess and her two immediate successors died within six months in 1349.[2] Slater states that 27 nuns were resident there in 1324 and that only 4 nuns and 4 novitiates survived 'The Great Pestilence'. Russell assigns an even more terrible mortality-rate to the monastery of Ivy Church where, he affirms, 12 of the 13 brethren perished.[3] By contrast Mullett notes that at that of Christchurch only 4 of the 80 monks then resident died.[4]

DIOCESE OF ROCHESTER

Lunn affirms that the Rochester diocesan institutions show that plague entered the diocese in December 1348 and that the peak of the subsequent epidemic was reached in May 1349.[2] The city of Rochester may have been attacked by it because out of his small household the bishop lost 4 priests, 5 esquires, 10 attendants, 7 young clerics, and 6 pages, and was left without any help.[5] The distinct implication is that they all died of the pestilence, but it is possible

93

that the episcopal household scattered as soon as plague appeared in it. In spite of his domestic loss, Lunn says that the bishop's register is continuous throughout the period of 'The Great Pestilence', but unfortunately it has two serious defects as a record of clerical mortality. The first of these is that after March 1349 no cause is given for the voidance of a benefice; the second is that the deanery of Shoreham, as already noted, was under the jurisdiction of Canterbury.[1] Lunn concludes his study of this diocese with the declaration that in spite of the many vacancies in its three deaneries there was no difficulty in meeting the demand for clergy.[1]

Institutions to vacant benefices in the county of Norfolk

Deanery	Before 1348	During 1349
Brooke	6	33
Brisley	1	24
Burnham	3	25
Depwade	4	16
Fincham	3	17
Flegg	6	18
Heacham	0	14
Holt	1	23
Ingworth	5	28
Redenhall	1	11
Walsingham	1	11
TOTALS	31	220

Throughout its recorded history bubonic plague, by reason of its immutable nature, has been constantly a maritime and urban disease. Jessopp[2] is certainly at fault in his assertion that more than half the population of East Anglia was destroyed by 'The Great Pestilence'; but he is indisputably correct in his affirmation that 'in no part of England did the towns occupy a more important position relatively to the rest of the population. In no part of England did three such important towns as Lynn, Yarmouth, and Norwich lie within so short a distance of one another.'[2] And nowhere around the coast of Britain, he could have added with equal force, were so many busy seaports and river-ports so closely together as on the East Anglian coast, or serving as many important fairs as those of Boston, Stamford, King's Lynn, Ely, Bury St Edmunds, St Ives, Sturbridge and Northampton.

Simkins states that plague appeared in Norfolk in 1348 but did not assume epidemic proportions until 1349, when its ravages 'are testified by the enormous number of institutions to the benefices in the county that year'.[3] She presents a table of institutions in support of this affirmation, and more-

over in several of the deaneries listed there were multiple institutions to the identical living in 1350. Thus in the deanery of Brooke there were three in succession to one church; in that of Brisley, two in succession to each of four churches; in Holt there were repeat institutions to four benefices void once in 1349, and in Ingworth there were as many as seven.[1] In October 1349 the bishop of Norwich obtained a papal licence to dispense 60 clerks of his diocese to hold parish churches void 'by reason of the pestilence. It is impossible', Simkins continues, 'to compute the number of deaths of unbeneficed clergy this year, but this also must have been extremely large; it is recorded that all the canons but one of the abbey of Hickling died; and every one of the Dominican friars of Norwich died, so that their houses were left empty and deserted.'[2] On the other hand Lunn declares that 'the Cathedral monks enjoyed startling immunity'.[3]

Jessopp asserts that at least 15 of the incumbents of the 23 parishes in the hundred of Depwade fell victims to plague during the summer and autumn of 1349.[4] In April 1349 a dispute entered for hearing between a husband and wife was never settled because before the day of hearing arrived (the courts were held at two-month intervals) all the wife's witnesses were dead and her husband was dead also.[5] At the manor court of Hunstanton held on 20 March 1349 only one death was registered for the preceding month, so the manor had evidently not been invaded by plague up to that date. At the next court held on 23 April five disputes were entered for hearing, but of the 16 men engaged as principals or witnesses, 11 had died before the court assembled. The next court on 22 May had three suits for debt down for hearing; but in one the defendant was dead, in the second the plaintiff was dead, and in the third both parties were dead. No court was held in June or in September, and when the court met on 16 October it was reported that in the space of two months 63 male and 15 female inhabitants had been killed by the pestilence, and in 9 cases the families had been exterminated.[6] 'Incredible though it may sound', Jessopp exclaims, 'the fact is demonstrable that in this one parish of Hunstanton, which a man may walk round in two or three hours, and the whole population of which might have assembled in the church then recently built, 172 persons, tenants of the manor, died off in 8 months; 74 of them left no heirs male, and 19 others had no blood relations in the world to claim the inheritance of the dead.'[7] No court was held at the manor of Raynham Parva between 1347 and 1350, though the lord of the manor had died in the interval. When the court was held in July 1350, it recorded that 14 men and 4 women, all holders of land, had died without leaving any heirs.[8] Jessopp declares also that he has not found a single roll of any Norfolk manor after April or May 1349 which does not provide abundant proof of the ravages

of the pestilence.[1] Thus at a court of an insignificant little manor at Croxton, near Thetford, held on 24 July, it was reported that 17 tenants had died since the previous court and that 8 of them had left no heirs. At a court held simultaneously at Raynham, at the other end of the county, 18 tenements were reported to be empty and in eight cases there were no survivors to inhabit them. At Bunwell, a hamlet in the manor of Hadeston, about twelve miles from Norwich, 'which could not possibly have had 400 inhabitants, 54 men and 14 women were carried off by the pestilence in 6 months, 24 of them without a living soul to inherit their property.[2] At a court held at Lessingham on 15 January 1350 the steward reported that only 30s. was to be levied from the customary tenants by way of tallage 'because the greater part of those tenants who were wont to render tallage had died in the previous year by reason of the deadly pestilence'.[3] Finally Jessopp asserts that in manor after manor the lord was carried off together with his steward and his tenants, and that 'in a single year upwards of 800 parishes lost their parsons, 83 of them twice, and 10 of them three times in a few months'.[4]

Lunn reports the visitation by plague of two religious houses in this county during 1349, to wit, the Austin priory of Mountjoy—where the prior and all the canons died—and the Benedictine monastery of St Bennet of Hulme, which was a larger house than Mountjoy, where one canon survived according to the *Chronica Minor*.[5]

Assuming that Stow's record is accurate, both Norwich and Yarmouth would appear to have suffered more severely in proportion to their populations than the county as a whole, for he states that

there died from the first of Januaire, to the first of July, in the Cittie of Norwich 57104 persons, besides Ecclesiasticall Mendicants and Dominikes. There was buried in the Church and Church-yard of Yarmouth, in one yeere 7052 menne and women, before which time the parsonage there was worth seven hundred marks by yeere, and afterwards was scarce worth fortie pound the yeere.[6]

A manuscript in Norwich Guild Hall gives the still higher figure of 57,374, 'besyd Relygius and Beggars', as the toll of plague in Norwich.[7] Blomefield argues that from the number of parishes it contained Norwich must have had a population of about 70,000 in 1348. Creighton dismisses these mortality figures for Norwich as wholly incredible and suggests that a death-roll of 17,000 would be nearer the truth because Norwich was less populous than London in the fourteenth century.[8] Indeed the manuscript figure would still be incredible for an epidemic of bubonic plague if Norwich had had in 1348 its 1958 population of 121,226.[9] Creighton's figure is still far too high for the fourteenth-century city, because if Russell's figure for its population in 1377 is approximately correct, Norwich could not have had a population in excess

of 10,000 in 1348. A possible explanation of the manuscript mortality figure is that it refers to the county of Norwich [otherwise Norfolk] and not to the city alone, for in some old records and in the title of Blomefield's history the name of the county town is used to signify the county. If this explanation is accepted, the figure of 57,374 plague-deaths during a severe epidemic of bubonic plague in a population of about 245,000 people is consistent with modern knowledge of its destructiveness.

Although Stow's mortality figure for Yarmouth is as incredible as his figure for Norwich, Creighton is not so emphatic in his rejection and suggests that 'it may be assumed to have lost more than half its people',[1] an assumption for an epidemic of bubonic plague that is not warranted. A possible explanation of the Yarmouth figure is that through a transcriber's or a printer's error a figure which was originally 1 became 7. If Yarmouth had a population of about 4,000 in 1348 it might have lost as much as a third of it from a devastating epidemic of bubonic plague.

Cox avers that the pestilence 'laid grievous hold on Suffolk' and refers to an enormous increase in the number of institutions to vacant benefices in confirmation of his statement.[2] He says that during the five years immediately preceding 1348 the annual average of institutions throughout the diocese was 81, but from 25 March 1349 to 25 March 1350 no less than 831 are recorded in the episcopal register. He remarks that there were 15 religious houses in the county whose superiors required episcopal institution and of these 8 of the superiors died during 1349, namely, those of Alnesbourne, Bungay, Chipley, Flitcham, Redlingfield, Thetford (St Sepulchre's), Woodbridge and Snape, of which the last was vacant twice. Jessopp notes that on the manor of Cornford Parva, which could never have had more than 50 tenants, the deaths of 6 women and 3 men were registered at a court held on 31 March 1349 as having occurred during the previous two months.[3] He implies that their deaths were due to plague, but it is possible that some at least of them were due to other causes, especially in view of their winter incidence. At a second court held on 1 May 15 more deaths (13 men and 2 women) were registered, 7 of whom left no heirs.[4] At the next court held on 3 November 36 more deaths were registered and 13 of these represented households that had been exterminated.[4] As these mortality figures add up to 60, either the dead were not all tenants or Jessopp's population figure of the tenantry is faulty.

Lunn comments that 'in the county as a whole, the effects of the Black Death, interpreted by the institutions, appear to have been heaviest in the north-east, along the water-course of the Waveney (see figure 15), though Stowe deanery, at the source of the Gipping, suffered severely'.[5] If, as seems

probable, the Waveney was then navigable for much of its length, Lunn's finding is consistent with the epidemiology of bubonic plague.

A royal decree, issued in December 1353, emphasizes the heavy incidence of bubonic plague among fisherfolk which is a consequence of the bionomics of *R. rattus*. It granted a respite to the men of Dunwich 'until the quinzaine of Michaelmas next for the payment of their ferm and the arrears thereof...' [because] the town which was almost entirely inhabited by fishermen before these times, has 'been so wasted and depressed by the late mortal pestilence'.[1]

DIOCESE OF NORWICH

Lunn remarks that in the fourteenth century this diocese possessed far more churches in proportion to its size than any other see in England. This abundance of churches surely implies that the diocese was a populous and a comparatively opulent one. Unfortunately all the institutions recorded in the bishop's register for the period of 'The Great Pestilence' are, he says, unspecified, and therefore no information is available about the number of vacancies that were caused by the deaths of their incumbents.[2]

In his analysis of the institutions in the archdeaconry of Suffolk, Lunn points out that the three deaneries of Orford, Dunwich, and Lothingland were all seaboard ones, 'sharing a similarity of physical features, with their broad expanse of reedy flats'. He notes that South Elmham deanery 'appears to have been a plague spot',[3] but regrettably he supplies no reason for its unenviable condition. As the bishop did not institute to the benefices in the deanery of Ipswich, his register is of no help in assessing the truth of the traditional ravages of 'The Great Pestilence' in Ipswich and its surrounding villages. If Unwin is correct in his assertion that Ipswich had a population probably in excess of 1,500 at the beginning of the fourteenth century, it is possible that it either escaped or was only lightly attacked by the pandemic, because he states that the poll-tax returns of 1377 assigned to it a population of 1,507 persons over 14 years of age.[4]

Lunn comments upon the good order in which the episcopal register was kept at this time, and affirms that there was no shortage of clergy in the diocese in spite of the enormous increase in the number of institutions during 1349. He opines that great credit is due to the bishop for his governance of the diocese, especially as he was often employed by Edward III on political business. For instance he was in France from the end of September 1348 to the end of May 1349, acting as a royal commissioner in the negotiations for a truce. Although the epidemic of plague reached its peak in the month after his return according to Lunn, it does not appear to have interfered with his

diocesan routine—at any rate he pursued a varied itinerary in his see through-out June and July.[1] If this is correct, it very strongly suggests that the pandemic was neither as extensive nor as intensive in this diocese as writers about the 'Black Death' have alleged.

Lincolnshire, conjoined with Oxfordshire, Bedfordshire, Buckingham-shire, Huntingdonshire, Rutland, Northamptonshire, Leicestershire, and the

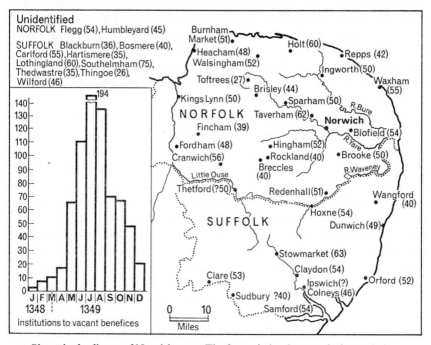

Unidentified
NORFOLK Flegg(54),Humbleyard(45)
SUFFOLK Blackburn(36),Bosmere(40),
Carlford(55),Hartismere(35),
Lothingland(60),Southelmham(75),
Thedwastre(35),Thingoe(26),
Wilford(46)

Institutions to vacant benefices

15. Plague in the diocese of Norwich, 1349. The figures in brackets attached to each deanery represent the maximum possible percentage mortality among the beneficed clergy.

northern half of Hertfordshire, formed the fourteenth-century diocese of Lincoln, the second largest of the English sees.[2]

The county was apparently not invaded by plague until the summer of 1349, but in the latter half of that year there was a huge increase in the number of institutions to vacant benefices.[3] There were 302 in the arch-deaconry of Lincoln compared with an annual average of between 30 and 40 before 'The Great Pestilence', while the archdeaconry of Stow had 59 compared with 6. The cathedral church suffered heavily from the pandemic, losing its dean, precentor, treasurer, 3 archdeacons, 14 prebendaries, and probably also its sub-dean. However, as Calthrop finds that only 2 of the incumbents of the city's 50 additional churches died during the pestilence,

it would seem that for some reason the cathedral clergy suffered an exceptionally heavy mortality. The deanery of Corringham may have been scourged by the pestilence as 14 of its incumbents are reported to have died, including 3 vicars of Redbourne and 2 rectors of Southorpe. Calthrop cites Massingberd for the statement that the number of deaths among the Lincolnshire clergy rose from 15 in June to 60 in July to 89 in August, then fell from 61 in September to 29 in November to 13 in December.[1] The district of Holland was less severely afflicted than Kesteven or Lindsey, and Stamford was the worst afflicted of the county's towns, losing 6 of its beneficed clergy. At least one religious house, Louth Park abbey, was involved and lost its abbot and many of its monks.[2] By contrast, Graham declares that there is no record of the visitation of the abbey of Crowland by plague at this time.

Thompson asserts that plague was certainly present in the neighbourhood of Lincoln in May 1349 and he opines that it was synchronously active on the Nottinghamshire border of Kesteven, because on 9 June the bishop consecrated a cemetery at Stragglethorpe for the reception of the bodies of the plague-dead.[3] He declares that North Lincolnshire was unmistakably the chief focus of plague-mortality as exemplified by the number of institutions, though he admits that the evidence these provide is, at the best, 'of a very imperfect kind'. It is indeed clear from his findings and conclusions that little reliance can be placed on the institutional statistics as an index of the ravages of plague among the clergy, and even less reliance on them as an index of its destructiveness among the commonalty. He also records the visitation by the pestilence of only one of the county's religious houses. This was the nunnery of Wothorpe, situated a mile or two south of Stamford, where only one of the sisters survived the visitation. The significance of this record is unfortunately impaired by lack of information about the size of the convent; but the hurt it suffered was apparently so serious and permanent that a few years later it was united with St Michael's priory at Stamford.

Plague apparently entered the county of Leicestershire as early as the second half of April 1349, because on 4 May the bishop consecrated the churchyard at Great Easton for the burial of the plague-dead in that locality.[4] As Great Easton is situated in the south-eastern tip of the county, between Rutland and Northamptonshire, *P. pestis* may have reached the district either by riverine transport up the river Welland or by a northward creep of an epizootic of rat-plague. Possibly Great Easton was not the first place in the county to be involved in the pandemic, because Thompson notes that on 30 April the bishop wrote to the vicar of Melton Mowbray to demand his fee for the consecration of an addition to the churchyard there.[4] Sister

'The Great Pestilence' in Britain

Elspeth,[1] after remarking that some doubt has been thrown upon Knighton's parochial mortality figures, comments: 'The records of the borough of Leicester a few years later show a degree of prosperity which is hard to understand if nearly one-third of the population had been swept away.' She cites Bateson[2] for the suggestion that Knighton's totals are the sums of several successive years. I have already stated that in my judgement, based on the known killing power of bubonic plague, Knighton's figures of plague-deaths in a population of the size of Leicester's in 1349 are unacceptable, although Creighton believes that 'Knighton's round numbers for the three parishes are not improbable, considering that Leicester was a comparatively populous town at the time of the poll-tax in 1377: the numbers who paid the tax were 2101, which would give, by the usual way of reckoning, a population of 3939'.[3] Apropos of the collapse of law and order, which was one of the most serious concomitants of 'The Great Pestilence', Sister Elspeth writes: 'The reckless grew more wild and reckless than ever: the year following the pestilence is specially marked by daring thefts and acts of sacrilege' in Leicestershire.[4]

A royal notice in December 1359 mentions that 5 tenements in Pattishall, about 10 miles south-west of Northampton (see figure 16), vacant owing to the deaths of their tenants during 'the time of the last pestilence', had remained uncultivated for a great while' for lack of tenants willing to take them.[5]

The pandemic was apparently most violent in the county of Northampton-shire from May to October 1349, 'during which period 148 of the beneficed clergy died, inferentially from plague'.[6] As the bishop instituted only to 281 livings in the county, this supposititious plague-mortality means a rate of nearly 53 per cent in a particular class of fourteenth-century society for which, by reason of its aetiology, bubonic plague could not have shown any preference. In any case proof that all these clergymen died must be forth-coming before their deaths from plague can be presumed, whereas Serjeant-son and Adkins have taken it for granted that they all died of plague. They assert that 'the clergy of the county town, where the plague was fiercest in October, suffered terribly, out of the 9 parochial benefices of Northampton, 7 were rendered vacant, the vicarage of All Saints being twice emptied'. They report that the abbey of Peterborough lost half its convent of 64 monks during 'The Great Pestilence' and that Luffield priory is said to have lost its prior, its monks, and its novices. If these reports are authentic plague would seem to have been widespread in this county in 1349, for Peterborough is at its north-eastern tip and Luffield Priory was at its south-western extremity.

Rees states that there was a considerable decrease in the rents of the manors of Eston, Torpell, Upton, Westwarden, Earls Barton and Grafton, immedi-

ately after 'The Great Pestilence';[1] but presents no evidence to show that the decrease in any one of them was due to the deaths of the tenants from plague.

In 1349 the deaths of 8 rectors, 2 vicars, and 1 chantry priest in this county are recorded in the episcopal register, a mortality-rate of nearly one-quarter of the clergy of the deanery of Northampton.[2]

The experience of the manor of Whissendine was probably typical of many others. At a manorial *post mortem* inquisition held in 1350 the jurors found that 15 virgates of land, each of which used to be worth 24*s.* a year, were then worth nothing because all the tenants were dead. At another inquisition five years later they found that the arable land of the manor was then worth by the year only 3*d.* an acre, 'and not more since the time of the aforesaid pestilence, because of the small number of workers'.

Rees[3] notes that 9 villeins died during the pandemic on the manor of Wissenden, and that the only bondman of Seyton (Seaton) died, supposedly from bubonic plague.

The pandemic was apparently severely felt in Huntingdonshire, 79 institutions to vacant benefices being made in 1349 compared with 15 in 1348. The abbot of Ramsey, the priors of Huntingdon, St Neots, and Stonely, and the prioress of Hinchinbrook died during 'The Great Pestilence'. Bedfordshire suffered as severely as its neighbours from the pestilence, and the plague must have been especially violent in and about the town of Bedford, as the names of the masters of both hospitals, and the priors of both Caldwell and Newnham, are found amongst those who died in 1349.[4] The prior of Bushmead, the prioress of Markyate, and the rectors of Biddenham, Sutton and Shillington died in the same year. The Dunstable chronicler records that the townsmen of Bedford hung a new bell in the church in 1349, an event which may have been commemorative of the cessation of the pestilence in that town.[5]

Ransom states that at Cranfield and Stevington there were plague-deaths among the tenants.[6]

Rickards reports that a water-mill at Pabenham, belonging to the manor of Stevington, which was worth a rent of 70*s.* before 1348, was worth nothing at an inquisition held in 1349 because of the pestilence.[7] The parish seems to have been impoverished, as shown by the findings of the above inquisition that the fulling-mill was empty, the dovecote in ruins, and the garden worth nothing; but the manor was assessed at £49 7*s.* 7*d.*, 'no marked diminution in value from about one hundred years earlier'.[8]

Lea records the ruin of Harvies Manor in the hundred of Stodden. When the owner died in 1351 he was seized of 300 acres of arable land which, at the *post mortem* inquisition, were reported to be worth nothing because they were uncultivated and nobody wanted them.[9] He infers that all the tenants had

been killed by plague. But in modern times there have been English land-lords who have allowed their land to become derelict two hundred years after bubonic plague disappeared from this country. Manfield relates the changes in the value of the manor of Kempston Daubney which she believes were caused directly by 'The Great Pestilence'. In 1296 it was valued at £32 8s. 8½d.; in 1358 at £16 2s., and in 1386 at £20, at which figure it remained for the rest of the century.[1] In 1346 Peter de St Croix held a fourth part of the manor of Millbrook until his death, probably from plague, in 1349, when a *post mortem* inquisition recorded that all his bondmen and cottars were dead of the pestilence.[2] The bondmen and cottars on the manors of Caynho, Clophull, and Ampthill are also said to have died of plague during 1349.[3]

There appear to be therefore authentic records of the extermination of most or all of the adult, able-bodied males on 5, possibly 6, Bedfordshire manors, presumptively by bubonic plague, and as there must also have been a heavy mortality among the womenfolk, it is possible that this county was as severely afflicted by 'The Great Pestilence' in proportion to its population as any county in England.

The episcopal register records the deaths of 4 beneficed clergy in the archdeaconry of Buckingham in May 1349 and a steady increase in the number during the summer months to give a total for the year of 77. The deaths of the prior of Bradwell and Luffield and of the prioress of Anker-wyke were reported during the summer, but no mention is made of any mortality among the other inmates of these houses. As the violence of the pandemic abated, the first overt signs of the great religious upheaval en-gendered by Wycliff—which had its most lasting effects in the east Midlands —were manifested at Oxford.[4] Besant affirms that 'it is not impossible that the spread of Wyclyf's opinions among the citizens of London may have been partly due to the shock' of the successive epidemics of the latter half of this century.[5] Jamison[6] asserts that 'The Great Pestilence' was at its peak in this county from May to September 1349, and she declares that it inflicted an equal mortality upon the clergy and the manorial tenants. At Salden all the tenants, both free and villein, died except one man who held one virgate in bondage. Rees also records the virtual extermination of the tenantry of Salden and adds that half the rents of the manors of Great and Little Kimble, Weston Turvill, and Hoggeston, could not be levied on account of the pestilence, inferentially because of the deaths of some of their tenants from plague.[7]

Though there is no extant record of its visitation of High Wycombe, plague attacked the adjacent parish of West Wycombe very severely, as is

testified by a special section in the manor rental of 1350 which records the names of more than 40 tenants who apparently died during the pestilence.[1]

Knight notes that the rolls of the Manor of Winslow, which belonged to the abbey of St Albans, reveal that during 'The Great Pestilence' 153 holdings changed hands, and she adds that 'from other evidence gained from the same rolls, three out of every five adult males in that manor must have perished.[2]

DIOCESE OF LINCOLN

Thompson[3] remarks that a very strict computation of the number of institutions to benefices in this diocese—exclusive of chantries—yields the figure of 1,857. Between Gynewell's consecration as bishop in 1347 and 25 March 1349 he instituted to 212 vacant benefices; but between the latter date and 25 March 1350 he made 1,025 institutions, of which 201 benefices were void by the resignation and 824 by the death of their incumbents. Judging from the monthly figures of institutions that Thompson presents (see figure 16), plague assumed epidemic proportions in some parts of the diocese in April 1349. It rose rapidly to a peak in July, declined slightly in August, rapidly in September, and progressively during the autumn to extinction in the winter of 1349/50. For the period from 25 March to 31 December 1350 only 161 institutions were recorded in the episcopal register, and of these only 41 were required on account of the death of the incumbent. Thompson concludes his study with the statement that 'the percentages of vacant benefices in each rural deanery work out with such unanimity that the mortality of the beneficed clergy...may be taken as a fair guide to the general death-rate'.

Unfortunately the biological nature of bubonic plague contradicts his conclusion, because if there is one characteristic of the disease that is absolutely constant it is the erratic manner of its spread and consequently its haphazard attack in every community. It is in fact the unanimity of these clerical statistics which precludes their use as a guide to the national death-rate from bubonic plague; but their unanimity might represent the activity in England of another lethal disease during the normally cold months from December to March when the rat-fleas, *X. cheopis* and *C. fasciatus*, hibernate in temperate climates. The characteristics of this other manifestation of 'The Great Pestilence'—for such it would have been to contemporary recorders— must have been the similarity of its clinical picture to that of bubonic plague: its winter incidence; its high infectivity; its transmission by direct human contacts; its preference for the well-fed and, especially with regard to the death-rate among the clergy, its high mortality in the middle-aged and elderly. Classical epidemic typhus fever completely fulfils these requirements.

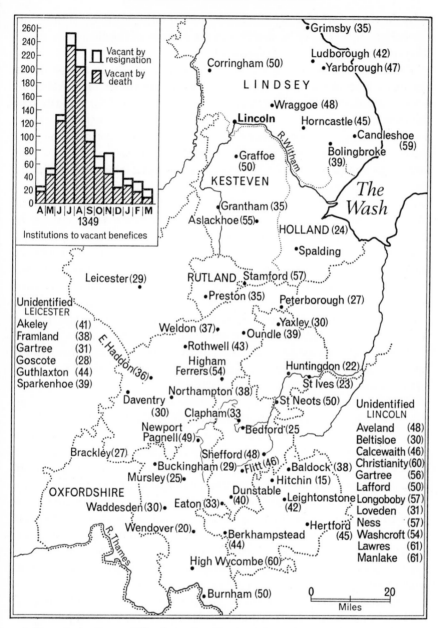

16. Plague in the diocese of Lincoln, 1348–9. The figures in brackets attached to each deanery represent the maximum possible percentage mortality among the beneficed clergy.

In the fourteenth century the county of Cambridgeshire constituted the diocese of Ely, but 13 of its churches in the deanery of Fordham were under the jurisdiction of the see of Norwich.[1]

There was a great mortality in the diocese in 1349 which, though it was unequally distributed, was heavy enough to invoke the grant in March of a papal indulgence for plenary remission of sins during the continuation of the pestilence.[2] There were 90 institutions to vacant benefices in 1349, a number which was some eighteen times greater than normal. Hampson asserts that the pestilence severely afflicted the monastery of Ely which housed 53 monks just before 'The Great Pestilence', whereas immediately after its cessation there were only 28.[3] There was no rent from a street in Ely because all the houses in it had been made tenantless by the pestilence.[4] Regrettably how many houses the street contained is not mentioned, for in the medieval city there may not have been more than half-a-dozen in it.

Wood-Legh remarks that the exact time of the appearance of plague in the diocese is not ascertainable, but she suggests that it was hardly serious before the end of March as April was the first month with an excessive number of institutions.[5] The monthly numbers of these from April to December inclusive were respectively 6, 6, 18, 24, 12, 9, 6, 3, and 4, from which figures she deduces that the epidemic reached its peak in July and then gradually declined to its cessation in December. She says that there is no evidence to indicate where the clergy died, but as 41 of the 90 were vicars she presumes that they died at their posts.

Cam cites Levett for the notice that 'about 1349 the accounts of St Mary des Prés show heavy expenditure at Sturbridge Fair on fish, horseshoes, mats, baskets, and cloth'.[6] If this notice is correctly dated, it very strongly suggests that Cambridge was free from plague at that time and that the county was hardly affected by it, because Sturbridge Fair was invariably cancelled when there was merely a threat of plague in its vicinity. Nevertheless Berodis[7] affirms that between April and August 1349 the pandemic killed 16 of the 40 scholars in residence at Trinity College. It is regrettable that the assertion that 3 Cambridgeshire villages were bereft respectively of 47, 57, and 70 per cent of their populations by 'The Great Pestilence' is not supported by their names and a reference to the contemporary source from which these guesses were obtained.[8]

Lunn records that in Cambridge 'the mastership of St John's Hospital fell void by death three times in quick succession' in May and early June 1349.[9]

Salzman[10] relates that on the manor of Crowland 35 of the 50 tenants at Oakington, 20 of 42 at Dry Drayton, and 33 of 58 at Cottenham, died during 1349. 'To these figures', he continues, 'must be added

the deaths of wives, children, and landless men.' He remarks that there is also evidence of severe mortality among the commoners at Soham and among the tenants on the manors of Ditton Valence, Bottisham, and Toft. 'On the other hand the records of Great Shelford and Elsworth, which cover this period, show no traces of the pestilence.' The Burwell accounts for 1348–9 also show no traces of it. With respect to the 3 Crowland manors, Lunn deduces that plague was epidemic among their tenantry in April 1349 because the deaths of 10 of the Oakington tenants were recorded at the manorial court held in May. He opines that the epidemic reached its peak in this county in June, as exemplified by the episcopal institutions and by the record of the Crowland manorial court in July that 40 tenants had died on the three manors. He notes that these manors were situated in the deanery of Chesterton, which had the second highest rate of presumptive plague-deaths among the beneficed clergy in the see of Ely.[1]

THE DIOCESE OF ELY

The diocese of Ely is supposed to have had 145 incumbents in 1348, and the episcopal register shows that the bishop made 92 institutions to vacant benefices in the twelve months from 25 March 1349 to 25 March 1350, though a few of them were void twice. It is said to have been in consequence of the mortality among his clergy that the bishop of Norwich founded the college of Trinity Hall at Cambridge in order to secure a supply of priests for his diocese.[2] At the abbey of Ely 15 of the 43 brethren perished in 1349.[3]

The disease did not reach Nottinghamshire until February 1348/9.[4] Cox states that its religious houses were attacked with dreadful severity, adding as confirmation: 'The superiors with their more commodious rooms and better food, suffered as heavily as any class', a statement that reveals a regrettable ignorance of the nature of bubonic plague, though it conforms to the epidemiology of typhus fever. He notes that coincident with the prevalence of the pestilence two priors each of Thurgarton and Shelford; the abbot of Welbeck; the priors of Blyth, Newstead, and Fellery; the warden of Sibthorpe, and the master of St Leonard's Newark died—inferentially from bubonic plague. He affirms that the pandemic destroyed more than half the beneficed clergy in the county because 65 of the 126 benefices were rendered void, and because the mortality among the laity at Newark was so great that the bishop was constrained to consecrate by licence a new churchyard there for the burial of the plague-dead.

Wallis-Chapman suggests that 'The Great Pestilence' and the subsequent pestilence of 1360 probably contributed to the fall in the land values in this

county. 'The fact that this fall is by no means universal suggests', she deduces, 'that it was partly the effect of a disease, which might possibly desolate one township and leave another untouched'—a pertinent contribution to a proper understanding of the nature of bubonic plague. 'For example',

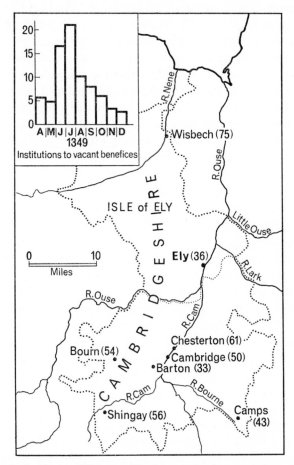

17. Plague in the diocese of Ely, 1349. The figures in brackets attached to each deanery represent the maximum possible plague mortality among the beneficed clergy.

she continues, 'some manors, like Langar, absolutely increased in value; others, like Warsop, fell in value, in this instance from about £17 to £4 15s. 4d.' Altogether she finds that of about 12 manors with relevant records 6 show a marked decrease in value.[1]

Thompson,[2] in his discussion of the significance of the clerical mortality figures in the deaneries comprising the archdeaconry of Nottingham—

which was a part of the diocese of York in the fourteenth century—(see figure 18) suggests that the comparatively low mortality rates in the Vale of Belvoir and other low-lying districts may be due to the enforced evacuation of many of the villages by floods. As the summer of 1348 was excessively wet his suggestion is a reasonable one. In October 1350 a royal warrant granted a 'release, for two years, to John de Bekeryng, of 10 *l.* out of 40 *l.* which he has to render yearly for the lands of Osewardesbekone, co. Nottingham...because of the great diminution in the value of those lands on account of the mortal pestilence lately prevailing'.[1]

Miller[2] assigns a population of something over 8,000 to the city of York in 1334, and Russell gives it a population of 10,872 in 1377 (see table 1), so that it seems probable that the population of Yorkshire did not exceed 12,000 in 1348, in which case a violent and prolonged epidemic of bubonic plague could have destroyed as many as 4,000 of its citizens. As York was the only town of any size in the county in 1348, and as bubonic plague is essentially an urban disease, a generous estimate of the plague-mortality in the county's widely scattered population is one-twentieth of its inhabitants between the ages of 10 and 35 years.

Miller[3] affirms that 'The Great Pestilence' appeared in this county in March 1349; that the disease was at its peak in the city from 21 May to 25 July, and that it persisted in York for nearly a year.

Salzman[4] reports that nearly half the parish priests of the archdeaconries of York and Cleveland are said to have perished during its prevalence, and Fallow[5] adds the note that between 24 July and 3 August 1349 two priors of North Ferriby died in succession, supposedly of bubonic plague.

'It is probably owing to the preponderance of information from ecclesiastical sources', Sellers writes, 'that the belief has become so general that the clergy suffered more than any other class of the community [from 'The Great Pestilence'], but a careful study of the limited material other than ecclesiastical does not bear out this assumption.' As she had previously asserted that Seebohm's[6] careful statistics—compiled from the Torre MSS—*prove* that more than two-thirds of the parish priests in the West Riding, and 35 of 95 in the East Riding, died during the pestilence, the inescapable inference from her statements is that—at any rate for the West Riding—more than two-thirds of the population died of bubonic plague, which, in view of the nature of that disease and the wide dispersion of the county's population, is an impossibility.[7] In August 1349 the abbey of Meaux lost 22 clerks and 6 laymen (the abbot and 5 monks dying in one day); only one-fifth of its 49 monks survived the pestilence, and the abbots of four of the largest Yorkshire monasteries succumbed to it. Sellers then remarks that the collection of wills

published by the Surtees Society, which cover the period of the pestilence, 'show few traces of the plague', only 9 wills being registered between 1348 and 1351. Nevertheless the *post mortem* inquisitions reveal, she affirms, a great mortality among the tenantry—presumably in York—and that of the 21 parish priests in the city, 17 died. As confirmation of the civic mortality, she states that the annual average number of freemen enrolled in York during the fourteenth century ranged between 50 and 60; but in 1349 the number was 208; for the succeeding three years it was respectively 117, 132, and 104, and it was not until 1353 that it returned to normality.

Finally, commenting upon the epidemics that afflicted Hull in the seventh decade of the fourteenth century, she writes: 'But there is one marked difference between these attacks of plague of the second half of the century and the Black Death. They were localized in towns, escape by flight was possible to the wealthy, but in 1349 death was in the soil, town and country suffered alike, the fortunes of the wealthy and poor were equalized.'[1] If such a 'marked difference' had existed, then the 'Black Death' was certainly not an eruption of plague; but the statement unfortunately betrays only a sad ignorance of the immutable aetiology of that disease, which can no more change its nature than 'the Ethiopian his skin, or the leopard his spots'.[2]

Lunn opines that plague was present in York in August 1349,[3] and the contemporary account of an incident, which is better described by Sellers, supports his opinion. She relates that the Coroners' Rolls of the city record that four parishes met and viewed the corpse of one, William Needler, found dead. They certified that he died 'a natural and not a violent death by reason of the pestilence in Coppergate, York, on 7 August 1349'.[4] Lunn comments that this case 'must have been typical of scores of others. Prisoners in the jails died off like flies. On this same roll of York (P.R.O. '*Coroners' Rolls—Yorkshire* 1349)—one of the very few surviving for 1349—no less than five inquests are found on prisoners who died in their dungeons.'[5] But typhus fever, popularly known as 'goal fever', killed the inmates of British prisons far more often than bubonic plague from early times to the end of the seventeenth century. Prisons as a rule were not congenial haunts for the house-rat, whereas the human body-louse, which transmits typhus fever, flourished under the conditions in which the prisoners were kept.

Lunn also remarks, in connexion with the office of coroner, that 'the Close Rolls show that in normal times the coronership was very rarely vacated by death. A man advanced in age pleaded inability to perform the duties. On an average in a normal year something like four new coroners were appointed; but in 1348 there were eight and in 1349 twenty-nine vacancies due to death, not including resignations.'[6]

Rees reports a reduction in the rents of the manors of Cotyngham, Wyve-ton, Kirkby, Morsheved, Alton, Hemelyngton, Cropton, Yapum, Castel-levyngton, Tampton, Nenby, Kildale, Darthyngton, Emeley, Sprotburgh, Cathwayt, Scorby, Sutton, and Skelton,[1] which he attributes to the mortal effect of 'The Great Pestilence'. He adds that

Osgodly was badly attacked, also Bulsham (Yabeton), all the tenants here falling victim and the rents (20s.) were lost...At Middleton, 12 bovates of the *nativi*, at Kebelyngcotes 10, at North Dalton 14, at Sledmere 40, at Wynstow 11, were by 1350 either waste or rented out. At North and Eastgaveldale there were 9 bovates waste. Conditions were similar at Hundemanby, Siwardby and Ruddeston, 10 bovates out of 14 being idle at Bruyngton.[2]

Thompson believes that the epidemic of plague was at its peak in York-shire during June, July and August 1349, because during those months the chapels and new churchyards of Egton, St Thomas's Chapel by Beverley, Fulford (a suburb of York), Cleasby, Wilton, Seamer, Brotton, Guisborough (an extension to the churchyard), Barton, Easby, and Thorpe-in-the-Street, were dedicated for the burial of plague-dead. In several instances the dedication was only made under the stress of an unusual mortality, for it was expressly limited to the duration of the pestilence.[3] Of the places named, eight are located in the extreme north of the county.

After giving a detailed account of the institutions to vacant benefices in the archdeaconries of Nottingham and York, Thompson remarks: 'The general conclusion that the two extremes, mountainous districts on the one hand and marshland on the other, were comparatively immune from pesti-lence, while normal agricultural country and the lower highlands suffered most heavily, is borne out by the figures for the three deaneries of the Cleveland archdeaconry', [shown below].[4]

		Percentage mortality of the beneficed clergy
Bulmer	Arable and pasture	51·51
Ryedale	Hilly	28·28
Cleveland	Moorland	21·42

Thompson's conclusion is consonant with the bionomics of *R. rattus*, with the important qualification that in agricultural country and upland the density of the house-rat population would vary directly with the distribu-tion of human aggregates in villages and townships.

Sellers[5] quotes a report by Clarkson that Richmond was so grievously ravaged by 'a plague and epidemic disease' about this time that about 2,000 of its inhabitants were destroyed. She rightly adds the warning that this report is not supported by any evidence and it would certainly appear to be

a spurious one, because it is improbable that Richmond had a population of more than 1,000 persons of all ages at any time in the fourteenth century. Its population in 1931 was only 6,165.[1]

'The Great Pestilence' may have entered the county through its port of Kingston-upon-Hull as a maritime importation by coastal shipping from East Anglian ports. Hull was certainly attacked by plague, and it would seem severely, for in March 1353 Edward III made a grant to its townsfolk because a 'great part of the men' had 'died in the late pestilence and the survivors are so desolate and poor that without succour they cannot pay the farm...and other charges on their town'.[2] Moreover the fact that many of the manors named by Rees were situated in either the district of Holderness or the Vale of Pickering strongly suggests that they were involved in the characteristic radiating spread of bubonic plague inland from the port of Hull.

Episcopally considered, Westmorland was a divided county in the fourteenth century, the southern half belonging to the see of York, the northern half to that of Carlisle.[3]

In view of its geographical features, its relative isolation from the rest of England, its scanty population, and its frequent experience of Scottish raids, it is extremely unlikely that *P. pestis* managed to penetrate during 'The Great Pestilence' even to its most populous part, the valley of the Eden, and it is pleasant therefore to find a local historian affirming that according to tradition the people of Ravenstonedale completely escaped 'The Great Pestilence'.[4]

DIOCESE OF YORK

Thompson argues convincingly[5] that the episcopal register of York is of much less value than that of Lincoln as an index of the presumptive plague-mortality rate of the beneficed clergy during 'The Great Pestilence', because there are three serious drawbacks to its use for that purpose. The first of these is that the number of non-resident clergy was very considerable.

A medieval rector [he declares] was frequently little more than the impropriator of his benefice; and the richer benefices were practically monopolized by clerks in the service of the king or some noble patron, who held dispensations for more than one benefice, and were otherwise well provided with prebends in cathedral and collegiate churches...The notice of the death of a parish priest does not therefore mean that he died in his benefice.

He then neutralizes this declaration by asserting that the number of rectors who can be proved to have held more than one benefice in either of the sees of York or Lincoln is so small that it is hardly worth recording.

The second drawback is that under the pressure of the rapidly accumu-

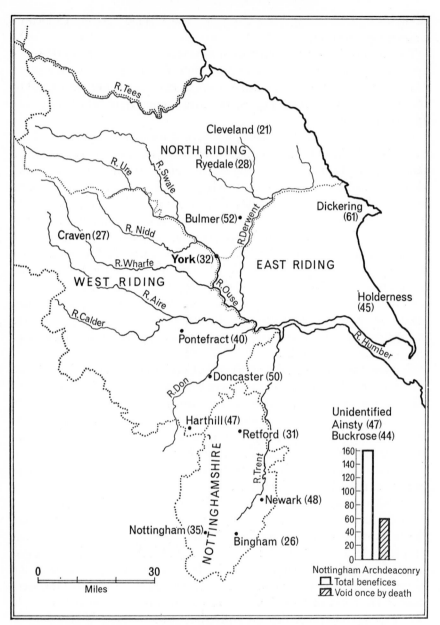

18. Plague in the diocese of York, 1349. The figures in brackets attached to each deanery represent the maximum possible plague mortality among the beneficed clergy.

lating institutions during 'The Great Pestilence' some were not entered in the episcopal register.

The third is that the total number of benefices in any given area of the see—upon which the percentage plague-mortality rate depends—is difficult to ascertain because certain churches had two or more distinct benefices, and in addition there were free chapels, the actual number of which can only approximately be ascertained.

If, as seems extremely probable, the bulk of the scanty population of the county of Durham in the fourteenth century (see table 3) occupied the valleys of the Tees and the Wear, the rest of the county must have been virtually desolate, with no conceivable possibility of the spread in it of bubonic plague. In all probability the only microbial diseases that could have spread outside those valleys under the prevailing conditions were small-pox, typhus fever, and epidemic influenza. Nevertheless Gee[1] declares that the county was not spared by 'The Great Pestilence' and he asserts that there is documentary evidence that its death-roll was heavy. For example, he says that in the Cursitor Roll special provision for a land title was made in the event of the death of the assigns during the pestilence which was then raging. Moreover, he adds, 'the papal registers for the next forty years give in their concessions to monastic houses conclusive proof of the virulence of the outbreak in the north'.

Comford[2] states that in the priory of St Cuthbert in Durham city so many of the clergy died of plague that there were not enough priests left to ad-minister the sacraments, and she affirms that the tenants of the Hospital of St Giles Kepier also suffered severely. Their visitation by the disease was accompanied by a failure of their crops and a murrain among their domestic animals, and this conjunction of misfortunes reduced the house to such dire poverty that in 1351 the bishop 'granted an indulgence of three hundred days to all who contributed to its relief'.

Bradshaw[3] opines that the pandemic crept up the North Road from Norfolk during the spring and early summer of 1349, with the result that the peasants living along the *Salters' Track* (see figure 19) were the first people in the diocese to experience it. He suggests that it may have reached Sunderland before the middle of July, because by that time 'four of the bishop's tenants at Wearmouth, who had broken the Assize of Ale, were dead'.[4] He notes that the business at the summer halmote at Chester le Street on 14 July proceeded normally; but at the halmote at Houghton le Spring on the 15th the peasants were in a state of panic, and a similar panic was manifest at Easington on the 16th. There was no alarm at Middleham halmote on the 17th, however, possibly because this village lay off the main

19. Plague in the diocese of Durham, 1349. The places marked are specifically mentioned in Dr Lunn's work on the bishops' registers or in monastic records as being involved in 'The Great Pestilence'.

road, and the halmotes of Stockton on the 17th, Sadberge and Darlington on the 20th, Wolsingham on the 21st or 22nd, and Lanchester on the 23rd of July, all seem to have been conducted normally. After this last meeting Bradshaw finds that there is an ominous silence in the records lasting until the halmote at Wolsingham on 7 April 1350.[1]

He deduces from the contemporary records that plague erupted as an epidemic disease at first in the south-eastern part of the county, and he believes that it raged with especial virulence at Billingham, where 48 tenants of the prior died of it. Although Billingham was not a large village he is convinced that at least half of its population perished. In the three parishes of Wolviston, Newton Bewley, and Norton, 28, 15, and 20 tenants respectively died of plague, and he opines that fugitives from these parishes carried the disease to neighbouring ones. The three hamlets of Shields, Harton, and Westoe had a combined death-roll of 41 people, and 16, 16, 8 and 11 deaths were recorded respectively in the villages of Jarrow, Wallsend, Southwick, and Monkwearmouth. At Stockton only three-quarters of the usual number of autumn works were performed because of the pestilence, which spread up the east side of the bishopric until it reached Newcastle and passed into Northumberland. He affirms that 'practically every vill belonging to the prior (of Billingham) was attacked more or less severely and in the case of the two Heworths two-thirds of the tenants disappeared. It was impossible for the bishop's vills to escape, and we know that some of them, especially Easington and Sunderland, suffered rather severely.'[2]

Bradshaw says that plague subsided in the winter

but it left behind a ruined and dispirited people. Every rank in life suffered—freemen, clergy, peasant. Such of the serfs as escaped often left their native villages in panic. Sometimes the people deserted the old site of the village in a body and built the village elsewhere. 'No tenants came from West Thickly because they are all dead' is one entry on the bishop's rolls, and in another place we are told that only one tenant was left at Rowley...whilst across the river at Bishopwearmouth 'a very large number of houses were fallen in ruins for want of tenants'.

He adds that the mortality was so severe in some parishes that no attempt was made in them during the winter and spring of 1350 to sow the land.[3]

With regard to Durham city, Gee remarks: 'It does not seem conceivable that the city escaped, but numerous and pathetic as are the details of the ravages in the bishopric at large no very clear tradition has survived in Durham itself.'[4] The exemption of Durham city is, however, quite conceivable when the aetiology of bubonic plague is understood. It just happened that by chance, in the natural erratic spread of the disease, *P. pestis* was not introduced among the city's house-rats when the epizootic of rat-plague was

prevalent in other parts of the bishopric. Durham city's escape from 'The Great Pestilence' was therefore neither inconceivable nor unique; it shared its good fortune with many English towns.

It is noteworthy that Bradshaw states that plague subsided in the winter. It almost invariably did so in temperate climates, because as soon as the normal cold weather of that season set in the plague-fleas hibernated in the rats' nests.

As one of the two English Border counties, the history of Northumberland from the Conquest to the accession of James VI of Scotland to the English throne is so full of Scottish rapine, loot, and arson, and of English reprisals in kind, that it is extremely improbable that, apart from Newcastle-upon-Tyne, *R. rattus* was established in this county in the fourteenth century in sufficient density to support an epizootic of rat-plague. It is significant that the contemporary record of its involvement in 'The Great Pestilence' is apparently confined to three references in the royal archives to the visitation of Newcastle-upon-Tyne by the pandemic.

The first of these, dated 20 November 1350, grants a pardon 'to the burgesses and other men of Newcastle-upon-Tyne, in consideration of their losses as well on account of the deadly pestilence as by various other adversities in these times of wars, of 250 marks of the 600 marks due from their town.'[1]

The second is contained in a royal order of 1 December 1350 that the triennial tenth and fifteenth shall be borne by the rents as well as by other goods of the town of Newcastle-upon-Tyne, even though 'several merchants and other rich men, who used to pay the greater parts of the tenths and fifteenths and of other charges incumbent upon the town, have perished in the mortal pestilence raging'.[2]

The third, dated 12 November 1352, is another pardon for the burgesses and townsfolk 'in consideration of their damages and losses sustained on account of the pestilence lately affecting the town as well as by various adversities coming upon them in these times of wars, of 100 *l.* of the 600 marks which they owe the King of the last tenth and fifteenth for three years. to wit for each year of the three 50 marks'.[3]

DIOCESE OF DURHAM

Lunn emphasizes that as the episcopal register does not cover the period of 'The Great Pestilence' it is useless for the evaluation of the possible plague-mortality of the beneficed clergy in this diocese.

Carlisle and its vicinity, and the lower reaches of the Eden valley, together

with a narrow coastal strip, would seem to have been the only habitable parts of Cumberland in the fourteenth century.

Wilson[1] finds little contemporary information about the effect of 'The Great Pestilence' upon the beneficed clergy in this county; but he notes an ominous gap in the diocesan register of Carlisle for the six years 1347 to 1352, which he assumes signifies a severe plague-mortality among the clergy. It is improbable that such an assumption is justifiable because the geography of this county, the sparseness of its population, the unease of its living conditions, and the aetiology of bubonic plague, conjoin to make it unlikely that *P. pestis* penetrated farther into the county than Carlisle at this time.

Evidence that Carlisle was involved in 'The Great Pestilence' is contained in a royal grant of various liberties made to its citizens in February 1352 in recognition of its importance as a frontier fortress against the Scots and because 'it is now wasted and more than usually depressed as well by the mortal pestilence lately prevalent in those parts as by frequent attacks'.[2]

DIOCESE OF CARLISLE

This consisted in the fourteenth century of most of the parishes in the county of Cumberland, together with those in the northern half of Westmorland; but as the episcopal register is blank for the duration of 'The Great Pestilence', nothing is known about the plague toll of the beneficed clergy in this diocese.[3]

As the king was in all probability one of the best-informed contemporaries of the extent and destructiveness of 'The Great Pestilence' in England, it is apposite to quote here his order of 28 January 1350 'not to permit men at arms, pilgrims or any others of the realm to cross from that port without the King's special order...*as no small portion of the people has perished* [my italics] in the present plague and the treasure of the realm is much exhausted, as the King has learned',[4] which was sent to the mayor and bailiffs of Sandwich, Winchelsea, Rye, Faversham, Great Yarmouth, King's Lynn, Maldon, Ipswich, Harwich, Dunwich, Heth, Oreford, Romney, Colchester, Hastings, Shoreham, Chichester, Southampton, Portchester, Hamelhouk, Melcombe, Weymouth, Swanage, Poole, Lyme Regis, Exeter, Topsham, Dartmouth, Plymouth, Sidmouth, Fowey, Barnstaple, Totnes, Exmouth, Bristol, Tynemouth, Halyeland, Newcastle-upon-Tyne, Boston, Scarborough, Grimsby, Hartlepool, Yarm, Raveneser (?Ravenglass), Saltfleetby, Kingston upon Hull, Berwick-on-Tweed, and London.

The sheriffs of London, Northumberland, York, Lincoln, Norfolk and Suffolk, Essex, Kent, Sussex, Southampton, Somerset and Dorset, Devon,

Cornwall, and Gloucester, were ordered to make an identical proclamation in their respective jurisdictions.

It is significant that the great majority of these seaports and river-ports lie south and east of the York–Exeter line. It is also noteworthy that Edward III did not state that one-half of the English people had been destroyed by 'The Great Pestilence'—or even one-third! He used a phrase which may generously be construed to mean about one-tenth, because 400,000 deaths in a population of 4,000,000 people would be 'no small portion'.

The references to the presumptive activity of bubonic plague in Wales have mostly been supplied by Rees,[1] who affirms that Snowdonia, especially Anglesey, was overrun by 'The Great Pestilence'. He may be correct for Anglesey, which appears to have been populous in the fourteenth century, but it is extremely improbable that Snowdonia was sufficiently colonized by the house-rat to support an epizootic of rat-plague. In any case he nullifies his affirmation by his succeeding statement that while certain hamlets had a heavy mortality others were little affected 'and even entire commotes escaped lightly'.

The lead miners of Englefield paid only 4*s.* of their dues in 1351 because most of them were dead and the survivors refused to work there.[2] A remission of rent was granted in 1351 to the burgesses of Rhuddlan on account of the poverty of the people as a result of 'The Great Pestilence'; but Rees says there is no record of any unusual mortality in that town.

In the lordship of Denbigh there is a record of the deaths of several tenants 'in the time of the pestilence' in the *villatae* of Barrok and Petrual. In the lordship of Ruthin there were two periods of severe mortality among the tenants during the weeks intervening between 12 March and 23 October 1349. As table 4 shows, one of these occurred during the last week in June and the other during the last week in August. Rees reports that the death-rate in this lordship 'continued well above the normal during succeeding years, one death being definitely attributed to "the Pestilence" in 1351, about nine in 1354, two in 1357, two in 1359, one in 1360, in addition to other deaths'. It is practically certain, however, that the deaths attributed to 'the Pestilence' in 1354, 1357, and 1359 were not due to bubonic plague but most probably to typhus fever.

In the commote of Creuddyn 7 of 9 advowry tenants were killed by 'the Pestilence' in 1351, and in the commote of Nant Conway either all the advowry tenants or the bulk of them was destroyed by it. Rees notes that it killed also many of the tenants of the manor of Hirdref and apparently exterminated the villeins there.

Rees reports that when William de Hastings died in March 1349, an

20. The distribution of 'The Great Pestilence' of 1348 in the principality of Wales.

TABLE 4

The course of the pestilence of 1349 in the lordship of Ruthin

Court	12 March	25 March	11 June	29 June	20 July	10 August	29 August	21 September	9 October	23 October
Colyan	—	—	—	10	25	8	44	12	Several	Several
Llanfair	—	1	1	13	29	14	45	7	Several	Several
Dogg	1*	1	—	25	11	13	20	9	3	2
Abergwillar	—	1	7	14	4	2	19	1	—	—
Ruthin Town	2	—	—	77 +	14	17	44	4	Few	Few
TOTALS	3	3	8	139 +	83	54	172	33	?	?

TABLE 5

Revenue losses on the manors of the lordship of Abergavenny

	Rents of assize of free and customary tenants		Additional losses due to the murrain and the mortality
	Before 1348	On 17 April 1349	
	£ s d	£ s d	
Penros	12 0 0	4 0 0	1 fulling-mill, reduced from 33s. 4d. to 6s. 8d., and 27 acres of wood 'of no value'
Trefgaer	4 6 8	1 10 6	
Henllys	5 9 1½	2 9 1½	
Trefgoythel	3 10 6¾	6 0	'The pleas and perquisites of the courts are of no value because the tenants are dead'. 111 acres of wood of no value in underwood
Bryngwyn	3 14 6½	1 8 2½	
Coyd Morgan	9 5 1¾	4 0 0	28 acres of wood of no value; three parts of one water-mill reduced from 14s. 6d. to 3s. 0d. 'The pleas and perquisites are worth nothing'
Werneryth	13 10 3½	1 14 6	
Llanwytherin	4 4 0	2 12 0	Pleas and perquisites worth nothing
Llandover	12 0 0	4 0 0	Organ mill reduced from 40s. to 10s. A fulling-mill reduced from 66s. 8d. to 13s. 4d., and another one from 20s. to 3s.
Ebboth fawr	6 13 4	2 13 4	12 acres of wood of no value
Ebbothfechan	7 0 0	3 0 0	10 acres of wood of no value
TOTALS	£81 13 8	£27 13 8	

* This death is dated 25 November 1348.

inquisition of his estate disclosed that the revenues of all his manors had diminished, and in every case except that of Penros the reason for the reduction given by the jurors was 'because of the mortality'. They recorded that in Penros many of the tenements were empty and derelict for lack of tenants, but there is no mention of any mortality on this manor. In some cases the values of other properties such as mills and woods had declined because of the murrain which was slaughtering the cattle while the pestilence was killing the people. Table 5 shows the reductions in the manorial revenues of this estate reported by Rees. They amount to £54 or nearly two-thirds of the total revenue of the estate before 'The Great Pestilence'.

Rees notes that at Llanllwch, near Carmarthen, the 12 villein tenants died during the pestilence, and he declares that the whole district of Carmarthen suffered seriously from it. He opines that 'the disease probably came by sea, for even as early as March 1349 the two Collectors of Customs of the King's Staple at Carmarthen had fallen victims' to it.

On 20 April 1350 Edward III granted a pardon and a remission of taxes to Sir Richard Talbot, the elder,

on his petition showing that the castle and town of Pembroke, with their members of Kyngeswode and Gwydon, and the commote of Coytrah, the castle and town of Tymby, the manor of Castlemartin, and the rent of castle-guard of the castle of Pembroke [see figure 20] are so deteriorated by the deadly pestilence which lately raged in those parts that he will be unable to answer for the whole of the said farm without grave loss.[1]

Clapham,[2] discussing the mortality of 'The Great Pestilence', remarks:

Possibly the traditional figure of a third of the population dead may be correct: many scholars have accepted it. But modern experience of plagues suggests a fair number of spots which would remain immune and affect the total. Perhaps 20 or 25 per cent may be nearer the mark than 33·3...We hear of depopulated but not deserted villages. When villages can be studied in groups, what surprises us is the continuity of their life. On the vast estate of the Bishop of Winchester in Wessex there is 'no sign of chaos or complete depopulation';[3] and following the Pestilence there is 'no revolution either in agriculture or in tenure'.[4] Across the country, on the East Midland and Fenland manors of Crowland, it is just the same: the estate accounts run on, and what is most important, there seems always to be someone ready to take over a vacant holding.

Trevelyan,[5] after describing the changes in population and land tenure that preceded 'The Great Pestilence', opines that 'a third or possibly a half of the inhabitants of the Kingdom died of plague in less than two years'.

Here, then, we have two acknowledged authorities whose estimates suggest a mortality range for 'The Great Pestilence' of from 20 to 50 per cent of the total population of England. That population most probably did not exceed

4 million souls in 1348, and it is suggested that of that number from 800,000 to 2,000,000 individuals—the majority between the ages of 15 and 40—died in two years without leaving any deserted villages, without causing any revolution either in agriculture or land tenure, and without any appreciable interruption of the political, commercial, and social life of the nation.

Obviously there is a fallacy somewhere—and it must be in the greatly exaggerated estimates of mortality because there were no deserted villages; there was no interruption in agriculture or land tenure; there was no appreciable change in the manner and customs of English life, and no interruption of the war with France!

Bubonic plague, by reason of its immutable nature, is principally an urban disease—but there were relatively few urban aggregates in England in the fourteenth century. There was not even a profusion of villages, thickly sprinkled over the land and linked by outlying farms, to enable *P. pestis* to be spread by haphazard rat contacts, erratically and unpredictably, among the colonies of house-rats which could only maintain themselves in close association with human aggregates. Yet without that fundamental epizootic spread of rat-plague no epidemic of the human disease could possibly have occurred.

Moreover England in 1348 was predominantly an agricultural society, with its national economy dependent upon the manpower available for agricultural needs—and bubonic plague tends to select for its attack the age-group which provided the major part of that manpower. When dispassionately reviewed, without assistance from the bogy of the 'Black Death', the contemporary records demonstrate conclusively that over the country as a whole there was no collapse of agriculture, no disruption of the economic life of the nation, for the simple reason that bubonic plague was biologically incapable of destroying under the social conditions existing in fourteenth-century England as much as 20 per cent of its population of some 4 million persons *of all ages* inhabiting, mostly in small village communities, a land area of 32,544,640 acres—an average density of population of 1 individual, adult, child, or infant, to every 8 acres. In all probability the national death-roll from 'The Great Pestilence' did not exceed one-twentieth of that population.

If 'The Great Pestilence' had been in its entirety a disease with a malignity approximately equal to that of bubonic plague—such as haemorrhagic smallpox—that was spread by human contacts, a death-roll of one-third of the nation might conceivably have been achieved. But bubonic plague was not so spread; had it been 'The Great Pestilence' would not have excited anything like the terror it aroused. The people of England were inured to epidemics of diseases which were obviously spread by human contacts. These

they could and did guard against with considerable effect by segregating the infected areas or by isolating their own home villages. Moreover experience taught them that recovery from the deadliest of these, smallpox, usually protected the survivor against the disease for life, and there was always a reasonable chance of recovery from it. It was the fact that they could not relate the spread of bubonic plague to human contacts; that recovery from one attack of it did not protect from a subsequent fatal attack; and that it tended to select the mothers and fathers of young families, that made it so terrible. Its high case-mortality rate, conjoined with its incomprehensible nature, imprinted a fear on the national mind which still lingers there today. The psychological effect of 'The Great Pestilence' upon the British people was far more harmful and more persistent than its mortal effect. It is still manifest in some of the modern literature about the 'Black Death', much of which is hypothetical.

There is not the slightest doubt that during the late spring, summer, and early autumn months, 'The Great Pestilence' was an epidemic of bubonic plague, engendered and sustained by an unrecognized epizootic of rat-plague. The house-rat could subsist during the cold weather of temperate climates in the warmth and shelter of human dwellings because it was a mammal; but its plague-fleas, much more susceptible to atmospheric temperature, invariably hibernated with the arrival of frosty weather. It is conceivable that in London and other towns in the south of England the plague-fleas might remain sufficiently active throughout an exceptionally mild winter to keep rat-plague smouldering, with the consequent production of sporadic cases of the human disease, and undoubtedly such winters occurred occasionally during the centuries of its invasion of England. Indeed Pepys' entries in his diary for 21 January 1660/1,[1] 15 January 1661/2,[2] and 28 November 1662,[3] show that for three successive years London, and part of England at least, had exceptionally mild winters. As it happens, bubonic plague was not epidemic in England then because *P. pestis* was absent. North of the Thames valley, however, it is doubtful whether any winter was consistently mild enough to permit the plague-fleas to continue their predatory activities.

But the rat also transmits to man the causal agent of typhus fever which, in its epidemic form, 'is a disease of great antiquity',[4] and which—in combination with dysentery and relapsing fever—was responsible for the *famine-fevers* of history. It manifests itself in man in one of two forms, the *classical*—which is spread by the body-louse, occurs in widespread epidemics, and 'has been in the past one of the great scourges of the world'[5]—and the *murine*, which is transmitted from the rat to man by *X. cheopis* and is self-limiting—

that is to say it does not spread from man to man by human contacts. However 'there seems very little doubt that, under suitable conditions, the disease may become epidemic in man and be spread by the body louse'.[1] In other words, the *murine* form can change to the *classical* in persons infected by *X. cheopis* who are infested with the body-louse. Snyder[2] states that the factors that favour the prevalence of typhus fever are the crowding together of people, lack of fuel, inadequate facilities for washing, 'and weather so cold that the same garments are worn continuously day and night for months at a time', because such wearing predisposes to louse infestation. 'Persons of all ages are susceptible to typhus...As age increases, the case-fatality rate rises sharply...There is considerable variation in the severity of typhus in different epidemics. Overall case-fatality rates for various epidemics range from less than 10 to more than 40 per cent.'[2] Although the body-louse lives on the clothing that is worn next to the body and not on the skin of infested individuals, transference or exchange of lice commonly occurs when people are crowded together under any circumstances. Moreover the inhalation of the powdered dry excrement of infected lice will produce the disease in man.

Langland,[3] introducing 'Covetise', describes him as wearing 'a tawny cloak upon him, twelve months old, all torn and rotten and full of creeping lice'. Zinsser[4] asserts that 'the manner of living throughout the Middle Ages made general lousiness inevitable. In England, in the twelfth and thirteenth centuries, the houses of the poor were mere hovels...and in cold weather the families were huddled together at night without changing the simple garments...which they wore in the daytime.' And some three hundred years after 'The Great Pestilence', Mrs Pepys found it obligatory to cleanse her new housemaid of her body lice and give her 'good, new clothes',[5] after which the girl promptly ran away. During the whole of the intervening period the body-louse flourished among all classes of English society, attaining its maximum infestation rate among the poor crowded together in the medieval slums of the towns, the exact places where bubonic plague struck first and fiercest, and persisted longest. There is evidence that in the sixteenth and seventeenth centuries the two diseases of bubonic plague and typhus fever alternated seasonally, and there is no reason why 'The Great Pestilence' should not have consisted of a similar alternation. Indeed such an alternation supplies the only satisfactory explanation of its continuance throughout the years 1348–9 and 1349–50, and also the apparent high mortality among the beneficed clergy, who, in all probability, were as infested with body lice as their parishioners.

Typhus fever was not differentiated from bubonic plague until about the middle of the nineteenth century.[6]

CHAPTER 5

PLAGUE AND PESTILENCE IN THE YEARS FROM 1350 TO 1500

THE LATE FOURTEENTH CENTURY

Had 'The Great Pestilence' caused anything like the devastating mortality in England and Wales ascribed to it by so many writers about the 'Black Death', the royal archives would surely have been full of petitions to the king in the years immediately succeeding its cessation for relief from taxation and for grants in aid. The paucity of the recorded royal pardons and grants indicates that this alleged mortality of the 'Black Death' exists only in the imaginations of its subscribers.

Some of the royal reliefs have been noted in the previous chapter, and to these only four more can it seems be added. In March 1354 the nunnery of Wyrthorp in the diocese of Lincoln petitioned the king for relief because of its impoverishment by the late pestilence.[1] In July of that year the mesne tenants of the royal manors of Newcastle Lyonns, Tassagard, Cromelyn, Outhard, and Castlemarny in Ireland petitioned for relief, alleging their complete impoverishment by the pandemic.[2] In August 1355 Edward III granted a remission for ten years of the annual farm of 6s. for a tenement in Winchelsea to the master and brethren of St Bartholomew, Winchelsea, because of that house's great depression by the late pestilence,[3] and in October of that year he received a petition from Henton priory in Somerset which stated that the greater part of its land had lain uncultivated since 1349 for want of labour.[4]

After 'The Great Pestilence' subsided in 1350, England appears to have been free from a major eruption of epidemic disease for ten or eleven years. Then in 1360 or 1361 there was a widespread pestilence which seems to have been prevalent—at any rate in the north of England—from mid-August 1361 to May 1362,[5] though some annalists record its eruption in other parts of the country in the preceding year. This epidemic was generally designated by contemporary writers the 'Second Pestilence', and later writers have tacitly

assumed that this and the succeeding pestilences in the second half of the fourteenth century were each and all recurrent outbreaks of bubonic plague. There is no warrant for such an assumption. There is no doubt that smallpox, measles, typhus fever, and dysentery were repeatedly epidemic in fourteenth-century England; pneumonia undoubtedly occurred in epidemic form in the winter months, and whooping-cough, the enteric fevers, and influenza in all probability were also epidemic at times. It is certain that tuberculosis, 'the white scourge', was responsible for many deaths annually, because one form of it, *scrofula*, then called the 'King's Evil', for which the royal touch was supposed to effect a cure, was so treated by Henry II, Henry III, and the first three Edwards.[1] It is probable that diphtheria, erysipelas—under the name of St Anthony's Fire—and poliomyelitis were locally epidemic from time to time and that, as Wilde suggested,[2] some of the great medieval epidemics of 'colic' that afflicted the British Isles may have been maritime importations of cholera. Wilde's suggestion is not the fantastic one that some readers may deride, because cholera could easily have been imported into south-western Europe from its Indian home by the return of Moslem pilgrim carriers of *Vibrio cholerae* from the great religious concourse at Mecca. The pandemic of the disease which introduced four deadly waves of it to the British Isles in the nineteenth century was almost certainly not the only incursion of cholera in these islands.

The identification of the English pestilence of 1360–1 as an epidemic of bubonic plague is open to several objections. The royal proclamation of 1361 that all slaughtering of food animals for the inhabitants of London must be done in the outlying townships of Stratford or Knightsbridge, in order to protect the citizens from the 'plague' then prevalent in France,[3] does not signify that the French pestilence was an outbreak of bubonic plague, because any widespread epidemic of disease with an appreciable mortality was a 'plague' to fourteenth-century recorders. De Chauliac's description of this French pestilence[4] refutes its identification as bubonic plague, even though he evidently regarded it as a recurrent manifestation of the pestilence he had survived in 1348, for bubonic plague did not change its nature between 1348 and 1360, and of this later pestilence he wrote that 'whereas in the first epidemic it was chiefly the poor who suffered, in the second many rich and noble persons, a multitude of boys, and a few women were attacked'. As Creighton justly remarks, it is unsafe to conclude 'that all the outbreaks of *pestis* in England subsequent to the Black Death, were of bubo-plague itself'.[5]

Contemporary English chroniclers also ascribe social and age incidences to this pestilence that are at variance with the characteristic incidence of bubonic plague. Adam of Murimuth calls it a great mortality and records

that 'of it there died in England some outstanding people and noblemen, and a very large number of churchmen, both secular and regular'.[1] Knighton later writes of it as the Second Pestilence in which 'great and less died, but especially young men and children'.[2] *The Brut* notes that it especially slaughtered men, whose wives 'as women out of control,' proceeded to consort with any men that were available, irrespective of their class or their state,[3] while the York chronicler says that it was known at the time as 'the mortality of children'.[4] With respect to this reference Galbraith remarks that 'the pestilence of 1361 is described by *John of Reading* as "sexum masculinum valde consumens". Knighton says with the *Anonimalle* writer that it was especially fatal to children. Compare the chronicle of Melsa, "secunda pestilentia...que dicta est puerorum"; evidently this was the north country name for it. The social effects of this pestilence are thus described in the B continuation of the *Polychronicon*: "foeminae...sumpserunt maritos tam extraneos quam alios imbeciles et vecordes, pudoric non parcentes...se cum inferioribus copulare".'[5]

Whatever was the true nature of this pestilence, it was evidently widespread and aroused great alarm in England. It may have erupted in London in the autumn of 1360 or the winter of 1361. It was certainly epidemic there in May 1361, because on the 10th of that month Trinity term was adjourned to midsummer as '*great multitudes of people are suddenly smitten* with the deadly plague now newly prevailing as well in the city of London as in neighbouring parts, and the plague is daily increasing'.[6] The italics are mine to draw attention to two features that are characteristic of epidemic influenza, to wit, its well-nigh universal incidence in the community attacked and the unique suddenness of its onset. Readers who are unacquainted with the potential lethal power of this disease may be surprised to learn that the 1918–19 pandemic of it was authoritatively estimated to have caused a global death-roll of more than 50 million, including 200,000 registered deaths from it in England and Wales. If epidemic influenza was a component of the pestilence of 1361, its extent then could have been proportionately as great as in 1918–19, but its case-mortality rate would certainly have been much higher. In the twentieth-century epidemic 'healthy young adults were specially affected',[7] and the fourteenth-century records suggest that the pestilence of 1361 possibly chiefly affected that age-group.

This pestilence evidently persisted into June in London, for a second proclamation on the 23rd of the month extended the adjournment of the term to Hilary.[8] As no further adjournment is recorded, it seems evident that the disease subsided some time during the summer, just when an epidemic of bubonic plague would be mounting to its peak. According to one

chronicler[1] it killed about 1,200 people in London in 2 days—24 and 25 June—and though he says that it was 'something like' the pandemic of 1348, he adds that it was 'nothing near so Dismal and Universally Fatal as the Former; but much more Destructive of the Nobility and Prelacy, where ever it went... but especially it raged among Young Men and Children, being less fatal to Women'.

In the diocese of Exeter 64 institutions to vacant benefices were made in 1361 and 128 in 1362.[2] Of the former number 46 or practically 72·0 per cent were made during the three months October–December; of the latter number 66 or 51·2 per cent were made during the three months January–March. If all the vacancies were caused by the deaths of the incumbents from the pestilence, 58·2 per cent of the diocesan clergy died during the six autumn and winter months when bubonic plague is usually either extinguished or rendered quiescent in temperate latitudes by the hibernation of the plague-fleas of *R. rattus*. If Pickard's figures are accurate and represent actual deaths, they afford conclusive evidence that the pestilence of 1361 was not an epidemic of bubonic plague in the diocese of Exeter.

The wide spread of this pestilence is attested by the records that the revenues from the royal stannary and the Cornish tin mines were much diminished in December 1361 'by reason of the plague',[3] and that men had died of it on 'divers farms'—presumably royal demesnes—in Essex.[4] It seems evident also that the royal grant in October 1366 to John le Mareschall of a reduction in the annual farm of his land in 'Southampton county' from £10 to 51s. 9½d., 'because of the last pestilence and the great storm', refers to the mortality of this pestilence and the destruction wrought by the tempest on St Maurice's Day, 14 January 1361.[5]

Leicestershire appears to have suffered severely from this pestilence as 43 parish priests, the dean and 7 canons of Newark, and nearly all the brethren of St John's Hospital, Leicester, are said to have died of it.[6] By contrast the adjoining county of Rutland was not so severely afflicted by it.[7] It was in his castle at Leicester that Henry of Lancaster died of pestilence on 24 March 1361 according to Kelly;[8] but Stow asserts that he died in London and was buried at Leicester.[9] Its involvement of Cambridgeshire is shown by the notices that Great Shelford, which escaped 'The Great Pestilence', suffered severely in 1361,[10] and that 9 of the residents of the King's Hall in the University died of it.[11]

Proceeding northwards, the epidemic appears to have invaded the county of Lincolnshire in 1362 as a monk of Thornton tells of 'a great and wonderful mortality of men in Lindsey, in South Ormsby, from Easter to Michaelmas' in that year, and of 'another mortality of children about Michaelmas'.[12] This record suggests that two distinct diseases were concurrently epidemic, and

this possibility is heightened by Cox's note about the abbey of Merivale in Warwickshire. There the bishop of Worcester 'commissioned a monk in June to act as a penitentiary for the pilgrims who frequented the chapel of St Mary at the gate of the monastery; it was stated in the licence that the bishop was informed that "large numbers of both sexes were coming to the chapel, and by reason of the crush and various prevalent diseases, many were brought to the point of death"'.[1] Warwickshire may in fact have been one of the worst afflicted counties in England, for the pestilence was apparently 'terribly severe' in the south and south-west parts of the county, where the mortality had been comparatively light in 1349.[2] In the afflicted area the incumbents of Claverdon, Morton Bagot, Aston Cantlow, and Bidford, and the abbot and parson of Alcester, died of it, and there were two consecutive institutions in August 1361 to the living Temple Grafton. The clergy of all these parishes had previously escaped 'The Great Pestilence'. In the central part of the county the incumbents of Ashow and Leek Wootton, the prior of Kenilworth, the vicar of Stoneleigh, two of the priests of St Nicholas, Warwick, and the prior and vicar of St Michael, Coventry, died during the summer of 1361.

Returning to the diocese of Lincoln, a 'further spate' of vacancies was recorded at Islip in Oxfordshire during the manorial year of 1362–3, and it has been assumed that they were caused by 'plague-deaths'.[3] The pestilence was mortal also in the adjoining county of Berkshire, where Edward III was building Windsor Castle, for it killed so many of the workmen that 'in 1362 writs were issued to the sheriffs of several counties, to impress 302 masons and diggers of stone, to be employed in the king's works'.[4]

In the neighbouring diocese of Lichfield the pestilence aroused great alarm in 1361, although it had apparently done no damage in that see before July of that year, because in July the bishop voiced his anxiety about it on account of the reports he had heard of its depopulation of many other parts of the kingdom.[5] As in 1349, rumour was a greater destroyer in 1361 than the pestilence. To encourage his flock to bear its approaching affliction with Christian fortitude, he granted an indulgence of 40 days to all who attended the prescribed masses and processions, and plenary remission of sins to those who died of it. This penitentiary licence was only to be valid, however, until Michaelmas, by which date he evidently expected that the pestilence would have subsided.[5] In this expectation he seems to have been disappointed, for in September according to Ramsay Muir the burgesses of Liverpool obtained a licence from him to bury their dead in the churchyard of St Nicholas instead of the parish church at Walton.[6] Further north York was attacked, but Miller supplies no detailed information about its visitation of that city.[7]

Wales

The pestilences of both 1361 and 1369 severely scourged south-eastern Wales, especially Monmouthshire.[1] In 1361 very heavy rent losses were recorded at Llantrisant, Trelech Town, and Hodenach Manor. By 1362 there was a loss of 142 'works' of the customary tenants at Caldecote Manor, 4 of the tenants dying that year. Rees gives a specified list of the 'workers' who had died by 1366 comprising 48 persons, together with certain holders of assort; but most probably some of these would have died from causes other than the pestilence. He adds that by 1372 the number of the dead had been increased to 55 and that the manor was almost devoid of bond tenants. 'But it must be remembered', he comments, 'that such a proportion of deaths is exceptional and that in many parts few or no losses are recorded.' Rees also reports a rapid increase of mortality in the lordship of Ruthin, in the north of the principality of Wales during the autumn and winter of 1361, which ceased in the ensuing spring.[2]

As I have already affirmed, contemporary references to this pestilence provide no justification for its identification as an outbreak of bubonic plague. It seems extremely probable that several distinct diseases were epidemic in different parts of England during the years from 1360 to 1362 inclusive, and that the royal grant to the nuns of Shaftesbury abbey in 1364, 'in relief of the state of the abbey which is much depressed by a tempest of wind and mortal pestilences lately prevailing in the realm',[3] seems to signify that authority recognized that the 'plague' of 1360–2 was a composite of different manifestations of a divinely engendered, punitive, pestilential state.

Though the exact composition of this pestilential state is obscure, the contemporary notices of it suggest that one component may well have been a wave of a European pandemic of epidemic influenza, which spread by human contacts from France to England. The mortality of children about Michaelmas at South Ormsby could have been caused by a local outbreak of diphtheria. The references to an apparent general mortality of children cannot be elucidated in the absence of specific information about the seasonal incidence of the mortality and the precise age-group of the children involved. The four chief lethal, epidemic diseases of children in England, in the age-group from birth up to 5 years of age, up to the end of the nineteenth century, were smallpox, measles, whooping-cough, and diphtheria, with scarlet fever as the chief killer of the survivors between 5 and 10 years of age. Diphtheria did not become a national menace, however, until urban aggregates grew and multiplied consequent upon the Industrial Revolution and compulsory

school attendance at the age of 5 was instituted; but any one of the first three diseases in this group could have been the 'child' component of the 'Second Pestilence'.

Scotland

The Scottish chronicler John of Fordun identifies the pestilence of 1362 in his country with 'The Great Pestilence' and affirms that it caused a similar mortality.[1] As Skene says that John was born about the beginning of the fourteenth century, was an ordained priest by 1327 and died in 1385,[2] he lived through both 'The Great Pestilence' and the one of 1361–2. That fact does not prove that the 1362 pestilence was an epidemic of bubonic plague; it merely indicates that it appeared to John to be another manifestation of the pestilential state that created 'The Great Pestilence', such as typhus fever for example. But if his record of it is accepted as one of bubonic plague, the disease could have been epidemic in Scotland when it was absent from England.

Ireland

After the cessation of 'The Great Pestilence' Ireland appears to have been free from a major epidemic of disease for many years. The royal remission of the payment of 86 marks from 'the king's city of Cork', because it had been so impoverished by the last pestilence and other misfortunes,[3] obviously refers to the second pandemic of bubonic plague. There seems to be no record of the 'Second Pestilence' in Ireland, but under the date of 1361 one of the Irish Annals records: 'Cluithe an righ' [The King's Game] throughout all Ireland in general, and Richard Savage died of it'.[4] As there appears to be only one other notice of this disease in those Annals, to wit, in 1504, when it is recorded as 'the pestilence' which killed 'Gilla-Patrick O'Connolly',[5] it seems unlikely that it was an epidemic disease. The rare mention of it is suggestive of a disease endemic among the commonalty, which on rare occasions killed the better-fed and housed members of the Irish aristocracy and prelacy. An Irish transliteration of the English 'King's Evil' would fit the scanty records of it, and O'Donovan opines that the Irish name 'had its origin in some similar notion'.[6]

It may have been a retarded spread of one of the diseases epidemic in 1361, or a local eruption of a fresh disease, that struck the abbey of Cockersand in 1363. At any rate its attack was so severe that 'a dispensation had to be obtained for several of the canons to be ordained in their twenty-first year'.[7] The abbey's affliction was apparently only an incident in a widespread prevalence of the disease in Cumberland, for it killed so many of the parish

priests in the diocese of Carlisle that the pope granted the bishop a faculty to secure 58 additional priests.[1] Wilson remarks that there is more explicit evidence of clerical mortality in Cumberland caused by this pestilence than by 'The Great Pestilence'.[2]

There are fewer records of the pestilential period of 1365–71 than of the 'Second Pestilence' and none concerns Scotland. According to the St Albans Chronicle, cited by Blomefield,[3] 'a sickness that men call the Pockes slew both Men and Women' in 1365, and two years later a London chronicle records that 'in this yere manye men and bestes were enfect with pokkes where thorugh they deyden'.[4] It is possible that through faulty chronology these records actually refer to the one outbreak of this 'pock' disease, but they provide an opportunity to discuss briefly its identity, because there are more records of it in the next hundred years.

The earliest reference to it in the fourteenth century comes from Ireland, where under the date of 1327 the *Annals of the Four Masters* has the entry: 'The Galar Breac raged throughout Ireland, of which many died.'[5] Concerning this record O'Donovan remarks: 'Throughout the province of Connaught, galar breac means the smallpox; but, in the south of Ireland, where bolzac is used to denote the smallpox, galar breac is used to denote the spotted fever',[6] which was typhus fever. In 1494 the *Chronicle of Lynn* records: 'In this yer begane the ffrence pockes',[7] or syphilis, which was vulgarly known as 'the great pox', variola then obtaining its present name of smallpox to distinguish it from the even more loathsome cutaneous lesions of syphilis. Flenley is incorrect, however, in his assertion that 'none of the English chroniclers record the outbreak of the disease',[8] because in the *Early Chronicles of Shrewsbury*, under the date of 1493–4, is the entry: 'And about thys tyme began the fowle scabbe and horryble syckness called the freanche pocks'.[9] As there was constant intercourse between Ireland and England during the fourteenth century, and as smallpox is the most highly contagious of all diseases, there is not the slightest doubt that the English records of the 'pock disease' refer to smallpox in spite of Creighton's obsessional denial of the existence of the disease in England at this time.[10] As the causal virus of smallpox is a member of a group of related viruses that affect most mammals —for example, cowpox, horse-pox, and sheep-pox—and as cross-infections of man and horned cattle with the viruses of smallpox and cowpox occur, there is no reason to doubt the veracity of the entry in the *London Chronicle*.

An epidemic appears to have erupted suddenly in London in April or early May 1368, because on the 22nd of that month Trinity and Midsummer terms were adjourned to Michaelmas, 'as a sudden deadly plague is

anew increasing in the city of London, and greater peril is thereof shortly to be feared'.[1] This epidemic may have been confined to London, or that city may have become involved in a widespread outbreak of disease that erupted some time in 1367, for one chronicle records: 'And in this same yer there fill so mich reyne in hey-time, that it wasted & distroyed bothe corne & hey... And ther fill also such a pestilens, that never non such was sene in no mannes tyme alyve; for many men, anone as they were go to bed hool & in good poynt, sodeinly they deiden.'[2] It mentions also that a concurrent outbreak of 'the pocks' killed both men and women.

The *Murimuth Chronicle* notes that in 1369 there was a pestilence which afflicted both men and the larger animals—which may be either a recurrence of the 'pock diseases' of 1367 or a wrong dating of that outbreak—and severe floods that caused a great loss of grain.[3] *The Brut* records a great pestilence of men and large beasts, and great floods, in 1371.[4] The York chronicler records a pestilence in 1369 which he numbers the 'Third Pestilence' and which he affirms was called at the time 'the pestilence of children';[5] but Galbraith comments that the reference to children appears to have been added owing to confusion with the pestilence of 1361. He notes that an identical reference to children is used again by this chronicler with respect to the 'Fourth Pestilence' in 1378.[6] Creighton identifies the 'Third Pestilence' as primarily a famine-plague, which possibly included an out-break of bubonic plague because 'an unusual mortality of the richer citizens, points to the plague proper'.[7] It seems probable that there was a dearth of cereal foods in 1369, though not necessarily also of root crops; but the objec-tions to his identification of it are that none of the 'famine-fevers' affects the larger animals, that they are all refractory to infection with *P. pestis*, and that an unusual mortality of the richer citizens eliminates bubonic plague as a component of this pestilence.

In Ireland there must have been a prevalence of smallpox in 1368 because the son of Sir Edmund Burke died of it,[8] and when the Irish Annals record the death of a notable personage from a communicable disease, it is certain that an unknown number of the expendable common folk also died from it. The English epidemic of it in 1369 may well have been imported from Ireland and then returned to that country in 1370 to cause what Wilde asserts was the 'Third Pestilence' in that island.[9] He opines that it was an importa-tion of the English pestilence of 1369 and he affirms that it persisted in Ireland for three or four years. It was therefore most probably the 'plague' that killed 'Amlain Mac Senaigh, accomplished emperor of melody' in 1371[10] together with an unknown number of his poor compatriots.

Short[11] alleges that the West Country was worse afflicted by the 'Third

Pestilence'—which he dates to 1370, in agreement with the *London Chronicle*[1] —than other parts of England. He asserts that it apparently recurred in 1375 after a period of excessive heat and drought, and that innumerable people then died of it. He also affirms that smallpox was widely epidemic in 1366 with a heavy mortality of all ages and both sexes, and it is quite possible that the disease was epidemic in different areas in England in both 1366 and 1369.

Whether the Irish returned the pestilence of 1371 with interest to England or not, a pestilence which one chronicle numbers the 'Fourth Pestilence' is said to have ravaged many towns in the south of England in 1374 and to have persisted in that region for a long time.[2] The next year, according to this chronicle, the pestilence destroyed 'a great number of the most notable and richest citizens of London and many of the chief officials of the Chancellory, the Commune Bank, and the Exchequer',[3] in which case it was almost certainly not an epidemic of bubonic plague despite Creighton's identification of it as such.[4] It may have been part of a global pandemic of a communicable disease if its record in *The Brut* under the date of 1376 is reliable, for the entry reads: 'So great and so persistent heat and therewithal a great pestilence in England, and in other different parts of the world, which killed violently and strongly, both men and women without number.'[5] Such a prolonged 'heat wave' in a temperate climate would immobilize the 'plague-fleas'. The identity of this pestilence is uncertain, but from the above records cholera would seem to have a claim to be the disease in question.

In 1373 a destructive epidemic is stated to have killed great numbers of the citizens of Exeter,[6] and the poll-tax of 1377 is said to have been levied in Devonshire 'immediately after a great plague, by which this county, and particularly the great towns of Exeter and Plymouth, had been much depopulated'.[7] Jenkins in his *History of Exeter*, cited by Pickard,[8] gives 1373, 1378 and 1398 as epidemic years in Exeter. It was evidently the two earlier epidemics that were responsible for the petition that Truro sent to the king in 1378 to plead for a reduction in its assessment for taxation because of the heavy loss of its population 'by plagues'.[9] The use of the plural suggests that more than one disease had been epidemic there in the years from 1373 to 1377.

Under the date of 1377 Fabyan reports 'many wonderfull sykenesses among the people, wherof ye people dyed wonderly faste as well in Italye as in Englāde'.[10] This was evidently the pestilence that afflicted Devonshire, which *The Brut* assigns to 1376,[11] and which are all references to the so-called 'Fourth Pestilence'. Whatever the true nature of this pestilence was, it so scourged England that a papal indulgence with plenary remission was granted to all who died of it—in 1376 according to *The Brut*[11] or a year later

according to Fabyan.[1] Either in 1375 or 1376 this pestilence, or some other disease, ravaged the north of England,[2] and in 1378 the York chronicler records that that city was visited by a pestilence which 'began before Michaelmas and persisted for a whole year, more or less'.[3] This is most probably the great mortality in the north of England, the like of which had never been seen before, that Stow assigns to 1379.[4] It was undoubtedly the 'plague' that induced the Scots to raid the north with the prayer: 'God and Sen Mungo, Sen Ninian and Seynt Andrew scheld us this day and ilka day fro Goddis grace and the foule deth that Ynglessh men dyene upon'.[5] Creighton remarks that the epithet 'foul death' was given by the Scots to the 'Black Death', which he regards as sufficient justification for him to identify this pestilence as an outbreak of bubonic plague.[5] Furness affirms that the Scots raided Penrith in 1380 at the time of its fair and carried off an immense booty from Cumberland; but they also carried away with them the 'plague' which, he adds with evident satisfaction, killed one-third of the people of Scotland 'wherever it came'.[6] If that is actually what happened, then it was almost certainly a communicable disease, transmitted by human contacts, and not bubonic plague that the raiders carried back with them, for they certainly would not burden themselves with the bulky transport that only could harbour *R. rattus*. On the other hand the raid and an outbreak of bubonic plague in Scotland may have been coincidental, in which case Creighton may well be correct in his assertion that 1380 ushered in one of the two plague-periods which afflicted that country in the second half of the fourteenth century.[7] This Scottish visitation is only mentioned by the poet Wyntoun and was thus possibly less disastrous than its two predecessors.[8] It was certainly the conjunction of this pestilence with the Scottish raid that made many of its townsfolk flee from Appleby and leave that town 'grievously impoverished'.[9]

Support for Creighton's assertion is possibly provided by the disastrous war that England was waging at this time with France and Spain, in which she had just lost two fleets,[10] because about this time Scotland and France concluded a military alliance against England, which undoubtedly led to considerable maritime intercourse between them and the importation from French and probably Spanish ports of munitions and merchandise, shipments which England could not prevent because of the loss of her navy, and which may have unwittingly included ship-rats infected with *P. pestis*.

Two years later a great earthquake on 20 June heralded or coincided with the eruption of a 'very pestilential fever' in Norfolk,[11] where it is reported to have been confined to young persons.[12] It was probably identical with the disease that was synchronously prevalent in London where, according to the

Polychronicon as cited by Creighton,[1] it affected chiefly boys and girls. In 1383 Walsingham, cited by Creighton,[2] records 'a great pestilence in Kent and other parts of England [that] destroyed many, sparing no age or sex', in which case it must have been a different disease from the one that was prevalent in 1382.

Whether Ireland was invaded by this pestilence from England, infected by shipping from continental ports, or involved in the Scottish epidemic, will never be known; but the various annals agree in declaring that 1383 was a year of widespread suffering and heavy mortality from epidemic disease in that country. The *Annals of the Four Masters* for example records that 'a great and virulent plague raged universally throughout Ireland [killing] Art Magennis, Lord of Iveagh', and a number of notable Irish men and women.[3] The *Annals of Clonmacnoise* also declares that this pestilence was universally dispersed in that land and then names 10 notable persons, of whom 4 were women, who died of it.[4] Among these names that of 'Don Magmahon of the neck, prince of Corckovaiskin', must surely satisfy the most precise historian that the record is authentic, for could even an Irish annalist invent such a name?

The next year the 'plague' killed the son of 'Turlough O'Connor, King of Connaught',[5] and as in this year two sons of Sir William Burke died of small-pox,[6] it is possible that an epidemic of that disease was a component of this 'plague'; but whatever diseases killed these Irish notables it is unlikely that bubonic plague was one of them. In all probability an epidemic of typhus fever was the chief component, for the medieval Irish had an international reputation for their cultivation of both head and body lice. Boorde begins the third chapter of *The Introduction to Knowledge* with the statement: 'I am an Iryshe man...I love to weare a saffron shert...Pediculus other whyle do byte me by the backe',[7] and emphasizes the constancy of the association with an elegant woodcut showing a woman picking lice from a man's scalp. And in the Irish epic of Cúchulainn the hero is discovered on one occasion sitting naked in the snow picking lice out of his shirt.[8]

After the subsidence of this Irish epidemic in 1384 the British Isles appear to have enjoyed five years of freedom from a major outbreak of epidemic disease; then in 1389 a disease of unknown nature erupted at Cambridge.[9] It may have been the start of the 'grete pestilence in England' in 1390,[10] which seems to have spread over much of the country during this and the succeeding three years. Creighton, who opines that it possibly began in the south of England in 1389,[11] says that it was active in 1390 concurrently with great heat from June to September; that it caused a great mortality; that it persisted in some parts of the country, but not everywhere, until Michaelmas,

and that it attacked the young more than the old.[1] He cites Walsingham for the statement that it was 'a great plague, especially of youths and children, who died everywhere in towns and villages in incredible and excessive numbers'.[2] He affirms that it reached the peak of its mortality in 1391, concomitant with a general dearth of food, in consequence of which 'many poor people died of dysentery'.[3] It extended to the north of England, where York suffered a death-roll from it of 1,000 citizens 'in a little space' in 1390, according to Stow,[4] and to the west in 1391, both regions suffering severely from it. Blomefield[5] and Creighton[6] both opine that this pestilence was essentially a 'famine-fever', though the latter cannot resist adding to it a probable complement of bubonic plague.[7] As that disease does not exhibit a selective preference for 'youths and children', it can be dismissed from this pestilence if Walsingham's statement is correct.

Whatever was the true nature of this pestilence, Creighton avers that its death-roll in Norfolk and many other counties was comparable to that of 'The Great Pestilence',[8] and the north of England seems to have been equally afflicted because Sellers states that according to the Rolls of Parliament this region was almost decimated.[9] She rightly dismisses as an exaggeration Drake's figure of 11,000 deaths in York—almost four-fifths of the city's population—but she and Salzman[10] agree that York was severely scourged by the pestilence in 1391.

The petition that parliament sent to Henry IV in 1399, praying him to send sufficient men to defend the Scottish marches because of the great pestilence in the northern parts of his kingdom,[11] seems obviously to have been prompted by the aftermath of the epidemic of 1390–1; but the opening year of the fifteenth century witnessed a disastrous pestilence in England. Adam of Usk describes it as a great plague which 'prevailed through all England, and specially among the young, swift in its attack and carrying off many souls'.[12] He adds that the abbot of Chertsey and 13 of the monks died of it.

In Ireland 'O'Brien Maol died of the plague in the English Pale'[13] in 1398, and two notable persons died of that disease in 1399,[14] so whatever it was it was probably epidemic in that country. As Edward III employed Irish troops in his French and Scottish campaigns, opportunities occurred for disease transmissible by human contacts to be shipped from one country to the other with any movement of men; but the shipment of bubonic plague would depend upon whether the type of vessel used in the commerce between the two countries, and the nature of the cargo carried, provided the requisite shelter for the transport of *R. rattus*.

The English chronology of pestilence in the second half of the fourteenth

century is so confused that it is difficult to distinguish individual epidemics and define their extent. Their identification is largely conjectural and a matter of personal opinion, based on one's knowledge of epidemiology, in the absence of explicit descriptions of their clinical characters. I consider that most of them were not outbreaks of bubonic plague. The governing factor in the persistence of this disease in England was the length of time that an imported strain of *P. pestis* retained its virulence among the house-rats, and that factor is unknown. Sooner or later, however, each strain died out spontaneously and then bubonic plague disappeared from the country until a fresh, virulent strain was imported. In the intervals between successive importations local epidemics affecting individual towns and villages occurred; but the importation of a fresh strain was required for the production of a major, *national* outburst of bubonic plague, and after 1350 the next outbreak of this magnitude was in my judgement that of 1563.

The second half of the fourteenth century witnessed a remarkable activity on the part of the medical profession in the production of plague-tractates. Sarton[1] describes 18 which were written between 1370 and 1398. Two only of these were possibly written by Englishmen, to wit, the one written by John of Bordeaux in 1390 and the anonymous epistle *Dilectissime Frater*, neither of which was an original work. Undoubtedly the most popular and important of these tractates was the one written by John of Burgundy. In England especially it was the authoritative work on 'plague' for the greater part of 200 years, and the version of it by John of Bordeaux—possibly a pseudonym for John of Burgundy—was immensely popular according to Singer, who mentions that there are 22 copies of it in the British Museum alone, 17 of which are English versions of the original Latin text.[2]

The gist of John's treatise—British Museum, Sloane MS 3449—is that a pestilential state of the atmosphere is created by the interaction of certain cosmic and terrestrial forces, and this corrupted atmosphere then affects those persons whose bodily humours induce in them a requisite susceptible state. Their humours are in turn corrupted, and the exhalation and emanation of these corrupt humours from their bodies, living or dead, aggravate the pestilential state of the atmosphere. This is really quite an ingenious explanation of the fact that certain individuals in a population, of which all the members are equally exposed to the pestilential atmosphere, escape the disease.

In common with most of his contemporaries John believed that the pores of the skin were the main channel of entry of the atmospheric poison into the body, and he therefore utters an emphatic warning against those activities which were reputed to open the pores, such as physical exercise, bathing,

luxurious living, and sexual intercourse. To disinfect the atmosphere bonfires must be lit out-of-doors and house-fires indoors and aromatic substances burnt on them. Internal disinfectants should also be used to destroy any virulent vapours which may penetrate into the body. Vinegar, possibly on account of its part in the Crucifixion, was in universal favour, as both an internal and an external disinfectant.

If the proper regimen of living as described in detail in his treatise is neglected, the pestilential poison can overwhelm the body very rapidly and the disease becomes *confirmed*—which means refractory to treatment—within twenty-four hours. The explanation of this disaster is that the evil vapours in the atmosphere, after entering through the pores, are conveyed by the blood to one of the three principal members, the heart, the liver, or the brain, each of which 'has an emunctory or place at which it seeks to expel its noxious superfluities. Thus, when the heart is attacked, we may be sure that the poison will fly to the emunctory of the heart, which is in the armpit. But if it find no outlet there, it is driven to seek the liver, which again sends it to its own emunctory at the groin. If thwarted there, the poison will next seek the brain, whence it will be driven either under the ears or to the throat. If still no relief is brought by the blood-letter, the case has indeed become urgent, for the poison, having taken twelve hours to perform its circulation and sought an issue in vain, will now within the next twelve hours indubitably "fasten itself", throwing the patient into an ague and forming an apostume at or near one of the emunctories; and then indeed the evil will be hard to eradicate.'[1]

The best treatment for the disease John asserts is bleeding, and as each principal member and its emunctory has its specific superficial vein, the withdrawal of blood from this vein will relieve the related member of its 'noxious superfluities'. As he belonged to the school of medical thought which believed that the two sides of the human body were in only imperfect relation with each other, he insists that bleeding must be performed on the diseased side. If the blood is withdrawn from the wrong side the gravest consequences may ensue, because not only will the patient lose healthy blood but its place will be taken by empoisoned blood from the diseased side, with the result that the body will become wholly corrupted.[2]

It is important to appreciate that John had no conception of bubonic plague as a specific disease entity. The pestilential atmosphere, after entering a person's body, could engender a variety of morbid manifestations, depending upon the precise state and interactions of the individual's humours at the time of his poisoning. If a large number of people showed similar manifestations within a relatively short period of time, then a 'plague' was recorded;

but the actual disease might be any one of a dozen or more communicable or transmissible diseases of man. It is therefore quite unrealistic to accept the record of a 'plague' before the middle of the seventeenth century as synonymous with an outbreak of bubonic plague, and even after Sydenham's day, up to the middle of the nineteenth century, bubonic plague and epidemic typhus fever were clinically indistinguishable.

THE FIFTEENTH CENTURY

As already noted, this century opened with a severe and widespread epidemic of some disease, according to Adam of Usk. After its subsidence England appears to have been free from another major epidemic until 1405, when Nash reports that many homes were decimated[1]—presumably in Bristol—by some unspecified disease which persisted until 1470, in which year there was certainly a major outbreak of an epidemic disease, for in the summer of that year, 'through corruption of the ayre, so great a plague [erupted] as had not been seen for many years'.[2] Creighton cites Walsingham's dubious report that it quickly destroyed 30,000 men and women in London, and that 'in country villages many families were almost exterminated'[3] by it. Stow adds the information that Henry IV dared not enter London and fled from Leeds Castle in Kent to 'Plashery' [now Pleshey?] in Essex, where he stayed until the pestilence was extinguished in his capital.[4]

If numerous country villages were synchronously involved in it, it must have been a disease of high infectivity that spread rapidly by human contacts, or indirectly by human contamination of foodstuffs, including drinking water, which in the summer were largely consumed uncooked. The most virulent epidemic of bubonic plague could not destroy much more than one-third of the population of London which, according to Creighton, was estimated at 44,770 in 1377,[5] and which certainly had not reached 90,000 by 1407. Moreover bubonic plague is essentially an urban disease and only those villages in the near vicinity of an infected town would be involved in the fundamental rat-epizootic, although occasionally a village at a distance from the epizootic focus would be infected by urban fugitives harbouring 'blocked' fleas. The figure of 30,000 deaths in London seems to have had a fascination for fifteenth-century recorders, for it is repeatedly quoted for different outbreaks of disease in that city.

There is some doubt about the precise date of the eruption of this pestilence, because on 24 October the term was adjourned to St Hilary 'as a deadly plague has suddenly broken out in the city of London, and is now newly spreading, wherefore it is feared that graver peril is likely to happen

shortly'.[1] If the disease did not erupt until mid-October it is extremely unlikely to have been bubonic plague; but assuming that it was, it must have been rapidly extinguished if the record of a great frost starting on St Andrew's Day (30 November) and persisting unbroken until 14 February is authentic.[2] In the few weeks available for its activity, the most malignant epidemic of bubonic plague could not conceivably have killed 30,000 people in London; but a water-borne epidemic of cholera or typhoid fever, or an epidemic of malignant dysentery, could have killed that number along the lower reaches of the river Thames during a summer epidemic. Gregory also records that 'men and bestys were grettely infectyd with pockys' this year,[3] and as small-pox would not be suppressed by a great frost, an outbreak of virulent small-pox may have been the great plague.

After this pestilence had subsided, England apparently enjoyed a relatively long period of freedom from epidemic disease, a period that provides an opportunity to present a preview of trouble to come, because the numerous pestilences that afflicted England during this century must be viewed against a background of war—foreign in the first quarter, internecine in the third—of the collapse of the church as a spiritual support, of the derogation of law and order, and of national impoverishment aggravated, as Trevelyan remarks, by the recurrence of 'plague' most frequently in the part of the community where wealth was chiefly made—the towns and the ports.[4] Green avers[5] that the one aim of the church in this century was to preserve its enormous wealth. 'All spiritual life seemed to have been trodden out in the ruin of the Lollards.'[5]

Diseases that are transmissible by human contacts would have been facilitated in their epidemic spread by the recruitment and movements of the opposing armies during the Wars of the Roses; but, supposing a fresh strain of *P. pestis* was imported during that period, bubonic plague is not so aided and no army would venture near an area where it was known to be prevalent. Individual soldiers, coming from places where unnoticed rat-plague was smouldering, might occasionally harbour 'blocked' fleas in their clothing; but there were no sieges to enable the insects to generate rat-epizootics of the disease, and they were likely to perish quickly with their hosts in the sanguinary battles of that war. Trevelyan refers to the Wars of the Roses as 'those brief occasional campaigns conducted by 2,000 to 10,000 men a side',[6] and the movements of such small bodies of men would not disperse the house-rat. Even Towton, in which battle Burne estimates[7] that 75,000 men were engaged, would not have distributed that rodent because neither army had the requisite bulk or type of wheeled transport for *R. rattus* to hide in.

Paradoxical as it may seem, when *P. pestis* was next imported into England, the dissemination of bubonic plague may have been assisted by the scanty use of road transport, since this meant that rivers were the main highways within the country, and after maritime carriage, riverine transport of the plague-rat in the dark holds of barges or safely hidden in their bulky cargoes was the most effective means of distributing bubonic plague.

To return now to records of pestilence, Short affirms that London sustained a death-roll of 30,000 of its citizens from pestilence in 1406,[1] but Noorthouck transfers this figure to 1407.[2] Creighton and Vine each cite Walsingham for the report that 30,000 people died of plague in London some time between 1405 and 1407, both dates inclusive.[3] Grafton declares that 'the plague of pestilence'—by which phrase he means bubonic plague— 'reigned so sore' during the summer of 1405 in London and the surrounding country that Henry IV dared not reside in his capital.[4] Paterson affirms[5] that this epidemic occurred in the summer of 1406. Gordon cites Macgowan for the statement that London was afflicted synchronously with Bordeaux, Aquitaine, and Gascony with a deadly epidemic of malignant dysentery in 1406.[6]

I make no apology for leaving this chronological tangle and statistical absurdity for the reader to unravel, and pass on to the next record of an unspecified pestilence in Norfolk in 1420,[7] mentioning in passing that Walsingham, cited by Creighton, says that 'numbers of Englishmen' were killed by plague in 1413, presumably in some foreign land, possibly France.[8]

The next record of pestilence—which was apparently restricted to the north of England—comes from a parliamentary record of a petition from the Scottish Border to Henry IV about the destruction caused by a 'plague' that had raged there for 'three years past and still reigns'.[9] The Lysons, adding a year and possibly some embroidery to their report, remark: 'In 1421 we find the men of Cumberland representing to parliament that all the country within twenty miles of the borders had been so depopulated by war, pestilence, and emigration, that where formerly there were 100 able men, there were scarcely 10.'[10]

After an apparent break in the records of some 12 or 13 years, there was another pestilence in either 1433 or 1434. Creighton states that in 1433 Parliament was prorogued on 15 August because of the eruption of a severe pestilence in London and its suburbs.[11] He notes that a London chronicle reports 'a grete pestilence and a grete frost' this year; but that conjunction was recorded by Arnold in 1434,[12] in agreement with which dating *The Brut* records that this pestilence attacked men, women, and children in London, and notably many worthy men such as aldermen. 'Also', it continues, 'in

England the people died sore, both rich and poor.' Finally it says that a great and hard frost, which began on 22 November and persisted to the succeeding Candlemas, (2 February) destroyed old people of both sexes and also young children.[1] On account of the concomitant pestilence the term was adjourned on 27 October to the octaves of St Hilary.[2]

This pestilence seems to have been a severe one and it may have been responsible for the production of 'The Articles of the good Gouvernaūce of the Cite of London'.[3] Only one of these articles has any bearing upon the control of epidemic disease, namely, the injunction against casting 'ony rubyes dunge or rycsshes or ony other noyce thinge in Thamys at Walbrok or at the Flete or other diches in ye citee or in opyn stretis in lanes off ye wardes'.[4] It was a useless injunction as far as bubonic plague was concerned, and in the absence of an organized civic system of scavenging it could not be enforced. The collections of dung and vegetable refuse that littered the streets of fifteenth-century London were, however, breeding grounds for the house-fly which is a dangerous disseminator of several microbial diseases of man, and in the summer months the homes of the English commonalty in both towns and villages were certainly fly-blown as well as flea-ridden. The presence of the house-fly in swarms in medieval London and other towns ensured that diseases such as typhoid fever, dysentery, cholera, bacterial food-poisoning, and infantile 'summer diarrhoea' were epidemic at times during the summer months. All these diseases are potential killers and their case-mortality rates in the fifteenth century would indubitably be far higher than in modern times. Epidemics of them in the summer months—which were also the season of bubonic plague—would be regarded in the fifteenth century as manifestations of a pestilential atmosphere—in other words as 'plagues'.

England seems to have experienced some bitter winters at this time. Fabyan records a great frost in 1436 which commenced on the eve of St Katherine's Eve (23 November) and persisted until 10 February, with such intensity that the Thames was frozen down to its mouth and a shipment of wines from Bordeaux had to be unloaded onto the ice.[5]

The next year the Chief Justice of the Common Pleas took refuge in St Albans abbey from an 'epidemic plague which was then reigning in the city of London'.[6] In 1438 one chronicle states that there was a great dearth of corn so that men 'were fayn to ete rye bred and barley, the whiche nevere ett non before',[7] which notice, if true, would seem to be of sociological interest. Another chronicle affirms that the general dearth was associated with a 'year of pestilence' during which 'many worthy people died...and of the commonfolk men, women, and children throughout the realm, and principally at York and in the North Country'.[8]

Both 1438 and 1439 were famine-years, consequent upon three wet harvests in succession.[1] Fabyan affirms that there was a great dearth of corn in both England and France in the latter year, and that in Paris the people 'dyed sore of the sykenesse of ipydyme',[2] the nature of which is anybody's guess. He says that wheat was so scarce in England that in many places people made bread of vetches, peas, and beans, and even of fern roots if they were too poor to buy the other breadstuffs. Creighton opines that the famine was accompanied by pestilence, which 'may have been fever and dysentery first and plague afterwards'.[3] Parliament petitioned Henry IV this year to cancel the ceremony of kissing the king in the performance of nightly service, because 'a sickness called the Pestilence universally through [England] more commonly reigneth than hath been usual before this time' and is 'most infective'.[4] Creighton accepted the wording of this petition as proof that the pestilence was bubonic plague, upon which he comments: 'But plague henceforth is seldom universal; it becomes more and more a disease of the towns, and when it does occur in the country, it is for the most part at some few limited spots.'[5] As I have already emphasized, it is biologically impossible for bubonic plague ever to have been a universal disease; but in justice to Creighton's erudition and his masterly handling of historical material, his faulty concept of bubonic plague was written before the aetiology and epidemiology of the disease were fully known. Vine, with less excuse, asserts that London experienced four epidemics of plague between 1430 and 1440, the last of which involved the whole kingdom.[6]

After a lull of some three years a grave pestilence erupted early in June 1444 according to Creighton,[7] but he omits to mention where it erupted. The civic archives of Lincoln supply the next notice of pestilence with the statement that there was a severe epidemic of some disease there in 1447—possibly in 1446 also—as a mayoral petition to Henry IV craved relief from taxation on account of the prolonged affliction of the city by 'a great pestilence...and other worldly misfortunes', which had driven so many citizens away that scarcely 200 remained in the city.[8] Presumably the mayor meant only 200 who were opulent enough to be taxed, for the poor had not the means to flee.

The years from 1447 to 1454 appear to have been pestilential ones in England. In 1448 there was a severe pestilence at Oxford,[9] and on 30 May 1449 parliament adjourned to Winchester to avoid 'the pestilential aire of Westminster'.[10] It adjourned again on 30 March 1450 to Leicester for an identical reason.[11] Two years later it adjourned to Reading on account of the 'plague' on 20 November—a time of the year that disposes of bubonic plague—but was soon after adjourned again until 11 February because of a great mortality in Reading,[12] and on 6 September 1454 William Paston

wrote from London to his son, John: 'Here is great pestilence. I purpose to flee into the country.'[1]

When this epidemic—which may have been confined to London—subsided, England seemingly had a well-earned rest from pestilence until 1463, when there was 'a greate pestilence wth a dry soomm' all England over and a harde wynter'.[2] It was in this year Fabyan relates that Queen Margaret, having landed in Scotland from France, invaded England. She fled back to France, however, when Edward IV marched north to challenge her, and he then planned to invade Scotland in retaliation; but 'he was then vysyted with the sykenesse of pockys',[3] which forced him to abandon his plan. It is possible therefore that it was an epidemic of smallpox that ushered in the series of pestilential years that Creighton ascribes to bubonic plague, which he affirms was prevalent in one part of the country or another, with few intermissions, until 1478.[4] Smallpox and not plague could have been responsible for the 200 weekly deaths in London which Venetian merchants reported—and most probably exaggerated—on their arrival in Bruges on 26 September 1454.[5] It was possibly in connexion with this metropolitan epidemic that Margaret Paston wrote to her husband: 'For Goddys sake be war what medesyns ye take of any fisusyans of London; I shall never trust to hem be cause of your fadr and myn onkyl, whoys sowlys God assoyle.'[6] Margaret regrettably had cause for her lack of faith in the medical profession in her day—London physicians were no more ignorant than those in other towns—in view of the remedies that Wilson notes[7] were advocated by Elizabethan physicians a century later. Here, for example, is the recipe for the famous plague-remedy invented by Edward IV, which was very popular in England during the latter half of this century.[8]

Jhesus. Thys ys the medesyn that the Kyngis grace usythe every day for the raynyng seknys that now raynthe the wyche hathe ben prowyd & be the grace of god yt hathe olpyn thys yere lxxi personys. he most take a hanfull of rewe, a hanfull of marygoldis, halfe a hanfull of fetherfeu, a hanfull of burnett, a hanfull of sorell, a quantyte of dragonys—the crop or the route:—then take a potell of rungyng water, Fyrst washe them clene & let them sethe esely tyl yt be a-moste cum from a potell to a quarte of leker: then take a clene clothe, & strayne ytt & drynke yt; & yt be byttyr, put ther-to a lytell suger of candy, & thys may be dronkyn oftyme; & yf yt be dronkyn be-fore eny purpyl a-pere, By the grace of God there schall be no perell of no dethe.

In medical prescriptions up to the middle of the seventeenth century the quantity or weight or volume of each ingredient was of less importance than the addition of the ingredients in the exact order specified in the formula. The fact that a handful of an ingredient might vary widely in amount,

according to whether the hand belonged to a small woman or a big man, did not affect the efficacy of the remedy as long as the ingredients were commingled in the proper sequence. If Edward's remedy was really an efficient purgative he would have made a fortune if he had patented it, for either history repeats itself or human credulity is unchanging, as today a large section of the population spends a huge sum annually on patent purgatives as a prophylactic against all evils of the flesh.

There was an epidemic of some disease in August 1465,[1] which was 'so fervent in Norwych' that Margaret Paston's mother and cousin fled from the city.[2] The next year parliament adjourned to Reading because of some infection in London,[3] and in 1467 it again adjourned to that town after certain members of the House of Commons had died late in June from a disease that was prevalent in London.[3] The continuator of the *Croyland Chronicle* is more prolix about this pestilence, the news of which reached him in all probability exaggerated by rumour, 'for', he writes, 'an infection prevailed in the pestilent air over the dwellers in the land, to such a degree, that a sudden death consigned to a wretched doom many thousands of people of all ages, just like so many sheep destined for the slaughter'.[4]

Four years seemingly passed in sickly England without incident until the beginning of August 1471, when the residentiary canons of Southwell Minster voted themselves a month's leave of absence because of a deadly pestilence in Southwell.[5] Some six weeks later Sir John Paston wrote from somewhere near Winchester: 'I cannot hear from pilgrims that pass the country, nor none other man that rideth or goeth any country, that any borough town in England is free from that sickness',[6] whatever it was. Pilgrims were notorious rumour-mongers and Sir John seems to have had 'Midas ears' for rumour! If it was anything like as extensive as he was told, it may have been the pestilence which has been assigned to Hull in 1472.[7] The pestilential scene certainly shifted northwards in that year to Hull, which was scourged again in 1476, and yet again in 1478, in which year more than 1,500 of its townsfolk are said to have died.[8] Creighton attributes all these epidemics to bubonic plague and remarks that they almost ruined the town.[9] The last one may have been a local eruption of that disease if, as he affirms, it was prevalent during the autumn and ceased with the approach of winter.[9]

Hull was not alone, however, in its affliction. In 1475 Edward IV invaded France

and in that journey...lost many a man that fell to the lust of women, and were burnt by them;* and their members rotted away and they died. And after that,

---

* They contracted gonorrhoea, and the complication of a secondary streptococcal or staphylococcal infection of a gonococcal balanitis resulted in destruction of the glans penis, and ultimately in a fatal septicaemia.

there fell a great disease in England called the 'styche', from which much people died suddenly. Also another disease reigned after that, called the 'fflyx', that never was seen in England before; and people died hugely of it for three successive years, in one place or another. And after that there bred a Raven on Charing Cross in London; and never had one seen breed there before. And after that came a great death of pestilence, that lasted three years; and people died mightily in every place, man, woman, and child.[1]

So, if this record is authentic, there were at least three and possibly four distinct diseases epidemic in England from 1475 to 1481 or thereabouts, for Edward's soldiers who survived their 'burning' would assuredly have disseminated gonorrhoea widely on their return to England.

The Middle English word, *stiche*, derived from the Anglo-Saxon *stice*, a pricking sensation, became restricted to mean a pain in the side,[2] and the most probable explanation of the 'styche' is that it was an acute infection of the lungs, complicated with pleurisy. Acute lobar pneumonia could have been the disease in question, possibly as a well-nigh constant sequel to a widespread distribution of the virus of the common cold. The 'fflyx' may have been an invasion of cholera, for had the disease been dysentery it would have been called the 'bloody flyx' or 'flux'. A virulent epidemic of cholera would have been quite capable of causing the mortality that occurred in 1477 according to Holinshed, who avers that fifteen years of war did not kill one-third of the number of people that the pestilence destroyed in four months.[3]

Two or three years before the raven bred at Charing Cross there was, Creighton asserts, a serious epidemic of plague in London,[4] and the 'great death of Pestilence' would accord with a local eruption of the disease in the City and its immediate neighbourhood. This had been preceded by 'a gret hote, somere, bothe for manne and beste; by the whiche ther was gret dethe of menne and women, that in feld in harvist tyme men fylle downe sodanly and unyversalle feveres, axes, and the blody flyx, in dyverse places of Englonde'.[5] It must indeed have been exceptionally hot weather to cause so many cases of 'heat stroke' in the harvest fields, and it is not surprising that typhoid and the paratyphoid fevers, dysentery, and other intestinal infections were epidemic, because hot weather in the summer, with its consequent dust, flies, increased drinking of water—often drawn from surface waters—and consumption of fly-contaminated, uncooked foodstuffs, would favour and facilitate the dissemination of these diseases from the human carriers of their causal bacteria.

In 1478 Newcastle-upon-Tyne was visited by a 'plague' and the canons of Southwell Minster voted themselves another leave of absence because of a pestilence in their vicinity.[6] It may have been the 'grete pestilence' which

caused the term to be adjourned from Easter to Michaelmas.[1] The next year there was a great mortality in London and many other parts of the realm which commenced towards the end of September 1479 and persisted to the beginning of November 1480.[2] This could have been a recurrence or recrudescence of cholera, which is conserved by human carriers of the causal vibrio. It cannot have been an outbreak of bubonic plague because of its seasonal incidence. In connexion with this epidemic it is of interest and possibly of significance that the *Annals of the Four Masters* has the entry under the date of 1478: 'A great plague was brought by a ship into the harbour of Assaroe.* This plague spread through Fermanagh, Tirconnel, and the province in general...and great injury was done by it through all the province.'[3] In the absence of a description of the clinical characters of this 'plague', its maritime importation is suggestive of one or the other of two diseases, namely, bubonic plague or cholera, each of which has its natural habitat in India and is capable of doing the great injury recorded. If there was a relatively slow, rat-epizootic spread of the disease, radiating inland from the port of Assaroe, the disease was bubonic plague: if its spread was relatively rapid, due to its dissemination by human contacts, the disease could have been cholera. And if it was quickly transported from Ireland to England to cause in this country the pestilence of 1479, as seems possible, cholera is more likely to have been the disease. Richard Cely reports a 'great sickness' in London in 1479 in three letters to his son, George, in Calais. The two last of these were written from 'Brytys plase in Esekys', whither he had fled from the city, in company with many other citizens who were stampeding out of London 'for fere of the sekenesse'.[4] His report provides no clue to its identification, except that in the sixteenth century the term, 'the great sickness' was generally used to imply bubonic plague or its pestilential counterpart, typhus fever.

The terminal decade of this century was apparently free from pestilence in England after November 1480 until one erupted at Oxford in 1499.[5]

Scotland

There had been a pestilence in Scotland in 1392, which Creighton affirms was an epidemic of bubonic plague,[6] after the subsidence of which the country seems to have been free from pestilence for some ten years. Then, some time in 1402, there was an outbreak of some disease that kept the custumars of Stirling from attending the annual audit and caused several deaths among those of Dundee,[7] so it was apparently widespread, at any

* Ballyshannon, in the south of the county of Donegal.[8]

rate north of the Firth of Forth. Another lengthy period of freedom appears to have succeeded this outbreak, because it was not until 1420 that another major epidemic of disease was recorded. In this year a pestilence that was called 'Quhew' by the commonalty killed many well-known nobles and multitudes of the common people.[1] The records are then silent again about epidemic disease until February 1431, when an epidemic that was called the 'flying pestilence' erupted in Edinburgh and the next year visited Haddington.[2] Creighton, who cites Fordun's record of it as *pestilentia volatilis*, remarks that 'it can hardly have been plague and may have been influenza'.[3] It was almost certainly an outbreak of epidemic influenza and possibly a recurrence of the 'quhew' of 1420. The pseudonym 'flying pestilence' is in fact a very apt name for epidemic influenza, which seems to spread with almost lightning rapidity, though no communicable disease of man can ever spread faster that the speed of human transport.

After an apparent interval of freedom of eight years, a pestilence erupted which is described in the ancient chronicle, *Ane Addicixoun of Scottis Cornicklis and Deidis*. Creighton, borrowing from Chambers, quotes its account of this pestilence:

The samen time there was in Scotland a great dearth...and verily the dearth was sae great that there died a passing [number of] people for hunger. And als the land-ill, the wame-ill, was so violent, that there died mae that year than ever there died, owther in pestilence, or yet in ony other sickness in Scotland. And that samen year the pestilence came in Scotland, and began at Dumfries, and it was callit the *Pestilence but Mercy*, for their took it nane that ever recoverit, but they died within twenty-four hours.[4]

Creighton identifies the 'wame-ill' as dysentery and the subsequent pestilence as bubonic plague;[5] but the British peoples in the fifteenth century had had a long acquaintance with the 'bloody flux', and even septicaemic plague rarely kills within twenty-four hours, while the bubonic form takes at least three days. The three diseases that commonly have killed within this time limit are pneumonic plague—'invariably fatal in one to four days'[6]— cholera, 'from two or three to twenty-four hours',[7] and the English 'sweating sickness'. Of these cholera is the one that best fits the record for it is certainly a 'wame-ill', and, as the records of the 1832 epidemic in England conclusively show, the case-mortality rate of the disease can be 100 per cent in the early stages of a virulent epidemic. As I interpret the Scottish record, cholera was imported by a human carrier, probably in a ship bringing food from a foreign port to relieve the famine, and at first the strain of *Vibrio cholerae* was moderately virulent. Then, in Dumfries, it acquired an exaltation of virulence and killed before the classical symptoms of 'colic' or 'wame-ill' had time to develop, so that to fifteenth-century observers it

was a different pestilence. 'The samen time', in the above record refers to the synchronous famine in England.

A period of seeming freedom succeeded the subsidence of this pestilence. It was broken in 1455 by a great pestilential mortality of men throughout the country, which may possibly have been an importation of the English pestilence of 1454.[1] There is little doubt that the two major epidemics of 1439 and 1455 must each have been succeeded by 'trailer' outbreaks of the diseases in Scottish towns and villages that were not involved in the major epidemics; but the records of these are hidden in local archives that have not yet been published. There would seem to be an interesting field here awaiting the research activities of local historians.

In 1475 a meeting of the Scots parliament was adjourned from September to Epiphany on account of a pestilence[2] which may have been confined to Edinburgh and its outlying townships. If it did not erupt until September it is unlikely to have been an outbreak of bubonic plague, because in the latitude of Edinburgh the 'plague-fleas' would probably be hibernating by that date. In March 1493 the civic authorities of Edinburgh issued orders to isolate the city from 'plague',[3] which they evidently feared as an importation of bubonic plague. Some five years later, in November 1498 to be precise, they repeated these orders because the 'perilous seikness of pestilence' had then 'rissen in the eastern parts' of the city, and they immediately sent all the scholars then residing in Edinburgh back to their homes,[4] thereby ensuring a wide dispersion of the pestilence if—as is probable from its eruption so late in the year—it was an outbreak of typhus fever erupting in the slums on the east side of the city. Whatever the pestilence was, it was certainly widespread in the subsequent year, when the efforts of the civic authorities to prevent its re-entry to Edinburgh indicate that they thought it was bubonic plague. In April 1499 they decreed that no citizen was to shelter any incomers from Haddington or Kelso, and that any citizens going to Peebles would be quarantined on their return.[5] In June they ordered that any dogs and pigs found straying in the streets were to be destroyed; they appointed 4 cleaners of infected houses at a daily wage of 12*d*. each,[6] and finally they ordered that all parts of the city were to be cleared of goods suspected of harbouring infection and prohibited all intercourse with Leith until St Giles' Feast.[7]

Ireland

'The references to plagues in Ireland after the invasion of 1349 are extremely meagre', wrote Creighton,[8] and as far as bubonic plague is concerned he is indisputably right; but the records in the Irish Annals of notable personages

dying of smallpox and other 'plagues' are almost embarrassing in their profusion; and if, as I contend, the records of the deaths of such personages imply a synchronous mortality among the commonalty, the fifteenth century was a pestilential one in Ireland.

The records begin in 1402 with the death of 'Brian, the son of Niall Oge'[1] from smallpox. There is then an interval of presumptive freedom from epidemic disease until 1414, when 'Donell, the son of Tiernan More O'Rourke' also died of smallpox.[2] Three years later 'David, the son of Tany O'Mulcomy, died of the plague in his own house'.[3] Why that fact should have been worth recording is puzzling, unless it was extremely rare for an Irish aristocrat to die of an epidemic disease in his own house, possibly because when any notable personage sickened with such a disease he was promptly placed under the care of the family or clan ollave in the fifteenth-century Irish equivalent of a private nursing-home. Five years after David, 'Melaghlin MacCabe',[4] and 'Hugh Magennis'[5] both died of the 'plague', to be followed a year later by the earl of March,[6] and after another year by 'Feradhach, the son of Brian O'Kelly'.[7] It seems evident that 'the plague', whatever it was, was prevalent in Ireland—intermittently at least—from 1424 to 1426.

'Plague came in Fir-Manach' in 1431,[8] and there was a famine in the summer of 1433, 'called, for a very long time afterwards, Samhra na mearaithne (i.e. the summer of slight acquaintance), because no one used to recognize friend or relative, in consequence of the greatness of the famine'.[9]

If bubonic plague happened to be smouldering anywhere in Ireland about this time, it was certainly extinguished by the severe winter of 1435 with its 'unusual frost', which was so severe and prolonged that lakes and rivers were frozen and pack-horses crossed Lough Erne on the ice.[10] If it was bubonic plague that killed two Irish prelates in 1438,[11] it must have been a fresh importation of *P. pestis*; but as 'John, the son of Edmund Burke' died of smallpox that year,[12] it may have been the haemorrhagic form of that disease, killing before the typical pustular rash developed, that was the 'plague' which killed both abbot and vicar. The next year 'the plague [raged] virulently in Dublin, so that three thousand persons, both male and female, large and small, died of it, from the beginning of Spring to the end of the month of May'.[13] If it was identical with the disease which killed 'Meyler, son of MacFeorais',[14] it must have been prevalent in some part of Ireland outside Dublin. The seasonal incidence of this 'plague' denies its identification as an outbreak of bubonic plague, but it could have been an epidemic of either typhus fever or relapsing fever, more probably the former in view of its reported mortality, although in some modern epidemics of relapsing fever the case-mortality rate has been as high as 30 per cent.[15]

After another interval of presumptive freedom, 'a great plague' erupted in 'the town of Ath-truim' in 1447[1] and evidently spread widely, because in the summer and autumn it raged in Meath, Leinster, and Munster, killing a great number of people including, it is said, 700 priests.[2] This 'plague' appears to have been associated with a severe famine, according to a footnote added by O'Donovan,[3] in which case it was a composite of dysentery, typhus fever, and relapsing fever in all probability. 'Felim, the son of John, son of Philip O'Reilly', who was taken prisoner by the English this year and 'afterwards died of the plague',[4] may have contracted his infection in captivity or have been incubating it when he was captured, in which case if he was incubating one of the 'famine-fevers' the English may well have had cause to rue his capture.

The note that 'O'Cassidy of Cuil, Ollave of Fermanagh' died in 1450[5] shows that even Irish physicians could not always heal themselves. He may of course have succumbed to old age, that irresistible angel of Death, or to the inadvertent exhibition of one of his own Irish remedies. Two years later he was followed to the grave by 'O'Coffey...a learned poet, who kept a house of hospitality' and died 'of the plague in Feara-Tulach'.[6] The significance of 'a house of hospitality' is obscure, especially when kept by an Irish poet; but if he was allowed the licence commonly accorded to a poet, it has an ominous ring about it of 'burnings'.

Happily, Ireland appears to have been free from major outbreaks of communicable disease after his death until 1464, when there was a minor holocaust of notable Irish personages, five men and three women dying of 'the plague'.[7] This entry immediately precedes one that makes the identification of this 'plague' particularly puzzling, for the second entry reads: 'Murtough ...and his wife, and three other besides, died in one day from having seen a horse that perished of the same spasms'.[8] The well-known passion of the Irish for horses is surely insufficient to explain the deaths of five spectators from remorse, and 'grease' (horse-pox), influenza, and glanders, appear to have been the only equine diseases transmissible to man in the British Isles. None of these is characterized by 'spasms', that character belongs to tetanus, a disease to which the horse is peculiarly susceptible; but tetanus is not a communicable disease and it is therefore impossible for it to be an epidemic disease, a 'plague'.

In 1467 four notable Irishmen 'died of the plague',[9] and the next year 'O'More and Mac Gillapatrick' also 'died of the plague'.[10] As, however, two different Irish words are used for 'plague' in these entries, it is possible that they were different manifestations of the pestilential atmosphere responsible for the 'plague'. The next record is of a 'great plague', namely Airaing in

Fir-Manach' in 1470,[1] which caused a heavy mortality. As MacCarthy says that the meaning of 'Airaing' is unknown to him,[2] it is useless to speculate about its identity. The next year a notable died of the disease that killed O'More and his companion in death.[3]

The record in the *Annals of the Four Masters* of the maritime importation of a great plague in 1478 has already been quoted. After raging 'throughout all Ireland', in the course of which it killed 'the Baron of Devlin and Mac Maurice Airig',[4] it apparently became rapidly extinguished and Ireland enjoyed a welcome exemption from 'plague' for nearly four years. The notice that a nobleman 'died of the plague after the feast of [Holy] Cross in Harvest',[5] may mean that there was an outbreak, possibly quite localized, of one of the intestinal infections such as typhoid fever or bacterial food poisoning, but this is just guesswork.

In 1488 'a great plague [raged] in Machair-Chonnacht',[6] and 'Brian, the son of Hugh Boy...died of the galar breac',[7] which was either smallpox or typhus fever, depending upon the part of Ireland in which he died. As a gloss to the first entry, O'Donovan quotes the entry in the *Annals of Ulster* under the date of 1487: 'Great rain in the summer of this year, which was like an inclement Winter, so that much of the crops of Ireland decayed in consequence.'[8] It seems evident therefore that the 'plague' of 1488 was a famine-fever. It apparently persisted in 1489, in which year 'great numbers died. It was so devastating that people did not bury their dead throughout Ireland.'[9] Concurrently with the 'famine-fever' there was an epidemic of smallpox as 'Brian, son of Aedh the Tawny [and] Mary, daughter of Domnall Mac Domnaill the Freckled' died of it in the spring of 1488.[10]

The stricken country had only a short respite after the famine ceased because in 1492 'an unusual plague [raged] in Meath, i.e. a plague of twenty-four hours' duration; and anyone who survived it beyond that period recovered. It did not attack infants or little children'.[11] This was undoubtedly an importation of the English 'sweating sickness' of 1485, an identification confirmed by the simultaneous entry in the *Annals of Ulster*: 'The baron of Slane...died this year [20 March] of the plague of sweating that came recently into Ireland.'[12] It is of interest that this disease took at least six years to spread from England into Ireland in spite of the constant intercourse between the two countries, because its slow rate of spread renders it highly improbable that *the sweat* was influenza, the identification generally favoured by medical writers.

Five years after this visitation of the 'sweating sickness' there was a 'great famine through all Ireland in this and the following year, so that people ate food unbecoming to mention, and never before heard of as having been

introduced on human dishes'.[1] Is there a veiled hint here of cannibalism? The concomitant 'famine-fever' was again accompanied by an outbreak of smallpox, of which disease 'Niall, son of Ua Niell', died 'between the two Nativities' (25 December and 6 January);[2] but the glandular disease from which 'Cathal, son of Toirdelbach, died...about Lammas'[3] was in all probability one of the adenopathies—either lymphatic leukaemia, lymphadenoma or generalized tuberculous adenitis—and had no connexion with either bubonic plague or typhus fever.

Smallpox was again prevalent in 1498, as 'Domnall, son of Nechtain, and Mac Maghnusa' died of it that year, the latter at the age of 60.[4] His death from it at that age emphasizes the fact that no age is exempt from this deadly and disabling disease in unprotected persons. A 'plague' was also prevalent this year as 'Mac Ward of Oriel' died of it,[5] but there is no clue to the nature of the particular manifestation of the pestilential state that killed him.

As this work is primarily a history of bubonic plague, an attempt must now be made to pinpoint the possible outbreaks of that disease in the British Isles during this century. As none of the records of 'plague' presents a clinical description of the disease that was prevalent—with the exception of *the sweat* —the identification of an outbreak of bubonic plague must be based on the immutable nature of its aetiology and epidemiology, a cardinal feature of which was its conditioned activity during the months from June to October inclusive, provided the weather during that period was neither excessively hot nor unusually cold. The rodent disease, often associated with sporadic cases of the human disease, sometimes commenced as early as April in mild springs, but the epidemic disease rarely attracted attention before June and usually not until July. Remote deaths from complications and sequelae of the human disease were frequently reported as late as January or even February.

In England the epidemic of 1478 at Hull appears to conform in its seasonal incidence and its reported proportional mortality to an outbreak of bubonic plague, and this conformation is strengthened by the fact that Hull was an important seaport and therefore always exposed to the risk of a maritime importation of *P. pestis* from the Continent. It would be entirely possible for Hull to experience a severe epidemic of bubonic plague in 1478 while the rest of England remained completely free from the disease. For an identical reason there may have been a local epidemic of the disease in London some time between 1477 and 1479 inclusive, but this surmise is less substantial than in the case of the outbreak at Hull.

There does not seem to be any outbreak of epidemic disease in Scotland that presents any circumstantial evidence for its identification as an outbreak of bubonic plague, with the doubtful exception of the epidemic of 1499.

In Ireland there was a possible importation of the disease through the port of Assaroe in 1478, but apart from this none of the Irish records of 'plague' presents any evidence that the disease in question was bubonic plague.

The picture presented by 'plague' and pestilence in the British Isles in the fifteenth century is—with the exception of the possible importation of cholera—one of epidemic outbreaks of communicable diseases indigenous to the islands, either alone or in conjunction with famines. The spread of each and all of these diseases was regulated by human contacts, either direct or indirect, and it is therefore of significance to find Kingsford asserting about this century: 'It is remarkable to note how easy communications were. The barges plied regularly from London to Henley in four days. A messenger covered the distance in a day's ride, and Dame Elizabeth [Stonor] took the journey as a matter of course. Even from Exeter to London there seems to have been a regular service of carriers, by pack-horse.'[1]

All these modes of conveyance of persons and goods would serve to spread a communicable disease; only the barge traffic would serve to transport *R. rattus*. It is true that occasionally 'blocked' fleas might be transported on the clothing of travellers or hidden in the horses' packs if they contained materials suitable for harbouring fleas; but the spread of bubonic plague was governed almost entirely by the spread of the infected house-rat.

CHAPTER 6

THE SIXTEENTH CENTURY

In this century the pattern of bubonic plague becomes manifest in England after and as a result of the institution of the parochial system of recording marriages, baptisms, and burials in 1538. Although these records are not by any means the equivalent of the modern system of registration—for instance with respect to burials the alleged cause of death is only occasionally recorded in the parish registers—they nevertheless show clearly that the epidemic disease had a seasonal incidence in the summer and early autumn months, with a peak mortality usually either in August or September; that it was peculiarly a 'household' disease—a feature which it derived from the house-rat—and that London with its great port was its chief focus and principal disseminating centre in England. Indeed there is strong evidence that London was the scene of local outbreaks of the disease in the intervals between national outbursts of it, and for a similar reason but much less often each of the important seaports of the British Isles experienced at some time an outbreak of bubonic plague which was localized to it. Bubonic plague was always an exotic and impermanent disease in these islands. It could only be introduced to them through their ports; its spread in them was governed by the breeding and predatory activities of the 'plague-fleas' of the house-rat, and those activities were hampered by the alien and uncongenial climate of the islands.

P. pestis travelled to these islands at irregular intervals along the 'rodent pipe-lines' from its Indian home and from the enzootic centre of the rodent disease in the mountainous region of Asir in south-western Arabia to Black Sea, Mediterranean, and Baltic ports, and then converged from them upon the port of London. Once the overland portion of its travel had been permanently disrupted in the seventeenth century by the establishment of direct trans-oceanic trade between Indian and British ports, bubonic plague disappeared from the British Isles. It lingered for a considerable time in eastern Europe while that region still maintained overland trade contact with India; but eventually disappeared there also when the long, dangerous,

and costly overland haul of oriental goods across Persia and southern Russia was replaced by sea-carriage around Africa into Mediterranean and Black Sea ports.

Of course *P. pestis* sometimes boarded ships that were loading in Indian ports in the bodies of infected rats and engendered epizootic plague among the ship-rats on board, and that in turn sometimes led to an outbreak of the epidemic disease among the crews of infected ships; but it was much more difficult for 'blocked' fleas from the rats' nests in the depths of a ship's holds to make contact with the crew than it was for such fleas in the thatched roofs of dwellings to make contact with their occupants, and it must be emphasized that *X. cheopis* rarely leaves a rat's nest until the occupants are dead or have deserted it. Moreover the 'blocked' fleas in the rats' nests have only a short infective life after their immediate hosts are gone; only 12 per cent of the potential 'plague-fleas' become 'blocked', and these would not attempt to attack the humans on board ship until all their preferential rodent hosts had been destroyed. It is theoretically possible that an entire ship's company in the seventeenth century might have been exterminated on voyage by bubonic plague; but in fact the great majority of 'Black Death' yarns about 'plague-ships' drifting about the oceans with not a living soul on board have as much substance as Vanderdecken's ghost ship. As far as the rodent disease is concerned, the seventeenth-century trans-oceanic voyages were so slow that it was invariably extinguished through the destruction of its rodent fuel before the ships reached their British home ports.

From London bubonic plague normally spread by haphazard rat contacts as a creeping epizootic or, less often, by the passive transport in merchandise of infected rats, especially by coastal shipping and riverine traffic. In inland towns the arrival of *P. pestis* often but not invariably engendered an epizootic of rat-plague, which sometimes led to an epidemic of bubonic plague or only to the infection of one or two households, especially if their dwellings were either spatially or compulsorily isolated from the rest of the township. The appearance of the human disease in a single household was usually sufficient, however, for the town or village to be credited in contemporary records with a visitation of plague. These urban foci invariably became spontaneously extinguished after variable periods of time in consequence of a natural loss of virulence by *P. pestis*, and the particular township was then free from both the rodent and the human disease until a fresh strain of the plague bacillus was introduced to its house-rats. From each temporary urban focus the disease might radiate by haphazard rat contacts for a variable distance into near-by villages and hamlets, and occasionally it might be transported to another town at a distance without involving any of the intervening townships.

THE BEGINNING OF THE CENTURY
England and Wales

The sixteenth century opened with 'a great pestilence throughout all England',[1] concerning which Holinshed relates that 'men died in manie places verie sore; but speciallie and most of all in the citie of London'.[2] He declares that London suffered a death-roll of 30,000; but Fabyan reduces this figure to the more credible though still probably exaggerated one of 20,000 'of all ages'.[3] Creighton, who believes that the population of London was less than 60,000 at this time, accepts Fabyan's figure as the most credible one, adding 'that a fourth or a fifth part of the inhabitants was as much as the severest plagues cut off'.[4] The epidemic erupted in the capital during June according to a Spanish report,[5] and London certainly seems to have suffered severely though its 'enormous mortality...has left few traces in the records of the City or of the State'.[6] The epidemic was evidently not responsible, however, for driving Henry VII and his queen to take refuge in Calais as one chronicle reports,[7] because Stow affirms[8] that they left London early in May—before the epidemic erupted—most probably to meet the duke of Burgundy at Calais, and that they returned there in June. Another Spanish report,[9] despatched at the end of December, states that the disease had by then 'entirely disappeared in England'. Creighton assumes that it was an outbreak of bubonic plague,[10] but there does not appear to be any contemporary evidence to support his assumption, apart from the fact that it occurred during the 'plague-season', and if he is correct in his assertion that 'in London it lasted through the winter'[10] it could not have been an epidemic of that disease, unless the autumn of 1500 was unusually mild and free from frost.

In October 1501 an epidemic at Gravesend, which may have been a 'trailer' of the metropolitan one, prevented Catherine of Aragon from disembarking there,[11] and in 1503 'there was a plague at Oxford...and at Exeter'.[11] There is no evidence to support Creighton's assumption that either of these 'plagues' was an outbreak of bubonic plague, and Pickard, who records that the mayor and two bailiffs died during the Exeter epidemic,[12] does not identify it as bubonic plague.

According to Creighton bubonic plague was certainly active in London in 1504 or 1505—perhaps in both years[11]—and he may be correct in view of the city's maritime activities, although there is no clinical evidence that the 'plague' was bubonic. After the cessation of this outbreak London appears to have been free from epidemic disease for the next four or five years, unless it was involved in the second outbreak of the 'sweating sickness' in the

summer of 1506.[1] It was possibly involved three years later in the 'great plague' that afflicted various parts of England in 1509,[2] and was undoubtedly involved in the European pandemic of influenza in 1510, which spread from France—where it was called *coqueluche**—all over England. Short relates that 'it attacked at once, and raged all over Europe, not missing a Family, and scarce a Person', but 'none died [of it], except some Children'.[3]

The next year (1506) London experienced an epidemic of some disease—possibly a recurrence of the influenza of the previous year—because Erasmus promised his friend Ammonius that he would visit him in London when the 'plague' was extinguished.[4] As Ammonius assured him at the end of November that the 'plague' had entirely disappeared, the outbreak may have been stopped by the onset of frosty weather.[5] This year also Creighton affirms that Cambridge and its university were attacked by 'plague', according to him while Erasmus was visiting there.[6] Two years later the university passed in the Michaelmas term of 1513 a grace to dispense with lectures 'for fear of the plague',[7] a fear that was probably excited by the epidemic which erupted in London in the summer and was reported to be raging among the sailors in the Fleet in September.[8] On the 3rd of that month it attacked the Venetian ambassador's household;[9] by the middle of the month it was said to be raging in London,[10] and in October it was reported to be causing between 300 and 400 deaths a day.[11] The seasonal incidence of this outbreak and its reported mortality suggest that it may have been a local epidemic of bubonic plague consequent upon the arrival of *P. pestis* at the Port of London; but this identification is purely conjectural in the absence of metropolitan parochial records of burials. 'This Year a great Mortality prevailed in England, say our Historians; they call it (as indeed all Diseases) the Plague; but to know what it was, we must consult Foreigners.'[12] On the Continent it was described as 'an epidemic contagious Fever, with a Dysentery, and black spots over the whole Body',[12] a description that is suggestive of the 'black' or haemorrhagic measles which ravaged London in 1674, attacking adults as well as children. Erasmus evidently feared that it was bubonic plague when he wrote on 1 November to Colet to apologize for his failure to visit him because of it.[13] If it was bubonic plague the autumn must have been a very mild one, similar to the 'wonderfull easy and softe wynter, without stormys or frostes'[14] of 1508, because on 6 December Bavarin reported to the Pesari that 'the plague' was still bad in London.[15] According to Stow twenty-seven of the nuns of 'the Minories without Ald-gate' died of the disease, 'besides other that were laie people, and servants in that house';[16] but as a

---

* Or *coccoluche*, a name given to it because the sick wore a close-fitting cap or hood over their head.[3]

contemporary chronicle[1] records this tragedy as happening in 1515 there is some doubt about its exact date.

It may have been an outbreak of typhus fever that drove Erasmus from London in February 1514[2] and deterred Henry VIII from riding in procession to St Paul's the following May;[2] but it was a metropolitan stirring of bubonic plague which drove him at Whitsuntide to retreat to Eltham as 'certain near the Court were dead of the great sickness',[3] because in this phrase we encounter the first attempt to recognize bubonic plague as a specific manifestation of a pestilential state. On 1 July Convocation was adjourned on account of the epidemic and the heat.[4] If that summer was exceptionally hot bubonic plague would have become quiescent with the enervation of the plague-fleas, but the rodent disease may have smouldered on as a desultory enzootic because Erasmus noted in April 1515 that the human disease had reappeared in London.[5]

The year 1517 produced 'a very droughty and frosty Winter [and] a very hot summer',[6] both inimical to the development of bubonic plague. Ormerod affirms that there was a terrible outbreak of plague in Chester this year, which so disrupted its civic life and paralysed its trade that 'grass grew a foot high at the market cross and in other parts of the City.'[7] Most likely this 'plague' was an incident in the third epidemic of the 'sweating sickness', which attacked London in September[8] and drove Henry VIII from his capital.[9] He moved to Windsor and withdrew from 'all business on account of the pestilence'.[10] He must have had a nasty shock when the disease followed him there and killed some members of his household.[11]

Gervis asserts that this epidemic of the 'sweating sickness' erupted in July 1517 and persisted for six months,[12] so it cannot have been the 'fearful sickness' which broke out suddenly in London at the end of April 1516[13] or the 'new malady' that frightened the Venetian ambassador early in 1517.[14] It was certainly the most deadly of the five epidemics of this disease. Macgowan says it was so malignant that it killed in 3 hours[15] and Gervis opines that its mortality was as great as the worst epidemic of bubonic plague.[16] He writes of it: 'Mourning supplanted the hilarity and brilliancy of the Court, and the King, while in miserable solitude, received message after message from different towns and villages, announcing that in some a third, in others even half the inhabitants, were swept off by the pestilence.'[17] Regrettably he evidently borrowed this account from one of the many apocryphal descriptions of the 'Black Death' because there do not appear to be any records of these calamitous mortalities in the royal archives. This epidemic of the 'sweating sickness' confuses the history of bubonic plague in England during the years from 1516 to 1518 because it was called 'the plague' by the Venetian ambassador

and other contemporary recorders. As it made 'great ravages in the royal household' and killed some of the pages who slept in the King's chamber,[1] it came near to altering the course of English history. Henry VIII escaped it; Anne Boleyn survived an attack of it![2]

It may have been typhus fever that killed three of Henry's pages in March 1518 and kept him in retreat at Richmond,[3] but it was plague which drove him from there to Woodstock in July and then chased him from his refuge,[4] for Wolsey's scout, who was either accompanying or trailing Henry, reported to him from Wallingford: 'Tomorrow the King leaves for Bisham, as it is time; for they do die in these parts in every place, not only of the small pokkes and mezils, but also of the great sickness.'[5] This record provides incontrovertible evidence that epidemics of smallpox, measles, and bubonic plague co-existed at times in sixteenth-century England, and it forced Creighton to admit that smallpox was present in England in 1518, though he does his best to belittle its significance.[6] Incidentally it should be noted that measles was a deadly disease then for adults as well as for children. It is a cardinal mistake to assume that diseases with which we are familiar today were as mild then as they are now.

Four days after Pace's report to Wolsey, Henry was at 'The More', 8 miles from Tittenhanger and 12 from Hatfield,[7] on the sparsely populated Hertfordshire uplands, whither 'the great sickness' had driven him from the Thames valley with its riverine spread of *P. pestis*. There is a distinct note of exasperation in his Privy Council's wish that Wolsey would devise 'such gistes as shall be most for the King's surety and my Lady's in this time of contagion.'[7] The contagion was raging in Lambeth[8] and possibly in other parts of the Liberties as well. Stow records that in the winter of 1518 there 'was a great death of pestilence, almost over all England in every towne more or less',[9] so that the epidemics of the autumn were succeeded by the eruption of yet another disease which, judging from its reported distribution, was most probably epidemic influenza.

Creighton affirms that plague was active at Nottingham and Oxford in April 1518,[10] and that it was a report of plague-deaths in the former town that caused Henry VIII to postpone his projected visit to the north,[10] as that would have entailed riding up the Great North Road through Nottingham; but there is uncertainty about the true nature of this disease. From Oxford Sir Thomas More reported to the King on 28 April that three children had died of 'plague' there 'but none others',[11] a report that eliminates bubonic plague as the disease. Nevertheless he ordered the mayor, 'in the King's name', to ensure that the 'plague sick' were confined to their houses and that these were marked with 'wispes'—i.e. bundles of straw—in accordance

with the regulations devised by Wolsey for the control of plague in London.[1] Whatever the disease was, it evidently became more violent after More's report, as the university informed Wolsey in November that it had raged there for 3 months.[2]

According to Creighton plague-deaths were reported on board one of the Venetian galleys at Southampton at the end of March 1519,[3] and if *P. pestis* managed to slip ashore on that occasion it was possibly responsible for the epidemic of disease in the Thames valley in the summer of 1520, especially 'at Abingdon and other villages towards Woodstock' in August.[4] It may also have slipped in through the port of Hull this year to cause the visitation that made the Corporation of Beverley disburse 16s. 2d. in relief to its sick poor.[5] Evidently there was either a recrudescence of the disease two years later or a fresh visitation of it, because the corporation then distributed 5s. in 'plague-relief'.[6]

The record of 'a great plage in London and many other places in the realme' in the Shrewsbury chronicle[7] presumably refers to the epidemic of 1521, which Grafton calls 'a great pestilence and death' whereof 'many noble Capitaynes died'.[8] Stow supplies the additional information that there was a great dearth in London and other places this year with wheat at 20s. a quarter,[9] so it seems very likely that the 'plage' was a famine-fever, especially as it was still prevalent in November, when it was not much feared though it was 'universal in every parish'[10] in London. The fact that it was not much feared, and was therefore not bubonic plague, is confirmed by the royal intimation to Wolsey to keep Michaelmas term in the city 'notwithstanding the continuance of the plague'.[11] Creighton has accepted this and other reports of 'plague' in London as certainly indicative of outbreaks of bubonic plague to substantiate his declaration that 'from 1511 to 1521 there is not a single year without some reference to the prevalence of plague' in the city.[12] His declaration is contradicted by the epidemiological character of the disease, for a number of these outbreaks of 'plague' occurred during the late autumn, winter, and early spring months when bubonic plague was usually inactive in England. It was presumably fear of this metropolitan 'plague' that caused Cambridge University to postpone its Michaelmas term 'to the morrow of St Martin'.[13]

In 1523 there was 'a great Dearth and Mortality in England and...after long and great Rains and Winds...there followed so severe a Frost, that many died of Cold'.[14] Such weather would certainly extinguish any focus of bubonic plague in England and there does not appear to be any record of that disease in 1524, yet it seems that it was fear of plague that made Cambridge University postpone its Easter term to the feast of St Barnabas.[15] The 'great

death in London' in the winter of 1525,[1] which impelled an adjournment of the Michaelmas term and drove Henry VIII to keep Christmas at Eltham with a small retinue—'for to eschue the plague'—[1] was most probably a virulent epidemic of typhus fever. Apparently the absence of king and court from London at Christmas had such a depressing effect upon the public enjoyment of the festive season that this particular anniversary was remembered as 'The Still Christmas'.[2] This year also there was a 'vehement plague' at Oxford which erupted in Cardinal College (now Christ Church) and involved the halls or colleges of St Alban, Jesus, St Edmund's, and Queen's, and forced the college that Wolsey founded to disperse for 3 years.[3] There does not seem to be any clue to its identity.

Scotland and Ireland

Ritchie[4] opines that the bulk of Scottish overseas trade during this century was with France, Flanders, and the Baltic states, and he remarks that it was difficult to prevent the importation of bubonic plague because Scotland was poor and its attention was so often fixed on war with England or distracted by bitter religious controversies. The significance of this observation is that *P. pestis* could therefore enter Scottish ports without any corresponding appearance in English ports and that, despite the geographical union of the two countries, bubonic plague could be widely epidemic in the one without any spread of the disease to the other.

Creighton affirms[5] that plague was epidemic in various places in the Lowlands and in the region between the Firths of Forth and Tay in the closing years of the fifteenth century, and that in 1500 it extended to involve Peebles, North Berwick, Edinburgh, Aberdeen, and numerous other towns and parishes. It reappeared in Edinburgh in 1502, whereupon the civic authorities decreed that no person was to communicate with the plague-sick except in the company of an official, or to be in the street after 9.0 p.m. 'without a byrning licht or a rationabill caus'.[6] The duration of this visitation is not recorded, but the disease had evidently abated by 1504 when the authorities promulgated in October an order about the cleansing of infected houses and goods in accordance with the old statutes.[7] These were presumably the ones that were incorporated in the *Rule of the Pestilence of 1456*, which Ritchie[8] avers is the earliest Scots law about plague.

This year plague was also epidemic in Ireland, where it 'swept away many people, almost everywhere, but especially in Ulster'.[9] Ware adds the note that the meeting of the provincial synod was transferred from Drogheda to Louth in July because the disease was 'very rife' in Drogheda, and that later

in the summer it was abruptly abandoned when plague appeared in Louth. None of the Irish Annals mentions this outbreak, but the deaths of two noblewomen from plague are recorded in one of them in 1505.[1] Ware declares that the disease was extensively epidemic in this year also,[2] but he quotes no contemporary record to support his statement.

Comrie opines that plague either attacked or threatened Dunfermline in 1504 because the queen's gear was removed from there to Lindores on account of it at a cost of £41 8s.[3] At this time the penalties for disobeying the Edinburgh regulations were branding on the cheek and banishment for a woman, amputation of a hand and banishment for a man.[4] The disease evidently reappeared in Edinburgh in the spring of 1505 because in July an order was made that the plague-stricken must not leave their houses without permission from the pest officers, and that every case of sickness—irrespective of its nature—must be reported to the authorities within 24 hours.[5] This order appears to be the first attempt to make infectious disease compulsorily notifiable in Scotland. It seems to have been largely ignored, because it was repeated in October with the time limit shortened to 12 hours and with additional regulations, including the prohibition of the purchase by women of any kind of material for clothes and the ejection of every beggar from the city within 24 hours.[6]

Except for a possible brief visitation of Edinburgh in 1509,[7] plague appears to have been absent from Scotland from 1505 to 1512, and there is no record of its presence in Ireland during this period, although the occurrence of outbreaks of epidemic disease in that country may be inferred from the report on the state of Ireland that was sent to Henry VIII in 1515, in which 'the pestylens' is blamed for some of the decline in the relative strength of the king's subjects in that land.[8]

When plague broke out again in Edinburgh in 1512 the authorities promulgated a fresh set of regulations against it. Every case of the disease must be notified immediately; no persons were to leave infected houses without official sanction; no citizen was to harbour an incomer from any suspect place; every part of the city was to be searched by officials who would report the plague-sick to the baillies, and no dogs or swine were to be allowed to roam loose. Relief payments were to be made to poor folk who were incapacitated from working, but all the remaining poor must either work or be ejected from the city.[9] However in spite of these orders 'the contagious plaige of pestilence'—which was now most probably typhus fever seasonally replacing plague—continued to spread, and in mid-January a royal proclamation was therefore issued to confirm the civic order. After reiterating the prohibitions about the movements of persons and goods, it prescribed an

isolation period of 40 days for convalescents from the pestilence, unless they carried a white wand or bore a white cross on their breast so that healthy people could avoid them if they wished. Stray dogs, cats, and pigs were to be summarily slaughtered without compensation.[1] Comrie states that copies of the proclamation were sent as 'Kyngis lettres' by messengers to all the Scottish burghs and that from 1513 they were the standard municipal anti-plague ordinances throughout the country.[2]

Although Edinburgh seems to have been free from it, plague appears to have been active in the surrounding country in 'Dene and other suspect places'[3] in June 1513, and the next year it was prevalent in the country around Aberdeen,[4] where the municipality took the precaution to erect huts on the Links and Gallow-hill in which any plague-sick and suspects were to be confined for 40 days.[4] After the subsidence of this outbreak Scotland appears to have been free from plague—or from epidemic disease recorded as 'plague'—until 1519, in which year there a was great outburst of epidemic disease in Ireland which persisted—in all probability with intermissions—until 1525.

Contemporary evidence suggests that this pestilential period began with an epidemic of bubonic plague in Dublin which killed 'a great number of the Foreigners of Ath-Cliath'.[5] The Lord Lieutenant's decision to remain in Dublin with his family 'notwithstanding the great plague'[6] may have been inspired by devotion to duty or enforced by the knowledge that death at the hands of the Irish outside the Pale was a greater risk than that of death by plague inside it. After the customary winter quiescence the disease re-crudesced in the spring of 1520 and evidently spread over a considerable area of the country during the ensuing summer, when it raged in Machaire-Stefanach[7] and in Fir-Manach.[8] It was epidemic in the English Pale in July,[9] and in August it was so widespread in the four counties occupied by the English that it was reported that there were hardly four places free from it, while its mortality in Ireland generally was said to be so great that the panic-stricken people were vacating their houses for the fields and woods, where they were still dying in large numbers.[10] If this report is true, the disease that killed them there was much more probably typhus fever than bubonic plague, for the house-rat would certainly not have accompanied them into the fields and woods but the body-louse would.

People were still dying of plague in the Pale in September,[11] and after the usual winter intermission, it was again epidemic in the summer of 1521 among the English occupation forces, concurrently with an epidemic of dysentery.[12] The next year it was prevalent in the south-west of Ireland, the town of Limerick being sadly scourged by it.[13] Creighton states that plague

raged also in Munster this year.[1] According to Ware[2] plague was rife in some places in Ireland, especially in Dublin, in both 1523 and 1524, but after the subsidence of this outbreak the country appears to have been free from it for the next ten years. It is probable that the activity of bubonic plague during the years from 1519 to 1525 was intermixed with epidemics of contagious diseases such as typhus fever, smallpox, dysentery, and influenza, which would be recorded as 'plagues' in the Irish Annals.

The year 1519 saw plague active also in Scotland in some parts of Lothian and in Edinburgh, where it was so prevalent that the lords could not meet and the young king was conveyed for safety to Dalkeith.[3] It may have recrudesced in the capital in April 1520 as the civic authorities attributed its yearly renascence to the existence of infected persons hiding in the buildings on 'the Borrowmure'.[4] But bubonic plague is not transferable from one human to another so the disease could only have been conserved in these buildings if they were infested with *R. rattus*. Comrie explains[5] that the 'Burgh Muir' was used for the burial of the plague-dead and for the disinfection of infected goods, for which purposes a number of buildings had been erected on it. These had evidently been occupied by squatters, who were ordered to dismantle them within 20 days and remove all their stonework within a further 20 days.[6] A woman who was caught redhanded by the watch in May 1521 in the act of hiding infected goods was branded on the cheek and banished from the city during the corporation's pleasure.[7] After this discouragement of other potential offenders the city fathers seem to have been free from anxiety about plague until 1529.

THE MID-CENTURY—I

England and Wales

The death in London of the Venetian ambassador in May 1526, possibly from bubonic plague,[8] heralded an epidemic of the disease of sufficient violence to provoke a panic exodus of the citizens up to a distance of 60 miles from the city.[9] It seems to have driven Henry VIII to spend the summer outside his capital, for he was at Guildford in July,[10] from which town he intended 'to have stopped at Stanstyd and Southwike; but as the parish in which the former stands is infected with plague'[11] he went to Warblington and thence to Porchester Castle.[12] Cambridge, where the Easter term of the University was prorogued 'till the morrow of Trinity',[13] and Guildford,[14] also reported visitations by plague this year. The disease may have persisted with winter intermissions in Cambridge until 1529; it was certainly the fear of plague, if not its actual presence, that caused the postponement of the Easter term that year 'till the morrow of the Visitation of the Virgin'.[15] That year

Shrewsbury was attacked by the disease, probably after the 'incessant rain day and night' that endured in England from 12 April to 3 June[1] had ceased, for the house-rat was averse to getting its fur wet.

It was most probably the fourth epidemic of the 'sweating sickness' that drove Brian Tuke from London to Stepney in June 1528,[2] but plague reappeared in the city early in June 1529[3] and was epidemic in the summer when the French ambassador's principal servants died of it in spite of repeated changes of lodgings.[4] This outbreak apparently subsided rapidly during September but the disease was not extinguished, only rendered dormant through the winter hibernation of the plague-fleas, because towards the end of March 1530 five of the Venetian ambassador's servants succumbed to it.[4] Their deaths seemingly prompted its rapid expansion, because parliament was prorogued on 26 April until 22 June 'on account of the pestilence in London and its suburbs'.[5] It was still active in the city in September[6] and parliament's reassembly had consequently to be deferred to October.

An epidemic of some disease, possibly bubonic plague, was violently active in London in the early autumn of 1531, driving the king to take refuge at Hampton Court at the end of November,[7] and causing earlier in the month an average weekly death-roll of from 300 to 400.[8] Henry VIII's Privy Purse expenses for 1530 and 1531 indicate that plague was active in London in the former year, and that it or some other epidemic disease confused with it was active there in 1531 and 1532. He moved to Greenwich in the summer of 1530 and paid £18 8s. in the autumn to compensate 'such poor folk as were expelled the town of Greenwiche in the tyme of the plague'.[9] As Henry would certainly not have gone to Greenwich, let alone stay there if plague were present, the poor folk must have been expelled as a precaution against the spread of the disease from London, because it was common knowledge in his day that it almost always appeared first in the hovels of the poor. As similar payments were made in 1531 on 13 January, 10 and 26 April and 8 November,[10] some epidemic disease other than bubonic plague must have been isolating Henry at Greenwich during this time.

There is evidence that plague was active in the summer of 1532. A Venetian despatch in mid-September reported that it was ravaging Kent and attacking London.[11] A second despatch a month later stated that the disease was increasing daily and making everybody uneasy,[12] a euphemism probably for panic-stricken. Fleet Street was apparently the worst affected area of the city in September,[13] but by mid-October 'the sickness' had much increased in London and Westminster and the mortality from it was universal, although the hardest hit part of the city was still the area around Fleet Street and the Temple.[14] There is supporting evidence that the disease was widespread,[15]

but if the mortality figures for London up to 21 October—99 deaths from 'plague' and 27 from other causes[1]—are accurate, either the terror of plague had grossly exaggerated its malignity on this occasion or 'the sickness' was some disease other than bubonic plague. As late as 29 October Chief Justice Fitzjames was declaring that 'plague' was increasing in London,[2] whereas an authoritative report eleven days later stated that it had abated.[3]

The fear of plague constrained 'the fellows, scholars, and bachelors of St John's College,' Cambridge, to isolate themselves somewhere in the country during the Easter term of 1532,[4] and because of that fear 'Michaelmas term was postponed till the morrow of St Martin, and then further postponed till the feast of St Nicholas';[5] but there is no record of an outbreak of the disease either in the university or the town that year. It invaded the parish of Much Wenlock, however, to produce one of the kindliest records to be found in the parish registers of England, for the death from it of the parish clerk drew from the vicar the testimony that he was 'a full honest server of the Churche and taught scolers playne song & prick song full well so that the churche was well served in his tyme'.[6] Plague was also widely prevalent in Kent in September, in and around Rochester[7] and 'at Dover and on the road thither'.[8] The next year, according to Creighton,[9] Oxford experienced a severe epidemic of it; but he supplies no details about it and the university archives apparently contain no record of it.

From 1533 to 1535 England seems to have been free from a serious epidemic, but about midsummer in the latter year a 'plague' erupted in London, although the disease was not widely distributed before August.[10] That month was evidently warm and wet, for the fear was expressed that 'these great humidities will engender pestilence at the end of the year',[10] and the foreboding was apparently quickly fulfilled because by mid-August 'plague' was reported to be raging in every London parish.[11] Before the end of the month it had spread to Stepney[12] and was said to be violently active all over the city.[13] These reports were all exaggerated, and when the Lord Mayor announced that Bartholomew Fair would be held as usual at Smithfield, he declared that the toll of the disease in London had been magnified.[14] The fact that the fair was held proves that these reports were fallacious and that the disease was not bubonic plague, because it was invariably cancelled when plague appeared in London. Undoubtedly the disease gave cause for apprehension for two independent witnesses,[15,16] reported that its activity was augmented in September, an exacerbation which provided Cromwell with an excuse to stop the Spanish ambassador's projected visit to Princess Mary.[17] However it declined rapidly during October and by the end of the month it had disappeared from London.[18]

In the spring of 1536 bubonic plague erupted in London[1] and evidently became epidemic there during the summer.[2] Its invasion of Westminster, where it was 'even in the Abbey',[3] threatened the coronation of Jane Seymour; but apparently early October frosts made the plague-fleas hibernate until the spring of 1537, when a report about it stated: 'They died here in every corner, but no very great death.'[4] The interpretation of this report is that though plague was busily killing the poor in the slums few deaths had as yet occurred among the better classes of society. The prisoners in the Fleet Prison were terrified of it,[5] and with justification, for its death-roll continued to grow during July and it spread along the Thames valley and into the Home Counties. By mid-July Archbishop Cranmer's fear of it constrained him to beg for royal permission to leave London, 'for they die', he moans, 'almost everywhere in London, Westminster, and Lambeth'.[6] Yet on the same day Lady Lisle was assured that the mortality was not as great as in the previous year because only 112 plague-deaths had been recorded in the city during the preceding week.[7]

By midsummer plague was widespread among the townships in the Thames valley and before September ended Kingston,[8] Windsor,[9] and Croydon[10] were involved in this extension of the disease. Meanwhile there had been no noticeable decline in the violence of the epidemic in London; indeed in October the mortality was 'extremely sore' in the city[11] and the Law term was postponed to Hallowmass, coincident with a royal proclamation prohibiting attendance at the christening of the future Edward VI without special authorization 'on account of the plague'.[12] However the christening was performed without interference from *P. pestis* although that microbe was still very busy at the end of the month in the country around London, as the warning that a traveller to escape it must ride 'twenty-six miles without baiting'[13] testifies. This warning contains two matters of interest. It suggests that plague was associated with places rather than with persons, so that the risk of contracting it was minimized if a traveller did not stop at a house or an inn while he was in the plague-area. It also suggests that the approximate limit of distance to which a 'blocked' flea might be transported by human agency in this century was a day's ride on horseback of some 25 miles.

Whether or no there was 'a greate plage in Shrewsberye' in 1535,[14] bubonic plague was so active there in the summer of 1536 that the election of knights to represent Shropshire in parliament could not be held in the town.[15] Creighton affirms that the disease was also so prevalent at Oxford that the university dispersed[16] and that by September hardly any place in Somersetshire was free from it.[17] It seems probable from the wording of a report that was sent from Penryn early in September[18] that Devonshire and part of Cornwall

were equally involved with Somersetshire in an extensive epidemic of it. There is, however, some ambiguity about this report; there is none about the report late in October that 'plague' was ravaging Doncaster, but the identity of the disease is uncertain.[1] The duke of Norfolk, who made the report, was engaged in suppressing the Northern Rebellion, and he has been accused of cowardice and has been censured for negotiating with the rebels instead of destroying them by force of arms. His reasons for his action were given to the Privy Council. 'It was not fear which made us appoint with the enemy, but the cold weather and the want of room to house more than a third of the army, and of fuel to make fires. Pestilence in the town was fervent, and where I and my son lay, at a friar's, ten or twelve houses were infected within a butt's length.'[2] If the weather was cold enough to interfere with military operations, then it was certainly too cold for plague-flea activity and the pestilence was not bubonic plague. It might have been typhoid fever from a polluted local source of drinking-water, but most probably it was louse-borne typhus fever. On the other hand the duke may have exaggerated both the cold and the billeting difficulty in order to conceal the real cause of his decision to treat with the rebels, namely, the refusal of his troops to enter a town in which 'plague' was present.

Towards the end of October 1537 bubonic plague disappeared from London, but it was replaced by typhus fever because a report in February 1538[3] stated that people were dying all over the city and in the country to the west of London. As was to be expected of typhus fever, this outbreak collapsed suddenly with the coming of warmer weather in the spring, which induced people to stop huddling together indoors and even perhaps to shed some of their louse-infested underclothes.

If London escaped an outbreak of bubonic plague this year Exeter was not so fortunate, for in June its townspeople were dying 'sore of the sickness',[4] and Exeter was only one of a number of places in England which were involved in an outbreak of epidemic disease that occupied the years 1537 and 1538. Hull was the scene of a severe epidemic at the beginning of July[5] which was probably one of bubonic plague. A fortnight later 'plague' was reported to be epidemic at Reading, near Buckingham, at Towcester—where the people were dying 'very sore'—probably at Thame, and certainly at Teddington.[6] Towards midsummer an epidemic at Launceston prevented the assizes from being held there[7] and in September another erupted in Kingston-on-Thames and drove Henry VIII from there to seek safety at Esher.[8] Some weeks earlier, apparently about mid-August, what may well have been bubonic plague erupted at Portsmouth and raged there for the next month or six weeks. It was still prevalent among the workmen in the

dockyard at the end of September.[1] It is not wise to assume that all the epidemics recorded in England between 1500 and 1539 that are reported as 'plague' in contemporary writings were outbreaks of bubonic plague. Until the parish burial registers permit of an examination of the seasonal incidence of a 'plague' mortality, the identification as bubonic plague of contemporary records of 'plague' is largely a matter of personal opinion, unless an outbreak is specifically referred to as 'the great sickness'.

Devonshire was extensively and severely afflicted by 'plague' in 1537,[2] and a disease that may have been bubonic plague was so violent at Chester that the Council of the Marches forbade the mayor and aldermen of Chester to resort to its court at Ludlow for fear that they would bring the disease with them.[2] The adjournment of the Easter term of Cambridge University to the feast of Corpus Christi[3] seems to have been caused solely by the fear of plague, however, as there is no evidence that Cambridge was attacked by any epidemic disease in 1537.

It seems probable that typhus fever was responsible for the 16 'plague-deaths' which were recorded at the beginning of March 1538 in Abingdon,[4] where the death-roll rose to 26 five days later.[5] If bubonic plague was the 'pestilence' which was reported to be ravaging Torrington and villages around Bovey Tracey as early as 8 February,[6] the winter of 1538 must have been exceptionally mild and warm in Devonshire. Certainly bubonic plague rather than typhus fever is the more likely cause of a mortality which was said to be so general in the county by the middle of the month that the timber trade was at a standstill,[7] while a report in mid-March stated that 'there was a great death at every place'.[8] Undoubtedly the witnesses believed it to be bubonic plague because several reports refer to the disease as 'the great sickness'; but epidemiological analysis of this 'pestilence' suggests that a virulent epidemic of typus fever in the winter was replaced surreptitiously by one of bubonic plague in the spring. Support for this view is provided by the fact that the 'pestilence' was prevalent synchronously in the eastern counties, where the winter is usually colder than in the West Country. For instance Colne in Huntingdonshire was visited by it early in the year,[9] and in January Thorpe in Derbyshire was so 'sore vexed with the plague' that 'almost no house' was free from it.[10] It was prevalent in Norfolk by the middle of March[11] and by the end of the month the mortality was increasing daily in that county.[12] Early in April it broke out at Buckingham and Willoughby,[13] and a little later Cambridge was attacked and the university was obliged to pass a grace 'for the intermission on account of the plague, of all ordinary lectures, disputations, and other public exercises till the feast of St Barnabas'.[14]

The report of a conversation between two king's visitors and the abbot of Pershore towards the end of April[1] contains the statements that there was then no mortality from 'plague' north of Doncaster, but from that town to Pershore not a single town or village had escaped the disease. The first of these statements was untrue and the second was certainly a gross exaggeration. As early as March plague was killing the citizens of York, and by the beginning of April its activity was so fierce that the corporation ordered that all the plague-sick should be removed to certain houses outside the Lathrop gate that had been specially set aside for their reception, that the gate should be closed, and that no infected person was to move about in or to enter the city.[2] Later in the year plague spread further north and the Council of the North informed Henry VIII towards the end of August that it was prevalent in Durham and Newcastle-upon-Tyne,[3] while a second report, early in December, affirmed that it was still active at various places in the two counties.[4] However the winter of 1538–9 was evidently cold enough all over England to arrest the rat-flea transmission of *P. pestis*, as there does not appear to be an authentic record of plague anywhere in the country in 1539.

A contemporary chronicle[5] records that the summer of 1540 was hot and dry and that no rain fell from the end of June until eight days after Michaelmas. 'Also', the chronicler continues, 'their rayned strang sicknes among the people in this realme, as laskes and hott agues, and also pestilence, whereof many people died.' He relates that Henry VIII sent commissioners to every bishop to 'exhort the people to fall to prayer and to go in procession in everie parish in the hole realme'.[6] It is evident from the royal concern that this pestilential summer must have engendered an alarming amount of sickness and a heavy mortality. Fabyan reports 'a greate laske',[7] which may well have been an eruption of cholera, and Stow relates that the drought was so severe that 'wells and small rivers were dried up, so that much cattell died for lacke of water'.[8] The excessive heat would certainly immobilize the plague-fleas in England, so whatever the 'pestilence' was it was not bubonic plague. In view of the fact that such a summer would almost certainly produce a 'plague' of flies, typhoid fever has a strong claim to be the 'pestilence'. There seem to be only three references to 'plague' in England this year—the two men from Gloucestershire who were taken ill at Dudley in March[9] were probably cases of typhus fever—namely, at Windsor,[10] Liverpool, and Watford. Morely[11] declares that Liverpool was nearly depopulated by the disease that afflicted it, but he is careful to explain that its population was small as the town had only 138 households in 1555. Creighton has extracted from the parish register of Watford the record of 40 'plague-burials' in a total of 47 burials during the months of July to September inclusive.[12] As these occurred

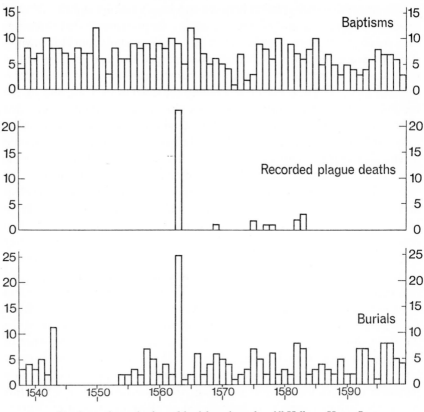

21. Baptisms, plague-deaths and burials registered at All Hallows, Honey Lane, London, 1538–99.

during the 'plague-months' it is possible that Watford was the exception to the general rule in 1540 and that it experienced an outbreak of bubonic plague.

After this hot summer there was apparently a lull until 1542 before bubonic plague advertised its presence again. Bishop Bonner's injunction about church burials in plague-time[1] may have been merely a precautionary measure as it was issued in February, but the parish register of Wragby[2] in Yorkshire contains a record of burials in 1542 that is very suggestive of a local outbreak of bubonic plague. From an annual average of 10 for the four preceding years the burials rose to 97, of which there were 33 in July and 27 in August, so that these two 'plague-months' contributed practically 60 per cent of the total burials in that year. When a parish register shows an excessive number of burials in a year and a monthly analysis reveals that

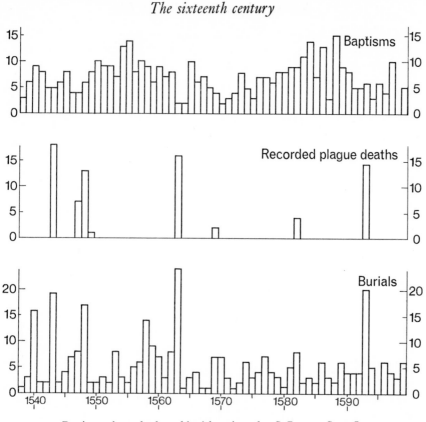

22. Baptisms, plague-deaths and burials registered at St Pancras, Soper Lane, London, 1538–99.

more than 50 per cent of them is contributed by any successive three months of the plague-season, June to October inclusive, the record is suggestive of an outbreak of bubonic plague in the parish. When more than 66 per cent of the total annual burials occurs in the three months of July to September inclusive, the record is almost certainly indicative of an outbreak of bubonic plague.

The accompanying figures are presented as illustrations of this thesis. Numbers 21 and 22 represent the burials recorded in two London parishes in which plague-burials were specifically entered in the registers, and numbers 23 and 24 those of two provincial parishes, namely, the town of Ludlow and the village of Colyton in Devonshire, in which no specific entries of plague-burials were made. The metropolitan parish registers show that plague was responsible for most of their excessive annual mortalities in this century. The parish of All Hallows, Honey Lane[1] was involved

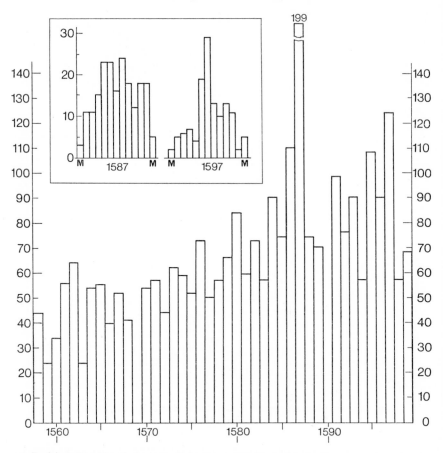

23. Burials registered at Ludlow, 1558–99. Inset: monthly burials for the years 1587 and 1597. (From 'Ludlow', ed. H. J. Weyman, *Shropshire Parish Register Society, Hereford diocese*, XIII, Shrewsbury, 1912.)

in the great epidemic of 1563, but not in the local outbreak of 1547–8 or the major epidemic of 1593, while sporadic plague-deaths were recorded in it in 1569, 1575, 1577, 1578, 1582, and 1583. The parish of St Pancras[1] was involved in all three of the major metropolitan outbreaks and recorded sporadic plague-deaths in 1543, 1549, 1569, and 1582. These records, which are representative of the London parishes, indicate that the behaviour of bubonic plague in the sixteenth-century city was that of a disease smouldering enzootically among the house-rats for limited periods of time, during which scattered, sporadic cases of the human disease were recorded in various parishes; dying out with the natural progressive loss of virulence by *P. pestis*;

176

receiving repeated infusions of fresh, virulent strains of the microbe by maritime importations of it through the port of London, and then erupting in unrecognized epizootics and subsequent epidemics of varying extent and malignancy from time to time when these fresh strains arrived.

The Ludlow register exhibits an excessive mortality in 1587[1] but the monthly analysis of the burials reveals that the seasonal mortality is not typical of bubonic plague, and in that year a strange disease, the 'Burning

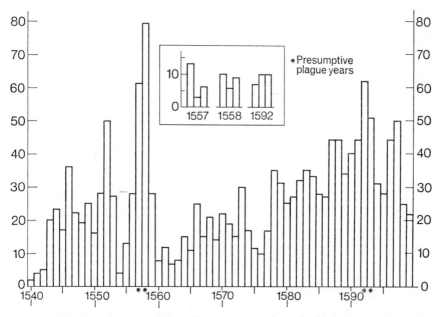

24. Annual burials registered at Colyton, Devon, 1540–99. Inset: burials in August, September and October for each of the three dated years. (From A. J. P. Skinner, 'Colyton, Devon, 1538–1837', *Publications of the Devon and Cornwall Record Society*, II, Exeter, 1928.)

Ague', was reported to be extensively epidemic in England and especially severe at Shrewsbury.[2] As Ludlow is only 26 miles from Shrewsbury and there was constant intercourse between the two towns, it is a reasonable presumption that it was the 'burning ague' which was responsible for the excessive mortality at Ludlow in 1587. Later in the century Ludlow was involved in the major English outburst of bubonic plague which raged intermittently from 1592 to 1598, and the monthly analysis of the excessive burials recorded in its register in 1597[3] is typical of an epidemic of bubonic plague.

The register of Colyton shows at least six occasions in this century when the burials were much in excess of the annual average.[4] In three of these

years, to wit, 1557,[1] 1558,[2] and 1592,[3] the monthly analysis of the burials affords a strong presumption that these excessive mortalities were due to outbreaks of bubonic plague. The reason why Colyton was more frequently visited by plague than Ludlow was because it was only about 3 miles inland from the fishing port of Beer and midway between the coastal ports of Lyme Regis and Sidmouth, whereas Ludlow was a central inland town and too far up the river Severn to be a river-port.

Plague returned to London in 1543 as the parish register of St Pancras testifies, for 18 of the 19 burials registered during the year are entered as plague-burials.[4] Other metropolitan parishes undoubtedly had similar plague-mortalities as an archiepiscopal mandate issued towards the end of August speaks of 'the raging pestilence',[5] and towards the end of October Michaelmas term was removed to St Albans because London was 'sore infected with the pestilence'.[6] Additional evidence of the severity of this metropolitan visitation is provided by Wriothesley's record that 'this sommer was great death in the citie of London and the suburbs of the same, wherefore the King made proclamation in the Courte that noe Londoner should come within seven miles'[7] of his country residence, and by a creditor's explanation that he had not dared to demand payment of a debt because of the epidemic.[8]

Outside London Berwick-upon-Tweed was the scene of a 'great plague' this year. It was ascribed by two contemporary recorders to 'the great multitude of people and the straitness of the little church',[9] a quaint combination which suggests that the God-fearing people of Berwick constantly packed themselves so tightly into their church that a pestilential vapour was generated by the commingling of the offensive humours emanating from their unwashed, over-heated, and louse-infested bodies. To a sixteenth-century reader this explanation of the origin of the epidemic would have been acceptable, and entirely convincing if simultaneously Saturn was in the sign of Cancer, the Moon was eclipsed, and the wind was in the east. At the opposite end of England plague was also busy this year in the parish of Lydden, where it destroyed most of the parishioners according to Vallance.[10]

There were several scattered, localized outbreaks of plague in England in 1544, which may have derived from or been independent of the severe metropolitan epidemic of the previous year. Bristol experienced a serious outbreak of it,[11] while Dover and Rye were each so seriously afflicted that in Henry VIII's absence in France the Privy Council refused to allow any soldiers to be shipped from those ports[12] in spite of urgent royal demands for men and horses to replace those lost in the siege of Boulogne. *P. pestis* could have been transported to each of these ports from London by coastal shipping,

but Bristol was more probably independently infected from a Continental port.

Plague was also prevalent simultaneously in and around Calais, and in view of its activity on both sides of the Channel and the transport across that water of men and munitions to sustain the English campaign in France, it is not surprising that it was active at numerous places in Kent, including Canterbury,[1] and that rumours of its presence in Sussex, Essex, and the Home Counties were frequent. Among the Crown expenses during the king's absence in France, these payments in connexion with those rumours are recorded.

July	Amyas Hill, for riding to Otelonde, Wynsore, and the More, to search the coasts there for sickness, 3s.
August	Amyas Hill, for riding to Oking and Gylford to search the country there for sickness, 12d.
September	John Brampton, for riding into Essex to make enquiry of sickness there, 4s.
	Jas. Stamforde, for riding into Kent to make enquiry of sickness there, 4s.
	Hugh Lighe, for searching the country about Greenwich, Eltam, Otford, Darteford and Knoll by the space of three days for sickness, 3s.[2]

These records reveal vividly the grave handicap under which every central authority in sixteenth-century Europe laboured in its efforts to control epidemic disease within its borders. Evidently Queen Catherine Parr was disturbed by the rumours about plague that reached her, and it is equally evident that any plans she made to combat the disease would need to be revised with each fresh report that her agents brought to her.

Synchronously with its activity in the south, plague was prevalent in the north of England in 1544. Newcastle-upon-Tyne was invaded in the summer and by mid-August the town was sorely afflicted.[3] The epidemic seems to have increased in violence during September; at any rate when ships were collected at the beginning of October to discover the strength of a Scottish fleet which was hovering off the coast, none sailed from Newcastle because 'all the honest inhabitants' had fled from the stricken town and no ships or seamen were available.[4] Simultaneously plague was said to be raging over most of Northumberland 'and sundry other places in the North'.[4]

Apart from the entry of 2 plague-burials in the register of one London parish in 1545,[5] the city appears to have had a respite from plague until the

summer of 1547. Grafton[1] blames soldiers returning from Haddington in the Scottish campaign for bringing it into London, but it was active in the city before their arrival as the burials register of St Pancras testifies.[2] During this outbreak the occupiers of infected houses were ordered to mark them with 'a cross upon their street doors',[3] and Creighton explains that this mark, which was a St Anthony's cross coloured blue, was to remain in position for 40 days.[4]

Plague recrudesced in at least one of the metropolitan parishes in the spring of 1548, for the register of St Pancras records 1 plague-burial in April, 7 in August, 4 in September, and 1—a remote death from sequelae in all probability—in December,[5] 13 plague-burials in a total of 17 burials during the year or more than 76 per cent. It is probable that the excessive mortalities shown in the registers of St Michael, Cornhill,[6] and St Antholin, Budge Row,[7] in 1548, and in those of All Hallows, Bread Street,[8] and St Mary le Bowe, Cheapside,[9] in both 1547 and 1548, were largely due to plague.

Possibly on account of the great drought in the summer of 1548 the disease was slow to become epidemic, but in July it 'raigned sore in London with great death of people, wherfore tearme and Parliament were adjourned from *Octavis Michaelis* (7 October) to the third daie of November'.[10] The adjournment of both the Law term and parliament indicates that the epidemic continued during August and September, and it drove Edward VI from his capital to keep his court out in the country—at Hatfield in September and at 'Lighes' in October.[11] Evidently frosty weather in the autumn extinguished this outbreak because, as far as its epidemic manifestation is concerned, plague seems to have been absent from London for the succeeding 9 years. The register of St Pancras records 1 plague-burial in 1549[12] and that of Saynte De'nis Backchurch 1 in July 1551;[13] but as 3 burials 'of the Sweat' are also recorded, (2 in July and 1 in August) the 'plague-entry' most probably represents a fourth death from the 'sweating sickness', which was epidemic in London that year.

After the customary intermission during the winter of 1544–5, plague resumed its activity in the north of England in the spring of 1545. It began 'to reign somewhat vehemently' at Berwick-upon-Tweed towards the end of April,[14] and by 10 May the quarry for supplying the stone for the fortifications of Berwick was 'full of lodges' for the plague-sick.[15] Throughout the summer plague continued to ravage the town and by the beginning of October it was reported to have destroyed most of the townsfolk[16]—a typical horrific rumour because all who could would have fled from the town to safety in the country. The disease was also reported to have spread over most of Northumberland during the summer—although most of that county was then too

desolate to harbour man or house-rat—and it was active in Newcastle-upon-Tyne at the beginning of October.[1]

In the south, in and around Portsmouth, plague was widespread in the summer of 1545 and by September many of the ships in the fleet guarding the Channel were infected and could not be kept at sea, because 'none will willingly enter them'[2] and their crews could not be transferred to other ships. By the end of the month plague was 'very sore in the town of Marlborough'[3] and epidemic at Oundle, which had a heavy death-roll from it in October,[4] and early in November a plague-death occurred in a family living at Glapthorne in Northamptonshire.[5] For about a fortnight after this death the family seemingly had no cause for alarm. Then, the epizootic among the house-rats having been established, plague struck again and within ten days 8 or 10 more plague-deaths occurred among members of the household.[5] This is a typical example of the epidemic character of bubonic plague —its constant manifestation as a house disease—and it is quite likely that no other family in Glapthorne was attacked by *P. pestis* on this occasion, simply because by a fortunate chance that microbe was not introduced among the rats infesting other houses in the village. The interval recorded between the first plague-death and the subsequent family holocaust is also characteristic of the disease—it represents the time required for a 'blocked' flea, after infecting one person, to engender an exterminating epizootic among the house-rats and for their starving 'blocked' fleas to attack other members of the household. Every epidemic of bubonic plague in the British Isles from 1348 to 1665 was invariably and inevitably a summation of such house incidents.

Concurrently with Oundle Cambridge was attacked, and the university accordingly dissolved the Michaelmas term 'till the morrow of St Martin on account of the plague'.[6] At Portsmouth some soldiers were dropping dead, 'full of the marks' of plague, as they paraded to receive their pay, 11 of a total of 34 named warships were infected, and from them 903 plague-sick sailors and marines had been removed.[7]

The next year Cambridge was again attacked—or to be accurate, in all probability plague recrudesced there after the usual winter intermission—and the university passed a grace 'for suspending the mathematical lecture till the feast of St Dennis [9 October], on account of the plague and the absence of scholars'.[8] Plague also erupted at several fresh places in Northamptonshire, namely, Polebrook, Holdenby, Southwick, and Northampton,[9] and it seems evident that it was widely dispersed in the county during the summer and early autumn of 1546, Synchronously it was extensively dispersed in Devonshire, so widely prevalent in fact that the musters in the

county had to be postponed.[1] In Wiltshire Salisbury was invaded by it at Whitsuntide, and the subsequent epidemic caused 'great sickness and death'[2] there until the third week in August, when it began to decline.

Plague may have been moving westwards this year as a creeping epizootic disease transmitted by rat contacts, because in 1547 it was epidemic in

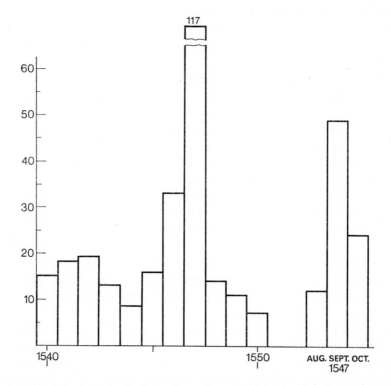

25. Annual burials registered at Camborne, Cornwall, 1540–50. Inset: burials in August, September and October 1547. During the epidemic of bubonic plague in 1547, plague mortality represented 72 per cent of the total mortality for the year. (From 'Cranborne, 1538–1837', ed. H. Topley-Soper, *Publications of the Devon and Cornwall Record Society*, Exeter, 1945.)

Cornwall at Stratton and Camborne. The parish register of Stratton records 153 burials of plague-dead this year[3]—an appalling mortality for that small township—and Camborne suffered severely as its register records 117 burials during the year.[4] Although there is no specific mention of plague in this register, the excessive mortality and the burial of 85 corpses in the three 'plague-months'—72·6 per cent of the annual total—render it practically certain that bubonic plague was responsible. (See figure 25).

182

Apart from its probable visitation of Banstead in Surrey, plague does not seem to have been active anywhere in England outside London in 1548. The parish register of Banstead[1] shows an average of less than 2 burials a year for the 9-year period 1549–57. There were 23 burials in 1548, of which 16 or practically 70 per cent occurred in the three 'plague-months',[2] (see figure 26) and three families, Unwyn, Pett, and Crowthere, provided 11 or practically 69 per cent of the presumptive plague-burials.

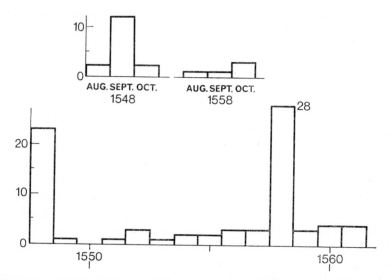

26. Excessive mortalities at Banstead, Surrey, in 1548 and 1558. Inset: the burials in August, September and October in 1548 and 1558. (From F. A. H. Lambert, 'The registers of Banstead in the county of Surrey', *The Parish Register Society*, 1, London, 1896.)

Lincoln was visited in 1549 according to Creighton,[3] but he supplies no information about the severity of this visitation. Plague was probably replaced by an outbreak of typhus fever in the ensuing winter, because in February 1550 the corporation decreed that certain poor people, who were then 'visited with the plague',[4] should be confined to their houses; that it was the duty of each alderman of a plague-ward to ensure that such people were so confined, and that it was also his duty to ensure that they obtained poor relief. A similar plan to cope with the epidemic of 'plague' that afflicted it in 1550–1 was adopted by York. The disease—which as at Lincoln was most probably typhus fever—attracted no official notice until January 1550,[5] when the corporation ordered all the people, 'dwelling in Laythrop' to evacuate their houses, which were needed for the accommodation of the sick.

These houses had been built by the corporation twelve years before for the reception then of the plague-sick and evidently they had been occupied by tenants or squatters in the interval. As the Laythrop accommodation now proved inadequate, the corporation erected two buildings in February on Hob Moor,[1] and later in the month it levied a fund on the four wards of the city for the relief of the sick poor.[2] In the spring of 1551 plague appeared in the city and by the beginning of May it was causing the authorities much trouble. Apparently the buildings at Layerthorpe and on Hob Moor were full of patients by this time, because on 7 May the corporation ordered all the plague-sick to keep in their own houses,[3] and as the disease continued to grow it cancelled the Corpus Christi play on the 18th.[4] After June the outbreak seems surprisingly to have subsided spontaneously, for the civic measures could not have arrested it, especially as they were hampered by lack of co-operation on the part of the commonalty and by the refusal of the leading citizens to accept civic positions of responsibility in plague-time, For instance six citizens elected to the office of bridge-master successively refused to undertake the duty and paid a fine of £4 each for their refusal.[5] It was during this pestilential period that the city council decreed that every infected house 'shall have Rede Crosse sat uppon the Dower',[6] which appears to be the first use of this colour as a plague-sign in England. Laycock avers[7] that in the two summers of 1550 and 1551 the parish of St Martin *cum* Gregory lost more than half its population from epidemic disease, and as this was one of the city's healthy parishes in his opinion, he considers that York lost at least half its population at this time.

At Stround in Middlesex a coroner's verdict was returned that the death of a tapster in November 1549 was due to 'the pestylaunce or plagg';[8] but an isolated case such as this may have been due to some disease simulating plague. On the other hand it could have been a case of bubonic plague resulting from the bite of a 'blocked' flea which attacked the man in London, where plague was smouldering in at least one parish, St Pancras,[9] this year.

According to Barnard[10] plague was active at Evesham in 1550, but its activity can only have been sporadic as the burials registers of the town's two parishes, St Lawrence and All Saints, show no excessive mortalities.[10] Cox[11] affirms that parts of London were attacked this year, instancing a number of plague-burials in the register of St Martin-in-the-Fields; but there is no plague-burial marked among the 10 burials registered between 21 January— when this register begins—and 14 March 1550.[12] In 1551, however, in a total of 51 burials during that year, 3 (all in July) are marked *ex sudore*,[12] and he may have confused these deaths from the 'sweating sickness' with plague.

The next year witnessed the last recorded outbreak of the 'sweating sick-

ness' in England,* and as it was a 'plague' to contemporary writers it is difficult to distinguish between it and bubonic plague in some of the reports of epidemic disease in 1551. It was probably plague 'which raged from Easter to Michaelmas' in Bristol and 'carried off many hundreds every week'.[1] If this report is not grossly exaggerated, so severe an epidemic would provoke a panic exodus from the city, and it may have been two of the fugitives who caused a clerical squabble in the parish of Standish in Gloucestershire. Early in September two strangers died in that parish and the incumbent, supported by his churchwardens, refused to allow their corpses to be interred in the churchyard 'for fear of the plague',[2] so they were buried in the king's highway. There they would have rested peacefully if someone had not informed the bishop, who promptly ordered their corpses to be exhumed and re-buried in the churchyard before 6 o'clock the next morning. Cooper notes that the 'sweating sickness' 'prevailed to a great extent in Cambridge' this year, killing at Buckden, whither they had fled from it, the two sons 'of the famous Charles Brandon, Duke of Suffolk'.[3]

A vague notice of its presence at Ulverston[4] appears to complete the record of bubonic plague's activity in England in 1551, and the next year seems to be devoid of any reference to its presence in this country, including London.

Scotland and Ireland

Bubonic plague returned to Scotland in the summer of 1529, causing the civic authorities of Edinburgh to ban from admission to the city the residents in certain suspect towns,[5] all of which were apparently situated north of the Firth of Forth, St Andrews in particular being severely visited.[6] A woman from St Andrews who entered Edinburgh 'with infected gear' was branded on both cheeks, her clothes were burnt, and she was banished from the city on pain of death.[7] The disease evidently continued to spread during the early autumn because in mid-October the Edinburgh authorities published a proclamation banning all the people of Dundee, St Johnstone, Cupar, and all other

---

* The parish register of Loughborough has the entry: '1551. The swat called *New acquaintance, alias Stoupe knave and know thy Master*, began 24 June.'[8] Hancock remarks in his autobiography: 'God plaged thys realme most justly for our sinns with three notable plages: The first was the posting swet, that posted from towne to towne throughe England, and was named *stope gallant*, for hytt spared none, for ther were dawncyng in the cowrte at 9 a'clocke thatt were deadd or eleven a'clocke'.[9] Waters notes that 'the "*stup-gallant* or the *hote sickness*" is also mentioned in the registers of Uffcolme, Devon, in August 1551. This quaint name was taken from the French, for the epidemic which ravaged France in 1528 was called the "*trousse gallant*", because it chiefly attacked young men in full health and strength.'[10] This is not the place to discuss the identity of the 'sweating sickness', but it may here be suggested that it was almost certainly a virus and not a bacterial infection. Present-day medical opinion appears to be divided between epidemic influenza and the French 'miliary' or 'Picardy sweat'.

towns north of the Firth of Forth from attendance at the 'next fair of Hellomes'.[1]

These outbreaks were the heralds of the widespread and destructive epidemic of 1530, which appears to have been one of the worst outbreaks of bubonic plague in Scotland in this century. It was prevalent in St Monance towards the end of February—if it was bubonic plague and not typhus fever —and in Edinburgh in May, when all the citizens were commanded to clean the drains in front of their dwellings 'under pain of banishment at the Provost's pleasure'.[2] Simultaneously two women were each branded on the cheek and banished from the city for contravening the anti-plague orders, and during June several more citizens were similarly punished.[3] An aggravated offence was committed by a tailor who concealed his wife's plague-sickness and attended mass on a Sunday when she was moribund. As the authorities opined that he had done his best thereby to infect the whole city, he was sentenced to be hanged on a gibbet before his own door. However he escaped by 'the will of God' as the rope broke, and as he was 'ane pure man with small bairns' the authorities relented and commuted his sentence to banishment for life.[4]

The epidemic in Edinburgh apparently subsided during September because on 8 October the council noted that no fresh case had been reported for the previous 8 days.[5] Nevertheless it decided to enforce for the remainder of the year the compulsory notification of every case of sickness, and it evinced no tendency to mitigate the severity of its punishments with the cessation of the epidemic; indeed two of the sentences passed in October are two of the harshest in the archives of plague. Two women were summarily drowned in 'the Quarell hollis at the Grayfrere port', one for stealing two 'stekis of bukrum' and importing plague from Leith to Edinburgh;[6] the other for attending mass and moving about in the city 'while the pestilence was on her'.[7] This month also three women were banished for opening a feather bed and selling the feathers while they were confined to their houses on suspicion of plague.[8] Many people fled from Edinburgh during this epidemic.

It seems probable that much of Scotland between the Firth of Forth and the Moray Firth was involved in this outbreak, for at the end of July Aberdeen closed all but three of its gates as a precaution against the 'contagious pestilence rengand in the contre',[9] and these three gates were each to be watched day and night to prevent any stranger from entering the town, while a night patrol of 6 men was to search every part of the town for strangers and cases of sickness.[10]

In the second quarter of this century 'plague' reappeared in Ireland in

1535. Ware records 'a raging Pestilence' that year which killed many people, especially in Ulster,[1] and in August Henry VIII was warned not to expect to obtain many Irishmen for his service 'in consequence of the plague'.[2] A few days later an important meeting which normally would have been held in Dublin was held 'at the hill of the Lions, for all the towns of this country are sore infected with the pestilence, and especially Dublin'.[3] By the phrase 'this country' in this context the recorder evidently meant the English Pale, as the meeting was one of the high English officials, and it is practically certain that the word 'pestilence' here means bubonic plague. The outbreak of it in the Pale was evidently a very severe one[4] and the disease seems to have been raging concurrently in other parts of Ireland. Creighton affirms that there was a most violent epidemic of it in Cork,[5] and one chronicle records that there was a 'great plague and smallpox throughout Ireland this year'.[6] In 1536 'many diseases and maladies raged, namely, a general plague, galar breac, the flux, and fever, of which many died'.[7] There is no certainty, however, that bubonic plague contributed to Ireland's misery this pestilential year. It is extremely probable that the 'general plague' was a 'famine-plague' and that the 'fever' was either typhus or relapsing fever or quite possibly a concurrence of them. After this year the country seems to have been free from epidemic disease until, in 1540, 'there was a plague in the Ard of Muintir-Luinin and Nehemias O'Luinin and his wife and children died',[8] presumably of it, together with an expendable number of the peasantry in all probability. Five years later there was 'a great dearth',[9] which was possibly associated with an outbreak of the 'famine-fevers', but for the remainder of this quarter Ireland appears to have been relatively healthy.

Apart from the record of 'mallochis pest' at Perth in September 1537[10] Scotland appears to have been free from plague between the winter of 1531 and September 1538, when the promulgation of 'Syndrie acts anent the pest' by the City Council of Edinburgh[11] indicates that that authority believed that bubonic plague had reappeared in the country. Aberdeen was also alarmed and its council simultaneously enacted certain statutes against the 'contagious infeckand pest, callit the boiche, quhilk ryngis in diverse partis'[12] of the country. Creighton asserts that the Gaelic *boiche* is synonymous with the English *botch* and that this was the old English name for bubonic plague.[13] Our word, which comes from the Old French *boce* through the Middle English *boche* means simply 'a swelling',[14] irrespective of the nature of the swelling, and it seems very doubtful if it was ever used specifically for the bubo of plague. Henslow, with reference to medicinal works of the fourteenth century, describes 'a playstre for to breke a boche or apostym or a felon',[15]

and these alternative names were in common use in England up to the end of the seventeenth century for non-specific, localized, inflammatory swellings occurring anywhere in the human body. Harvey, in his treatise on syphilis, repeatedly uses the word *botch* for the inflammatory swellings of that disease.[1]

The next year Ayr was alarmed at midsummer by a rumour that plague was present in that part of Scotland and took the precaution of guarding its gates and closing all unauthorized entrances into the town.[2] It escaped the disease on this occasion and again in 1544, but the threat recurred 'and the next year the ports were watched daily, the vennels closed, and thornis and stakis fixed in the oppin parts of the town'.[3] This time Ayr did not escape an epidemic visitation of a disease which was called 'the plague'; but as Pryde affirms that it prevailed from September 1545 to March 1546 it was not bubonic plague. Its seasonal incidence is strongly suggestive of typhus fever, especially if September was colder than usual in 1545. Whatever it was it cost Ayr a large sum of money to isolate the sick on the moor outside the town, to repair its gates, to build 'a lodge at the bridge', and to meet other expenses incurred by the epidemic. Pryde gives a detailed list of these expenses, which amounted to £353 7s. 2d., and adds that as late as 1550 the town was still paying for services rendered during the epidemic.[4]

There was 'ane violent peste in Edinbourghe and Leyt'[5] in July 1545, which appears to have been an epidemic of bubonic plague. It was more extensive than this notice suggests, for in October 1546 it was reported to be raging 'in sundry parts of Scotland'.[6] As the Court of Sessions was moved from Edinburgh to Linlithgow in June 1545 on account of the pestilence,[7] plague evidently erupted in the capital in the spring of that year. Aberdeen was possibly attacked by it during the summer, as in September the Dean of Guild was authorized to disburse money for the relief of suspect cases of plague.[8] Possibly it only manifested sporadic activity there up to mid-September, because on the 10th of that month the Town Council decreed that only four of the gates were to be left open during the daylight hours as plague was 'now ragand in certane partis of this realme'.[9] Some epidemic disease, possibly typhus fever, was epidemic in the late autumn of 1546 in both Aberdeen and Edinburgh, because in December a man in the former town was branded on his left hand for concealing the illness of his child,[10] and on the 30th 'the men of Weir', who had come from St Andrews, were commanded to leave Edinburgh at once on pain of death 'quhill the pest be repressit'.[11] It was possibly this disease which erupted in Perth in November 1548.[12]

The next year an extensive epidemic of what was most probably bubonic

plague afflicted many places in Scotland, including Edinburgh, Aberdeen, and Stirling.[1] Edinburgh's visitation seems to have been a severe one, for a report from the English camp at Stichel speaks of a great plague there and the departure of the governor to Glasgow 'and ther dothe kepe a Parlement'.[2] The disease was said to be raging also at Haddington and Berwick. It was evidently epidemic in Aberdeen at the end of September because on 11 October a distribution of St Nicholas braid silver was made to the plague-stricken,[3] and it was still active in mid-October when the council issued fresh regulations against it.[4] These included compulsory notification of every case of sickness within 6 hours of its onset, irrespective of its nature, and the segregation of the entire household—when a case of plague occurred in a house—until the authorities were satisfied that the house was free from infection.

THE MID–CENTURY–II

England and Wales

Creighton's comment that there is very little notice of plague in the first five years of Elizabeth's reign[5] is true for London, as the only notice of its presence there during that quinquennium seems to be the entry of 60 'plague-burials' in a total of 195 burials in the parish register of St Martin-in-the-Fields in 1558.[6] The accuracy of these entries is, however, very doubtful because only 18 of them occurred during the four 'plague-months' of July–October, whereas 34 of them occurred during the months of December–March inclusive, and these were most probably deaths from typhus fever. In the last year of Mary's reign 4 'plague-burials' are entered in this register during July and August 1557 in a total of 119 burials,[7] and these may well have been sporadic deaths from a smouldering rat-enzootic of bubonic plague.

For another four years or so London appears to have been free from bubonic plague. Then in 1563 the disease erupted in that city, indubitably as a consequence of the maritime importation of a fresh, highly virulent strain of *P. pestis*, exploded in what was probably the worst of the great metropolitan epidemics of the disease, and then extended as a major national outburst of it. The first notice of its presence is the entry of a 'plague-burial' on 27 March in the parish register of St Michael, Cornhill, with the note appended: 'The beginning of the plague in this p'ishe.'[8] It may have developed slowly at first, especially if the spring was colder than usual, but in June it was epidemic, as Machyn records that a blue cross was ordered to be affixed to the door of every plague-infected house.[9] By the end of the month it was raging, as the civic order of 200 headless, blue

crosses* on 3 July[1] testifies and repeat orders for more crosses on the 6th and the 8th emphasize.[1] Indeed the extent and malignity of the outbreak had aroused such apprehension by this time that a strenuous combined effort by the state and the civic authorities was made to control it. All householders were ordered to light bonfires in the streets and lanes at sunset in order to 'consume ye corrupte ayers' and to repeat the act three times a week.[2]

Contemporary writers incriminated the English garrison of Newhaven (Havre)—where a deadly epidemic of bubonic plague undoubtedly materially assisted the French to capture the last English possession in France—for importing it into London on their return to England, but as Creighton clearly shows plague was epidemic in London two months before their return.[3]

By mid-August the plague death-roll in London was reported to be 'above one thousand and in a weke'.[4] Some time prior to this report, either at the end of July or early in August. Elizabeth I left her capital for the refuge of Windsor, where she had a gallows erected in the market place of the town on which to hang anyone coming there from London. She also ordered that no goods of any kind should be brought from London either to or through Windsor by road or river, and any people in Windsor who had received any goods from London before her arrival at the castle were ejected from their houses and the houses were shut up.[5] Even at the end of July plague was not universally dispersed in London, however, for the parish register of St Andrew, Holborn contains the entry, opposite the date of 23 July: 'Here began the great plague',[6] and it is a reasonable assumption that there were other metropolitan parishes that were still free at this date. As far as this parish is concerned its register records 490 plague-burials in about 28 weeks.[7] The parochial incidence of this epidemic is illustrated by the record in the burials register of the church of St Mary the Virgin, Aldermanbury, which, as figure 28 shows, experienced an average proportionate plague-mortality among the metropolitan parishes. The total burials in the year were 119[8] of which the four months of July–October inclusive accounted for 99 or more than 83 per cent of the total. One one day, 27 September, 6 burials were registered,[9] a number so excessive that it is noted in the register. At least one family in the parish, of the name of Ynch, appears to have been exterminated with the deaths of 6 members between 26 September and 14 October.[10]

The epidemic increased in fury during the first fortnight in September and by the end of the third week of that month the plague-deaths exceeded

---

* The headless or 'tau' cross, coloured blue, was the constant emblem in medieval art of St Anthony the Great, who was the tutelary saint invoked for the epidemic disease known in the Middle Ages as 'St Anthony's Fire'.

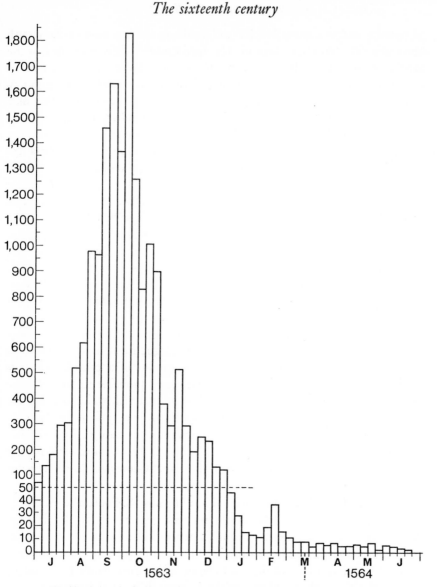

27. Weekly plague-deaths in London, 1563–4, as originally recorded by John Stowe. (From *Three fifteenth-century chronicles*, ed. J. Gairdner, London, 1880.)

1,600 a week. (see figure 27) It then declined slightly to the end of the month, when it exacerbated in a burst of furious activity which culminated in its peak mortality of more than 1,800 in the first week of October. Thereafter it declined again until the third week in November, when a transient spurt

of renewed activity accounted for 300 deaths in the last week of the month and caused the term to be kept in 'Hartford Castell'.[1] It is probable that the arrival of the autumn frosts shortly afterwards induced the plague-fleas to hibernate and that the deaths attributed to plague in December were remote deaths due to complications and sequelae of a *Pasteurella* infection that may well have been acquired as far back as early September. The disease had certainly been extinguished by January as no more plague-deaths were recorded in the second half of that month. The metropolitan mortality-curve of this epidemic is shown in figure 27; it is typical of a major epidemic of bubonic plague in a temperate climate.

Stow affirms[2] that the city's death-roll from all causes in 1563 was 20,372, of which 17,404 were returned as plague-deaths. These figures represent the mortality in 108 parishes in the city and liberties and to them must be added those of the 11 out-parishes, respectively 3,288 and 2,732. Assuming that these figures are correct, 23,660 people died in London during 1563, of whom not less than 20,136 or 85 per cent succumbed to bubonic plague. The burials register of St Martin-in-the-Fields conforms to this percentage with one of 82 per cent, for of 177 burials registered this year 145 are marked as plague-burials.[3] As it seems unlikely that the population of London and its out-parishes in 1563 exceeded 80,000, bubonic plague must have destroyed at least one-quarter of it, and when the panic exodus of a considerable part of the population is taken into account, it seems probable that the disease exterminated one-third of the available human material, which is about the maximum degree of destruction that a major, virulent epidemic of bubonic plague can accomplish in a community ignorant of its nature. Stow emphasizes that the poor bore the brunt of the mortality—an invariable feature of the disease—for 'the rich by flight into the Countries made shift for themselves'.[4]

Jones[5] avers that the worst afflicted locality was 'S. Poulkar's* parish by reason of many fruiterers, poor people, and stinking lanes, as Turnagain-lane, Seacoal-lane, and such places'. From his personal experience of two London epidemics of plague he asserts that the slums of this parish were the soonest invaded by the disease and the last to be rid of it.[6] Fortunately for London, even in the slums the incidence of the human disease was uneven because it was governed by the variable factors of the density of rat-infestation of the individual dwellings, and the haphazard attack of the 12 per cent of 'blocked' fleas upon their occupants. Moreover where some of the occupants worked outside their homes during the daytime their risk of contracting the disease was lessened, for the 'blocked' fleas did not confine their attacks to the night-

---

* St Sepulchre's.

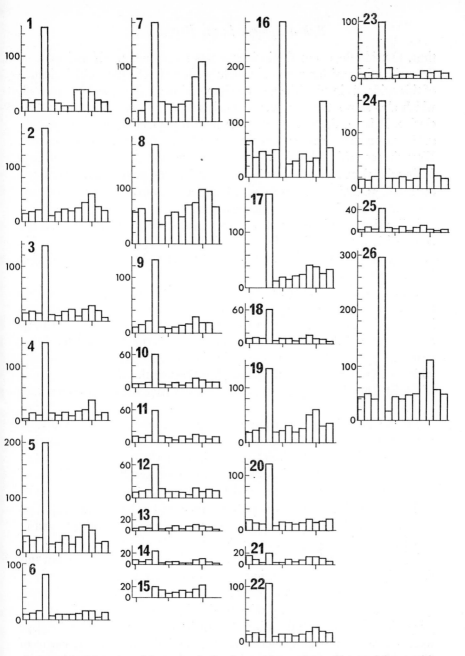

28. Annual burials registered in twenty-six London parishes, 1560–72. (Extracted from parish burial registers in the publications of the Harleian Society.) All Hallows, Bread Street (11); All Hallows, Honey Lane (13); Christ Church, Newgate (16); Kensington (15); St Antholin, Budge Row (6); St Clement Eastcheap (23); St De'nis Backchurch (2); St Dunstan in the East (26); St James, Clerkenwell (7); St Lawrence Jewry (22); St Margaret Moses (10); St Martin-in-the-Fields (8); St Mary Aldermary (3); St Mary the Virgin, Aldermanbury (20); St Mary le Bowe, Cheapside (12); St Mary Magdalen (25); St Mary Somerset (19); St Matthew, Friday Street (21); St Michael Bassishaw (24); St Michael, Cornhill (5); St Olave, Hart Street (17); St Pancras, Soper Lane (14); St Peeters upon Cornhill (1); St Stephen's Walbrook (18); St Thomas the Apostle (4); St Vedast, Foster Lane (9).

time. Outside the slums the incidence was more uneven still and some of the residential parishes were only slightly affected. The parochial incidence of this epidemic in 26 of the metropolitan parishes is illustrated in figure 28, which also shows the total annual burials in them from 1560 to 1572 inclusive. It is worthy of note that the human population was not the only sufferer from this visitation. The churchwardens of the parish of St Margaret, Westminster paid 'John Welch, for the killing and carrying away of dogs during the plague, and for putting of them into the ground and covering of the same, 3s. 2d.'[1] At 1d. per dog, which seems to have been the standard payment at this time, John Welch slaughtered only 38 dogs, but there was a similar slaughter in many of the other metropolitan parishes, so that the dog, which was incriminated as a distributor of plague, suffered heavily in every outbreak of that disease although it is naturally immune to infection by *P. pestis*.

Except for a doubtful one in April,[2] which might have been a death from lymphadenoma or one of the other adenopathies,* no plague-burial is entered in any of the 26 metropolitan parish registers that I have examined in 1564. Stow's return of the weekly mortality in London during the first half of that year (see figure 27) confirms the extinction of bubonic plague in the city which, except for a presumptive, sharp outbreak of the disease in the parish of Christ Church, Newgate, in 1565,[3] seems to have been free from it until 1568.

Two vague references to its presence appear to constitute the notices of bubonic plague in England during the years from 1551 to 1555 inclusive. Barnard says it was epidemic at Evesham in 1553, albeit 'with no great effect on the local burial rate'[4]—in which case there was certainly no epidemic of bubonic plague there that year—and Furness quotes[5] an entry in the parish register of Penrith recording its presence there and in Kendal in 1554. Two years later, at Cambridge, 'in consequence of a scarcity of victuals, and in anticipation of the plague during the summer',[6] the Easter term of the university was dissolved until 6 July. There is something queer about this dissolution for the term was instructed to re-start when an epidemic of plague would have been mounting to full activity. It is very doubtful therefore if there was any stirring of bubonic plague at Cambridge in 1556 in spite of the record that 'all suche as had their houses infected with the plage were before them'—the vice-chancellor of the university and the mayor of Cambridge—'and were sent to prison open hedded over the markett hill, and the Sargeante goying before them for not obeyinge the proclamacion',[7]

* Diseases that are characterized by enlargement of lymphatic glands, which, in this century, would be confused in many cases with plague buboes.

because it was December when the infected houses were ordered to be shut up with their occupants inside them. A week later the mayor fined three transgressors respectively 20s., 10s., and 5s. each 'towardes the relyffe of the poore, and the rest to go agayne to prison and there to remayne all night'.[1] Justice would have been seen to have been done if the mayor had had them stripped of their louse-infested underclothes. Fortunately for the citizens of Cambridge the town appears to have remained free from another outbreak of epidemic disease for nearly seven years after the subsidence of this one, which was in all probability an outbreak of typhus fever.

During 1557 bubonic plague or a disease that was confused with it was active at four widely separated places in England, namely, Lincoln,[2] Evesham, Colyton[3]—see figure 24—and Solihull. Evesham had a death-roll of at least 170 this year, compared with an average annual burial-rate of 22, in a population which Barnard avers could not have exceeded 2,000.[4] Unfortunately he does not supply the monthly figures of burials which are essential to confirm that this excessive mortality was caused by bubonic plague. In their absence it is not wise to assume that the mortality was due to plague. If it occurred outside the 'plague-season', it could have been caused by typhoid fever smallpox, typhus fever, or some other epidemic disease.

There is some doubt about the identity of the disease which afflicted Colyton in 1557 and 1558,[5] though the balance of probability is that it was an outbreak of bubonic plague. There is less doubt about the identification as plague of the disease that afflicted Solihull during those two years (see figure 29). In 1557 the registered burials in the 4 'plague-months'—July to October inclusive—comprised 50 per cent of the annual burials.[6] In 1558 the 'plague-month' burials constituted 47 per cent of the annual total and if 8 burials registered in November are included as remote deaths from plague the percentage rises to 60. The identification of this mortality as due to bubonic plague is not conclusive but I am unable to suggest another disease as its cause. Pemberton declares that there was an exceptionally heavy mortality at this time in the neighbouring parish of Sheldon* and that at least two rectors of Solihull died of the disease that was epidemic in their parish.[7]

The parish register of Darley Dale records 7 'plague-burials' in 1558,[8] but as one of these occurred on 1 March, and the remainder in April it is possible that they were really deaths from typhus fever. However bubonic plague was active in England this year, repeating its performance of the previous year in its distribution. Chester may have been mildly attacked by it as Ormerod

---

* In a footnote (no. 3) he gives the figures of the burials registered annually from 1553 to 1561 inclusive as 15, 15, 6, 8, 56, 68, 41, 23, and 16.

notes that 'few died, but many fled to escape the same',[1] meaning plague. Some 18 miles to the north Liverpool seems to have had a severe visitation, judging from the council's order that all the plague-stricken must 'depart out of their houses and make their cabbins on the heath, and there to tarry from the feast of the Annunciation of our Lady (25 March) until the feast of St Michael the Archangel (29 September); and from the said feast of St Michael until the said feast of the Annunciation of our Lady to keep them on the back side of their houses, and keep their doors and windows shut on the street side until such time as they have licence from the Mayor to open them, and that they keep no fire in their houses, but between 12 and 3 of the clock at afternoon, and that no other person or persons be of family conversation or dwell with them upon pain of imprisonment.'[2] This visitation of Liverpool is stated to have been so destructive that no market was held in the town for three months and that more than 240 persons or one-quarter of the population died of it.[3] Creighton notes that plague was epidemic at Loughborough at some time during the period 1555–9 and that 295 deaths were registered in the parish during those years.[4] Stratford-on-Avon had an excessive mortality in 1558 with 145 burials registered during the year,[5] but as only 45

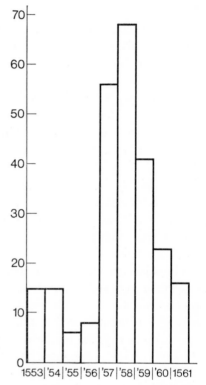

29. Annual burials registered at Solihull, Warwickshire, 1553–61. (From R. Pemberton, *Solihull and its church*, Exeter, 1905. Based on information contained in 'The registers of Stratford-upon-Avon in the County of Warwick', transcribed by R. Savage. *The Parish Register Society*, VI, London, 1905.)

or 31 per cent were registered in the three principal 'plague-months' (see figure 30), the mortality must have been caused by some disease other than bubonic plague, especially as it increased through the autumn to a peak of 33 burials in January. Smallpox would seem to be the most likely cause of this mortality.

Kelly asserts that there is no doubt of the epidemic activity of plague at Leicester in 1559, and he declares that the disease recrudesced there in 1560

196

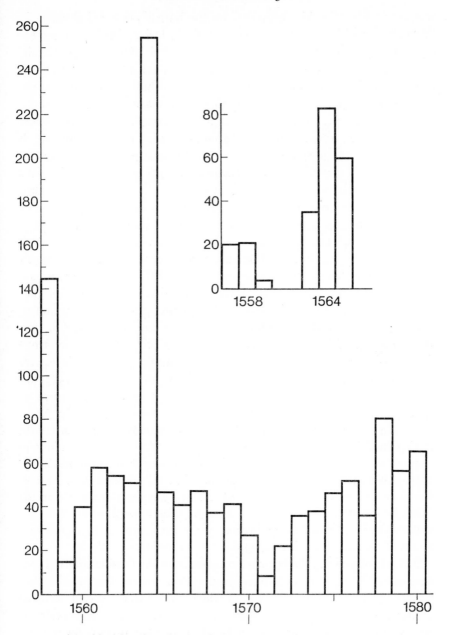

30. Annual burials registered at Stratford-upon-Avon, 1558–81. (Inset: the burials in August, September and October in 1558 and 1564.)

and 1561.[1] He bases his statements on the burials registered annually in St Martin's parish during the years 1558–62 inclusive, which were respectively, 12, 57, 37, 39, and 23.[1] He presents no analysis of the monthly burials, however, and it cannot be too strongly emphasized that an excessive annual mortality itself is not indicative of an epidemic of bubonic plague; it is the seasonal occurrence of that mortality that is diagnostic, and in the absence of evidence that more than 50 per cent of the burials registered in any one of those years occurred during the 'plague-months', his statements are of dubious value because diseases other than bubonic plague could account for the triennial mortality. Unfortunately even today professional historians make the mistake of assuming that an excessive mortality in an English sixteenth-century town or parish must have been caused by plague. For example Rowse, with reference to the growth of its population, remarks of Halifax: 'Then came the plague and the two years 1586 and 1587 show 566 more deaths than births.'[2] But analysis of the monthly burials registered in the parish of Halifax during those years reveals that in 1586 there were only 51 burials or 23·3 per cent of the annual total registered during the 'plague-months' of July–October inclusive, whereas the 4 months of December–March (to the 24th) record 97 burials or 44·5 per cent of the total.[3] In 1587 the corresponding figures are 168 or 22·8 per cent and 417 or 56·6 per cent.[4] It is therefore obvious that bubonic plague was not the cause of the excessive mortality; the most likely cause—especially as the spring of 1587 was 'exceeding cold and late' and 'September was intensely cold'[5]—was an epidemic of typhus fever which erupted as a 'famine-fever', for Short records of 1586; 'This Year, and till Harvest in the next, was a great Dearth in England.'[5] Once the disease has started the body-louse will continue to transmit and disseminate *Rickettsia prowazeki* as long as the members of the affected community continue to wear their infested underclothes. An epidemic of typhus fever in the sixteenth century was therefore only arrested either by the arrival of weather hot enough to force people to discard their underclothes or by the extermination of the body lice in the community by the *Rickettsia*, which invariably destroys every louse it infects.

Bubonic plague was the principal component of the terrible epidemic that devastated Oswestry in 1559 (see figure 31) causing the huge total of 557 burials registered during the year, of which 371 or 66·6 per cent occurred during the months of July to October inclusive.[6] The disease evidently erupted in the town towards the end of June or early in July, for the first burials marked as 'supozed plague' are entered in the register on 11 July[7] and from that date it raged furiously until the coming of the autumn frosts.

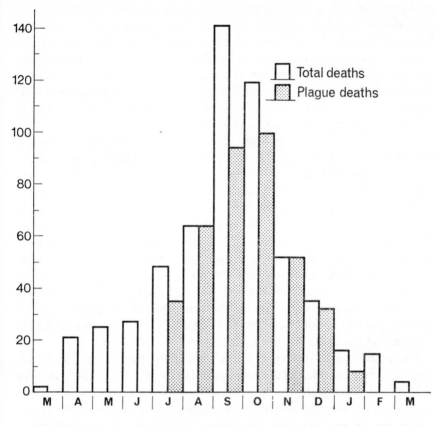

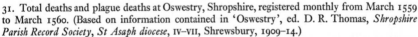

31. Total deaths and plague deaths at Oswestry, Shropshire, registered monthly from March 1559 to March 1560. (Based on information contained in 'Oswestry', ed. D. R. Thomas, *Shropshire Parish Record Society*, St Asaph diocese, IV–VII, Shrewsbury, 1909–14.)

The epidemic reached its peak towards the end of September, in which month 142 burials were registered, and its ferocity may be gauged from the fact that on two occasions, the 6th and the 12th, 9 victims were buried in the day, while on two other occasions, the 18th and the 26th, 8 victims were buried in the day. It is highly probable that in an epidemic of such violence some victims—especially among families living near the perimeter of the parish—would be buried in unconsecrated ground in gardens and fields and their deaths would therefore not be entered in the parish register. The continuing heavy death-roll of 103 in the 3 months of November–January[1] suggests either that many remote deaths occurred from complications and sequelae of plague or that another deadly disease with a seasonal incidence

in the late autumn and winter months—such as smallpox, typhus fever, or pneumonia—replaced bubonic plague as that became arrested with the hibernation of the plague-fleas with the October frosts. Plague was also so widely prevalent in the counties of Cheshire,[1] Staffordshire,[2] and Notting-hamshire[3] this year that difficulty was experienced in taking the musters in those counties. Until all their parish registers have been examined and their monthly burials records analysed, however, the incidence and distribution of bubonic plague in them in 1559 will remain unknown.

The next appearance of bubonic plague in the English provinces was its outburst in 1563, probably the severest national outbreak of it in this century. From Hastings in the south to Helmsley in the north it was epidemic during this and the two succeeding years in many towns, villages, and parishes, although the western half of the kingdom seems to have been comparatively free from it. Its activity extended to the English possession of Newhaven (Havre) in France and to the Channel Islands. It broke out at Newhaven early in the summer and 'slue daily great numbers of men, so that the streetes lay even full of dead corpses, not able to be removed, by reason of the multitude that perished'.[4] It evidently invaded the Channel Islands about midsummer as it appeared among the occupants of the castle of Jersey towards the end of July,[5] and by mid-August it was 'very sore in Jersey, especially in the castle'.[6]

Greenhill remarks that 1563, with a total of 191 burials, was 'by far the most fatal year recorded in the registers of Hastings'.[7] He correctly ascribes this excessive mortality to plague as most of the deaths occurred in the months of August, September, and October, and he adds that plague was raging simultaneously at Rye. Creighton records that it was epidemic at Derby, where 21 plague-burials were entered in the register of St Michael's parish during the period May–August,[8] and that it appeared at Leicester—where a household was segregated on account of its presence—although the first registered plague-burial there apparently did not occur until 11 May 1564.[9] Kelly supplies some interesting information with respect to this visitation from the chamberlains' accounts:

> Item, paid to Bagnall's wief when she was vyzited with the plagge, the space of vij weeks, vij s.
> Item, paid to Inglysshe's wief, of Anstye, for kepynge Kyrckame's house, beying visited with the plage for x weeks, at xvj d. a week, xiij s. iiij d.
> Item, paid to Izabell Frere for the lyke for x weeks, x s.[10]

He refers to 'An Act agaynst them that are vysytt with the plague, and will not kepe their houses' (6 Eliz., June 30), entered in the 'Town Book of Acts', which gave the council authority to fine anyone leaving an infected

house within two months of the last plague-death in it £5, with the alternative of permanent banishment from the town if the fine was not paid.[1] Because of this epidemic the summer assizes were removed from Leicester to Loughborough.[2] Nash affirms that plague was synchronously active at Stratford-on-Avon, Lichfield, and Canterbury,[3] but as the parish register of Stratford-on-Avon shows unequivocally that there was no epidemic of any disease in that town this year (see figure 30), his date for these visitations should have been 1564. There is no doubt, however, about its presence at Deptford during the summer,[4] or at Barking[5]—where 288 burials were registered in the parish of Allhallowes compared with 53 in 1562 and 27 in 1564—and it may have been responsible for doubling the annual mortality in the parish of Stoke Newington.[6] It certainly invaded the parish of Kensington, where 'John, a strainger, out of the red Lyon',[7] who was buried on 3 July, may have imported it from London in a 'blocked' flea roosting in his clothing, for of the 20 burials registered during the year 16 or 80 per cent occurred during the 4 'plague-months' of July–October. Cambridge also seems to have been visited, as the university term was adjourned in October 'on account of the plague then prevailing'.[8] It must have been extinguished during the ensuing winter because in August 1564 Elizabeth I visited Cambridge[9] in the course of one of her progresses, for which honour the university presented her with 'a cupp of silver gilded with a cover gilded, xvj$^{li.}$ij s.', containing 'fourty anngells, xx$^{li.}$'.[10]

With plague active in contiguous counties, the town council of Shrewsbury decreed in September that if any inhabitant went to London or any other plague-area, he would not be allowed to come within 4 miles of any part of the council's jurisdiction until at least two months had passed since he was in the infected place.[11] It would be interesting to know why 4 miles was chosen as the safe limit, especially as this appears to be the first notice of an attempt to protect an English town from bubonic plague in space as well as in time. York also took precautions to prevent plague from invading its precincts. Acting upon 'the credible report' that plague was prevalent in London, the corporation decreed in July that no resident was to shelter any Londoner or other plague-fugitive and that any such fugitive already in the city must be immediately ejected.[12] York appears to have escaped this year although plague may have been active a few miles away if the note in the 'Hensley [misprint for Helmsley] Register' is authentic. It reads: 'The reason as some think, that nothing is written in the year of our Lord God 1563, because in that year the visitation of plague was most hot and fearful, so that many fled and ye town of Hensley, by reason of the sickness was unfrequented for a long season, as I find by an old writing dated 1569.'[13] Although plague seems to

have extended the area of its activity in the county in 1564 York appears to have escaped it again. The disease came near enough to that city to excite alarm, however, and about mid-June the corporation accordingly ordered that no stranger or vagabond was to be allowed admission until the gate wardens discovered from which place he had come, and that no inhabitant of 'Ferybrig, Aberforth or Rippon or other place thereabouts nerby visited with the sykenesse'[1] was to be allowed to enter the city. A few days later a mayoral order prohibited any tradesman or craftsman in York from attending Moorchurch Fair, which was held on Midsummer Day in the parish of Kirkby-upon-Wharf, about 4 miles from Aberford.[2]

In the Midlands Leicester, Stratford-on-Avon, and Bristol experienced epidemics of bubonic plague of varying severity in 1564, and it was possibly responsible for the excessive mortality in the isolated parish of Cubert in Cornwall. This small parish with a population which did not exceed 290 persons in 1810, lost 70 parishioners from a pestilence this year.[3] The Lysons affirm that this death-roll was recorded in an old register,[3] but as they do not give the figures of the monthly burials the identity of this pestilence remains obscure.

Kelly notes that 4 'pest burials' are entered in the register of St Martin's Church, Leicester between 11 May and 3 June this year.[4] If these represent the only plague-deaths that occurred in the town Leicester was fortunate to escape so lightly. The duration of the epidemic which afflicted Stratford-on-Avon this year can be measured by the entries in the parish burials register.[5] The first half of the year with a monthly average of between 3 and 4 burials was the normal rate for the town; but July with 17 entries shows an excessive mortality, and the fact that this excess represents the eruption of the epidemic is confirmed by a note in the register that 'the plague' began on 11 July.[5] The epidemic increased in destructiveness during August to reach its mortality peak in September, after which it declined slowly in October (see figure 30) and rapidly during the rest of the autumn to its extinction towards the end of December. In 1564 Stratford lost 254 of its townsfolk whose burials were registered and possibly another 30 or so whose burials were not registered, while at least 176 victims died during the 6 months of the epidemic. Although Stratford was an important Warwickshire town at this time it is doubtful if its population exceeded 800 souls. Plague may therefore have destroyed as much as one-quarter of its population so that England has reason to be profoundly thankful that William, son of John Shakespeare, who was baptized in the parish church on 26 April 1564,[6] survived this slaughter. Perhaps he was sent for safety to his mother's girlhood home at Wilmcote[7] during the epidemic, for his father was then a

substantial citizen who could afford to remove his family from the stricken town.

Sometime during 1564-5 Bristol suffered a severe attack of bubonic plague if the records presented by Hudd[1] are authentic. One states that in 1564 'a very hot Plague', which killed upwards of 2,500 people, lasted the whole year in Bristol; the other reports a great plague in the city which endured from September 1564 to September 1565 and destroyed 2,070 of the citizens. These records require to be checked against the burials registers of the city's parishes before they can be accepted. It is to be hoped that this study will be made when a comprehensive history of the city of Bristol is eventually written, because there can be no doubt that a mortality of such magnitude exerted a much more important effect upon the civic life of Bristol than any other event that occurred at that time. A similar study of a parish register is needed to ascertain if bubonic plague invaded the parish of Leverton in Lincolnshire in 1565 when the church-wardens purchased books 'of the order of prayer & fastyng in the tyme of plage'.[2]

According to the Lysons plague 'is said to have been very fatal in 1569' at Exeter,[3] but Pickard avers that 1570 is the date of the first reliable record of the disease in that city.[4]

Plague was certainly active in London in 1569 as the entries of plague-burials in the registers of the parishes of St Pancras,[5] St Michael, Cornhill,[6] All Hallows (Bread Street),[7] St Mary le Bowe,[8] All Hallows (Honey Lane),[9] and St Olave, Hart Street,[10] testify. In the registers of the third and fifth of these parishes only a single plague-burial is entered and the first has only two such entries, but each of the remaining registers has multiple entries. For instance, St Michael's register records 10 plague-burials in a total of 20 burials during the year; St Olave's has 6 in 40, and all the 15 burials in the register of St Mary le Bowe are marked 'plague', one family contributing 5 of them. If these records comprise the whole extent of plague's activity it can only have been sporadically active in London this year. Nevertheless its presence aroused so much official apprehension that the Court would not stay in the capital[11] and Michaelmas term was adjourned first to 3 November and then to next Hilary.[12] The next year two of these parishes had entries marked 'plague' in their burials registers, to wit, 5 in St Michael's[13] and 6 in St Olave's,[14] although there is some doubt about the identity of these as they occurred in the late autumn and winter months. They may have been remote deaths from bubonic plague or deaths from typhus fever. Apparently 'plague' was active in the city in the summer of 1570 to judge from contemporary correspondence.[15] At any rate the court evidently kept away from London because the Spanish ambassador complained that it was difficult to discover

what was happening as 'in consequence of the plague, they have given order forbidding, under pain of death, anyone going from London thither'.[1] As there are no burials marked 'plague' in 24 of the registers of the 26 parishes represented in figure 28, and no evidence of an excessive mortality in any of them this year, either some other disease than bubonic plague was epidemic or a rumour of plague was being used as an effective counter to Spanish espionage. Support for this speculation is supplied by the ambassador's report, about a fortnight later, that plague was not increasing in London but there was a 'great sickness of fever all over the country'.[2] Outside London, Exeter was severely scourged by bubonic plague this year, a death-roll of 684 being recorded in the city's eight parishes, with an additional 40 from the parish of St Thomas. Pickard, who gives these figures,[3] also records the monthly burials, a rare forethought by a local historian. The peak month was September with 195 burials and the three months of August–October contributed 497 burials or 72·6 per cent of the annual total. His remark that 'the sudden rise in July, with a steep ascent in August, September, and October, followed by a sharp drop at the end of the year, will be seen to be characteristic of plague',[4] is to be commended to other local historians. There was a slight recrudescence of the disease—after the usual winter intermission—in the summer of 1571, with a peak again in September of 23 burials, the 3 previously mentioned months contributing 60 or 37 per cent of the annual total of 162 burials registered in the eight parishes.[4]

London seems to have been free from even a rumour of plague in 1571, but in 1572 the register of St Olave's parish has 5 burials marked 'plague',[5] and Creighton affirms that the disease was so prevalent in 1573 that the queen ordered the new lord mayor to cancel his inaugural feast.[6] He states also that the register of St Andrew's parish, Hertford, records numerous burials of London fugitives who he evidently believes were plague-victims.[6] Cox notes that the churchwardens of St Christopher-le-Stocks expended 6*d*. on the purchase of 'red wandes and bylles for the plague'[7] this year. This seems to be the earliest metropolitan notice of the change in the official plague-warning colour from blue to red, which remained the official warning colour for bubonic plague up to its disappearance from England towards the end of the seventeenth century. The disease cannot have been as active in London as these reports suggest, however, because no plague-burial is marked in 1573 in any of the 26 metropolitan parish registers examined and most of those parishes show no excessive mortality as figure 28 confirms. The register of St Olave's parish is the only one of the 26 which contains a specific record of plague in 1574. In a total for the year of 59 burials 31 are marked 'plague', of which 17 are entered in the three 'plague-months' of August–

October, 11 in the remaining two months of the autumn, and three in the winter months of the old calendar year. These were probably deaths from typhus fever, as were possibly also some of the late autumn ones. There was a burial in January marked 'the blody fflix',[1] which may have been an intestinal haemorrhage from cancer of the bowel as it is improbable that dysentery was the cause at that time of the year. If all the plague-burial entries are assumed to be correct the parish had a plague-mortality rate of 52·7 per cent, which would mean that the disease was active in it. Presumably plague was present in some of the other metropolitan parishes also to justify Walsingham's warning to the Privy Council that it would be wise to prohibit plays in London this year 'for fear of the plague'.[2] Creighton notes that plays and shows were banned in Southwark 'at that time of contagion' and he quotes a Bill of Mortality for the week ending 28 October, to support his assertion that this visitation was a major epidemic of plague.[3] In this bill the deaths from all causes in the city and liberties are given as 166, of which 65 or nearly 40 per cent are returned as plague-deaths. This is considerably less than the assumptive rate in St Olave's parish and refutes the idea that there was a major outbreak of bubonic plague in London in 1574.

There were 9 plague-burials marked in a total of 32 in St Olave's parish[4] and 2 in a total of 7 in that of All Hallows, Honey Lane[5] in 1575 as defined by our calendar, while St Martin-in-the-Fields has 51 marked 'plague' in a total of 154 for the old calendar year.[6] Of the marked burials 40 are entered in the five months of June–October and are presumably correct entries; they represent a plague-mortality rate of slightly more than 33 per cent. The remaining 11 entries are of doubtful accuracy. On the other hand it is possible that not all the plague-deaths in this parish were recorded as such in the register because, while the burial of 'Margareta s' to Jamye ye Scots bagpipe' on 5 September[6] is marked *peste*, Jamye's burial on 14 October is not so marked, although it is very probable that he also died of plague. Incidentally it would be interesting to know what a Scots piper was doing in London in 1575 when his queen was languishing in and English prison. Was bubonic plague by chance on this occasion a 'liquidating' English 'secret agent'?

Jamye's death occurred in one of the western out-parishes of London which was involved in the epidemic of plague that afflicted the city and liberties of Westminster in the latter part of the summer. A Westminster Bill of Mortality for the week ending 9 September 1575 reads: 'In St Margaret's Parish, 25, whereof 13 with the plague. In St Martin's Parish, 3 of the plague. In the Savoy-with-Strand Parish null. In St Clement's Parish, 3, of whom 2 were with the plague.'[7] Thus plague claimed 58 per cent of the burials registered in Westminster during the first week in September and it

is possible that the true rate was higher. Creighton, who also quotes this bill,[1] remarks that 1575 was a singular year because plague was present in Westminster and absent from London; but he was unaware of the records of plague in the burials registers of some of the metropolitan parishes. A *News Letter*[2] suggests that the Westminster epidemic was extinguished in October with the coming of the autumn frosts.

Scotland and Ireland

After its extinction in the winter of 1550 bubonic plague appears to have been absent from Scotland until 1564, when there may have been some sporadic cases of it in Edinburgh because a furrier, 'after being cleansed, was ordained to pass to some quiet house outside the town for the space of eight days and thereafter, if in good health, to be allowed to return to the town'.[3] The civic authorities were certainly afraid of its maritime importation from Denmark, where it was reported to be raging at the end of June,[4] and they accordingly appointed three officers to keep a day and night watch at 'the Newhavin' upon all shipping and merchandise arriving from Denmark.[5] Simultaneously the government, equally apprehensive, ordered that all persons and goods lately come from Denmark were either to stay on board the ships or to shelter—presumably on land—in places remote from Scottish ports.[6] It is noteworthy that the government regarded 'lynt' as the most dangerous stuff with respect to the importation of plague of all the goods coming from Denmark.[7] A Privy Council order specified that it must be unloaded on the rock islet of 'St Columb Inch'. (Inchcolm), unpacked there, and then spread out and exposed to the wind every other day until next Martinmas by officially appointed cleaners, the expense of this disinfection to be borne by the owners of the 'lynt'.[8] Pitch, tar, iron, and timber were to be cleansed by allowing one or two tides to wash over them; 'barrellis of asse' were to be singed with burning heather, and the ships themselves were to be broached so that the sea filled them 'to the owir loft',[9] a treatment that would certainly force *R. rattus* to swim ashore, much as it disliked getting its fur wet. When two 'foul' ships entered Leith harbour without licence towards the end of September, the Council ordered their masters and crews to be arrested and imprisoned.[10]

No further notice of plague in Edinburgh is reported until September 1568, when a merchant is said to have imported it into that city.[11] The promulgation of two anti-plague orders in October, together with a *Statute of Pestilence*, suggests that the civic authorities were then striving to control its activity. The first order forbade anyone to visit the plague-sick on the 'Borrow Muir'

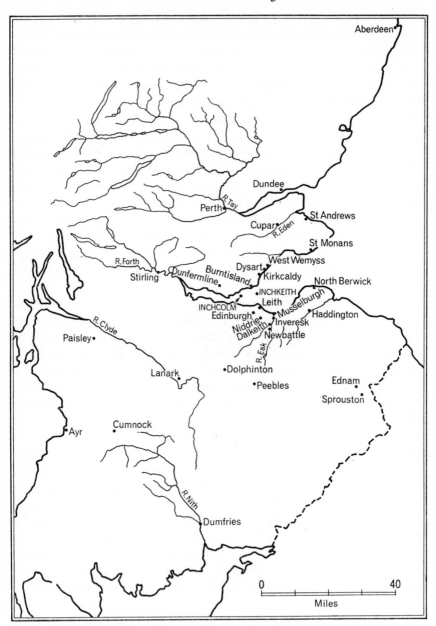

32. The distribution of bubonic plague in sixteenth-century Scotland.

or to go there for any purpose before 11 a.m., and then only in the company of an official who would be on duty every day at that hour at the West Port to convey people to the moor and back again. It also prohibited anyone from tending the plague-sick without licence from the 'baillie of their quarter' under pain of death.[1] The second order provided for the appointment of two officers at a monthly salary of £8* each to supervise the plague-sick on the moor, the cleansing of their clothes, and the cleansing of infected houses in the city. Two men and two women were also appointed to bury the plague-dead, each man being paid a monthly wage of £5, each woman one of £3. The treasurer was enjoined to procure as quickly as possible 'ane goun of grey with Sanct Androis cors, quhite, behind and before', and a staff with a white cloth fixed to one end of it for each of the supervisors, cleaners, and sextons. Also two closed biers were to be made, covered with a black cloth, and with a white cross and a bell at the head of each to warn people that they carried plague-corpses.[2] This order seems to be unique in the British Isles in this century in its provision of a special uniform for the attendants on the plague-stricken.

The *Statute of Pestilence* contains these regulations: (1) Sickness of any kind must be notified immediately to the appropriate officials. (2) The plague-dead must be buried in 'Grayfreir' churchyard and each grave must be 7 feet deep. (3) All sales of cloth, especially wool and linen, are absolutely prohibited. (4) The removal of any article from 'the caldrone' is absolutely prohibited. (This was the cleansing station on the moor for the clothing and other personal articles of the plague-stricken.) (5) As soon as any house is infected, all the members of the household with their chattels must be removed as quickly as possible to the moor, the dead must be buried, and the house cleansed. (6) The cleaners on the moor are forbidden to enter the city without permission. (A special officer was appointed to wait upon them and ensure that they did not communicate with any person or exchange any goods on the road leading from the moor to the city.) (7) If a cleaner is granted permission to visit his house in Edinburgh, he must not leave it again for 20 days. The penalty for disobeying the fourth, sixth, and seventh regulations was in each case death.[3] Plague was apparently still active in Edinburgh in November as the council allocated £500 for poor-relief 'in this present pest' on the 10th[4], and a report from Berwick five days later stated that the

* Comrie says that this and other salaries mentioned are 'given in pounds Scots, which in the sixteenth century were equivalent to about one-fifth of the value of the English pound, but, in order to obtain an idea of the comparative purchasing power of money in the sixteenth century and at the present day, [1932] it is necessary to multiply by ten. Accordingly a salary of eight pounds Scots per month would equal thirty-two shillings *English*, or about one shilling per day. The latter would have the purchasing power of about ten shillings at the present time.'[5]

plague-deaths in Edinburgh were more numerous than before.[1] The out-break must have subsided during December as the four sextons were dis-charged on the 22nd,[2] but after the usual winter quiescence the disease recrudesced in the spring of 1569 and the cleaners were ordered to be on duty at the 'Grayfreir port' every evening to bury the dead, cleanse infected houses, and remove the plague-sick and their chattels to the moor.[3] The civic authorities evidently feared a fresh importation of it in September, because on the 25th all ships arriving from Denmark were ordered to dis-charge their cargoes on Inchkeith and other adjacent places.[4] This visitation may only have been a slight one as an official announcement on 30 December that 'the pest was over, and that all who had been sick in the hospital of Senys Convent were to be taken to the Muir and cleansed',[5] indicates that it was extinguished during the autumn of 1569. The hospital mentioned was located in the nunnery of the Sciennes. Creighton opines, however, that this outbreak of bubonic plague—which lasted he says from 8 September 1568 to February 1569—was one of the severest experienced by Edinburgh up to this time.[6] His opinion is endorsed by Chambers, who asserts that the reported mortality of 2,500 'could not be less than a tenth of the population'.[7] What-ever the true degree of this epidemic of plague may have been, it is important in the Scottish history of plague because it induced Dr Gilbert Skeyne to write his treatise, 'Ane Breve Description of the Pest',[8] which was the first medical work on plague to be written in Scotland. It contains no original matter in its 46 pages,[9] but it is meritorious for the fact that it was written in the vernacular for the benefit of common folk who could not afford medical advice. He ends his work with a peroration that is as pertinent today as when he wrote it.

As there is diversity of time, country, age, and consuetude to be observit in tyme of ministration of ony medicine preservative or curative, even sae there is diverse kinds of pest, whilk may be easily known and divided by weel-learnit physicians, whose counsel in time of sic danger of life is baith profitable and necessar, in respect that in this pestilential disease every ane is mair blind nor the moudiewort in sic things as concerns their awn health.[10]

Plague did not disappear from Scotland on this occasion until sometime in 1570 as Lanark was attacked by it that year. Comrie notes that the town evidently did not possess a resident doctor at this time as it paid 5s. 'to the doctor the minister brocht', and he was also paid 2 merks 'for fouir Monon-dayis custum in tyme of pest'.[11] After this outbreak subsided Scotland appears to have been free from plague for about four years. Then a fresh importation of *P. pestis* occurred sometime in 1574, probably towards the end of Septem-ber and almost certainly through one of the ports of the Firth of Forth. It

was present in Edinburgh, Leith, and Kirkcaldy in October,[1] and on the 27th all vagabonds and idle persons were ordered to leave Edinburgh within 24 hours. The plague-sick were to be taken to the Sciennes hospital if the disease increased in extent.[2] It does not seem to have increased in Edinburgh, but in mid-November it was reported to be active in parts of Fife and the Court of Session was adjourned until 8 January.[3] The Privy Council had previously complained that plague was being spread 'landward' by fugitives from places 'where they were bound to remain', and it therefore ordered that no one was to conceal the disease when infected or to 'remove landward on pain of death'.[4] Apparently it threatened to persist in Edinburgh throughout the autumn because in December the Kirk Session ordered a public fast and humiliation for eight days in order to stop it.[5] However it was certainly extinguished before mid-February 1575 as the cleaners and their gear were then officially removed from the town moor.[6] Leith seems to have been more severely afflicted than Edinburgh on this occasion; at any rate the capital sent 40 bolls of meal to Leith at the end of November 1574 to be distributed among the poor and the plague-stricken there.[7] It seems probable that the two visitations ended simultaneously as Leith was officially proclaimed to be free from plague by mid-February.[8]

After an apparent absence of 18 or 19 years bubonic plague invaded Ireland in 1574 to produce the second of its major outbreaks there in this century. Two years before there had been 'a great mortality of men and cattle' in the country,[9] but the nature of the causal disease is unknown. Ware avers that plague erupted in the summer of 1574 and raged in Dublin until the end of October,[10] when it was checked by frosty weather to remain dormant during the winter. It recrudesced in the spring of 1575 to rage again, 'not only in the City and County of Dublin, but also all over the English Pale'.[11] It seems probable that this epidemic had a disastrous effect upon the population of the English Pale, in which case it possibly exerted an effect upon the subsequent course of Irish history. Its immediate effect was to cause the cancellation of the general hosting for the cesse,* which was planned to begin on 10 April 1575 but was abandoned 'by reason of the plague which followed'.[12] It delayed the departure of the Lord President from Chester to assume office in Ireland,[13] and when in mid-September he landed at Skerries[14]—about midway along the coast between Dublin and Drogheda—he found 'the infection of the plague so generallie dispersed, and especiallie in the English Pale, that he could hardlie find a place where to settle himselfe without danger of

---

* In Ireland *cess* was the 'obligation to supply the soldiers and the household of the lord deputy with provisions at prices "assessed" or fixed by government'.[15] The general hosting was a muster of the English garrison of the Pale for an expedition into the surrounding Irish lands to enforce the *cess*.

infection'.[1] It was as well that he went at once to Carrickfergus, for the epidemic persisted in some parts of the Pale to the end of October, when plague was reported to be active in Drogheda.[2] Outside the English Pale plague severely afflicted many places in Ireland this year. The record of its activity in one of the annals reads:

Intense heat and extreme drought in the summer of this year; there was no rain for one hour, by night or day, from Bealtaine [1 May] to Lammas [31 August]. A loathsome disease and a dreadful malady arose from this heat, namely, the plague. This malady raged violently among the Irish and English in Dublin, in Naas of Leinster, Ardee, Mullingar, and Athboy. Between those places many a castle was left without a guard, many a flock without a shepherd, and many a noble corpse without burial, in consequence of this distemper.[3]

This notice cannot be accepted without question, however, because intense heat would immobilize the plague-fleas. Yet bubonic plague was certainly epidemic in Ireland this year. A reasonable explanation is that the heat was coincident with the drought and when that broke on 1 August cooler weather enabled the plague-fleas to resume their predatory activities. Creighton assumes that plague was solely responsible for this violent and extensive outburst of epidemic disease, which he affirms desolated Ireland this year, ravaging especially Wexford, Dublin, Naas, Athy, Carlow, and Leighlin;[4] but it seems evident from the record in the *Annals of the Four Masters* that at least two distinct diseases, a loathsome one and a dreadful malady, were prevalent, and in view of the heat and the drought it is extremely probable that dysentery was epidemic, either prior to or concurrently with bubonic plague.

Dublin's involvement in it provides the bulk of the anti-plague regulations enacted in sixteenth-century Ireland. In June 1575 a general assembly of the townsfolk complained of the flight from the city of aldermen, sheriffs, and wealthy residents, and promulgated an order that the deserters would be permanently deprived of their citizenship unless they returned or sent a deputy by 31 July to discharge their civic responsibilities.[5] In January 1576 another general assembly complained that concealment of the plague-sick was largely responsible for the maintenance of the disease. It accordingly decreed that failure to inform the authorities within 24 hours of the appearance of plague in a house would be punished by imprisonment for 80 days, closure of the offender's house for 80 days, perpetual banishment from Dublin, and permanent loss of freedom and franchise. Simultaneously it recognized that the community had a responsibility to care for the plague-stricken and authorized the erection of buildings for the accommodation of the plague-sick in 'the great gardinge in Allhallowes', together with the

acquisition for the same purpose of Mr Edward Peppard's house and 'the steapell'. The mayor was instructed to pay for this accommodation out of the city's revenues. It was also decided that honest householders should be appointed to care for the plague-sick; that those responsible for sending the sick to the 'great gardinge' must provide meat, drink, and all other necessaries for them, and that a gate, locked and guarded by watchmen appointed by the mayor, should be made 'uppon the utter gate of Allhallowes'.[1] Nine months later a third assembly decided that in future 'two callodors and two visitors' should be appointed from time to time to attend upon and bury the plague-stricken 'as occasion shall serve', and that each of these officials should receive a daily wage of 6*d*.[2] This Dublin epidemic of bubonic plague has a particular medical and social interest because it secured the first appointment in Ireland of the sixteenth-century equivalent of the modern medical officer of health. This appointment was made by a general assembly of the townsfolk in July 1575. The conditions of the appointment were

that Dennis Collier, phisician and surgien, shalbe and is admitted to the fraunches, fryudomes and libertyes of the cittie of Dublin, in consideration that he nowe adventured his life in this contagious tyme of plague into the cyttye, attendyng upon the Maire and every other that shalbe in danger or neede of phisicke or surgrye; that he shall continue duringe his life in service of the cittie, as well in the time of plague as in all other tymes, doying his duty, taking for his fee as the patient and he shall agree, or as the Maire for the tyme being shall resounablye order or adward.[3]

The map, figure 33, shows the location of the towns named in the English records as having been visited by plague in this century in Ireland. With the exception of Limerick and Cork they are all situated on the eastern side of the island and most of them are either on the coast or in the valleys of navigable rivers. There is little doubt that *P. pestis* chiefly entered the island through its east coast ports, and as Ireland had no mercantile marine English shipping was probably mainly responsible for the importation of plague, although the disease was almost certainly not imported solely from England. Some of its importations undoubtedly originated from Continental ports in France and the Low Countries, while both Cork and Limerick were possibly infected directly from Spanish ports.

THE END OF THE CENTURY
England and Wales

The panic fear which bubonic plague excited in the public mind is clearly shown during the four years of 1576 to 1580, when the disease was evidently smouldering as an enzootic among the house-rats of London with the pro-

ULSTER

CONNACHT

Louth
LOUTH
Ardee
R.Boyne
Athboy
Drogheda
Mullingar

Dublin

Naas

LEINSTER
Athy

Carlow

Leighlin

Limerick

R.Barrow

Wexford

MUNSTER

Cork

Approximate area of
the English Pale

0   50
Miles

33. The distribution of bubonic plague in sixteenth-century Ireland.

TABLE 6

Plague-burials recorded in some of the London parish registers

Parish	Year	Mar.	Apr.	May	June	July	Aug.	Sept.	Oct.	Nov.	Dec.	Jan.	Feb.	Mar.	Total plague-deaths	Total deaths	Percentage plague-mortality rate
St Michael, Cornhill	1578	—	—	1	—	1	3	9	4	—	—	—	—	—	18	—	—
	1582	—	—	—	—	—	—	—	2	7	6	2	—	—	17	47	36·2
	1583	—	3	2	4	3	3	4	—	—	—	—	—	—	19	41	46·3
St Martin-in-the-Fields	1576	—	1	—	—	—	1	1	1	—	—	—	—	—	4	69	5·8
	1577	1	—	3	—	—	3	7	—	—	—	—	—	—	14	116	12·0
All Hallows, Honey Lane	1576	—	—	—	—	—	1	—	1	—	—	—	—	—	2	26	8·0
	1577	—	—	—	—	—	—	1	—	—	—	—	—	—	1	—	—
	1578	—	—	—	—	—	—	1	—	—	—	—	—	—	1	—	—
	1582	—	—	—	—	—	—	—	—	1	1	—	—	—	2	8	25·0
	1583	—	—	1	—	1	—	1	—	—	—	—	—	—	3	7	43·0
St Olave, Hart Street	1577	—	—	—	—	1	2	—	—	—	—	—	—	—	3	24	12·5
	1578	—	3	—	—	1	1	13	12	5	2	1	—	—	38	77	49·3
	1579	—	—	3	3	7	—	2	—	—	—	—	—	—	15	26	58·0
	1581	—	—	—	1	3	1	4	7	3	2	—	1	—	22	48	46·0
	1582	—	—	—	—	—	2	8	7	1	1	—	1	—	20	49	41·0
	1583	—	2	—	—	1	1	1	—	1	—	—	—	—	6	22	27·3
St Peeters upon Cornhill	1583	—	2	—	—	—	—	—	—	—	—	—	—	—	2	25	8·0
	1585	—	—	—	—	—	—	1	—	1	—	—	—	—	2	28	7·0
Christ Church Newgate	1582	—	—	—	—	1	—	—	—	—	—	—	—	—	1	73	—
	1583	—	—	—	—	—	—	1	4	1	2	3	—	1	12	121	10·0
All Hallows, Bread Street	1584	—	2	5	1	1	—	—	1	1	1	—	—	—	12	51	23·5
	1582	—	—	—	—	—	1	—	—	—	—	—	—	—	1	16	6·2

duction of sporadic cases of the human disease in the city, its liberties, and its out-parishes. The burials registers of four only of the city parishes contain entries marked 'plague' during this period. These are presented in table 6, from which it will be seen that St Olave's parish experienced a local ebullition of it in 1578–9.[1] Although this was not an extensive outbreak it was enough to drive the gentry from the city[2] and its apparent involvement of the Duchy of the Savoy drew a sharp reproof from Lord Burghley upon the Recorder of London. Smarting under what he considered to be an unjust censure the Recorder replied with a defence of his conduct which reveals the standard of plague-control that was accepted as satisfactory by high authority at this time. 'I have weekly myself surveyed the Duchie', he wrote to Lord Burghley,[3] 'and have taken that order there, that if the like had been executed elsewhere, I think the plague had not so greatly increased as this last week it did. And truelie, my Lord, I did twice passe with all the constables betwene the barres and the tilt-yard, in both the liberties, to see the howses shutt in.' As he acquired a knighthood shortly afterwards, the public health conscience of both the state and the municipality must have been favourably impressed by this bi-weekly inspection of the exteriors of plague-infected houses. His courage failed him, however, when there was a sharp augmentation of the disease in September and he took refuge in Buckinghamshire, whence he wrote in extenuation of his flight that 'he was hardly troubled every day with such as came to him having plague sores about them; and, being sent by the Lords to search for lewd persons, in sundry places he found "dead corses" under the table, which, surely, did greatly amaze him'.[4] His excuse is of importance because it reveals that spontaneous recovery from bubonic plague occurred after the buboes suppurated and burst—an event which was increasingly likely to occur as the virulence of *P. pestis* naturally declined— and that many plague-deaths were not reported to the authorities. There is an element of macabre humour in the tragic history of bubonic plague in London in the spectacle of the city's Recorder touring the stews for prostitutes and other lewd persons and finding plague-corpses littering the premises. Confirmation that there was concealment of plague-dead and that the records in the parish registers are incomplete is provided by the report that there were 180 plague-deaths in London in the first week of October 1577;[5] but as the disease was 'not very great' three weeks later,[6] that figure may represent the peak-mortality of plague in that year. Nevertheless the state was terrified by it. On 1 August, 'for thavoiding of the sicknes likelie to happen through the heate of the weather and assemblies of the people of London to playes', all plays in the city were suppressed until after Michaelmas.[7] Three weeks later the lord mayor was severely admonished to discover

all the infected houses forthwith and shut them up, 'be they persons of what degree or qualities soever', and set a special mark on them to warn that they were infected. Simultaneously he was enjoined to see that the plague-stricken poor were given monetary relief.[1] A report of the presence of plague in Southwark, Kingston, and Lambeth Marsh in September caused the postponement of the 'Training of Shot' in Surrey until the ensuing spring,[2] and a few days later the lord mayor was censured by the queen for his careless performance of the segregation of infected houses.[3] In November he was

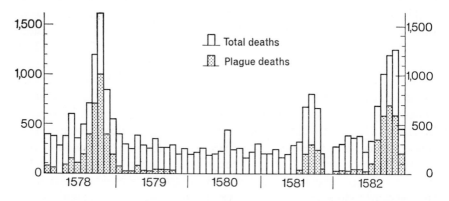

34. London bills of mortality, 1578–82. (Based on information contained in Creighton's *History of epidemics in Britain.*)

ordered to close 'all suche innes, taverns, and ale-houses as are knowen to have been infected since Michaelmas laste'.[4] Then frosty weather did what neither government nor municipality could do and plague subsided for the winter, to recrudesce in the summer of 1578. Thanks to Lord Burghley's preservation of the London Bills of Mortality for the quinquennium 1578–82 and Creighton's extraction and publication of them,[5] the behaviour of bubonic plague in the city during those years can be presented graphically in figure 34. Creighton blames plague for the fact that the registered baptisms in London were 33 per cent less numerous than the registered burials in this quinquennium, although plague manifested only two flares of activity in it.[6] As a study of the metropolitan parish registers clearly demonstrates, however, plague in this *endemic* state exerted singularly little effect upon a population the size of London in 1578, especially as —*unlike smallpox, measles, whooping-cough, and 'summer diarrhoea'*—it was not selectively deadly to the infantile population. It was the summation of these and other communicable diseases,

particularly tuberculosis, conjoined with poor feeding and defective hygiene, that created the excess of burials over baptisms in the London of the first Elizabeth. The parish registers present occasional records of smallpox, measles, and dysentery, and the analysis of their monthly burials shows that diseases other than bubonic plague were epidemic and lethal during this quinquennium.

During September, October, and November of 1578 the Lord Mayor received a succession of orders, to wit, to ban Londoners from attending Michaelmas Fair at Canterbury because of plague in that city;[1] to prohibit all unnecessary assemblies in London 'till the sicknes be slaked';[2] to cancel Guildford Fair because it was a favourite resort of Londoners and plague was still 'rageng both in the said Cittie and diverse other townes and thorowfares near adjoining therunto',[3] and to stop the players in Southwark from acting because the assemblies at their plays augmented the disease in London.[4] On 11 October Lord Mayor's Day was cancelled;[5] a month later the term was adjourned,[6] and the queen censured him again because plague was daily increasing in the city and the weekly death certificates were being carelessly compiled.[6] The office of Lord Mayor of London was certainly no sinecure in plague-time in the days of Elizabeth I. To her credit the queen made an original move to curb the activity of the disease which was progressively afflicting her realm and had so far resisted the efforts made to control it—she commanded the President of the College of Physicians to call the best-experienced physicians of the college together to devise with all speed advice and regulations to be published to help the populace to combat plague, and with shrewd commonsense she instructed him that the matters to be considered were:

1. The provision of convenient remedies, which must be cheap enough for the poor to buy 'and to be had in all places where no potecaries are', for the protection of the healthy.

2. The provision of cheap and equally available curative medicines for the plague-sick.

3. The pronouncement of a time-limit for the confinement of convalescents in segregated houses, and

4. As the infection 'is commonlie seen to take hold on clothes, beddinges and garments, and to leave also a contagion in the howses and places where the sicke are and have ben', to advise on some safe and quick way of disinfecting houses and garments.[7] What keen observation the Elizabethans showed and how near they came to understanding the aetiology of bubonic plague! The recommendations of the college were presented in the book of orders and remedies published by royal command to which reference is made

in September 1592.[1] Three days after this royal 'broadside', Cobham Fair at Kingston-upon-Thames was postponed and the bailiffs were ordered to keep the town free from plague as the queen proposed to remove to it.[2] Then on 2 December, royal letters were sent to the authorities of 15 counties about the 'stayenge of the infection of the Plague'.[3] Fortunately about this time Nature decided it was time for the plague-fleas to hibernate and on the 23rd stage plays were accordingly resumed in the city and liberties.[4]

The metropolitan outbreak of 1578 coincided with a widespread activity of bubonic plague in Hertfordshire and East Anglia, a culmination of its intermittent activity since 1570 in different parts of England. Exeter's visitation in 1570 has already been described and two contemporary reports,[5,6] sent from that city during August, confirm the severity of its ordeal. Northampton was invaded either towards the end of the summer or early in the autumn of 1570, for in October a town assembly 'ordered all the infected houses to be marked on the doors with "Lord have mercye uppon us". This inscription was to be kept on the doors for 20 days after any death, the visited inmates confined strictly to their houses, and victuals distributed to them at the public cost.'[7] Earlier in the year Rotherham and Selby were evidently attacked, for on 2 June the corporation of York ordered a continuous day and night watch to be kept at the city gates to prevent any 'suspect persons' from either town, where 'the sykenesse' had recently been active, from entering York.[8] Plague may have been present in Rotherham as early as mid-May or it may have been a rumour of its presence there then that made Mary Queen of Scots complain of the danger to her health that would accrue by her removal from Bolton Castle to Chatsworth, as 'the pest is in Rodrem'.[9] Farther north plague was 'very sorry at Newcastle' in August, and Cowper, who quotes this report, declares that it was never absent from the northern counties during the years from 1570 to 1598.[10] Regrettably, as is only too common in the history of bubonic plague, he presents no evidence to substantiate this sweeping statement, although a careful study of the burials registers of the parishes in the four northernmost counties would seem to be an essential prerequisite for such a declaration. Creighton asserts, with a similar lack of confirmatory evidence, that both Oxford and Cambridge were visited by plague in 1571, the latter place severely.[11] As Cooper apparently found no notice of its activity that year in the *Annals of Cambridge*[12] and as the French ambassador paid an official visit to the university on 30 August,[13] it is certain that plague was absent from Cambridge then. Incidentally it is of interest to learn that the university numbered 1,630 students on 4 November 1570.[14]

Although 1572 appears to have been free from any recorded outbreak of

bubonic plague in provincial England, it raged in Southampton in 1573 according to Attwood,[1] but his statement needs to be confirmed by an analysis of the monthly burials registered in the Southampton parishes. Chester, Cambridge, and Peterborough are said to have been attacked by it in 1574. Chester's visitation seems to have been a slight one as Ormerod affirms that plague disappeared from the city after the deaths of a few people 'in the Crofts'.[2] At Cambridge on the contrary the disease struck heavily. Cooper relates that a Londoner who came to Midsummer Fair was blamed for its introduction to the town and that the university and municipal authorities agreed to use conjointly 'the Old Clay Pits' as an isolation camp for the plague-sick and their keepers. 'The expense of enclosing this ground with ditches was £14 8s. 4d.: £3 12s. 0d. was paid to labourers for carrying earth to fill up the pits and low places: and £3 6s. 8d. for the timber, thatch, and claywork, of a house and bridge framed to be there set. The ground was rented at 1s. per annum, of Edward Ball, the town clerk, from whom it acquired the name of Ball's Folly.'[3] Cooper opines that the site of this camp was occupied in 1842 by the houses known as Gonville Place.[4] The university was apparently free from plague by the end of September although the disease may still have been lingering in the town. In a letter to Lord Burghley the vice-chancellor explained that the principal reason for the visitation was divine punishment for their sins; but the immediate cause was not in his opinion 'the corruption of the ayer as the Phisitians saieth at this tyme'. He believed that the true causes were its importation by a London visitor who died of it in Barnwell and 'the corruption of the King's dytch the which goeth thorough Cambridge', which he purposed to have cleansed 'so sone as we shall have any hard frost'.[5] As the ditch was then in all probability the town sewer, its cleansing must have sweetened the summer air of Cambridge to the satisfaction of *R. rattus*, who dislikes nasty smells. The vice-chancellor reported that from 26 July to 4 September, 115 persons had died of plague in Cambridge.[6] These must have been townsfolk because at its appearance the university promptly dispersed to safer quarters in the country until the disease was extinguished by the autumn frosts.[7]

From London a surgeon apparently carried a 'blocked' flea into the parish of Chipping Ongar, as he died there of plague towards the end of July. His and 9 more burials are marked 'plague' in the register.[8] Quite possibly these plague-deaths were confined to the hostelry or house in which he lodged and the rest of the parish escaped the disease. Stamford was less fortunate because it was 'very sore visited' by plague in the summer of 1575. Between 8 August and 7 September 40 victims were buried there, and the town's failure to cope with the epidemic was reported to be so gross that it was

doubtful whether any resident would escape infection.[1] The reporter added that 17 houses were infected; that the town was impoverished, and that 'but that the good people of the country send in victuals daily, there would be many die of famine'.

'This yeare the queenes mtie went a p'gresse towards Shrosbery but because of deathe wthin a iiij myles of the same she cam no further the' Lychefilld and from thence went to Worcester.'[2] None of the east Shropshire parish registers with burial records that cover this period shows any excessive mortality in either 1575 or 1576, a fact which arouses the suspicion that it may have been desirable, either for her own sake or for the sake of certain other people, that Elizabeth I should not visit Shrewsbury in 1575. No more effective deterrent to such a visit could have been found at that time than a credible rumour of bubonic plague in the way thither. It was probably during this progress that Elizabeth rode from Worcester to visit the squire of Elmley Castle, a visit that is commemorated to this day in the finely painted inn sign of the 'Queen's Head' and a living tradition of her visit in the village. From there or from Worcester she planned to ride to Woodstock, but as she was informed 'that the plague was at Chipping Norton and other places of that countie',[3] the sheriff of Oxfordshire was ordered to make sure that all infected houses were shut up with their occupants inside them, 'provideng, nevertheless, that they be relieved of foode and other necessaries',[4] an order that reveals Elizabeth's care for her subjects. Northwards from Stamford, Hull was visited by plague this year. Sykes notes that the register of the parish of Holy Trinity records 131 burials in 1575, of which 50 are marked 'died of the plague'.[5] The next year the disease invaded Shrewsbury and the bailiffs ordered all swine and dogs to be removed from the town, all cats to be killed, the streets and alleyways to be cleaned regularly by the townsfolk, and fires to be lit every other night in numerous places in every street.[6] St Matthew's Fair, which was held annually on 22 September, was transferred to the common at Kingsland and the County Court was held at the village of Meole Brace.[6] Some 43 miles to the north, at Northwich in Cheshire, the near-extermination of the Antrobus family by *P. pestis*[7] may have been brought about by the importation of a 'blocked' flea roosting in the clothing of a member of the family. If the house in which the family lived was an isolated one plague may easily have been confined to it and the parish register will show no excessive mortality during the 'plague-months' of 1576. Plague may have recrudesced in the summer of that year at Hull, or the action taken by the corporation of York against Gregory Burgeous may refer to the outbreak of the previous year. He was accused of attending and treating the plague-sick at Hull, wherefore 'his doores

shalbe shutt uppe, and his shoppe also; and that from hensforthe he shall not be suffred to resorte anie more unto this Citie' without the permission of the corporation.[1] Acting the Good Samaritan in plague-time in sixteenth-century England was regarded by officialdom as a crime against the community.

Cowper alleges that plague spread from Newcastle-upon-Tyne, where it was prevalent this year, southwards through Cumberland—as it had done on a previous occasion in 1570—to attack Hawkshead in 1577. He quotes from the parish register the note, entered in November: 'In this monthe begane the pestelent sicknes in or pishe wch was brought in by one George Barwicke wherof is dept all those yt are thus marked ✱.'[2] The first of these marked burials is dated 19 November, the last 25 February, and there are 38 of them with monthly incidences of 2 in November, 16 in December, 16 in January, and 4 in February. Eight families are represented among the marked names, among which the Tomlinsons contributed 12 deaths, the Hodgsons 8, the Barwicks 6, and the Kirkbys 5.[3] This record is one of a localized epidemic of typhus fever, and it is noteworthy that whoever made the entry in the register apparently recognized that the disease was somehow different from bubonic plague.

The plague-burials registered in St Olave's parish[4] (see table 6) probably represent the bulk of London's plague-mortality in 1579 because, before the summer warmth energized the plague-fleas, 'God be thancked, the Citie was now well cleare'[5] of the disease, and to keep it clear the people of Norfolk were forbidden to come to Bartholomew Fair 'if Plague be so great as it is reported'[6] in the county. Outside London there was at least one plague-death in Hackney where, according to the official record of her death, a woman died of it by 'Divine Visitation',[7] and it was prevalent at Bury St Edmunds.[8] The next year it erupted at Norwich in April[9] and two months later it was epidemic at Plymouth, whence a report dated 17 July stated that 'the most of the inhabitauntes, bothe of the better and meaner sorte, ar departed out of the towne, leaving it defenceles',[10] or in plain English there was a panic exodus of all who could fly from the stricken town. In July 1581, almost twelve months to the day later, all plays were forbidden in London until the end of September as plague had 'laitlie increased' in the City,[11] and it is practically certain that the ban was not lifted then as 75 plague-deaths were recorded in the city during the second week in that month,[12] and early in October it was 'muche dispersed within the Cittie and Liberties'.[13]

The earliest marked metropolitan plague-burial in 1582 appears to be the entry on 21 July in the register of Christ Church, Newgate.[14] The evidence supplied by the metropolitan parish registers suggests that plague did not

become truly active before mid-August and that at its peak, early in October, its distribution was markedly uneven, so that while some of the city parishes were rather severely attacked others were hardly touched by it and some escaped altogether. It is possible also that the fatality-rate of this outbreak was lower than usual as it does not seem to have attracted much civic notice; indeed the first reference to it in the state archives relates to its activity at Windsor and Eton.[1] However before the end of September the Law had fled from the city and the Michaelmas term was kept at Hertford.[2] During this outbreak plague spread into Westminster, where it was still active towards the end of November according to a Bill of Mortality for the week ending the 22nd, which records 13 plague-deaths in a total of 20 from all causes.[3] Maitland affirms that from 28 December 1581 to 27 December 1582 there were 6,930 plague-deaths in London,[4] but Creighton records only 2,976 in a total of 6,762 deaths from all causes.[5] The plague-burials marked in the registers of 6 London parishes for the years 1581 to 1585 inclusive are shown in table 6. Although the activity of plague was probably only sporadic in the summer of 1583 it was sufficient to prompt the lord mayor to enquire of the College of Physicians how many doctors were required to treat the plague-sick in the city.[6] Four, he was told, which suggests that there cannot have been a large number to treat. In 1584 the removal of a case of 'plague' to 'Glomesburie'[7] —presumably the modern Bloomsbury—suggests that a plague-hospital had been established there. But the disease which killed four prisoners in Newgate Goal in January of that year was almost certainly typhus fever, even though officially they died 'by Divine Visitation of the pestilent disease called the plague'.[8]

From the autumn of 1585 London appears to have had a respite from plague, until the importation of a fresh strain of *P. pestis* in the summer of 1592 supplied the spark for the great metropolitan and national epidemic of 1593. The first official notice of its arrival seems to be the warning on 13 August that plague was 'dailie increasing in London'.[9] Some three weeks later the disease had 'greatly increased within the City',[10] and six days later— on 12 September—two city parishes, those of St Martin-in-the-Fields and St Michael, Cornhill, registered its presence in their burial entries. The former records 5 plague-burials in September, 14 in October, and 3 in November;[11] the latter has the marginal note: 'Ye first of ye plage, out of ye red lyon Taverne'.[12] Although its presence is not specifically noted in their burials registers, plague was undoubtedly active this autumn in other metropolitan parishes as figure 35 shows, and the expenditure incurred* by the churchwardens of the parish of St Alphege, London Wall,[13] suggests that it

* 'For redd wandes for the plage...ij*d*. For two searchers for the plage...iij*d*'.

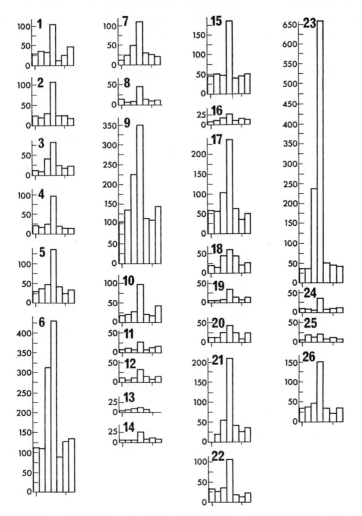

35. Annual burials registered in twenty-six London parishes, 1590–6. All Hallows, Bread Street (11); All Hallows, Honey Lane (13); St Clement Eastcheap (20); St De'nis Backchurch (2); St Dunstan in the East (21); St Helen's, Bishopsgate (10); St James, Clerkenwell (6); St Katherine by the Tower (23); St Lawrence Jewry (22); St Margaret Moses (8); St Martin-in-the-Fields (9); St Mary Aldermary (3); St Mary the Virgin, Aldermanbury (18); St Mary-le-Bowe (12); St Mary Magdalen (25); St Mary Mounthaw (24); St Mary Somerset (17); St Matthew, Friday Street (19); St Michael Bassishaw (26); St Michael, Cornhill (5); St Olave, Hart Street (15); St Pancras, Soper Lane (14); St Peeters upon Cornhill (1); St Stephen's Walbrook (16); St Thomas the Apostle (4); St Vedast, Foster Lane (7).

had invaded or was threatening that parish. On 17 September Thame Fair was postponed to the fifteenth day after Michaelmas on account of 'the generall infection' in London,[1] and on 11 October the lord mayor was pointedly advised to forgo the ceremonies of his appointment and 'converte that chardge towardes the releyfe of those persons whose houses are infected'.[2] There is ample evidence therefore that plague was active in London in 1592, which means that it was epizootic among the house-rats. Cold weather in the autumn rendered it quiescent as far as the human population was concerned, but in the warmth of the rats' nests the fresh, virulent strain of *P. pestis* was conserved through the winter in a smouldering enzootic which blazed into a raging epizootic again with the arrival of warm weather in April 1593, and this epizootic then engendered a major epidemic of the disease. 'It was an ominous sign', remarks Creighton, 'that the infection lasted through the winter; even in mid winter people were leaving London.'[3] It seems evident that the winter of 1593 was unusually mild, because on 21 January it was officially noted that after diminishing for some weeks plague was increasing again in the city,[4] and its continuing increase provoked the prohibition on the 28th of plays, bear-baitings, bowlings, bullfights, and all sports and like assemblies within the lord mayor's jurisdiction. Simultaneously the prohibition was extended to cover the outer Liberties in Middlesex and Surrey within 7 miles of the City.[5] Yet the earliest marked plague-burial in the metropolitan parish registers appears to be the one dated 23 April in the register of St Olave's parish.[6] The eight parish registers which contain marked plague-burials this year are presented in table 7. This table suggests that the epidemic began —as was to be expected—in the dock area on the east side of London and spread westwards; but this movement was neither uniform nor continuous because some parishes which escaped the first wave of the epidemic were visited by plague after the epidemic had apparently missed them. This erratic behaviour of the disease, due to the haphazard nature of the rat contacts, is characteristic of epidemics of bubonic plague.

The spring of 1593 seems to have been unusually favourable for the breeding and predatory activities of *X. cheopis* because May witnessed an extraordinary augmentation of the epidemic which was recognized by the notice: 'The plague is very hot in London and other places of the realm, so that a great mortality is expected this summer.'[7] That expectation was unfortunately fulfilled for when June ended plague was dangerously dispersed, not only in London 'but in many towns and villages about the City', so widely dispersed in fact that all the fairs held in and around London— Bartholomew, Southwark, Uxbridge, St James, Brainford, Waltham Abbey,

1a   *Rattus rattus* (the old English black rat; the house- or ship-rat)
1b   *Rattus Norvegicus* (the grey or brown rat; the field- or sewer-rat)

(*facing p.* 224)

2   Rats (*Rattus rattus*) hanging a cat. A drawing
on a late thirteenth-century manuscript

TABLE 7

Plague-burials recorded in the registers of some London parishes in 1593

	First entry	Mar.	Apr.	May	June	July	Aug.	Sept.	Oct.	Nov.	Dec.	Jan.	Feb.	Mar.
St Peeters upon Cornhill	8 May	—	—	1	—	2	2	—	—	—	—	—	—	—
St De'nis Backchurch	22 June	—	—	—	2	2	—	—	—	—	—	—	—	—
St Mary Aldermary	10 July	—	—	—	—	12	2	—	1	—	—	—	—	1
St Michael Cornhill	6 June	—	—	—	2	5	14	12	8	9	1	2	1	1
St Martin-in-the-Fields	12 June	—	—	—	3	7	24	50	41	28	10	1	—	—
All Hallows, Bread Street	—	—	—	1	—	1	—	1	—	—	—	—	—	—
St Pancras, Soper Lane	—	—	—	—	1	—	1	9	2	1	—	—	—	—
St Olave, Hart Street	23 April	—	1	3	—	7	26	19	6	2	3	3	1	—

St Giles in the Bushe, Ware, Croydon, and Katherin Hill near Guildford—were cancelled.[1] Throughout July the epidemic mounted in violence, and the lord mayor's plea that Bartholomew Fair should be held in spite of the epidemic because of its trade value was countered by the Privy Council's reproof that in place of painting on the doors of infected houses crosses 'which are wiped awey in short space, you shoulde do well to cause redd crosses to be nayled fast upon the dores of those whose houses are infected and some watche appointed to looke unto them that they do not abrode'.[2] Mid-July evoked from the queen and her council the acknowledgement that the epidemic was a divine punishment for the nation's sins—nevertheless every effort ought to be made to arrest it, and London should copy the action of Kingston, 'where the infection did begin very hotleye' but had been stopped by the immediate removal of infected persons to a 'house' erected in the fields at a distance from the town.[3] Two days later a muster of the London levies was cancelled as plague was then 'so spredd over all the parishes as there are few places that are free'.[4] On 29 July Sturbridge Fair was cancelled;[5] but still the epidemic grew in fury and August brought another great increase in its toll of deaths.[6] At this juncture the state gave up the fight and left the capital to its fate, apart from the continuance of the royal chorus of accusation of the lord mayor, whose alleged slackness in his execution of the anti-plague regulations was held to be responsible for the failure to arrest the disease.[7]

Stow affirms that from 29 December 1592 to 20 December 1593 the deaths registered within the walled city totalled 8,598, of which 5,390 were ascribed to plague. Outside the walls and in the liberties a total of 9,295 deaths was registered, of which, 5,385 were ascribed to plague.[8] According to him London therefore suffered a death-roll of 17,893, of which plague was responsible for a trifle over 60 per cent. Creighton presents figures which differ widely from those given by Stow. He affirms that the total of deaths in the city, the liberties, and the out-parishes was 25,886, of which 15,003 were ascribed to plague.[9] These figures are identical with those in a marginal note in the burials register of the parish of St Peeters upon Cornhill.[10] This register also contains the note:

> In a thousand five hundred ninety and three,
> The lord preserved my house and mee.
> When of the pestilence theare died,
> Full manie a thousand els beeside.[10]

This note is of historical value for the proof it affords that even in a violent and extensive urban outburst of bubonic plague entire households escaped

attack, either because their houses were not rat-infested or because by chance *P. pestis* was not introduced among their house-rats.

A reputed Bill of Mortality for 1593—covering the old calendar year from March to March—is extant.[1] It is divided into three sections—(1) the 97 parishes within the walls; (2) 16 parishes which presumably constituted the liberties, together with the pesthouse, and (3) 9 out-parishes in the Home Counties. These are here tabulated:

Section	Total burials	Plague-burials
1	13,404	6,976
2	19,144	11,707
3	9,878	7,234
TOTAL	42,426	25,937

Although the figures of these mortality records differ, their respective plague mortality-rates are in reasonably close agreement, to wit, a trifle over 60 per cent, a trifle under 58, and a trifle over 61. It is practically certain that none of these records is accurate because in all probability many plague-deaths were not entered in the parish registers as the dead were hastily interred in unconsecrated ground, especially in the outer parishes. The mean of these records gives a figure of 28,735 deaths from all causes, of which 17,238 were ascribed to plague, yielding a plague-mortality rate of practically 60 per cent. Whatever the true figures were, it seems probable that bubonic plague was responsible for about two-thirds of the deaths that occurred in London from the beginning of September 1592 to the end of December 1593. Incidentally, in the third bill only 5 plague-burials are entered in the register of St Peeters upon Cornhill in an annual total of 112 burials,[2] so it is not surprising that the vicar's household escaped. In fact his parish had the lowest plague-burial rate (4·4 per cent) of any of the London parishes, the next lowest being St Helen's (Bishopsgate) with 16·0 per cent.[3] Of the parishes within the walls 22 registered more than 100 plague-burials and the plague-burial rates among these ranged from 35·6 to 92·8 per cent. At the Pesthouse the rate was 93·7 per cent (see table 8); among the 16 parishes in the liberties it ranged from 35·2 to 73·6 per cent, and in the 9 out-parishes its range was from 63·5 per cent in the parish of St Giles in the Fields to 83·5 in Lambeth, with St Magdalen Bermondsey a close second with 80·3 per cent. The maximum number of plague-burials registered in any one parish in each of the three sections was 337 in St Clements Eastcheap, 2,502 in St Sepulchre, and 2,095 in St Magdalen Bermondsey.[3] As these figures stand they reveal that it was in the dreadful Tudor slums around the docks and in the 'new housing-estates' of sixteenth-century London that plague was most destructive. In those slums, where the inhabitants were packed together

TABLE 8

Burials registered in certain London parishes in 1593*

	Total burials	Plague-burials
S. Gabriel Fen-church	300	107
S. Michael Crooked-lane	139	129
S. Hellens	25	4
S. Botolph Algate	1,771	624
S. Bartholomew the Great	254	187
S. Sepulchres Parish	3,440	2,502
Trinity Minories	109	78
St Giles in the Fields	894	569
Lambeth Parish	1,569	1,308
S. Magdalens Bermond	2,606	2,095
S. Clements Eastcheap	506	337
The Pesthouse	208	195

in hovels that were inevitably heavily rat-infested, *P. pestis* was easily transmitted from house-rat to man. It is no accident therefore that bubonic plague was pre-eminently the disease of the poor in the British Isles. As the sizes of the populations in these three sections of the metropolis are unknown, the implications of these mortality records must be treated with caution, for proportionately plague may have been as destructive in 1593 within as without the walls of London. All that can safely be affirmed is that this was a calamitous visitation of bubonic plague.

Creighton declares that the neighbourhood of the Fleet Ditch was the worst afflicted area in the city.[1] He derived this belief from an opinion expressed in 1595 that 'in the last great plague more died about there than in three parishes besides'.[2] Judging from the burials registered in the parishes represented in figure 36, however, the epidemic raged most violently in the parish of St Katharine by the Tower,[3] which appears to have been more than twice as heavily attacked as any of the other parishes. The actual number of burials entered in its register in 1593 is 525, of which 333 occurred in the three 'plague-months' of August–October. There were almost certainly plague-deaths in the parish in June and July, possibly also in May and November; but assuming that only 333 of its parishioners died of plague the plague-mortality rate in this parish was 63·4 per cent. Undoubtedly many metropolitan parishes had lower rates and a few were probably not attacked at all. Freshfield remarks that while plague was 'very deadly in most parishes in the City it was apparently of no strength in St Bartholomew's parish'. This was the parish of St Bartholomew-by-the-Exchange.[4]

* Extracted from *A collection of very Valuable and Scarce Pieces*, Anonymous (London, 1721).

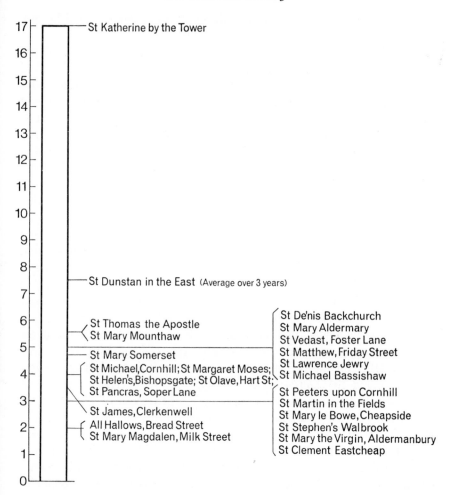

36. Excessive mortalities in twenty-five London parishes in 1593 (arranged in the order of the multiples by which their total burials in that year exceeded their average annual burials for the four years 1590, 1591, 1595 and 1596).

The peak of this epidemic seems to have been reached about the third week in August—rather earlier than usual for a major English epidemic of bubonic plague—and opposite the date of 17 August in the parish register of St Pancras there is the marginal note: 'Ostes par la pyte. L'Arc de Dieu enflammes a l'encontre la ville.'[1] September witnessed little diminution in its violence, and it was towards the end of the month that a plague-sick Londoner made a will which Jewers reproduces,[2] and which he rightly describes as a pathetic

appeal that reveals the loneliness of the plague-stricken, deserted in very many instances by family, kinsfolk, and friends.

Synchronously with its augmentation in violence during August, plague spread widely around London. Westminster was evidently severely involved as the Privy Council opined early in October 'that the greatest number for the most part are dead out of such houses as were pestered with inmates'.[1] In other words plague had practically exterminated the poor folk of Westminster, clustered together in their overcrowded dwellings. To the east of London the disease was epidemic in Greenwich in September[2] and it radiated outwards from the city through Middlesex into Essex, Hertfordshire, and Buckinghamshire. Creighton says that Watford and Hertford were two of the commonest resorts for fugitive Londoners in plague-time and that in each town there were many deaths from plague during the three years 1592–4.[3] He notes that at Watford there were 124 burials in the first eight months of 1594, many of which are marked 'plague', and that plague-burials are specified in the registers of the Hertford parishes of All Saints and St Andrew in both 1592 and 1594.[3] The metropolitan epidemic collapsed in October 1593, but it left numerous plague-stricken persons whose remote deaths are recorded as plague-burials in several of the London parish registers during the remaining autumn months. The disease recrudesced feebly in the summer of 1594, when 421 plague-deaths were registered in London in a total mortality for the year of 3,929.[4] Apparently it lingered as an enzootic disease among the house-rats into 1595, because Creighton reports 29 registered plague-deaths in a total mortality for that year of 3,507.[5] By the end of the year, however, either the requisite rodent fuel was exhausted or *P. pestis* had suffered a natural loss of virulence, as nothing more is heard of bubonic plague in Tudor London. This review of the activity of bubonic plague in sixteenth-century London may fittingly be concluded with a quotation from the churchwardens' accounts of the parish of St Mary Woolnoth,[6] which epitomizes the efforts of the state, the church, and the people to control the disease.

1593–4. Item for setting a crosse upon one Allen's doore in the sickness time...ij *d.*
Item paid for setting two red crosses upon Anthony Sound his dore...iiij *d.*

Its metropolitan history from 1543 to the end of the century, as revealed in the burials registers of the London parishes, is summarized in figure 37.

The opening years of the last quarter of this century witnessed the prevalence of bubonic plague at opposite ends of England. In 1576, as Rowse notes,[7] it invaded the Cornish moorland parish of St Breward, where in a total of 29 burials registered that year—more than three times the annual

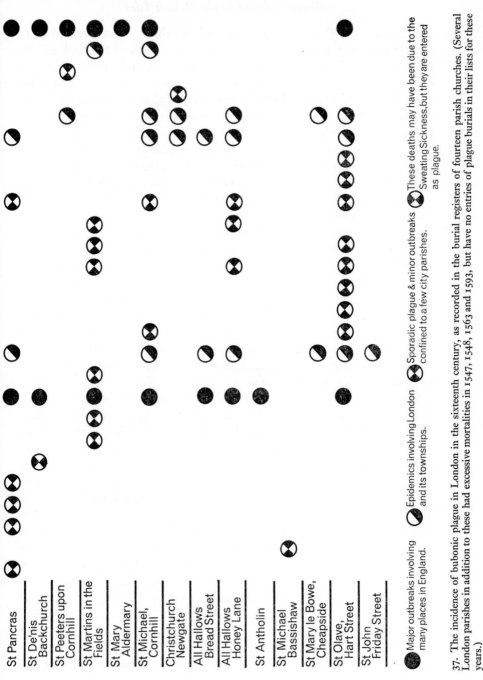

St Pancras

St Denis
Backchurch

St Peeters upon
Cornhill

St Martins in the
Fields

St Mary
Aldermary

St Michael,
Cornhill

Christchurch
Newgate

All Hallows
Bread Street

All Hallows
Honey Lane

St Antholin

St Michael
Bassishaw

St Mary le Bowe,
Cheapside

St Olave,
Hart Street

St John
Friday Street

Major outbreaks involving
many places in England.

Epidemics involving London
and its townships.

Sporadic plague & minor outbreaks
confined to a few city parishes.

These deaths may have been due to the
Sweating Sickness, but they are entered
as plague.

37. The incidence of bubonic plague in London in the sixteenth century, as recorded in the burial registers of fourteen parish churches. (Several London parishes in addition to these had excessive mortalities in 1547, 1548, 1563 and 1593, but have no entries of plague burials in their lists for these years.)

average—24, or 82·7 per cent occurred in the 3 'plague-months' of August–October.[1] In 1577 it struck hard in the north of England and for the next two or three years it spread panic and death in the Border counties. Barnes affirms that it attacked Newcastle-upon-Tyne in 1576[2] and Allen infers that it was the 'pestilent sickness' recorded in the parish register of Hawkshead as the cause of death of 38 parishioners in the autumn of 1577;[3] but as the first marked burial occurred on 19 November and 16 are entered in each of the months of December and January, the disease in all probability was typhus fever. However Armitt avers that plague was present in the valleys of the Lake District this year[4] and it may have preceded typhus fever in the parish of Hawkshead, where 85 burials were registered compared with 48 in 1576.[5] This visitation of the Lakeland dales by epidemic disease— whatever its nature—gave the death-blow to a one-time flourishing industry, the manufacture of woollen cloth, which possibly reached its peak during Henry VIII's reign. The industry began to decline soon after the accession of Elizabeth I as Kendal cloth lost favour with the people of London, who provided its main market, and the mortality caused by this epidemic among the Lakeland weavers and fullers extinguished it.[6] The Lakeland weaver's sedentary life, imposed upon him by the operation of the handloom in his cottage, rendered him equally prone to the attacks of plague-fleas—if *P. pestis* was introduced to the house-rats that infested his dwelling—and of the body lice that infested his person.

In 1577 plague interfered with the Michaelmas term of the University of Cambridge[7] and is reported to have caused a great mortality at Bury St Edmunds[8] in 1578–9, when 194 plague-deaths were registered in St Mary's parish and 'entire families were swept away'.[8] The summation of the mortality of these two years must have been calamitous. As a consequence of the concurrent invasion of Rye and Dover by plague in 1577 the French marines —who were presumably prisoners of war—were allowed to leave those towns.[9] Its involvement of a Westmorland parish in 1578 provides an example of its household incidence, for of the 20 plague-deaths entered in the register 10 were contributed by one family.[10] Synchronously plague was mortally busy in the summer of this year in East Anglia, Essex, Hertfordshire, and Cambridgeshire. Norwich suffered a disastrous epidemic of it, which erupted shortly after the termination of the queen's visit to the city and destroyed 4,817 of its citizens between 20 August 1578 and 19 February 1579.[11] At Cambridge its appearance caused the Lent term to be dissolved on 18 March 1579,[12] and after 2 students of Queen's College had died of it there was a general exodus from the university.[13] Earlier in the summer it visited Ware[14] and St Albans.[15] Creighton affirms that the Hertford parish registers record

TABLE 9

*Burials in Northamptonshire**

	Burials registered in 1578	Annual average of quinquennial burials	Burials registered in 1603	Burials registered in 1605	Annual average of quinquennial burials	Burials registered in 1638	Annual average of quinquennial burials
All Saints	134	47	107	411	91	247	76
St Giles	21	10	20	123	22	185	21
St Peter	9	4	16	26	6	19	7
St Sepulchre	16	7	88	65	20	114	18
TOTAL	180	68	231	625	139	565	122

plague-burials in both 1577 and 1578[1] and that in September 1578 plague visited the 'Bull' Inn at Hoddesdon.[2] In Essex either Colchester or Chelmsford—probably the former town—was attacked by a pestilence which Morant declares persisted there from December 1578 to the ensuing August.[3] It is unfortunate that he seemingly omitted to examine the relevant parish registers, because until their burial entries have been critically examined the identity of this pestilence will remain obscure. Judging by its seasonal incidence as implied in his note about it there is a strong possibility that it was an epidemic of smallpox.

In the Midlands bubonic plague may have been responsible for the excessive mortality recorded in 1578 in the four Northampton parishes, especially the parish of All Saints (see table 9). Serjeantson, cited by Cox,[4] states that in many cases *plague* is written before the entries while others are marked *p* or *pest*, but regrettably he did not count the marked entries so that it is not possible to compare their number with that of the annual burials. Plague may also have been active in Worcestershire this year because Barnard notes that the burials throughout the county were 33 per cent in excess of the christenings.[5] It was certainly active in the adjoining county of Warwickshire where the parish register of Stratford-on-Avon records 4 plague-burials in a total of 9 burials in October.[6] It may have visited Tewkesbury in the neighbouring county of Gloucestershire, for 'the supposed sickness of Pestilence' appeared there about Michaelmas and caused 30 deaths in 6 weeks; 'but by the diligent care of the bailiffs in shutting up the suspected houses, a general infection was prevented'.[7] As the rat would not be affected by 'the diligent care of the bailiffs', it is very probable that the supposed

* Reference: J. C. Cox, *The Parish Registers of England* (London, 1910).

sickness of pestilence was a localized outbreak of either typhoid or typhus fever. Whatever was its nature it flickered again in the summer of 1579 to kill five of the occupants of the 'Swan' Inn at Tewkesbury.[1] It was plague, however, that delayed the county musters in Cornwall in the spring of 1578.[2]

For the next two years bubonic plague maintained an extensive activity with outbreaks dispersed over England from Rye in the south to Newcastle-upon-Tyne in the north, and from Yarmouth in the East to Plymouth in the west. Sometime in 1579 it may have visited Eltham, for the churchwardens paid 3*d.* that year for 'a booke for ye plague to be reade in ye churche'.[3] It is a pity that Corner did not include a study of the parish burials register in his examination of the parochial finances. To the west of Eltham it was 'hotte in or neare the streates adjoynenge to St Edmund's Church' in Salisbury,[4] and still further to the west Plymouth is reported by Creighton to have suffered an estimated loss of 600 of its townsfolk from plague,[5] a mortality that should show some evidence of its happening in the parish registers. Apparently it recurred at Norwich in 1580,[6] and Creighton affirms, without producing any confirmatory parochial evidence, that in the previous year it was prevalent in Ipswich,[5] at Colchester,[5] and at Yarmouth, where he says it was reported to have killed 2,000 persons between May Day and Michaelmas,[5] a death-roll probably greater than the population of that town. It is possible that this mortality was wrongly assigned to Yarmouth, however, because Cox avers that Newcastle-upon-Tyne was so scourged by plague in 1579 that 'the municipal authorities wrote to the bailiffs of Yarmouth that the plague had carried off about 2,000 persons between May and Michaelmas, and they warned them to refrain from sending vessels for coal'.[7] But, as already noted, plague was active in Norfolk this year[8] and Yarmouth may have been one of the places involved in that county.

Cox presents evidence from its parish registers that Howden in Yorkshire was attacked by bubonic plague this year, for the burials registered during the three months May–July were 127 in 1579 compared with 23 in 1577, 25 in 1578, and 25 in 1580.[9] Similarly from the register of All Saints, Barnard presents evidence that Evesham suffered severely from it,[10] because in this parish alone—which cannot have had a population in excess of 900—the burials registered in 1579 were 148. 'Doubtless no visitation', he comments, 'ever took heavier toll in the little town, and the entries reveal some remarkable instances of mortalities in families.' The epidemic reached its peak in October when 30 deaths were registered, including those of 8 members of one family within 12 days.[10] Simultaneously plague attacked Wolverhampton[11] and a little later in the year it visited Milborne Port in Somerset and killed 9 of the parishioners.[12] The next year it was prevalent in Norfolk in the spring

and in Herefordshire and Gloucestershire in the summer, causing the county musters to be delayed in the first two counties[1,2] and postponed in the third.[3] It probably attacked Gloucester, as the County Assizes were held in July at Tewkesbury;[4] it was active at Bury St Edmunds,[5] and its eruption at Rye during the summer frightened some of the freemen from the town and they were absent at the mayoral election.[6] It may also have recurred at Stamford because Creighton notes that a corporation order was made early in September forbidding the townsfolk to leave the town.[7]

The only record of its activity in 1581 seems to be its appearance at Worcester,[8] though a critical study of English parish registers might well reveal its activity in other places, but in 1582 it was epidemic in a number of widely separated places. It erupted at Baston towards the end of July, destroying during the three months August–October 59 of the inhabitants, though the burials marked 'in the Plage' total 71 between 17 August and 14 February, comprising 33 males, 37 females, and 1 infant, sex unknown.[9] An excess mortality of females is to be expected, in view of the aetiology of bubonic plague, in a society where the women do not leave home to work. Further north Hull received a short visit from it in October which may have been confined to the parish of Holy Trinity, where 12 of the 32 burials registered during the month were those of supposed victims of plague.[10] Dover seems to have had similar good fortune earlier in the year if Creighton's report that 6 houses were shut up there then[11] represents the only activity of plague in the town. At Cranbrook in the same county there was a prolonged prevalence of plague, however, extending intermittently over the three years 1581–3, for the parish register records respectively 18, 41, and 22 marked plague-burials in those years.[11]

In 1583 Norwich appears to have been the principal provincial focus of bubonic plague. Blomefield affirms that for several weeks the plague-deaths ranged from 20 to 25 each week, chiefly among 'the Strangers', and that the death-roll of this epidemic was between 800 and 900.[12] In Yorkshire Wadworth must have suffered heavily as the parish register records 26 plague-burials in the hamlet in the autumn of this year.[13] In sharp contrast the parish register of Hailsham has a solitary plague-burial entry[14] and the victim, a woman, may have contracted the disease elsewhere. During the winter a disease which was most probably typhus fever was epidemic in the country southwest of Bath, for the chamberlain of that city paid 8*d*. to two men in March 'for seeing that none should cum into the cittie from Palton and other places which were infected with the plague'.[15] It was undoubtedly bubonic plague, however, which killed 770 members of the Walloon community in Southampton this year.[16] Creighton states that Yarmouth was visited by the

disease in 1584[1] and it was prevalent in the Isle of Sheppey from Michaelmas to the onset of the ensuing winter.[2] A third reference to its alleged activity in 1584 reads: 'Thys yeare in Ap'll the plage was in Oswestre so that the Walshe clothe & market was kept at the Knockyn beinge 9 myles from Shrewsberie and thyder the Drapers of Shrewsberie ev'y Moonday dyd resort to buy theyre clothe.'[3] A study of the Oswestry parish register shows, however, that of the 92 burials in that year 40 per cent occurred in the three months January–March; 30 per cent in the period 18 March to 31 July, and less than 16·5 per cent in the three 'plague-months' August–October.[4] Obviously there was no visitation of Oswestry by bubonic plague in 1584 and the fact that the record in the chronicle is wrongly dated is apparent from the note in the parish burials register under the date of August 1585: 'This yere the 18th daie of M'ch the Plague began in this towne and contynued untill the 20th of July, whereof died three-score and foure p'sons and no more.'[5] Possibly the chronicler was bemused by the strange disease which broke out in Shrewsbury in May 1584 which was 'mutche lycke the plage but was not the plage'.[6] It certainly lacked the lethal power of bubonic plague because the burials register of St Mary's parish shows no evidence of any unusual mortality either in 1584 or 1585 with 12 burials in the first year and 14 in the second.[7] The chronicler describes it as a disease that started suddenly with either vomiting or diarrhoea, followed by a cramp in the legs and a stitch in the side. The majority of patients, he says, recovered with good nursing; 'but manye dyed sodenly in a man' soom well overnyght and dead before morninge soom ij houres soom in one hour som in more soom in lesse and it fell in ev'y p't of the towne the lycke hathe not been seene it towchid pore and ryche it was properly termyd stowp gallants broother'.[8] The clinical description is suggestive of an epidemic of gastro-enterocolitis, either water-borne or from a contaminated foodstuff of general distribution.

Although many writers seem to be unaware of the fact, an excessive mortality in a sixteenth-century English parish could be caused by numerous diseases other than bubonic plague. The mortality in Oswestry in 1587 was higher than in 1585 and in 1587 the parishes of Shrewsbury St Mary and Stratford-on-Avon—and possibly other English parishes—experienced excessive mortalities. Examination of the monthly burials registered at Oswestry[9] and at Stratford[10] shows seasonal mortality curves that eliminate bubonic plague; but the two curves are sufficiently alike to render it probable that they are the products of one particular disease. The mortality curve shown by the monthly burials registered in the parish of Shrewsbury St Mary[11] could be a 'plague-curve' as its peak occurs in the 'plague-months'. There is an alternative explanation of it, however, in the contemporary record

that 'this yeare and in the moonthe of Julii a strange sickness namyd the burninge Agewe raignid all England ov' and especially at this tyme in the towne of Shrewsberie of the wch there discessid at the begynninge many of the woorthiest occupiars and p'perist p'soonns leavinge greate chardge of childre' behynde them'.[1] The social incidence of this disease is reminiscent of the 'sweating sickness', the last epidemic of which erupted first in Shrewsbury; it is certainly at variance with the characteristic social incidence of bubonic plague. But not all the excessive mortalities shown in English parish registers about this time were due to the *burning ague* because bubonic plague was busy in numerous places in England in the years from 1585 to 1587 inclusive.

In 1585 it was reported at Boston, King's Lynn, Guyhirn, and Ipswich. At Boston this year, and again in 1588, 'a number of houses belonging to the corporation, in St John's Row, appear to have been used as pest-houses'.[2] Creighton remarks that Boston appears to have been continuously infected with plague during the four years 1585–8,[3] and he notes that the burials from all causes registered in the parish were 372 in 1587 and 200 in 1588 compared with annual averages of 122 for the preceding eight years and of 84 for the succeeding twelve years.[3] He adds that plague prevailed within a radius of 10 miles around Boston. 'At Leake there were 104 burials from November, 1587, to November, 1588, the annual average being 24; at Frampton there were 130 burials in 1586–7, the average being 30; at Kirton there were 57 burials in 1589, and 102 in 1590.'[3] It is to be hoped that the next history of Lincolnshire will include a critical study of the burials registers of these parishes because the above figures by themselves afford no proof that the mortalities were caused by bubonic plague. Creighton is the authority also for the statement that plague was active at Guyhirn and Ipswich this year.[3] The supposition that King's Lynn was visited rests upon a note in the municipal archives that a mayoral proclamation towards the end of May ordered all owners of dogs and cats to kill their animals forthwith and bury the carcasses outside the town, excepting 'onlie such as have a dog of accompte', which must be kept fastened at home and only allowed out on leash.[4] It is possible that Cambridge was involved either this year or the next—when Lincoln was evidently attacked[5]—because in September 1586 the town treasurers paid 10s. to a builder 'for the use of the tymbre for the visited houses'.[6] Chesterfield undoubtedly suffered a calamitous visitation of bubonic plague in 1586–7. The disease erupted in the town early in October 1586, and after the usual period of quiescence during the winter, blazed up again in the spring of 1587 to develop into an epidemic which was designated in a marginal note in the parish register 'the great plague of Chesterfield'[7]

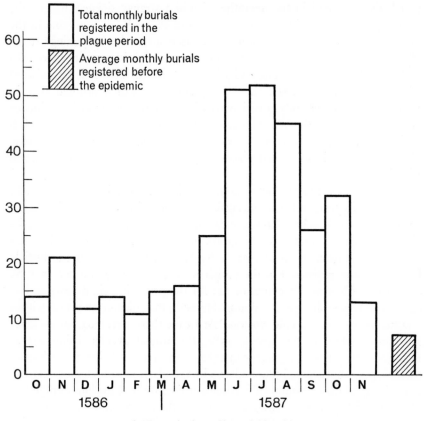

38. Plague deaths at Chesterfield, 1586–7.

to distinguish it from the lesser visitation of 1608–9. Godfrey points out that because of this grievous epidemic, which possibly destroyed as much as one-sixth of the population of Chesterfield and its outlying villages, no troops from the hundred of Scarsdale attended the Derbyshire muster of 1587, although the attendance of the large Scarsdale contingents was of importance on account of the threatened Spanish invasion.[1] From 1562 to 1635 Chesterfield's annual burials averaged 82, and for a period of fourteen months immediately preceding the epidemic they numbered 85. The epidemic extended over fourteen months also, from October 1586 to November 1587, and during this period 358 burials were registered. Eleven of these must be excluded as 9 were plague-dead from the chapelry of Calow and the other 2 were not cases of plague. Godfrey calculates that of the remaining 347 burials bubonic plague accounted for between 275 and 290, and that during

238

the plague-period the borough's death-rate rose by more than 300 per cent. 'On the assumption', he comments, 'that there were some 300 families in Chesterfield from which to account for some 347 deaths due to plague and normal causes together in the fourteen-month period, an examination of the burial list discloses that a likely maximum of 175 families bore the whole of the deaths on both accounts, and that about 125 families had therefore no single death among them. Then, of the 347 deaths, almost half the deaths occurred in some forty-odd of the families...which...must have been virtually wiped out of existence.'[1] He gives full details of a number of these family holocausts, which emphasizes more clearly than any previous English writing on bubonic plague its characteristic feature of a *house disease* and exposes the nonsense that has been written about 'ghost villages' exterminated by the disease. Figure 38 shows the mortality curve of this epidemic as manifested by the registered monthly burials. Godfrey supplies the significant explanatory note that the big drop in the number of burials registered in September 1587, which was succeeded by an increase of some 20 per cent in October, was due to 'an almost unprecedented spell of cold weather, consisting of cold winds, hard white frosts and falls of sleet and snow. When the weather became milder again in October the rate at once went up.'[1] This is a most valuable unsolicited testimonial to the susceptibility of *X. cheopis* to cold weather in England. It should also be noted that this freak weather was not a unique event in the centuries when bubonic plague afflicted England. To anyone who aspires to be a local historian, Godfrey's account of the 'great plague of Chesterfield' can be heartily commended as something to emulate.

The outbreak of presumptive typhus fever in November 1586 in the hamlet of Bottesford, about 10 miles south of Newark, provides a vivid illustration of bureaucratic notions of plague-control in sixteenth-century England. 'The sickness' had appeared in a family which was accordingly segregated in its house. The official responsible then reported: 'I have kept the suspected persons in one house this five weeks and it remains there only. We cannot learn certainly whether it is the plague or not, but it is very suspicious. Six have died and four remaining have had "rysings" some between their shoulders and necks, some between their thighs and bodies.'[2] The aetiology of typhus fever ensures that the segregation of this unfortunate family would confine the disease to the one house and make certain of the infection of every one of its inmates, because no lice could leave the dwelling except on the persons of the inmates, whereas if the disease were bubonic plague the segregation of the human occupants would not confine the house-rats to the house.

After Chesterfield Lincoln may have been the worst sufferer from bubonic

plague in 1586.[1] The Lysons affirm that Derby was visited by plague this year[2] and Creighton asserts that St Peter's parish was the scene of this visitation,[3] but he supplies no confirmatory evidence from the parish burials register. He also fails to supply such evidence to support his note that plague was prevalent at Norwich in 1588.[3] At Lincoln plague may have recrudesced in 1587 after the usual winter intermission, as its reappearance seems to have been responsible for the Common Council minute of 1 March that a certain Father Willyman be given the freedom of the city, together with fishing rent free, a house belonging to the corporation, and an annuity of 46s. 8d., for as long as he dwelt in the city, provided always that he should not at any time go to any infected towns or places in the country without the licence of the mayor or his deputy.[4] Regrettably the city archives are silent about the service he rendered in plague-time to win this handsome reward from the people of Lincoln. Creighton states that at Wisbech 42 burials were registered in September and 62 in October 1587—inferentially in consequence of an epidemic of bubonic plague—numbers that are three or four times greater than the annual average of these months in that town.[3] Plague may have been the cause also of the excessive mortality at Hart, where 89 burials were registered this year, 10 of which were those of strangers,[5] possibly fugitives from the epidemic of the disease then raging in Durham City.[6] Creighton affirms that plague was prevalent at this time in the neighbouring parish of Stanton.[3]

On the other side of the Pennines Penrith was desolated by excessive mortalities in successive years. Cox reports that 203 burials were registered there in 1587 and 592 in 1588,[7] making a total of 795 compared with its normal annual burial-rate in this century of 50, so that the town lost about 700 of its inhabitants in these two years in excess of its normal loss. As it is improbable that its population exceeded 2,000 persons at this time, it must have lost at least one-third of its population. It is very probable that bubonic plague was mainly responsible for this destruction, an assumption that an analysis of the registered monthly burials might confirm. It was certainly plague that earned a severe censure for the sheriff and justices of Derbyshire for their failure to relieve Chesterfield in its sore need.[8]

The annual average of burials registered in the parish of Leominster from 1560 to 1598 was 60, but in 1587 there were 218, of which 41 occurred in October alone.[9] This figure is suggestive of a visitation of bubonic plague, although to make that disease responsible for this excessive mortality we need to know the burial figures for the three 'plague-months' of July–September, which the vicar unfortunately does not supply. It is especially necessary to know what proportion of a particular annual mortality was

The Manner of Dissecting the

PESTILENTIALL BODY.

3 The frontispiece to G. Thomson's *Loimotomia:*
  or the pest anatomised

4   *Rescued from the plague* by F. W. W. Topham, R.I.

contributed by the four 'plague-months' in 1587 because of the prevalence of the *burning ague*. For example there was an excessive mortality at Bury St Edmunds that year which might have been due to this disease, but of the 89 burials registered in St James' parish during the eight months of April–November, 78 or more than 87 per cent occurred in the three principal 'plague-months',[1] a finding which identifies bubonic plague as the cause of the mortality. Tymms reports that the plague-sick were removed from their homes to tents erected for their reception in the fields outside the town.[1]

It was fortunate for Elizabeth I and her England that bubonic plague was not extensively epidemic during the critical year of 1588. Creighton avers that it was prevalent in the Spanish ships as they sailed up the English Channel, so that after their panic flight from their anchorage off the coast of Flanders 'the broken remnants of the Armada which reached Corunna were like so many floating pest-houses'.[2] This may be true; but his companion assertion that dysentery and typhus fever 'utterly crippled' the English fleet and rendered individual ships 'so weak that they could not venture to come through the Downs from Margate to Dover'[2] does not appear to be justified by the facts of history. It was surely Elizabeth's 'proverbial parsimony'— a parsimony which 'was as a general rule necessary to the bare survival of her government'[3]—and the consequent shortage of powder, shot, and other provisions, and not sickness among their crews, that crippled the English ships, for Howard trailed the Spanish fleet well up into the North Sea without having the means to attack it. And it was the southerly gale, which drove the Spanish ships northwards, and not the sickness of their crews that prevented the English ships from venturing through the Downs from Margate to Dover, for no sixteenth-century ship, however well-manned, could have made that passage in the teeth of a southerly gale.

Nevertheless it was well for England that plague confined its activity during 1588 to the northern half of the kingdom and came no nearer the great camp at Tilbury than Norwich, which may have been only slightly attacked.[4] Boston's importation of a cleaner to disinfect the pest-house in St John's Row[5] must surely signify that plague was no longer present in the town, in which case the excessive mortality in the town this year was apparently caused by some epidemic disease other than bubonic plague, possibly by the *burning ague*. It was bubonic plague, however, that erupted at Newcastle-upon-Tyne in May and in the succeeding months destroyed 1,727 of the townsfolk.[6] The register of St John's parish records that the plague-dead were distributed among 5 burial grounds, to wit, 340 in St John's; 509 at the Chapel; 300 at Allhallows; 400 at St Andrew's, and 103 at St Nicholas'.[7] These figures add up to 1,652 burials, leaving 75 corpses

which were presumably interred in ground that was afterwards consecrated. As the population of Newcastle probably did not exceed 5,000 persons at this time, this epidemic of bubonic plague destroyed upwards of one-third of its population. In August 1589 'Edward Errington, the *Towne's Fooll*...died in the peste'.[1] Alas, poor Yorick! This year plague also attacked Durham City and the register of St Oswald's parish records its extermination within 10 days of the 7 members of the 'maysterman' family.[2] Creighton relates that huts for the accommodation of the plague-sick were erected on Elvet Moor outside the city.[3] From the summer of 1589, apart from the usual winter intermissions, there was a progressive expansion of the area of activity of the disease, culminating in the great national outburst of 1593, which was un-doubtedly one of the most serious major epidemics of it that England experienced between 1348 and 1666.

In 1590 Plymouth and Exeter were attacked, as incidents probably in a widespread prevalence of bubonic plague in the West Country, for Somerset was so generally and grievously infected that the musters could not be held in the county.[4] Apparently the disease overwintered in Plymouth and re-crudesced in 1591.[5] On account of its prevalence at Exeter the assizes were transferred to Honiton.[6] Pickard opines that Exeter's toll of 1,030 burials was borne by a population of 9,100, so that this epidemic of bubonic plague decimated the city. Of the total burials 675 or 65·5 per cent occurred in the three 'plague-months' of August–October, with September as the peak month with 311 burials. If November with 179 burials is included in the 'plague-season' in this instance the mortality-rate rises to 82·9 per cent. A study of the monthly burial figures for the autumn of 1590 and the year 1591, which Pickard laudably supplies,[7] suggests that there may have been an unusual prolongation of mild weather in Devonshire that enabled plague to smoulder among the house-rats, for the monthly burials recorded for December 1590 to December 1591 inclusive are respectively 94, 62, 55, 47, 43, 42, 24, 18, 47, 26, 21, 15, and 18. On the other hand these excessive figures, which Pickard ascribes to bubonic plague, may represent deaths from a winter and spring epidemic of either typhus fever or smallpox, with a slight recrudescence of plague, after its customary winter intermission, in July 1591. The correct interpretation of the monthly burial figures in 1591 depends upon the atmospheric temperatures in Exeter during the winter and spring of that year, about which no information appears to be available. As Pickard justly remarks, the combined mortality of these two years must have gravely injured the city because, added to the loss of life, there was the loss of fugitives who never returned to Exeter. Nevertheless he asserts that by 1600 the population had risen to 8,900 by the influx of people from rural

areas.[1] During this visitation 12*d*. was paid 'to one of the waytes for making white crosses on the doors where the plage was', and a little later 6*s*. was paid for additional crosses.[2] In the parish of Allhallows the annual burials registered from 1586 to 1594 inclusive were 1, 4, 3, 5, 14, 21, 4, 5, 6.[3] Excluding the years 1590 and 1591 the average annual burial rate was 4, so in 1590 the burials were threefold and in 1591 fivefold the average rate in this parish. It is obvious that this epidemic of bubonic plague must have exerted a considerable effect upon the social and economic life of Exeter. Many English towns and villages had similar disastrous experiences of bubonic plague in the centuries from 1348 to 1666, yet most of the local histories scarcely mention plague—apart from horrific references to the 'Black Death'—or the other deadly epidemic diseases that played a part in moulding the history of the English people.

Undoubtedly plague did not confine its ravages to Devonshire's two chief towns during these mournful years. It was possibly widely active in villages and parishes scattered around the central moorland area; but a comprehensive study of the county's parish registers is needed to ascertain the extent of its activities. Such a study would seem to be a worthwhile one for a history graduate working for a higher degree. Some idea of the extent of the disease at this time is provided by its invasion of Widecombe-in-the-Moor, one of the most secluded hamlets in the county prior to the development of modern road traffic. In 1590 the parish register records 59 burials,[4] the largest number in any one year recorded in the parish. The burials registered in the four months June–September number 29 or practically 50 per cent of the annual total. South of Widecombe the river-port of Totnes suffered a grievous visitation, the mortality curve of which is illustrated in figure 39. The deaths from all causes entered in the parish register number 270, of which 237 are marked as 'plague-deaths', giving a plague-mortality rate of practically 88 per cent.[5] As figure 39 shows, the epidemic reached its peak in August, after which it declined steadily to its extinction towards the end of January. This slow decline, which is suggestive of an unusually mild autumn, renders the mortality-curve somewhat atypical for an epidemic of bubonic plague in England.

Creighton infers from a burial entry in the parish register of Totnes that plague first appeared at Dartmouth and he implies that it was transported from there to Tiverton,[6] a probable chain of events. Harding quotes a note in the parish register of Tiverton which states that 553 persons 'dyed of the pestilence' there in 1591.[7] He calculates that because of the stocking industry the population of Tiverton in 1590 was nearly 5,000, so that this epidemic of bubonic plague decimated it. He adds that there was a panic exodus from

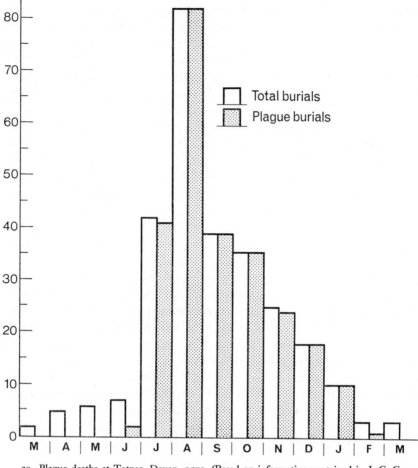

39. Plague deaths at Totnes, Devon, 1570. (Based on information contained in J. C. Cox, *The Parish Registers of England* (London, 1910).

the town, during which hundreds of the townspeople fled, some never to return, and he avers that the combined loss from death and flight destroyed the stocking industry and thereby completely altered the history of Tiverton and indirectly of Devonshire.[1] It seems much more probable, however, that it was the invention of the stocking-frame in 1589 by the incumbent of Calverton in Nottinghamshire, the Rev. W. Lees,[2] that was responsible for the decay of the Tiverton industry. It is a pity that Harding did not give the figures of the monthly burials in his history, but it is pleasing to find a local historian showing an interest in the parish registers of his subject. The Lysons note that the summer assizes were held at Tavistock this year on

account of 'the plague raging at Exeter',[1] and in the adjoining county Redruth was visited by it.[2] It erupted there in August 1591 according to a note in the parish register quoted by Cox,[2] and after the customary winter quiescence recrudesced in the spring of 1592, causing 27 deaths in June alone compared with an annual rate of less than 10.[2] A second note in the register quoted by Cox states that the epidemic ceased in November 1592. Peter supplies the additional information that for 30 years prior to 1591 the maximum number of burials registered in any one year in Redruth was 16, whereas 96 were registered in the 11 months of this visitation.[3] He also reports that in the neighbouring parish of Illogan 122 plague-burials were registered in 1591.[3] Regrettably both writers omit the relevant monthly burial figures. In the north of England Morpeth and Alnwick were 'infected with the sickness of the plague'[4] in the spring of 1590, and in the eastern counties Norwich and Kirton are reported to have been attacked by it. The former place suffered severely, sustaining a death-roll of 672 in less than 4 months;[5] the latter may proportionately have been even worse afflicted as 102 burials are entered in the parish register.[6]

The Shrewsbury Chronicles, after recording that in 1592 London was afflicted with plague and 'a pestelent burning ague', continue: 'The sayd plage was in Darby, Lichfilld, Bewdley, Worcester, Glocester, Tewksbery, Wem, Bishopps Castell and wthin three myles of Shrewsbery, so that watche and warde was kept for longe tyme at all the gates there that non infected p'son or any others shulld com from those places except they kept them sellves owt of the towne for a monthes space at least.'[7] The inclusion of Wem in this list is a mistake, probably due to a false rumour, as its parish register shows no excessive number of burials in any one of the three years 1592–4. The annual average of burials for the nine years 1583–91 is 30 and the burials registered in each of the succeeding three years number respectively 34, 35, and 20.[8] The reference to the visitation of Tewkesbury would seem to be at fault also in its chronology because Dyde affirms that though plague appeared in the town in November 1592 only two or three houses in Barton Street were infected until April 1593. Then the disease erupted in a fierce epidemic which raged furiously throughout the summer and autumn, smouldered through the ensuing winter and spring of 1594 until the middle of May, and then suddenly ceased.[9] The Norfolk parish of Holt has a note in its burials register in 1592 which reads: 'A greate plage wch beganne the 4 of Auguste continnued unto ye 26 of Feb. followinge.'[10] Cox remarks that whereas the annual burials averaged 6 prior to 1592, in only 7 months of that year 64 were registered.[10] Some time during this year plague paid a brief and comparatively harmless visit to Bury St Edmunds,[11] and it was almost as

innocuous at Derby, which suffered severely, however, from a violent recrudescence of it in the following year.[1]

In 1593, as already mentioned, Tewkesbury was the scene of a grievous epidemic of bubonic plague. Dyde reports that 560 plague-burials were registered during that year, that upwards of 150 houses were infected, that many people fled from the stricken town, and that from before Whitsuntide until 1 November no market or fair was held in the town.[2] Creighton affirms that Canterbury, Nottingham, and Lincoln were all attacked by the disease this year,[3] but until confirmation is forthcoming from a study of their diocesan and parochial burial registers his statement must be accepted with reserve. This year was also a 'plague-year' in the parish of Stoke Newington if the figures extracted from its burials register are accurate. In 1592 the registered burials were 18; the next year they were 34, and of these 19 or practically 56 per cent occurred in the three principal 'plague-months'.[4] Although Burford in Oxfordshire was not involved, the fear excited by this outburst of bubonic plague incited the Privy Council to forbid its townspeople to hunt in the Forest of Wychwood because of the queen's express prohibition of all unnecessary assemblies 'in this dangerous tyme of infecon of the plauge, which spredeth yt self in many places'.[5] The Council explained that the reason for this injunction was that 'many people of dyvers townes whereof some are infected, as wee are informed, wilbe drawen together, to the hassard of many her Ma[ts] subjects'.[5]

Among the towns involved in this outburst, which 'hath greatly touched many other parts of this land',[6] was Cambridge. It and the university were attacked towards the close of the year, whereupon the colleges dispersed into the country and all public assemblies in the university were postponed until 20 February.[7] Cooper has extracted the appended items relating to this visitation from the municipal treasurer's accounts for 1593.

> Item, for a locke, nayles, hookes, & hingins & workmanship of a dore to keepe in the visited persons, iij *s*. xj *d*.
> Item, for carryinge boothe tymbre to Mydsomer Green for visited, iij *s*. iiij *d*.
> Item, charges for carryenge a letter to the Busshope of Lyncolne concerning the man that shold cure the visited, iij *s*.
> Item, for the charges of Williams the surgion for the visited being in towne, iiij *s*. vj *d*.[8]

Evidently a pesthouse-cum-lock-up hut was erected at Midsummer Green for the isolation of the plague-sick poor, while the better class patients were visited in their own homes by the surgeon. It is to be regretted that we have no record of the testimonial that the bishop of Lincoln may have given about

the competence of the man 'that shold cure the visited'. Was he, one wonders, Father Willyman, seeking fresh fields of plague to conquer?

Kelly affirms that Leicester was invaded during the summer of this year and that it was scourged by bubonic plague until late in the spring of 1594.[1] At a Common Hall meeting in September 1593 weekly payments of 2s. and of 12d. were allocated to the plague-stricken and a petition was lodged for a county levy for their relief. Late in October a mayoral letter reported that 21 houses were infected; that *about* 35 plague-deaths had occurred; that some adjoining houses were suspect, and that a continual day and night watch was being kept in the town. A little later the number of plague-dead had risen to 44, of which 9 were named Messenger—probably signifying the extermination of a family—that in three houses 4 persons were dead in each house, and that between 500 and 600 poor people were receiving relief. Towards the end of November another mayoral letter reported at least 46 houses infected with at least 107 plague-deaths, and a week later the town was reported to be incurring a weekly expense of at least £6 in plague-relief, plus the pay of 20 watchmen from the previous Michaelmas.[2] As Kelly found the burial entries in each of the three Leicester parishes to be much below the usual average, he concluded that the plague-dead must have been buried in open fields outside the town.[3] He extracted from the municipal archives an item that is of relevant interest, to wit, a *certificate of health*, dated 6 October 1593 and signed by the mayor, which was issued to Alice Stynton to enable her to leave Leicester to join her husband who was travelling in Northamptonshire, 'gaytheringe under the Great Seale of England, by lycence, for a poore house at Waltam Crosse'.[4]

At Derby plague seems to have struck with particular violence the parish of All Saints, the register of which contains this notice of it: 'October, 1592. The plague began in Derby in the house of William Sowter, bootcher, in the parish of All Saints...and it continued in the town the space of twelve months at the leaste, as the register may appeare. October, 1593. About this tyme the plague of pestilence, by the great mercy and goodness of Almighty God, steyed past all expectation of man, for it reasted upon a sodayne at what tyme it was dispersed in every corner of this whole parish; ther was not two houses together free from it';[5] yet, adds Waters, 'it never entered the house of a tanner, a tobacconist, or a shoemaker'.[6] If these exceptions really happened they may have been merely by chance, as bubonic plague strikes so haphazardly, or because the particular premises, with their distinctive odours, may have been obnoxious to the house-rat. Alternatively the dusts of tan-bark, tobacco, and leather, filtering into the rats' nests, may have been inimical to the subsistence of *X. cheopis*. The Lysons state that 237 plague-

TABLE 10

Plague-mortalities in the parishes of Derby in 1593

	Total burials	Plague-burials	Annual average for the quinquennium preceding 1592
All Saints	—	255	—
St Alkmund	—	91	—
St Michael	—	21	—
St Peter	50	Bulk	5
St Werburgh	57	Bulk	5

deaths were registered in the parish of All Saints in 1593.[1] Even at the peak of this epidemic, however, when 'no two houses together' were free from it in the parish of All Saints, the distribution of the disease must have been fearfully inexplicable to the townsfolk of Derby. Some families were probably exterminated; other lost some of their members, and others escaped unscathed. Cox says that both parents and 5 children of the Sowter family died, and he gives some information about the burials registered in the five Derby parishes between September 1592 and October 1593.[2] This information is presented in table 10.

'With the consent of ye most p'rte of the chiefest of ye inhabitaunts', the town of Godmanchester raised an emergency fund of £6 in 1593 'to be paid to one Willyman, wch did undertake to be painfull and carefull about ye people infected wth ye plage wthin this towne.'[3] The surname Willyman can scarcely have been a common one and its recurrence here in association with plague arouses the surmise that the man who was paid to attend the plague-stricken at Godmanchester was identical with the man who was rewarded by the city of Lincoln in 1587. If this surmise is correct he appears to have shed his priestly prefix in the interval, and as neither authority credits him with a medical qualification the suspicion arises that he was a charlatan who found it advisable to leave Lincoln for the good of his health.

Creighton affirms that Lichfield sustained a plague death-roll of 1,100 of its citizens this year,[4] and in the contiguous county of Shropshire the ancient borough of Bishops Castle was devastated by an epidemic of the disease that is well-attested. The parish register contains two notes about it that were written by the vicar. The first records his conviction that the epidemic was a divine chastisement for the heinous sin of holding the annual fair on the Sabbath because its date, 24 June, happened to fall on a Sunday in 1593.[5] He

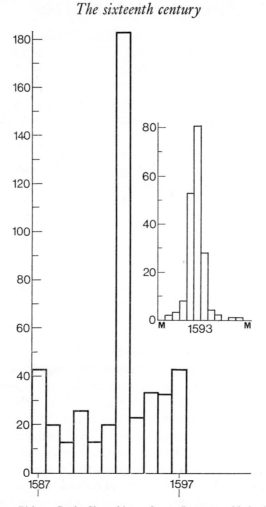

40. Plague deaths at Bishops Castle, Shropshire, 1587–97. Inset: monthly burials for year March 1593–March 1594. (Extracted from the Bishop's Transcript of the parish burial registers in the possession of the Borough of Shrewsbury Public Library.)

protested vigorously against this profanity but he was overborne by the determination of the aldermen and townsfolk to hold the fair on its proper date. The second note records the cessation of the epidemic. An examination of the parish burials register reveals that in the interval of less than 21 months between these two notes, 174 inhabitants of the little town were destroyed by bubonic plague in a total death-roll for 1593 of 183—an average of more than 8 burials each week compared with an annual average of 18 during the preceding quinquennium. Figure 40 illustrates the calamity that befell

Bishops Castle and shows that the peak of the epidemic occurred in August, in which month 81 burials were registered. The burials registered during the five months June–October were exclusively those of the victims of plague, and the mortality curve is typical of a severe epidemic of bubonic plague in an English township during normal weather for the season of the year.[1] It is very probable that additional victims were interred in unconsecrated ground and their burials were therefore not entered in the parish register. The population of Bishops Castle is given as 1,302 persons in 1958[2] and it is improbable that it exceeded half that number in 1593, even though it was relatively a much more important place then than it is today. It is possible that the true plague-death-roll was about 200, so that the borough may then have lost one-third of its population, a proportion which is about the maximum that bubonic plague *alone* was capable of inflicting. A loss of this magnitude—which assuredly included the extermination of some families —must have had some effect upon the subsequent history of the borough that some future historian may care to assess. Some 16 miles due south of ravaged Bishops Castle plague also struck savagely at Presteigne. Southall says that prior to 1593 the annual burials registered in the parish averaged about 50, but in that year considerably more than 300 were attributed to plague alone, and he opines that this terrible mortality was borne by a population of less than 2,000.[3] Barnard's statement that plague was synchronously active at Evesham requires confirmation from the parish burials register,[4] but Medland's report that the parish register of St Nicholas, Gloucester records 81 plague-burials this year indicates that the disease visited that city.[5] Far to the north plague was 'so sore' in each of the cities of York and Durham that 'none of worth' remained in either city,[6] because there was the usual panic exodus of all who had the means to flee from those cities.

Towards the close of 1593 the activity of bubonic plague appears to have declined considerably although the disease was not extinguished because, as so often happens after a major outburst of any epidemic disease, there were numerous 'trailer' outbreaks of it in 1594. For instance it was reported to be 'very hot' at Sherborne in Dorsetshire,[7] and Creighton states that the parish register of Watford shows many burials marked 'plague' among the 124 burials which were registered during the first 8 months of the year.[8] He adds that plague-burials were also registered this year in the Hertford parishes of All Saints and St Andrew.[8] The year is noteworthy in the English annals of bubonic plague because the Privy Council ordered the justices— wherever plague was active—to ensure that the parson and three or four 'substantial householders' viewed all corpses before burial and certified the *probable* cause of death in each case to the minister in charge of the parish

or to a churchwarden, who must make a weekly return of (*a*) the number of persons dead of plague and (*b*) the total number of dead, with their *probable* causes, to the justices. The collected parish returns must then be entered by the Clerk of the Peace in a special book, and every three weeks the justices must assemble and send the returns to the Privy Council.[1] Here is the conception of our modern system of civil registration of the causes of death; but this product aborted before it was embedded in the national womb because the panic fear of plague was such that no 'substantial householders' could be obtained to view the corpses of the plague-dead.

The next year, apart from an unsupported statement by Creighton that it was prevalent at Tregony in Cornwall,[2] plague seems to have been absent from England. However it was only dormant and 1596 witnessed a renewal of its activity in various places. The register of St Mary's parish in Haverfordwest shows an excessive mortality in the eighteen months from September 1596 to March 1598 which may have been caused by plague. Phillips finds that 80 burials were registered during that period whereas only 13 were registered in the succeeding eighteen months.[3] He affirms that the excessive mortality in the parish began in the autumn of 1596 and that that year and 1597 were both years of exceptionally bad harvests, in which case the excessive mortality may have resulted from destitution and 'famine fever'. He opines that St Mary's parish could not have contained more than one-third of the population of Haverfordwest and he estimates the town's death-roll during the sickly eighteen months at not less than 250 or about one-eighth of its population. He adds that 1596 was a very sickly year also in the adjoining county of Carmarthen, where the estuarine township of Ferryside suffered a mortality proportionate to that of Haverfordwest, as 76 burials were registered in St Ishmael's parish in 1596 compared with 13 in 1593 and 18 in 1594–5.[3]

It is possible that the main focus of bubonic plague in the closing years of this century was in the north of England, however, especially in the Lake District. The annual burials registered in the parish of St Bees during the fifteen years 1589–1603 reveal that there were two years of excessive mortality during that period, to wit, 1592 and 1596–7;[4] but in the absence of the monthly burial figures it is not possible to tell whether either of these excessive mortalities was due to bubonic plague. There were excessive mortalities also in 1597–8 in the parishes of Crosthwaite, Penrith, Newton Regny, Kendal, Kirkby Lonsdale, Crosby Garrett, Cartmel, Heversham, and Middleton, which Lees avers ranged from 3 to 5 times greater than the annual average of burials in those parishes,[5] and there were other Lakeland parishes that had similar mortalities. For instance 85 burials were registered

TABLE 11

Annual burials in some Lakeland parishes in 1596–8

	1596	1597	1598	Average annual burials
Gosforth	56	116	—	About 13
Langwathby	8	17	24	—
Kirkoswald	—	10	51	—
Greystoke	—	182	—	Less than 30
Crosthwaite	—	267	84	About 30
Newton Regny	—	30	—	8
Kirkby Lonsdale	—	82	—	Less than 50
St Leonard, Cleator	—	—	28	5
Lamplugh	—	26	—	12
Hawkshead	—	85	—	—
Millom	22	13	17	—
Dean	7	Missing	—	—
Ravenstonedale	—	27	16	15
St Bees	65	63	14	About 20

at Hawkshead in 1597,[1] a number at least double the average annual registration, and at Gosforth 56 were registered in 1596 and 117 in 1597 compared with 10 in 1595 and 17 in 1598.[2] Nicholls affirms that the bishop of Carlisle died of plague at Rose Castle in 1597[3] and the parish of Great Orton, Carlisle was devastated by an epidemic of some disease in 1596–7 according to Gillbanks.[4] Barnes gives some burial figures extracted from the registers of 14 Lakeland parishes[5] which are presented in table 11. His data are regrettably incomplete, however, and the true nature, extent, and destructiveness of this invasion of the Lake District by an epidemic of disease will not be known until all the relevant parish registers have been exhaustively studied and analysed with especial reference to their seasonal mortalities. Bubonic plague could have been responsible, but so also could smallpox, typhus fever, epidemic influenza, dysentery—as a 'famine-fever'—or one of the enteric fevers.

There seems to be no doubt, however, about the ravages of bubonic plague in a part of this region in 1598. An inscription in Penrith Church records that in that year the disease killed 2,260 persons in Penrith, 2,500 in Kendal, 2,200 in Richmond, and 1,196 in Carlisle.[5] Barnes opines that this inscription was copied from an older one when the church was rebuilt in the eighteenth century which, according to Bishop Nicholson,* gave identical figures except for Penrith (2,266). Considerable doubt has been cast on the accuracy of these figures—Barnes declares that the parish register of Penrith records only

* *Miscellany Accounts of the Diocese of Carlisle.*[5]

TABLE 12

Monthly burials at Richmond, Yorkshire

1597	August	23	65
	September	42	
1598	May	93	568
	June	99	
	July	182	
	August	194	

583 burials in 1598[1]—and it certainly looks as if they were in excess of the populations of the first three towns. He believes that the rural deaneries and not the towns were named in the original inscription, but even if this explanation is correct the figures are still inaccurate because there is evidence that an unknown number of plague-dead were interred in unconsecrated ground in fields and on the fells. The Penrith parish register has a note after a burial entry dated 27 September 1597 which reads: 'Here begonne the plague (God's punishment in Penrith). All those that are noted with P. dyed of the infection, and those noted with F. were buried on the fell.'[2] In these two categories there are respectively 608 and 213 entries, but Cox opines that in all probability many more were buried in their own gardens and elsewhere whose burials were not registered.[2] During the old calendar year of 1596–7 there were 4 burials registered in the parish of Edenhall. The next year there were 8, of which 6 were plague-dead, all from one family, and a note in the register states that one of the victims was buried in 'flatts close' and the other 5 in 'their Lodge on Edenhall Fell at a place called Shaddowbourgh'.[3] Barnes cites Nicholson and Burn* for the statement that between 1 August 1598 and the ensuing 25th of March 128 persons died, inferentially of bubonic plague, at Appleby, Scattergate, Colby, and Colby Leathes.[3] Whatever the true nature of the disease was, these records suggest that the region suffered grievously and that that suffering was aggravated by the desertion of the sick which seems to be implicit in the phrase accompanying many of the burial entries in the Greystoke register—'who died of want of means to live'.[4]

Creighton, who has no doubt that the disease was bubonic plague, opines that the epidemic which ravaged the Lakeland counties erupted at Richmond in the autumn of 1597;[5] but if it was plague that was active at Gosforth and St Bees in 1596 (see table 11) his view of its origin is questionable. Richmond certainly experienced a terrible death-roll as the figures of the monthly burials there which he supplies convincingly demonstrate (see table 12). Walker

* *History of Cumberland and Westmorland*, vol. I.

TABLE 13

Plague-burials in the city of Durham, 1597

Elvet	More than 400
St Nicholas	215
St Margaret	200
St Giles	60
St Mary	60
St Gaol	24
TOTAL	959 +

presents some additional information about Penrith's visitation that is very suggestive of bubonic plague. He avers that the initial activity of the disease in the town was confined to a few families, most of whose members were destroyed in a few days, and he gives several examples to support his assertion.[1]

The year 1597 seems to have been one of near famine in the north of England[2] and many places in the North Riding of Yorkshire, in Durham county, and in Northumberland were involved in an outburst of epidemic disease which may have been a concurrence of bubonic plague and 'famine-fever'. The former disease was certainly epidemic during the year in New-castle-upon-Tyne, Darlington, and Durham City. Creighton notes that the assizes were not held in Newcastle that year on account of the prevalence of plague there and he records that 340 plague-burials were entered in the parish register of Darlington up to 17 October.[3] He supplies also the figures of the plague-burials registered in the city parishes of Durham that are presented in table 13. These are minimal figures for the parishes other than that of St Nicholas, however, because they give the plague-deaths only up to 17 October and because many victims were undoubtedly buried on the moor and elsewhere. It seems evident from these minimal figures that this epidemic must have seriously disorganized the economic and social life of the city, which certainly lost one-quarter and possibly one-third of its population on this occasion.

South of the Humber–Mersey line Ludlow, Leominster, Tewkesbury, Cranbrook, and Hastings appear to have been the recipients of the final outbreaks of bubonic plague in sixteenth-century England. At Ludlow 124 burials are entered in the parish register in 1597,[4] and an analysis of the monthly burials reveals a seasonal mortality that is suggestive of bubonic plague as the three principal 'plague-months' contribute practically 50 per cent of the annual burials. Plague may also have been active in two other

Shropshire parishes this year, namely Wem[1] and Newport,[2] for the burial registers of both parishes show excessive mortalities and the monthly burial figures in each case are suggestive of plague. On the other hand, although the Oswestry parish register exhibits excessive mortalities of 213 and 193 burials in 1597 and 1598 respectively,[3] the analysis of the monthly burials in each of those years indicates that some disease other than bubonic plague was responsible for them. Now Weyman mentions 'a great sickness of small-pox in Shrewsbury' in 1595, and he states that in that year and in 1597 there were over 100 burials in each year, inferentially from smallpox.[4] It is possible therefore that the excessive mortalities in the Shropshire parishes in 1597 may have been caused by smallpox, for the seasonal incidence of variola is not as exact as that of bubonic plague and outbreaks of it may occur during the summer months, especially if the weather is cooler than usual.

At Leominster 180 burials were registered in 1597 compared with an annual average of 60,[5] but in the absence of the monthly burial figures it is not certain that this excessive mortality was caused by bubonic plague. Tewkesbury's visitation in 1598 was a comparatively light one as Dyde reports that only about 40 plague-deaths were recorded there,[6] but both Cranbrook and Hastings were fiercely attacked. In the former place 181 plague-deaths are entered in the parish register in a total of 221 burials that occurred during the 15 months of the epidemic.[7] Hastings, with a total mortality of 114 during the year, was not as severely afflicted as Cranbrook.[7] Its parish register contains the curious notice about this visitation that plague 'was in all quarters of the Parish except Hartley quarter' and that it 'gott almost into all the Inns and Suckling Houses of the Town, places then of much misorder'.[7] The register also contains the note: 'Now also this year others of the plague were buried near to their several dwellings, because they could get none to carry them into the Church, for it was the beginning of this infection, so that none would venture themselves.'[8] And if no volunteers could be found to discharge this last Christian duty to the dead in a parish such as Hastings, there must have been many parishes with more difficult geographical features where large numbers of the plague-dead were interred hurriedly and unceremoniously in unconsecrated ground.

Scotland and Ireland

In October 1579 the Scottish authorities decided to take precautions against the approach of bubonic plague from England. A proclamation read at the market crosses in Edinburgh, Coldinghame, Duns, Kelso, Jedburgh, and other towns prohibited Scotsmen from visiting Berwick-upon-Tweed or

other infected places in England and banned Englishmen from entering Scotland.[1] The next year a ship arrived in the Firth of Forth in September from Denmark having had several presumptive plague-deaths on board during the voyage. Its crew and passengers were ordered to land on the islet of Inchcolm and remain there on pain of death until free from infection.[2] Simultaneously a proclamation was read in all the coastal towns warning the inhabitants not to permit any of the ship's crew or passengers to land, or any of its cargo to be discharged, or to have any trade or communication with the vessel whatever under pain of death.[3] On 3 October a ship arrived from Bruges, where plague was then prevalent, having among its passengers three pregnant women. They, together with the ship's crew and passengers, were isolated at Newhaven.[4] Towards the end of November the Privy Council was notified that the company on the first ship had been isolated on Inchcolm for nine weeks; that the master of the ship and numerous other persons were dead, and that the ship was leaking badly and its cargo deteriorating. Nevertheless, the remaining members of its company were not released until mid-January, after 115 days' quarantine.[4] The quarantine in this instance seems to have been effective as, apart from Creighton's report of an outbreak of plague in Perth in 1580[5]—which is not mentioned in the *Chronicle of Perth*[6]—Scotland appears to have been free from the disease until the major outburst of it in 1584–5, which Creighton considers was one of the most serious epidemics of it ever experienced by that country.[5] This epidemic erupted in July 1584 in the small seaport of Wester Wemyss,[7] probably as a maritime importation from Flanders, because the civic authorities of Edinburgh decreed that month that no merchandise was to be shipped from Flanders on account of the prevalence of the *pest* there.[8] From Wester Wemyss the disease evidently spread to Perth as about the end of September James VI, who was then staying there with his retinue, was informed that plague had appeared in 5 or 6 houses in the town and promptly fled to Stirling.[9] The town chronicle records that the subsequent epidemic lasted from the end of September 1584 to August 1585 and that 1,427 citizens were destroyed by it.[10] Chambers opines that this toll could not have been less than one-sixth of the population of Perth.[11] This death-roll must have cast a deep gloom over the town, a gloom that was not lightened by the ordinance promulgated by the Kirk Session in May 1582 that no persons should marry, under pain of a fine of £10; that no wedding-feast should be held during the plague-time, and that a fine of £40 would be imposed on anyone who invited more than 4 persons 'on the side' to a banquet or a wedding.[12] As the kirk was convinced that the epidemic was a divine chastisement for the sins of the people of Perth, it was horror-stricken about the deity's reaction to such a flagrant sin in

plague-time when, on 11 October 1585, 'being the first Sunday of the holy communion, and of public fast and humiliation, appointed by the Kirk to be holily observed, that God of his mercy might remove this miserable plague from this town, George — and Elspeth Cudbert were both apprehended in naked bed together, in filthy fornication'.[1] George and Elspeth had been sent to the 'plague-lodges' as suspect cases of the disease and had evidently come to an agreement during their quarantine, as they were caught in the act in Elspeth's house after their discharge from the pest-house. The record is silent about the identity of the 'Peeping Tom'.

Later in the year Dysart, Kirkcaldy, and other places in Fifeshire were attacked[2] and Dysart seems to have suffered severely because on 26 October the civic authorities of Edinburgh sent an unspecified number of 'chalders meill, twenty stayne of butter, and half ane last of saip' to the people of Dysart.[3] From these ports plague spread inland in its usual radiating fashion between the Firths of Forth and Tay and possibly also to the north of the latter, as the Aberdeen authorities published an ordinance at the end of September 1584 for avoiding 'the contagious pest ringand in dyverss partis, townis, and places of the southt contrie'.[4] It included the usual watches to prevent strangers entering the town; the mooring of the ferryboat on the town side of the ferry during the hours from 4 p.m. to 8 a.m.—with the injunction that the ferryman must 'luge in the blokhous'—and the prohibition of an Aberdonian from travelling south without a special licence. The congregation of people at a 'wake' was forbidden. All beggars of Aberdonian birth must wear the arms of the town openly on their breasts and all other beggars were to be ejected from the town within three days.[5] Aberdeen apparently remained free, but the progressive extension of plague in the country to the south so aggravated the fear of the municipal authorities that in May 1585 they enacted the savage ordinance—'in caice onye infeckit persoun aryve or repair be sie or land to this burght or fredome thairof, or in caice ony induellar of this burght ressave, hous, or harbrie, or giff meat or drink to the infekit persoun or persounis, the man to be hangit, and the woman to be drownit'.[6] That this was no idle threat was manifested a few days later when two women were condemned to death for harbouring fugitives from the plague-area, although the death sentence was subsequently commuted to banishment from the borough.[7]

On 1 May 1585 'the Pest brake up in Edinburgh in the Flesh Mercat Closse, by the infectioun of a woman who had beene in Sanct Johnstoun, where the plague was',[8] and the civic authorities immediately ordered her house and the adjoining ones to be segregated.[9] Simultaneously the citizens were ordered to clean their privies and prevent them from discharging their

TABLE 14
Extracts from the records of the burgh of Edinburgh concerning the epidemic of plague in 1585

1585 May	9	The three remaining occupants of the infected house to be transported forthwith to 'the hows at the acres of umquhill Adam Purves, bewest St Rochis chapell'. The infected house to be cleansed with diligence.
	18	The city treasurer is authorized to erect 5 or 6 big huts on the moor for the accommodation of the plague-sick, 'and namelie for Walter Ochiltrie and his wyfe and bairnis', because one of their children has died of plague 'in thair house at the mylnis'. Instructions issued to cleansers. Swine, dogs and cats to be slaughtered.
	19	Three persons to be selected in every quarter to assist the baillies. The council to be convened every day. Relief to be provided for the poor and needy.
	20	Authorization of the provision of the necessary gear and materials for cleansing infected houses and goods. The Greyfriar port to be used exclusively as the exit for 'foul folks' proceeding to the moor.
	21	Irons equipped with shackles to be sent to the moor. All persons concealing the presence of plague to be executed, and the official executioner appointed. Thomas Wilsoun, 'presentlie infeckit with the pest and in poynt of deyth', together with Margaret Russell and his daughter, are to be tried for concealment and, if convicted, summarily executed.
	22	The 4 cleansers are to wear a uniform consisting of 'ane jowpe of black with a...of quhyte clayth sewit about the sam...'. A sum of £244 13s. 10d. has been collected for plague-relief in Perth.
	28	The University is to be closed. A distribution of sustenance is to be made among the plague-sick on the moor.
June	12	Owing to the prevalence of plague among the tenants of Innerleithen, the laird and the city council have agreed that the sick shall be sent to the moor.
	19	The markets in Leith must be stopped because they are 'contrair to the privileges of this burgh'.
	25	An emergency tax of £1,000 is to be levied for plague-relief, because 'throw the vehemencie of the pest the number of puir incressis dailie', the city's finances are already exhausted, and the rates and customs yield no revenue. As so many citizens have fled from the city, leaving their houses and shops in danger of being burgled, a town watch of 24 men is to be appointed, of whom 12 will watch by day and 12 by night. Each man will be paid £3 a month.
July	8	In order to secure good order on the moor, and to control the pest, all the 'fowle lugeis, fowle folk, and fowle geir [are to] be placeit be eist the greitt fowle luge, quhilk is at Purvessis Acres, and the clene folk, thair lugeis and geir to be west the samyn;...'. If any infection appears among the clean folk, the sick and their chattels are to be removed immediately to the foul side of the moor.
December	15	Because of the flight of the citizens from the pestilence, the kirk is now destitute of elders and deacons.
	17	The number of cases of plague is now so greatly diminished that the few remaining can be confined 'with thair kepers in the Quhyte hous,...'.
	22	Now that the frost has arrived, everyone having infected or suspect goods, even though they have been cleansed, must expose them in the open air, either by night or by day, and if any infection derives from any goods, their owners will be executed.
1586 March	23	Official announcement that the epidemic is extinct, the watchmen are discharged, and the city is replenished with inhabitants.

contents into the streets; to refrain from sheltering vagabonds, travellers, or strangers unless they notified the baillie of their ward within 3 hours of the arrival of a lodger, and to provide three persons in every quarter to assist the baillies to enforce the regulations. Pigs, dogs and cats found in the streets were to be slaughtered forthwith, and anyone concealing a case of plague was to be summarily executed. The progress of the epidemic and the further efforts of the civic authorities to arrest it are recorded in the city's archives,[1] from which source table 14 has been compiled. Chambers says that this epidemic sometimes destroyed as many as 24 people in a single night[2] and Birrel records that even though 'the haill people whilk was able to flee, fled out of the town; nevertheless there died of people which were not able to flee, fourteen hundred and some odd'.[3] Although Birrel was a burgess of Edinburgh this mortality figure can only have been a rough estimate in the absence of any municipal registration of death. Nevertheless it indicates a heavy proportionate death-roll, possibly as much as one-tenth of the population of the city.

It was in this month that James Henrysoun, a surgeon, was officially appointed to take care of the sick, to visit all the hospitals of the burgh and the poor who were sick or hurt, whatever their sickness might be. He was to be at the disposal of the City Council day and night, and the city contracted to supply him with any 'unguents, drogs, implasteris and uther medicaments' he might require. In return for his services he was to be paid an annual salary of £20 for the rest of his life.[4] It is pleasant to be able to record that in December 1585 he was thanked by the civic authorities for his good services, during which he had contracted plague himself and had lost his wife from the disease, and was exempted from all burgh taxes for the rest of his life.[5] Meanwhile the council made provision to house homeless children in the chapel of St Mary's Wynd and procured a heavy bier for the carriage of the plague-dead to burial on the moor to obviate the transport of corpses there on mens' backs.[6] Evidently conditions on the moor where the plague-sick were quartered in huts gave rise to concern because of the misbehaviour of some of the officials there, for in July 'the fowle hangman'—who was apparently the chief officer there—was laid in irons and sentenced to be bound to the gibbet until further orders, while the rest of the offending officials were discharged. The contacts of plague-sick people were also sent to the moor for an isolation period which in August was increased to 15 days, and any of these contacts who were allowed to return from the moor after that period must still confine themselves in their houses for another 15 days before they were free to mix with the townsfolk. The council also banned all gatherings in the city except at kirk and market and it imposed a curious prohibition upon the sale of chives, leeks and onions.[7]

The king repeated his behaviour at Perth and fled from his capital immediately the first alarm of plague was sounded in it. He went to Stirling, from which town he was chased in November 'by reason of the great plague there'.[1] He had moved first to Falkland, together with his Exchequer, but when plague appeared there in August he and the Exchequer went to Stirling.[2] By this time most of the coastal townships in the sheriffdom of Fife were involved in the epidemic and it was feared that the disease would be carried to the towns farther inland, especially Falkland where the king was in residence, by rascals and other miscreants. Accordingly all persons who were not entitled to be in that town by special permission or occupation were ordered to leave it for their homes within 6 hours of the publishing of the order on pain of death.[3] As the disease continued to spread around Perth, in Fifeshire, and to various places in Lothian, precautions—which needless to say were ineffective—were next taken to protect Stirling. All 'idle vagabonds and sturdy beggars' were to be expelled from the town and no one was to be admitted who came from beyond 12 miles east of Stirling who could not produce a 'clean testimonial', that is a certificate of freedom from any contact with plague. Furthermore the townsfolk were forbidden to leave Stirling or to return to it without official permission if they had been more than 12 miles east of it.[4] Chambers affirms that St Andrews was invaded in August and that plague raged there 'till upwards of four hundred people died, and the place was left almost desolate',[5] in all probability as much by desertion as by death. Dundee was involved in the epidemic in October; Dunse is said to have been scourged by it during 1586,[6] and Barbé asserts that Leith was ravaged by it that year.[7] This outburst of bubonic plague declined in the autumn of 1586 but *P. pestis* was not banished from Scotland. In 1586 it visited Niddrie, which may have suffered severely because on 22 June the Edinburgh authorities, 'in consideratioun that the seiknes of the pestilence is rissin and heavilie spred in the toun of Nudrie',[8] sent there 4 loads of meal to be distributed among the poor. Their action does them credit as 12 days before they had been told that plague had appeared in the Potteraw.[9] The next year Leith was attacked and Edinburgh experienced a nasty visitation of it. It was 'very grievous in Leith' in the autumn of 1587 and simultaneously many houses in Edinburgh were reported to be infected[10] The civic authorities were doubtful at first about the identity of the pestilence that was scourging Leith, so they sent 8 commissioners at the beginning of November to Leith to 'visy the deid corpssis for the mair certaintie'.[11] Their doubt was speedily dispelled by the eruption of the disease in the city within a few days. Chambers cites a legend that the disease started in Leith in September 'by opening up of some old kists' and he affirms that it persisted

there and in Edinburgh until February 1588, creating 'a great terror in Edinburgh and all the coast-side'.[1] If this disease was truly bubonic plague and not typhus fever the autumn of 1587 must have been exceptionally mild in Midlothian.

Although this outbreak seems to have been confined to a strip of country along the south shore of the Firth of Forth, the terror it excited spread much farther afield. A rumour of its presence at Old Cumnock constrained the town council of Ayr to repair the town gates at a cost of £7 19s. 6d. and pay 4s. 'to ane boy to rin to Cumnok for the pest.'[2] There is no evidence that Ayr's fear had any foundation in fact and in 1588 plague came no nearer to it than Paisley, which Creighton affirms was attacked in October of that year.[3]

Scotland appears to have had a respite of 8 or 9 years from bubonic plague after the subsidence of this outbreak. To guard against its importation from England in 1593 the Edinburgh City Council decreed in August of that year that all packages of cloth coming from London must be put 'in the overhous in the new hospitall' and that the owners of the cloth must stay in the building till further order.[4] Towards the end of the month, when a ship arrived from London, its crew and passengers were quarantined in the Newhaven at Leith.[5] There is no evidence that plague entered Scotland at this time, but four years later its maritime importation—probably through the port of Musselburgh—produced another extensive invasion of the country. Its presence was first recognized at Inveresk at the end of June 1597[6] and it apparently made rapid progress there, as a fortnight later the Edinburgh authorities gave 100 merks for the relief of the plague-stricken poor of the town.[7] It spread rapidly up the Esk valley and Dalkeith and Newbattle were invaded almost concurrently with Inveresk. On 22 July Edinburgh gave £20 for the relief of the plague-sick in Dalkeith and £50 for the relief of those in Musselburgh.[8] Early in August plague had 'greitly spred in the south parts'[9] and Dolphinton, Ednam, Sprouston, the 'toun of Sesforde', and 'Lyntoun' are officially named as involved in the epidemic. At this juncture the Edinburgh authorities prohibited all unauthorized intercourse, on pain of death, between its citizens and the inhabitants of the 'houssis about the Mostone, Borthwick Water, Ousnam water, others quha hes continuall repair in this burgh and in Leith'.[10] Four days later plague erupted in Leith and soon afterwards the civic authorities appointed 4 men to administer Leith during the epidemic as the baillies of that town were failing to do their duty. Simultaneously they ordered a ditch to be dug across the road in an attempt to isolate Leith from Edinburgh;[11] but they were not indifferent to the unhappy state of that town because on 17 August they made a loan of 500 merks to Leith for plague-relief, a laudable act as

TABLE 15

Extracts from the records of the burgh of Edinburgh relating to the epidemic of plague of 1597

August	5	Six neighbours appointed to watch at 3 gates, to inspect incomers and to keep out beggars.
	9	Order issued that 'nane be fund gangand throw the toun with mands, creills of heyring, fruitt, sybois, flouris or siclyk with claythis, weddis or ony geir to sell', under penalty of banishment.
		Beggars and able-bodied vagabonds, not residents of Edinburgh, ordered to leave the city.
		'Paul's Wark' to be repaired for the accommodation of poor children and others to be lodged and fed there at the city's expense.
	19	All segregated persons to be fed, if necessary at the city's expense. A. Ur and his wife appointed to be 'clengers'.
	22	No plague-dead to be buried in coffins in the common plague ground for lack of room.
	24	All poor persons segregated on account of plague to be given 16d. a day. A man and his wife appointed as 'clean cleaners'.
September	23	Nicoll Gilmure and his wife, convicted by an assize, of concealing the plague sickness of their child, are to 'be keipit ane quhyle in the vines and banist this burgh for evir...'.
		A paid watch of 24 men to be appointed, of whom 12 are to watch each night.
October	11	'Understanding that the woman clenger in Leyth, callit Lang Meg, is convict for conceilling of the pest and beand the caus of infectioun of sundry personns, ordanis the dome of hanging to be...execut upoun hir;....'

plague was then epidemic also in Edinburgh.[1] The efforts of the civic authority to control the disease are presented in table 15.[2] To these records must be added the sum of £145 8s. 11d., which includes an item of £8 for the provision of herrings, ale, coal, and other necessaries for 21 adults and an unspecified number of children who were either segregated in their houses or isolated in the pest-house. A further 45s., representing a rate of 3s. a day for 15 days, was paid to a family of the name of Symontoun. The fact that official provision was made for the subsistence of the plague-stricken poor indicates an important advance in the attitude of British society to a public calamity. Bubonic plague is answerable for an incalculable volume of human anguish, suffering, and loss; but it is responsible also for the conception of the social principle that a community has a moral responsibility for the welfare of its members. At the same time the city fathers of sixteenth-century Edinburgh were not befuddled with the false notion that everyone must receive equality of treatment, irrespective of his or her social position and value to the community. They made what they considered to be adequate provision for their indigent fellow-citizens, commensurate with their status

in the community, and they provided a larger relief for the Symontoun family, evidently because that family had won a higher standing in their society. In the final year of this century Perth is reported to have sustained 'ane great dead',[1] but there is no mention of 'plague' in connexion with this mortality. The absolute immunity of Aberdeen from bubonic plague in the second half of this century is, as Creighton pertinently comments,[2] a remarkable fact in the history of the disease in Scotland. Basically that immunity resulted from the fact that the house-rat population of Aberdeen was not dense enough to support an epizootic of rat-plague, and this sparseness of rodents resulted in turn from the early use of stone for the building material of the ordinary dwelling-house in Aberdeen and the contemporaneous absence of thatch as the roofing material.

The situations of the different places mentioned in the Scottish records as having been visited by bubonic plague in this century are shown on the map, figure 32. It is noteworthy that a majority of the places attacked were either sea- or river-ports and that the area of the country affected was relatively small. It is obvious that these Scottish visitations by bubonic plague were almost entirely consequential upon the maritime importations of *P. pestis* from English and European ports, most often in all probability from Baltic ports. It is also obvious that the restricted area of the activity of the disease in Scotland exposes the nonsense, so often encountered in the literature, of plague sweeping like a 'Black Death' at terrifying speed universally over this—or any other—land.

After the cessation of the epidemic at the close of 1576 or early in 1577, the Irish records that are accessible to English students appear to be silent about bubonic plague for the remainder of this century. It is possible, however, that there were localized 'trailer' outbreaks of it during this period which are hidden in municipal archives, local chronicles, and personal papers and have not been considered of sufficient importance by Irish national and local historians to merit their attention.

CHAPTER 7

THE FIRST QUARTER
OF THE SEVENTEENTH CENTURY

England and Wales

The pattern of the behaviour of bubonic plague in this period was a repetition of its behaviour in the preceding century. There were several major outbursts of the disease, separated by intervals during which it gradually became spontaneously extinguished because of a natural loss of virulence by *P. pestis*. These outbursts succeeded the maritime importations of fresh, virulent strains of the bacillus, and they were succeeded by 'trailer' epidemics affecting one or more urban concentrations of humans and house-rats, with or without some extension to villages in the surrounding neighbourhood. In some places plague smouldered as an enzootic disease among the rats for variable periods of time in the intervals between its major outbursts. The transmission of *P. pestis* from these enzootic foci to urban concentrations of house-rats previously free from it, either by haphazard rat contacts or by the chance, passive transport of infected rats or 'blocked' fleas, produced scattered, localized epizootics of rat-plague which often but not invariably engendered outbreaks of human plague. Sometimes the epizootic led only to the appearance of the human disease in a few households in the affected town. Each and all of these visitations subsided spontaneously, either because of the induced hibernation of the 'plague-fleas' by frosty weather or because of the reduction of the particular house-rat population below the minimal density necessary to sustain an epizootic of rat-plague.

The first notice of bubonic plague in the British Isles in this period occurs in Scottish records, which may explain why some contemporary writers accused James I and his retinue of transporting it from Edinburgh to London, where there was a major outburst of the disease in 1603. In Scotland it was reported to be active in 1600 at Findhorn and other places in Morayshire,[1] and the publication by the Dundee authorities of regulations to prevent its extension[2] suggests that it may have been widespread in the surrounding countryside. The next year it erupted in the summer: 'none knew how or

whence. Some suspected it to have had its rise upon the Buchan Coast out of a Dutch cask with onyons and hops cast ashoare; but, not to disput, the pestilence spread from Forth to the North, and raged here the length of Glenelg. None dyed there nor in our farr Highlands and north isles; most of our people run to the hills, the purer aire.'[1] Craill in Fifeshire, the parishes of Eglesham, Eastwood, and Pollock in Renfrewshire, and Glasgow are said to have been involved in this outbreak;[2] but it was probably typhus fever which provoked the royal proclamation[3] against the pestilence which was afflicting Glasgow in mid-December 1601.[4] Towards the end of January, the infected people of Craill, who had been driven out on to the neighbouring moor, began to wander about the countryside seeking food and shelter, and as their wandering portended the spread of the disease—which was un-doubtedly typhus fever—the sheriff of Fife was ordered to ensure that they were provisioned.[5]

Comrie[6] notes that a visitor was appointed to go from Stirling to Glasgow to report upon the prevalence of plague in that city and that synchronously the town council imposed restrictions upon intercourse with Edinburgh, St Andrews, Kirkcaldy, Kinghorn, and Tonybane, which were evidently thought to be infected. Glasgow's pestilence was quickly extinguished, for on 6 January a cleaner was allowed to go there from Edinburgh 'to clenge the persouns infectit thair with the pest'.[7] There were numerous cases of what passed for plague in Edinburgh in January 1602, according to the tenant of the Whitehouse where the disease first appeared.[8] He lost five of his children from it and all his goods, for these were burnt when his house was disinfected. By the end of the month the alarm in Edinburgh was such that the meeting of the Secret Council at Holyrood House was suspended until 1 May,[9] when it met at Dunfermline. Early in February, as 'the pest had laitlie rissin in Wardlaw's Close', the civic authorities appointed a foul cleaner at a wage of 20 merks a month and a clean cleaner at 8 merks.[10] About three weeks later the city treasurer was directed to appoint and pay four watchmen for the Sciennes, whither the sick people had apparently been removed, and to build huts for them.[11] Some time during the next two months this outbreak of typhus fever must have ceased, because on 19 May a pension of £10 was awarded to William Ur, the foul cleaner, for his services during the outbreak,[12] and a week later James Henrysoun, the plague-surgeon, had his pension increased by £40 in recognition of his services.[13]

Plague seems to have been somewhat widespread in the south of Scotland from June 1603 until the end of the year,[14] and its appearance in Edinburgh in the early autumn made the household at Holyrood House decidedly apprehensive.[15] Prestonpans and North Berwick appear to have been more

severely attacked in the summer as £468 17s. 6d. was collected in Edinburgh in September for the relief of their plague-stricken inhabitants.[1] Plague was possibly active also in Ayrshire as the corporation of Ayr paid 9s. 'to two boys who came from Mauchline and Ochiltree with news of the pest'.[2]

James I and his retinue can be exonerated from the charge against them because plague was active in a number of English towns in 1602 and present in London, according to Wilson,[3] at least two months before James entered the city; it was certainly active in Stepney in March.[4] It was raging in the Low Countries and it is very probable that it was imported from Amsterdam in the summer of 1602 along with refugees from that city, because the Privy Council's prohibition of their landing[5] ignored the ship-rat. Plague may also have been introduced from Danzig to Wapping, where two houses were reported in October as infected and all their occupants dead.[6] Yarmouth, where 80 plague-deaths occurred in one week in September, seems also to have been infected from Amsterdam.[7] As in 1593, London was the principal focus for the outburst of 1603 and suffered grievously from it, although as the Allyn letters[8] show there were families living within the walled city that passed unscathed through both those epidemics of bubonic plague. Wilson notes that plague appeared in Southwark early in March,[9] but the death of Elizabeth I diverted official attention from it, and it 'attracted little or no attention before the end of April'.[10] He reproduces a Bill of Mortality which shows that no plague-death was recorded among the 78 burials returned for the first week in January but 32 were included among the 122 burials in the last week of May.[11] James I reached London on 7 May[12] and the first specified plague-burial in the register of a city parish is dated the 11th,[13] from which date the epidemic increased in violence and extent according to the Venetian secretary[14, 15] until its peak during the last week in August. It is noteworthy that he reports that the weather in May was unusually hot and that it aroused a fear that plague would spread, especially as the authorities had taken no action against it 'except to kill the dogs and mark the houses by fastening upon them a great printed paper with these words, "Lord have mercy upon us"'.[15] Towards the end of May, however, they made some efforts to control the epidemic. On the 29th they ordered all gentlemen not in attendance at court or having special reason to be in the city to leave it.[16] On 23 June they adjourned Trinity Term,[17] and on 6 July the King's state entry into London was postponed until the winter.[18] Five days later St James' Fair—which was held on 25 July, the day chosen for the coronation—was postponed for 8 or 10 days,[19] and on 8 August they cancelled Bartholomew and Sturbridge Fairs 'and all others within fifty miles of London'.[20] According to the Venetian secretary, they issued strict orders in mid-September that no one was to

leave London,[1] and he added that after a temporary abatement of the epidemic a few hot days had so revived it that 3,056 persons had been destroyed in one week,[2] many of them so rapidly that they were 'well and merry, dead and buried the same day'.[3]

Plague continued to rage in London throughout September and it was still so prevalent in mid-October that Michaelmas Term was adjourned until

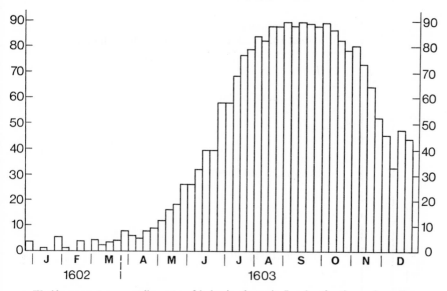

41. Weekly percentage mortality-rates of bubonic plague in London for the weeks ending 23 December 1602 to 22 December 1603. Total deaths in the seventeen weeks from the beginning of July to the end of October were 32,754. Total deaths in each of the seventeen weeks in July, August, September and October were: 445, 612, 1,186, 1,728, 2,256, 2,077, 3,054, 2,853, 3,385, 3,078, 3,129, 2,456, 1,961, 1,831, 1,312, 766, 625.

St Martin's Day.[4] Indeed it did not subside until the onset of very cold weather in December[5] (see figure 41). Stow, cited by Creighton,[6] gives the figure of 38,244 as the total number of burials registered from 23 December 1602 to 23 December 1603 in the city and liberties and assigns 30,578, or practically 80 per cent of them, to bubonic plague. He also states that fugitives from London were kindly received and treated in some places but bitterly reviled and denied help in others, and that many died near good towns in fields and barns and by the roadside.[7] Another authority declares that in this epidemic the total and the plague-mortality figures for the period equivalent to that in 1593 were respectively 37,294 and 30,561,[8] which give a plague-mortality rate of nearly 82 per cent. A marginal note in the burials register

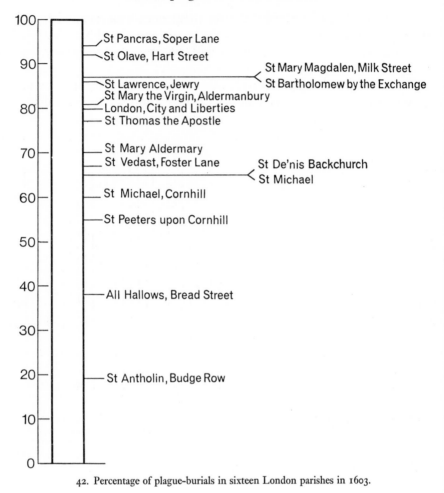

42. Percentage of plague-burials in sixteen London parishes in 1603.

for May of St Peeters upon Cornhill gives the identical figures[1] cited by Creighton from Stow.

As is customary with bubonic plague, the distribution and intensity of this epidemic in the metropolitan parishes were both uneven. Whereas it was recorded in St Mary Magdalen on 11 May,[2] the first plague-burial entered in the register of St Michael, Cornhill is dated 24 June and has the marginal note, 'the first of the plague'.[3] The variation in its intensity is shown by the difference in its mortality-rates, which range from 19 per cent of the total registered burials in the parish of St Antholin, Budge Row,[4] to 94 per cent in that of St Pancras, Soper Lane.[5] Figure 42 illustrates the variations

in its intensity in fifteen London parishes whose burials registers are complete for 1603.

The spread of plague to Westminster discovered a 'very unruly' body of citizens 'near St Clement's Church and the fields' who had to be forcibly imprisoned in their infected houses.[1] Cox asserts that the disease raged in St Margaret's parish from June 1603 to September 1604, an impossible continuity for bubonic plague if the winter of 1604 was a normal one, but there is no doubt that the parish was scourged because he records that its churchwardens paid £151 17s. 7d. 'for the graves of 451 poor folk'.[2] They also paid for the slaughter in the parish of 502 dogs at a cost of 1d. each animal.[3] Creighton states that from 14 July to 20 October 1603, 832 burials were registered in Westminster, of which 723—or more than 86 per cent— were victims of plague.[4] He gives also the figures for the total and the plague-burials in Stepney, Newington-Butts, Islington, Lambeth, and Hackney, which yield respective plague-mortality rates of 94·5, 89·7, 84·5, 97·0, and 88·0 per cent. If the mortality figures are accurate they indicate that the epidemic was much more deadly in these overcrowded suburbs of London than in the city itself. In the parishes in the liberties the worst hit were those of St James Clerkenwell[5] and St Martin-in-the-Fields[6] with registered burials during the year of 811 and 588 respectively, to which in the former August contributed 336. The degree of their excessive mortalities while bubonic plague was epidemic in them is revealed by comparison with their average burials for the three years immediately preceding and succeeding 1603. These figures are for St James 111 and 187;[7] for St Martin 87 and 147.[8]

Among the out-parishes the register of Kensington[9] contains the note that this year was the year of 'the great plague' in the parish, and 31 burials are recorded compared with an average of 8 for the preceding three years. In the parish of Stoke Newington the burials register shows 65 entries—compared with 11 in 1602—of which 16 are in September and 10 in October;[10] in Tottenham 79 burials were registered, of which 44 are marked as victims of plague,[11] while in Wandsworth more than 100 plague-deaths were recorded.[12] On the opposite side of London most of the out-parishes seem to have been more or less involved in the epidemic and it extended eastwards along both banks of the Thames into Essex and Kent.

In the Home Counties it appeared at Datchet[13] and at Hampton Court, where 2 or 3 plague-deaths occurred each day for an unspecified period among the retainers who were living in tents pitched around the round tower.[14] In Essex it 'swept off great numbers' of the townspeople of Colchester.[15] In Kent it invaded the parishes of West and East Malling, Offham, Addington, Ryarsh, Wateringbury, Yalding, and East Peckham,[16] and at

Maidstone the burials register of All Saints parish records the names of 136 plague-dead,[1] compared with its average annual burial-rate of less than 60. The parish registers of Chislehurst and Strood also record an excessive number of burials this year, to wit, 63 compared with an annual average of 10 in the former; in the latter 44 compared with 14.[2] Unfortunately Cox does not give the monthly burials for these parishes and in their absence it is not certain that these excessive mortalities were caused by bubonic plague. A report in October stated that Kent was so generally infected with plague that few towns on the road from London to Dover were free from it.[3] In the neighbouring counties of Surrey and Sussex the epidemic involved Dorking— where the parish register records 108 burials with the ominous note that 'many were buried in gardens or fields'[4]—and Pycombe, where the parish register lists 15 plague-burials;[5] but a study of the parish registers of these counties would probably reveal more visitations.

Westwards from London plague spread along the Thames valley to Oxford, where the colleges and halls kept their gates constantly shut day and night, the shops were all shut, the market closed, and the streets emptied of people.[6] From some point in the valley it spread south-westwards into Wiltshire, causing an order to be made at the Devizes Sessions in mid-October 'for avoydinge the greate infection of the plauge dispersed almoste in all the countries of this realme'.[7] This order directed that a watch should be kept in every town and village in the county for the arrest of all vagrants, who were to be summarily ejected if they were suspected to be 'dangerous for infection'. No ale or drink was to be sold outside corporate and market towns, and in them only by licence. A payment of 40s. a week was to be made to the poor of Westbury, because most of that town's inhabitants were weavers and spinners and, as various houses were infected, they were 'utterly impoverished'. Upon the receipt of a certificate of the weekly quantity required, corn was to be delivered from Warminster and Lavington, at market prices, to persons from Westbury deputed to receive it. The terror aroused by plague is revealed by the complaint that William Batt of Crofton gave shelter in his house for three nights to 'a wandering woman and her child, coming from London as it was supposed, to the great danger of the inhabitants of Crofton'. When told he must not shelter them William, to his credit, 'did irreverantly abuse them with most sclanderous speeches'.[8] Some three months later a second order committed to prison for one month people in infected places in the county who refused to remain segregated in their infected houses. It also directed that weekly sums of money were to be paid to many weavers in Salisbury, Devizes, and Fisherton Anger, who were losing work because plague was prevalent in those places.[9] Marlborough was

also infected at this time, and in Salisbury the disease augmented so seriously in September that on 4 October a special rate was levied on the county for plague-relief there.[1] Farther west plague was raging, according to a contemporary chronicle, in Bristol, which suffered the most calamitous visitation from plague at this time in its history, losing more than 3,000 of its citizens between July 1603 and January 1604.[2] A companion chronicle, dating the visitation from 28 July 1602 to 20 February 1604, declares that the plague-mortality comprised 2,440 deaths.[3]

In the Midlands Tewkesbury, with 23 plague-burials entered in its parish register,[4] and Walsall with 16,[5] experienced comparatively mild visitations. Dullingham may have suffered more severely, but Sweeting regrettably merely states that there was an excessive mortality in the parish this year.[6] Plague appears to have been active in the neighbourhood of Melton Mowbray as the churchwardens paid two men 6d. 'for keepinge the townsfolke of Tythe and Asswell out of o^r market being suspected for the plague'.[7] It must have been violently epidemic at Stamford because Creighton affirms that the town sustained a plague death-roll of nearly 600.[8] Presumably it was the Nottinghamshire village of Stamford therefore which was declared to be still free from plague in October although the disease was spreading in the surrounding district.[9] Cambridge seems to have been fortunate to escape with a slight invasion of a single parish, St Clement's, 10 of whose parishioners were buried on Jesus Green, which had been appropriated by the municipality for the interment of plague-dead.[10]

In East Anglia several places had excessive mortalities in 1603, but it is not certain that bubonic plague was wholly or even partly responsible for all of them because smallpox was simultaneously epidemic in the region, notably in Ipswich,[11] where the corporation took action to prevent plague from being imported from London. As early as May it ordered the removal of all persons in houses infected with 'the sickness'—which was possibly smallpox and not bubonic plague in this instance—to the Sick House, and in July a Great Court elected four bailiffs who were to select four of the most reliable townsmen to supervise the infected houses, the burial of the dead, and the provision of meat and drink to the sick, and two women to attend the sick and act as undertakers. At a wage of 6d. a day two gravediggers were also appointed, conditional upon their acceptance of isolation in a house specially built for them, to which food and other necessaries would be brought by an attendant appointed at a wage of 7s. a week. In September the corporation prohibited any ship from coming nearer the town than Greenwich Ness, about 1½ miles distant, and placed a day guard at Stoke Bridge, where the London waggons entered the town, and at Stoning Cross to prevent the entry 'of persons

suspected of the Plague'.[1] It must be noted here, however, that the register of the Ipswich parish of St Nicholas records 4 deaths 'of the plague' in a total of 50 burials in 1603.[2] The analysis of the monthly burials shows that there were 33, or 66·0 per cent, in the four 'plague-months' of July–October. In 1604 there were 55 burials in the parish, of which 26 or 40·7 per cent occurred in the four 'plague-months' and 22 or 40 per cent between 26 March and 1 July. There seems little doubt therefore that outbreaks of bubonic plague and of smallpox overlapped in Ipswich during the years 1603 and 1604.

If, as seems probable, Ipswich experienced a mild visitation of plague at this time, Lowestoft appears to have been less fortunate. Jones affirms that there were 35 burials in the parish in each of the years 1600 and 1601, that the number rose to 81 in 1602 and to 316 in 1603, 280 of which occurred within a period of 5 months.[3] Unfortunately he omits to name the particular months and in the absence of a monthly analysis of the registered burials this excessive mortality cannot certainly be attributed to bubonic plague, especially in view of his report that smallpox was simultaneously present in the county. Perhaps some future historian of Suffolk will determine the incidence and assess the effects of these two epidemic diseases upon the county in 1603–4 by a study of its parishes' burial registers.

It was bubonic plague, however, that destroyed 3,076 of the citizens of Norwich—in 1602 according to Blomefield[4]—and was still increasing in its epidemic violence there in September 1603[5]. As this death-roll probably represented one-quarter of the city's population, its effect upon the civic life of Norwich would seem to merit the attention and judgement of any future historian of that ancient city.

Returning to the Midlands, plague was epidemic at Northampton in September[6] and the burials registered in the town's four parishes were 107 in All Saints; 20 in St Giles; 16 in St Peter, and 88 in St Sepulchre, making a total of 231.[7] Regrettably Cox does not give the figures for the monthly burials, but he does note that 'in many cases *plague* is written before these burial entries; in other instances *p.* or *pest*'.[8] At Boston the market was closed because of the prevalence of plague[9] and Chester experienced a disastrous visitation of it about this time because Creighton avers that in the three years of 1602–5 it destroyed 1,313 persons there.[10] This mortality figure does not agree, however, with his previous notice[11] of an unspecified number of plague-deaths in 1602; 650 in 1603; 986 in 1604; 812 in 1605, and about 100 up to January 1606, when he says the epidemic ceased. Some future historian of Chester will perhaps resolve this discrepancy by a critical study of the city's parochial burial registers.

It erupted at Chester 'in one Glover's house, in St John's-lane' and killed 7 of the inmates in a short time.[1] The subsequent epidemic increased in intensity until 60 deaths occurred weekly, and Ormerod quotes a contemporary manuscript* as stating that plague accounted for 650 deaths in a total death-roll of 711 in 1603, a mortality-rate of more than 92 per cent. It is convenient to continue the history of bubonic plague at Chester to the end of the quinquennium now, because if Ormerod is correct in his chronological details both the Lysons[2] and Creighton[3] are at fault in theirs. He reports that in 1603 many plague-sick persons were removed from their houses to cabins built at the riverside, close to the New Tower. The next year the disease was 'very hot' in the city and a great many people were sent to the cabins. Some of the justices and 'a great number of citizens' fled into the surrounding countryside,[4] but the mayor stayed at his post and gave noble service while plague ravaged his household. The Court of Exchequer was removed to Tarvin, the Michaelmas Assizes were held at Nantwich, all the fairs were cancelled, and the watch was not kept on Midsummer Eve. During this epidemic 812 plague-deaths were recorded.[5] He affirms that it did not subside until the middle of 1605 and that plague was not extinguished in Chester until the ensuing February—February 1606 by our calendar. He quotes from the Rogers MS the statement that the eventual total of plague-deaths was 1,313 and that additional deaths from other diseases—a fact that local historians might note with advantage—occurred during its prevalence.[6]

Other places attacked by plague in the north Midlands this year were Brimington, a chapelry of Chesterfield,[7] Congleton,[8] and Leicester, where Kelly says that the disease broke out immediately after the departure of the royal family on the 24th of June. He opines that it was possibly imported by visitors from Stamford, where it was then epidemic, crowding into the town to see the royal party.[9] Fortunately Leicester's visitation on this occasion seems to have been a mild one and of short duration—the registered burials in the parishes of St Martin and AllSouls [*sic*] were only about 10 more than the annual average[10]—but it is of historical interest as it was responsible for the first use of hurdles to cordon infected houses.

In the northern counties plague was epidemic at Hull, Newcastle-upon-Tyne, and probably at York in 1603. Hull evidently experienced a grievous epidemic as the expenses incurred by its corporation testify. Commencing on 23 July 1603, payments ranging from 17s. to £2 18s. 8d. were made every week for 56 weeks for the relief of the plague-stricken poor, the total sum disbursed amounting to £97 12s. 7d. To this sum must be added further relief payments for 31 weeks amounting to £53 7s. 2d. Then there were

* Rogers MS.

payments for 'reparying of the lodge and houses in the carr for infected persons and for loss and damage of grasse...and waisted £5 6s. 8d.'.[1] Other expenses were the weekly wages of the wardens and watchmen of the isolated plague-sick, which amounted to £7 6s. 0d., and the cost of removing the plague-sick and their necessary goods and chattels to the isolation camp amounting to £67 19s. 3d. Altogether 788 persons received relief to some extent during this outbreak.[2] The disease spread to the outlying village of Hessle, where additional plague-relief expenses were incurred by the municipality of Hull. These amounted to £67 11s. 5d. and comprised these payments:

> To visited people in Hessle, £46 7s. 5d.
> For stronge watter, turfes, soape, and other nessacaryes, £2 15s. 5d.
> Allowed unto a Crier of the visited, 4s. 6d.
> Payd to Wardens, £7 14s. 0d.
> Allowed per monyes assessed upon familys infected and shutte up, £4 15s. 1d.
> Mr. Parrot pd. in monye to the towne, £5 15s. 0d.[3]

Concerning York, Sellers avers that it suffered more severely from plague in the seventeenth century than at any previous time in its history. She says that it erupted in Newcastle-upon-Tyne in July 1603 and that two months later it had spread south to several villages in the Tadcaster and Wetherby district, some 10 miles to the south-west of York. Stringent protective measures were thereupon enforced in that city. The feasts of the trading companies were prohibited and public begging was forbidden. An officer was appointed to kill all cats and dogs found wandering in the streets at a rate of 2d. for each animal killed plus their pelts. Suspect cases of plague were to be removed at once either to Hob Moor, about a mile outside Micklegate Bar, or to Bootham Stray, about the same distance from Bootham Bar, where tents or some sort of temporary buildings had been erected for their accommodation.[4] Needless to say these measures were ineffective against the introduction of *P. pestis* to the city, but the exact time of its entrance is unknown. After the customary winter intermission plague recrudesced there in the spring of 1604 and rapidly blazed up into another violent epidemic which caused a panic exodus of all who could fly from the city, including the civic officials, and a death-roll estimated to be about 3,512.[5] Sellers adds that the registers of 17 of the most populous parishes of the city show a total of 2,000 burials between 1 May and 31 December 1604. Scaife notes that the first entry, presumably of a plague-burial, in the register of the parish of St Mary, Castlegate in 1604 is dated 23 July, and that between this date and 24 March 114 burials were registered.[6] Laycock, who states that plague was transported from London to Pontefract in the autumn of 1603 and thence to York in the spring of 1604, relates the tradition that it erupted in 'The Hag-worm's

Nest' or Beedham's-court on the west side of the river Ouse; that the low-lying parishes were first affected, the order of their invasion being St John, Micklegate–St Michael, Spurriergate–St Mary, Castlegate–All Saints, Pavement–All Saints, North Street.[1] He notes that the first plague-burial was entered in the register of St Michael, Spurriergate on 4 June and that plague destroyed at least one-quarter of the city's population, which he estimates as 11,000. The two parochial dates of 4 June and 23 July are of great significance because they reveal how slowly bubonic plague spreads by haphazard rat contacts in an urban population. Laycock affirms that all communication between the city and the surrounding countryside was severed and that stone crosses were erected on the principal roads from 1 to 2 miles outside the city so that markets could be held at them.[2] In spite of these precautions the disease spread so widely in the county that the archbishop reported mournfully in October that his diocese was 'sore visited with the sickness'.[3] There are discrepancies about the exact time, duration, and severity of this visitation in the accounts given of it by different authors. These could probably be resolved by a comprehensive study of the episcopal and parochial registers in a thesis for a higher degree of the University of York, and it is to be hoped that such a study will be made, for an epidemic which may have destroyed upwards of one-quarter of the city's population must have exerted some effect upon its social and civic development.

It must be mentioned that Creighton[4] and Mullett[5] record numerous other English towns and villages that were visited by bubonic plague in 1603, and the interested reader is referred to their works.

During 1604 plague extended the area of its epidemic activity in England and Wales and Creighton avers that there were 'few parts of England from which evidence of plague does not come in the years immediately following the great plague in London in 1603'.[6] In the course of its spread southwards from Newcastle-upon-Tyne it was probable that Durham City would be involved, and the burials register of St Giles's parish records 18 plague-deaths between the beginning of September 1604 and the ensuing 25th of January.[7] There is also a note in this register about the extermination by plague of a family of the name of Ourd.[8] South of York the parish of Monk Fryston was severely attacked in September 1604. Between the 10th of that month and 16 April 1605 there were 39 burials, 24 of which (61·5 per cent) are marked as plague-burials, and of these 2 families contributed 11.[9]

Just as York seems to have been a focus for the dissemination of plague in Yorkshire, so Chester seems to have exerted a similar influence in Cheshire, in which county Nantwich and Malpas are reported as attacked by the disease. The former town is said to have been invaded from Chester towards

the end of June. It was precipitately abandoned by all its well-to-do inhabitants and among those who remained about 430 deaths from all causes were registered between June 1604 and March 1605.[1] As no information is given about the monthly burial figures it is not possible to say how many of the deaths may have been plague-deaths. Ormerod states that Malpas 'suffered severely from the plague in the early part of the seventeenth century', but as he quotes only 2 entries of plague-deaths in the parish register in June 1604[2] there is some doubt about the severity of its visitation at this time. In the contiguous counties of Shropshire and Staffordshire there are records of plague in 1604 at Shrewsbury, Myddle, Condover, and Mucklestone; but it is probable that the disease was more widely dispersed in these counties. Towards the end of the year a petition from the townsfolk referred to the grievous and lengthy visitation of Shrewsbury by plague,[3] and in St Mary's parish 119 burials were registered between 2 June—when plague appeared in the parish—and the ensuing March.[4] As most of these occurred before November they were in all probability plague-burials. The excessive mortality experienced by this parish in the year 1604 by our calendar is shown by a comparison of the 122 burials then registered with the annual average of 25 for the 10 years immediately preceding[5] and of 26 for the equivalent succeeding period.[6] At Myddle the parish register records the plague-deaths of 4 members of one household; but as there is no evidence in the register of any excessive mortality in the parish during the first quinquennium of this century,[7] its invasion by plague was evidently restricted to this one house. According to the parish register plague erupted at Condover in August,[8] but the visitation was fortunately a slight one. Compared with annual averages of 19·5 and 17 for the decennial periods immediately preceding[9] and succeeding[10] 1604, the 30 burials registered in that year do not represent a severe epidemic of plague, even though 16 or rather more than 53 per cent of them are marked 'plague'.[11] In 1605 there were 17 burials in this parish, of which 5 are marked 'plague' in the register,[12] so it seems that after the usual winter intermission there was a feeble recrudescence of the disease, possibly confined to 1 or 2 dwellings. The parish register of Mucklestone contains this notice about the rumoured distribution of plague in 1604: 'Note that this yere was an Universall plage. U.Z. Srowesberry, Wichchurch, Lichefeld, Eccleshall, Chebsey, Panckriche, Staffard, Stone, Olton, Addersly, Chester cyty, Nauntwich, Weddensbury, Northwiche, Alldringgain, Anlym, Hodnet, Usxenton Pochshe, The cyty of Coventry, Warwicke, Bristol, York, London, Glocester cityes.'[13] Plague appeared in Coventry about the middle of May and some time during that month it invaded Rugby,[14] and in the parish register of Stratford-upon-Avon 7 burials are marked *de peste* (2 in

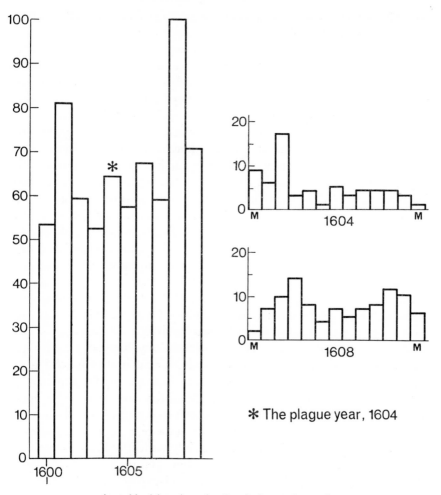

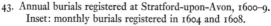

43. Annual burials registered at Stratford-upon-Avon, 1600–9.
Inset: monthly burials registered in 1604 and 1608.

March and 5 in April), this year. As at least 5 of these marked burials appear
to be those of children, 'the plague' in this instance was undoubtedly one
of the childhood fevers, possibly diphtheria in view of its seasonal occurrence.
Moreover, there was no excessive mortality in Stratford in 1604; in fact the
total of registered burials, 64, was lower than the annual average of 66 for the
decennium commencing at 1600.[1] Furthermore an analysis of the monthly
burials shows a seasonal curve that is not indicative of bubonic plague (see
figure 43). It is noteworthy that there was an excessive mortality in Stratford

in 1608 and that bubonic plague was not responsible for that mortality either.[1] The most likely cause of it would seem to be an epidemic of smallpox.

In the Gloucester parish of St Nicholas, 42 plague-burials were registered in 1604[2] and in the adjoining counties Bath[3] and Kidderminster[4] are said to have been attacked. A report from Bath declared that plague erupted there early in May and that 50 deaths from it occurred in the succeeding 14 weeks.[5] In a Bill of Mortality for the period from mid-May to 20 September 88 deaths from all causes are recorded, of which 77 are ascribed to bubonic plague.[6] It also records that in each of 3 houses 8 of the occupants died of plague, which probably means that those families were exterminated. The register of the Abbey Church shows 51 burial entries this year, of which 86·2 per cent were registered in the four months of June–September. The peak of the epidemic occurred in July, much earlier than usual, and the outbreak was extinguished in October. One family, which was almost certainly exterminated, lost both parents, two daughters and a son, in thirty days from 14 July.[7] With Bath involved it is not surprising that Bristol was attacked. Plague was reported to be raging there early in July;[8] but until the city's parish burials registers have been critically studied the duration and mortality of this visitation will remain unknown. Other places in the Midlands said to have been attacked this year are Sandridge, Nassington, Shelton, Stamford Baron, and Oxford. The first of these may, however, have escaped because an entry in the parish register reads: 'Found in the Church box the 17th of June xxvys vid whereof gyven to Cattines wif for searching of Lambard suspected of the plague vs.'[9] No information is available about the result of her search and the authors who record this note evidently did not consider it necessary to include a study of the registers in their history of the parish. Nassington, however, was certainly visited by plague because the parish register shows 68 burials between June and the succeeding January and the inference is that most of them were plague-burials.[10] At Shelton it seems probable that plague was confined to one household,[11] but the burials register of St Martin's parish at Stamford Baron contains the names of 125 people 'wch departed by the sicknes namely the plague',[12] a mortality that may well have been a dire calamity in that parish, the population of which probably did not exceed 500 souls. At Oxford plague erupted according to Boase[13] after the king and his court had left that city. It is to be regretted that he supplies no information about either the severity or the duration of this visitation, but it is known that it claimed one victim of local importance, namely, '(John) Eveleigh, Principal of Hart Hall'.[14]

South of the Thames plague was active in 1604 in varying intensity in numerous places in Sussex, Hampshire, Wiltshire, Dorsetshire, Somerset-

shire, and Devonshire. At Horsham, where the parish register shows no excessive number of burials this year, it was possibly confined to a single household.[1] By contrast Southampton is reported to have been ravaged by it, even more grievously than by the terrible visitation of 1583 according to Shillington,[2] who reports that there were 161 deaths in the small Flemish colony alone. Plague apparently erupted at Cranborne in Dorsetshire towards the end of June and from then until its last victim was buried on 11 December its toll was 71 lives.[3] The analysis of the monthly burials (see figure 44) shows that a majority of these deaths, 62 per cent in fact, occurred in the two months of July and August. Smart[3] remarks that several families were seemingly exterminated. One family contributed 8 victims, another 6, and two others 5 each. As the annual burials at Cranborne averaged only 14 for the two years immediately preceding and succeeding this visitation, it is evident that it suffered severely from bubonic plague on this occasion.[4]

Salisbury also suffered severely. Merriman says that the table of burials in the 3 city parishes—supplied by Hatcher—shows that in August alone the deaths numbered 235. At the Hilary Sessions it was reported that plague was simultaneously active at Devizes, Marlborough, Fisherton Anger* and Calne, and the justices accordingly levied a rate of 40*s.* weekly on each of the first two towns and one of 30*s.* on Fisherton Anger for the relief of their plague-stricken poor.[5]

The visitations of Bath and Bristol have already been noted. In the adjoining county Exeter experienced a small outbreak which Pickard considers is of particular interest 'on account of Exeter's successful control measures'.[6] These were started in November 1603 with the issue of notices warning people from infected places not to come to St Nicholas Fair. A week later the importation of goods from any infected place was prohibited on pain of a fine of £5 and disfranchisement, and the townsfolk were forbidden to lodge or receive strangers into service on pain of a fine of 40*s.* for each offence. Some time later 8 persons were chosen from each of the city's wards to act as watchers, and on 1 May 1604 a poor rate was levied and the pest-house made ready for the reception of patients. In July Lammas and St Nicholas Fairs were cancelled. Needless to say these precautions did not prevent plague from creeping into the city and of 62 burials registered during 1604 it was held responsible for 26.[7] As the annual burials for the decennium 1594–1603 averaged 35, it is obvious that plague was not really epidemic in Exeter on this occasion, although that fortunate fact owed nothing to the municipal precautions. It is possible that the disease was for some reason, now unknown, confined to a particular group of houses.

* Fisherton Anger or Auger was a tiny parish, situated about 1 mile west of the centre of Salisbury. Since the seventeenth century it has disappeared by absorption into a contiguous parish.

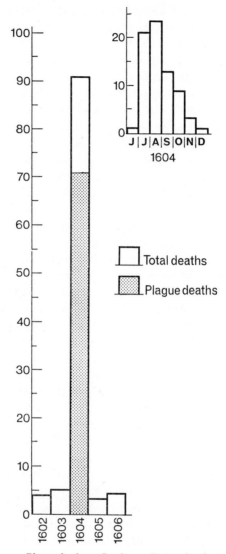

44. Plague deaths at Cranborne, Dorset, in 1604.

In London plague seems to have smouldered throughout the first 9 or 10 months of 1604, with short, intermittent spasms of activity in the spring and summer. It was typhus fever and not plague, however, that was active in January 'owing to the carelessness with which bedding and clothes of persons who died of the disease are being used by the living'.[1] There are numerous

short references in the *Calendar of State Papers, Venetian* to the decline of plague in the winter of 1604;[1] to its temporary recrudescence in the following spring;[2] to its decline again;[3] to another brief recrudescence in the late summer,[4] and to its extinction in the autumn.[5] The city as a whole can only have been slightly affected because only one parish, that of St Michael, Cornhill records 1 plague-burial in August.[6] By comparison Westminster seems to have experienced a more severe attack of plague this year. A report at the end of April censured the merchants who were clothing the army in Ireland because the persons who were packing and despatching the clothes 'had sores running on them',[7] a statement which suggests that plague had recrudesced after its winter intermission early in April and that the virulence of *P. pestis* had declined. A Bill of Mortality for the week ending 15 December certified that 35 deaths had occurred in the 'liberties of Westminster and Duchy of Lancaster at Strand', of which 27 were attributed to plague.[8] While some of these may have been remote deaths from complications of that disease, it is probable that others were deaths from typhus fever.

It is probable that Carmarthen was not the only place in Wales to be involved in the widespread activity of bubonic plague during the first quinquennium of this century, but it is the only place in the principality to which I have found any reference in English notices of the disease. Spurrel asserts that it suffered severely in 1604[9] but he supplies no supporting evidence for his assertion, and Philips[10] is equally uninformative in his notice of its visitation.

The 'trailer' outbreaks of 1605 represent the natural subsidence of the first invasion of Stuart England by bubonic plague. The notices of it in some of the London parish registers indicate that it was sporadically active in the capital in the summer and early autumn of this year. It may have been responsible for the slaughter of the Hullinges family in the parish of St Lawrence Jewry,[11] although there is no mention of it in the register, for in addition to John Hullinges—who was a barber-surgeon and therefore liable to encounter 'blocked' fleas in the discharge of his professional duties—two sons, two daughters, and two servants died in his house in the space of six weeks. It was certainly active in St Antholin's parish, the register of which records 4 plague-burials in an annual total of 21,[12] and 3 plague-burials in an annual total of 8 burials were registered in the parish of All Hallows, Bread Street.[13] It was presumably active also in the parish of St Alphege, London Wall, as the churchwardens paid 1s. 8d. this year 'for settinge 5 red Crosses on the doores of vyseted houses'.[14] In the 'liberty of Westminster and the Duchy at Strand' 2 plague-deaths were registered during the week ending 5 July, 1 in each of the parishes of St Martin and St Clement.[15]

The relative freedom of London is confirmed by the lord mayor's report

to the Privy Council. In April the king requested him 'to test the efficacy of a remedy for the plague, invented by Henry de Ommeren et d'Ashenbroke, a German; and if it be found effectual, to give him some living, to induce him to abide in the city'.[1] In his report a fortnight later the lord mayor replied that the civic authorities could not test De Ommeren's invention 'for there has not died of late of the sickness within the City or Liberties above 2 or 3 a week at most, and those have been dead or past all remedy before it was known what sickness they had'.[2] But if London escaped, some of its outlying townships may have experienced severe attacks of the disease. Twickenham, for instance, reported 67 plague-burials this year,[3] a mortality which may have been three or four times greater than usual.

At Oxford a recrudescence of the disease again compelled the removal of the plague-sick to 'Port-mede house, the cabins near it, and others by Cheyney Lane, near Hedington Hill',[4] buildings which were evidently temporary pest-houses. It was active at Godmanchester, where 30 plague-burials were entered in the parish register,[5] and in the neighbouring counties of Northamptonshire and Cambridgeshire it visited Northampton and Grendon in the former county and Cambridge in the latter. Northampton may have experienced a severe attack because Cox notes that many of the entries in the burial registers of its parishes are marked 'plague',[6] but regrettably he did not count them. He states that the parish register of Grendon lists the names of 12 victims of the disease.[6] At Cambridge a grace was passed in October to cancel the sermons and public exercises of the university as plague was present in the town, and Cooper relates that in the churchwardens' accounts of the parish of Great St Mary there is this charge: 'Item, paid for a double guilt boule which was given to Mr Watts our minister for his extraordinary paines taking amongst us in the parishe at two severall tymes when the sicknes was amongst us, viijlivs. vjd.'[7] It is pleasant to discover this grateful appreciation of noble pastoral service in plague-time.

To the north of Cambridge Methley and Monk Fryston in Yorkshire were visited, while to the west of them Stockport, Macclesfield, Chester and Manchester were attacked. Methley was scourged as 51 burials were registered there, compared with an annual average of 14 for each of the decennia immediately preceding and succeeding 1605. The first plague-burial entry in the parish register is dated 5 August, the last 3 December, and during those sixteen weeks at least two families were exterminated. Moreover the register does not reveal the full death-roll because the rector noted in it that 'a number of the plague-stricken died and were buried at the Lodges',[8] the 'plague-huts' outside the village. Monk Fryston was fortunate as it had only one plague-death and the victim was possibly a fugitive from Methley or elsewhere.[9]

Axon affirms that Stockport lost 51 of its townsfolk from plague between 9 October 1605 and 14 August 1606,[1] a report which suggests that the disease was introduced too late in 1605 to become epidemic, that it smouldered through the winter among the house-rats, and that it flared up to become epidemic in the late spring or early summer of 1606. He declares that Macclesfield was more severely afflicted as upwards of 70 burials—presumably plague-burials—were registered there between 3 September and 3 October and 'whole families appear to have died'.[2] Mullett says that from 1603 to 1606 inclusive the annual deaths from plague in Chester were 650, 986, 812, and 100 respectively.[3] Manchester was afflicted with 'a sore pestilence' in 1605.[4] The register of the Collegiate Church shows that by 21 July the burials numbered 500; by 20 August the number had risen to 700, and by 17 January to 1,000.[4] Axon adds that until November most of these were plague-deaths, but towards the end of that month 'those who had died from other causes are distinguished by the words "not of ye plague" after their names'.[4] It is a pity that he did not count these marked burials and give also the monthly figures of burials in 1605. He notes that some of the plague-sick were sent to the pest-house and others to cabins built for their reception on 6 acres of land at Collyhurst Common, where also the dead were buried. The twin borough of Salford was evidently involved in this epidemic as in July a tax was levied on the hundred of Salford for the relief of its plague-stricken.[5] During the first week of August 1,157 persons received pecuniary assistance from this tax,[5] but they were not certainly all cases of plague; the number probably includes all the contacts who were segregated with the plague-sick in the cabins or their houses. Moving south plague struck at Shrewsbury, where 667 persons died—presumably of it—among the town's five parishes between 2 June 1604 and 6 April 1605.[6] In the near-by parish of Condover, which may well have been infected from Shrewsbury, several burials are marked in the register with an asterisk in the years 1604 and 1605 and are stated to be plague-deaths. In the former year 16 are so marked in a total of 30, but as 4 of them occurred in the months of December to March inclusive, it is doubtful whether they were even remote deaths from plague—more probably they were deaths from typhus fever. In the months of April and May five burials were registered and all these are marked with an asterisk.[7] In view of their seasonal occurrence these may have been deaths from smallpox.

In Wales Carmarthen was certainly attacked by plague in 1605, whether or not it was visited by the disease in 1604 as both Spurrell and Phillips assert, because the deputy-lieutenants of the county reported in July that the town of Carmarthen and 24 other parishes in the shire were 'grievously infected with the plague'.[8]

The closing decennium of the sixteenth century and the opening one of the seventeenth were each marked by a great national outburst of bubonic plague in England. Each of these outbreaks undoubtedly exerted some effect upon the national life, but an assessment of their social and economic consequences is the province of the social historian. Barrett, after an exhaustive study and analysis of the earlier mortality, concluded that 'all that may safely be said is that the year was one of grave infection, with some diminution towards the very end. The next year was much less seriously affected, the deaths from plague being 421, and in 1595 only 29.'[1] Although it is indubitable that the true mortality of the 1593 epidemic will never be known, there would seem to be a reasonable probability that for London it lies somewhere between the figures given by the vicar of St Peeters upon Cornhill[2]—of which Barrett was seemingly unaware—and those supplied by Bell*;[3] and it is possibly a significant fact that their mortality rates are nearly identical, to wit, 57·9 and 59·6 per cent respectively. In all probability Barrett's criticism of the validity of the mortality figures of the 1592–3 epidemic is applicable to those given for the 1603–4 epidemic, although there is less confusion over these figures. Dekker, in his contemporary account of this epidemic, declares that more than 40,000 people in London were destroyed by it;[4] but in a later pamphlet[5] he repeats the figures given in the parish register of St Peeters upon Cornhill. Wilson also quotes these figures, but he remarks that the inclusion of the mortality figures for Westminster, Lambeth, Newington Butts, the Savoy, Stepney, Hackney, and Islington bring the total death-roll for London and its liberties to 43,154, of which 35,104 were ascribed to plague.[6] These figures yield a mortality-rate for plague of just over 81 per cent, indicating as we should expect that the disease was much more deadly in the crowded slums of the liberties than in the walled city. Wilson adds that as the mortality figures for the 8 out-parishes and the 7 outlying districts are not given for the whole year the true death-roll was somewhat greater.[7] Unfortunately the exact size of London's population in 1603 is unknown. Wilson opines that it could hardly have exceeded 250,000,[8] but it may not have exceeded 200,000. It certainly increased between 1593 and 1603, probably rapidly, because the repeated efforts of Elizabeth I to stop the jerrybuilding and the overcrowding on the fringes of the city indicate a continuous increase in the size of London's population. If this outburst of bubonic plague is credited with the destruction of one-quarter of the population that was forced to stay in London, the population in 1603 would have

* John Bell, clerk of the Parish Clerks' Company. He declared that the records of the Parish Clerks showed that from 21 December 1592 to 20 December 1593 the total of burials in London amounted to 17,884, of which plague accounted for 10,662.

been about 160,000. What seems to be indisputable about these two great eruptions of bubonic plague is that, relative to the size of London's population at the time, the mortal activity of the disease on each occasion was almost constant and its panic effects were identical.

The spasmodic efforts made by the state to control this outburst of plague were mainly directed to the prohibition of public assemblies, for which reason all the annual fairs in and near London were cancelled, and to the protection of the king and his court. The common people were left to their own devices, although attempts were made to stop their overcrowding. A proclamation issued in mid-September 1603 reads:

Whereas the number of dissolute and idle persons, and the pestering of many of them in small and strait rooms hath been a great cause of the plague, no new tenants are to be admitted to reside in any houses which have been so infected until it shall be thought safe: none of the rooms are to be pestered with multitudes of dwellers, and such of them as were pulled down are to be razed accordingly and not rebuilt.[1]

Although it was based upon the faulty notion that bubonic plague was caused by a pestilential state of the atmosphere, there was good sense in this proclamation because where people were crowded together in small dwellings the 'blocked' fleas had greatly increased opportunities to transmit *P. pestis*. In October James I and his court fled to Winchester, to which city Michaelmas Term was adjourned until Martinmas, and from there he issued a proclamation forbidding persons who had had plague in their houses since 20 July to come to Winchester. Simultaneously the Justices of the Peace within 8 miles of that city were enjoined to observe the regulations designed to keep the disease away,[2] which in effect meant the arrest of any strangers found in their districts who did not have authentic certificates of health. In July 1604, as plague had then apparently subsided in London, a proclamation forbade any Londoner to go to St James' Fair at Bristol, where plague was then raging,[3] and on 1 November, as there had been a recrudescence of plague in September—which caused the adjournment of Michaelmas Term—a proclamation forbade any inhabitant of London or Westminster, 'or any place where the Plague is or hath been six weeks' before that date to come to the court without a pass, 'except bishops, judges, King's counsel, the magistrates of London and Westminster, and the household'.[4] It was well for his peace of mind that James did not know that *X. cheopis* is no respecter of persons.

Scotland and Ireland

As early as September 1600 plague was active at Findhorn and the townsfolk were forbidden to go into the country on pain of death.[5] As the disease was then raging 'in Danzig and other ports in the Baltic, where a great number

of Scots are now trading', no ships coming to Scottish ports from suspect places were to be allowed to land either passengers or goods without special licence.[1] This precaution was taken too late, however, for plague had already been imported into the country, and by late autumn it was prevalent in various places in the 'West country', notably the parishes of Eglishane, Eistwood, Pollock, and the town of Craill.[2] At the end of November it was reported in the barony of Calderwood,[3] and in January 1602 it was stated to be daily increasing in intensity in Craill.[4] The disease responsible for this report was typhus fever. Because of the inadequate provisioning of the sick poor of Craill, isolated on 'the Mure', they and their families had wandered away and scattered over the county of Fife, with the consequent danger of infecting the entire county.[5] They were therefore to be rounded up and isolated and proper measures were to be taken for their provisioning.[5] This report is illuminating because neither *R. rattus* nor *X. cheopis* would have accompanied these people on their wanderings; but the body louse would have gone with them of necessity. There are several more references to this 'plague' outbreak of typhus fever, which spread to Glasgow in December 1601[6, 7, 8, 9] and which significantly ceased in Edinburgh in May 1602[10] with the presumptive arrival of warmer weather. Later in that month, however, bubonic plague resumed its activity in 'sundry parts of the country'[11] and seems to have persisted—with the usual winter intermissions—for the next two years, because in May 1604 it was so prevalent in Edinburgh that the Scots parliament was transferred to Perth.[12] During June the epidemic in Edinburgh increased in violence and its concealment by the populace undoubtedly hampered the civic authorities in their efforts to control it. One man was fined £20 early in June 'for not reporting the sickness of one of his children until it was dead'[13] and he was certainly only one of many offenders among his fellow-citizens. Warm weather in July further increased the activity of the disease and the baillies were ordered to select quartermasters to serve for the duration of the epidemic.[14] As enough of the *Common Good* could not be collected, owing to the flight of people from the city and the increase in the numbers of the plague-sick and the destitute, the civic authorities decided to raise a loan of between £1,000 and £2,000.[14] By mid-August this loan was exhausted and they were constrained to appropriate to their own plague-relief the fund of £24,000 which Edinburgh had collected for the relief of plague-stricken Geneva.[15] This visitation cost the city £5,229 16s. 10d. in cash[16] and an incalculable sum in lost trade, industrial paralysis, and the disorganization of its commercial and social life, which encouraged immorality and crime. In December a man was hanged 'for opening of honest mens lockis and dores, they being out of

town fled for the pest',[1] and in all probability there were other burglars and looters.

Comrie remarks that from 1603 to 1609 'plague was present in one place or another throughout Scotland, but there was no serious epidemic'.[2] He mentions that a man was fined 40s. at Lanark for admitting fugitives from Edinburgh to his house and that another was gaoled on his return from that city. The townsfolk of Paisley were forbidden to go outside the sheriffdom of Renfrew. Anyone entering the town 'by back ways' was to be fined £5. The walls on wastelands near the gates were to be built up and covered with thorns to prevent people from climbing over them. The watchers at the town gates were each to be provided with a sword and a Jedburgh staff and no one coming from Glasgow, who had not been absent from that city for 6 weeks, was to be admitted.[3] This hint that Glasgow was attacked by plague in 1604 appears to be the sole reference to its visitation. Chambers declares that Aberdeen was attacked in the spring of that year, that plague became widely dispersed in the town during May, and that the epidemic was augmented by hot weather in July.[4] Among the control measures which the civic authorities of Edinburgh devised during this epidemic was one that the 'clengers' should wear 'leverary coits', possibly in order that a strict watch could be kept on their activities. At the same time all citizens were forbidden to send clothes to the common washers for laundrying and no one was to visit the segregated or go to 'the Seynis' without licence from a baillie. Furthermore all tavern doors were to be closed from 9 p.m.[5]

The notice of plague in Ireland appears to refer only to its invasion of Dublin, but there was most probably some extension of the disease into the English Pale. The panic flight of its wealthy and influential citizens had left the city so weak and impoverished by Easter 1604 that a General Assembly decreed that such deserters were to be punished by disfranchisement and loss of freedom, and that in future no freeman who was a householder was to leave Dublin without licence from the mayor.[6] The notice that two men each received a grant of 40s. 'in respecte of their service and attendans, this dangerose tyme of infection',[7] suggests that the outbreak was a severe one, and there are other records that support this suggestion. For instance the general muster of the citizens, which was annually held on Easter Monday, was cancelled,[8] and the civic authorities decided to build a pest-house for the isolation of the plague-sick.[9] After its usual winter intermission plague recrudesced in the spring of 1605 and in May the Lord Deputy ordered the pest-house to be moved farther from the city.[10] Five days later either he or the civic authorities decreed that four strong men should be appointed

to attend and looke to the pest house, and stop the infected from running abrode; which men shall bury the dead, both in the pest house and in the cittie as occasion shall happen; and uppon theire cominge into the cittie they are to carry white staves of an ell longe, and shall not come in but by Mr Maiors privity. It is agreed that, for better purgeing of the aire, Mr Maior do command that every inhabitant shall burn a fagot at his dore every Wednesday at night, Satterday at night, and Monday at night, and such other nights as Mr Maior shall thinke fit, and occasion shall happen.[1]

The 'running abrode', of the plague-sick was a distressful compulsion of the disease, enforced by delirium or by the agonizing pain of buboes in process of suppurating. 'All the Sick likewise quickly after Seizure grew delirious, running wildly about the Streets, if they were not confined by Force.'[2] 'The pain of the swelling was, in particular, very violent and intolerable' so that 'some, for want of help to hold them down in their beds, or look to them, destroyed themselves; some broke into the streets, frequently naked, ran directly to the river if not stopt, and plunged themselves into the water wherever they found it'.[3] The four 'calledors' appointed by the city to take charge of the pest-house were each to be paid '12d. Irish' for the burial of every householder, man, woman, or servant, and 6d. for every maid, boy, or child.[4]

Plague seemingly pursued a similar course in Edinburgh, for its recrudescence there in the spring of 1605 caused the meeting of the Session to be prorogued to 1 December,[5] and precautions were taken to ensure that no person entered the city without a certificate of departure from a place that was free from plague. Its recrudescence was attributed by the populace to the imprisonment of 6 ministers who were to be prosecuted for attempting to convene a General Assembly at Aberdeen in July.[6] The disease was reported to have appeared simultaneously this year in Edinburgh, Leith, and St Andrews[7] and each of those towns seems to have been severely afflicted by it. It was also epidemic in 1605 at Roxburgh and Peebles[8] and in a number of 'small towns about Edinburgh'.[9] From St Andrews Archbishop Gledstanes wrote to the council towards the end of August to excuse his absence because 'of the gryte continewing infection of this citie, insamekill that hardlie can any that dwellis heir promeis clerinnes and saifetie from this seiknes'.[10] He added: 'This berar remains in landwart without the toune tua mylis, and thairfor is onsuspect';[11] an illuminating testimonial to the terror excited by plague, for without this assurance the letter would have aroused consternation among its recipients. Comrie records that the town council of Peebles decreed that every case of sickness of any kind must be notified to the baillies on pain of death, and that the Glasgow authorities imposed a fine of £20

on any inhabitant who received into his house anyone coming from Lanark, Peebles, Peddert, Leith, Linlithgow, and Edinburgh.[1]

Creighton declares that 1606 was Scotland's worst plague-year in the first decennium of this century[2] and the Lord Chancellor of Scotland's report confirms him. After commenting that Scotland was quiet and in better state than ever before in living memory, he continues:

The onlie truble we haiff is this contagious sicknes of peste, whilk is spread marvelouslie in the best townes off this realme. In Edinburght it hes bene continuall this four yeares, at the present not verie vehement, bot sick as stayes the cowmoun course of administration of justice, whilk can not be weill exercised in naa other plaice. Air and Striveling ar almoste overthrowin with the seiknes, within thir twa monethes about twa thousand personnes dead in ane of thame. The maist of the peple fled, and the tounes almost left desolat. Dundee and Pearthe, otherwayes called St Johnstoun, the twa best tounes in this kingdom nixt to Edinburght, vearie wealthie and merchand tounes indeed, are baithe also infected within theis twa monthes, and in great truble. Glasgow and manye other tounes and paretes are in the same distres.[3]

Chambers cites Balfour for the assertion that plague 'raged so extremely in all the corners of the kingdom that neither burgh nor land in any part was free. The burghs of Ayr and Stirling were almost desolate; and all the judicatories of the land were deserted.'[4] Balfour's statement was a typical 'Black Death' plague-extravagance, begotten of the age-old fear of the disease; but there can be no doubt that many towns and villages in Scotland were involved in this epidemic.

By the middle of June plague was so prevalent in Edinburgh that Parliament was adjourned and directed to reassemble on 1 July at Perth,[5] which must therefore have been free from plague at that time. As the Lord Chancellor's report was written on 3 October, Perth must have been infected some time in the interval, possibly early in August. At Edinburgh the epidemic reached its peak either late in August or early in September, and it evidently had not subsided by mid-October because on the 23rd the Session and other judicatures were suspended on account of its persistence.[6] As the Secret Council was in session at Linlithgow when this suspension was promulgated, it seems probable that that town was not involved in this outburst of plague, for it was certainly free in August when the Diet of Council was transferred to it from Stirling, where plague was then epidemic.[7] It was still prevalent at Stirling in September, causing the cancellation of the annual fair.[8] Comrie says that two cases of plague were notified in Glasgow in 1606, but it is scarcely credible that they were the only cases because the corporation voted £100 for the relief of the plague-stricken who were segregated on the Town Moor. It also ordered all beggars to leave the town and all dogs and cats to

TABLE 16

Expenses incurred by the burgh of Ayr in consequence of its visitation by plague in 1606*

1606–7	£	s	d
To a kettle for cleaning the pest clothes on the foull mur,	28	0	0
To John Broun, officer of Alloway, for bringing coals to the cleaning cauldron on the muir,	6	15	0
To a poor woman, suspect of the pest,		16	8
In arrears (including £56 13s. 4d. for the late John McQuattie for the custom of the firlots† and pecks in the pest yeir),	107	14	10
1607–8			
For a ship's main sail to bed the kill appointed for drying of claithis the Tyme of the lait infectioun,	40	0	0
To a boy, for running to Kilmarnock anent the tryell of the pest thair,		12	0
To Helen Crawfurd, for entertaining twa little barnes the tyme of the infectioun,	1	18	8
TOTAL	£184	17	2

be confined by their owners, and these anti-plague regulations were seldom enforced until the disease was epidemic in a town.[1]

Of all the Scottish towns that were attacked by plague in 1606 and 1607, Ayr may have been proportionately the worst afflicted, for by the end of August it had sustained 'a verie grite mortalitie of all degreis and rankis of personis',[2] and for the next two years, as table 16 shows, the municipality was paying the expenses incurred by its visitation. These expenses present several points of interest in relation to the municipal handling of an outbreak of bubonic plague in the seventeenth century. For instance the clothes of the plague-stricken were apparently disinfected by boiling or by immersion in hot water, a process that would certainly destroy the body louse but would probably not affect *X. cheopis*, even if it were temporarily roosting in clothing, as that agile insect would not wait to find itself in hot water. The use made of a ship's mainsail is unexpected and its cost would seem to be unduly high. As Kilmarnock is about 12 miles from Ayr, the boy who was paid 6d. a mile for the round journey must have been a potential marathon runner if he actually covered the entire distance without a rest. If Helen Crawfurd was paid at the customary English plague-relief rate of 1s. a head a week, the two little children must have been in her care for at least 19 weeks, which may have been the period during which plague was scourging

* Extracted from *Ayr Burgh Accounts, 1534–1624*; transcribed and edited by G. S. Pryde, Scottish Historical Society (Edinburgh, 1937), XXVIII, 232–6.

† *Firlot*. A basic measure of grain, approximately equal to one bushel.

the town. As a direct result of this visitation Ayr engaged a town surgeon at a yearly fee of 50 merks.[1] Pryde comments that 'in this respect the burgh was about a generation behind the chief towns in Scotland, but well in advance of the smaller burghs'.[1] Glasgow's first town surgeon was engaged in 1577, Edinburgh's in 1585—in each case at a yearly stipend of £20—but it was not until 1637 that Dumbarton appointed a surgeon at a salary of £40 a year, with a house, yard, and burgess-entry free, to practise 'the science of *phisik, pottingerie* and *chirurgie*'.[2] The treasurer of Dunfermline also had to pay expenses incurred by the town during its visitation in 1606. These included a grant made to the baillies to enable them to reward subordinates who gave particularly valuable service during the epidemic, and the hire of a horse to enable a baillie 'to ryde to Culros in tyme of plague'. Bread and ale were purchased for the sustenance of a man who spent a night repairing the town gate. As late as November 1607 the treasurer paid 40s. to 3 men who came to Dunfermline to seek relief for the plague-stricken in Wemyss,[3] a pleasing reminder that British townships rendered mutual assistance in plague-time.

Concerning Perth, the town's chronicle records on 9 August 1606: 'The same nycht there was blude fyre, and the pest come in, quhilk continewit till May thereafter.'[4] If the epidemic ran true to form it attained its peak some time in September or early in October, declined during the succeeding autumn months, became quiescent with the arrival of frosty weather, remained dormant during the winter months and recrudesced in the spring of 1607, to be extinguished by a recurrence of cold weather in May, a not uncommon happening in more southerly latitudes than Perth. The nature of the 'blude fyre' is obscure; but as it was seen at night it may have been a particularly impressive display of the Northern Lights. Whatever was its nature it was evidently regarded by the people of Perth as an evil portent of pestilence. 'A vehement frost', which endured from 11 November 1606 to 20 February 1607,[5] undoubtedly constrained *X. cheopis* to hibernate.

A recurrence of plague in Dublin in the late summer of 1606 may explain why the civic authorities were petitioned in October to maintain the pesthouse 'to avoid danger in this contadgiose tyme'.[6] On the other hand, as plague is not specifically mentioned in the petition, some other epidemic disease aroused the public alarm. Creighton records that there was a 'most dreadful pestilence' in Cork during the winter of 1607 and the spring of 1608,[7] but he expresses no opinion about its nature. As its seasonal incidence excludes bubonic plague, it was probably either a malignant epidemic of typhus fever or of smallpox.

In Scotland plague appears to have recurred in 1607 in some of the towns

that were attacked by it the previous year. In Edinburgh the Court of Session was prorogued on 15 October until 17 November[1] and again on 5 November[2] because of its sporadic persistence in the city; but the disease evidently disappeared towards the end of November as the provisional re-assembly of the court on 15 December[3] was confirmed by a proclamation on the 10th.[4] 'Trailer' epidemics were undoubtedly scattered about the country during the spring and summer of that year, the aftermath of the outburst of the previous year, which was blamed for the excuse offered to the king that any neglect occurring in the royal service was due to 'the desolate estate of the country in regaird of the universall plague'.[5] Elsewhere plague may have been more active than in Edinburgh, for the Synod of Fife was prorogued in April 'on account of the plague in those parts',[6] and Stirling may have experienced a severe visitation as it was forced to borrow official cleaners from other towns.[7]

Although Dunfermline appears to have escaped plague in 1607 the presence of the disease on the other side of the Firth of Forth kept the town on tenter-hooks, and Nance Somervell was therefore fortunate to be let off with a fine of £5 when she was convicted of disobeying 'the lait Acts in passing over the firth to Tineadill and oyir pairtis in Louthiane wtout leve of the Magistrats'.[8] Nevertheless plague must have crossed the Firth if Chambers is correct in his statement that it erupted in April in Perth, Dundee, and other places there-abouts.[9] Dundee was certainly infected in July 1608 because on the 28th the General Assembly of the church, which was to have met there, was transferred to Linlithgow and Chambers adds that a great many houses in the town were then infected.[10] The contemporary report from Perth that 'mony of the speciall inhabitantes thairof ar removit af the toun and reteint thameselffis to some placeis of grittair suirtie'[11] indicates that plague was epidemic there in the summer of 1608. Chambers states that the disease erupted in the town at the end of August, that it persisted there until May 1609, and that 500 people died of it.[12] As Perth's population at this time possibly did not exceed 2,000 it may have lost at least one-quarter of it.

The involvement of the little port of Burntisland caused the ferries across the Firth of Forth to be closed[13] and with plague so near at hand the Dun-fermline magistrates ordered all the town gates to be closed and guarded.[14] The officers responsible for that guard must have had a difficult job because they were ordered to ensure that no one was to be allowed to go more than 3 miles outside the town in any direction without a licence from the magis-trates. The reason for the imposition of this limit is obscure and it is difficult to see how a gate-guard could enforce it once he had let a person leave the town. The magistrates attached so much importance to its observance, how-

ever, that a fine of £5 was the penalty for its disregard. They also ordered all householders in the town to make their 'backsyds & head roumis fensible that na passage be haid yrthrow w^t in 23 days nyxt heirefter'.[1] Evidently the outbreak at Burntisland subsided with the arrival of autumn frosts because the watch was withdrawn from the town gates of Dunfermline early in December 'in respect of the short day, early nyt, and evil weddir and that (praysed be God) the plaig is sumqt stayit in yer nyxt adjacient partis'[2] and the next year witnessed a marked decline in the activity of plague in Scotland. Indeed in 1609 only 3 places, Perth, Kinghorn, and Inverkeithing, are named as the sites of its activity.

At Kinghorn 2 of the town cleaners, a man and a woman, were arrested on a charge of deliberately trying to spread plague to their pecuniary advantage by cutting the winding-sheet of a plague-corpse in pieces and scattering them about the town.[3] This vicious but innocuous effort links Scotland with Switzerland and Italy in connexion with known records of nefarious attempts to spread bubonic plague. At Geneva in 1530 the keepers of the pest-house concocted a 'plague-poison' by drying and powdering poultices they applied to plague-sores and mixing the powder with pulverized white euphorbia (*veratrum album*), itself a deadly poison. The poison was then impregnated in handkerchiefs which were dropped about the streets of Geneva.[4] In Milan in 1630 a barber, Giangacomo Mora, was accused of manufacturing a 'plague-ointment' which confederates smeared on walls and buildings. The appalling brutality of the manner of his execution is a terrible testimony to the insensate terror inspired by plague.[5]

In January 1609 Inverkeithing 'and sundry oyer places heirabout'[6] were reported to be infected with plague; but as in the latitude of Inverkeithing the temperature even in a mild winter would be low enough to force the plague-fleas to hibernate, this alleged outbreak of plague was in all probability an epidemic of typhus fever.

There does not appear to be any record of plague in Scotland during the next 4 years, 1610–13, and apart from a reference to it in the municipal accounts of Ayr[7]—which is most probably a belated acknowledgement of services rendered during the visitation of 1606—the years from 1616 to 1623 are equally silent about it. Ireland also appears to have been free from plague throughout this period of fourteen years; in fact it was more fortunate than Scotland because, whereas the disease reappeared in that country in 1623, the next record of its presumptive presence in Ireland is in 1650.

England and Wales

For several years after the subsidence of the great outburst of 1603 plague smouldered more or less sporadically in the twin cities of London and Westminster. The registers of 9 London parishes record plague-burials in each of the years from 1606 to 1610 inclusive (see table 17) but their annual percentage plague-mortality rates for the years 1606-9 inclusive—respectively approximately 36·0. 20·0, 17·5, and 16·0—show that there was a progressive decline in its activity in those parishes. The percentage mortality rate of 21·0 in 1610 may represent a slight exacerbation of the disease, but even so it shows that plague was relatively no more active in 1610 than it had been in 1607.

In London and its liberties 50 plague deaths were registered during the last week of July 1606[1] and another 70 during the first week in August.[2] Some time during this month the lord mayor was evidently censured for his failure to control the disease because early in September he reported that he had given strict instructions that the red crosses on the doors of plague-infected house must be 'laid in oil to the intent that they may not easily be put out'.[3] As the plague-order of 1603 had specified that the cross was to be painted in oil,[4] it is probable that his officers had been substituting the quicker and cheaper method of chalking the cross on the doors. In a riposte he urged the Privy Council to direct the Justices of Peace of the Home Counties to enforce the London anti-plague regulations in their respective shires on account of the daily influx of their countyfolk to shop in London.[3] It is interesting to find that London had become a national shopping centre as early as 1606. Early in October plague was reported to be increasing in London[5] and the lord mayor added to the measures in operation an order for the more stringent segregation of the inmates of plague-infected houses.[6] Prior to the publication of this order Michaelmas Term had been adjourned on account of the spread of the disease.[7] Although plague was not truly epidemic in London this year it was widely dispersed in the metropolitan area and it was active on both sides of the English Channel in October.[8] The exact number of plague-deaths in that area this year is unknown and Creighton's estimate of 2,100 (see figure 47) seems to be too high, as the scanty evidence available suggests that a figure around 1,500 would be nearer the mark. It is of interest that the monthly plague-mortality figures he gives[9] indicate that the peak occurred in October, because this is late in the year for bubonic plague in England and suggests that the early autumn of 1606 was unusually mild.

Outside London there was a rumour of plague at Windsor early in

TABLE 17

	1606		1607		1608		1609		1610	
	Total	Plague	Total	Plague	Total	Plague	Total	Plague	Total	Plague
St Michael, Cornhill	41	13	—	3	—	1	44	13	—	—
St Helen's, Bishopsgate	23	4	19	4	33	7	40	7	21	4
All Hallows, Bread Street	10	5	19	9	—	—	20	2	—	—
St Pancras, Soper Lane	2	1	—	—	—	—	—	—	—	—
St Mary Somerset	72	38	52	5	55	6	51	6	55	6
St Michael Bassishaw	37	6	37	7	47	10	47	4	—	6
St Olave, Hart Street	—	—	40	4	38	4	77	4	—	—
St Stephen, Walbrook	—	—	—	1	—	—	—	—	—	—
St Mary the Virgin, Aldermanbury	—	—	—	—	27	7	34	15	—	—
TOTALS	185	67	167	33	200	35	313	51	76	16

Extracted from the burial registers of the parishes in the Publications of the Harleian Society, respectively volumes VII (1882); XXXI (1904); XLIII (1913); XLIV (1914); LX (1930); LXXII (1942); XLVI (1916), XLIX (1919), and LXI (1931).

September[1] but the townsfolk declared that it was false.[2] However there is a record of its visitation of Eton,[3] just across the river, though no details of this visit are given. Clarke affirms that Tamworth was attacked by it[4] but he supplies no evidence to support his statement. A Londoner is blamed for introducing the disease to a Peterborough household of which the father, son, daughter, and servant died of it; 'only his wife and her mayde escaped with soars'.[5] If, as is quite possible, the culprit unwittingly brought with him a 'blocked' flea roosting in his clothing, the sequence of events would then have been an outbreak of rat-plague in the dwelling; the transference of *P. pestis* by starving 'blocked' fleas deprived by death of their natural hosts to the unfortunate family; the creation by chance contacts of an epizootic among the house-rats of Peterborough, and a consequent epidemic which persisted for 9 months according to Sweeting.[5] The wife and her maid survived because their buboes became secondarily infected with pyogenic cocci and ruptured, and the resulting suppuration destroyed and discharged the plague bacilli.

Manchester experienced an epidemic of disease in the late autumn of 1606 and the winter of 1607 which Axon records as an outbreak of plague,[6] and which was evidently regarded as such by contemporary Mancunians, but which was much more probably an epidemic of typhus fever. Whatever was its true nature its patients were sent to the pest-house and, as the *Constables'* *Accounts* show, the sum of £3 8s. 10d. was expended on their removal to it and their maintenance there.[6] Included in these payments 5s. 4d. was ex-

pended on 4 lots of 'coales to ye Pesthouse'; 4*d*. on straw 'for Marshalls ffolkes'; 6*d*. for drink on the night Widow Marshall was taken there [? by force]; 8*s*. 5*d*. to the porters who carried her and her goods there; 10*s*. 5*d*. for her winding sheet and burial, and 3*s*. 3*d*. as rent for the building to a Mr Cox.[1] This last item suggests that the pest-house was simply an isolated dwelling-house requisitioned for use as a temporary isolation-house. The

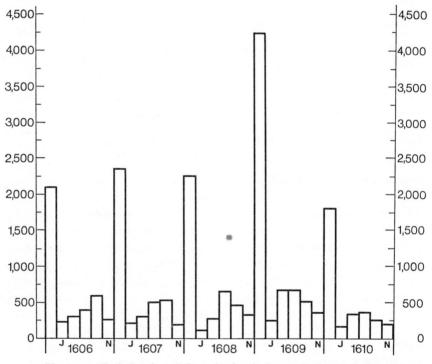

45. Plague mortality in London, 1606–10, showing the increase in the months from July to November. (Composed from Creighton's *History of epidemic disease in Britain*.)

epidemic was severe enough to justify the levy of a tax ranging from 6*d*. to 6*s*. a person for the relief of the stricken.[1] The local authority seemingly had trouble on this occasion with a man from Moston who had been chained in his cabin by the local constables but had escaped, and who persisted in wandering about the district at all hours, 'lying in the out-houses of divers inhabitants of Moston, to their grief and danger'.[2] An order was therefore made for his committal to Manchester gaol at the cost of Moston town until further notice.[3] There is no evidence that he was suffering from any communicable disease.

In Wales Carmarthen was so severely visited by plague again in 1606 according to Spurrell that the Great Sessions were held at Golden Grove.[1]

Plague was active again in London, in 1607 much as it had been in the previous year, for 2,352 deaths were ascribed to it according to Creighton.[2] As figure 45 shows, it was at its maximal activity in September and October with an unusually late peak in the latter month. Apart from London England was almost free from plague this year. It appeared in Leicester but Kelly says its mortality there was not large.[3] However it was sufficient to cause the municipality to pay the expenses of a messenger to ride with letters 'to one Mr Willyam Motte, a fizition at Bourn in Lincolnshire, to request hym to come over to Leicester to the vizited people to help cure them'.[3] Regrettably no information is extant about the outcome of this invitation and the 'Motte cure' for bubonic plague has perished with its inventor. Payments were also made for painting red crosses 1 foot in height on the doors and windows of infected houses, with 'Lord have mercy upon us' in big letters written over them; for a nurse to attend the sick; for searching the dead for plague-signs; for provisioning the plague-stricken segregated in their houses, and for placing hurdles around 30 infected houses. The sum of £3 8s. 9d. was expended upon these efforts to control the disease,[4] which were of course ineffectual, and plague persisted in Leicester and gradually gathered strength to erupt in 'The Great Plague' of 1610–11. This started at the beginning of June 1610 and an early consequence was the removal of the Assizes to Hinckley. A municipal certificate, dated 31 March 1611, states that since May 1610 the corporation had expended £306 2s. 2d. in plague-relief. A pest-house was built in a garden in St Nicholas' parish, the tenant's interest being bought out for 10 guineas, and a similar sum was paid for the pitch-boards, timber, and construction of a number of huts which constituted the pest-house. This evidently proved inadequate as people were segregated in their infected houses which were surrounded with hurdles and watched day and night. Chains were placed across the bridges and the town gates were continuously guarded to prevent all egress and ingress. The watchmen were armed with crossbows and authorized to shoot at those 'vizited people' who 'would not be kepte in theire howses'. By the act of 1 James I, c. xxxi,[5] which enacted that 'any infected person having any infectious sore upon him who should contemptuously go abroad' committed a felony punishable by death, local authorities were legally entitled to use any force necessary to confine people in their infected houses. The death-roll of this epidemic was the heaviest sustained by Leicester since its visitation in 1349. A note in the register of All Saints' parish records that more than 600 plague-deaths occurred, and the register of St Martin's parish notes

that there was 'a very great mortality' and that entire families were exterminated.[1] The parish registers do not reveal the full mortality of this
calamitous visitation because, although the bulk of the plague-dead was for
the first time buried in the churchyards, an unknown number of victims
found graves in gardens and fields. Kelly cites Throsby for the report that
when at a later date a canal was dug through St Margaret's Cow Pasture
a number of skeletons were unearthed which Throsby opined were victims
of this epidemic.[2] Kelly records an incident in this epidemic which illustrates
the inhumanity aroused by the panic fear of bubonic plague in seventeenth-
century England. 'On a Saturday night a young man came from Leicester
to Lutterworth,' he writes, 'and on Sunday night the fellow sickened of the
plague, which rose in his groin, which being discerned by the people of the
house where he lay, they put him forth, whence he departed to return home,
but fell down and died in the fields.'[3] The Worcestershire parish of Ribbesford appears to provide the only other report of plague in England in 1607.[4]

Three metropolitan Bills of Mortality for the weeks ending respectively
21 October, 28 October and 11 November 1608[5] returned figures for the
total and the plague-deaths of 247 and 127, 240 and 102, and 47 and 0
respectively.[6] If there was no plague-death during the second week in
November, it seems probable that frosty weather put a sudden stop to the
predatory activities of the plague-fleas. As smallpox was concurrently active
in the capital,[7] it may have been that disease or the eruption of an outbreak
of typhus fever which caused the prorogation of parliament from 27 October
to 9 February even though 'the Plague' was officially blamed for the prorogation.[8] Creighton records 2,262 plague-deaths in London this year with
a peak of activity in September,[9] and according to his figures there were 320
deaths from the disease in November. During October it spread to Hampton
Court, where two of the royal retainers died of it on the 16th[10] and 2 more on
the 20th,[11] fatalities which prompted the queen to leave that palace. South of
London typhus fever was most probably responsible for the note of 'plague'
in the parish register of Horsham against the burial entry of a woman on
28 February.[12] Then follow identical notes against the burial entries of 8 more
victims, 4 of whom were children. North of London plague was reported this
year at Leicester, Ludlow, Chester, Manchester and Cambridge.

The parish register of Ludlow records 8 plague-burials in a total of 72
burials registered during the year.[13] Chester seems to have experienced a
similar mild visitation as Ormerod affirms that only about 14 plague-deaths
were recorded there that year.[14] The presence of the disease in Manchester
is an inference only from a document dated 16 May 1608 which states that
a weekly tax was levied for the relief of the plague-stricken;[15] but it may have

been levied for the relief of some other town. In October 1608 the University of Cambridge passed a grace 'to discontinue sermons at St Mary's and exercises in the schools on account of the plague'.[1]

The next two years, 1609 and 1610, witnessed several severe outbreaks of bubonic plague in English towns and in all probability the conjunction of epidemics of it with those of typhus fever and smallpox. The alleged plague-mortality in London in 1609 increased to a total of 4,240 deaths,[2] nearly double its mortality in each of the two preceding years and more than double its mortality in 1610.[2] The figures that Creighton gives show a total of 2,090 deaths in the four 'plague-months' of July–October. There were 330 deaths in November. Ignoring these, the total deaths in the months of December to June inclusive were 1,820, so that of the alleged plague-deaths 49·2 per cent occurred in the 'plague-months' and 42·9 per cent in the months when bubonic plague was usually dormant but typhus fever and smallpox were active. It is probable that some of the November deaths were remote deaths from bubonic plague and equally probable that others were deaths from either typhus fever or smallpox, which was certainly active in London in April 1609.[3] With all due respect to a great medical historian, it is a mistake today to accept Creighton's plague-figures implicitly. Doubt about the accuracy of his figures for 1609 is supported by the fact that the number of registered plague-burials in 7 of the City parishes (see table 17) was less than in any one of the three preceding years. Wilson avers that plague—or what passed for plague—was more widespread in January 1609 than ever before in London at that season, in spite of its coldness as he remarks,[4] and that by the end of the month the 'plague-deaths' (so-called) amounted to 60 a week and the epidemic was spreading rapidly. The significant observation that excludes bubonic plague as the cause of this epidemic is contained in the Venetian ambassador's despatch, dated 13 February,[5] in which he remarks that the disease was prevalent in spite of very cold weather. A week later he reported that the deaths from it had increased by 50 per cent although it was 'the height of the winter cold'.[6] Undoubtedly the Londoners believed that the disease was plague because, as the ambassador remarks, 'everyone is trying to get a house in the country, as they fear a great scourge in the city when the heat begins'.[7] But there was no great scourge of bubonic plague in London in the summer of 1610, and with the arrival of warmer weather the epidemic of typhus fever subsided. Bubonic plague did recrudesce in April 1610 after its customary winter intermission, but its feebler activity—1,803 alleged deaths[8]—coincided with a severe epidemic of smallpox which rivalled plague in its mortality.[9] Wilson adds that by early June London was deserted by a large part of its inhabitants, but to

everyone's surprise St Bartholomew's Fair was held as usual on 25 August.[1] with the result that the 'plague'—which could only have been smallpox as bubonic plague is not spread by human contacts—was widely dispersed about the country around London. The Venetian ambassador was extremely surprised that the fair was held because, as he explained, 'the plague, fostered by the unripe fruit the poor eat has been more deadly than at any time in the last three years'.[2] During September Wilson affirms that more than 200 plague-deaths were reported in London and 'the infection had spread to the best and most open streets',[3] and on the 22nd Michaelmas Term was adjourned.[4] However the epidemic declined rapidly in October and plague was extinguished for the time being early in December with the onset of cold, dry weather. Cox asserts that London suffered a total death-roll of 11,875 this year,[5] a surprisingly light toll for concurrent epidemics of bubonic plague, typhus fever, and smallpox, and one which, if Cox's total is correct, disposes of any claim that there was a major outbreak of plague in the capital this year.

Needless to say James I and his court deserted London as soon as plague became active there, and by the beginning of October he and his ministers were scattered about the country in their efforts to evade it, for by that date it had 'spread to many villages'.[6] It continued to spread in its characteristic radiating fashion from its metropolitan focus, so much so that towards the end of the month the queen is reported to have complained that royalty was not safe from it anywhere,[7] a complaint that was given substance early in November when there were several reputed cases of it among the royal retinue.[8] The example set by the king was copied by most of the wealthy citizens and the high civic officials; but the lord mayor remained at his post of duty, as did also the Archbishop of Canterbury, the Lord Chancellor, and the Chancellors of the Exchequer and the Duchy.[9] The last-named seems to have carried off the honours because he stayed in London although he was 'shrewdly frighted' by plague-deaths among his household.[10]

South of London plague was reported this year from Strood, Canterbury, and Horsham. At Strood it exterminated a family of 4 persons in May;[11] but it may have been confined to this household on this occasion in contrast with its presumptive visitation in 1603, when Cox says the parish register recorded 44 burials, 'though the average yearly mortality of the period was only fourteen'.[11] The epidemic at Canterbury began in a house in which 5 children were orphaned by it, and it was three weeks before the civic authorities realized that the parents had died of plague.[12] Gardiner avers that the subsequent epidemic was a severe one, and she notes that the civic authorities twice paid 'visiting companies of actors, Lord Chandos' players [and] Lord

Berkeley's players, a solatium of twenty shillings to leave the city without giving any performances, because of the danger of spreading the sickness when a crowd collected'.[1] Proportionately Horsham appears also to have experienced a severe visitation of an epidemic disease in 1609—which was contemporaneously called 'plague'—for between 25 March and 21 June the parish register records 39 'plague-burials' in a total of 66 for the year up to 21 December.[2] Rice notes that 22 of the dead were stated to be children and he adds that two families were exterminated. The seasonal incidence of this alleged plague-mortality and the high proportion of child victims, 56·4 per cent, rule out bubonic plague as its cause. It could have been a virulent epidemic of measles, which in the British Isles attains its maximal activity in December and June,[3] and which was much more deadly in seventeenth-century England than it is today. It was very probably bubonic plague, however, which visited Westbourne this year as Sperling reports that 68 burials were registered there during the summer months, compared with an annual average of 13 for the decennium 1550–9 and of 21 for the years 1600 to 1650 inclusive.[4] He justifiably suggests that though plague is not named in the parish register the excessive seasonal mortality is indicative of that disease. It was certainly bubonic plague that attacked Bradford-on-Avon this year in a visitation which lasted 20 weeks according to a petition presented by the town for relief.[5]

Among the Midland counties which were invaded by plague in 1609 Worcestershire seems to have been possibly the worst afflicted. In January the constables of Salwarpe were ordered to collect 3s. 4d. weekly for the relief of the plague-stricken poor living in Foregate Street, Worcester—these were most probably cases of typhus fever—and in September they were instructed to double that sum.[6] At Bedwardine plague may have been confined to the inhabitants of St John's parish, but it was apparently more widely dispersed at Leigh, where the inhabitants, in addition to providing relief for 140 of their own plague-stricken poor, were required to relieve also a number of sufferers in the neighbouring parish of Suckley.[7] The worst outbreak of the disease may have been experienced by Castlemorton, where it erupted in the late spring or early summer and recrudesced in 1610, with the consequence that a levy had to be raised in April of that year for the relief of the plague-stricken.[8] In the adjoining county of Shropshire plague, after lying dormant during the winter, erupted at Ludlow in April 1609, and an analysis of the registered monthly burials there (see figure 46) shows that the outbreak reached a first peak in June, developed a second peak in September, and was extinguished in December.[9] In a total of 155 burials registered during the year—compared with annual averages of 68 and 77

respectively for the quinquennia immediately preceding[1] and succeeding 1609[2]—96 or 65·7 per cent are marked with a cross and Weyman presumes that these represent plague-burials.[3] He remarks that a number of families were exterminated during the epidemic and my examination of the burials register indicates that one family—of which both parents and their 5 children were buried in a period of 19 days in September—was certainly exterminated and 4 others probably suffered the same fate. The mortality curve of this

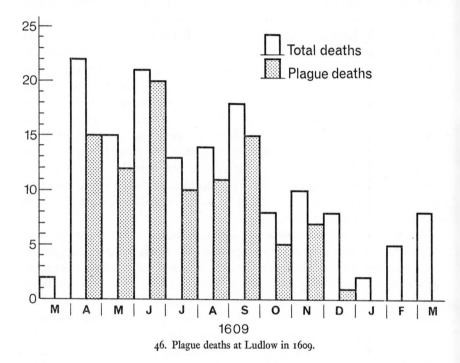

46. Plague deaths at Ludlow in 1609.

epidemic differs from the usual seasonal curve of bubonic plague in England but the reason for this difference is not now discoverable. Its sudden onset and rapid progress in the spring suggest that it might have been a much more serious visitation but for some repressive influence in the early weeks of the summer, possibly the occurrence of a spell of cold, wet weather in July. To the north-east of Ludlow Belper was also visited by plague this year, and as it lost 53 members of its small population between 1 May and 30 September,[4] it may have suffered a minor calamity. Cox affirms that the disease can be traced in other Derbyshire parishes in 1609, although none of them suffered as severely as Belper.[5] In the contiguous county to the

south Leicester's disastrous visitation has been described, but it is to be hoped that some future historian of that city will make an exhaustive study of it, including a comprehensive examination of the parish registers, because it seems evident that it was a calamity which must have exerted some effect upon the civic, social, and economic life of Leicester. Moving east into the adjoining county, the Lincoln Corporation archives mention under the date of 15 December 1609 that some citizens were shut up in their houses 'for fear of the sickness' and that a levy was authorized for their relief.[1] In view of the time of the year it is probable that 'the sickness' was on this occasion an outbreak either of typhus or relapsing fever, each of which is louse-borne. Blomefield is uninformative about the duration of the outbreak of plague in Norwich this summer, but he does state that its death-roll was small and he mentions that 'the River was watched least they should bring Stuff or Infected Persons from Yarmouth'.[2] There is little doubt that municipal authorities in seventeenth-century England recognized that navigable rivers played an important but obscure part in the spread of bubonic plague, and the river-watch organized by the civic authorities of Norwich was a wise measure in view of Cox's assertion that 'evidence can be obtained, though by no means always from the parochial registers, of plague attacks during the sixteenth and seventeenth centuries at almost every seaport of the King-dom, small or large'.[3] It was a tragedy of ignorance that rendered the Norwich watch and all other river-watches in this century incapable of arresting the riverine spread of plague.

Also in 1609 plague was reported from Liverpool, Aberford, and Newcastle-upon-Tyne, although it was most probably its winter alias that afflicted Liverpool, whose mayor acknowledged in March the receipt of £160 for the relief of the 'poore and visited people of that city',[4] adding the informa-tion that 28 cases and suspect cases of the disease then remained in 'the Cabons'. These were presumably temporary huts erected outside the town to serve as a pest-house. At Aberford, where it was apparently confined to a single family, it was undoubtedly typhus fever that killed 4 of the 5 members in December.[5] Newcastle-upon-Tyne may have lost some hundreds of its citizens from bubonic plague this year for Cox reports that about 20 plague-burials were registered in the parish of All Saints in 1609 and 160 between April and December 1610.[6] Perhaps some future historian of Newcastle will examine all its parish registers and give a full account of the duration and severity of this visitation.

Bubonic plague disappeared as an epidemic disease from London in 1610 and did not reappear as such until 1625, and it also declined in activity in the provinces. Four only of the metropolitan parishes appear to show specific

references to the presence of plague in them this year and the registers of 3 of these,* which are included in table 20, muster only 16 plague-burials between them. The fourth was the parish of St Giles, Cripplegate, where a parishioner was summoned in April to appear at the next sessions to answer 'for receivinge people into his house sick of the plague brought from other parts to the prejudice of the parish' and for having 'at the same tyme another sick of the French pockes [who] liveth incontynently with one Fayth Langley'.[1] Was he running the seventeenth-century equivalent of a nursing home? In view of the paucity of references to plague in London in 1610, and Creighton's figure of 1,803 alleged plague-deaths[2]—of which only 1,090 occurred in the plague-months of July–October inclusive—Keys is at fault in his assertion that 1610 was a severe plague-year in the city.[3] He seems to have based this erroneous statement on his belief that Ben Jonson wrote his play, *The Alchemist*, which is built round the disease, because of its severe epidemic activity in 1610; but the precise date of Jonson's completion of this play is uncertain. It is one of a group of plays which he produced between 1605 and 1615[4] and a more likely explanation of his introduction of plague in this play is that his son, the first Benjamin, died of the disease in 1603 at the age of seven.[4]

As London and Westminster were so little troubled by plague during the next 14 years, it is convenient to deal now with their records of the disease up to and including 1624. In 1610 the churchwardens of St Margaret's, Westminster paid 6*d*. to 'Goodwife Wells for salt to destroy the fleas in the churchwardens' pew'.[5] Evidently the Anglican worshippers of the seventeenth century were as tormented by this ectoparasite as the monks had been in Salimbene's day.[6] Most of the fleas, which undoubtedly were equally devout and attentive in most English parishes, were the human flea, *Pulex irritans*, which rarely, if ever, transmits *Pasteurella pestis* from man to man and never from rat to man; but some of them, especially in plague-time, were *X. cheopis*, carried into churches in the outer clothing of people seeking divine protection from the dreaded scourge, and their presence explains the closure of many churches in plague-time, especially as some churches probably also harboured *R. rattus*. The general ignorance of personal and domestic hygiene and the lack of facilities for the regular laundering of clothes and bed-linen, which encouraged the conservation of fleas, lice, and bed-bugs, explains why the churchwardens also found it necessary in 1610 to expend 10*d*. on the purchase of 'a pound of orris powder† to put among

---

* St Helen's, Bishopsgate,[7] where 4 plague-burials were registered in a total of 21 in 1610; St Mary Somerset,[8] where 6 were registered in a total of 55, and St Michael Bassishaw,[9] where 6 were registered in a total of 47. Their respective percentage plague-mortality rates of 19, 10·9, and 12·7 confirm the comparatively feeble activity of the disease in London that year.

† The powdered rhizome of three species of Iris, which has a fragrant odour like that of violets and is credited with insecticidal properties.[10]

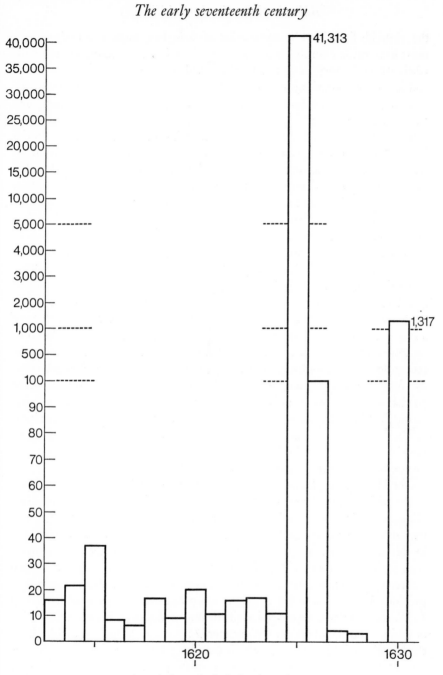

47. Annual plague-deaths in London, 1613–30.

the churche linon'.[1] The summation of fleas, lice, bugs, and body-odours must have made church attendance, especially in hot weather, a true test of Christian endurance in Stuart England and it is not surprising that Pepys and his contemporaries used to roam from church to church during the protracted sermons—the desire for a breath of fresh air and a good scratch must have been irresistible.

The register of St Michael Bassishaw contains one entry of a plague-burial in 1611[2] and during the 12 years from 1613 to 1624 only 192 plague-burials were recorded in the metropolitan area (see figure 47). It is probable that many of these were deaths from typhus fever which was endemic by reason of its aetiology in most English towns in the seventeenth century during the winter months. Yet it was during this lull that a proclamation in 1615 praised among recent public works the building of what was evidently a permanent pest-house.[3] The civic authorities cannot have foreseen the great outburst of 1625 but they were obviously apprehensive about the probability of another maritime importation of bubonic plague. The wider diffusion of that disease in England this century, especially in connexion with the great metropolitan epidemics of 1603, 1625, 1636, and 1665, may have been a consequence of an increase in the bulk of merchandise carried by road and in the speed of its transport about the country. A proclamation in July 1618 blames 'the recent decay of the highways and bridges [on] the common carriers, who now use four-wheeled wagons, drawn by 8, 9, or 10 horses, and carrying 60 or 70 cwt. at a time, whereas heretofore they used two-wheeled carts carrying 20 cwt.'.[4] Undoubtedly *R. rattus* would find it much easier to conceal itself in the larger wagons, and when these were loaded with certain kinds of merchandise they would offer attractive hiding-places for rats seeking to escape from an area of epizootic rat-plague.

Outside London plague appeared at Horsham but with a restricted activity, as the parish register records only 7 plague-burials and a suspect one.[5] The Gloucestershire hamlet of Tredington was by contrast ravaged by it and may have suffered comparatively one of the most grievous visitations of it in this decennium. Maclean opines that the hamlet did not contain more than 80 inhabitants in 1610, in which year 24 burials were registered there between 5 September and 2 December compared with a total of 11 during the previous decade, and of the 24 plague was presumptively responsible for 22.[6] In Worcestershire it appeared in 'the tithing of Whitsons between the parish of Claines and the liberties of Worcester'.[7] No information is available about the severity of this outbreak, which may have been considerable as Sinker states that a levy was raised for the relief of the plague-stricken.[8] Its eruption at Evesham provoked the usual flight of the well-to-do inhabitants from the

town and a consequent order by the corporation that 'no member of the body corporate should leave the town during "the tyme of this Visitacon" under a penalty of £10; [and] that no burgess should leave without the Mayor's license under a penalty of £5'.[1] Barnard adds that watchmen were appointed to assist the Justices of the Peace to enforce this order. Southall notes that on account of the prevalence of plague in Hereford the assizes were transferred to Leominster this year and he asserts that Presteigne was synchronously ravaged by it.[2]

On the eastern side of England Cambridge seems to have been proportionately as badly scourged as Leicester as Cooper reports that 429 burials were registered there, excluding the parishes of St Andrew the Great and St Andrew the Less.[3] He remarks that early in September the corporation, 'by reason of the great visitation & infection now in this town very rife and dangerous', dispensed with the bailiffs' dinners at Sturbridge Fair and on Michaelmas Day.[3] Independent testimony to the gravity of this epidemic of plague is provided by a report sent from Cambridge on 7 September to Sir John Wynn.[4] If plague actually invaded Cambridge in 1608 it may have persisted as an enzootic disease among the house-rats there, possibly with sporadic cases of the human disease, until a spontaneous increase of virulence of *Pasteurella* engendered an epizootic with a consequent epidemic of it.

Chester appears to have experienced a severe visitation in 1610 as Ormerod affirms that many died of plague there[5] and Liverpool may have been equally unfortunate as 'a lay of half a fifteenth' was levied on towns in East Lancashire for the relief of its plague-stricken people.[6] In the other 'Rose county' the register of St Mary's parish in Beverley is unfortunately incomplete for 1610—probably because of plague—but it shows nevertheless that the town was scourged by the disease. Radcliffe says that the epidemic erupted there in June, in which month 23 plague-burials were entered in the parish register, 'besides 40 that was shuffled into graves without any reading over them at all'.[7] There were 30 plague-burials in August, he reports, 12 in September, 2 in October, 5 in November, and when the outbreak was extinguished later in that month the plague death-roll amounted to 114.[7] At Lamesley 28 persons died of plague this year,[8] a mortality that may have represented at least one-quarter and possibly one-third of its population. At Whickham 'the plage began (in July) at Storye's in the South field, whereof died Storye and his three children'.[9] On this occasion plague was not confined to this household as Surtees notes that several entries of plague-burials follow this record in the register.[9] Unfortunately he did not trouble to count them.

The next year, 1611, saw the last reported flicker of bubonic plague in

England until 1615. It recrudesced slightly at Tredington in April in one house in which 3 members of the family died of it.[1] It behaved in a similar fashion at Leicester, reflecting in its feebleness the earl of Rutland's 'benevoleunce unto the poore visited people of Leicester';[2] he gave 'for one weeke' in September 20*s*. to be distributed among them. One feels that his lordship might have been somewhat more generous, especially as he had no income tax to pay and no death duties loomed ahead to impoverish his heirs. The only serious appearance of plague this year was at Chippenham, which was apparently so badly visited by it that the customary levy for plague-relief upon places within a 5-mile radius of the stricken town proved insufficient to meet its needs. Justices of the Peace were empowered by the statute 1 James I, c. 31 to assess any parish within 5 miles of a town or place infected with plague at so much money a week.[3] Accordingly a weekly rate of £40 was levied on all townships within a 10-mile radius of Chippenham, excluding Bradford-on-Avon and Westbury which had themselves been 'lately infected with the plague'.[4] The reason given for this levy was 'lest great famine be bred in the said town, and the poor inhabitants be thereby enforced to disperse themselves abroad, and endanger the country by the further spreading of the same contagious sickness'.[4] The widespread poverty that existed among the urban communities of Stuart England was an important factor in the conservation of bubonic plague. The poverty of Sheffield is a representative example. In January 1615 it is said to have had a population of 2,207 persons, of whom 725 were 'all begging poor'. One hundred householders in the town were poor artificers but able to relieve other needy citizens, whereas 160 householders were too poor to help others and would be driven to beggary by a fortnight's sickness. The population included 1,222 children and servants of the householders.[5] The little market-town of Shipston-on-Stour, which cannot have had a population of more than 600 in 1618, may have been proportionately even more poverty-stricken. In that year it petitioned against its taxation for the relief of the plague-stricken poor at Worcester because it had to support 140 households of its own and there were not more than 30 households in the town financially able to contribute to this relief.[6]

In 1615 plague was active at Twickenham, where the parish register recorded 24 plague-burials during the year,[7] and it may have visited High Wycombe in 1617 and again in 1624. Downs notes that in the former year 112 burials were registered compared with an annual average of 67 for the preceding quinquennium, and in the latter year there were 109 compared with an annual average for the preceding 6 years of slightly less than 70.[8] Regrettably he does not give the figures for the registered monthly burials

in those years and in their absence his view that the increased mortalities were caused by bubonic plague is not acceptable. In 1617, however, Dudley may have been sorely afflicted by the disease as a petition from it for relief avers that 'sickness' had persisted in the town for 'almost three-quarters of the year', that it was still active, and that there were then in the town 'seaven score children by reason of this sickness who either want father or mother or both'.[1] The parental loss is suggestive of plague; but until Dudley's parish registers have been critically studied the true nature of the 'sickness' will not be certainly known.

Minehead, Worcester, and possibly Shipston-on-Stour, appear to be the only places in England where plague occurred in 1618. The Somerset county archives merely state with respect to Minehead that a levy was ordered in July for the relief of its plague-stricken inhabitants, but a hint at the severity of its visitation is contained in a note that a certain Francis Pearce, who had undertaken 'to victual and provide the necessaries of life for the infected people', was owed £20.[2] As that debt represented a considerable sum of money in 1618 it is possible that there were several score of plague-stricken people in Minehead. There seems now to be a break of some 3 years in the English records of bubonic plague because its next appearance, according to Cox, was at Little Marlow in July 1621, when it killed 19 people.[3] The parish register dates this visitation to 1625, however, with a note recording the burial of Lady Mary Borlase, who 'died of plague, as did 18 more'.[4] The apparent absence of references to plague elsewhere in England in 1621 suggests that Cox is at fault in his chronology in this instance, because it is not until 1623 that excessive mortalities suggestive of bubonic plague are encountered in parish registers and notices of it occur in municipal archives. Apart from Leicester, where Kelly affirms that plague reappeared 'in a virulent form',[5] the presumptive parochial outbreaks of it are all located in the north of England, particularly in the counties of Cumberland and Westmorland. Cowper, who asserts that 1623 was 'a very severe plague-year in the north', quotes Slinger (*Lancaster Guardian*, 11 April 1896), as his authority for the report that there were 270 plague-burials in Lancaster that year.[6] The parish register of Middleton, near Heysham, records an excessive mortality, to wit, 181 burials compared with 63 in 1621, 51 in 1622, and 48 in 1624;[7] but until the monthly burial figures in 1623 have been studied it is not certain that the excessive mortality there was caused by bubonic plague. In the Lakeland counties there were excessive mortalities in the 11 parishes shown in table 18, and a critical study of other parish registers in this region might reveal other excessive mortalities and determine their causation. Stockdale cites the Rev. T. Lees for the statement 'that in some parishes the

TABLE 18

Annual burials in eleven Lakeland parishes, 1623

	1623	Annual average	Authority
Kendal	762	—	
Greystoke	163	Under 30	
Crosthwaite	257	About 30	
Penrith	227	30 to 35	Stockdale
Newton Regny	35	8	
St Bees	145	30	
Kirkby Lonsdale	120	Under 50	
Cartmel	219	—	
Millom	93	18 to 27	Knowles*
Camerton	92	10	Barnes
Hawkshead	98	—	Cowper

TABLE 19

Monthly burials at Camerton and Hawkshead, 1623

	Mar.	Apr.	May	June	July	Aug.	Sept.	Oct.	Nov.	Dec.	Jan.	Feb.	Mar.
Camerton	4	4	3	7	12	15	20	16	6	4	2	3	—
Hawkshead	1	3	7	5	5	21	10	9	13	7	1	11	2

death rate in 1623 exceeded five times the average'.[1] Regrettably the vicar omitted to name these parishes. 'From entries in the Greystoke register', he continues, 'it is evident that one cause of the mortality was a famine among the extremely poor—"tramps" as we now call them: as deaths occurred in the village street, at the cross, in "hog-houses" in the fields, and many of the entries are supplemented by the affecting statement that death took place "for want of means to live".'[1] If the local harvest failed in the Lake District a famine may well have occurred there because there was no state recognition of a distressed area in Stuart times; but if there was famine, the 'famine fevers' were a more likely cause of an excessive mortality than bubonic plague. There is evidence which supports this contention for Stockdale remarks that the burials in the afflicted parishes were spread more or less evenly over the year, with the exception of October and February which each had about one-third more burials than the other months. It is of course

* Rev. Canon Knowles. 'The Earlier Registers of Waberthwaite and Millom', *Trans. Cumb. West. Antiq. Archaeol. Soc.* III (1878).

possible that both plague and the 'famine fevers' were killing the Lakeland folk. Barnes for Camerton and Cowper for Hawkshead give the figures for the monthly burials registered in those parishes in 1623[1,2] (see table 19). These figures show that at Camerton the four 'plague-months' of July–October contributed more than 68 per cent of the annual death-roll, and if the burials registered in June and November are added the six months during which plague and its complications and sequelae could have been responsible for the deaths contributed 82·6 per cent of total burials. Bubonic plague was therefore responsible for the excessive mortality at Camerton, a conclusion that is supported by Barnes' note that multiple deaths commonly occurred in each infected house during the epidemic.[1] At Hawkshead, where the total of registered burials was 96, the corresponding percentages are slightly more than 47 and a little over 66. It seems probable that dysentery as a 'famine-fever' was largely responsible for Hawkshead's death-roll.

Nicholson affirms that no burial was registered in the parish of Orton during the 5¼ months preceding January 1625 but 61 were registered in the succeeding fourteen months, a mortality which he says was nearly 3 times greater than the usual mortality in the parish.[3] It is evident that some cause other than bubonic plague was responsible for the excessive mortality because the monthly burial figures which he presents give a percentage rate of less than 30 for the four principal 'plague-months'. Presumably the missing month of March supplied the 5 burials required to provide his total of 61 burials as his monthly figures add up only to 56. South of the Lake District Lancashire was severely afflicted by epidemics of disease this year, some of which may have been outbreaks of plague, some visitations of smallpox, and some epidemics of typhus fever, though the true nature of the county's morbidity trial will not be known until all its parish registers have been critically examined. In 1623 the parish registers of Blackburn reveal a great mortality according to Axon. He notes that the annual burials about this time averaged from 110 to 120; but from January to December 1623 there were 410 registered. The monthly burial figures for the three months of October–December were respectively 60, 55, and 66, so that just over 44 per cent of the total deaths occurred during this period, which he affirms was the period of maximum mortality when 'numerous members of the families of the local gentry died'.[4] Smallpox would seem to be the most probable cause of this mortality. This year Bolton also sustained a disastrous mortality, nearly 500 burials being registered at the parish church, a figure which Axon opines may represent one-third of its population.[4] Rochdale parish register also records a great mortality between August 1623 and the subsequent February. In 1622 the burials numbered 201, a figure which rose to 587 in

Places afflicted by multiple
visitations of plague
• London

• DURHAM Places involved in the epidemic
of A.D. 1603

• Malpas Other places visited

Whickham 1610
•Newcastle-upon-Tyne
•Lamesley 1610
DURHAM•

Greystoke 1623•
Camerton 1623•
Penrith 1623•
St Bees 1623•
•Orton 1623
Hawkshead 1623•
Cartmel 1623•
Scarborough 1624
KirkbyLonsdale 1623
•Lancaster 1623
•York
Aberford 1609
MONK FRYSTON•
•Beverley 1610
Methley 1604• •Hull
Middleton 1623•
Liverpool 1607• Salford
1604• •Manchester 1604•
•Stockport
1604
Northwich 1604 Dronfield 1608
•CHESTER-
FIELD
Lincoln
Chester• MACCLESFIELD
Nantwich 1604
Malpas 1604• •Belper
Whitchurch 1604• Mucklestone 1604 1609
Hodnet 1604• •Stone 1604
Myddle 1604• •Stafford 1604
Eccleshall 1604•
Shrewsbury 1604• Chelsey 1604 Lichfield 1604 STAMFORD
Condover 1604• Tamworth Peterborough 1606
Penkridge 1604 •WALSALL •Leicester
Wednesbury 1604 •Olton 1604 •Nassington
1604
Stowe 1610• Ludlow •Coventry 1604 Godmanchester 1604•
1604 •Warwick 1604
Presteign 1610• Ribbesford •Grendon 1604 •Cambridge
Leominster 1610• (1606
Suckley 1609 Worcester 1609 NORTHAMPTON
Hereford 1610• •Tredington 1610
Castlemorton 1609 •Evesham 1610 COLCHESTER
Carmarthen 1604 •Tewkesbury
Gloucester 1604• •Sandridge 1604
Oxford
Chippenham 1611 High Wycombe Westminster
WINDSOR• •DATCHET Greenwich
BRISTOL• MARLBOROUGH •London 1610
Bath 1604• •Calne 1604 CHISLE- STROOD
Bradford-on-Avon 1611• •DEVIZES HURST Canterbury
Westbury 1611 •DORKING 1609
Minehead 1618 •MAIDSTONE
SALISBURY
Southampton 1604 •Horsham 1604
Cranborne 1604• •PYECOMBE
•EXETER

2• •1
5• •3 •4
6• •7
8•

1.RYARSH 2.ADDINGTON 3.WEST MALLING
4.EAST MALLING 5.OFFHAM 6.WATERINGBURY
7.YALDING 8. EAST PECKHAM
0 50 100
MILES

48. The reported distribution of bubonic plague in England and Wales, 1600–24.

1623 and fell to 124 in 1624. Of the burials registered in 1623 close on 500 occurred between 1 July and the end of February,[1] a seasonal incidence which suggests that plague and typhus fever may have combined to scourge Rochdale.

Plague was active in 1624 over a wider area than in the previous year for it was reported at Scarborough, Yarmouth, Tamworth, Tewkesbury, and High Wycombe, and these outbreaks were the forerunners of the great outburst of 1625. Scarborough was 'sore grieved' by it in the summer and a levy was made for its relief;[2] but the visitation seems to have been extinguished in the autumn as the levy was cancelled at the Helmsley Sessions in January. In February the Privy Council was informed that 'Yarmouth and some places of the county thereabouts' were suffering with plague,[3] but it is unlikely that bubonic plague was active then and the disease was probably typhus fever. The visitation of Tamworth may have been a calamity as it was designated 'the great plague at the town of Tamworth' in an order made about the collection of relief money for the town.[4] The justices ordered a levy of £32 from the county of Warwick, from which £8 a week for one month was to be distributed in Tamworth, but the levy had not been completed by Michaelmas 1627. By contrast Tewkesbury was lightly attacked, the visitation causing less than 20 plague-deaths, a fortunate escape which Dyde attributes to 'the care of the bailiffs in removing infected families into Oldbury-field, where houses were built for their reception'.[5] Reference has been made to the visitation of High Wycombe by plague this year but no mention was made of the excessive mortality there which Downs inferentially ascribes to bubonic plague.[6] Unfortunately he does not give the monthly burial figures in support of his surmise and as Creighton avers that the summer of 1624 was unusually hot and dry,[7] the excessive mortality in High Wycombe and in other towns and villages could have been caused by fly-borne outbreaks of bacillary dysentery or water-borne outbreaks of typhoid fever. The accompanying map, figure 48, shows some of the places in England and Wales which appear to have been visited by bubonic plague during the twenty-five years from 1600 to 1624 inclusive. Their relative concentration in the west Midlands counties may, however, be a fault of this history and not a true representation of the incidence of the disease.

Scotland

Although Scotland was free from plague in 1619, it had been exposed to the risk of a fresh maritime importation of *P. pestis* in the previous year when a ship from Norway entered Dunbar harbour in July with 'some infectioun of the pest' on board.[8] The master of the ship was ordered to sail back to

Norway immediately, wind and tide permitting, and to re-ship any goods he had already landed on pain of death. A later proclamation ordered strict precautions to be taken against the importation of plague by ships coming from Denmark 'and other parts of the Eastern Seas',[1] and a ship which arrived from Königsberg—where plague was then raging—was ordered to quarantine at St Colme's Inch.[2] One result of the alarm raised by these maritime dangers was the issue of an order by the Privy Council to the Edinburgh magistrates to improve the sanitary condition of the city. It certainly needed cleaning, for the Council declared that it was

so filthy and unclean, and the streets, vennels, wynds, and closes thereof so over-laid and coverit with middings, and with the filth of man and beast, as that the noble, councillors, servitors, and others his majesty's subjects wha are lodgit within the same burgh, cannot have any clean and free passage and entry to their lodgings; wherethrough their lodgings have become so loathsome unto them, as they are resolved rather to make choice of lodgings in the Canongate and Leith, or some other parts about the town, nor than to abide the sight of this uncleanliness and filthiness; whilk is so universal and in such aboundance through all parts of this burgh, as in the heat of summer it corrupts the air, and gives great occasion of sickness.[3]

A correct observation although it was not applicable to bubonic plague, which is not a 'filth disease' like typhoid fever, the bacillary dysenteries, and cholera. It would be unfair to regard seventeenth-century Edinburgh as the queen of Scottish dirt because there is no doubt that most Scottish towns were then as filthy as the capital. Half-a-century later an English visitor commented:

Their cities are poor and populous, especially Edinburgh, their metropolis, which so well suits with the inhabitants, that one character will serve them both, viz. High and dirty. The houses mount seven or eight stories high, with many families on one floor, one room being sufficient for all occasions, eating, drinking, sleeping, and sh—. The most mannerly step but to the door, and nest upon the stairs. I have been in an island, where it was difficult to tread without breaking an egg; but to move here, and not to murder a t—, is next to an impossibility.[4]

Bubonic plague had vanished from Scotland in a major epidemic role before this comment was written; but the enteric fevers, the dysenteries, and the louse-borne fevers remained to afflict its people, and the morbidity and mortality rates of these diseases were undoubtedly aggravated—as also they were in England—by the public indifference to the need for urban and domestic sanitation and cleanliness.

Plague invaded Scotland again in the autumn of 1624. Reliable information was received early in November that the disease was raging in Dutch and Baltic ports,[5] and it was most probably imported from one of them simul-

taneously with its maritime importation into England, because 'upon the 28th of November the Pest brake up in sundrie houses in Edinburgh, to the great terrour of the whole toun. It began in Paul Hay a merchant's hous a moneth before, and was not knowen till now; therefore the more dangerous, because hard to descerne the uncleane from the cleane.'[1] Its appearance so late in the year precluded it from developing epidemic activity; but after so long an absence the occurrence of sporadic cases—as *P. pestis* was spread slowly by a creeping epizootic among the house-rats—created a panic and the meetings of the Privy Council, of the Court of Session, and of all the inferior judicatories were adjourned until February.[2] Sporadic cases of the human disease may possibly have occurred as late as mid-December, because on the 15th a man was granted a licence 'to go to Edinburgh, to attend to his wife and family during the visit of the plague there, and to remain there until the 15th of January next'; and in his petition for the licence the applicant stated that the appearance of plague had made 'the inhabitants thairof to provyde and foirsee for the saulftie and transport of thair families incase anie forder growth of the said plague sall happen to continew in the said burgh'.[3] However there was no augmentation of its activity; on the contrary it was evidently extinguished even among the house-rats by the arrival of cold weather in December, for there is no notice of its presence anywhere in Scotland for another eleven years.

England and Wales

A fresh, virulent strain of *P pestis* probably arrived in England in the late summer or early autumn of 1624. It arrived at a time when England was already suffering from the ravages of other epidemic diseases as Creighton emphasizes,[4] because during the previous two years London had been a focus for spreading epidemics of dysentery, typhus fever, and smallpox. A Londoner reported in December 1623: 'Here is a contagious, spotted, or purple fever, that reigns much, which, together with the smallpox, hath taken away many of good sort, as well as meaner people';[5] and in August 1624 he wrote: 'We had 328 died this week, a greater number than hath been these fifteen or sixteen years, and yet no mention of plague...But this spotted fever* is cousin-german to it at least, and makes as quick riddance

---

* The modern use of the name, *spotted fever*, is as a synonym for the septicaemic form of epidemic cerebrospinal meningitis, which is manifested by the occurrence of multiple haemorrhages in the skin. This meningococcal infection may attack and kill children, but it is more commonly encountered in its epidemic form among young adults who are crowded together in camps, barracks, hostels, and on ships, especially under the stress of war. It is almost certain, however, that the disease which was mortal in London in 1624 was typhus fever, which was often called *spotted fever* in the past because it is accompanied by a characteristic skin rash that assumes the appearance of multiple flea-bites.

315

almost.'[1] Again, early in September, after remarking that 407 deaths had been returned in the city's Bill of Mortality for the previous week, he wrote: 'And yet we will be acknown of no infection. Indeed, by the particulars, we find about 250 of them to be children,* most of the rest carried away by this spotted fever, which reigns almost every where, in the country as ill as here ...and takes hold of whole households in many places.'[2] Wilson notes that the mortality in London during the second half of 1624 was exceptionally high, due to the prevalence of spotted fever, which the public ascribed to the marketing of a bumper crop in September of cucumbers that had been poisoned by having been watered from 'low, noisome and stinking' ditches.[3] He remarks also that parliament was prorogued from November to February 'on account of "a general sickness and disease which proves mortal to many and infectious to more", which was dispersed in London and Westminster'.[4] It is possible that cerebrospinal fever and typhus fever were concurrently epidemic in London in the winter of 1624 as they may be clinically indistinguishable. Their absolute distinction today depends upon the microscopical and chemical examination of the cerebrospinal fluid.[5] The annual burials registered in 30 London parishes during the eleven years 1620–1630 are shown in figure 49. In some of these parishes there was an increase in the number of burials in both 1623 and 1624. An analysis of their monthly burial figures reveals that there were more burials in the autumn and winter than in the first half of the year in general, although this seasonal distribution is not a constant feature of their registers. It is significant that cerebrospinal meningitis, the louse-borne fevers, and smallpox all exhibit a preference for cold weather conditions for their epidemic manifestations in the British Isles.

Although neither bubonic plague nor typhus fever exhibits a mortal predilection for children, one London parish register, that of St Michael Bassishaw, credits plague with just such an age incidence in 1625. In a total of 164 burials registered during the three summer months of July–September, 49 were those of children and 37 of these are entered as plague-burials.[6] As

* In August 1620 'the Earl of Dorset's young and only son died of measles'[7] and it is probable that an epidemic of malignant measles was responsible for this child mortality.

---

49. Annual burials registered in thirty London parishes, 1620–30. All Hallows, Bread Street (12); All Hallows, Honey Lane (15); Kensington, Middlesex (13); St Antholin, Budge Row (6); St Bene't Paul's Wharf (10); St Clement Eastcheap (23); St De'nis Backchurch (2); St Dunstan in the East (24); St Helen's, Bishopsgate (8); St James, Clerkenwell (14); St Katherine by the Tower (30); St Margaret Moses (7); St Martin-in-the-Fields (25); St Martin Orgar (29); St Mary, Aldermary (3); St Mary the Virgin, Aldermanbury (21); St Mary-le-Bowe (16); St Mary Magdalen (28); St Mary Mounthaw (26); St Mary Somerset (20); St Matthew, Friday Street (22); St Michael Bassishaw (27); St Michael, Cornhill (5); St Olave, Hart Street (18); St Pancras, Soper Lane (17); St Peeters upon Cornhill (1); St Peter, Paul's Wharf (11); St Stephen's, Walbrook (19); St Thomas the Apostle (4); St Vedast, Foster Lane (9). (*see opposite*)

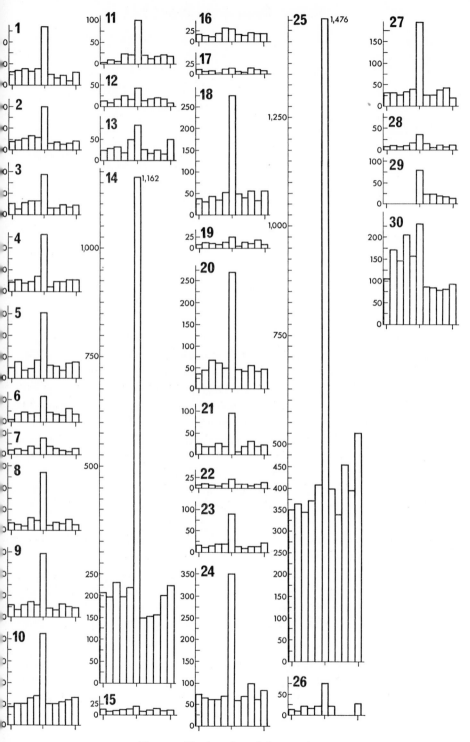

Figure 49 (For legend see facing page.)

TABLE 20

Plague-burials in the registers of twelve London parishes, 1625

St Michael, Cornhill	July 15	Hew Pinninge, servt to Mr John Woddward, scrivener; plague.
St Antholin, Budge Row	July 12	Robert Parker; plague.
All Hallows, Bread Street	August 5	Sarah, servant to Mr George Abdy, drawer of cloth [*in Polles church yard, of the pestilence*, xii d]
St Thomas the Apostle	July 26	Robert Stevenson (brought from ye Pest house).
St Helen's, Bishopsgate	June 8	Jane d. of Thomas Haypell.* [* 'Pla' in margin.]
St Be'net, Paul's Wharf	July 15	George Blunt; plaugue.
St Peter, Paul's Wharf	July 8	Elizabeth Tew, servant to Mr Franckham, dier, in the churchyarde at the east end, without a coffin; Plague.
St Pancras, Soper Lane	August 2	Thomas Reave, cittizen & salter of Londō, aged 25 years, in the midle of the ile.* [* Plague].
St Mary Somerset	May 27	Henry Exton. Plague.
St Martin-in-the-Fields	July 4	Edward Johnson a poore boy in the fields. *peste.*
St Mary Magdalen, Milk Street	July 12	Gregorie Penton, clothworker, p.
St Michael Bassishaw	May 27	Susan Wharton, infant. Plague.

none of the other metropolitan parish registers supplies any information about its child-burials at this time, it is not known whether the experience of St Michael's parish was unique or common to the London parishes. In the absence of modern diagnostic methods the identification of this particular child-mortality is not possible, but pointers to the nature of the responsible disease are that it may have been confined to a single parish and that it certainly occurred during the 'fly-season'. At a guess it could therefore have been a virulent outbreak of *Salmonella* food-poisoning. 'In the Middle Ages, regulations were in force in England forbidding the use of tainted and diseased meat in public cook shops along the banks of the Thames. The slaughter and sale of sick animals, however, was not supervised, and the results can be imagined.'[1]

Creighton avers that plague was prevalent in London in the spring of 1625[2] and that it was violently epidemic in July.[3] The dates on which the first plague-burials are marked in the 12 parishes which seem to be the only ones that specifically mention plague (see table 20) support his statement. The weather in March must have been unusually mild, however, if it was truly bubonic plague which earned the lord mayor a reprimand from the Privy Council.

We understand [wrote that august body] that the plague doth daylie encrease in the citty and that ther dyed this last weeke seven of it in one parrish and although it hath beene thus encreasing divers weekes yet wee cannot heare that any good

course hath beene taken for preventing it either by carrying the infected persons to the pesthouse or setting watch upon them or by burning of the stuffe of the deceased which being of little or noe value might easily be recompensed.[1]

Seven deaths in one parish hardly seems to merit this reprimand, but it exemplifies the dread in which bubonic plague was held by the highest mandatory authority in England. As no entries of plague-burials apparently occur in the metropolitan parish registers before the end of May, it is doubtful if the disease was active in March; but the Privy Council had been informed early in February—most probably wrongly—that plague was then prevalent in Yarmouth and its vicinity,[2] and it knew from past experience that if the disease invaded any of the East Anglian ports it would almost inevitably invade the port of London, especially when plague was raging in Holland.

The death of James I on 27 March; his funeral with great pomp on 7 May; the arrival in June of Henrietta Maria—to whom Charles I had been married by proxy in Paris on 1 May—and the opening of Parliament on the 18th, combined to distract official attention and public alarm and delay the customary panic flight of the wealthier citizens from the mounting activity of plague in London. Some of the citizens were becoming apprehensive about its progress, however, because one wrote from Fleet Street on 21 May to his wife: 'The plauge doe much increase heare, which make my cosin & I to keepe our selves in our chamber but when we must needs.'[3] The progress of this destructive epidemic is described in the contemporary correspondence collected by Birch.[4]* Early in April the number of infected parishes rose from 4 to 10 in one week, in which 25 plague-deaths were recorded.[5] Towards the end of the month a correspondent remarked that though the reported plague-deaths did not exceed 25 a week, 'yet the apprehension is more than usual, and startles us very much, as well in regard of the time of the year, and great concourse that of necessity must be,† as that it is already dispersed in more than a dozen several parishes'.[6] He added: 'The physicians do in a manner agree that this sickness is not directly the plague, as not leaving any sore, or any such like accident, but only contagious in blood or kindred.'[7] It may have been this note that induced Wilson to allege that pneumonic plague was more prevalent in 1625 than in 1603 and that the absence of buboes from many of the corpses led the physicians and 'searchers' to mistake the cause of death.[8] There does not appear to be any contem-

---

* The correspondence collected by Birch consists largely of letters written by the Rev. Joseph Mead from Christ's College, Cambridge, to Sir Martin Stuteville, transmitting reports received from correspondents in London.

† The coronation of Charles I, which was postponed to October soon after this letter was written.

TABLE 21

The progress of the epidemic of plague in London in 1625*

					Within the walls	
Correspondence source	Date	Total burials†	Plague-burials†	Parishes infected	Plague-burials	Parishes infected
Dr Meddus to Rev. Joseph Mead	29 April	305	26	9	3	2
John Chamberlain to Sir Dudley Carleton	6 May	292	30	—	—	—
Rev. J. Mead to Sir Martin Stuteville	14 May	332‡	45	13	—	—
	28 May	401§	78	17	14	9
Chamberlain to Carleton	12 June	434	91	25	—	—
Mead to Stuteville	18 June	—	165	31	—	—
Chamberlain to Carleton	25 June	640	239	32‖	30‖	—
Mead to Stuteville	2 July	942	370	50	57	—
	9 July	1222	593	57	109	—
	30 July	3583¶	2471¶	—	—	—
	27 August	Abatement of 364 in reported plague-deaths				

porary evidence that either of these major outbursts of bubonic plague was accompanied by any appearance of the pneumonic form of the disease. The absence of buboes was due in all probability to the extremely high virulence of the responsible strain of *Pasteurella pestis* at the start of the 1625 epidemic, the victims succumbing to a fulminating septicaemia before the characteristic localization of the plague bacillus in the lymphatic glands had time to develop. Pneumonic plague is invariably associated with bleeding from the lungs, which would have been a dramatic symptom to seventeenth-century observers, but there is no notice of any such bleeding in any contemporary account of this epidemic to my knowledge. Moreover the infectivity and mortality of pneumonic plague are so great that the death-roll in each of these outbreaks would have been far higher if that form of the disease had occurred.

As table 21 shows, the plague-burials registered in the city and its liberties

* Compiled from *The Court and Times of Charles I*, T. Birch (London, 1848), I, 17–45.
† Registered during the previous week.   ‡ Supplied by Chamberlain.
§ Supplied by Chamberlain, who gives 16 as the number of infected parishes.
‖ Supplied by Mead, who adds that 115 plague-burials were reported from Shoreditch, White-chapel, and two parishes in Southwark.
¶ In Westminster, Stepney and Lambeth '(places not counted in the bill), near 840'.

did not exceed 100 until the middle of June and up to that date only 25 of the 122 parishes had been invaded; but on 13 June it was reported that plague had spread 'into all parts of the city' and had invaded Westminster.[1] It is probable that this report was exaggerated although the disease was undoubtedly exciting widespread alarm, as a gloomy comment in Birch's collection testifies. The French retinue of Henrietta Maria had 'come in an ill time', a correspondent writes,

for the sickness increases and is spread far and near...So that, if God be not merciful to us, this town is like to suffer much, and be half undone. And that which makes us the more afraid is, that the sickness increaseth so fast, when we have had for a month together the extremest cold weather ever I knew in this season. What are we then to look for when the heats come on, and fruits grow ripe?[2]

That week's Bill of Mortality had returned 434 deaths from all causes, of which 91 were ascribed to plague.[2] As events were to show his apprehension was unfortunately fully justified, and if it had not been for that spell of unusually cold weather in the late spring there is little doubt that the epidemic of 1625 would have been even more extensive and destructive than it was.

With the arrest of this cold weather plague speedily assumed epidemic proportions and the increase of the registered plague-burials above the 100-mark (see table 21) was officially acknowledged by the adjournment of Trinity Term on 18 June.[3] Two days later the reception by the Privy Council of a petition from Godalming to cancel the fair held there at the end of June as plague was then 'dispersed into divers parishes within the saide countie',[4] reveals the rapidity with which the disease was spreading with the coming of warmer weather. During July the registered weekly plague-burials rose to nearly 2,500 (see table 21) and the public panic increased to an even greater degree. On 11 July Parliament adjourned to Oxford[5] and five days later a report from the city said that this adjournment 'and the increase and general spread of the plague, cause such distraction and consternation, that the like was never seen in that age. The number of deaths for four weeks was answerable to those in the first year of the late King, but this last week it is near a thousand greater, which makes all men hasten away.'[6] Prior to these notices William Wynn, writing from Westminster College to his father on 3 July, had remarked upon the extraordinary increase in the number of plague-deaths, 500 having occurred during the previous week. He added: 'The Towns upon the Thames side are also infected...[and] it is dangerous to visit any doctor just now, or to buy or sell anything.'[7] A postscript written by his brother begs their father to stop the bearer of the letter from coming to their house at Gwydir for a month for fear of his introducing plague there.

The dreadful augmentation of the plague-burial figures in London made

one Cambridge don wonder whether the metropolitan mortality returns were being falsified.[1] They probably were but in the opposite manner to his surmise because forty years later Pepys discovered proof of their falsification.[2] About the middle of July the don wrote to a friend, transmitting a report he had received from the rector of a London parish:*

Henceforth, you must not look to be supplied as you were wont. The plague is in the doctor's parish, and the rest of our intelligence is fled, and it grows very dangerous on both sides to continue an intercourse of letters, not knowing what hands they pass through, before they come to those to whom they are sent. Our Hobson† and the rest should have been forbidden this week but that the message came too late...We are yet, God be thanked, free of the plague here; nay fewer burials and tolling of bells than all this year before.[3]

The writer enclosed with his letter the London Bill of Mortality for the week ending 9 July which is reproduced in table 21.[4] It was the first of a series of 8 he sent, the remaining 7 of which are presented in table 22. Incidentally he mentions that the bills were compiled on Thurdsays,[5] so their dates do not always correspond with the dates of his letters. The general belief that letters could transmit bubonic plague testifies to the contemporary ignorance of the nature of the disease and resulted in the adoption of ludicrous measures for the disinfection of mail in the British Isles and in many European countries.

On 20 July the lord mayor was notified that the king and the Privy Council were leaving or had already left London and he was exhorted 'to continue zealously and rigorously' to execute all measures requisite for the abolition of plague.[6] It is greatly to his credit that John Gore, like the boy in *Casabianca*, remained faithful to his duty, and on 30 July he was able to retort to the pusillanimous Privy Council that 'he had used all diligence to prevent the spreading of the infection' and that the epidemic had consequently not been so destructive within the walls as it had been outside them.[7] Meanwhile the rector of St Gabriel Fenchurch repeated in a letter to the Cambridge don two stories about plague that were current in his parish in July. Their invention aptly illustrates the credulity and ignorance of the Londoners about plague. One tells of a man living in Leadenhall Street who fled into the country with his 7 children to escape it but buried them all there and returned to the city[8] The other tells of a woman who fled from London

for fear of the plague, [who], when she was come on the hill near Streatham, in the way to Croydon, turned back, looked on the city, and said, 'Farewell, London,

---

   * St Gabriel Fenchurch.

   † Tobias Hobson, 'a carrier who lived at Cambridge in the seventeenth century. He kept a livery stable, but obliged the university students to take his hacks in rotation. Hence the term *Hobson's choice* came to signify "this or none"'[9].

and farewell, plague'; but soon after was taken sick, had the tokens on her breast, and these words to be distinctly read: 'It is in vain to fly from God, for he is everywhere.'[1]

In a letter from Cambridge dated 30 July the don remarked that the malignity of this outbreak already greatly surpassed that of 1603 and the month of August, 'the month of corruption' was yet to come. 'I send you a corranto', he continues, 'brought me besides expectation and almost against my will; but it was well aired and smoked before I received it, as all our letters used to be; nor was the plague then at St Paul's Churchyard, whence it came.'[2] He was not alone in doubting the truth of the official returns of plague-deaths, for as early as 20 June the Tuscan Resident in London confided in a despatch his belief that the true plague-mortality was being concealed 'in order to detain the nobility as long as possible' to provide the proper welcome for Charles's queen.[3] He added the interesting observation that the average weekly mortality from all causes in London ranged from 130 to 180 at that time. The total death-roll in the week preceding his despatch was 445 and he opined that the excess of deaths above 180 could certainly be attributed to plague, although officially the plague-deaths were returned as 165[3] (see table 21). In an earlier despatch dated 6 June he referred to a royal proclamation that no person other than a member of the court or someone named by their majesties was to go to any place where 'their Majesties may be this summer, or to approach their persons within a distance of twelve miles...on account of the plague which every day gains force'.[4] A month later he noted that the court had moved to Hampton Court[5] and on 11 July he reported that he was moving 14 miles outside London as his house was then surrounded by plague.[6] He added that the disease was then universally distributed in London and that it had spread to other parts of the kingdom. On the last day of July, 'owing to the increase of plague', the Exchequer was transferred from Westminster to Richmond until further order.[7]

Throughout August London suffered a grievous destruction of its citizens although a large part of its inhabitants had deserted it. On the 4th Bartholomew and Sturbridge Fairs were cancelled,[8] and the preamble to an Order in Council published on the 5th records 'the lamentable informacions which wee daily receave of the great spreading of the contagion of the plague through the Kingdom'.[9] This order requested the Archbishops of Canterbury and York to instruct their bishops to notify the churchwardens of infected parishes to stop public assemblies and exhort their parishioners to observe the public fast—which Wilson says was proclaimed on 2 July[10]—privately in their own homes. He remarks that the Tuscan Resident commented 'with some surprise and irony on this fast, "which is performed in all the parishes

and consists in staying in church all day, singing psalms, hearing sermons, the one shortly after the other, and making I know not how many prayers, imploring God for the stoppage of the plague and the ceaseless rain which for a month past has fallen to the detriment of all kinds of crops ".'[1] Had they known how averse the house-rat was to getting its fur wet they would have welcomed the rain for its undoubted limitation of the speed of spread and of the extent of the epizootic of plague. Wilson relates that the king and the Lords heard two sermons in Westminster Abbey to inaugurate this fast; that a collection for plague-relief was taken at the service, and that all those peers who had absented themselves were ordered to double their contribution.[2] It seems probable that the amount of the contribution had been prescribed for each class of the congregation. Additional fasts were proclaimed for 20 July and succeeding Wednesdays. Most of the aldermen and minor officials fled from London and the lord mayor was forced to absent himself from his duties in June because his own house was infected.[3]

The Tuscan Resident, who had found refuge at Richmond, reported on 8 August that 3,400 deaths had been registered in London during the week,[4] and on the 16th he reported a death-roll of 5,000 adding:

I will send my letters to London, although no one is allowed to go there at present, and it can only be done secretly and by payment of money...The Magistrates, in desperation, have abandoned every care; every one does what he pleases, and the houses of merchants who have left London are broken into and robbed...Plague having broken out here also, I must depart and go at least forty miles farther.[5]

Five days prior to this despatch a royal proclamation had ordered all churches in the kingdom to take a collection for the relief of the plague-stricken poor in London.[6] It seems probable that this order was ignored by those parishes which were themselves experiencing the ravages of plague; but even so a large sum of money must have been collected and it would be of interest to know how and by what authority it was disbursed. Possibly it was administered as an early example of a lord mayor's fund with which we are familiar.

On 14 August an Order in Council cancelled the mustering of the train bands throughout England,[7] an action which indicates that the epidemic was by then widespread in the country, and simultaneously a correspondent reported: 'The sickness is so violent in London, that there is no intercourse of boats from Kingston. Those that go to London must not return into the country. At Woodstock, where the Court is, none may go from thence to return, nor any come thither, and for contraveners a gibbet is set up at the Court gate.'[8] He added that the total deaths registered in London during the past week were 4,855 including 4,133 of plague, 'not counting West-

minster and the outlying parishes, where there died above one thousand'.[1]
A fortnight later the Privy Council warned the Bishop of London that
plague-corpses must be interred at least 3 feet deep because 'the contrairie
whereof being generally observed to be now practised cannot choose but be
a greate occacion of increase of the infeccion by corrupting of the ayre in
greater measure'.[2] The previous day a gossiper had passed on the rumour
that the Lords were about to direct the lord mayor of London to send the
plague-sick out of the city to tents and cabins in the fields, and he added:
'No man comes into a town without a ticket, yet there are few places free.
Only one house infected in that town [Southampton] but one died that day
without the town, in the fields. He came from London. He had good store of
money about him, which was taken before he was cold.'[3] This day also the
Cambridge don, in a renewal of his correspondence after a silence of nearly
a month, remarked on the coincidence of the decline in the plague-mortality
curve with that of the 1603 epidemic.[4] He expressed the fear that the decline
was rather for lack of human material than for any other reason because it
had occurred 'only without the walls', whereas within them there had been
an increase of about 160 deaths.[5] His fear is understandable in view of the
fact that the plague-deaths in London during the second week of August
amounted to 4,855, to which must be added 'the better part of 2,000 from
Westminster and Stepney',[6] and even this number did not represent the
peak week of the epidemic.

For the next two months we have the evidence presented by the Bills of
Mortality shown in table 22. They reveal that the epidemic continued to
rage, but with lessening violence, during the first ten days of September;
that it declined abruptly during the first week in October, and that this
decline was succeeded by its gradual recession during the remainder of that
month and the first ten days of November. From Cambridge a letter dated
4 September joyfully reported that the registered plague-burials in London
had decreased by nearly 1,000 that week and that the abatement was general.[7]
The writer added: 'I had no mind to send you a bill, finding of late that
there is danger in them...howsoever, *the carrier perfumes them all*' (my
italics).[8] The bill he enclosed, which recorded the mortality returns for the
week from 25 August to 1 September inclusive, gave these figures:

Buried in all 97 Parishes within the Walls, 1,360; of plague, 1,144:
Buried in the 16 Parishes without the Walls part within and without the Liberties,
1,688; of plague, 1,439:
Buried in the 9 Out-Parishes, 846; of plague, 761:
Total burials, 3,897; of plague, 3,344:
Parishes clear [of infection], 5; Christenings, 117.[8]

TABLE 22

*London Bills of Mortality in 1625 sent by the Rev. Joseph Mead to Sir Martin Stuteville**

Week ending	97 Parishes within the walls		16 Parishes of the liberties		9 Out-parishes		Total	
	Total	Plague	Total	Plague	Total	Plague	All causes	Plague
1 September*	1,360	1,144	1,688	1,439	846	761	3,897	3,344
8 September	1,216	859	1,305	1,055	726	636	3,157	2,550
6 October	288	199	291	174	251	165	838	538
20 October	181	98	270	107	200	126	651	331
27 October	132	44	130	32	113	58	375	134
3 November	98	29	152	25	107	35	357	89
10 November	78	26	135	34	106	32	319	92

The respective percentage plague-mortality rates of these three divisions are a trifle over 84·0, 85·2, and practically 90·0, so that the crowded, jerry-built slums on the outskirts of the capital were the area where plague struck fiercest. After another six days the don was able to report that the total weekly burials had decreased by 740 (see table 22) and the burials within the city walls by 234.[1] He mentions that a Bill of Mortality covering twenty weeks, which had come into his possession, gave the total number of burials registered in the city and its liberties as 39,569.[2]

I saw [he continues] the last week a letter from the doctor,‡ dated September 1; wherein he signifies his preservation hitherto, and wonderfully deplores the state of the city, whereof one passage is this; viz.— 'The want and misery is the greatest here that ever living man knew; no trading at all; the rich all gone; housekeepers and apprentices of manual trades begging in the streets, and that in such a lamentable manner as will make the strongest heart to yearn.'[3]

To some employees who were left behind in London when their masters fled plague brought, however, a time of luxury and relaxation. William Lilly describes with gusto the enjoyable time he had after his master fled into Leicestershire, leaving him and a fellow-servant to look after his house. He bought a bass-viol and took lessons on it; went bowling in Lincoln's Inn Fields, and sometimes to church to hear funeral sermons, 'of which there was a great plenty'. All those Londoners who could do so fled into the country; no person of any consequence remained in the capital, and the

* Compiled from *The Court and Times of Charles I*, T. Birch, (London 1849), I, 46–61.
† From 25 August to 1 September.
‡ Dr Meddus, rector of St Gabriel Fenchurch.

desolation was calamitous. The Sunday before the peak Bill of Mortality was published for the last week of August, 'which was of five thousand and odd hundreds' (see figure 50) he attended a sacramental service at St Clement Danes. Three ministers officiated because the number of communicants was so great. One of them fell sick of plague as he was giving the sacrament and died on the Thursday after, and another was stricken at the close of the service but recovered after an illness of thirteen weeks. The third escaped completely although Lilly says 'he officiated at every funeral, and buried all manner of people, whether they died of plague or not'.[1] These clergymen and some others named by Wilson[2] redeemed the honour of the churches they served; but regrettably many deserted their parishioners and

the flight of clergymen from the City was resented as bitterly in 1625 as in 1603. Those who had two benefices, and whose usual practice in the summer was to discharge their office to their 'Countrey sheep' were excused, but for the runaways whose only cure and whose only care was a London parish there was neither excuse nor sympathy.[3]

In mid-September the Tuscan Resident reported from his refuge at Melchbourne near Bedford that almost as many people were dying of plague 'within the circuit of three miles' from London as in the capital itself, and that the disease was so widespread throughout the kingdom that it was impossible to go anywhere without a danger of contracting it.[4] A fortnight later he noted that the epidemic was declining in London but plague was still so prevalent in the provinces that few cities, boroughs, or villages had escaped its visitation.[5] This was a typical 'Black Death' exaggeration, founded on ignorance of the aetiology of bubonic plague, distorted by rumour, and magnified by terror of the disease; but it was not confined to the fearful imagination of the Tuscan Resident; indeed it has been repeated and elaborated by many subsequent writers on bubonic plague, even in our own time.

The metropolitan epidemic of 1625 was largely contained within the three summer months of July–September and table 23 shows that the epidemic reached its zenith in August. It is not possible now to verify the accuracy of these parochial records, but it is certain that they understate the plague-mortality. Nevertheless the figures they give demonstrate that the disease was almost universally dispersed in the London area and that it was everywhere gravely destructive of human life. With the subsidence of the epidemic in October the population began to return and a traveller who passed through London in mid-October records that 'he found the streets full of people and the highways of passengers—horse and foot'.[6] The rapid reflux of the population made the government apprehensive about a recrudescence of

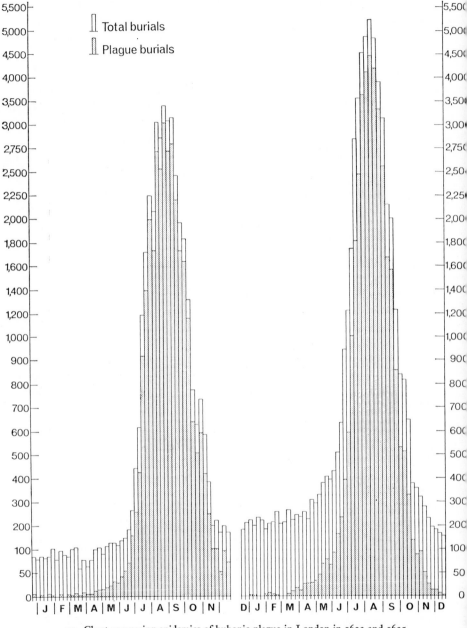

Total burials

Plague burials

| J | F | M | A | M | J | J | A | S | O | N |　　| D | J | F | M | A | M | J | J | A | S | O | N | D |

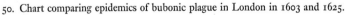

50. Chart comparing epidemics of bubonic plague in London in 1603 and 1625.

TABLE 25

Showing the summer incidence of bubonic plague in twenty-five London parishes in 1625

	Public. Har. Soc. vol. nos.	Registered burials				Total summer burials	Percentage of annual total	Total burials marked plague
		1625	July	August	September			
St Peeters upon Cornhill	I	136	17	53	33	103	75·7	—
Saynte De'nis Backchurch	III	102	6	46	23	75	73·5	—
St Mary Aldermary	V	92	1	32	30	63	68·4	—
St Thomas the Apostle	VI	136	26	65	28	119	87·5	—
St Michael, Cornhill	VII	154	14	49	49	112	72·7	78
St Antholin, Budge Row	VIII	60	6	14	13	33	55·0	29
St James, Clerkenwell	XVII	1,103	329	454	168	951	86·2	—
St Vedast, Foster Lane	XXX	147	20	71	25	116	78·9	—
St Helen's, Bishopsgate	XXXI	141	17	54	11	82	58·1	44
St Bene't, Paul's Wharf	XLI	217	8	42	24	74	34·1	74
St Peter, Paul's Wharf		98	11	43	2	56	57·1	48
All Hallows, Bread Street	XLIII	43	2	19	12	33	76·7	9
St Mary le Bowe	XLIV	28	2	8	5	15	53·5	—
St Pancras, Soper Lane		13	0	4	3	7	53·8	6
St Olave, Hart Street	XLVI	277	66	104	42	212	76·5	—
St Mary Somerset	LX	270	55	118	30	203	75·1	9
St Mary the Virgin, Aldermanbury	LXI	95*					—	
St Martin-in-the-Fields	XXV	1,476	155	403	414	972	65·8	992
St Clement Eastcheap	LXVII	88	12	41	21	74	84·0	—
St Martin Orgar	LXVII†	88†	16	26	23	65	73·8	47
St Dunstan in the East	LXIX	347	62	101	69	232	66·8	—
St Katherine by the Tower	LXXV	237	52	56	25	133	56·1	—
St Mary Magdalen, Milk Street	LXXII	35	9	9	6	24	68·5	25
St Michael Bassishaw	LXXIII	190	23	88	53	164	86·3	105
St Mary Mounthaw	LVIII	69‡	6	41	17	64	92·7	—
St Gregory by Paul	—	232	30	92	87	209	90·0	200
TOTALS		5,874	945	2,033	1,213	4,191	71·3	1,666

Notes in Registers: * 'Names of such as dyed in the yeare 1625 beinge the yeare of the great plague wherein by reason of the death of the minister and of the clarke, and for want of some bookes and notes in their hands which cold not be had this booke for this yeare cannot be better p[er]fected.' For the same reason, no months or days are entered in the register this year.

† The burial entries total only 81 for this year, although the annual total of 88 is given in the register.

‡ The burial entries in this register only begin for 1625 on 21 July.

the epidemic and on 11 October a proclamation adjourned the term to Reading; forbade persons to resort to London unless they lived there, and prohibited any carriers from taking goods there until the cold weather was established. Simultaneously the inhabitants of Reading and everyone living within a radius of 3 miles of it were ordered to receive nothing from London.[1] The progressive decline of the epidemic in October[2] did not save the lord mayor from receiving a metaphorical 'kick in the pants' from the absent Privy Council, which censured him on the 12th for negligence in enforcing the anti-plague regulations.[3] He was told that plague-infected houses must be marked with a red cross and the inscription 'Lord have mercy upon us', and that convalescents must not be allowed to leave their houses until they were completely recovered. The next day an Order in Council confirmed that Michaelmas Term was to be held at Reading because of the 'great infeccion' still present in London.[4] Still flushed with anti-plague zeal now that the disease was declining and possibly yearning to return to the 'flesh-pots' of the capital, the Privy Council censured on the 21st 'the undiscreet and unruly caryage of the inhabitants of Westminster of whom those who have the sore running upon them goe as freely abroade conversing promiscuously with others as if they were not infected'.[5] These convalescents were of course quite incapable of transmitting bubonic plague to their healthy fellow-citizens. They would not have transmitted pneumonic plague—if that form had appeared in this outburst—although it is spread by 'droplet' infection among human contacts and has an extremely high infectivity, because pneumonic plague has practically a 100 per cent case-mortality rate and the rare convalescent from it does not bear a running sore on his body.

The spontaneous extinction of this great metropolitan outbreak of bubonic plague was the product of a combination of factors, to wit, the local near-extermination of its essential rodent reservoir, the house-rat; the enforced hibernation of the rat's plague-fleas by cold weather; the lack of human host material consequent upon the terrible mortality and the flight of a large section of the population from the plague-area, and a natural loss of virulence upon the part of *P. pestis*. It is of particular interest that there is a contemporary notice of this loss of virulence in the report that Sir John Coke sent on 18 October to Lord Brooke, 'On Monday next the Court removeth towards Windsor and then to Hampton Court if the sickness shall abate. We are full of hope that God beginneth to stay his hand, because now in London the *tenth person dieth not of those that are sick, and generally the plague seems changed into an ague*.'[6] (The italics are mine.) This mild form of bubonic plague is technically known as *pestis minor*. It can occur independently of

TABLE 24

The incidence of plague in six central London parishes in the weeks ending 20 and 27 October 1625*

	Registered burials		Percentage plague-burial rate	Registered burials		Percentage plague-burial rate
	Total	Plague		Total	Plague	
St Andrew, Holborn	33	22	66·6	—	—	—
St Bride	24	16	66·6	—	—	—
St Saviour, Southwark	32	10	31·2	—	—	—
St Mary, Whitechapel	44	30	68·1	31	20	64·5
St Clement, Temple Bar	53	43	81·1	18	11	61·1
St Martin-in-the-Fields	36	22	61·1	31	22	71·0

a decline in the virulence of an epidemic of *pestis major* and several distinct epidemics of it have been recorded in modern times.

The subsidence of the epidemic progressed unevenly in the London parishes as table 24 shows, because small aggregates of house-rats that had been missed by *P. pestis* in its major wave of infection became infected as the ravenous 'blocked' fleas migrated from the empty rats' nests in a desperate effort to survive. As late as the week ending 26 November (see table 26) the parishes of St Andrew, Holborn, St Mary, Whitechapel, and St Clement, Temple Bar, were contributing 37 per cent of the registered plague-burials in London,[1] though it is highly probable that these were mostly remote deaths from the disease. The decline in the number of plague-burials in November was, however, on the whole rapid and continuous, with the area within the walls having a marked advantage over the liberties and the out-parishes, but many of the artisans who returned to London were infected by 'blocked' fleas still surviving in their dwellings and died of plague.[2] Dr John Donne, the dean of St Paul's, replying on 25 November to the British ambassador in Constantinople, who had told him that 2,000 people were dying of plague each day in that city, wrote:

Your number was so far attempted by us, that in the city of London, and in a mile compass, I believe there died 1,000 a day. The citizens fled away as out of a house on fire, and stuffed their pockets with their best ware, and threw themselves into highways, and were not received so much as into barns, and perished so, some of them, with more money about them than would have bought the village where they died.[3]

* Copied from *The Court and Times of Charles I*, T. Birch (London, 1849), I, 57.

TABLE 25

Statistics supplied by the Rev. J. Mead to Sir M. Stuteville, 1625–6*

	Burials registered in the city of London and its liberties		Plague-burials within
Week ending	Total	Plague	the walls
24 November	231	27	—
1 December	190	15	—
8 December	181	15	2
15 December	168	6	2
12 January	159	4	1
19 January	137	3	—
2 February	125	4	—
9 February	160	10	7
16 February	146	10	4
23 February	185	8	—
2 March	173	1	—
9 March	142	0	—
23 March	165	3	—
30 March 1626	133	2	—

Towards the end of the month the weather apparently became so cold that the surviving rat-fleas hibernated, with the result that in December plague practically vanished from the area within the walls (see table 25). Its disappearance inspired the Privy Council to exhort the lord mayor and the Justices of the Peace of Middlesex and Surrey to strive their utmost to ensure that plague-infected houses were carefully cleansed, 'and especially the household-stuffs in them and namely the beddinge both by frequencie of fyer and exposeing them to the frostie and kindlie weather which it may please God to send'.[1] It was just about this time, remarks Masson,[2] that the English learnt of the disastrous failure of the expedition to Spain under the command of Viscount Wimbledon. That failure resulted from incompetent leadership and the indiscipline of the troops, but it was an outbreak of either plague or typhus fever on board the ships of the fleet that forced the expedition to return to England early in December. It is noteworthy that Plymouth must have been free from plague early in October because Charles I went there then to inspect the expedition.[3]

As 1625 drew to its close the termination of this disastrous outbreak was officially announced by an Order in Council published on 20 December[4] and ten days later a royal proclamation removed all the restraints on travel,

* Compiled from Birch, *op. cit.* I, 63–92.

communication, and the transport of merchandise that had been imposed in attempts to control the epidemic.[1] The deaths attributed to it in the winter months (see table 25) may in a few cases have been remote deaths, but in all probability most if not all of them were sporadic deaths from typhus fever which was endemic in seventeenth-century London. The terminal figures of its alleged mortality are supplied by Birch[2] and conclude with the report of a correspondent on 11 March 1625 (old calendar) that no plague-death was included in a total of 142 from all causes, and the comment: 'It is just a twelvemonth since it was so.'[3] The true total of lives destroyed in London and its suburbs by this epidemic will never be known, for the mortality figures that are extant are certainly inaccurate. Creighton, who gives the figures of 54,265 as the total death-roll and 35,417 as the plague-toll, remarks that the latter figure indicates that many plague-deaths were concealed. He emphasizes that the figures do not represent the full mortality suffered by the city and its liberties as a separate record was kept by a number of parishes, and he declares that the grand totals were respectively 63,001 and 41,313.[4] The Tuscan Resident reported that from May 1625 to the beginning of the ensuing February the recorded plague-deaths within a radius of 1 mile from the centre of London amounted to more than 60,000.[5] According to the *Remembrancia* the total of plague-deaths in 1625 as returned in the Bills of Mortality was for London, within and without the walls, 35,403, and for England and Wales, 68,596.[6] A Bill of Mortality for London and its out-parishes for the year from 16 December 1624 to 15 December 1625 gives Creighton's figures for the total and the plague-burials.[7] To these figures must be added the supplementary ones of 8,736 and 5,896 respectively that are given in a separate bill for Westminster, Lambeth, Newington, Stepney, Hackney, and Islington,[8] which make the grand totals identical with Creighton's figures. They represent the deaths that were officially returned for a particular period of 52 weeks, and it is of interest to compare them with the figure for the plague-deaths in the twenty weeks ending 8 September, when the epidemic was still raging in the city and its environs, supplied by the Cambridge don.[9] His bill covered the period back to the week ending 2 May and can therefore be reasonably assumed to include the greater part—probably four-fifths—of the true plague death-roll. If this assumption is correct the plague-deaths for the 52 weeks from March 1625 to March 1626 (by our calendar) should have totalled 49,461 and, if the proportionate relationship of Creighton's figures is correct, the deaths from all causes should have amounted to 71,943. The percentage plague-mortality rates calculated from these two sets of figures are nearly identical, to wit, 70·3 for Creighton's figures and 68·7 for the other set, and both are close to the

figure of 71·3 per cent shown in table 23. It seems a reasonable presumption therefore that whatever the true mortality figures are, bubonic plague was responsible for about 70·0 per cent of all the deaths that occurred in the metropolitan area in 1625. As regards the total mortality, taking into account that typhus fever and smallpox were also probably killing in the same period, it may have approached 100,000, and as the population of the metropolitan area probably did not exceed 300,000 in 1625, this epidemic of bubonic plague played the major part in destroying about one-third of the population of London, Westminster, and their suburbs. There are numerous references in churchwardens' accounts and in the registers of parishes in and around London that reveal the attitude of both clergy and laity to plague, and the efforts of municipal and parochial authorities to control it at this time. For example the churchwardens of St Alphege, London Wall expended 6s. 8d. on the marking of infected houses with red crosses,[1] which at 2d. a cross represents 40 houses in that small parish, while those of St Margaret, Westminster paid £2 17s. 8d. for the slaughter of 466 dogs,[2] which represents approximately 1½d. a dog. 'Little can be gleaned of the part played by doctors in this calamity. Many, as in 1603, fled into the country',[3] but a few remained faithful to their professional duty and at least one of them, Raphael Thorius, died of plague in July or August having 'acted more for the publick (by exposing his person too much) then his most dear concern'.[3] No medical man could have a nobler epitaph. Wilson has dealt fully with the plague-orders and regulations of both 1603 and 1625 and the interested reader is referred to his book as it would be a plagiarism to reproduce them here.

On 1 May 1626 Elizabeth Comer (or Cunnier) was buried at St Martin-in-the-Fields and in the burials register there is this note against her name. 'Paied the First daye of Maye 1626 to [*blank*] Haukes barbor Surgion for his paines openinge & vieuing the bodie of a frenche woeman who deceased in Hartishomlane to see of what decease shee dyed, ij s. vj d.'[4] It is improbable that murder was suspected and plague would certainly not have supplied the reason for the post mortem, which seems to have been made because she was a French woman and might therefore be expected to reveal some morbid process of a Gallic and sensational nature. It is much to be regretted that Mr Haukes' autopsy report was not copied into the register even if, as is possible, he found no obvious cause of her death, because this record of an official post mortem is the first one in England known to me. About a month before this plague was discovered in the parish of St Margaret Lothbury when the 'searchers' found a child who had—according to them—died of it. The result was that the family was strictly segregated in their house. After a week had passed £3 was lent to the father as he was unable to pursue his

trade as a brazier and the family of 8 persons was destitute. His application for additional relief after another eight days had elapsed was considered by the vestry to be 'very strange to the whole parish, having spent so much money in so short a time'. At its suggestion he agreed to be removed with his family to the pest-house, to be kept there 'at the charges of the parish, paying for every particular person 7s. per week, which did amount to 11 *l*. odd money, and there to continue for a month'.[1] The vestry explained that this uneconomic action was taken to prevent plague from spreading, but as the house-rats were left undisturbed it was ineffectual and before the subsequent epidemic subsided 103 parishioners had lost their lives from it. Freshfield says that at this time there were about 70 houses in the parish of St Christopher-le-Stocks, about 115 in that of St Bartholomew-by-the-Exchange, and a slightly larger number in St Margaret's. He opines that the population of St Christopher's did not exceed 500 and that neither of the other parishes had a population of more than 600. The first of the three contained very few poor folk; the second had a considerable number of poor residents, while St Margaret's was almost exclusively occupied by destitute poor, which explains why bubonic plague picked it out in 1626.

As was to be expected from its nature, bubonic plague exterminated many families in London and other towns during its great outburst of 1625. Alington records several instances in the parish of St Gregory by Paul[2] and Underhill, after noting that of 847 deaths registered in the parish of St Dunstan-in-the-West 647 were ascribed to plague, relates the extermination of a household of 7 persons in about ten days.[3] Table 26 contains some other instances extracted from the burials registers of some of the London parishes and a comprehensive study of all the metropolitan parish registers would undoubtedly discover many more. The burials in this table total 80 and the time elapsing between the first and the last of them is fifty-eight days. The speed of extermination ranges from the 2½ days required to destroy each member of the Lawrence household to the 14 days for each member of the Abbot family. The average lethal speed of bubonic plague (*pestis major*) appears to be about 3 days. It is possible that in the case of the latter family the two sons had been sent into the country as soon as plague became epidemic in London or were absent from home for some other reason during July and August. There would be sufficient 'blocked' fleas still alive in the house to infect them when they returned in September. If this family is excluded the speed of extermination ranges from 2½ days to the 6 days required to kill each member of the Tickell household, assuming that all its members died of plague. The only other epidemic diseases with a comparable killing speed of which there are historical records in England are the 'sweating sickness'

TABLE 26

*Some examples of the household incidence of plague in London during the epidemic of 1625**

Parish	Name of householder	Occupation	Burials registered during the summer months of 1625		
			July	August	September
St Clement Eastcheap	Lawrence	Tailor	15, M; 26, S; 27, S; 28, 2 S; 30, F	—	—
St Thomas the Apostle	Dike	—	—	20, 2 S; 25, G-M; 28, D	2, S
	Wood	—	—	—	7, S; 13, S and D; 22, D; 25, D; 27, F; 28, D
St Michael, Cornhill	Wilkinson	—	25, S	3, D; 7, S; 19 M†	—
	Evance	—	—	8, D; 16, D; 19, D†; 29, S†	1, S
St Michael Bassishaw	Rothwell	—	10, M; 14, S†; 17, S; 19, S†	—	—
St Bene't, Paul's Wharf	Burt	—	—	23, S; 31, S†	3, S†; 5, S†
	Vidler	—	11, D†; 22, S†; 23, S†; 24, F and D†	—	—
	Todd	—	—	—	7, D; 8, S†; 11, F†; 20, 2 C†
St Peter, Paul's Wharf	Franckham	Dyer	8, Md†; 18, D†; 22, M†; 24, F†; 26, D†‡; 23, Md	1, B†; 17, F†	—
St Helen's, Bishopsgate	Browne	(Widow)	—	9, D and L; 10, L; 11, L	—
	Haward	Joiner	1, D; 12, 2 S†; 14, S†; 15, M†	—	—
	Watson	Clothworker	7, D; 12, Mn†; 20, S†; 23, F and D†	—	—
	Tickell	Leatherseller	—	4, Mn; 5, S; 18, S†; 20, F†	3, S†
	Abbot	Merchant-Tailor	19, F†; 30, D	—	—
	Slynne	—	—	—	6, S†; 14, S†; 11, F†; 24, D; 26, S; 27, Mn
St Mary Mounthaw	Smallwood	—	22, D; 29, W-L	13, S and D; 15, D; 17, F and D	—

* B = Brother; C = Child; D = Daughter; F = Father; G-M = Grandmother; L = Lodger; M = Mother; Md = Maidservant; Mn = Manservant; S = Son; St = Servant; W = Widow.

† The girl who died on 26 July was the daughter of the man who died on 17 August; both were lodgers. The lodger who died on 9 August was the wife of the one who died on the 11th; their daughter

in the epidemic of 1485 and cholera in the great epidemics of 1832 and 1848.

In the Home Counties there are records of this epidemic involving Stoke Newington, Bromley, Enfield, Ashford and Kennington, Richmond, Chiswick, Kingston-on-Thames, Windsor, Little Marlow, and Godalming; but there is not the slightest doubt that a study of the appropriate parish registers would reveal that many more places were involved in these counties. The parish register of Stoke Newington records 40 plague-burials—'marked in the register with a red cross'—in a total of 52 burials registered in 1625. As there were only 15 burials registered in 1624 and 10 in 1626[1] the assumption is that plague trebled the mortality of this parish. It is possible that the parish of Tottenham was simultaneously attacked as Robinson states that 54 burials were registered there in 1625, an excessive number for the parish.[2] As smallpox was concurrently epidemic in the area, however, it is regrettable that he did not give the monthly burials figures for these parishes. The fact that Bromley was involved is contained in the report to the Privy Council that it had 'ben long tyme visited with the infection of the plague'.[3] Pegge assumes that the 67 burials—of which 26 were female—registered in the parish of Enfield this year were those of plague-dead, although this mortality was only about one-third of the plague-toll there in 1603 when 180 burials were registered.[4] He records that the justices levied a sum of £1 19s. 6d. for the relief of the plague-stricken in Ashford and Kennington and that the levy was raised to £3 in August to provide a month's rations for the poor of Ashford 'to prevent them from breaking forth of the town'.[4] The notice of plague at Little Marlow has been mentioned. The Tuscan Resident was driven from Richmond by the disease in mid-August.[5] From Chiswick, as plague was then raging there, Lord Francis Russell removed his family in August to Woburn Abbey.[6] The manor house at Chiswick had been specially reserved in an Elizabethan lease as a refuge for the Master of Westminster School and its 40 King's Scholars in times of plague in London and in 1625 it may have been imported by them or by other fugitives from London.[6] A few cases of the disease occurred at Woburn but no one in the Bedford household contracted it. In July it was reported to be epidemic in Kingston and its neighbourhood[7] and there are two reports of its activity at Windsor[8] and a note of its involvement of Stoke Poges.[9] Its appearance at Windsor denied Charles I his enjoyment of the royal residence there and his further efforts to evade the disease present an undignified picture. Moreover they were unsuccessful because, as Wilson notes[10] though the Court did its best to dodge the disease it was repeatedly introduced through the medium of 'blocked' fleas in all probability by the attendant rabble, with the result that

all the places it fled to became infected. From Whitehall Charles moved to Hampton Court, thence to Oatlands, and from there in mid-July to Windsor, whence he was soon chased to Woking; and then Bisham, Rycote, and Woodstock in succession received the royal dodger and his retinue. At Woodstock, as has been noted, Elizabeth I's custom of erecting a gibbet at the entrance to the royal retreat was revived to discourage potential importers of plague; but the true importers were never suspected let alone hanged. In any case how can you hang a flea? From Woodstock Charles moved to Oxford, where the eruption of plague gave him an excuse to dissolve Parliament,[1] thence to Beaulieu in September, from there to Southampton, then to Plymouth, and finally to Wilton.[2] None of England's sovereigns, with the exception of Charles II, emerges with any credit from their encounters with bubonic plague.

Most of the counties bordering on the English Channel seem to have been more or less extensively involved in this outburst of plague. In Kent the disease was reported at Dover[3] and Canterbury;[4] in Sussex at Rye;[5] in Hampshire at Portsmouth[6] and Southampton;[7] in Devonshire at Exeter, Plymouth, and Ashburton; but while at least one of these reports is faulty it is extremely probable that a critical study of the burials registers of the parishes in these counties would reveal numerous other locations of plague in 1625.

Plague was allegedly raging at Canterbury in July[8] although it does not appear to have invaded the city until about the middle of June, because the first notice of its presence seems to be 2 plague-burial entries in the latter half of that month in the register of the Strangers' Church.[9] The burials registered at this church in 1625 numbered 51 and of these 22 or slightly more than 43 per cent occurred in the four months of June–September, the word 'contagion' being attached to 18 of them. There is some doubt about the identity of the disease that was prevalent in Canterbury this year for the annual burials registered at the Strangers' Church in the years from 1622 to 1630 inclusive are respectively 20, 71, 54, 51, 62, 31, 31, 49, and 21, so that in 1623, 1624, and 1626 the recorded mortality was greater than in 1625. Canterbury may have experienced a comparatively mild visitation of bubonic plague this year or an epidemic of some less lethal disease; only an analysis of the monthly burial figures will discover the true cause of its mortality. Greenhill affirms that plague was epidemic at Rye in 1625 but less virulent then than in either 1563 or 1580.[10] Regrettably he does not present any mortality statistics from the parish burials register to substantiate this comparison. Portsmouth was reported to be 'grievously afflicted with the plague' in September and the Privy Council was informed at the beginning of

October that a town assembly to elect a new mayor could not therefore safely be held.[1] By the middle of November the epidemic had 'so much abated', however, that the townsfolk petitioned the Council for authority to hold the mayoral election.[2] Southampton may have escaped lightly as only one house in the town was infected at the end of August,[3] but Bath was somewhat more severely afflicted and Exeter seems to have suffered a calamitous visitation. In the register of the Abbey Church of Bath 5 burials in August and 7 in November 1625 are marked with an asterisk, and of the 34 burials registered during the year 53 per cent occurred in the four 'plague-months' July–October. All the marked burials in August were of members of the Tucker family—which lost the mother, 2 sons, and 2 daughters in 14 days—and all those in November were of members of the Smith family, 5 daughters and 2 sons of which died in 16 days.[4] It seems practically certain that this visitation of Bath by bubonic plague was fortunately confined to a small number of houses because there was no excessive mortality there. The registered burials at the Abbey Church this year numbered 34 compared with an annual average of 30·7 for the decennium immediately preceding[5] and of 28·8 for that immediately succeeding[6] 1625. Concerning Exeter Pickard remarks that from 1615 to 1624 the annual burials registered in the twelve city parishes averaged 175, whereas the registrations in 1625 and 1626 were respectively 1,807 and 506. He notes that with an estimated population of 12,300 in 1625 the death-roll in that year represents a mortality-rate of 14·6 per cent. He opines that the epidemic erupted in the spring because on 27 April the civic authority agreed to pay £28 for the use of a house and garden as a pest-house.[7] It must have been kept fully occupied for as late as 29 October plague was reported to be 'grievous at Exeter'.[8] When plague crept into his palace and killed 6 members of his household the bishop at first 'removed awhile into his garden and despatched business at a window; but later he decided to move to a safe place 4 miles out of Exeter'.[8] Hamilton asserts that this visitation was so terrible that Exeter was left almost destitute of inhabitants,[9] a typical exaggeration about plague which may be corrected to read—according to Pickard's figures[7]—that the city lost about one-seventh of its population in 1625. He states that the County Sessions were held at Crediton, where the justices ordered that any residents of Crediton who visited Exeter or any other infected place, or consorted with persons coming from such places, should be shut in their houses for one month. Plague nevertheless spread to Crediton, which suffered severely from it, and concurrently it invaded Chulmleigh, Moreton Hampstead, St Thomas, Dawlish, Withycombe, Chudleigh, Lidford, Barnstaple, Honiton, and Plymouth, where 80 persons died in one week. He notes that a sum of £40 was allotted

to Plymouth and Stonehouse for plague-relief.[1] There is a mystery, however, about the involvement of Plymouth in this epidemic. As early as 16 May the Privy Council received information that 8 suspect plague-deaths had occurred 'in Osen, over against Plymouth'.[2] If 'Osen' was the seventeenth-century synonym of Oreston, the modern township on the opposite side of the Cattewater from Plymouth, it is quite possible—if these were really plague-deaths—that the disease was active in Plymouth also in May 1625. On the other hand it does not seem to have been epidemic there that summer because on 20 September the mayor was ordered to proclaim 'with sound of drum' that while the king was in residence and the Fleet was concentrated there 'all persons lately resided, sojourned, or slept in any place infected with the plague, and particularly in or about Exeter',[3] were prohibited from entering Plymouth or its environs. It is extremely unlikely that Charles I would have gone to Plymouth if plague had been epidemic there and in-conceivable that he would have stayed in the town; yet the borough archives state categorically that plague visited Plymouth in 1625.[4] The disease was said to have been introduced by the troops concentrating there for the Spanish expedition. Moreover in the corporation's accounts for 1626 there is the record of a payment of 28s. 11d. 'for the charge of the setting upp of the house in the fields out of the Towne wherein the Mayor was chosen being wholly occasioned by means of the plague then in towne'.[5] It is to be hoped that some future historian of Plymouth will solve this problem by a com-prehensive study of the borough archives and the parish registers. If Cox's chronology is accurate the disease was certainly epidemic in Plymouth in 1626 as he affirms that it killed 1,600 of the townspeople that year.[6] All over Devonshire 'watches were set at the entrance to towns, and especially on bridges, to turn back any that were suspected of infection'[7] and levies were made for the provision of plague-relief to stricken towns. Hamilton gives these sums as the weekly allocations for plague-relief, to wit, Cullompton, £20; Dartmouth, £15; Tiverton, £100; Totnes, Ashburton, Buckland, and North Bovey, £150 between them. He comments: 'That these grants repre-sent a vast number of individual cases may be inferred from the instance of Northam. In that parish it is mentioned that 633 persons were "shut up". Yet only 32 l. 18s. 8d. a week was granted.'[7] However that sum would suffice to relieve the number of recipients mentioned at the customary contem-porary rate of 1s. a head each week.

In the adjacent county of Somerset Bath—as already noticed—and Bridg-water were visited and probably some other towns and villages were involved in the epidemic. Bridgwater may have been severely attacked because the Michaelmas Quarter Sessions were transferred to Taunton, where regula-

tions were made 'for the examination and detention of strangers in an isolation camp near to the town, and for the closing of houses suspected of infection'.[1] Harbin adds that 'Frome also had trouble with infected strangers, who were shut up in a remote house, where they all died'. These strangers included a man, his wife, and their child, fugitives from London, who cost the townsfolk of Frome 'the sume of eight pounds and upwards' for their segregation. They seem to have been upset by this unexpected burden upon their municipal finances as they petitioned the county authorities for authorization to levy a tax for poor-relief.[2] At the Sessions to which this petition was presented another was received from the inhabitants of Bridgwater, recalling that at the previous Sessions the authorities had been notified of the great misery and distress created in the town by the visitation of plague, which was still prevalent there in October.[3] In the previous July the magistrates had ordered the constables of Taunton to erect 'Boothes or Tents' in the close known as 'Tunwayes' in the parish of Westmuncton, 'for sequestringe and keepinge in of persons either infected or suspected to come from London or any other infected places'. They were also directed to appoint watchers to keep all suspect persons, whether Taunton-born, residents in the town, or strangers, in this isolation camp for at least 20 days.[4] As there does not appear to be any record that Taunton was attacked by plague on this occasion, the corporation no doubt congratulated itself on its scientific and successful preventive work; but if Taunton escaped it was very fortunate because plague seems to have raged in the surrounding countryside. The medical officer of the Langport Union some 200 years later contributed this note to Chadwick's report: 'It is stated in a very old history of Somerset that, about 300 years ago, nearly the whole of the inhabitants of Kingsbury, Muchelney, and Long Sutton were carried off by a pestilence, and that for many years afterwards it [*sic*] was considered so unhealthy that it was inhabited solely by outlaws and persons of the worst character.'[5] Harbin suggests that this tradition could refer to the 1625 outbreak of plague; but if the doctor's chronology is correct it would seem to refer more probably either to the plague epidemic of 1563 or to the last epidemic of the 'sweating sickness' in 1551.

On its way from London to the West Country plague may have struck hard in Wiltshire. On 5 August Steeple Ashton Fair was cancelled because, as the Privy Council was informed, 'there are severall townes not farr from thence in which the sickness is already dispersed'.[6] Judging from this report it seems likely that Trowbridge, Westbury, Melksham, Bradford-on-Avon, and possibly Devizes were involved in this westward spread of the disease; but until the burial registers of the Wiltshire parishes have been comprehensively

studied the extent and severity of the county's involvement will remain unknown. More information is available about its visitation of Winchester which by mid-September was in great distress, 'all the principall and wealthiest inhabitants being retired into other parts of the countrey about and the markettes very evill served with necessary provisions for those who remaine'.[1] The date of its eruption in the city is not known, but once introduced it evidently rapidly became epidemic, although the dirt and insanitation described by Jacob[2] were not, as he opines, conducive factors. The civic toll of 35 deaths registered in 1624 rose to 82 in 1625, and of this number 62 or 75·6 per cent occurred in the three months of August–October. From the information he supplies it is evident that several families were exterminated and he notes that the college scholars were boarded out from October 1625 to May 1626. He relates that the election of civic officers was removed from the 'thickly populated' St Maurice quarter of the city—which would be the chief focus of the epidemic—to the Guildhall; that a cottage was burnt down by order because a man died of plague in it—a somewhat extreme method of eradicating *X. cheopis* but undeniably effective—and that £75 was raised in the city for the relief of the plague-stricken.[3] In Oxfordshire Oxford itself must have been free from plague up to mid-July as otherwise Parliament would not have been told to reassemble there on 1 August.[4] However, by 27 July, when the vice-chancellor of the university reported that All Souls College was closed on account of it, it was present in various parts of the city.[5] A week later, by which time two notable persons had died of it,[6] Owen Wynn remarked on its prevalence in a letter to his father,[7] in which he enclosed an infallible remedy for it prescribed by Sir Walter Raleigh's apothecary, who guaranteed that it would effect a cure within 24 hours. It was just another of the nostrums which were concocted in plague-time and which 'cured you dead'.[8] By contrast Cambridge and its university escaped this outburst of plague not, however, in consequence of the official stoppage of all scholastic activities on 1 August or the cancellation of Sturbridge Fair on the 4th,[9] although the latter act was a wise precaution. On 26 September the mayoral feast, held annually on Michaelmas Day, was postponed 'forasmuch as the infeccion of the Plague is dangerously disperced...in many Townes & hamletts neere unto the Towne of Cambridge', which was then 'altogither cleere from any such infeccion'.[10] Plague came perilously near though, for on 3 October it was reported to have killed 3 persons in one household in Trumpington and concurrently 2 houses were closed because of it in Royston and their occupants 'translated into the fields'[11]—a euphemism for driven forcibly out of the village. In February there was 'much talk' in Cambridge that it had erupted at Linton;[12] but if there was any epidemic of disease there

then it was probably one of typhus fever. According to Clarke Coventry was visited[1] but he presents no local evidence to support his statement. The fact that Redditch was attacked is confirmed by the record that the parishes of Kings Norton, Northfield, and Alvechurch were assessed for the relief of the plague-stricken there at weekly rates of 9*s*., 4*s*. and 5*s*. respectively.[2] According to another local record eight more parishes were included in this assessment, namely, Bromsgrove, 12*s*.; Feckenham, 7*s*.; Belbroughton, 6*s*; Beoley, 6*s*.; Inkberrow, 5*s*.; Stoke Prior, 4*s*.; Upton Warren and Cooksey, 3*s*., and Cofton Hackett, 1*s*.[3] As these assessments represent a total weekly sum of £3 2*s*.' which was a considerable amount of relief-money in 1625, it is a reasonable supposition that Redditch was severely afflicted, for at the customary seventeenth-century relief rate of 1*s*. a week to each recipient the town had 62 persons at this charge in a population that cannot have exceeded 500 persons of all ages.

In the hamlet of Bradley in the parish of Malpas in Cheshire the extermination of the Dawson family provides a notable instance of the axiom that bubonic plague was a disease of the dwelling-house in England. *P. pestis* appears to have been introduced among the house-rats in the Dawson's home by a son who arrived from London ill with plague on 25 July and died a day or two later.[4] He was buried either in the garden or in an adjoining field. Between 10 August when the next death occurred—note the 14-day interval required for the epizootic among the house-rats to develop—and 5 September, the other 8 members of the family died of plague, a total of 9 persons in 40 days or, if the interval between the first and second deaths is excluded, in 26 days, an average of about 3 days per victim. There is a glory in this domestic tragedy. Richard Dawson

being sick of the plague and perceyving he must die at yt time, arose out of his bed, and made his grave and causing his nefew, John Dawson, to cast some straw into the grave, wich was not farre from the house, and went and layed him down in the said grave, and caused clothes to be layed uppon, and soe dep'ted out of this world; this he did, because he was a strong man, and heavier then his said nefew, and another wench were able to burye.[4]

Richard Dawson's forethought in the shadow of death surely entitles him to a humble place in the company of those very gallant gentlemen, like Captain Oates of Antarctic fame, who have gone knowingly to their death in order to relieve their companions. Ormerod, referring to this family holocaust, quotes entries in the parish burials register to show that plague continued its ravages in Bradley until the middle of October, when a mother and her child were buried by other members of the family,[5] presumably either in the garden of the house or in an adjacent field.

Returning to the eastern Midlands, Melton Mowbray and Leicester were involved in this outburst of plague. At Melton Mowbray the churchwardens paid 7*s.* 8*d.* 'to Wydow Powlie for Vittelinge yonge Queniboroghe lodging in the field being suspected of the plague for hys dyet j month and watching some nights of hym'.[1] If this was truly a case of plague and there was no outbreak of it among the townspeople, Melton Mowbray purchased its exemption very cheaply. Kelly says that the corporation made strenuous efforts to prevent the importation of plague into Leicester from London, but it appeared in Leicester in the spring of 1625, although it was restricted to a small area of the town for the first half of the year. However it spread rapidly during the warm weather of the summer and the corporation was obliged to make many payments for the watching of infected houses and for the relief of their occupants. In addition it paid £40 3*s.* 4*d.* 'for the dayely relief of the visited people in the Soare Lane, at the North Gate, Red Crosse, and St Maries Close'.[2] The common carriers were ordered to stop carrying any wares or passengers to and from London until further notice, but at least one tradesman ignored the order. He was a haberdasher who had collected a great hamper of hats and other commodities from London at the village of Wykin, about 2 miles from Daventry, where the carrier who brought them was now ill with plague.[3] The Hinckley authorities who sent this warning to the corporation on 7 September reported in a second letter about a week later that the carrier had died.[4] Kelly notes that payments were also made for killing 10 dogs and 'for searchinge of xlj^{tie} dead corpes' at a cost of £1 0*s.* 4*d.*[5] It is highly improbable that these corpses represented the sum of Leicester's plague-toll because the money disbursed for plague-relief in the areas named suggests that there were more than 40 deaths in those districts alone.

The full extent of the invasion of East Anglia and Lincolnshire by bubonic plague in 1625 will not be known until all their parish registers have been studied, but there are contemporary notices of its infection of Norwich and Grantham.[6] The disease erupted in Norwich about the end of June and Blomefield avers that it was imported from Yarmouth. He says that it increased steadily in intensity up to the end of July, in the last week of which month 26 plague-deaths were registered and 'the Belman by publick Proclamation warn'd all Persons within the city to put away their Dogs and Swine out of the Walls, on pain of being killed'.[7] By mid-August 19 houses were infected in four parishes and during the week ending the 19th 77 burials were registered in the city, of which 67 were ascribed to plague.[8] The civic authorities ordered a watch to be kept on the infected houses and a whipping for every person found begging in the streets, but the epidemic continued

to grow throughout August and September, in which month more than 40 plague-deaths were registered each week. The peak was apparently reached in the third week of this month with a total of 91 registered burials, of which 73 were ascribed to plague. It was as a last, desperate civic effort to arrest the epidemic that 'the Black-Tower on Butter-Hills was made up for a Reception for infected poor, and Tho. Chambers appointed Keeper thereof at 4*s*. a Week'.[1] An identical weekly wage was paid to each of two widows who were appointed to search the infected poor and to each of four bearers who collected the plague-corpses and carried them to the burial ground, which was presumably somewhere outside the city. After its usual winter intermission plague seems to have recrudesced in March because on the 15th the 6 plague-attendants were ordered 'to reside in Norman's Hospital and carry red staves', measuring 1½ yards in length, whenever they went outside that residence.[2] From 22 July 1625 to 10 November 1626 Norwich is reported to have sustained a death-roll from all causes of 3,835, to which number plague contributed 1,431,[3] a mortality rate of 37·3 per cent. This is such a low rate for a major epidemic of bubonic plague that either there must have been widespread concealment of the disease in Norwich or this visitation of the city was not as severe as the extant accounts of it suggest.

There appear to be only a few notices of plague in the counties north of the Humber in 1625 and none of its presence in the Lake District. It is unlikely that Sowerby and Leminge were the only places attacked by it in Yorkshire; that it visited only Gateshead, Barnard Castle, and Sunderland in Durham County, and that Newcastle-upon-Tyne was the only sufferer from it in Northumberland; but the parochial history of these counties has not yet been compiled and until it is written their experiences of bubonic plague in 1625 will remain incomplete. It seems to have been the Sowerby near to Thirsk which was 'visited with the sickness of the Plague' in the late autumn of 1625—or perhaps early in the spring of 1626—with the result that the Quarter Sessions, due to be held at Thirsk in mid-April, were transferred to Allerton.[4] At Leminge plague erupted at the beginning of August and is said to have persisted until nearly the end of the ensuing February.[5] Cox is the authority for the reports that Barnard Castle and Newcastle were involved in this northward spread of the disease. He asserts that it was epidemic in both towns, though less deadly in each than in 1609 and 1610,[6] but regrettably he did not justify his assertion by presenting a statistical examination of the appropriate parish burial registers. Sunderland was officially reported to be 'dangerously infected with the Plague' in the summer[7] and a marginal note in the parish register of Gateshead records that plague accounted for 89 burials there in 1625.[8]

It is incontestable that this outburst of bubonic plague ranks as a national calamity. Its occurrence at the beginning of the reign of ill-starred Charles I may well have been regarded as an evil portent by many of his ignorant and superstitious subjects and it must have had a detrimental influence upon the national economy. It is a pity therefore that none of the histories of his reign attempts to assess its political, social, and economic effects. Creighton regards it as a national calamity and emphasizes the profound social confusion, the grave dislocation of trade, and the widespread impoverishment it caused.[1] He describes the panic exodus from London of all who could flee from the city and comments: 'As in 1603, the magistrates, the ministers, the doctors, and the rich men seem to have left the city to take care of itself.'[2] Wilson avers that the distress among the poor was acute and that many parishes were unable either to relieve their plague-stricken inhabitants or to maintain the essential parochial services. According to him the most striking feature of this visitation to contemporary observers was the stillness and desertion of the city. Westminster, Whitehall, the Strand, the Inns of Court, the Royal Exchange were all deserted, he says, and for every shop that was open sixteen were shut. Food was very dear and transport prohibitive to the poor, for a coach-ride of a few miles from London cost more than a week's wages. He declares that the mortality of this epidemic disrupted the maintenance of law and order with the result that burglary and looting were rampant. 'Segregation was impossible,' he remarks, 'for the healthy households would not half have served to keep the sick or bury the dead.'[3] But this statement is a regrettable exaggeration and inconsistent with the epidemiology of bubonic plague. Unfortunately segregation of infected households was the only notion of plague-control known to the municipal and parochial authorities in seventeenth-century England, and when it proved ineffective their anti-plague organization collapsed. Wilson affirms that there was a severe national trade depression after the outburst had subsided. For instance the clothiers in the provinces had large stocks on hand which they dared not bring to London, while the farmers had a whole year's produce which they could not sell in the stricken towns. The urban traders on the other hand were prevented from selling their wares in the country because of the fear that they harboured 'the contagion' of plague. As a consequence of the general trade depression there was serious unemployment among the artisans and a general rise in the cost of living that greatly aggravated the distress of the poor, which had already been made severe by a bad harvest after an abnormally wet spring.[4] In conclusion he opines that the entertainers, especially the players, were hard-hit, for few companies toured the provinces during this outburst of plague because few places would admit them,[5] and

the cancellation of fairs, markets, and entertainments intensified the public depression while rumour augmented its fear.

An accurate comparison of the severity and effects of the two major epidemics of bubonic plague of 1603 and 1625 is not now possible because so much of the requisite data about each of them is lacking; but the accompanying diagram (figure 50) shows that the plague-mortality curves of the two epidemics—as plotted from the figures of the recorded plague-burials in London—are identical in shape and practically identical in time. In view of the immutable aetiology of bubonic plague there is no reason to suppose that this common curve would differ appreciably for England as a whole or for the bulk of epidemics of the disease in individual towns, villages, or parishes. The student who wishes to study the influence that bubonic plague may have exerted upon the progress and development of a particular locality can therefore use this mortality curve as a reliable guide to the identification of any unspecified mortality that occurred anywhere in Stuart England.

CHAPTER 8

THE SECOND QUARTER OF THE SEVENTEENTH CENTURY

England and Wales

After the subsidence of the great outburst of bubonic plague in 1625, 'trailer' epidemics were reported from numerous places in England in 1626 and 1627. Creighton remarks that though a number of provincial towns—notably Plymouth, Colchester, and Newcastle-upon-Tyne—were visited by plague in 1626 there was no general diffusion of the disease, and the total number of plague-deaths in the provinces did not amount to one-fifth of its mortality in London in the previous year.[1] It manifested some sporadic activity in London in 1626, for in the week ending 30 March 2 plague-deaths were recorded in a total of 133 deaths from all causes,[2] but these may have been deaths from typhus fever. Then on 6 October corresponding plague-figures of 7 (in 6 city parishes) and 217 were reported.[3] The proclamation on 30 June of a general fast on account of its activity, to be observed in the capital on 5 July and in the provinces on 2 August,[4] suggests that it may have been more active in the metropolitan area than the above figures indicate; but the absence of specified plague-burials in the registers of the London parishes excludes its epidemic activity.

Colchester appears to have been severely attacked in 1626. Blomefield avers that plague was raging there in September[5] and on the 14th the inhabitants of Colchester and Sudbury were forbidden to attend Braintree Fair because their towns were then 'very much infected'.[6] As early as mid-July 20 houses were officially reported to be infected in Colchester[7] and the town may therefore have sustained a relatively heavy mortality which may be manifest in its parish registers.

Canterbury possibly experienced a recrudescence of plague this year as 12 of the 61 burials registered at the Strangers' Church are marked 'contagion',[8] and its reappearance at Portsmouth aroused the fear that its spread would endanger the Fleet, then 'riding at anchor neere thereunto',[9] as two seamen were reported to have died of it on board the *Greate Saphyre*.[10] It is

possible that the Fleet promptly left Portsmouth but, if so, it certainly did not sail to Plymouth, which was in a distressed state in mid-July because the prevalence of plague had caused a panic flight, 'not onely of the inhabitants in generall but alsoe of the principall magistrates and other inferiour officers'.[1] Creighton affirms that this epidemic of plague caused 2,000 deaths in Plymouth and that the disease was widespread in Devonshire this year.[2] As it was simultaneously widespread in Dorsetshire and Cornwall and probably also in Somersetshire, the West Country would seem to have borne the brunt of its activity in 1626. Its prevalence in Dorsetshire in August produced an alarmist report to the Privy Council[3] to the effect that it was so rife in 'Brideport and Blandforde and in manie places neare the seaside'[4] that it would be dangerous to billet the 1,000 soldiers from Devon and Cornwall in that part of the shire, and the Council had previously been warned that it would be unsafe to muster the forces of the Stannaries because plague was so widespread in Cornwall.[5] Bridport seems to have suffered severely as it was 'reduced to great distress and poverty'[6] and Dorchester was similarly reduced to destitution 'by a twenty weeks visitation of the plague'.[7] In Devonshire Ashburton experienced a calamitous visitation of epidemic disease this year, which possibly destroyed at least one-quarter of its population, because 366 deaths were recorded there compared with its average annual mortality of about 30.[8] This epidemic is of particular interest because it appears to have been an abnormal outbreak of bubonic plague. As figure 51 shows, the three spring months of April–June contributed 243 deaths or a trifle less than 64·0 per cent of the annual total, whereas the three 'plague-months' of July–September contributed only 11·7 per cent of the total mortality.[9] According to another recorder the disease caused 464 deaths in Ashburton and spread from there to Okehampton, having been originally imported into Ashburton from Plymouth by way of Ivybridge.[10] Its seasonal incidence is more suggestive of smallpox than of bubonic plague and an epidemic of malignant smallpox could have produced the death-roll recorded at Ashburton; but I believe that it was one of the rare epidemics of bubonic plague which occasionally erupted in England during an exceptionally mild spring because of the fact that plague was undoubtedly epidemic in Plymouth at this time. Indeed it was epidemic there in May, for early in June all commerce had ceased, all the 'best inhabitants' had fled from the town, and the 'infection' was reported in the surrounding parishes where the soldiers were billeted.[11] A report from Plymouth on 11 April stated that 40 plague-deaths had occurred during the past week, that 20 houses were segregated, and that some of the victims had been taken ill, had died, and been buried in less than 24 hours.[12] Septicaemic plague can kill with this rapidity but 'black' or

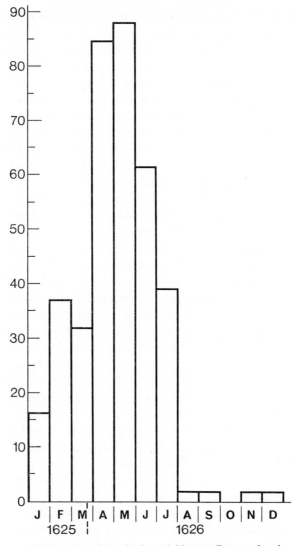

51. Presumptive plague deaths at Ashburton, Devon, 1625–6.

haemorrhagic smallpox can also kill as quickly. A previous report on 18 March had said that 'the sickness' was increasing daily in strength, that 14 or 15 people were dying each day from it, and that the townsfolk were fleeing from it into the country.[1] A plague-relief gift of £92 11s. 5d. from the people of Exeter was a most laudable instance of mutual aid for Exeter suffered a severe attack of plague itself this year.[2]

From Exeter the summer assizes are said to have been transferred to Tiverton,[1] although a contemporary report affirms that the city was reasonably clear' of plague at the end of July.[2] Judging from these records it would seem that the spring of 1626 was exceptionally mild in Devonshire, enabling plague to be epidemic at Plymouth, Exeter, Ashburton, and probably other places in the south of the county in April, May, and June. It is pleasant to record that on 27 April the corporation of Exeter gave £6 to William Kinge in appreciation of his constant care of the plague-sick in the city.[3] It is possible that the customary winter intermission of the disease did not occur there on this occasion as a civic report to the Privy Council stated that plague had been prevalent in Exeter for sixteen months.[4]

In Somersetshire the Ivelchester Sessions ordered a levy for the relief of the plague-stricken parishes of 'Hilbishopps and Staplegrove'[5] and in Warwickshire, because of the 'dangerous dispersion of the infection of the plague into many parts' of the county, the justices made an order at Trinity Sessions prohibiting feasts, wakes, May games, Morris dancing, bear-baitings, and 'like assemblies' for the remainder of 1626.[6] Simultaneously they made a weekly grant of 40s. to the parish of Allesley for the relief of its plague-stricken poor, and as this parish was then about 2 miles from Coventry it is possible that plague was concurrently active in that city. At the previous Epiphany Sessions they had showed a commendable humanity by granting a weekly relief of 12d. to a man who had lost his wife and a child from plague and had another child not 2 years old to care for, 'and he, being grown old, is by the said sickness utterly disabled to maintain himself and the said child.'[7]

At Horton in Buckinghamshire, where 34 plague-burials were registered in 1626, Ellis affirms that rags collected for paper-making brought the disease into the parish[8]. This is a possibility, but as the conditions under which the collected rags were stored would almost certainly have attracted *R. rattus* and facilitated its breeding, it is more probable that *P. pestis* was brought to Horton by rat contacts.

A report from Norwich to the Privy Council about the middle of May stated that plague had been present throughout the winter and that it was now increasing in intensity with the arrival of warmer weather, 'so that there die very manie weekly, there being 16 of the 32 parishes infected'.[9] The Council promptly cancelled the mayoral feast of St George and suggested that the money usually spent on it, together with the customary donations from aldermen and commoners, should be used to relieve the plague-stricken poor and to build a pest-house.[10] However it annulled the cancellation on receipt of a civic petition to hold the feast accompanied by a certificate that the outbreak of plague was not serious enough to arouse alarm and that 'good

order' had been taken to ensure that it would not spread.[1] Nevertheless it cancelled the annual fair at King's Lynn later in the year because of the appearance of plague.[2] This cancellation promptly drew a protest from the wholesale tradesmen of London who frequented the fair.[3]

There are reports of plague this year at Whickham in Durham County and in several Yorkshire parishes, but at Whickham the disease appears to have been confined to a single household.[4] The Yorkshire parishes which were invaded, to wit, Sowerby, Egton Bridge, Aytons Ambo, Wykeham, and Hutton Bushell,[5] are all situated in the North Riding. At New Malton, also in that district, a man was fined £40 and set in the stock for 3 hours 'with a scrowle of paper on his head written in Romaine capital letters—For bringing down [from London], receivynge into his house, and utteringe goods infected with the plague: And for contempte of the authoritie seekinge to suppresse his insolencies: And from thence to be taken to York Castle, there to remaine until the fine be paid.'[6] He threatened to shoot the Justices and such persons as sought to keep him and his goods in his house. New Malton was visited by plague this year, but it was probably infected by rat contact spread from Scarborough, where the disease was epidemic in 1626.[7]

There is no notice of plague in any of the available London parish registers in 1627. A 'plague-searcher' was buried in one parish,[8] but there is no evidence that she died of plague. The Home Counties also seem to have been free from the disease this year, which saw it make a brief appearance at Chichester in the autumn[9] and a recurrence at Portsmouth, where 'manie inhabitants of best ability (as well officers as others)' had fled from it into the country by the end of June.[10] It was apparently active in Wiltshire, however, as the musters could not be taken on account of its dangerous dispersion in the county[11] and Salisbury was severely attacked. At the end of June 27 houses were segregated and 2,674 persons were receiving relief at the rate of 1*d*. a head each day.[12] This relief was costing the municipality the sum of £77 19*s*. 10*d*. a week, a heavy financial burden at that time. The civic authorities complained that the city had 'only received £40 and 2*d*. in relief from the county since the plague began last March', while there were 'not twentie howsholders lefte within this cittye which are able to geve relyeffe'.[13] A second memorial, dated 30 September, records that 88 houses were then segregated, that more than 2,900 persons were receiving relief, and that there had been 72 deaths—presumably all plague-deaths—during the past month.[14]

There was a recurrence of the disease in both Devonshire and Cornwall in 1627; in the former county at Plymouth, Dartmouth, and Exeter, in the latter in and around Falmouth.[15] At Plymouth plague was active in at least one ward in the town, to wit, Vennar's Ward, the residents of which were

assessed for plague-relief.[1] The names of 67 persons are listed but against 27 of them is the note 'not in town'. Of the remainder 15 refused to pay, 6 are marked 'dead', and others are noted as 'not able'.[2] Altogether only about one-third of those named seem to have paid their share of the levy. Plymouth was probably no worse served in this respect than any other English town, and this record reveals the difficulty that every local authority encountered in its efforts to combat the ravages of bubonic plague. Some 24 miles to the east Dartmouth was concurrently severely afflicted, for plague was reported to be 'so hot' there at the end of June that all the inhabitants— that is to say, all who had the means to do so—had deserted the town.[3] A month later the mayor reported that in spite of letters from the Privy Council the inhabitants 'still forsake the town, although the plague has ceased'.[4] Towards the end of September the Council was informed that Dartmouth had been 'much weakened by the death of a great number' of its townsfolk during the recent epidemic of plague.[5]

During the next two years there appear to be few records of the activity of plague in England and some of these may really refer to its activity in 1627, so it may be correct to say that the country was practically free from the disease during 1628 and 1629. The petition for plague-relief from the parish of 'Aishweek', which was sent to the Ivelchester Sessions with the statement that 'the most sufficient and able people' in the parish had been destroyed by the 'late lamentable visitation of sicknesse...leaving many poore and impotent people and fatherlesse children',[6] almost certainly refers to the epidemic of 1627 in Somersetshire. As Ashwick is only some 3 miles from Shepton Mallet it is possible that that important market town was involved in this outbreak of plague, in which case an examination of its parish registers should reveal the extent of its involvement. In all probability the report that Farnham was 'greatly impoverished through the plague and many charges'[7] also refers to its visitation in 1627.

Towards the end of the old calendar year of 1629, on 12 March to be precise, the Privy Council warned the lord mayor of London that it had been informed of 'divers houses infected with the plague in the parishes of St Giles-in-the-Fields, Shoreditch, and Whitechapel, and other places near the city'.[8] Three days later, as it was beginning to spread in the liberties, it ordered the plague 'Book of Orders' to be reprinted,[9] and two days later instructed the Justices of the Peace for Middlesex to select an isolation-house for the plague-sick and free the county from 'the multitudes of poore Irish and other vagabonds who swarm and must increase the infection';[10] but on second thoughts it decided that a better plan would be for the lord mayor to empty all the infected houses, shut them up, and send their inmates to the pest-

house.[1] Simultaneously a royal command was sent to the College of Physicians to assemble and produce as quickly as possible a course of action to control the disease.[2] There is a significant reference at this time to the presence of the house-rat in London. In a letter written on 28 July from his town house in St Martin's Lane to his son-in-law, Viscount Conway remarks: 'I...have a quarrel with you, son Harvey, that you did not kill all the rats, for you left one that bit little Bridget [his grand-daughter] by the nose and the mark remains, but "without mayme of deformity".'[3] This notice links London with Indian cities and their 'bigge hungrie Rats, that often bite a man as he lyeth on his bed'.[4]

There are notices of an outbreak of epidemic disease, which may have been bubonic plague, at Cambridge in 1629. The town is said in a letter to have been visited with 'a most greivous sicknesse' which had, however, spared the colleges, probably because the university authorities gave both fellows and scholars permission to leave Cambridge for the safety of the countryside.[5] A second letter referred to a Bill of Mortality which certified that 343 persons had died or were suspected to have died of 'plague' between 28 February and 8 November.[6] A gift of £45 10s. 0d. from the people of Exeter was gratefully acknowledged by the vice-chancellor, who emphasized that the resources of Cambridge were few and its necessities many and great, for while 4,000 persons were receiving relief there were not 100 residents able to contribute to that relief.[7] There seems to be something queer about this visitation because Cooper makes no mention of an epidemic of plague or of any other disease in Cambridge in 1629.[8]

The next two years witnessed a sharp resurgence of plague both in London and in the provinces. Although Creighton calls the metropolitan epidemic of 1630 a small one because it caused only 1,317 deaths,[9] it accomplished something that previous visitations had failed to do, for it induced the civic authorities to decide to build and maintain a special plague-hospital modelled on the Hospital of St Louis in Paris 'for receiving, nourishing, keeping and dressing of all infected with the plague'.[10] There was no hospital like that one in London or elsewhere in England in 1630. The pest-houses provided in numerous towns were mostly domestic buildings, temporarily requisitioned for the isolation of the plague-sick and generally lacking medical attendance, nursing service, and the provision of adequate supplies of food and other necessities. In some cases surgeons were appointed to visit the patients and food supplies were nominally provided, but too often in practice the patients and their family contacts were left to fend for themselves. Unfortunately the metropolitan authorities discovered that they were unable to provide a plague-hospital like that of St Louis, firstly because there was no building in

London equivalent to that of the Hôtel Dieu in Paris—which was responsible for the maintenance of the Hospital of St Louis—and secondly because there was no possibility of securing a nursing service in any way comparable with the devoted service given by the French nuns. Nothing further is heard therefore about the establishment of a special hospital for the plague-sick in London, and several years were to pass before the state officially advocated the provision of permanent pest-houses in English towns. However, to keep the civic authorities 'awake', the Privy Council complained to the lord mayor in April that the anti-plague regulations were being ignored.[1] It directed him therefore to ensure that every infected house in which the occupants were segregated 'should have guards set at the door, and a red cross, or "Lord have mercy upon us" set on the door to warn passers-by'.[2] Next day it informed him that a butcher in Whitehcapel had turned his plague-sick boy out of his house to find a lodging elsewhere and that the boy had died that same night in a widow's house. 'In order, therefore, that others might not take example by the ill carriage of [the butcher], they required that he and his wife and children should forthwith be sent to the Pest-house.'[3] Three days later it ordered the lord mayor and the Justices of the Peace for Middlesex and Surrey to prohibit all meetings and stage-plays, bear-baitings, tumbling, rope-dancing and similar shows, 'and all other meetings whatsoever for pastime, and all assemblies of the inhabitants of [the] several counties at the common halls of London...and all assemblies of people at taverns or elsewhere'.[4] Then on 16 April, on receipt of information that a case of plague had been removed from an infected house in Lothbury to a garden-house in Finsbury Fields, it warned him that 'no infected persons should be permitted to be removed to any Garden-house or other place but to the Pest-house, or such common place as was provided for infected persons, and upon which a watch and guard were kept, and the doors shut up, and a "Lord have mercy upon us!" set thereon'.[5] By 16 April only 8 plague-deaths had been recorded in London during that week, and of these only one had occurred within the walls.[6] Next day the number had risen to 11, distributed in 6 parishes.[7] Although these figures probably belittle the true extent of plague and its mortality in mid-April, even if they were trebled they would scarcely seem to justify the Privy Council's orders to the lord mayor which show clearly the insensate fear aroused by the mere appearance of the disease. In the week ending 24 April only 7 plague-deaths were registered in London, but many places near the city were rumoured to be infected, 'especially towards the water-side, as Greenwich, Newington, Barnes, Ditton, by Kingston; and on this side Thames, Twickenham, by Isleworth, Hounslow; some say Hampton Court, Brentford, Etc....Others name Lam-

beth and Croydon also.'[1] The significance of the first phrase in this report is noteworthy.

London recorded only 3 plague-deaths in the week ending 1 May, but on that day news from Greenwich reported 6 or 7 plague-deaths there in 5 houses during the previous week-end,[2] and a few days later the number had risen to 12 with more than 20 houses segregated, 'partly infected, partly of such as have visited those which were'.[3] This stirring of plague, slight though it was, excited the government to issue fresh regulations for its arrest, and on 22 April a proclamation ordered all Londoners to wash their houses out daily and keep the channels in front of them flushed.[4] No vagrants or beggars were to be allowed to assemble at burials or lectures; no relief was to be distributed except by the proper officers; no meetings were to be held in halls or taverns, and no fruiterer or greengrocer was to be allowed to store any fruit in his house—it must be stored in the warehouses in Thames Street.[4]

Only three of the London parishes specifically mention plague in their burial registers in 1630, namely, St Vedast, 2 plague-burials in a total of 24 burials;[5] St Olave, 8 in a total of 56,[6] and St Martin-in-the-Fields, 41 in a total of 520.[7] There may have been some augmentation of plague in May,[8] at any rate in some parts of the capital, and it was sufficiently active there and in some other places in July to make the Government cancel Bartholomew, Sturbridge, and Our Lady Fairs at the beginning of August; to prohibit the holding of any fair within 50 miles of London, and to forbid Londoners to attend any fair in the kingdom until 'the plague is ceased'.[9] Later in the month Michaelmas Term was adjourned on account of its continued activity,[10] which evidently did not diminish during September because in the first fortnight of October the weekly plague-deaths in Smithfield rose from 60 to 77,[10] and even in December it was still active enough apparently to provoke the lord mayor to send a defensive letter to the Privy Council describing the measures he had taken to control the disease.[11] These included the burial of the plague-dead late at night; the driving away of mourners 'by threatening and otherwise', and the punishment of some persons for removing 'the inscriptions set on infected houses'. It was more likely typhus fever than bubonic plague which was responsible for the alleged plague-deaths after Christmas and for the segregation of 5 freshly infected houses in the Strand in March.[12] Table 27 contains the returns of the weekly plague-deaths recorded as such in London during the autumn and winter of the old calendar year of 1630.

Outside London and its environs Cambridge seems to have been the chief focus of plague in 1630, and Creighton avers that though the death-roll of this visitation was only 214 it was the worst epidemic of bubonic plague that

TABLE 27

Weekly plague-deaths in London in 1630, as reported in the letters written by the Rev. J. Mead to Sir M. Stuteville

Date of letter	Plague-deaths	Number of parishes infected		Remarks
		Total	Within the walls	
27 October	61	22	15	In Westminster, 3 plague-burials recorded in a total of 278
5 December	20	12	4	—
19 December	5	—	—	—
30 January	9	—	—	Up to 10 January no plague-death had been recorded since before Christmas
6 February	6	4	—	All out-parishes
27 February	9	—	—	—
7 March	7	—	—	—
13 March	10	7	1	9 deaths in 6 out-parishes

Cambridge ever experienced.[1] No previous visitation certainly ever produced such a minute description of its alleged introduction and progress as the Rev. J. Mead's account.[2] Plague seems to have appeared in Cambridge early in April and by the middle of the month 7 plague-deaths had been recorded there. According to Mead it was imported by a soldier 'who had a sore upon him',[3] who lodged in a shoemaker's house, and Cooper also blames a soldier for its introduction.[4] It was the shoemaker's wife who was, says Mead, responsible for the subsequent epidemic because she used the soldier's bed to accommodate subsequent occupants without changing the sheets and disinfecting the bed.[5] 'Some add, for a cause', he continues, 'a dunghill at the back of his house, in a little yard, in which the fool this Lent time suffered some butchers, who had killed meat by stealth, to kill it there, and to bury the garbage in his dunghill, so to avoid discovery, by which it became very noisome even to Magdalene College.'[6] The remainder of Mead's verbose and involved account can be read in Birch's work[7] by any who are interested in the psychology of fear, because it provides a vivid illustration of the terror inspired by bubonic plague in the mind of an educated seventeenth-century Englishman. Although plague was active in the town on 1 May Mead was able to report that 'all our parish, all the petticurie, all the market-hill and round about it, are yet (God be thanked) absolutely clear and unsuspected'.[8] Evidently fear was too strong for his piety, however, because when he next

357

TABLE 28

Plague among the lay staff of Christ's College, Cambridge in 1630

Dead	Endangered
The second cook 'and some three of his house'.	The minister's daughter has 3 sores, but apparently survived her attack.*
The gardener and all his house.	—
The porter's child.	The porter 'was at the Green'.
The butcher and three of his children.	—
Two of the baker's children.	—
The laundress's maid.*	—
One of the bedmakers.	Her son was lodging in an infected house in the parish.

wrote in mid-October it was from Balsham,[1] some 12 miles to the south-east of Cambridge, whither he had fled to escape the disease. To do him justice he was probably no more terrified than the rest of his colleagues and it is significant that the university early deserted Cambridge. Cooper records that a grace was passed on 19 May to stop all sermons and exercises and that the university officially dispersed 6 days later.[2] He quotes a letter from the Master of Sidney Sussex College reporting 61 plague-deaths in the town between 28 February and 15 May.[3] Mead returned some time in November, but Christ's College was still closed on the 27th, and he commented upon the very slow reflux of the university,[4] which did not reassemble in fact until the middle of December.[5] He records that about 108 people in his parish had died of plague and he supplies a list of the officials and retainers of Christ's College (see table 28) who had died of the disease or whose lives had been endangered by it.[6] In a letter to Lord Coventry the vice-chancellor wrote:

For the present state of the town the sickness is much scattered, but we follow your lordships counsell to keep the sound from the sick; to which purpose we have built nere 40 booths in a remote place upon our commons, whether we forthwith remove those that are infected, where we have placed a German physician who visitts them day and night and he ministers to them.[7]

As Cambridge was then quarantined by the surrounding countryside, the vice-chancellor felt it was incumbent to explain that to give their 'neighbours in the country contentment' the municipality had 'hyred certain horsemen this harvest-time to range and scowre the fields of the towns adjoining, to keep our disorderly pore from annoying them'.[8] By the end of September the epidemic had much abated and commons were resumed in Trinity

* Both women were residing outside the college precincts.

College on 20 November[1] but it was not until January that its extinction dispensed with the weekly relief payments to the poor. Cooper affirms that plague accounted for 347 deaths in a total toll of 617—a mortality rate of 56·2 per cent—and that 839 families, consisting of 2,858 poor persons, received relief.[2] An item in the municipal treasurer's accounts throws a sinister light upon the treatment accorded to the plague-sick in the pest-house. 'Item, for a key & mending the lock on the pesthouse dore on Midsomer grene, xij d.'[3]

A royal brief was issued late in June drawing attention to the severe visitation of Cambridge and the plight of its poor inhabitants consequent upon the closure and dispersal of the University, so that more than 2,800 persons were then in need of relief at a cost to the town of more than £150 a week.[4] The brief recommended the needy to 'all our loving subjects' in the sees of Canterbury, London, Winchester, Lincoln, and the city and liberties of Westminster.[5] Cooper mentions that some thousands of pounds were collected but there does not appear to be extant a record of the exact amount.[6] As London contributed several thousands,[6] Norwich £164 8s. 8d.,[7] and the village of Wye in Kent £4 4s. 7d.,[8] it is possible that Cambridge received as much as £5,000 for plague-relief in 1630. One result of the epidemic was to induce the municipality to provide a regular pest-house, which was erected by the end of June.[9]

To complete this record of what was possibly the greatest calamity Cambridge had suffered from epidemic disease up to that time, two anecdotes about this visitation are presented from contemporary writings. 'On Saturday last', reported the county justices on July 19, 'Cambridge being full of country people, the ostler taking or delivering their horses fell down dead of the plague.'[10] His sudden death naturally aroused profound alarm among those who had been in contact with him that day and some of them may have come from Great Chesterford, whose inhabitants complained to Lord Howard that they were greatly frightened by the conduct of a Cambridge printer who owned a house in the village to which he had brought his wife and two other women and their children while plague was raging in Cambridge. This was bad enough; but to make matters worse the husbands were coming every Saturday to see their families and were returning to the plague-centre on the following Monday.[11] However Lord Howard seems sensibly to have ignored the complaint as there is no record that the authorities took any action against the printer and his friends.

Canterbury, Aylesford, Norwich, Shrewsbury, and Preston are reported to have been visited by plague this year; it was so 'generally dispersed' in Bedfordshire that 'the training of the companies of horse and foot' had to

be postponed,[1] and in December it was reported that many parts of Nottinghamshire had been and still were 'so extremely visited with the plague' that the shire musters could not safely be taken.[2] At Canterbury it may have been typhus fever and not plague which was responsible for the 3 burials of a man and his 2 children that are marked 'de la peste' in the register of the Strangers' Church,[3] but plague was undoubtedly responsible for the infection of 17 houses at Aylesford in June.[4] Norwich fortunately escaped lightly on this occasion if Blomefield's account of its visitation is correct.

In April 1630 [he relates] the Plague broke out again in St Gregories Parish, one Child dying of it, upon which the Court met, and swore a Woman Searcher of the Infected, nail'd up the Door of the House, and by the Common Cryer order'd, all Dogs, Cats, tame Doves, Rabbits, and Swine to be put out of the City or killed, and in May, the Tower next Brasen-Door was appointed for the Buryers, and for a Prison for such infected Poor as would not be ruled: and the Distemper being much in Cambridge, the Carriers thither were prohibited; six houses were erected on Butter-hills near the great Black Tower there, which was fitted up with them for Pest-Houses, and an Acre of Land inclosed about them with tall Boards, and Watch-men were set Day and Night to keep any from going thither, or coming thence, and all that died there were ordered to be buried in the Church-Yard of St Peter at South-Gate; but it pleased God that this great Caution had it's desired effect, the Distemper not spreading, not above 1 or 2 died in a week.[5]

Apart from the fact that they were almost certainly built either of wood or of lath-and-plaster, the pest-houses on 'Butter-hills' were probably similar in size and plan to the plague-quarantine station which was built on St Helen's Isle in the Scilly Isles in 1764.* Although all ages and both sexes of suspect cases of plague were to be herded indiscriminately into one large room, the authorities, with true bureaucratic tenderness for official proprieties, provided separate small rooms for the female searchers and the male guards. As on a previous occasion, the Privy Council ordered the cancellation of the mayoral banquet at Norwich and again the corporation petitioned for the annulment of the order on the grounds that in the 34 city parishes only 9 plague-deaths had occurred in June, and these were confined to 5 houses in 3 parishes.[6]

The statement in a contemporary manuscript that 'the plague was in Shrosbury'[7] this year is chronologically incorrect because neither of the parishes of St Mary and St Chad shows an excessive mortality in 1630. The

---

* Lewis writes: 'St Helen's pool continued to be the usual anchorage as long as sail lasted, and in 1756 we find that all ships with suspected plague must make for here. St Helen's replaced Old Grimsby in 1764 as quarantine station, and on it was erected the Pest House. This was never a Hospital in the true sense. It was a well-built house to shelter the unhappy plague victims...It would be a primitive refuge at best, and we hope, as we are told, that it was never needed, and never used.'[8]

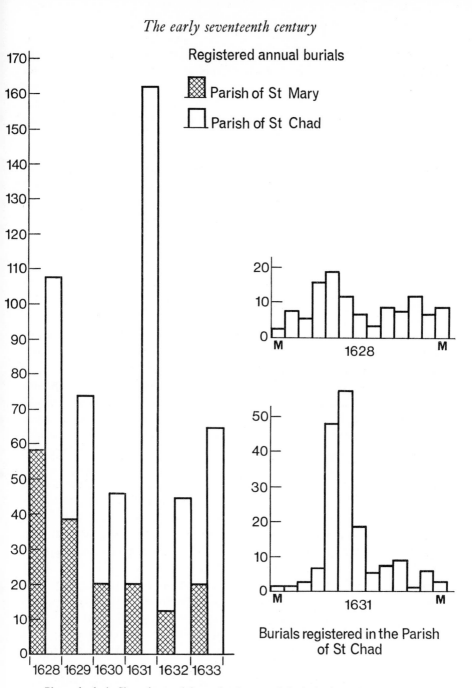

52. Plague deaths in Shrewsbury, 1628–33, showing annual deaths in the parishes of St Mary and St Chad and monthly deaths in the parish of St Chad for the years 1628 and 1631

register of the latter parish shows a great increase in the number of burials in both 1628 and 1631; but a study of this register shows that the earlier mortality was caused by some disease other than bubonic plague, whereas the later one undoubtedly resulted from an epidemic of that disease. (See figure 52.) In 1628[1] the burials registered in the three principal 'plague-months' comprised 32·7 per cent of the annual total; in 1631[2] they contributed 75·3 per cent of the annual total. There is also a note in this register, dated 23 June, that 'the plage be gane in Shrosbury',[3] and the register of St Mary has a note that 'the infection was suspected in 1631',[4] presumably in that parish. As its burial register shows no excessive mortality this year, however, it seems evident that plague was restricted on this occasion to the part of Shrewsbury contained in St Chad's parish, which probably harboured then the town's slums. Eighty of the people of Bishop's Castle voluntarily raised the generous sum of £16 5s. 6d. for the relief 'of the poor people of Shrewsbury, visited by God's judgment of the plague',[5] and to their credit forbore to speculate upon the nature of the sins that had brought this divine punishment upon their fellows. Either during this visitation or the succeeding one in 1650, Cadogan's Chapel at the end of Frankwell was adapted by the corporation as a pest-house 'and those dying there seem to have been buried in St Chad's churchyard'.[6]

Undoubtedly the worst urban sufferer from bubonic plague at this time was Preston in Lancashire, where 1,100 burials—mostly of victims of plague—were registered between 8 November 1630 and 4 November 1631.[7] Leech quotes a contemporary observer as recording that the epidemic so ravaged Preston and its neighbourhood that the town was depopulated and the corn rotted in the surrounding countryside for lack of reapers.[7] The appearance of 'plague' so late in the year puzzled the townsfolk and one of them wrote to his brother: 'The trueth is, wee have here amongst us a very infectious disease, which our tradesmen will not call the plage. There have dyed, within these fyve or six weekes, neere twentie; some three houses are shut up.'[8] After allowing for the understandable reluctance of tradespeople to invite the arrest of their means of livelihood, there is a distinct possibility that they were justified in their refusal to identify the disease as plague, because it seems probable that originally it was an outbreak of typhus fever like the one that preceded the London epidemic of plague in 1625. Indeed there seems little doubt that the pestilence that scourged Preston was a sequence of outbreaks of typhus fever and bubonic plague, the former erupting in the late autumn and persisting through the ensuing winter, the latter starting with some sporadic cases early in the autumn, lapsing into quiescence during the winter, and then erupting in the spring to develop as

a devastating epidemic in the summer of 1631. In all probability other Lancashire towns were involved in this sequence, a contention that is supported by the Lord President of the North's report in September 1631 that Lancashire was 'miserably distressed with the pestilence'.[1]

After its presumptive winter quiescence, plague erupted violently in Preston in March and in the old calendar year of 1631 the registered burials were 950 compared with an annual average for the preceding quinquennium of 74.[2] The epidemic developed with furious speed to reach a truly appalling mortality peak in July (see figure 53), after which it declined slightly in August and precipitately in September to its cessation in December. In June its ravages were so grievous that the Assize Judges authorized the Justices of the Peace of the hundred of Blackburn to arrange for the transport of fuel and victuals 'to some convenient place nearest to the town of Preston'[3] in order that the townspeople might buy what they needed. It is a measure of Preston's ordeal that in 15 weeks from the 16th of April £856 5s. 5d. was distributed for plague-relief at weekly rates ranging from 9d. to 1s. per person, and that during the weeks ending 16 April, 30 April, and 23 July the numbers of persons in receipt of plague-relief were respectively 1,372, 1,390, and 1,017.[4] Indeed this may well have been the worst calamity that Preston has ever suffered. It is probable in fact that it suffered proportionately as severely as any English town in the history of bubonic plague, and surely no history of the town can be authentic which does not present an appreciation of an ordeal that must have had an effect upon its growth and development. Even so it must be emphasized that there is no reason to suppose that the town was depopulated by bubonic plague on this occasion, simply because that disease was incapable of achieving such a state. Undoubtedly a large number of its inhabitants temporarily deserted it, and it is certain that more than half the population survived.

There is no doubt that 1631 was a severe plague year over a part of England, whereas London appears to have escaped very lightly and Westminster apparently equally so, for the churchwardens of St Margaret's parish paid only 1s. 'for bills for visited houses'.[5] Only one of the metropolitan parishes, St Martin-in-the-Fields, records any plague-burials, 10,[6] and in mid-October in a weekly total of 278 deaths, plague was credited with but 61, dispersed in 22 parishes.[7] Of the plague-deaths 16 occurred within the walls and 3 in Westminster.[7] Greenwich appears to have been even more fortunate. In mid-April two houses were segregated for fear of plague, their contents burnt, and their occupants removed to a pest-house; but a few days later it was reported that the suspicion of plague was unfounded.[8] In London the lord mayor was able to inform the Privy Council that plague had wholly

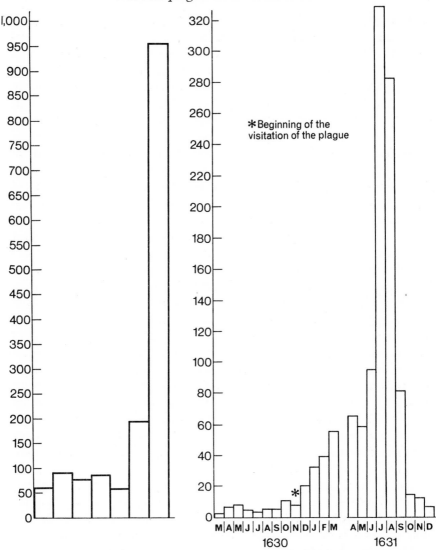

53. Plague deaths at Preston, Lancashire, from November 1630 to December 1631. Left: annual burials 1625–31. Right: monthly burials from March 1629/30 to December 1631.

ceased 'within the walls of the city; the infection which remains is for the most part in Middlesex'.[1] Downs affirms that plague was prevalent at High Wycombe in both 1631 and 1632, and the figures he gives of the registered burials in those years, respectively 109 and 146,[2] are certainly excessive compared with the annual average of less than 59 for the quinquennium ending

with 1630; but in the absence of the monthly burial figures it is not certain that either of these excessive mortalities was caused by plague.

In the Midlands plague was active in a number of places in 1631. It was possibly transported by a 'blocked' flea into a household in the parish of Condover, and the family appears to have been exterminated as the burials of its 5 members within 22 days in July and August are each marked in the register with the letter *p*,[1] although this is sometimes used to denote 'pauper' in seventeenth-century parish registers. As the burials register of Condover shows no excessive mortality this year there was no outbreak of plague in the parish. In Warwickshire Birmingham and a number of outlying townships were involved in the Midland spread of the disease, and in September the Justices of the Peace for the hundred of Hemlingford were forced to stop their monthly meetings because plague had broken out

verie dangerously in Deritend, w'thin the p'ish of Aston, and...it hath spread it selfe farr more dangerously and broken out in Birmingham, a great market towne, and in div'es other hamlets w'thin the s'd p'ish of Aston (vi'd:) in Eardington, Castell Bromwich, Saltley, and Minworth, in the p'ish of Curdworth, all w'thin the s'd hundred of Hemlingford, [the old administrative division for north-west Warwickshire] and manie have dyed thereof.[2]

It is interesting to find Birmingham described as a 'great market town' in 1631 because the Hearth Tax returns reveal that it contained only 501 house-holders in 1662.[3] Gill opines that this visitation of Birmingham was 'not much less disastrous than the Great Plague of 1665'[4] in Birmingham. Un-fortunately the burials register of St Martin's Church, the parish church of Birmingham, ends on 21 June 1630 and is defective until 1654,[5] so that no comparison is now possible between the parochial mortalities of 1631 and 1665. The Justices of the Peace in Leicestershire likewise stopped their meetings in the hundreds of both East and West Goscote as several towns in the former were infected with plague[6] and the disease was 'much raging' in the latter.[7] Kelly avers that Leicester escaped on this occasion, but Lough-borough was attacked with the loss of 135 of its inhabitants. Leicester sent £10 to Loughborough for plague-relief[8] and Cox notes that the parish of Stathern—some 12 miles south-east of Nottingham—several times contri-buted sums varying from 3*s*. 4*d*. to 20*s*. for the relief of the plague-stricken in Loughborough.[9] On 3 occasions this year it also contributed to the relief of the plague-stricken people of Plungar,[9] some 2 miles to the north of it. Sweeting reports that the parish register of Rampton in Cambridgeshire records 30 burials this year, compared with an annual average of 2 or 3, and he opines that this excessive mortality was caused by plague.[10] In Norfolk Wymondham was attacked in the latter part of the spring, apparently severely

as Norwich sent £103 5s. 7d. for the relief of its plague-stricken, but the disease had 'well abated' there by mid-July.[1] Norwich itself was visited during the summer, though only lightly as Blomefield states that not more than 20 or 30 plague-deaths were registered in the city.[2] Nevertheless all transport with both Wymondham and London was stopped; the city gates were shut and watched day and night; infected houses were segregated, and 2 pest-houses were made ready on Butter-Hills.[2] On the opposite side of the Wash, Louth experienced a visitation which proportionately closely approached if it did not equal Preston's prior calamity, for Creighton reports that in the 7 months of April–November 754 plague-deaths were recorded there, of which nearly 500 occurred in July and August.[3]

The epidemic of plague which erupted in the spring of 1631 was so widespread and severe in the two 'Rose Counties' by the beginning of July that the Scots were officially charged to abstain from all intercourse with the two shires.[4] In Lancashire Manchester had a narrow escape. Axon cites Hollinworth for the record:

Anno 1631. The Lord sent his destroying angell into an inne in Manchester, on which died Richard Meriot and his wife, the master and dame of the house, and all that were in it, or went into it, for certaine weekes together, till, at the last, they burned or buried all the goods in the house...no person else was that year touched with the infection.[5]

During the centuries of its presence in England, even during the 'Black Death', many townships in England were as fortunate as Manchester on this occasion—such is the behaviour of bubonic plague. Other Lancashire towns were not so fortunate. In Furness Dalton suffered 360 plague-deaths this year; 120 were recorded in the Isle of Watney, and Biggar was attacked, probably with equal severity.[6]

On the edge of Lancashire [reported the Lord President of the North] the town of Heptonstall has near forty houses infected, and Mirfield has lost nine score persons ...Redness and Armin are furiously infected, and 100 persons died, this being brought out of Lincolnshire as the other out of Lancashire, and is more taking and deadly. It was brought into the suburbs of York by a lewd woman from Armin, and in that street are since dead some four score persons. It has not yet got within the walls, except in two houses, forth which all the dwellers are removed to the pesthouses, but it has broken forth at Heptonstall and Acam[7]

—the modern Acomb, 1½ miles west of York. Stern measures were taken by the civic authorities of York at the instigation of the Lord President to keep the populace in order and thanks to these measures there were few deaths inside the city walls.[8] The authorities circulated prophylactic prescriptions, both for personal and domestic use, and prescriptions for topical applications

to plague-sores. Beeston and Holbeck were involved in the outbreak but Halifax and Leeds escaped.[1] There is a Latin inscription in Mirfield Church which records the deaths of 131 parishioners in 1631,[2] and Chadwick declares that Mirfield was so severely scourged that 'the entries of deaths from the plague occupy two and a half pages of the parish register'.[3] What a pity he did not count them! Perhaps some future local historian will rectify his omission and make a careful study of its parish register; the history of Mirfield will then be enriched with positive information about its ordeal by plague. In August plague was suspected at Wakefield and the Scots were ordered to give goods imported from that town a 'plague-trial';[4] but no further information seems to be available about this suspicion. In the parish of Pocklington the register contains the note, under the date of 29 September 1631: 'Here begins the sickness of the plague', and 49 burials are recorded as due to it. A second note on 26 July 1632 records the cessation of the outbreak.[5] On the other side of the Pennines, Fulwood, Cadeley, Broughton, and Kirkham are named as being centres of its activity this year.[6]

Scotland

After the subsidence of this outburst of plague England appears to have been comparatively free from the disease until 1636. Prior to its reappearance in England in that year plague appeared in the Scottish port of Cramond in 1635, imported according to tradition by a Flemish merchantman.[7] In a letter dated 2 October Lady Hamilton describes in somewhat incoherent Scots the manner of its introduction.[8] Rendered into English her story is that a sailor from the ship got drunk in Cramond and died on the road to Queensferry, or more probably was murdered by two rustics who robbed him of 8 or 9 dollars, and it was the distribution of this money in Cramond that was responsible for the infection of four or five houses in the town. Her husband, who was 'afrayit aneuch' of plague—in English, scared out of his wits by the mere mention of the disease—was already preparing to flee for safety to Teningham, 'and said yester nicht at the burd that the best remeid he kneu quhen any vos in supetion of the plaig vos to flit sum and far of, and to be long a cuming bak agane';[9] a remedy which the British upper classes employed with precipitancy and constancy. Brown affirms that plague appeared in Cramond towards the end of September,[10] which was fortunate for the town because cold weather extinguished it in mid-December after 10 houses only had been segregated.[10] He is the author of a maxim that every social historian might ponder with advantage, to wit, that the influence exerted by bubonic plague 'must ever be before us in any estimate of the social condition

of the people'[1]—provided that its malign influence is not exaggerated by 'Black Death' notions of its alleged omnipresence and omnipotence, and that evils are not ascribed to it that should properly be assigned to other diseases and other influences. Buchan asserts for instance that this century was

one of deep poverty for the common people [of Scotland]. The bonnet-lairds and the tacksmen, the labourers and shepherds, the petty craftsmen in the villages, even the burghers in the little towns, lived very near the edge of destitution... Idyllic pictures have been drawn of the Covenanting peasant as a stalwart in good homespun clothes and blue bonnet, and of his house as a snug dwelling like an illustration to the Cotter's Saturday Night. The truth seems to be that the physique of most was early ruined by poor feeding and incessant toil, that they had small regard for personal cleanliness, that their clothes were coarse at the best and generally ragged, and that their dwellings resembled a Connemara cabin. Recurrent plagues carried off their thousands, and foul habits and a diet of thin brose and bannocks weakened the survivors. Nasty, brutish, and short was the life of the seventeenth-century Lowlander.[2]

Buchan has possibly overdrawn this picture of the Scots, but it is undoubtedly true in its fundamentals of life in Scotland—and of the common folk in seventeenth-century England with some modifications—and if his phrase 'recurrent plagues' is amplified to mean recurrent epidemics of bubonic plague, smallpox, typhus fever, relapsing fever, influenza, dysentery, typhoid fever, pneumonia, measles, whooping cough, and possibly cholera—with tuberculosis as a steady, constant killer in the background—the individual influence exerted by bubonic plague from 1348 to 1666 upon the social condition and development of the peoples of the British Isles can be assessed in its correct proportion.

As long as plague was active in any of the European ports from which ships sailed to Scottish ports importations of *P. pestis* were inevitable in spite of the order to abstain from 'frequenting ships from the Low Countries'.[3] The Scots Privy Council undoubtedly did its best to keep plague out of Scotland, and its efforts reveal what many writers about plague in Great Britain have not appreciated, that in the seventeenth century British authorities recognized that the disease was not endogenous and that its presence was governed by its importation from foreign sources. Throughout 1636 the menace of plague threatened Scotland and towards the end of May the Council prohibited the entry into any Scottish port of colliers from Newcastle-upon-Tyne[4] where the disease was then prevalent. Late in July it cancelled the fairs held annually at Melrose and Coldstream[5] and early in September those at Roxburgh, North Berwick, and Selkirk.[6] In October it issued regulations 'anent the plague in Leberton'[7] because a sudden death had occurred at Stenhouse in that parish,

though there was no evidence that the death was due to plague. Brown affirms that in addition to the fairs already named St James's Fair at Kelso was cancelled and the weekly markets at Kelso, Jedburgh, Hawick, and Duns were prohibited.[1] Imbued with the notion that plague was spread by human agency, the Council appointed a commission in June to apprehend and try a man 'who, contrary to the prohibition brought from England a child affected with the plague'.[2] The child died and though the man must have known the cause of its death

yitt he most maliciouslie and unchristianlie, hes since the death of the barne, suffered sindrie persons to ryde upon the same hors and saddle whereon the infected barne raid, without acquainting thame with the danger and disease quherwith the barne was visite, whereby he hes done what in him lyes not onelie to bring the lyffes of these who raid upon the same hors and saddle in danger bot lykewayes to infect the haill countie thereabout.[2]

In spite of this and other efforts of the Council plague appeared in mid-autumn at Preston and Prestonpans, whereupon their inhabitants were ordered not to quit their bounds and the fairs at Haddington, Preston, Tranent, Musselburgh, and Dalkeith were cancelled.[3] Once again the maritime introduction of the disease so late in the year saved Scotland from an outbreak of plague, and its disappearance before Christmas removed the restrictions imposed by the Council.[4]

The next year there was a more serious influx of plague into Scotland; indeed Brown opines that the precautions taken to arrest it show that it 'virtually paralysed the life of the districts where it appeared'.[5] It is possible that on this occasion it may have entered Scotland both by sea and land because about the middle of May 1636 the Council was informed that it was prevalent on the English side of the Border.[5] The Council promptly attempted to sever all communication between the two countries by prohibiting first the markets and afterwards the fairs in all the chief Border towns, namely, Kelso, Jedburgh, Hawick, Melrose, Duns, Coldstream, and Selkirk.[6] It also appointed a special commission, composed of notables on its side of the Border, to enforce its regulations, with the warning that disregard of them would be punished by death.[7] It also decreed that in every parish in the threatened area 'sufficient honest men' were to be chosen who would supply the wants of the plague-stricken from their own possessions. A tax was to be levied for the support of the poor to prevent them from straying out of their own parishes, and every landowner was told to provide a 'lodge', with a constant guard, for the reception of the plague-sick. For the provisioning of plague-stricken parishes certificated persons were commissioned to travel to and fro to the nearest ports. There were to be no gatherings at

funerals, no burial feasts, and the company at 'lyke wakes' was to be rigorously limited to the family of the diseased.[1] As Brown remarks, it was one thing to decree and another to enforce, and he relates that James Murray of Selkirk invited 'a great part of the countrie' to celebrate his daughter's marriage in open defiance of the Council's orders. He was warned that the company must be limited to four or five witnesses and when he ignored this notice his defiance was officially notified to the baillies of Selkirk. They took no action and they also ignored the Council's subsequent request to place him under ward, and although between 80 and 100 guests attended the wedding Murray was not punished.[2]

Early in June 1637 the eruption of plague at Nisbet Mill was the herald of a widespread outbreak of the disease,[3] and two days later news reached the Privy Council that Jedburgh and other places near the Border were involved.[4] Numerous deaths were reported, not only of Scots people but also of English fugitives from across the Border where plague was raging.[4] On 21 June the Council cancelled Lauder Fair, as plague was then prevalent in the neighbouring districts,[5] and ordered a gate to be built 'at the entry to the Potteraw'[6] as a precautionary measure against the disease. Five days later it cancelled Moffat Fair;[7] but plague continued to spread and by the beginning of July Ancrum, Spittell, 'and other neighbouring parts of the middle marche' of Scotland[8] were involved in the epidemic. Then St Boswell's Fair, which was held annually on 7 July at Lessudden, was cancelled because 'manie parts of the countrie thereabout' were infected,[9] and a month later the Council issued a proclamation forbidding the promiscuous resort of people to Dunbar herring drive.[10] Happily the autumn frosts apparently came early in Scotland this year as there is no further notice of plague, and apart from a dubious report of its presence in January at Jedburgh and Craillinghall[11]— which was most probably a stirring of typhus fever—there is no mention of its presence in Scotland in 1638. That country remained free from it in fact until 1644.

England and Wales

Although Britain was comparatively free from plague from the end of 1631 until 1635, a few small outbreaks occurred in 1632 and Lincolnshire was the scene of a widespread prevalence of it. Wood affirms that the hamlet of Curbar in Derbyshire was visited with the extermination of several families.[12] He says that some of the victims were buried in a plot of ground that was known in his day [1865] as 'Elliott's Piece', while the rest were buried in different places within the precincts of the hamlet. The Lincolnshire references to plague in 1632 are contained in two reports which the Justices of the Peace

sent to the Sheriff of the county. In the first, dated 20 July, they notified him that measures had been taken 'for the relief of the poor within the hundred of Lawress, long visited with a most grievous plague'.[1] With a second, some 2 months later, they included a certificate of their expenditure on poor relief in the wapentake of Manley, adding as a justification for that expenditure that the county had been 'very much troubled with the plague'.[2] The petition which the vicar of St Alkmund's Church presented to the corporation of Shrewsbury this year obviously refers to the outbreak of plague in St Chad's parish in 1631. He pleaded 'to be admitted a burgess without fine, he being a widower, and not likely to have any issue, in consideration of his having ever since the plague began read morning prayer daily within his parish, where the people of the town daily resort in a great[er] number than they formerly did, to his great danger'.[3] No doubt some members of his congregation were ill-smelling and perhaps the reverend gentleman had a keen sense of smell; but unless a 'blocked' flea had managed to hop up into his pulpit he ran no risk of contracting bubonic plague during his morning prayer readings.

The years 1633 and 1634 constitute one of the few periods in the English annals of bubonic plague when the country was apparently completely free from the disease; but it is possible that an exhaustive study of the English parish registers would discover one or two isolated parishes in which rat-plague was smouldering during these years, with the consequent production of small, local outbreaks of the human disease. The latter year is noteworthy, however, for the publication of the seventh edition of P. Barrough's *The Method of Physick*, which, if it added nothing to contemporary knowledge about the nature of plague, is one of the most readable and competent medical books of its time.[4] In his account of plague he comments upon its seasonal prevalence towards the end of the summer and the beginning of autumn, and remarks that those cases in which buboes do not appear are the most dangerous. Flight from the plague-area offers the only protection because the disease is caused by the inhalation of pestilential air. It is instructive to find him using the term 'botch' as a synonym for bubo and interesting to find him recognizing what we know now to be a fulminating septicaemia as the most dangerous form of the disease.

In 1635 a fresh strain of *P. pestis* evidently entered England, apparently by a simultaneous maritime importation through the east coast ports of Hull and Yarmouth, and later in the year probably also through the port of London. Radcliffe quotes Gent's horrific account of its visitation of Hull and his assertion that it destroyed 2,730 of the townspeople, 'excluding those who fled'.[5] Gent declared that plague persisted in Hull until 1639 but it is much

TABLE 29

Records of bubonic plague in some London parishes in 1636*

	Date of first plague-burial	Annual burials	Plague-burials
St Peeters upon Cornhill	5 May	26	9
St Michael, Cornhill	24 May	32	9
St Antholin, Budge Row	19 October	21	6
St Peter, Paul's Wharf	21 July	17	7
St Bene't, Paul's Wharf	8 August	98	47
St Olave, Hart Street	13 June	64	15
St Mary Somerset	6 August	87	32
St Martin in the Fields	12 June	422	77†
St Martin Orgar	28 January	26	3
St Michael Bassishaw	17 August	41	8

more probable that there were 2 distinct epidemics of it in that seaport during this quinquennium; one of which erupted in 1635, recrudesced after a winter intermission in 1636 and was extinguished in the autumn of that year or the winter of 1637, while the other erupted from a fresh importation in the spring of 1638 and subsided late in 1639. The presence of plague in Yarmouth is implicit in the communication which the Lords of the Admiralty sent to the bailiffs of that port early in August,[1] but until its parish registers are studied the degree and duration of its visitation will remain unknown. Jones says that at Lowestoft the deaths increased from 25 in 1634 to 170 in 1635 and opines that the excessive mortality was caused by plague. He avers that Lowestoft suffered as severely from plague in the first half of this century as any place in England except London. He gives the figures for the annual burials there in the years from 1600 to 1603 inclusive as respectively 35, 35, 81, and 316, of which 280 occurred in 5 months; but unfortunately he does not name the months.[2]

From the spring of 1636 up to 'a very stormy and tempestuous day'[3] in August 1642, when the Civil War began, London was never completely free from plague, although there was no serious epidemic recurrence of it after the subsidence of the 1636 outburst. The earliest plague-burial registered in a city parish that year appears to be the one dated 5 May in the register of St Peeters upon Cornhill,[4] (see table 29) and the latest to be the one dated 28 January in that of St Martin Orgar.[5] Between these dates London lost at

* Extracted from the Publications of the Harleian Society, respectively volumes I, VII, VIII, XLI (2 registers), XLVI, LX, XXV, LXVII and LXXII.
† Recorded up to 30 September, on which date this volume of the parish register ends.

least 10,400 of its citizens from bubonic plague and sustained during the year a total death-roll of 23,359.[1] According to Godfrey the Venetian ambassador estimated the population of London to be about 300,000 souls in 1610,[2] so it is improbable that it exceeded 400,000 in 1636 although Noorthouck alleges that it was then about 700,000.[3] For this figure he cites Anderson's edition of Howell's *Londinopolis** in which that author relates that the king requested the lord mayor to ascertain the number of Roman Catholics and strangers in the city in 1636. His worship accordingly made a census of all the people and found that 'there were of men, women and, children, about 700,000 that lived within the bars of this jurisdiction alone'.[3] Noorthouck comments that this number seems large for the time and the boundaries, but he suggests that if the representations in the proclamations of Elizabeth I against new buildings were not exaggerated, the same limits might contain more people in Charles I's reign than they did in 1773.[3] Wilson estimates the population to have been 317,097 between 1632 and 1634, in which case it would probably not have exceeded 350,000 in 1636. He based his estimate on the 1801 census return of 745,000 and the proportion then of burials to population (1 in 30).[4] Accepting 350,000 as the maximum figure for its population in 1636, London lost about 6·6 per cent of it that year, of which bubonic plague accounted for just under 3·0 per cent.

Although no parish within the walled city appears to have been infected before the first week in May some of the eastern out-parishes were invaded some 3 weeks earlier, for a report in mid-April tells of the discovery of 8 plague-houses in Stepney and Whitechapel and of the deaths of 15 of their occupants.[5] Then on 22 April a royal proclamation promulgated 'orders for preventing the spreading of the Plague'.[6] These of course were ineffective and on 4 May a second report mentioned that in addition to the deaths in Stepney and Whitechapel one plague-death had occurred in Bishopsgate Street and another one at Aldgate,[7] which means that *P. pestis* had now entered the city. The civic authorities now petitioned the king to have the Stepney plague-deaths excluded from the weekly London Bills of Mortality and certified in separate bills.[8] The reason given for this petition was that the inclusion of the Stepney deaths in the London bills created a wrong impression in the country that the city was worse infected than was the case, with the result that not only were the countryfolk afraid of coming to London to shop but were afraid also of accepting merchandise from the city.[8] In other words the Stepney plague-deaths were bad for trade! The epidemic progressed slowly up to mid-June, possibly because the temperature was too

* J. Howell, *An Historical Discourse; or Perlustration of the City of London and Westminster; with the Courts of Justice, Antiquities, and New Buildings thereunto belonging* (London, 1657).

low for the optimal breeding and predatory activities of the plague-fleas, and by 13 June only 64 plague-deaths had been registered in the previous week and but few of those within the walls.[1] Cool weather seems to have

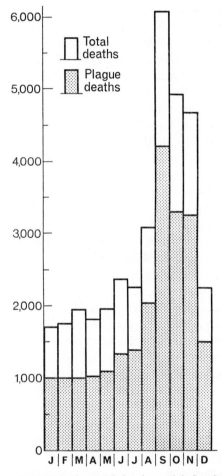

54. Total deaths and plague deaths recorded each month in London, January 1635 to December 1636. (Composed from Creighton's *History of epidemics in Britain*.)

continued into July as the plague-deaths increased only very slightly that month (see figure 54) but in August the epidemic increased rapidly and in September it climbed steeply to its peak. Even during August and September its spread was erratic and there were undoubtedly numerous parishes both within and without the walls that were either unaffected or only slightly

374

affected by it. For example in St Antholin's parish 5 of the 6 registered plague-burials were contributed by one family,[1] and one family in the parish of St Michael Bassishaw contributed 3 of the 8 registered plague-burials.[2]

On 22 April an Order in Council was issued for rates to be levied in Middlesex and Surrey to provide money 'for the erection of Pest-houses and other places of abode for infected persons'.[3] This appears to be the first indication of state interest in the isolation in separate buildings of the plague-sick; but it still regarded segregation of the plague-sick and their household contacts in their own houses as an indispensable method for the control of the disease because in May the Privy Council complained to the lord mayor 'that the *Red Cross* and the inscription *"Lord have mercy upon us"*, were placed so high, and in such obscure places, upon infected houses, as to be hardly discernible; and that they were so negligently looked to that few or none had watchmen at the doors, and that persons had been sitting at the doors of such houses'.[4] About a fortnight later Trinity Term was in part adjourned,[5] but no further official notice of the outbreak seems to have been taken for some 8 weeks. Then on 17 July Bartholomew Fair was cancelled,[6] on the 18th Tutbury Fair and its concomitant Minstrels' Court,[7] and on the 26th Our Lady Fair at Southwark.[8] The alarm created by the August augmentation of the epidemic then provoked the cancellation of Sturbridge Fair on the 20th of that month.[9] Also early in the month Michaelmas Term was adjourned[10] and its adjournment was extended at the beginning of October as there was no sign that the outbreak was subsiding.[11] On the contrary its continued activity inspired the king on the 18th to proclaim a general fast to be observed weekly,[12] evidently in a belated attempt to placate the wrath of a punitive deity. Presumably the autumn frosts were late in arriving this year for the toll of plague-deaths in November was practically identical with the October mortality (see figure 54) and it was not until December was well advanced that the epidemic began to subside. Even then plague was not extinguished; it continued to smoulder sporadically throughout the winter, unless it was mistaken for typhus fever, and in the spring of 1637 its recrudescence was sufficiently active to threaten a recurrent epidemic in the summer of that year.

The despatches of the Venetian ambassador this year exhibit the mixture of rumour and fact typical of many of the contemporary reports about bubonic plague. On 13 June he reported that the epidemic was making great progress in London and had spread into the surrounding townships.[13] Towards the end of August he stated that more than 800 plague-deaths were occurring each week in London,[14] and on 24 October he affirmed that more than 2,000 deaths were happening each week in the city,[15] inferentially from plague alone.

TABLE 30

The death-roll of London in the latter part of 1636

Week ending	Registered deaths		Percentage plague-mortality rate
	All causes	Plague	
14 September	1,069	650	60·8
26 September	1,200-odd	645	53·7
19 October	1,302	792	60·8
2 November	900	458	50·9
20 December	405	85	21·0

Finally on 26 December he produced this mixture of fact and fiction: 'The plague being confined by the very sharp cold, is beginning to lose the malignity with which for nine months on end it has troubled a great part of this Kingdom.'[1] He added correctly that the plague-deaths in London were then less than 200 a week, a statement confirmed by the figures from the London Bills of Mortality that Anthony Mingay (see table 30) sent to Framlingham Gawdy.[2, 3, 4, 5, 6] The appearance of plague in the eastern suburbs of London in 1636 is consistent with its maritime importation, probably from Holland. Once established among the ship-rats in the port of London, its natural direction of spread would be westwards along the Thames, which was the main highway of Stuart London, and northwards with the movement of traffic up the Great North Road. The contemporary notices of the epidemic indicate that the eastern suburbs and the walled city bore the brunt of the attack, which is to be expected for 'plague travels by the most frequented trade routes'.[7] Westminster was involved but to what extent is not known because Burke merely states that in August 1636 'the Plague-mark reappears, and continues till October 1638'[8] in the burials register of St Margaret's parish. Plague was present in the Tower Division of Middlesex at the end of April[9] and in Clerkenwell early in May.[10] Towards the end of the month it was reported that three houses had been segregated in Smithfield Bars and that the disease was spreading dangerously in that area.[11] At the end of the month the prisoners in the Fleet petitioned the king 'to be allowed to go into the country on securities' as the prison was in very great danger from the epidemic,[12] and simultaneously plague was reported to be sorely afflicting the parishes of St Giles-in-the-Fields, St Giles Cripplegate, St Sepulchre, Clerkenwell, Islington, St Katherine (by the Tower), East Smithfield, Whitechapel, Stepney, Shoreditch, and Isleworth.[13] Charles granted the petition of the prisoners in the Fleet; he could hardly do otherwise in view of the

directive which the Privy Council sent on his behalf to Sir Richard Lucy at the beginning of June.[1]

The Lords have been informed [it reads] that there are divers gentlemen, citizens of London and others, that send their children to be nursed and put to school at Enfield, Waltham, and other towns near his Majesty's house at Theobalds, whereby the parents of the said children take often occasion to repair thither or send their servants, which in this time of infection may prove dangerous to his Majesty's servants and others; Sir Richard is to cause the said children to be removed.

It is interesting to speculate upon the course of British history if Charles I had been as terrified of war as he was of bubonic plague.

This metropolitan epidemic seems to have had its principal focus in the parish of Stepney, which was so badly infected by the end of May that the Middlesex justices cancelled Greengoose Fair because its location was near Stepney, 'where the plague doth more increase than in any other parish within or without London'.[2] Concurrently with its spread in Stepney plague crossed the Thames and was active in Southwark early in June,[3] and by the 12th of that month its great increase and dispersion 'in the city of London and suburbs'[4] provoked an Order in Council cancelling both St James's and St Peter's Fairs.[4] The latter was held in Westminster. Table 31 shows that the epidemic continued to increase in intensity and extent during the summer and early autumn months; but before the end of June the Privy Council had dispersed into the safe depths of the country and its members were no longer apprehensive about the progress of plague in London. This table also shows the lingering, sporadic activity of the human disease after the cessation of its epidemic activity, which was a common feature of plague in British urban foci. These sporadic cases were caused by the prolonged survival of some 'blocked' fleas under the ideal conditions for flea-infestation provided by the ordinary dwelling-houses and especially by the hovels of the poor in the slums of London and other large towns. It is significant that the annual plague-mortality rates of the parishes listed in table 31 are low. They are, in their order in the table, respectively 18·2, 36·7, 17·0, 11·5, 23·4, 41·1, 28·5, and 34·6. Although these registers represent only about one-fifteenth part of the London parishes and they probably do not record all the plague-deaths within their boundaries, they nevertheless demonstrate that this epidemic was neither so violent nor so ubiquitous as the Privy Council's panic represented it to be.

South of the Thames valley Faversham appears to have been one of the few places visited by plague this year. According to Giraud plague was epidemic there from May to November, during which time 78 plague-burials were registered in the parish.[5] As the town was a riverport on the river Swale

TABLE 31

Total monthly and plague-burials registered in eight London parishes in 1636*

	Mar.	Apr.	May	Jun.	Jul.	Aug.	Sept.	Oct.	Nov.	Dec.	Jan.	Feb.	Mar.
St Martin-in-the-Fields	13	45	63	53 (iv)	72 (xvii)	75 (xxi)	101 (xxxv)	—	—	—	—	—	—
St Mary Somerset	2	7	1	7	2	9 (vi)	11 (iv)	20 (x)	10 (vi)	8 (vi)	6	3	1
St Michael Bassishaw	0	3	3	3	3	8 (v)	5 (ii)	2	3	4	1	2	4
St Martin Orgar	0	1	1	2	3	2	2	5	2	1	5 (i)	0	2 (ii)
St Olave, Hart Street	2	4	7	5 (i)	5	5	9 (vi)	16 (vii)	3 (i)	2	2	1	3
St Peter, Paul's Wharf	0	0	0	0	i (i)	0	8 (iii)	3 (i)	2 (ii)	2	0	1	0
St Bene't, Paul's Wharf	0	3	9	3	3	11 (v)	39 (xxx)	12 (vi)	4 (iv)	5 (ii)	3	2	4
St Antholin, Budge Row	2	0	3	1	2	0	2	3 (ii)	5 (iv)	1	1	0	1
St Peeters upon Cornhill	1	3	1 (i)	1	1	2	4 (iii)	4 (ii)	4 (i)	2	1 (i)	1	1 (i)

in the seventeenth century—a member of the Cinque Port of Dover—it may have been invaded by a maritime importation of *P. pestis* independently of the importation of that microbe into the Port of London. Giraud quotes the minutes of a Common Council meeting which was held at Faversham on 12 May 1630. These note the wide dispersion of the disease in Kent and prescribe precautions to be taken to protect the town from infection. These consisted of appointing three wardens to examine all incomers and refuse admittance to any person coming from a plague-area; the removal of all dunghills in the town and a ban on the making of any more in or near the town, and the appointment of a woman 'to searche all such as dye, and to have for the wakes 11s. a week'.[1] He does not make it clear, however, whether these precautions were adopted in 1630 and repeated in 1636 or whether they were first adopted in the latter year. Besides Faversham plague was active in at least two other places in Kent this year. The account of its importation from Sevenoaks into the hamlet of Kemsing, which was written by Leonard Gale in 1687 when he was 67 years old, is of sufficient historical value to merit quoting because it appears to be a unique personal description of a household visitation of bubonic plague.

* The Roman numerals represent the plague-burials included in, or comprising, the monthly mortality.

I was born [he relates] in the parish of Sevenoaks, in Kent, my father, a black-smith...had, by a former wife, two sons, and by my mother three sons and one daughter; and when I was between sixteen and seventeen years of age, my father and mother going to visit a friend at Sensom, in the said county, took the plague, and quickly after they came home my mother fell sick and about six days after died, nobody thinking of such a disease. My father made a great burial for her, and abundance came to it, not fearing anything, and notwithstanding several women layd my mother forth, and no manner of clothes were taken out of the chamber when she died, yet not one person took the distemper; this I set down as a miracle. After her burial, we were all one whole week, and a great many people frequented our house, and we our neighbours' houses, but at the week's end, in two days, fell sick my father, my eldest brother, my sister, and myself; and in three days after this my younger brothers, Edward and John, fell sick, and though I was very ill, my father sent me to market to buy provisions, but before I came home it was noysed abroad that it was the plague, and as soon as I was come in adoors, they charged me to keep in, and set a strong watch over us, yet all this while no one took the distemper of or from us, and about the sixth day after they were taken, three of them dyed in three hours, one after another, and were all buryed in one grave, and about two days after the two youngest both died together, and were buryed in one grave. All this while I lay sick in another bed, and the tender looked every hour for my death; but it pleased God most miraculously to preserve me, and without any sore breaking, only I had a swelling in my groin, which it was long ere it sunk away, and I have been the worse for it ever since, and when I was recovered, I was shut up with two women, one man, and one child for three months, and neither of them had the distemper.[1]

This account is typical of the experience that must have befallen many thousands of English families between 1348 and 1666. It is evident that Mrs Gale brought back in her clothing a 'blocked' flea from the visit to Sensom, where unsuspected rat-plague was present in the absence of the human disease, for it is certain from the nature of bubonic plague that rat-plague often occurred in England without the transmission of *P. pestis* to human beings because that transmission was always fortuitous. The strain of that microbe which infected the Gale family was one of lowered virulence as it took 6 days to kill her, although there was something peculiar about her infection because she obviously did not exhibit the usual signs of plague. As her husband made 'a great burial for her' her corpse would not be interred for several days, possibly not for a week. During this period and the suc-ceeding 7 days of freedom of the Gale family, the 'blocked' flea she intro-duced was engendering the requisite epizootic of plague among the house-rats infesting the Gale's dwelling, and when those rodents were exterminated after the usual interval of about a fortnight the hungry 'blocked' fleas attacked the family. It is noteworthy that *X. cheopis* did not leave the rats' nests to attack any of the visitors to the Gale's house as long as there were any of

their natural hosts alive to feed on. As Mr Gale was a blacksmith his house and forge may have been sufficiently isolated from neighbouring houses to prevent 'blocked' fleas from traversing the distance—in many English villages the blacksmith's forge, or its present site, is at one end of the village—and for some unknown reason no infected rat left the house. Consequently there was no outbreak of plague in the hamlet. It is also noteworthy that Leonard recovered spontaneously and without the suppuration of his bubo, a rather rare occurrence which indicates that he must have had a robust constitution and have been infected with a strain of *P. pestis* of lowered virulence.

Travelling westwards along the Thames valley plague invaded Isleworth in May and passed on to attack Reading. Isleworth was fortunate to escape lightly as its mayor certified that no more than 13 plague-deaths occurred there.[1] At Gloucester the magistrates prohibited 'Vincente that carries sightes and shewes with dauncing on the Ropp' from showing in the city, paying him £1 6s. 8d. as compensation, and they paid an identical sum to 'William Daniell one of the Kings Revells because he should not playe being in the contagious tyme',[2] so it seems possible that in its westward riverine spread plague was nearing the county; but there does not appear to be any evidence that Gloucester was invaded by it this year, although to the north-west of it Presteigne was attacked. In September the corporation of Bishop's Castle prohibited strangers from entering the town 'on account of the great danger of sickness and the infection that is in London and in other parts of the Kingdom, especially in the town of Presteigne',[3] and synchronously an order was made at the New Radnor Quarter Sessions 'for the relief of the poor inhabitants of Presteigne who were suffering grievously from the plague'.[4] In the east Midlands Leicestershire, Cambridgeshire, and the fen country were involved to some extent in this outbreak. Kelly asserts that though Leicester was attacked the visitation was a mild one. He notes that the mortality recorded in the parish registers did not exceed the annual average, from which observation he deduces that plague was not epidemic there. He remarks that the sporadic activity it manifested this year was repeated in successive years until 1639, when it reached a peak of activity and the pest-house was rebuilt at a cost of nearly £30.[5] Cambridge took the precautionary measures of cancelling Midsummer Fair, of prohibiting all goods from London from being sold in the town or within 3 miles of it,[6] and of cancelling Sturbridge Fair on 20 August because of 'the present increase and dispersing of the Plague into sundry parts of the Kingdom'.[7] The town appears to have escaped but plague sneaked into Gonville and Caius College at the beginning of November to kill a fellow and 3 scholars, while another recovered from it after his bubo suppurated and burst.[8] Probably its arrival

so late in the year saved the town from an outbreak of it; but this slight visitation was sufficient to induce the university to cancel its sermons until the first week in January.[1] Sweeting affirms that there are a number of references to plague among the notes on the register transcripts in Gibbons' *Ely Episcopal Records*, although comparatively few of the country parishes present any evidence of excessive mortalities at this time.[2] A local order published late in August indicates that plague was then active at some places in the wapentakes of Kirton, Skirbeck, and Elloe in Lincolnshire, and at a meeting of the county justices on 1 September Wiberton and Skirbeck were reported to be infected.[3] One item in this order records that Boston was also infected and that two 'able men', to be chosen by the mayor, were to be allowed to come to market to arrange for its provisioning. Another item warns 'that noe Tradesmen in Boston, Grantham, or any other Markett Towne or place infected, shall have recourse or commerce to utter any commodities whatsoever unto persons in any townes not infected dureinge the tyme of this Visitation'.[3]

In Norfolk Norwich, Yarmouth, and King's Lynn were visited. The last-named seems to have been the worst sufferer as a report in mid-September states that plague was 'very much increased in Lynn, and is feared to have begun anew in one house in Yarmouth', but Norwich was then 'sound and free, only 13 died last week, being the smallest number for three months'.[4] Early in October there was a rumour that plague had invaded Norwich although the magistrates denied its presence,[5] and about the middle of the month 7 deaths occurred from a disease which the physicians declared was not plague but 'some other contagious disease, "which die with spots"'.[6] It may have been a localized outbreak of typhoid fever with its eruption of 'rose spots'. Blomefield affirms that plague appeared in St Austin's parish in Norwich in September, causing very few deaths, however, until May 1637, when its lethal activity increased to 15 or 16 deaths each week. 'But', he adds, 'tho' it continued here near two Years, the Caution taken was so greate, that by God's mercy it never came to any considerable height.'[7] In the contiguous county to the south Bury St Edmunds was severely scourged by it in 1637. Tymms relates that 435 plague-deaths are entered in the register of St Mary's parish between July and December, with August and September as the peak mortality months.[8] He remarks that the entries are not so clearly marked in the register of St James's parish, but he gives the monthly plague-burial figures for August to December inclusive as respectively 28, 47, 34, 16, and 15, which indicate that the epidemic reached its peak in September in this parish. It is convenient here to give the additional information that Tymms supplies about this disastrous visitation. On 27 Novem-

ber 1638 the king granted a brief for a general collection to be made throughout the kingdom for Bury St Edmunds, 'almost all ye chiefest inhabitants and tradesmen being withdrawn into the country for fear of infection of the plague'. On that date there were 263 families infected, all of them on the town's charge at upwards of £200 a week. Although there were 4,000 persons in the town still healthy, 103 families were segregated in their houses, 117 persons were convalescing with plague-sores, 439 had completely recovered, above 600 had died from the disease, and the town had already disbursed more than £2,000 in plague-relief.[1] In his will, dated 26 April 1639, one of the citizens made several bequests to persons who, when his manservant died of plague during the 1638 epidemic, had come to his rescue when 'I cold gett noe body to help me, & that all my houshold fledd from me & left me both comfortles & helples, when my selfe & my wife were both lame.'[1]

In the north of England this outbreak of plague seems to have been restricted to the counties of Yorkshire, Durham, and Northumberland. Each of these counties was possibly invaded through its ports, probably by coastal shipping either from London or East Anglian ports. The regulation made by the corporation of Hull in September against 'seamen arriving from places infected with the sickness coming ashore against express command'[2] would apply equally to shipping from those ports and from foreign ports. Hull appears to have kept free from plague this year but the cancellation early in September of Howden Fair—much of the traffic for which would pass through the port of Hull—indicates that the authorities were apprehensive about its maritime importation. In the adjacent county Durham City, Gateshead, and Barnard Castle were visited this year and plague was possibly more widely dispersed in the county than these records suggest. Richmond affirms that plague raged at Barnard Castle in 1636 and that it caused 515 deaths at Gateshead.[3] However Surtees reports only 200 plague-burial entries in the parish register of Gateshead between 1 June and 30 September of that year.[4] This discrepancy cannot be resolved with certainty now but it is possible that Richmond's figure represents the deaths from all causes recorded in Gateshead and its parochial jurisdiction during the year 1636. Durham City may have escaped very lightly as Surtees quotes a contemporary report, written in July, that 'within Durham and for twelve miles to the South, only two houses were infected'.[5] By contrast Newcastle-upon-Tyne was devastated by a 'tremendous visitation' of plague, for Creighton avers that in a population of about 20,000 there were 5,542 registered plague-deaths in the eight months of May–December;[6] but this mortality figure is at variance with the one given in the 'true List of the weakly Buerials of such as Deyd

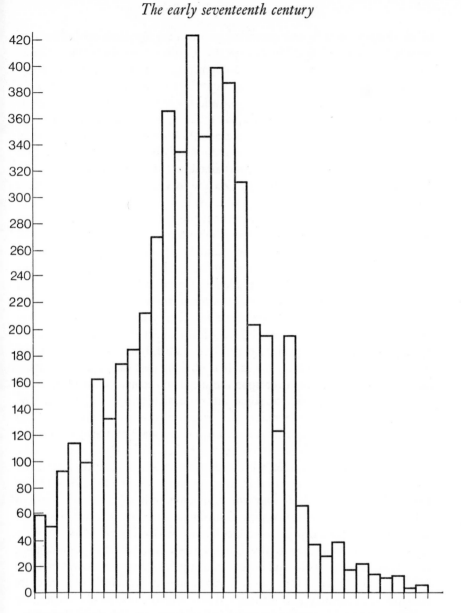

55. 'A true list of the weakly Buerials of such as Deyd of the Plague begune ye 14th May, 1636, onley within the Corperation of Newcastle upon Tyne.' *p* William Coulson of Jesmond.

of the Plague' which was compiled at the time by William Coulson of Jesmond[1] (see figure 55). Dendy says that Coulson 'kept in his family bible an account of the persons who died (from plague) in each of the thirty-six weeks during which it continuously raged'.[1] Coulson's record covers only 33 weeks, however, as figure 55 shows, and his death-roll for the epidemic is 5,082. Dendy gives the figure of 4,982 for it while Brand, cited by Denby, asserts that there were 5,037 plague-deaths.[1] Other guesses about the size of Newcastle's plague-toll in what was undoubtedly one of the most disastrous visitations by bubonic plague ever sustained by any town of comparable size in the British Isles are presented by Cox and by Clepham. Cox cites Fenwick for the statement that about 7,000 people died in Newcastle in 6 months and to substantiate this citation he declares that the parish registers record 5,552 deaths in some 8 or 9 months.[2] To resolve the discrepancy between these two figures he asserts that there were undoubtedly many more plague-deaths that were not entered in the parish registers.[2] Clepham avers that the combined plague-mortalities of Newcastle and Gateshead in 1636 totalled more than 5,500 and he remarks that the latter town was visited by plague in 1570–1.[3] The exact total of Newcastle's mortality in this direful year will probably never be known now, but it seems evident that it lost upwards of 5,000 of its inhabitants from a population that did not exceed 20,000 and may have been considerably lower. It is obvious that such a calamity must have exerted a profound effect upon the social and economic life of the town which it is to be hoped that some future local historian will assess. The course of the epidemic exhibits the characteristic summer incidence and mortality curve of a major urban outbreak of bubonic plague, although the peak in the second week of August occurs rather earlier than usual, and the marked fall in the next week with a secondary peak in the two succeeding weeks is peculiar and inexplicable. It is not surprising that the Scots Privy Council prohibited on 26 May the admission into any Scottish town of colliers and other persons coming from Newcastle[4]—which was described as plague-stricken at that date—and conjoined with this prohibition an order to the magistrates of seaboard towns to keep a strict watch on all ships coming from London, Newcastle, and other English ports where plague was present. It seems evident that plague must have erupted in Newcastle soon after its recognition in Stepney, and as the speed of overland transport of merchandise at this time could not have carried infected rats or 'blocked' fleas from Stepney to Newcastle in so short a time, the Newcastle epidemic must have taken origin from a maritime importation of *P. pestis*, most probably by coastal shipping. A ripple of terror radiating from Newcastle evidently reached Gilling in Yorkshire during the summer of 1636, because at Rich-

mond in January the justices arraigned 'the Constable of Gilling for compelling a poore old blinde man, not able to see the light of a candle, to watch the whole towne in his course of vicinitie, this last summer in the time of the visitation of Newcastle and the Bishoppricke of Duresme to the great dainger of the inhabts of Gillinge'.[1]

Although there was a considerable contraction of the activity of the disease in England in 1637, as usual after a major epidemic of plague there were some 'trailer' outbreaks of it scattered about the country this year. It recrudesced in London in the spring after the customary winter intermission and Creighton affirms that it was responsible for 3,082 deaths in an annual total of 11,763 from all causes.[2] The parish register of St Martin Orgar records a plague-burial on 29 March;[3] that of St Peeters upon Cornhill one on 15 April[4] and that of St Bene't, Paul's Wharf one on 26 May.[5] A second victim was buried at St Peeters in May,[6] but then the disease seems to have become temporarily quiescent, evidently because of cold weather as a letter written from the *Golden Anchor* in Fleet Street on 9 May indicates.[7] The arrival of warmer weather resuscitated it so that by mid-July it was sufficiently active to provoke the cancellation of both Bartholomew and Our Lady Fairs on the 23rd,[8] and a month later, as there was no sign of its cessation, Sturbridge Fair was cancelled together with all other fairs within 10 miles of Cambridge.[9] A study of the burial registers of the nine city parishes in which plague-burials are marked this year (see figure 56) reveals that its distribution in London was uneven in both time and space. The small number of deaths ascribed to plague (22) in these registers raises a doubt about the accuracy of Creighton's plague-mortality figure, which could be correct, however, if plague was only sporadically active within the walled city but simultaneously prevalent epidemically in the liberties and out-parishes. It may have been its restraint in the city which incited several citizens in the spring of 1637 to commit an offence that alarmed the Privy Council when it received on 3 May this report:

This day the doors of Stephen Smith, fishmonger, were, by the sufferance of the warder, broken open, and William Fenn, late servant to Smith, who already had been indicted for offences committed during the several infections of that house, entered thereinto and brought to the door for sale a quantity of salted fish without the privity of the officers, notwithstanding Susan Wheelyer, a maidservant of Smith's was then shut up and left infected with the plague at the time of Smith's unlawfully abandoning his house.[10]

In its immediate reply the Council ordered

that Stephen Smith be committed to Newgate, and there be kept under strong bolts till further order, and that William Fenn be sent to the pest-house and a

Total burials   Plague burials

1637 1638 1639 1640 1641 1642

386

weight of iron be put on his heels to keep him safe and quiet there. Further, that the warders, for their great neglect, be put in the stocks placed in the street before the door of Smith's house.[1]

Smith richly deserved his punishment for his callous desertion of his maid-servant even though he had innumerable precedents in plague-time for his behaviour.

As plague was sporadically active in London in each of the next 5 years, it is convenient to deal now with its behaviour there during this quin-quennium before continuing with its history in the provinces in 1637. Figure 56 shows that two parishes registered 8 plague-burials between them in 1638 and that in each of the years 1639 and 1640 three parishes registered totals of 6 and 19 plague-burials respectively. The next year witnessed a local stirring of the disease in one parish which caused 16 deaths, and 4 deaths in a second parish brought the total for 1641 to 20. Finally in 1642 a single parish registered one plague-burial. These parochial records show that the sporadic activity of the disease fluctuated from year to year, a fact noticed by Creighton who remarks that it was synchronous with an increased total mortality in the years from 1638 to 1642 inclusive.[2] Although he seems to have been loath to credit any disease other than bubonic plague with the lethal power to cause large mortalities, he was forced to ascribe these changes in London's death-roll to the effects of diseases other than plague. His statement that in 1638 only 363 plague-deaths were registered in the capital in a total of 13,624 from all causes[2] signifies that a decrease of 2,719 deaths from plague occurred simultaneously with an increase of 1,861 from all causes. He admits, albeit reluctantly, that smallpox was rife in London in 1641,[2] and he opines that typhus fever was continuously prevalent among the London poor and that from 1638 to 1666 it was closely associated with plague as a causal factor of London's mortality.[3] The sporadic activity of plague in London in the summer of 1638 was sufficient to provoke a proclamation in September prohibiting sufferers from the *King's Evil** from coming to the City to receive the royal touch before Easter or 14 days before that festival.[4] There is a notice that it was present in September 1639 in a house 'upon

---

* This was the old name for *scrofula*, an infection of the lymphatic glands in the neck by the bacterium that causes tuberculosis. *Scrofula* was at one time believed in both England and France to be curable by the pressure of the royal fingers on the lesion. 'Touching for the *King's Evil*' was begun in England by Edward the Confessor. The practice 'fell into disuse among the Norman Kings after the Confessor, but was revived by Henry II, Henry III, and the three Edwards'.[5] From the death of Richard II until the accession of Henry VII records of the practice are lacking. Henry added to the ceremony a gold coin, the *Angel*, to be worn hung round the neck as a touchpiece. The ceremony, which progressively became more elaborate, was a feature 'of all subsequent reigns to the time of William of Orange, who treated the practice cavalierly; but Queen Anne revived it, even touching Dr Johnson [without success]'.[5] It was finally abandoned in George I's reign.

'Clarkenwell Greene',[1] which the constables and churchwardens were ordered to mark with a red cross and a bill and set a guard on it as 3 members of the household had died of plague. In Westminster the churchwardens of St Margaret's parish paid 'Bummer the beadle'—a Dickensian character surely—8*d.* some time this year 'for watching a house all night in Gardiners Lane which was shut up and supposed to be infected'.[2] But it apparently was a false alarm, although Bummer probably shivered in his shoes throughout the night.

Plague was sufficiently active during the summer of 1640 'in and about London' to cause the authorities to close all the metropolitan playhouses and the Paris-garden on 11 September.[3] Richmond was also slightly visited by it either this year or in 1641, the visitation being apparently confined to two houses 'near to the pond at the entrance to the town'.[4] During 1641 the local stirring of the disease in the parish of St Michael Bassishaw (see figure 56) provoked a parliamentary decree on 21 October that all public and private business would be deferred until 30 November;[5] but in all probability it was a slight ebullition of typhus fever towards the end of the year that caused a further deferment of all such business until the first day of the Easter Term.[6] The House of Lords was so alarmed by this parochial sparkle of plague that early in September it ordered strict enforcement of the regulations about marking and segregating infected houses and added some new ones, to wit, that persons leaving an infected house without authority were to be followed by 'Hue and Cry' and segregated in the house in which they took refuge; that the city's pavements must be repaired, the kennels kept clean, and the night-soil removed; that ratepayers who failed to pay their rates were to be distrained on their goods; that persons turning sick servants out-of-doors were to be forced either to take them back or to maintain them, and that persons who were removed from infected houses on a magistrate's order were empowered to return to their old lodgings after their recovery.[7] In the last two orders there is the dawn of the concept that the freedom and rights of the individual must be preserved in any action taken to protect the community. They reflect credit on the humanity of the Peers in seventeenth-century England. The presence of plague in the metropolitan parishes in 1641, in addition to those shown in figure 56, is revealed by notices of it in the registers of St Michael, Cornhill—4 plague-burials in an annual total of 29[8]—and St Bene't, Paul's Wharf, 15 in 77.[9] Also the churchwardens of St Bartholomew-by-the-Exchange incurred these expenses on account of its presence:

Pd for sending Griffin's maid and child to the pest house, £4 5s. od.
Pd for the pest house man for searching, £4 10s. od.[10]

According to a report sent from London in September 1641, nearly 200 plague-deaths had occurred there in the last week in August,[1] the bulk of which must undoubtedly have been contributed by the poor crowded together in the slums. The reporter ascribed these deaths to the influence of Bartholomew Fair, but the Venetian ambassador correctly attributed them to a 'heat wave' in the last days of August.[2] Two more reports from London, dated respectively 3[3] and 24 October,[4] indicate that there was a slight, transient upsurge of plague in some part of the metropolitan area towards the end of the summer which reached its peak in the last week of September with the registration of 239 plague-deaths.[5] The activity of plague in London in 1641 caused Lady Harley anxiety for the safety of her son, who had been entered at Lincoln's Inn. Accordingly she wrote to him in May:

Deare Ned, I am very sorry to heare that the sikeness is so much increased...I could wisch your chamber were in Lincolnshire and not in the laine over against it; those lains weare the unsweatests places in Loundoun, and allways the siknes is in thos placess. I have sent you a piece of angelica rooat: you may carry it in your pocket and bite some times of it.[6]

In another letter dated 7 August she expressed her apprehension about the news from London 'that the sikness and smallpox dous so increes...'[7] Creighton's reluctant admission that smallpox was prevalent in seventeenth-century England was unavoidable with such contemporary proof of its presence.[8] The next year, 1642, seems to have been virtually a plague-free year for London. One plague-burial is entered in each of the parish registers of St Michael, Cornhill[9] and St Mary Somerset,[10] but it is not certain that these were true deaths from bubonic plague; they may each of them have been a death from tuberculous adenitis or one of the other diseases of the lymphatic system.

The records of bubonic plague in England in the six years from 1637 to 1642 indicate that the extent and degree of its activity in the provinces agree roughly with its behaviour in London. It was widely distributed in 1637 and a number of places experienced more or less severe visitations of it; but thereafter its activity progressively declined until in 1642 it was reported from five or six places only in the kingdom. According to Shillington Bishop's Waltham and Ringwood were severely afflicted by it in 1637[11] and it was evidently epidemic at Calne, where the expenditure on plague-relief suggests that the visitation was a serious one. In addition to numerous payments for the provision and maintenance of a pest-house, £2 was paid as compensation to a man for the slaughter of his sow and piglets because they had fed on the excrements of infected people, and £20 was paid to 'a phisition that came purposely from London and stayed two monethes attending one

the towne and parrish of Calne to adminester phisick in the time of the sickness'.[1] In the west Midlands Ross-on-Wye, Claines, Worcester, Kidderminster, Birmingham, Deritend, and Walsall are said to have been visited, and in the east Midlands Horton, Melton Mowbray, and Cambridge. In East Anglia there are reports of plague at Bury St Edmunds and Norwich, and in the northern parts of England at Chester, Derby, Hull, Aldborough in Holderness, and Barton-upon-Humber. Ross-on-Wye sustained a disastrous epidemic of it this year as an inscription on a stone cross in the churchyard records that 315 plague-dead are buried beneath it and their resting place will be preserved undisturbed in perpetuity.[2] To this day a considerable area of ground around the cross has been kept inviolate. As the population of Ross may well have been less than 800 persons of all ages in 1637, this calamitous epidemic of bubonic plague destroyed at least one-third of the population of the little river-port. After Ross Worcester may have been proportionately the worst afflicted place in England this year. Wood cites a Worcester schoolmaster's declaration that plague erupted in the city on 3 June and persisted until 9 April, during which time a total of 1,505 deaths was recorded in the city and its liberties;[3] but Willis-Bund affirms that 'between June 1637 and April 1638 no less than 1,551 persons died of it'[4]—presumably of plague alone. John Toy ascribed the visitation to God's punitive anger, because He had already twice warned the people of Worcester of their sins by inflicting slighter outbreaks of the disease upon the city; but it apparently never occurred to him that the Almighty would not thus degrade the Infinite to single Worcester out for such irrational punishment, for Worcester was certainly no more sinful than Lincoln, Salisbury, Canterbury, or any other English episcopal centre. It certainly never drew part of its revenue from brothels like the see of Winchester. Including the Cathedral Church there were eleven parishes in Worcester in 1637, but unfortunately only three of their registers have so far been published, namely, those of St Alban, St Helen, and St Peter the Great, and the register of the last one does not begin until 1686. As far as the available parochial records of this visitation are concerned therefore the only ones accessible outside Worcester are those of St Alban and St Helen. In the first of these there is the entry of a plague-burial on 4 June and then follow 17 more such entries up to 2 September, when the register ends abruptly, probably because of the death or desertion of the vicar.[5] It does not recommence until 5 May 1639. As the total burials registered in 1637 up to that date number 18,[5] the plague-mortality rate of the parish was 100 per cent. The register begins in 1630 and the average annual burials registered in the seven years preceding this visitation number 9.[6] Plague therefore doubled this number in a period of three months. It is noteworthy that one family

contributed 4 of the plague-burials registered in this parish.[1] The register of St Helen begins in 1538 and apart from the years 1633 and 1642, for which there are no burial entries, it is complete for the years from 1625 to 1645 inclusive.[2] The average annual burial-rate for that period—excluding the years 1636, 1637, 1644, and 1645—is 21. An examination of the registered monthly burials in each of these four years (see figure 57) shows that, except

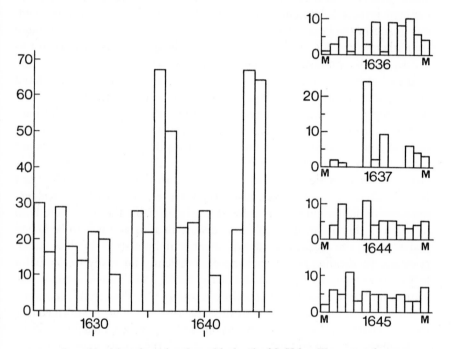

57. Annual burials registered at the parish church of St Helen, Worcester, 1625–45, with monthly burials for the years 1636, 1637, 1644 and 1645.

in 1637, bubonic plague was not responsible for the excessive mortalities recorded in the parish register. In 1637 the annual burials were 51. There was no burial in July, but the three months of August–October contributed 35 or 68·6 per cent of the annual total.[3] At Claines the constable asked the county authorities to suppress four unlicensed alesellers 'during the time of this dreadful visitation',[4] and the constables of Hanley Castle and Malvern reported that no rogues had recently been punished because in 'this dangerous time of infection' there are 'very few that walk'.[4] As is to be expected from its nature, plague evidently radiated from Worcester for a variable distance into the surrounding countryside, and a panic exodus of its citizens certainly

391

extended farther for on 31 July the warder on duty at Ludford's Bridge at Ludlow stopped a man 'who was apparently coming from Worcester, which was then infected with the plague, from entering Ludlow'.[1]

Kidderminster was seemingly not attacked until late in the third quarter of the year as the first plague-burial entry in the parish register is dated 8 September.[2] Burton adds the information that the register records 60 deaths from 'the sickness' in October, 62 in November, and 47 in December; but none is recorded in January and the subsequent winter months. Although this is late in the year for an epidemic of bubonic plague in England there are authentic records of its epidemic activity in the absence of frost in unusually mild autumns. In connexion with a previous visitation of 'the sickness' at Kidderminster in 1604, when 4 burials due to it were entered in the parish register between 29 April and 6 May, Burton suggests that typhus fever was the cause of their deaths;[2] but they may have been plague-deaths confined to a single household. He mentions in a footnote[2] that 115 persons died at Bewdley in five months in 1604 but regrettably he does not name the particular months although he uses the term 'goal fever' as a synonym for bubonic plague in his reference to this epidemic. The 'goal fever' of England was, however, always typhus fever. As Bewdley and Kidderminster are only 3 miles apart it is extremely probable that they were both involved in this outbreak of epidemic disease in 1604 and it is to be hoped that some future local historian will identify it by a study of their parish registers. In Birmingham plague raged so violently for many weeks that a levy on the county of Warwickshire of 100 marks a week was ordered by the justices for the relief of its plague-stricken people.[3] 'And whereas', continues the order, 'also since the making of the said order this court is informed that the said contagion hath lately broken out and begun in Deretend, a village next adjoining to the said town of Birmingham', the county must contribute an additional weekly levy of 20 nobles for the relief of its plague-stricken villagers.[4] It is perhaps incorrect to name Walsall as one of the towns which were attacked by plague this year as Willmore does not record its presence actually in the town; he says that contemporary accounts refer to the sad havoc it created in the neighbourhood of Walsall.[5] It was evidently prevalent so near at hand in June that the municipal authorities gave the constable of the borough an urgent mandate to stop the entry of any stranger who did not carry a certificate that he came from a plague-free area. He was told to report the names of any townsfolk who were disobedient, refractory, or negligent in the discharge of their duties and warned that he would be held responsible for any negligence. He was also instructed to warn all 'Innkeepers, Alehousekeepers, and Victualers' in his constablewick that they

must not admit any stranger into their houses who did not have a certificate of health.[1]

At the end of May 1637 the Privy Council notified the Justices of the Peace for Suffolk that Hadleigh was 'miserably afflicted with the plague'; that more than 40 families were affected, and that the bulk of the chief inhabitants had fled the town.[2] Hadleigh evidently experienced a severe outbreak of plague this year but Bury St Edmunds was probably even more grievously attacked. The information about its visitation supplied by Tymms has already been recorded, and it is not surprising that the assizes were transferred from Bury at the end of June to Ipswich which was then 'wholly free' from plague, although 'divers other towns' in the county were infected.[3] The high proportion of reported cures in Bury suggests that the infecting strain of *P. pestis* was less virulent than usual. Hirst, writing in 1938 when modern methods of treatment provided patients with a much better chance of recovery than in 1637, remarks that 'among Orientals the case mortality from bubonic plague has generally been about 80 per cent; among Europeans of recent years it has been considerably lower, about 30 per cent. Children between the ages of five and ten show the lowest mortality and pregnant females, who almost invariably abort, the highest.'[4] The Oriental case-mortality rate almost certainly applied to the usual epidemic of bubonic plague in seventeenth-century England because the general desertion of the plague-sick and their consequent lack of food, water, and nursing attention militated against their recovery. Concerning Norwich, two contemporary notices confirm Blomefield's statement that on this occasion its visitation was a slight one.[5] One report from the city in June informed Framlingham Gawdy that though the sickness had increased it was 'not nervous' and he could therefore safely attend the assizes.[6] A second report towards the end of the autumn mentioned that only 3 plague-deaths has been registered during the previous week in a total of 16 deaths from all causes.[7] In the adjoining county Midsummer Fair was cancelled on 4 June and Sturbridge Fair on 21 August,[8] but Cambridge may have escaped lightly if Cooper's account of its visitation[9] is correct. Cox reports that at Derby 59 plague-burials were registered this year at the parish church of All Saints and 9 at that of St Alkmund.[10] If these figures represent the full extent of Derby's plague-mortality on this occasion the town was fortunate. According to Southall Chester was the scene of such a desolating epidemic of plague in 1637 that grass grew knee-high in the streets,[11] but as Ormerod does not record any visitation this year it seems certain that Southall's date is a misprint for 1647, in which year there was a calamitous outbreak of plague in Chester.

An Order in Council published on 26 September 1637 records that plague erupted in Hull during the summer and that about 200 deaths from it had occurred there since 15 July.[1] In connexion with this outbreak there is an interesting reference to the disinfection of mail from plague-infected places, a practice which had been initiated by the Venetians in the last decade of the fifteenth century. It is contained in a letter dated 5 September and reads: 'For the letters which come weekly by post, the manner in other countries is to open and air before the fire all such letters as are bound up with silk-thread, pack-thread, or such like, but for letters of bare paper they use no such observance, but suffer them to pass.'[2] This visitation of Hull was serious enough to attract the attention and secure the assistance of local authorities throughout Yorkshire, and at the Richmond Sessions in January the justices ordered a levy on the North Riding for the relief of the plague-stricken at Hull, Barton, and Aldborough.[3] The corporation of Hull acknowledged the receipt of £100 from Durham[4] and of small amounts from a number of places in Yorkshire; but regrettably its archives apparently contain no information about the number of persons receiving relief or of the deaths from plague. At Patrington, some 13 miles south-east of Hull, the parish register shows 21 marked plague-burials in a total of 38 from all causes this year.[5] The fact that plague was active farther north than the district of Holderness would appear to be implicit in the notification received by the Scots Privy Council in the middle of May that it was prevalent on 'the English side of the Border'.[6]

In Wales Presteigne appears to have been severely scourged by plague in 1637. Southall affirms that in one month alone—which he unfortunately omits to name—148 deaths, presumably plague-deaths, occurred there.[7] The visitation seems to have implanted an evil but impracticable thought in the mind of an Upton-upon-Severn man, who was bound over to be of good behaviour at the Worcester Sessions in June 'for saying he could find it in his heart to go to Presteigne to fetch the plague and to bring it to his wife and children at Upton on Severn'.[8] It is evident that Presteigne's ordeal was a severe and protracted one because a letter of explanation about the delay in the payment of the borough's quota of ship money, which was sent to the Privy Council, blamed 'the plague, which continued there for two years together, and did not cease till about the latter end of April'.[9]

The marked decline in the activity of plague in London in 1638 seems to have emboldened some of the citizens of Westminster to flout the anti-plague regulations. At any rate an Order in Council, issued towards the end of September, complains that the occupants of some infected houses had refused 'to remove themselves and their goods into sheds, to be there aired

and cleaned'.[1] Such anti-social behaviour was intolerable and the council accordingly directed the justices to ensure 'that all such persons be shut up in their houses for two months longer than they are otherwise shut up, in order that fresh people resorting to the same may not be endangered by lying upon their beds'.[2] Brett-James avers that 'in 1600 Westminster was joined to London almost completely by houses great and small on both sides of Fleet Street and the Strand...The century was to show the covering of much of the available space round the Abbey with buildings, while the outlying parts nearer the main streets of London were quickly developed.'[3] He declares that Westminster was always a place of slums, of narrow dirty streets lined with wretched dwellings, and of numerous miserable courts and alleys.[4] 'In these streets, so narrow that people could shake hands across them, with ramshackle wooden hovels, with no drainage and with a deplorably evil population, it is not surprising that plague was rife.'[5] What is much more surprising, however, and what clearly reveals the erratic spread of the human disease, is that plague was not very much more rife in Westminster, for the conditions he describes would ensure the maximum degree of rat-infestation. Yet on numerous occasions when plague was active in London there was no spread of the disease to Westminster. It is also surprising to find a writer in 1935 apparently ascribing the prevalence of bubonic plague to lack of drainage and sinful living, neither of which conditions determines the intimate association of rat, flea, and man that governs the incidence of the human disease. Like the rain, bubonic plague falls indiscriminately upon the just and the unjust, the saint and the sinner! Table 32 presents a record of the activity of plague in Westminster compiled from the independent contributions of Brett-James[6] and Burke.[7]

Throughout 1638 plague seems to have smouldered sporadically in Norwich. In the week ending 24 April it was reported that 4 suspect plague-deaths had occurred there[8] and subsequent reports[9-14] give the figures presented in table 33. According to Jones Lowestoft was attacked by plague in 1638,[15] but as the details he gives about this visitation are identical with those given by Tymms for the 1637 epidemic at Bury St Edmunds, it seems evident that one of these authorities must be wrong; and as it is most unlikely that the royal brief quoted by Tymms would confuse Bury St Edmunds with Lowestoft, Jones's statement appears to be the faulty one. Moreover early in May 1638 the corporation of Bury thanked the city of London for the money which it had contributed to the relief of the plague-stricken poor in Bury.[16]

Cooper affirms that plague appeared again in Cambridge some time in May this year.[17] It seems to have increased with considerable rapidity because

TABLE 32

Bubonic plague in the city of Westminster up to, and including, 1642

	Authority	Plague-deaths	
1563		14+	First record of plague in city; disease persisted till end of November.
1574		—	Appeared in May, persisted till August.
1575	Burke	—	Appeared in April, persisted till 1 January 1575/6.
1576		—	Appeared in July, persisted till December.
1577		—	Appeared in June, persisted till June 1579.
1581		—	Appeared in July, persisted till January 1583
1592		—	Appeared in August, persisted till May 1594.
1603	Brett-James	900	Burials registered in St Margaret's parish church.
	Burke	—	Appeared in June, persisted till September 1604.
1605	Burke	—	Appeared in September, persisted till November 1607.
1608		—	Appeared in June, persisted till October 1611.
1625	Brett-James	1,500	Burials registered in St Margaret's parish church.
	Burke	—	Appeared in June; 38 plague-burials, 15 August; 557 in September.
1636	Brett-James	1,669	Money collected from all landlords whose tenants were infected.
	Burke	—	Appeared in August, persisted till October 1638.
1638		—	Pest-houses built; 'merely wooden sheds with the doors crossed with oak'.
1642	Brett-James		Pest-houses enlarged; in July, churchwardens of St Margaret's instructed to build 'tenne roomes in Tuthill ffeilds for Pesthouses neere the Shedde now there with Garrettes over the same according to a plott in that behalfe made of tenne houses in Rainge'.

TABLE 33

Sporadic plague in the city of Norwich, 1638*

	Deaths recorded during the preceding week	
Date of report	Total	Plague
14 May	18	7
25 June	17	4
13 August	23	5
20 October	?	2
10 November (about)	10	3
26 November	?	0†

* Compiled from the reports in the Gawdy MSS.
† During the preceding fortnight.

on 23 June the Senate passed a grace for suspending sermons and exercises,[1] and by the end of June members of the university were seeking safety in the country.[2] Nevertheless Sturbridge Fair appears to have been held[3] but the Michaelmas Day feast was cancelled on account of the persistence of the disease,[4] and on 2 October the university passed a grace to postpone all lectures as plague was still active in the town.[4] Sweeting declares that there are notices of plague in many of the Cambridge parish registers at this time and he quotes two records which indicate that some of the colleges were involved in this outbreak. He opines that the town was provided with several pest-houses, some of which were maintained until 1703, when the corporation had them demolished, and he remarks that the parish register of All Saints contains numerous entries of plague-burials in 1638.[5] Regrettably it apparently never occurred to him to count them. In the adjoining county of Northamptonshire plague struck heavily at the county town and the parishes of Holcot and Wold.* Cox asserts that this visitation of Northampton was worse than the epidemic of 1605. He says that plague erupted in the town on 29 March and that between that date and its extinction on 1 January the register of St Sepulchre's church alone records 114 burials, whereas the annual average of the preceding quinquennium was 18.[6] The mayor complained officially on 1 May, however, that the danger of plague in the town had been much exaggerated, with the result that the country folk were afraid to come to it to trade. Consequently the markets had decayed, provisions were scarce, and the tradesmen—even when they had certificates of health—were scarcely allowed to attend fairs or markets or trade outside the town. Moreover, owing to the restrictions imposed on the town, some of the townsfolk had fled from it and the day-labourers they employed were now out of work.[7] A report says that the mayor had been informed by the physicians that some of the cases of disease in the town were plague and some were spotted fever; but the reporter opined that they were all cases of the one disease because they died 'within three or four days, and *catch it one of the other*'.[8] The mayor's remonstrance seems to have been mis-timed because during the summer the activity of the disease caught up with the rumours, for early in September the sheriff of the county reported that plague had been 'so great and so long in Northampton' that the county was still giving the town £148 a week for plague-relief.[9] Assuming that this sum was distributed at the customary rate of 1s. a head each week, at least 2,960 persons were in receipt of relief in a population that cannot have exceeded, 5,000 persons of all ages. The parish of Holcot may have suffered proportionately even more

---

* As there appears to be no parish of this name in the county today, Cox's reference is presumed to be a misprint for Old, a village and parish about 2½ miles from Northampton.

severely than Northampton as 60 burials were registered there compared with an annual average of 7.[1] The parish register of Old records 18 plague-burials during April–May and contains a note to the effect that no other month in the whole register was so mortal.[2] A report towards the end of October states that Leicester was sadly afflicted by plague this year,[3] but it seems to have been an exaggerated rumour because Kelly avers that only sporadic cases of the disease occurred there in 1638.[4] By contrast Gloucester appears to have been heavily attacked as the Privy Council noted in September that the city was 'much visited with the plague'.[5] The most northerly focus of the disease this year seems to have been Thornton-in-Pickering, which was given a grant for plague-relief in July by the North Riding justices.[6]

Having entered Wales through Presteigne in 1637, plague extended its invasion of the principality in 1638, attacking numerous places in Montgomeryshire, where 'it pleased God', according to the sheriff, 'to visit a great part of the county with the plague, and three, the greatest towns, Machynlleth, Llanidloes, and Newtown',[7] suffered involvement.

During 1639 plague appears to have been reported from only three places in England, namely Haselor in Warwickshire, Leicester, and Hull; and from Taunton alone in 1640. The notice that 'the parish of Old Stratford and the town of Haselor' had been 'lately visited with the infection of the plague' occurs in the records of the county's Epiphany Sessions.[8] At Leicester an increase in the sporadic activity of the disease made the corporation appoint 8 warders in August to watch the town gates, and at the end of the month a night watch was added.[9] Kelly relates that an official report made some time before the Lent Assizes states that up to 2 February 1639 only 17 houses had been infected and 41 plague-deaths recorded. 'But it is impossible', he declares, 'to reconcile the foregoing return if it included all the deaths from plague, with the parish registers of burials, as the number of burials in St Martin's and St Margaret's parishes alone that year were 76 above the average, instead of the 41, as returned for the whole town.'[9] At Hull the extinction of plague this year ended what must surely have been a truly calamitous period in its history if Gent, as cited by Radcliffe,[10] is correct in his chronology of its visitations by bubonic plague. The fact that Taunton received £191 17s. 4d. from the corporation of Exeter in August 1640 for the relief of its plague-stricken poor[11] indicates that it must have experienced a severe epidemic of plague, because if Exeter's donation was the only one that Taunton received it still represents a grant for the relief of upwards of 3,000 plague-sick and their household contacts. Pickard reduces the amount of this grant to £185 17s. 4d.[12] He notes that the Exeter authorities cancelled

the Lammas Fair as a precaution against the importation of the disease from Taunton,[1] which suggests that plague was prevalent at Taunton in July. They simultaneously decreed that no person or goods coming from Taunton were to be allowed to enter the city.

Although plague appears to have been extinguished in Montgomeryshire during the autumn of 1638, it was active farther south in Wales in 1639 in Monmouthshire. It may have spread into that county from Gloucestershire and before the end of April it 'was very hot in divers parts of the county, as Caerleon, Abergavenny, Bedwellty, and many other places'.[2]

The advent of 1641 found plague still relatively subdued in London, where 1,375 plague-deaths were registered during the year;[3] but an increase in the number of its reported appearances in the provinces suggests either that a fresh importation of *P. pestis* may have occurred through some seaport other than London or that a smouldering focus of rat-plague in the provinces had somehow become activated. On the other hand it is possible that a fresh ripple of the disease did creep in through its common channel of the Port of London for in August a reporter writing from London commented: 'Both Houses grow very thin by reason of the small-pox and plague that is in the town; 131 dying here this week of the pest, and 118 of the small-pox, and 610 in whole of all diseases.'[4] There are also official notices of plague in both Westminster[5] and Southwark[6] this summer, and of the segregation of infected houses in the latter place. In the provinces Taunton and Wincanton in the West Country; numerous townships in the Midlands, and Shotwick, Chester, and Halifax farther north, were among the places visited by plague this year. Creighton opines that plague was bad in the Midlands in 1641, naming Thurmaston, Birstall, Whetstone, Oakham, and Stamford as places afflicted.[7] He cites Camden for the statement that at Stamford there were between 500 and 600 deaths,[7] inferentially from plague. Kelly affirms that it raged during the summer at numerous places in the neighbourhood of Leicester, notably at Market Harborough in addition to the places named by Creighton.[8] Leicester itself escaped, but not as he seems to imply because a continuous watch was kept at its gates to bar the ingress of people from the neighbouring infected townships.[8] The most probable reason for its freedom is that Leicester's house-rat population had been so thinned by the persistence of enzootic plague that its density was temporarily too low to support an epizootic of the disease. Simpson supplies a note about previous visitations of Stamford that is worth inserting here. He affirms that it was attacked by plague in 1574 and that in 1580—presumably because of a recurrence—the corporation made a severe enactment against deserters among the townsfolk. In December 1602 it decided to build a *cabbin* 'wherein p'sons infected wth

the sickness called the Plague should be kept and maynetayned'. The pest-house must have been kept fully occupied in 1603 because he says that in that year the parish register records nearly 600 deaths in the town.[1] Pickford records Congleton's visitation and quotes from an unpublished manuscript in his possession: 'According to an old tradition the plague was brought from London in a box of clothes sent down to a person at North Rode Hall, whose relation had died of the plague in London. On opening the box the family caught the infection and died.'[2] He adds the usual asseveration of a nine-teenth-century writer on plague that Congleton was depopulated by this visitation. Unfortunately for the tradition bubonic plague has never acted as a 'jack-in-the-box'. I have already explained the rare sequence of events when a 'blocked' flea survived transportation in a box of clothes. Usually when an outbreak of the human disease happened it was confined to the one household, but occasionally the infected house-rats spread *P. pestis* in the particular village or town. Apparently Chester was only lightly visited this year because a contemporary report, which was sent from the city at the end of July, states that 'the plague which broke out at Shotwick, and lodged at the Red Lion in Chester' had not spread from that hostelry.[3] A note in the parish register of Shotwick records that plague was prevalent there 'from Midsomer till Michmas', but Morrell regrettably supplies no further information about its visitation though he obviously examined the register.[4] Apart from a bare notice of its visitation,[5] no information is supplied either about the degree of Halifax's involvement.

In the fateful year of 1642 Malmesbury, Oxford, Cambridge, Stamford Baron, and Gateshead are named at provincial foci of plague. It seems prob-able that Malmesbury was invaded early in the spring, for on 7 June the corporation of Exeter ordered a 'watch to be kept at Eastgate and Southgate to prevent "wolles" being brought from Mamesbury and other infected places of the Plague"'.[6] Malmesbury was apparently badly scourged because a petition from it presented to the county Quarter Sessions in 1646 states that plague persisted there for fourteen weeks in 1642.[7] 'The plague had been so frequent a visitor to Oxford', writes Cannon, 'that many of the colleges maintained houses outside the town, to which they retreated during epidemics—Corpus to Witney, Oriel to Cowley, All Saints to Stanton Harcourt, Magdalen to Brackley, Trinity to Garsington—and, in spite of the new waterworks, in 1642 there was a worse outbreak than ever.'[8] It is a pity that no contemporary records are cited to substantiate this assertion and that no information is given about any of the lesser preceding visitations. It is unfortunate also that the writer did not trouble to acquaint herself about the aetiology of bubonic plague because that knowledge would have saved her

from making the irrelevant reference to the new waterworks. Cox reports
that 16 plague-deaths were entered in the parish register of St Martin at
Stamford Baron this year,[1] and with plague in Cambridge the university
passed a grace on 6 June for the cessation of all sermons and excercises.[2]

From July 1642 to August 1646 the Civil War to some extent distracted the
attention of the British people from the recurrent menace of bubonic plague;
but the one misfortune neither supplanted nor suppressed the other, for there
were numerous outbreaks of plague during the war years. The menace of
plague certainly hovered over some public bodies to the exclusion of war
alarms, however, because the parish of St Margaret, Westminster, expended
£200 in 1642 on the building of a new pest-house.[3] It is difficult to assess the
influence that plague may have exerted on the course of the war as exact
knowledge of the sites and extent of its eruptions during this period is lacking
and will not be known until all the parish registers of England have been
critically studied. What may safely be said about its influence, and that of its
alias typhus fever, is that neither of the combatant parties would knowingly
have entered an area where either of these diseases was epidemic. A possible
exception to this generalization occurred at Lichfield if Creighton is correct
in his surmise that it was plague which killed 821 people there in 1645 and
1646,[4] because Charles I went there after his defeat at Naseby. It seems
probable that the outbreak of typhus fever at Reading and Oxford in 1643[5]
exerted an important influence on Charles and his advisers. Clarendon
asserts that after the capture of Reading Essex, 'by the great decay and
sickness of his army, was not in near six weeks able to remove from Reading'.[6]
Essex was in fact immobilized, partly by the outbreak of typhus fever among
his troops, and partly by lack of money with which to pay them and without
which they were in no mood to move. The Commons sent £15,000 to Essex
on 17 May, but Gardiner affirms that 'even if Charles's army had been in
a far worse condition than it was, the money would have reached Essex too
late. Disease had broken out among his troops and was rapidly thinning his
ranks.'[7] Charles had received on 13 May the convoy of arms and ammunition
which the queen had collected for him and was therefore temporarily in a
better condition to fight than Essex. In Oxford he and his military council
deliberated upon their proper course of action. 'It was proposed by some',
writes Godwin, 'that they should march immediately for London, where
everything was said to be in confusion, where the earl of Essex's army
hovered baffled, weakened and dismayed, and where it was hoped that, either
by an insurrection of the citizens who adhered to the royal party...or by
victory, an immediate end might be put to the contest.'[8] It was actually
Charles's last opportunity to regain his throne, and if he had struck hard for

London it is possible that he would have succeeded; but he marched west-wards and besieged Gloucester. Why? According to Godwin because 'the admirable conduct of the parliamentary leaders awed the victorious royalists'.[1] This reason seems an exceedingly weak one in view of the state of Essex's army. There were two much more cogent reasons for Charles's move—the successes of the Royalists in the West Country and typhus fever masquerading as bubonic plague. It had already seriously weakened Essex's army and was now appearing in the king's army. It is extremely probable that it was the fear of leading his army into the epidemic area, rather than respect for the 'admirable conduct of the parliamentary leaders', that decided Charles to march west and thereby lose both his crown and his head.

The influence which the Civil War exerted upon the dissemination of bubonic plague is easier to assess, because the immutable aetiology of the disease renders it absolutely certain that only armies that are static for lengthy periods of time can provide the requisite conditions for the genera-tion of rat-plague, without which there can be no genesis and dissemination of the human disease. The Civil War, apart from some minor and com-paratively short sieges, was open warfare which precluded the passive transport of infected rats to engender epizootics of rat-plague, and when sieges occurred there were no siege-lines held for months on end to become rat-infested. Only two sieges appear to have been affected by epidemics of disease, to wit, those of Reading and Newcastle-upon-Tyne. During the former typhus fever—possibly followed by plague—erupted among the besieging parliamentary troops and spread from them to the besieged when the town surrendered;[2] during the latter plague erupted among the besieged and spread among the occupying Scottish army after the town surrendered.

In 1643 plague was more or less active in London, Westminster, Cambridge, and Bath. In Westminster it may only have killed the child 'in the Still-yard', for whose nursing and the relief 'of a poore woman that was shutt up in the house there' a payment of 10s. was made by the churchwardens of St Margaret's parish.[3] In London, as table 34 shows, plague was more active, although its activity was no more than sporadic if these parochial records represent the full extent of its mortality. It is possible that it was more widely dispersed in the city than these records indicate, however, for a wife wrote from Charing Cross in June to her husband: 'My dear love—I resevid your lettars from Dublin…The plag is very hote hear; it is next dore bot 2 to Ser Gregory Worrons overan aganst us. The hous is shut up.'[4] Although neither city experienced a severe visitation, plague occurred in one or the other or in both until 1648, after which year there do not appear to be any notices of its presence until 1664; but whereas in 1643 London was more

TABLE 34

Plague in certain London parishes, 1643–8

	1643	1644	1645	1646	1647	1648
St Mary Somerset	62 iii	48 i	—	—	—	—
St Michael, Cornhill	—	—	—	35 vii	31 i	—
St Peter, Paul's Wharf	—	—	—	28 vi	—	—
St Bene't, Paul's Wharf	54 ii	48 iii	107 xliii	78 ii	66 xii	55 i
All Hallows, Bread Street	—	—	—	—	15 ii	—
St Michael Bassishaw	74 xix	—	—	—	37 iii	27 iii

Total burials—arabic numerals; marked plague-burials—roman numerals.

affected than Westminster, in 1644 their condition was reversed, for while only 3 plague-burials were registered in London parishes the churchwardens of St Margaret's disbursed £59 4s. 4d. in plague-relief.[1] Plague recurred with progressively increasing activity in Westminster during the succeeding three years because the St Margaret's churchwardens distributed £81 1s. 5d. in relief in 1645, £154 13s. 9d in 1646, and £165 10s. 0d. in 1647.[2] The next year their expenditure fell to £73 and in 1649 it was only £1 16s. 0d.,[3] so that plague was evidently extinguished in the parish some time in 1649. It was apparently slightly more dispersed in London in 1646 than in 1645 (see table 34), but its activity was still sporadic and there is no contemporary evidence to support Radcliffe's assertion that plague raged in London in 1646.[4] It was more widely active in 1647 than the parochial records show because a London Bill of Mortality for the week ending 28 September reads: ' 1647. Buried in the ninety-seven parishes within the walls 76, whereof of the plague 26. In the sixteen parishes without and at the pest-house 210, whereof of the plague 120. In the ten out-parishes in Middlesex and Surrey 146, whereof the plague 66. The total this week 432, whereof of the plague 212. Decreased in the burials this week 62. The total this week in these 7 additional parishes 54, whereof of the plague 26.'[5] If plague had had a similar death-roll in the preceding weeks of the summer London would have experienced a minor epidemic of it with possibly some 2,000 plague-deaths; but it seems probable that this bill records the peak mortality of plague in London this year and by mid-October the city was free from it,[6] to remain free from it seemingly

for another sixteen years. Outside London Cambridge appears to have been the only town in England to report the presence of plague in 1643. Cooper notes that on 28 July the university passed a grace which was to remain in force 'till the Vice-Chancellor thought it safe for public meetings to be again renewed'.[1] It is possible that Bath had a slight visitation from plague this year as the register of the Abbey Church records 109 burials compared with an annual average of 34·5 for the preceding decennium[2] and an analysis of the monthly burials—with 52 registered in the three principal 'plague-months'—reveals a mortality curve that could signify a mild outbreak of plague. On the other hand an outbreak of dysentery or of typhoid fever might produce a similar low-mortality curve.

The next year witnessed the start of an epidemic of bubonic plague that undoubtedly contributed to the capitulation of Newcastle-upon-Tyne and heralded a considerable expansion of the area of its activity in England. Apparently plague did not appear in the town until the autumn was well advanced and in all probability it was a maritime importation through the port of Tynemouth. Adamson relates that on 28 October despatches from Tynemouth Castle reported that plague was then 'very hot' in the castle, that 8 soldiers of the garrison had died of it in one week and that about another 60 were ill.[3] Some time during the next fortnight the disease entered Newcastle, for a letter written on 7 November states that it was then 'in divers houses in Sandgate and some few in this town, and many places in the country'.[4] Terry mentions that there is a tract in the British Museum which contains this reference to the outbreak: 'The Plague is so hot in Tinmouth Castle, that divers of the Commanders there have left it.'[5] If this report is true plague played a decisive part in the surrender of the castle. If in Newcastle it followed its normal course in England—and there is no reason to suppose that it differed on this occasion—it became quiescent with the arrival of the autumn frosts, remained dormant throughout the winter of 1644, and then recrudesced in the late spring or early summer of 1645. As the municipal authorities were doubtless preoccupied with the siege, it is not surprising that there are seemingly no municipal notices of this visitation. In 1644 plague appeared also at Eaglescliffe, Whickham, and Durham City in Durham County; at Leeds, and at Banbury, Oxford, Colchester, Sandwich, Tiverton, and Yarkhill in Herefordshire. A note in the parish register of Eaglescliffe records the plague-deaths of 21 parishioners and adds that as they were not all buried in the churchyard all their names are not entered in the register.[6] Surtees relates that plague erupted in Durham City in November 1644 and 'raged nearly the whole year. Eighty-one persons were buried from St Nicholas' parish between 29th June and 30th September,

and twenty-seven others are recorded to have been buried at Shaw Wood from 2d September to 7th October, 1645'.[1] Surtees remarks that the toll of plague-deaths in Whickham was considerable but the entries in the parish register are strangely confused,[2] possibly because the vicar either died with his parishioners or deserted them.

The next year proved to be a fateful one for Leeds, which was cruelly scourged by an epidemic of plague that erupted probably about the middle of March and raged throughout the summer and autumn of 1645. In the early phase of the epidemic *P. pestis* seems to have possessed an exalted virulence, killing its victims with a fulminating septicaemia before the diagnostic buboes formed. This supposition is confirmed by a note in the parish register which records that 131 bodies were buried in August '*before the plague was perceived*'.[3] Many of these victims lived in 'Vicar-laine', where the epidemic originated. During June it increased so much in violence that on 2 July 'the ould church doores was shut up and prayers and sermons onely at Newchurch, and so no names of burials came to bee certified to us save these following, until Mr Saxton came to bee Vicar at Easter following'.[4] The subsequent confusion and gaps in the entries in this burials register tell more plainly than words[5] the disruption and disorganization of the parish by this epidemic of plague. Appended to the burial entries for this year, however, is a return that was made to the military governor of Leeds of the deaths that occurred during the period from 11 March 1644 to 25 December 1645 inclusive[6] (see figure 58). The total number is 1,325. In this return 71 deaths are stated to have occurred between 12 March and 1 June, and 127 between 1 and 26 June. Thereafter it records the deaths each week from the week commencing 26 June to the week ending 25 December. Figure 58 shows that the peak of the epidemic was reached in the last week in July when 216 deaths were returned, although the monthly figures reveal that August had a larger death-roll than July, to wit, 357 deaths against 302. The three principal 'plague-months' contributed a fraction under 66·0 per cent of the total deaths returned, and if the deaths in June and October are included in the 'plague-months' the percentage figure rises to 89·4. Whitaker, who estimates that this mortality represents probably one-fifth of the population of Leeds in 1645, remarks: 'I cannot discover that any person of name in the town died of the plague.'[7] His discovery is not surprising to anyone familiar with the reaction to bubonic plague of the English social classes in the seventeenth century. It was *the* disease of the poor, who were unable to fly from its proximity as the wealthier townsfolk invariably did immediately the suspicion was voiced that plague was in their town. And in Leeds as in other towns they took no chances; long before the official recognition of the disease

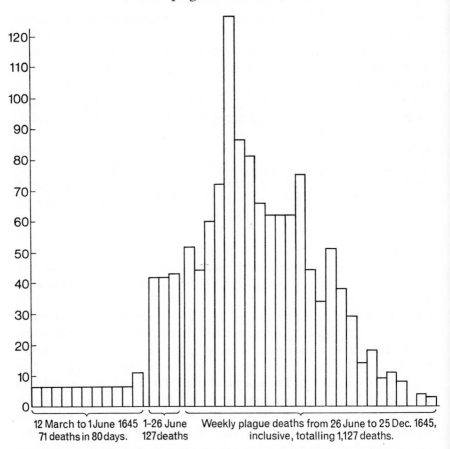

58. The epidemic of bubonic plague at Leeds in 1645. (Based on information contained in G. D. Lumb, 'The registers of the parish church of Leeds', *Publications of the Thoresby Society*, VII, 1895–7.)

in July the bulk of those who had the means to leave Leeds fled from the town. Whitaker also quotes what seems to have been a contemporary observation that in June 'the air was then very warm, and so infectious that dogs and cats, rats and mice died, also several birds in their flight over the town dropped dead'.[1] He is rightly sceptical about these avian deaths being caused by flight through a pestilential atmosphere and suggests that they were carnivorous birds which had fed upon animals dead of plague. As it happens birds are immune to natural infection with *P. pestis* though they are susceptible to infection by *P. avicida*, another member of the haemorrhagic septicaemia group of bacteria. The truth is that the birds were probably

introduced as an embellishment to the most interesting observation of a rat and mouse mortality during an epidemic of bubonic plague, the only mention of such an association in English writings on plague to my knowledge prior to the second half of the nineteenth century. Creighton is the authority for the notice that Banbury was visited by plague this year and that between April and November it lost 161 of its townsfolk from the disease.[1] The fact that Oxford was attacked is implicit in the royal proclamation of 1 August,[2] which recites the anti-plague regulations enacted in James I's reign and directs the vice-chancellor of the university and the mayor of Oxford to enforce them. A subsequent proclamation appointed 38 overseers for the fourteen Oxford parishes and decreed that all-plague burials were to be performed after 10 p.m.; that no plague-corpse was to be interred in a city churchyard, and that all dogs and cats were to be sent out of the city or slaughtered.[3] It also gave directions for the governance of infected colleges of the university. 'The plague, yt arrow of death, is sadly at Colchester, brought by a woman that came to visit her freinds; their have already divers died.' So wrote the Rev. Ralph Josselin in his diary under the date of 5 August 1644.[4] But he wrote it from hearsay for he was living at Cranham in Essex at this time. He notes that Cranham was free from plague on 26 August although the disease had augmented at Colchester, while the 'spotted fever' was killing people at Olney.[5] It is possible that when its parish registers are studied it will be found that Colchester experienced a severe outbreak of plague on this occasion, though it was probably no worse afflicted in proportion to its population than either Sandwich or Tiverton. In the former town a report in mid-August stated that 120 houses were shut up and the town was suffering 'an extreme visitacion of sicknesse';[6] in the latter 450 deaths were registered during the year, 250 of which occurred between the end of July and the beginning of December and 105 of these in October alone.[7] Harding ascribes this mortality to an epidemic of the 'sweating sickness',[7] but it has the characteristic seasonal incidence and mortality rate—55·5 per cent of the total deaths—of an epidemic of bubonic plague, and there is no authentic evidence that the 'sweating sickness' recurred in England after the epidemic of 1551. Southall affirms that his examination of the parish register of Yarkhill discovered the record of an outbreak of plague there in July 1644, and he opines that it was probably the last appearance of the disease in Herefordshire.[8] It is regrettable that he does not present confirmatory data from his study of the register, but his omission appears to be a common failing with English local historians.

The ordeal of Leeds has been described. It marks a year that witnessed a grievous extension of plague in England. In the south Winchester, Wootton

Bassett, and several places in Dorsetshire, including Dorchester, were visited. The West Country was involved in an extensive epidemic of it and plague was reported from Bristol, East Coker, Rode, Wiveliscombe, Dunster, Minehead, Ottery St Mary, and Totnes, though there is evidence that some of these outbreaks ascribed to plague were caused by typhus fever. It was plague, however, which attacked Worcester, Oxford, Derby, Kelvedon, King's Lynn, and Boston in the Midlands this year. North of the Humber–Dee line it visited Chester and Manchester, and numerous townships in the West Riding of Yorkshire were involved in a widespread epidemic of it, among which Halifax, Wakefield, Bradford, Leeds, York, and Whitkirke are named in contemporary records. In the northern counties it was prevalent at Gateshead, Bensham, Bishop Middleham, and Hurworth in Durham County, and at Newcastle-upon-Tyne. Clarke asserts that plague was prevalent in both Winchester and Bristol in June 1645, and in Worcester in September.[1] It is regrettable that he supplies no civic or parochial evidence of its activity in either Winchester or Worcester, but his reference to Bristol's visitation is supported to some extent by Harbin's questionable assertion that the largest plague-mortality occurring in Somersetshire during the Commonwealth was sustained by Bristol in the spring of 1645.[2] The fact that Wootton Bassett was attacked by plague is attested by the petition which the villagers sent to the Wiltshire Quarter Sessions in 1647.[3] It affirmed that plague was continuously present there for sixteen weeks after its appearance on 25 April, that 60 persons died from it during that period, and that plague-relief cost the parish about £100. Dorchester's visitation is of uncertain duration and severity in the absence of any published study of its parish registers. Ward cites a contemporary report that plague 'gleaned only a few...here and there, at that time when some other Townes were almost layed wast by the same stroak of God's hand'.[4] On the other hand the Speaker of the House of Commons received what would seem to have been an official report on 1 October that plague had seriously afflicted Poole, Sherborne, Dorchester, Perret, and Week.[5] Harbin, after his reference to Bristol's visitation, implies that both Ottery St Mary and Totnes suffered severely from plague in 1645–6. He may be correct with regard to Totnes, but examination of the parish register of Ottery St Mary reveals that bubonic plague was not responsible for the excessive mortality recorded in its burials register then.[6] The annual burials during the eleven years 1620–30 average 57 and for the six years 1640–5 they number respectively 81, 99, 84, 97, 104, and 199. The years 1646 and 1647 are missing and the burial record does not begin again until 14 May 1648, from which date to the end of the year 37 burials were registered. It is evident therefore that for several years prior to 1645 the

town experienced an excessive mortality the cause of which is unknown. The monthly analysis of the burials registered in 1645 shows that 15 occurred in October, 18 in November, 79 in December, and 37 in January; that is to say the three autumn months contributed more than 55·0 per cent of the annual total. If the burials in January are included the percentage rises to a fraction under 76·0. This seasonal incidence excludes bubonic plague as the cause of the mortality which probably resulted from a malignant epidemic of smallpox, as it reached its peak before typhus fever as a rule became epidemic in southern England. Harbin quotes a note in the parish register of East Coker which reads: 'From the eighth day of June until the tenth day of September, there died and were interred in the contagious Sickness, Plague and Pestilence, three-score and ten persons—and so it pleased the Almighty, suddenly, beyond all Men's Expectation to put an end to this fearful Visitation.'[1] It certainly seems to have been a 'fearful Visitation' because in all probability a number of victims were interred in unconsecrated ground, in which case the death-roll may have been 100 or more in a parish whose population probably did not much exceed 300 in 1645—and East Coker is in Somerset! Harbin also records that the parish of Rode petitioned for relief at the Ilchester Sessions in 1647 on the grounds that of a population of '800 soules in number at the least beinge very poore', 280 had died between August and February 1645.[2] Wiveliscombe may have been proportionately even more grievously scourged than Rode as 440 of its inhabitants were buried between 17 October 1645 and 9 August 1646.[3] Yeovil also seems to have been disastrously involved in this wave of plague according to a petition presented by four of its townsmen to Ilchester Sessions in 1647. They pleaded that 'in the tyme of the late greate contagion in Yevell, wherein manie hundred soules died, and the sicknes growing soe daungerous that noe living would undertake to bury the deade infected bodies', they were persuaded by the constables of the hundred and of Yeovil to carry and bury the plague-dead at 14*d.* each daily. They averred that they did this work properly for eleven weeks, 'to the greate hazard of their lives, and losse of earninge other better daily wages abroad'; but the constable of the hundred has since died and they cannot obtain their wages from the Yeovil constable.[4]

The epidemic which afflicted Dunster this year apparently started among the garrison of the castle, the royalist governor of which sent an account of it to Dr Thomas Sydenham, the famous Restoration physician. In his version of it he says that the infected soldiers died 'suddenly with an Eruption of Spots'. He then relates how a surgeon, who was serving as a common soldier there, persuaded the governor to let him treat the sick soldiers

and having obtained leave, he took away a vast quantity of Blood from every sick Person at first coming of the Disease, before there was any Sign of a Swelling; he bled them till they were like to drop down, for he bled them all standing, and in the open Air; nor had he any Porringer to measure the Blood; afterwards he order'd them to lie in their Tents; and tho he gave no Medicine at all after Bleeding, yet, which is very strange, of those very many whom he treated after this manner, not one died.[1]

> Wonderful little, when all is said,
> Wonderful little our fathers knew.
> Half their remedies cured you dead—
> Most of their teaching was quite untrue—
> Look at the stars when a patient is ill,
> (Dirt has nothing to do with disease,)
> Bleed and blister as much as you will,
> Blister and bleed him as oft as you please.
> Whence enormous and manifold
> Errors were made by our fathers of old.[2]

Sydenham evidently believed that the disease was plague; but the fact that it erupted early in the spring, among soldiers crowded together in the un-hygienic quarters of a medieval castle; that it first manifested itself with an eruption of spots, and that none of the soldiers who were bled subsequently developed buboes, makes a diagnosis of typhus fever indisputable. What is certainly 'very strange' about it is that the soldiers survived both the fever and the surgeon's treatment. Truly the human body has a remarkable capacity for self-healing in spite of medical intervention. Cox adds the information that there were 80 burials at Dunster in May alone this year. 'It was in May', he continues, 'that Charles I sent the Prince of Wales, then a boy of fifteen, to Dunster Castle "to encourage the new levies". The Prince had just been driven from Bristol by the plague, and the court was not aware, as Clarendon tells us, that it was raging just as hot in Dunster town immediately under the castle walls.'[3] As it well may have been, for epidemics of bubonic plague and typhus fever often overlapped and sometimes co-existed in seventeenth-century England. Cox is also the authority for the notice that Minehead was severely attacked by plague in 1645. He says that it caused a five-fold increase in the registered burials above the annual average;[4] but as he omitted to give that average, the size of Minehead's death-roll is anybody's guess until some local historian examines its parish registers and publishes the details of its mortality. He quotes an interesting entry in this register in 1597 that 'ye blouddye flux raged in this year',[5] a proof that dysentery as well as bubonic plague took its toll of lives in sixteenth-century England.

The parish of Colyton undoubtedly sustained a calamitous visitation of plague at this time. Between 16 November 1645—when 'the sickness' began

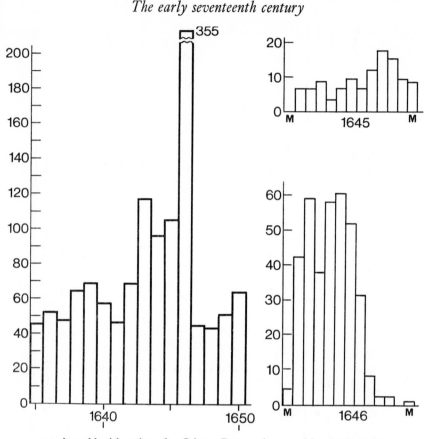

59. Annual burials registered at Colyton, Devon, 1635–50, with monthly burials for the years 1645 and 1646.

according to a note in the register—and 2 December 1646 the registered burials number 459[1] in a population that cannot have exceeded 1,000 souls and in which the average of the annual burials for the decennium immediately preceding 1645 was 65·5.[2] The visitation shows two distinct phases of epidemic activity—see figure 59—namely, the three months of November–January in the first phase and the 6 months of April–October in the second phase. There are alternative explanations to account for these phases. Either they represent two distinct epidemics or an unusual behaviour of bubonic plague. If two diseases were operating in the parish they must have been typhus fever and bubonic plague, because only those diseases would be given the name used in the marginal note in the register. If only plague was present the autumn weather must have been exceptionally mild to allow the plague-fleas to remain active into January, when cold weather induced

TABLE 35

Families involved in the epidemic that afflicted the parish of Colyton in the years 1645 and 1646

Family	1645					1646								
	Nov.	Dec.	Jan.	Feb.	Mar.	Apr.	May	June	July	Aug.	Sept.	Oct.	Nov.	Dec.
Daniell	2	1	—	—	—	—	—	—	—	—	—	—	—	—
Follett	—	2	2	—	—	—	2	—	—	—	—	—	—	—
Maplederham	—	—	—	1	—	—	—	4	—	—	—	—	—	—
Whicker	—	—	—	—	—	2	2	—	1	—	—	—	—	—
Pwyer	—	—	—	—	—	2	2	—	—	—	—	—	—	—
Hawker	—	—	—	—	—	2	3	—	1	—	—	—	—	—
Peaze	—	—	—	—	—	—	3	—	—	—	—	—	—	—
Percey	—	—	—	—	—	—	4	2	—	—	—	—	—	—
Widger	—	—	—	—	—	—	1	4	—	—	—	—	—	—
Ticken	—	—	—	—	—	—	3	2	1	—	—	—	—	—
Bird	—	—	—	—	—	2	1	—	1	7	—	—	—	—
Clearke	—	—	—	—	—	—	—	3	1	1	1	—	—	—
Spiller	—	—	—	—	—	—	—	1	5	1	4	—	—	—
Tirpin	—	—	—	—	—	—	—	—	5	—	—	—	—	—
Guy	—	—	—	—	—	—	—	—	3	2	—	—	1	—
Gill	—	—	—	—	—	—	—	2	1	2	—	—	—	—
Starr	—	—	—	—	—	—	—	—	—	3	1	—	—	—
Cockee	—	1	—	—	—	—	—	—	—	—	3	—	—	—
Banfield	—	—	—	—	—	—	3	—	1	3	1	—	—	—
Penny	—	—	—	—	—	—	—	—	—	—	3	2	—	—
Stocker	—	—	—	—	—	—	—	—	1	—	2	1	1	—

The figures indicate the number of the members of each family buried in a particular month.

their temporary hibernation. Possibly rat-plague continued to smoulder in a desultory fashion until the arrival of warm weather in April roused the plague-fleas to full activity. There would then be large numbers of 'blocked' fleas available to transmit *P. pestis* from rat to man, and the result was the eruption of a furious epidemic which reached its peak in August and provided the bulk of the appalling mortality recorded in the parish. The registered burials among 21 of the families living in the parish at the time of this visitation are presented in table 35, which shows even more clearly than the diagram the two phases of the epidemic, although it is not certain that all the deceased died from either typhus fever or plague or that all the burials from these families were registered. It seems likely that several of these families were exterminated, notably those of Bird, Spiller, and Banfield.

It is worth noting at this juncture the public apprehension about malodorous smells as progenitors of epidemic diseases, an apprehension which still persists today in the British Isles, especially when household drains start to stink. With plague active in several Devonshire towns, the municipality of Exeter decided that something must be done to prevent the city's atmosphere from being made pestilential by obnoxious vapours. Accordingly the council decreed that pigs must be removed 'outside the walls because the sickness or the plague is now raigning in manie parts and such infectious diseases are much occasioned by nastie and beastlie smelles'.[1] It is not certain that Exeter was attacked by either plague or typhus fever on this occasion and Oxford may have been equally fortunate, for although the authorities issued 'orders for preventing the spreading of plague in Oxford',[2] Wood does not mention any visitation of the city. These orders contain no new provisions and are simply a copy of the London orders, which had become by 1645 generally accepted by English municipal authorities. Derby may have been fortunate also to have had plague confined to one of its parishes, St Peter's, in which 63 plague-deaths were registered.[3] However, as Cox also quotes a statement that 'the plague was in Darby and the assizes kept in Fryers Close',[3] the disease may have been wider spread. Also in 1645 plague was reported at Kelvedon in October,[4] and in May at King's Lynn[5] and Boston.[6] The former town possibly experienced only a mild outbreak of it because the mayor reported on 20 May that no more than 12 houses in the town had been segregated and that not more than 14 plague-deaths had occurred.[5] In a letter sent to the mayor of Hull the mayor of Boston described the start of the outbreak in that port. It began, he says, with the usher of the town school, who was seized with a violent fever of which he died within 'two or three days having some Red spots'. After 3 more persons had been seized with a similar fever and had 'all died spotted', the municipal authorities took

fright, segregated the infected households, and appointed day and night watchers, searchers, and buryers.

> Our searchers [he continues] say the spots are like the spots which were in Plague time but none of them had any swelling or sores save only one that died on Friday last, the searchers affirmed he had a swelling on the outside of his thigh and had like spots also as the other, Our physicians seem doubtful whether it were the plague or not, but we for our parts are afraid and take it for granted to be the Plague.[1]

And rightly so, for this is as good an account of septicaemic plague as the seventeenth century provides. The mayor added that 5 families were then infected, of which 11 members had died in about six weeks. During the summer of this year plague also erupted violently at numerous places in Lancashire and Yorkshire with the consequent production of an extensive outburst in which Chester, Manchester, and many Yorkshire towns were involved. Manchester in particular appears to have suffered one of the severest epidemics of disease in its history. It had had a narrow escape from plague in 1630, when Preston and several other Lancashire towns were visited, and the disease actually invaded it in 1631 but was possibly confined to one hostelry where the master and his wife died of it 'and all that were in it, or went into it, for certaine weekes together, till, at the last, they burned or buried all the goods in the house; and yet, God in midst of judgement did remember mercy, for no person else was that year touched with the infection'.[2] At entry in the *Constables' Accounts* shows, however, that numerous plague-sick persons were segregated in the wooden huts erected on Collyhurst Common to serve as pest-houses.[3] Nine years later there was another alarm of plague and in November 1640 the constable paid 3*s*. to two men for watching one of the town gates for 3 days and 7*s*. to another two men for watching 7 days 'at hyde Crosse'.[4] The next year in spite of various precautions adopted by the municipal authorities Manchester was visited by epidemic disease. Axon evidently believed that it was plague; but as the epidemic did not erupt until mid-autumn it was more probably an epidemic of smallpox, especially as he asserts that it 'spread from house to house, carrying off whole families',[5] because to spread in that fashion the causal agent must have been transmitted by human contacts. One item in the *Constables' Accounts* at this time reads: '1641 Dec. 18. to Wm. Hollinshed ffor watching Laploves house too dayes and nights 2*s*. the sickness there appearing pd. for Inkle to lye the Ded corpes att Laploves 8*d*. and for cording 4*d*.'[6] The Laplove family seems to have been destroyed except for a little girl, and according to the Astbury parish register 5 of its members were buried in two days.[7] Axon quotes numerous extracts from the *Constables'*

Accounts which show how the authorities tried to control this epidemic. Two of these are worthy of note:

Dec 22. ffor Coales to the Cabins 5d., to little Bess for 5 days attendance to the people confined in houses and Cabins 1/6, oo.o1.11 Dec 28. to little Bess for a boll of Lickorise and wyne vinebar, oo.o1.o.[1]

Little Bess appears to have been the heroine of this epidemic, nursing the sick tenderly and faithfully when their own kinsfolk had deserted them. There are numerous entries in the accounts that testify to the constancy and value of her services:

> Paid Little Bess, for keeping Mary Houlden's boy, 6s. 8d.
> Paid to Little Bess her quarters wages, 6s. 8d.
> Paid to Little Bess for three days' serving to the infected, 1s.
> To Little Bess for one weeks' pay for attendance to the cabins, 2s. 4d.[2]

Axon says that there are other payments to her at various times

for balls of liquorice, wine vinegar, candles, pitch, frankincense, etc. Evidence is afforded that her ministrations were subsequently extended to wounded soldiers. It is interesting to meet in one entry with her name, which was Elizabeth Smith, otherwise 'Lancashire Bess'.[3]

If the city of Manchester ever decides to compile a roll of honour of its humble citizens who have served it well in peace, the name of 'Little Bess' should be high up on that roll.

It was four years later, however, that epidemic disease—this time bubonic plague—really struck hard at Manchester. A parliamentary ordinance, dated 9 December 1645, reveals that plague had raged there with such violence that for many months Manchester had been completely isolated from the rest of England. The effects of its ravages had been so dreadful that 'most of the inhabitants living upon trade, are not only ruined in their estates, but many families are like to perish from want, who cannot sufficiently be relieved by that miserable wasted country'.[4] Axon supplies the figures of the monthly burials registered at the Collegiate Church from October 1644 to September 1646 inclusive,[5] which are presented diagrammatically in figure 60. It is obvious from this diagram that the epidemic erupted in May 1645 and rose rapidly to a peak towards the end of August, after which it declined slowly in September and quickly in October to its extinction in November with the coming of the autumn frosts. It seems probable that the population of Manchester was reduced by one-third by this epidemic, which was a typical outbreak of *pestis major*. There are numerous contemporary records that testify to the destructive effect of this visitation. Successive notes in the baptismal register of the Collegiate Church in August, September, and

October explain the absence of entries in those months as due to 'the extremi-
tie of the sicknesse', and in the marriage register for September there is the
note: 'There was not anie at all by reasonn of the sicknesse was soe greate.'[1]
The appended extracts from the *Constables' Accounts* also testify to the
calamitous nature of Manchester's ordeal.

Sept 26. pd. to Doctor Smith for his charges to London and a free guift, 04.00.00
    pd. Doctor Smith for pte of his wages for his service in ye tyme of visitacon,
    39.00.00
Nov 22. Recd fro. ye Countie in ye tyme of the visitation for wch wee have given
    an accompte to ye Justices, 918.00.00.[2]

The payment of £918 is a striking testimony to the extent and degree of
Manchester's suffering. Distributed at the customary seventeenth-century
rate of relief it represents upwards of 3,000 persons in receipt of relief for
a period of 6 weeks. Undoubtedly many Mancunian families were exterminated on this occasion and Axon relates the tragedy of one, the owner
of 'the Pool, a moated hall, the site of which is indicated by the name of Pool
Fold'. His youngest child, a daughter, who was then 3 years old, was the sole
survivor of a family of 11 children born between 1627 and 1642. His will,
dated 19 June, 'is written entirely in the testator's own hand, even the
witnesses to this document not daring to come nearer to the infected house
than the "west side of the poole". From this position "they saw and heard"
the plague-stricken man "signe seale and publish the same" in their presence,
but separated from them by the width of the moat or pool.'[3]

In Yorkshire plague recrudesced with but slightly diminished violence
at Leeds this year. An account of this recrudescence is given in a letter written
by Fairfax—probably Colonel Charles Fairfax—dated 20 September, in
which he states that from 19 June to 18 September 859 deaths from plague
and only 11 from other diseases were recorded in Leeds.[4] The figures he
gives for the weekly deaths do not tally, however, with those entered in the
parish register.[5] He mentions that he had recently visited Bradford and
Halifax, 'where not many die, some days two or three', and then gives a
detailed account of the distribution of the plague-deaths in Leeds. He
remarks that about 270 householders of Leeds have left their houses and
many of them have 'removed their whole families into the Countrey'.
Finally he gives a long list of the towns and villages around Leeds that were
more or less involved in the epidemic, among which Holbeck, Wakefield, and
Halifax—since his visit—appear to have suffered the worst visitations.[6]
Confirmation of the severity of Halifax's involvement is contained in a
letter sent to the mayor of Hull from Colne on 24 August. The writer,
Fairfax, says that he

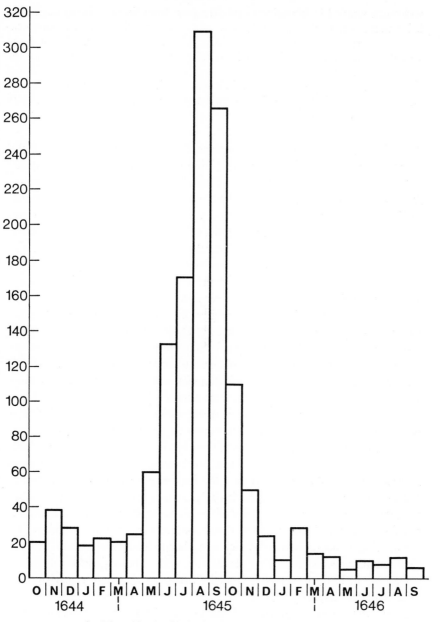

60. The epidemic of bubonic plague at Manchester in 1645.

417

was much wearied in labouring to rule the poor from rising to infect the Town, being in number above 2000, and almost £13 a day for relief, and the county backward to assist the town to keep them in. I paid till we had provided cabins and settled things, and then having prohibited all public assemblies, I had leave for the time to go out to Colne, where I am as yet safe, I praise God, though Skipton threaten us. Bradford parish is much infected. Most little towns about Halifax were safe August 19th, but such strict watch is kept now in every town in the county that we cannot hear one from another.[1]

An order made at the Quarter Sessions at Knaresborough on 7 October notes that 'very many towns' in the West Riding were infected with plague at that date, among them Wakefield which Chadwick says lost 245 of its townsfolk from it between 2 August 1645 and 2 August 1646.[2] He relates that a month earlier the constables in the wapentake of Skirack and Barkston Ash had been ordered to levy a rate for the relief of the plague-stricken at Whitkirke, which had then been suffering for several weeks from an epidemic of it. The constables of the wapentake of Claro were similarly ordered to provide a weekly sum of £250 for the relief of many afflicted towns in the West Riding. These townships and parishes each received an allocation of 10s. a week— Morley, Shelley in Kirkburton, Crigleston, Ardsley, Dewsbury, Stutton, Cowthorpe, Ferringsby, Ripon Bongate, Otterburn, Empsey, Wombersley, Carleton, Purston Jacklin, Castleford, Stapleton, Kirksmeaton, Brotherton, Shelley, Cunsborough, Newton, and Great Houghton and Houghton Robert.[3] The remaining places named in Chadwick's list received the allocations shown in table 36. As these grants were apparently assessed on a population basis, they provide a rough measure of the populousness of these Yorkshire towns and parishes in 1645. York seems to have escaped lightly on this occasion judging from a report sent from the city on 22 September,[4] as only 6 plague-deaths are mentioned in it. In the adjoining county of Durham several parishes were involved in a localized outbreak of the disease. The parish register of Gateshead contains a note that £7 17s. 5d. had been collected at the church door for the relief of the plague-stricken poor there and that relief had been paid for those in Bensham and for providing 'loudges' for them.[5] The parish registers of Whickham, Bishop Middleham, and Hurworth also contain specific notices of plague this year. The register of Hurworth has a note in Latin to the effect that by divine punishment 43 parishioners died of plague during July 1645.[6]

Next year, although plague did not extend the area of its prevalence, it visited a number of fresh places, so that on balance there was no contraction of the extent of its activity. In addition to its recrudescence at some of the places it attacked in 1645 it invaded numerous townships in the south-

TABLE 36

Towns in the West Riding of Yorkshire in receipt of plague-relief in 1645

Town or Parish	Weekly rate		
	£	s.	d.
Agbrigg and Morley	47	12	4½
Bradford	26	13	4
Pudsey	1	0	0
Wakefield	25	0	0
Halifax and Northoram	66	13	4
Middleton, Carleton and Rodwel	3	0	0
Walton in Sandal	1	0	0
Barkston Ash	23	16	2¼
Tadcaster	4	0	0
Grimston	1	10	0
Saxton	3	0	0
Brotherton	3	0	0
Claro	47	12	4½
Wetherby	5	0	0
Rigton	1	0	0
Usburne Magna	1	0	0
Sutton and Thorpe	3	0	0
Keighley	4	0	0
Stanecliff and Ewecross	47	12	4½
Skirack	23	16	2¼
Leeds	50	0	0
Whitkirke, Houghton and Coulton	10	0	0
Shadwell	1	0	0
Barwick in Elmet	2	0	0
Garforth	1	10	0
Osgodcross and Staincross	23	16	2¼
Campsall	1	10	0
Askrom	1	0	0
Pontefract	10	0	0
Ferrybriggs	2	0	0
Darrington	2	0	0
Ackworth	1	10	0
Knottingley	1	10	0
Strafford and Tickhill	35	14	3½
Doncaster	5	0	0

western counties, especially Devonshire. A petition presented to the Wiltshire Quarter Sessions stated that the villages of Marston and Potterne were grievously afflicted by plague, which had erupted in each of them towards the end of July and raged in both for three months.[1] Earlier in the summer the Sessions had been petitioned by the mayor of Wilton to provide relief for the plague-stricken inmates of the almshouse at Foulstone [now Fuggle-

stone] and for the sick poor in Wilton. Of the 40 poor people who had been admitted to the Hospital of St Giles at Foulstone, 10 had died—presumably of plague—by 13 July. 'The inhabitants of Quidhampton', he reported, 'are troubled with watching and warding day and night, to keep off those at Foulstone; perhaps Bemerton may be enjoined to assist them in their watch.' He added that the Overseers of the Poor at Wilton had totally neglected their duties and had deserted the town.[1] Later in the year, at the October Sessions, the justices received another petition from Wilton which stated that there were then about 30 infected houses in the town.[2] As it is improbable that the population of Wilton exceeded 500 persons in 1646, if an average of 5 persons is allowed for each house, the town would have contained some 100 inhabited dwellings. If 30 of these harboured plague Wilton must have suffered a severe visitation in 1646. Also at these Sessions Devizes and the parishes of Highworth, Maiden Bradley, Horningham, and Fisherton Anger were reported to be plague-stricken,[2] and at the January Sessions a petition from Twyford affirmed that that township had been afflicted with plague since the previous August.[3] Of the Somersetshire parishes of Hillfarrence, North Petherton, and Weare, which were attacked this year, the first named seems to have been the worst afflicted as plague was epidemic in it for eleven or twelve weeks.[4] Yeovil also appears to have been very badly infected as 'manie hundred soules' are said to have died there and the epidemic was so violent 'that noe living would undertake to bury the deade infected bodies'.[5] Confronted with this paralysis of an essential service two constables, as has been mentioned, persuaded four men to bury the plague-corpses with the promise of monetary payment which was afterwards not honoured.

Of the English counties invaded by bubonic plague in 1646, Devonshire appears to have sustained the most extensive and destructive visitation. Thornton, who cites Polwhele[6] for the affirmation that Devonshire suffered severely from plague in 1624, 1626, 1628, and 1646, relates that at its second visitation in 1646 276 plague-deaths were registered at Totnes, but many more were not registered because the corpses were buried in gardens and fields. He remarks: 'During this second epidemic the inhabitants fled, terror-stricken, in large numbers from the town, and the grass grew in the streets.' He opines that the epidemic was imported by parliamentary troops under Sir Thomas Fairfax in January—apparently under the common misconception that *P. pestis* is transmitted by human contacts. It is possible, however, that infected house-rats may have been introduced in the forage waggons that may have accompanied those troops. Tiverton was also the scene of a severe epidemic which, according to Polwhele, destroyed some thousands of its population, and both Barnstaple and Bideford were seriously involved.

Plague erupted at Bideford in June, introduced there according to local tradition in bales of wool landed from a Spanish ship. Such a maritime importation may well have occurred there as the simultaneous disembarkation of *R. rattus* would not have been noticed, especially as it most probably took place at night. Thornton affirms that the subsequent epidemic caused 228 registered deaths, a proportion only of the true death-roll which was much larger because many plague-deaths were not registered. He comments that the mayor's behaviour was culpable as he deserted the stricken town, an example that was immediately copied by many of the townsfolk.[1] At Hemyock the parish burials register reveals that it was involved in this outbreak. The register shows that 13 burials occurred in 1645, 59 in 1646, 9 in 1647, and 16, 11, and 12 respectively in each of the succeeding years.[2] All but one of the entries in 1646 are marked with an asterisk. There is also a note which implies that the register for this year was compiled after the epidemic had ceased. As 31 of the victims were buried in July and another 9 in August, these two months of the 'plague-season' contributed 67·8 per cent of the total burials registered at Hemyock this year. Incidentally the parish register of Totnes contains a note which records that 262 of its townsfolk died of plague between 6 December 1646 and 19 October 1647.[3]

In the Midlands Newark and Stafford were visited according to Heberden,[4] but he supplies no information about the duration and severity of their infections. Willmore asserts that 821 plague-deaths were recorded at Lichfield in 1646, a figure that needs to be confirmed by an examination of the cathedral and parish registers of that city, an examination that he regrettably failed to make. His statement that Tamworth suffered severely is equally unsubstantiated.[5] Middleton relates that

on the hill above Lyme Park [in Cheshire], near the ancient relics of antiquity known as the Bow Stones, are several grave-stones in memory of persons who died of plague in 1646. The victims were the members of two families—the Hampsons and the Blakewalls...Tradition tells us that the victims on being stricken with the plague, were driven from their houses in Kettleshulme by their terrified relatives and friends. They are said to have erected small huts in the angles made by the stone walls in the fields where they now lie; and food was regularly left for them by their friends at a safe distance until they were too weak to fetch it. When death came their bodies lay unburied for some time before anyone grew courageous enough to approach the spot and inter them. A distance of about half a mile separates the graves of the Hampsons from those of the Blakewalls.[6]

Cox adds the information that these graves are in the parish of Taxal and that the corpses were interred in July. He remarks that there is a similar memorial, the Riley Grave Stones, about a quarter of a mile from the village

of Eyam, which marks the burial place of the Hancock and Talbot families.[1] Fourteen notices of so-called 'plague-stones' can be found in *Notes and Queries* for 1852. Most of these stones are most probably either boundary stones or the bases of destroyed market-crosses. Axon affirms that plague erupted in Wistaston, a village 2 miles from Nantwich, a little after midsummer 1647 and continued for about nine weeks, during which time it killed 26 persons.[2]

In the eastern counties Blomefield states that plague was active in both Norwich and East Dereham in 1647,[3] but he supplies no confirmation of these visitations from contemporary records. Sweeting is more informative about its visitation of Threckingham as he quotes a contemporary notice of it in a Latin inscription on the wall of a farm-house in the parish, which translated reads: 'The devouring plague raged at Threckingham in the month of May, 1646.'[4] Cooper notes that plague erupted at Cambridge in May also this year; that a report dated 4 May records that 5 persons had died in two houses; that other houses had been segregated to prevent it from spreading, and that a plague-death had occurred at Jesus Green,[5] otherwise the pest-house. In confirmation Worthington notes in his diary that the news that plague was present in St Andrew's parish was published on 28 April.[6]

In the North Country plague recurred in the parish of Whickham, but it was evidently a transient recurrence as the parish register records only one plague-burial.[7] Surtees adds that 'entries of the pestilence still occur in 1647'.[7] Regrettably he did not consider it necessary to count them. In the adjoining county Newcastle-upon-Tyne was visited again in October as the result of the importation of *P. pestis* into the Tyne by a ship from London. Terry notes that by the 8th four houses were reported to be infected and that a week later the disease was said to be increasing.[8] Fortunately its arrival so late in the year evidently led to its early extinction by the autumn frosts as there seems to be no further notice of it.

The first year of the Commonwealth saw a marked contraction of the area of the activity of bubonic plague in England, and this shrinkage continued progressively during the next three years to the near-extinction of the disease in 1651. It evidently smouldered in scattered foci in the West Country in 1647 as the civic archives of Exeter record in April the need to keep 'watches and warders in regarde of the great sickness in soe many places and soe neare unto this Cittie'.[9] But the two places where plague appears to have struck hardest this year were St Ives in Cornwall and Chester. The Lysons affirm that at St Ives 535 plague-deaths occurred between Easter and the middle of October,[10] a mortality that must have had a shattering effect upon that little

town. Morris declares that between 22 June 1647 and 20 April 1648 'no less than 2,099 persons died of the Plague in Chester. Grass grew at the Cross and in the most frequented parts of the city. Cabins for the infected were erected under the Water Tower, and in the adjoining salt-marsh.'[1] The Lysons aver that 1,906 of these deaths occurred between 25 June and 22 October,[2] in which case more than 90 per cent of the city's mortality happened during the 'plague-season'. Ormerod adds the information that Parliament issued an ordinance for the nomination of the civic officers 'as the assembly of citizens could not be held without danger'.[3] The city's extinction as a port is generally ascribed to the silting up of the river Dee, but it would seem to be a reasonable supposition that this slaughter of the citizens contributed to that extinction. Coming so soon after the prolonged siege of the city, the impact of this epidemic of bubonic plague must have been a terrible one. Indeed it seems probable that the combined effects of siege and visitation decisively altered the history of Chester, dealing the city a blow from which it never fully recovered. In addition to Chester plague was active in the Midlands at Oxford, Great Hampden, Northampton, Loughborough, and Cambridge; while in the north it visited Whickham again and the parish of Bridekirk in Cumberland. With plague violently active so near it, it is not surprising to find the corporation of Liverpool at the end of June prohibiting the entry into the town of people and goods from Chester and Warrington.[4] Until its parish registers have been examined no information appears to be available about Warrington's visitation. Oxford seems to have escaped lightly again as Wood reports only 2 registered plague-deaths there.[5] Northampton on the contrary was hard hit according to Cox,[6] but as he reports that its parish registers for 1647 are missing it is difficult to understand how he obtained the evidence for his statement. To Loughborough the constables of Wymeswold sent 14*s*. 'for the poore visited people' there.[7] As in 1611 they paid 5*s*. 'towards the releiffe of the visited folke in Thurmaston' and an identical sum for the plague-stricken in Leicester,[8] they seem to have had an active social conscience. The corporation of Leicester employed one watchman on weekdays and four on market days to prevent people from Loughborough entering it and salved its conscience by sending £10 to that town for plague-relief.[9] At Cambridge plague was prevalent from 30 August to 18 December, 'during which time', Cooper records, 'the University and Town disbursed to, and on account of the sick, £66 6*s*. 1*d*.'.[10] He adds that booths for the plague-sick were erected on Jesus Green and Coldham's Common, though these could not have been much used if, as he asserts, not more than 8 or 9 plague-deaths were registered.[10] It is possible, however, that these were the only deaths that occurred in the pest-houses as the sum expended on plague-relief suggests

that the death-roll was much larger. On the other hand Worthington records only 4 plague-deaths, all of which occurred in September.[1]

The invasion by plague of the parishes of Great Hampden and Bridekirk provides tragic illustrations of its ability to exterminate the occupants of infected houses who stayed in them. Downs relates the sad story which Robert Lenthall, the rector of Great Hampden, recorded in the parish register. Here it is in his words.

My daughter Sarah Lenthall was buried ye eleventh day of August Ann: supra, [1647] she came from London to Whickham [High Wycombe] & on ye Saturday only to see us and so to returne ye morrow in ye afternoone to Whickham againe, but then fell sick & on Wednesday morning following being ye 11th of Aug. about an houre before Sun rise dyed of ye sickness & so in ye Evening we buried her in ye Meade called ye Kitchen-meade by ye hedgeside as you go downe into it on yor left hand, a little below ye pond at ye entrance into ye meade: She was aged 14 yeares eleven months & seaventeene dayes—had she lived to Bartholomew day she had bin full 15 yeares of age.

Susanna Lenthall my wife dep'ted this life Thursday evening about eight a clock ye 26 of August, she died of ye sickness comfortably & in peace & was buried ye 27 by hir daughter Sara.

John Gardiner a childe yt lived in my house died of ye sicknes & was buried August ye 29th.

Adrian Lenthall my sonne a hopefull yong man & neere one & twenty yeares dep'ted this life of ye sicknes, Thursday morning a little before day breake & was buried at ye head of his sister Sara's grave ye same day, being ye 2nd of Septe'b:

My cosen John Pickering a lad about 13 yeares of age, dying of ye sicknes, was buried the 25 of Septeb: 1647   Robert Lenthall, Rector.[2]

It is more than 300 years since this simple yet moving lament was written in the bitterness of his grief and loneliness by a man bereft by bubonic plague of wife, children, and kinsman within the space of one month. Because they were the victims of that dread disease he dared not bury them in consecrated ground and erect a monument over their resting place; but he has given his loved ones a more lasting memorial, one that will endure as long as the printed word is read and long after the costliest gravestone has crumbled to dust. Also he has bequeathed to us a classical account of the domestic operation of bubonic plague in seventeenth-century England. His daughter unknowingly introduced to her home one or more 'blocked' fleas roosting in her clothing. As the incubation period of the human disease is commonly from 2 to 5 days, although occasionally it may extend to 10 days, Sarah was already infected with *P. pestis* when she set out on her last journey home. The incubation period is symptomless, however, so she did not feel ill till she reached

home and her family therefore had no warning of their danger before plague declared itself in her. After her death there was the usual interval of about 14 days while the 'blocked' fleas engendered an epizootic of plague among the house-rats that infested the rectory, and then followed the human deaths. Why did the rector escape? Simply because the plague-fleas for some reason would not attack him—probably because his natural body-odour was repellent to them.

The second story is no less tragic. It concerns a family named Bromfield, the owners of a property in the parish of Bridekirk known as Hames Hill. Browne found that the registers of this parish were confused and defective in 1647. 'Two families', he comments, 'seem to have been destroyed by plague; they are entered "peste mortui". Knowing as I did when a boy, that the old ruins of Hames Hill were called haunted, I wondered, upon seeing these records, whether that idea had originated with this wholesale family destruction.'[1] He then relates the legend, which undoubtedly had some foundation in fact, that the last heiress of Hames Hill was the survivor of ten sisters, 'nine of whom died of the plague, caught from a man who merely called in at the house to light his pipe. She herself, being in London, escaped, but coming down, on hearing of their misfortune, was allowed by the magistrates to converse with her mother across the river Derwent only.'[1]

Although London was almost free from plague in 1648, Westminster appears to have had a serious outbreak of it as Cox affirms that the register of St Margaret's parish records 557 plague-burials in September alone.[2] Outside the metropolitan area its sphere of activity was further contracted this year and its seems to have been reported from four places only in England namely, Alborne, Leicester, Chester, and Liverpool. No information is given in the Wiltshire Quarter Sessions records about the severity of the outbreak at Alborne, [now Aldbourne] except that a levy was made on the county for the relief of the plague-stricken parishioners.[3] Leicester's visitation was fortunately only a plague-alarm, one house being shut up for six weeks because of a child's suspected death from plague.[4] The epidemic at Chester subsided during the autumn of 1647 but plague possibly lingered there until its final extinction in 1648, because on 24 June the civic authorities wrote to William Lenthall about 'the recent visitation' experienced by the city.[5] Morley asserts that there are several references in its municipal archives to the presence of plague in Liverpool in the early part of 1648, and he quotes an extract from the minutes of the Town Council which reads:

April 7th, Memd. that the 3rd Portmoote Court, wch shold have beene held at after Xmas, was deferred and put off by reason of the sickness and infeccon happe'ing in certaine houses in the Chappell Strete, wch through the blessing of

God (great care being taken) and much cost bestowed in buylding of Cabbans, and removing the said families forthe of the towne into the said cabins, it ceased in two months tyme, with the death of about 8 or 9 p'sons of meane qualities.[1]

Although Morley records this as an outbreak of plague, in view of its seasonal incidence, the ease with which it was arrested, and its slight mortality, it was more probably an outbreak of typhus fever. The removal of the infected families with their body lice would stop typhus fever from spreading in the town, but that removal would not stop the dissemination of bubonic plague by the infected house-rats left behind in the houses. Except for a reference of somewhat dubious value that plague broke out at Shrewsbury in 1649 and persisted to 1651,[2] England appears to have been free from bubonic plague in 1649.

Scotland

In the late spring or early summer of 1644 plague returned to Scotland, attacking Edinburgh, Borrowstounness, Kelso, Perth, and other places.[3] Chambers avers that it was imported into Edinburgh in October by Scottish troops returning after the capitulation of Newcastle-upon-Tyne and that it then spread rapidly from the capital to numerous towns, 'all of which were grievously afflicted by it during the next year'.[3] He notes that in a curious and rare pamphlet describing the siege of Newcastle, which was published at Edinburgh in 1645, there is the statement that during the siege plague was raging 'in Gateside, Sandside, Sunderland, and many country villages about'. The author, William Lithgow, also declared that it had been raging in Tynemouth for five weeks 'with a great mortality' and that it was responsible for the capitulation of that place. He says the garrison was glad to surrender and be allowed 'to scatter themselves abroad...to the great undoing and infecting of the country about'.[4] Support for Chambers' contention that plague spread overland on this occasion is provided by the proclamations made by the Committee of Estates 'anent the pest in Teviotdale'[5] and 'anent the plague'[6] which were published in the autumn of this year. The first of these prohibited certain fairs and markets and notified the appointment of commissioners to supervise all traffic in a prescribed region. The second carried the warning that the goods of any person who moved from the Border district to Edinburgh—or any other place outside the plague-area —without a certificate of health would be confiscated. On the other hand Wood points out that the municipal archives of Edinburgh reveal that it was the danger of the maritime importation of plague that the civic authorities feared, not its overland transport by the Scots army. She dates its eruption in Edinburgh to some time towards the end of the winter of 1644 by the old

calendar and records that in April 1645 the grammar school was closed on account of its prevalence.[1] The subsequent epidemic of it undoubtedly gravely harmed Edinburgh. Some of the city fathers to their credit stayed in the stricken city and did their best to control the epidemic and mitigate the distress it caused, but many fled into the country together with most of the nobility and the well-to-do citizens. On 10 April the town council made an agreement with Joannes Paulitius, M.D. that he should visit the infected at a salary of £80 Scots per month.[2] It removed a great number of the plague-sick to huts in the King's Park, segregated the others in their homes,[2] and ordered the return of the deserters under fantastic penalties.[3] Wood asserts that 'all business in the Town came to a standstill. The High School and College were dismissed, the Court of Session and Parliament left the city, and the trade, as is shown by the Common Good's yield, diminished by one-half where it did not utterly disappear.'[4] She opines that the epidemic ceased at the beginning of January 1646 and she notes that early in February a proclamation was published ordering absent councillors to return to the city. By the beginning of May the council had so far computed the cost of the epidemic to the city that it decided that a tax of 50,000 merks was required to meet it. In the Treasurer's accounts the cost of this epidemic to Edinburgh is recorded as £10,792 6s. 8d.[4] This must have been a very heavy financial burden, though it is a much smaller one than that imposed on the city for the provision and maintenance of the Scottish army, to wit, £62,458 17s. 6d. in 1643–4 and £22,989 7s. 6d. in 1649–50.[5] Dr Paulitius, whose salary had been raised to £100 on 6 June, died about that date, possibly of plague, and Dr Rae was appointed on 13 June to succeed him at the same salary.[6] Both these doctors worthily upheld the honour of their profession, for the first died on duty and the second lived to earn the commendation of his fellow-citizens. When in August 1661 he petitioned for the payment of arrears of salary amounting to £300, the council gave bond to pay that sum to him at Martinmas, with interest so long as the principal remained unpaid, because 'he did verie acceptable service in his tyme and had verie great losse of a good wyfe and familie'.[7] Another citizen who also won honour by his faithful and meritorious service during this epidemic was 'John Dickiesoun in Potterrow', the overseer in charge of the disinfection of infected houses, who in April 1646 was 'admitted burgess and gild-brother gratis for his services in plague-time'.[8]

Although no record appears to be extant of the death-roll inflicted upon Edinburgh by this visitation, it was undoubtedly a heavy one and the effect it must have exerted upon the civic and commercial life of that city was not confined to the Scottish capital. On 15 August 1645 the royalist army under

Montrose destroyed the last Covenanting army in Scotland at the battle of Kilsyth and its defeated leaders fled the field. 'So far as Scotland was concerned', avers Buchan, 'the forces of the Covenant were annihilated, and its leaders were in exile...For the moment he [Montrose] was undisputed master of all Scotland.'[1] But Buchan's conclusion needs to be amended with one important qualification—bubonic plague was master of the capital! Chambers asserts that 'the marquis was solely prevented by the plague from advancing and taking possession of the city'[2] and Buchan admits that though Montrose received the submission of Edinburgh, he halted his army 4 miles away and never entered it because plague was raging in it.[3] Perhaps it is idle now to speculate upon the course that British history might have taken if Montrose had established himself in Edinburgh and set up a royalist government there. Probably the final destruction of the royalist cause in England at Naseby in the preceding June had decided the fate of that cause in Scotland also—and yet if plague had not denied Edinburgh to Montrose it seems probable that the massacre at Philiphaugh would not have happened. In addition to Edinburgh, Glasgow, Paisley, Lanark, Peebles, Leith, Perth, Falkirk, Stirling, and Dunfermline are named as places that were visited by plague this year. Comrie affirms that Glasgow was scourged by an epidemic of it that raged there until 1648,[4] in which year bubonic plague disappeared from Scotland for the succeeding 2½ centuries, to reappear, a pale shadow of its former self, in Glasgow in August 1900, in a transient visitation that produced 36 cases with 16 deaths.[5]

Comrie notes that between 1644 and 1646 the municipality of Glasgow promulgated numerous anti-plague regulations.

Among these, quartermasters were elected to search out sick persons, visiting of the muir where the sick were kept was forbidden, and various doctors were appointed to visit the sick poor. Thus, Dr M'Cluir was appointed in 1647 'to attend the visitationne of the toun for ane monethe to come, and to geive him ten dollouris for bygaine service to incuradge him', and later in the same year, £40 was given to John Hall for visiting those dead of the pestilence.

As plague was still active in 1648 he was voted 100 merks 'for his service in attending the magistrates at all times anent with pestilence', and on 2 October he was awarded £40 'in complete payment of his services'.[6] Kelso declares that in 1645 Paisley was the scene of a violent outbreak of plague which persisted with unabated fury until 1646. He says that the population was estimated to be 1,140 in 1634 and he cites Brown's opinion that the sufferings of the townspeople were aggravated by a dearth of provisions of every kind.[7] At this time Renfrew was apparently a much more important trade centre that it is today and the people of Paisley were accustomed to shop there.

428

During this epidemic they were refused entry into Renfrew, but a special trading-post was established for them at the head of 'Hairst Loan', the way leading to Paisley. At this post 'a large fire was kept burning, with a pot suspended over it containing water, and a ladle in it. The Renfrew merchant having grasped the ladle, stretched it towards his Paisley customer, who deposited in it the price of his purchases; it was then immersed in the boiling pot, and brought out purified from all infection, and declared current.' Kelso adds that some of the plague-stricken were removed from the town to the 'moor', probably a part of the mosslands.[1] At Lanark the charter of the masons and wrights was ordered to be disinfected because it had been in the hands of a man whose family was exterminated by plague at this time. As Comrie supplies no more information about Lanark's visitation,[2] it is possible that on this occasion plague was confined to the household of that man.

Ritchie, writing about this national outburst of bubonic plague, describes the anti-plague measures that were practised by Scottish municipal authorities.[3] Compulsory notification of all kinds of sickness to the authorities was decreed at the approach of the disease in order to prevent concealment of cases of plague. The official diagnosis of individual cases of plague was the responsibility of the aldermen or baillies; but in the larger towns a surgeon was sometimes appointed to undertake this duty for the duration of the epidemic. When the presence of plague in a town was officially recognized an isolation camp was constructed outside the town to which the plague-stricken were removed and where they were attended only by the 'foul clengers'. Ritchie says that at first the conditions in these camps were deplorable; but by the middle of this century the larger towns had evolved arrangements for their supervision, for the medical care and treatment of the plague-sick, and for the regular distribution of provisions among their inmates. Suspect cases of plague and their contacts were segregated in their homes for 15 days, then disinfected together with their goods, and finally isolated for another 15 days. This disinfection was performed by male and female 'clengers' who were appointed for the duration of the visitation. He remarks that no details of their methods of disinfection are extant, although house disinfection was universally regarded as a matter of great importance. It is known, however, that the final stage of the disinfection process was prolonged airing and ventilation of the dwelling, the whole interior of which was often limewashed. 'Takin' the sey'—an assay or trial of infected goods of all kinds—was regularly practised. A person who claimed that his goods were free from infection was confined with them and compelled to handle them daily for a specified length of time under the surveillance of municipal officials. Town guards were always appointed in every Scottish town in

plague-time to check the incomings and outgoings of travellers, and to prevent anyone entering the town who did not carry a 'testimonial' from the magistrates of his home town that he had not been exposed to infection.

Plague is reported to have raged with great fury at Perth in 1645, many families being exterminated by it. The corpses of those who died in the plague-camps outside the town were interred deep in the open fields. The epidemic was not confined to Perth; it raged throughout the surrounding countryside and 3,000 people are said to have been destroyed by it in the district, 'besides many who died afterwards it not ceasing for several years, though not raging with such violence. It almost depopulated Perth.'[1] One of the Perthshire parishes involved in this extensive epidemic, that of Methven, is the traditional burial place of Bessy Bell and Mary Gray, the subjects of a one-time popular Scottish ballad. The tradition is that they were the victims of plague under particularly unfortunate circumstances. They were neighbours and intimate friends, Bessy being the daughter of the laird of Kinvaid and Mary that of the laird of Lednock. While they were together at the latter's home in 1645 plague erupted in the neighbourhood, whereupon they retired to a romantic spot called Bum Breas,* on the estate of Lednock. Here they lived safely for a while until they both contracted plague from a young man, an admirer of both, who came to visit them in their retreat.[2] The story is almost certainly apocryphal, although at the time at which it is said to have occurred it would have been quite normal for a young Scot of good birth and position to have had fleas, both human and rat, roosting in his clothing. Plague is reported to have raged violently also at both Falkirk[3] and Dunfermline[4] this year, but there does not seem to be any record of its mortality in either town. An innovation in the attempted control of plague that was practised at Falkirk on this occasion was the disinfection of houses, clothes, and furniture by fumigation at the change of the moon. This disinfection was performed by 'smeikers and cleansers' who were brought from Linlithgow and Borrowstounness for the purpose.[5]

There seems to be little doubt that this was one of the worst and most extensive invasions of bubonic plague that Scotland ever experienced and that many more towns and parishes were involved in it than have been named. As late as the middle of September the Commissioners of the Scottish Army were still bemoaning the 'great ragings of the Plague' in Scotland,[6] although in all probability the epidemic had by then passed its peak and was on the wane. It seems inconceivable that there was no interaction between these national calamities, the Civil War and this outburst of plague, but

---

* Perhaps the spot now known as the *Devil's Cauldron*, on the river Lednock, Perthshire, 1¼ miles north of Comrie.

a critical assay of the influence which each exerted on the other is perhaps not now possible. Certainly it would be more difficult than the assay of the remedy invented by Dr Burgess,[1] which was completely valueless either as a prophylactic against or a cure for plague, even though it was guaranteed that it was effective 'not only for the common plague which is called the Sickness, but also the smallpox, missles, surfeat and divers other diseases'.[1] The historical value of this alleged remedy is the claim that it was a cure for smallpox, measles, 'and divers other diseases', which indicates that they were sufficiently common and formidable at this time to vie with plague in the need for a certain cure. 'Surfeat' probably covered every abdominal disorder from cancer to a bilious attack induced by gluttony.

During 1646 the extent and intensity of plague's activity in Scotland began to decline, although it recrudesced fiercely after its winter intermission in several places—notably Glasgow, where Chambers asserts that it reached its peak towards the end of this year[2]—which Ritchie names as Edinburgh, Leith, Peebles, Paisley, Falkirk, Stirling, Lanark, and Perth.[3] It was active in either 1645 or 1646 in Dysart and Galashiels also. At Dysart a commission was granted to the baillies to take all necessary steps to suppress it in the town.[4] The treasurer of Edinburgh paid £16 10s. 0d. to cover the expenses of two men who went to Galashiels to disinfect the plague-houses there.[5] Apparently plague was still present in Edinburgh in the late autumn of 1646 because the £44 which was collected at Colinton, presumably during the first week in December, was almost certainly intended for the relief of the plague-stricken in the capital.[6]

A further contraction of the plague-area in Scotland occurred in 1647, but it struck hard at several places that year before it disappeared from that country. At Brechin for example it raged furiously, killing 600 people in a few months. An inscription on a monument in the churchyard, where most of the victims were buried, reads: '1647. Luna quater crescens, sexcentos peste peremptos (Disce mori!) vidit. Pulvis et umbra sumus.'[7] Comrie, who affirms that Inverbervie and other places in the neighbourhood were simultaneously attacked, remarks that this outbreak produced an important set of anti-plague regulations, including an instruction—apparently the first of its kind in Scotland—that poison was to be laid for rats and mice.[8] Another town which seems to have been grievously scourged by plague this year was Largs, as the records of the presbytery of Irvine contain several notices of its affliction during August and September, and towards the end of the latter month a representative was sent to Largs to report upon its state. The subsequent report that if the calamitous state of Largs was not immediately relieved 'the people wald be forcit to break out athort the countrie', roused

the presbytery to action and it urged its brethren who had already collected money or victuals to send them at once to Largs, simultaneously exhorting the rest to collect relief at once. The relief contributions from the parishes in the neighbourhood of Largs were—Newmylnes, £7 8s. 4d.; Stewarton, £111; Kilwinning, £100; Perston £40, 8 merks; Irvin, 200 merks, and Kilmaine, 102 merks,[1] amounts which testify to the devastating effect of the epidemic on Largs. Dunblane was evidently involved in this outbreak also because early in June the civic authorities of Edinburgh forbade any citizen to go to the fair of Dunblane as plague was reported to be raging there.[2] Plague was also active this year in the parish of Menmuir and in Aberdeen. In the former it stopped all worship in the church from the beginning of April to the end of September;[3] in the latter the plague-sick were removed to huts on the links, where they were strictly isolated.[4]

In 1648 plague appears to have been restricted to Glasgow and Montrose. In Glasgow it declined to its extinction, but an entry in the Kirk Sessions records at Montrose reads:

Because of ane fearfull prevailing pestilence entered into the city, enlarging and spreading itself, dailie destroying and cutting down many, which occasioned ane scattering and outgoing of all the members of session to landward, for their refuge and saiftie, therefore there was no session nor collection in this our church of Montrose betwixt the last of May 1648, and the 1st of Februarii 1649.[5]

A traditional story of plague, 'which has long had a general currency in Scotland',[6] concerning the black slug (*Arion ater*), may serve as a light relief to conclude the grim history of bubonic plague in Scotland. Two bonny young women, during the plague in Dundee, lived together 'in a remote cottage on the steep (indeed almost perpendicular) ascent of Bonnetmaker's Hill'. Though deprived of assistance and provisions, they still appeared healthful and well fed, even when famine succeeded to plague. Their remarkable preservation of blooming health under these circumstances exposed them to an accusation of witchcraft, which they were able to refute by showing that they had lived on the black slug.

No wonder the Scots are fey!

CHAPTER 9

THE SECOND HALF OF THE SEVENTEENTH CENTURY

THE LATE SEVENTEENTH CENTURY
Ireland

In 1650 bubonic plague invaded Ireland for the last time. For upwards of thirty years after the extinction of the outbreak of 1607 the island seems to have enjoyed freedom from the disease, for Heberden's unsupported statement that 'plague' caused a great mortality in Ireland in 1646 is of doubtful historical value,[1] and Wilde's note that Limerick was afflicted 'by a terrible plague' in 1648[2] may mean any epidemic disease with a high case-mortality rate, such as malignant dysentery, virulent typhus fever, or haemorrhagic smallpox. Indeed later in his chronological table, under the date of 1650, he opines that the 'plague' of Limerick 'appears to have been a Dysentery' which, in conjunction with the siege, destroyed thousands of the citizens and 'like wise severely afflicted all Munster', in which province 5,000 people were computed to have died of it.[3] He is the source also of the report that 'plague' was prevalent in Connaught and Galway in 1649,[4] the year in which Cromwell invaded Ireland. If dysentery was the disease that ravaged Munster in 1650 it may also have been 'the plague' which subsequently swept 'all Ireland', so that when Cromwell besieged Kilkenny in March 1650—too early in the year for bubonic plague to be epidemic—the original garrison of 1,200 men 'had through the ravages of Plague been reduced to three hundred men, and there had also been an immense mortality of the inhabitants of the town'.[5]

The first notices of presumptive bubonic plague in Ireland in 1650 are contained in the two petitions which the Commons of Dublin presented to its General Assembly in June. The first of these stresses the urgent need for the provision of relief to the poor sick and for the payment of expenses incurred in burying the dead 'in this time of mortalitie';[6] the second, after reiterating the immediate need of money 'for the reliefe of the poor at the

pest house, and to provide coales and fire with candlelight, for the court of guards', declares, that 'it is not convenient to lay a cesse on the cittie at present, by reason of the absence of the able inhabitants of this cittie and the greate mortalitie'.[1] Subsequent references to this epidemic in petitions presented in 1651 strengthen the presumption that it was a visitation of bubonic plague and suggest that it was a severe one. For example, a petition presented to the General Assembly on 27 June 1651 states that by reason of the past ten years of war, 'as also by the heavie plague whereby this cittie is exceedingly depopulated', at least half the houses in Dublin had been destroyed and the remainder, which were 'very much decayed and ruined', could not be repaired on account of the lack of artificers and workmen.[2] Three months later a surgeon petitioned the Assembly for some recognition of his services as plague-inspector. As he lost his family from the disease during the tenure of his appointment, the award of £5 'for his service done and to bee done untill the next Midsommer'[3] does not seem to be an unduly generous one. In July 1657 a petition was presented to the assembly by certain citizens of Dublin 'sheweinge…that there is very much of sweareinge, curseinge and blasphemie used and practised (as in the English tongue too much soe also in the Irish tongue), which as it is a breach of the good lawes of the land, soe it is a high provokeinge of God which may justly cause the plague and other judgments to sease uppon this cittie'.[4] A more immediate and natural cause of the ravages of plague and other epidemic diseases in Ireland, however, was man's inhumanity to man, for the social state of the Irish commonalty at this time was conducive to epidemics of the 'famine-fevers'. In May 1653 the commissioners published 'A Declaration touching the Poor'[5] which disclosed a terrible state of affairs. There were multitudes of vagrant poor consequent upon the devastation resulting from the rebellion who, they alleged, had acquired habits of licentiousness and idleness.

Some feed on carrion and weeds, some starve on the highways, poor children deserted or exposed by their parents are fed on by ravenous wolves and beasts and birds of prey. All means of stopping this must be tried. Impotent people are to be assisted and able-bodied vagrants sent to houses of correction till they are broken from their idle course of life, and willing to betake themselves to some honest calling. At present the number is too large, and the poverty of the country too great to effectually put the law in force.[6]

It is not surprising in the circumstances that early in June that year they were confronted with a great mortality in Ireland, which they ascribed to a recurrence of plague and attempted to arrest by enforcing the English anti-plague laws and orders of James I in conjunction with the provisions of the poor laws of Elizabeth I.[7] There is no certain evidence that bubonic plague

reappeared in Ireland after the extinction of the epidemic of 1650, and the 'greate mortality' of 1653 was undoubtedly a product of destitution, starvation, and the 'famine-fevers'. It is noteworthy that the history of bubonic plague in Ireland, which began in 1350 with the universal belief that the disease was the instrument of a punitive God, ended three centuries later in that persistent belief, because this belief governed man's attitude to plague and stultified all his attempts to understand and conquer it throughout the British Isles during the twelve centuries separating the sixth from the nineteenth. Finally, with respect to Ireland, it is of interest that the Dublin Census of 1659 recorded a total population in the Pale of 8,780 persons of all ages, comprising 6,459 English and 2,321 Irish[1] Sir William Petty, then physician to the English Army in Ireland and secretary to the Lord Lieutenant, estimated that the number of British personnel lost between 23 October 1641 and 23 October 1652 was 112,000, of which he opined that two-thirds perished by war, plague, and famine, while about 504,000 Irish persons perished from the same causes during that period. He estimated the population of Ireland at 850,000 in 1651.[2]

England and Wales

Phillips avers that there was a persistent tradition in Pembrokeshire at the beginning of the present century that plague was imported into that county by sea through the port of Milford Haven in or about 1650.[3] He believes that the tradition had a factual basis because, 'with the exception of Newport, obviously an independent centre of infection, the only localities reported as suffering from plague were Crundall, Hillblock, and Prendergast, adjoining the town on the east, and Great Pill, Honeyborough, and Waterston on the northern shore of the harbour'.[3] As plague was epidemic in Ireland this year, it is possible that it was imported from that country simultaneously into Milford Haven and Newport, Ireland having been invaded by a maritime importation of *P. pestis* from England, where it was busy infecting rats and men in a number of places in 1650.

Shropshire seems to have been the only English county to have been badly affected by plague this year, but the disease was also active at Appledore, Wellington in Somerset, and Cockerham. It erupted at Shrewsbury in June and the epidemic reached its peak in August. As figure 61 shows, the epidemic was unevenly dispersed in the town because the registered burials in St Chad's parish were 10 times more numerous than those in St Mary's, and whereas the mortality in the former parish was nearly 3 times larger than its average annual mortality in the preceding quinquennium,[4] in the latter it was less than the

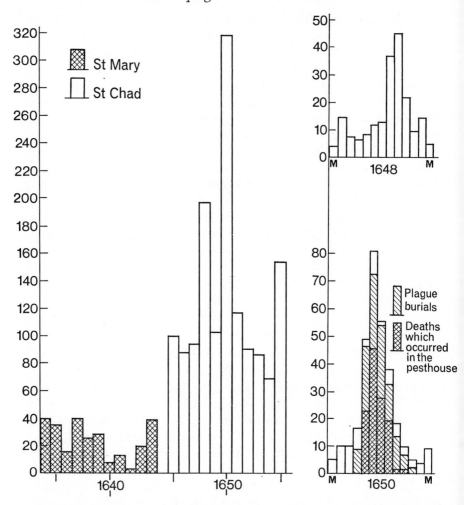

61. The epidemic of bubonic plague at Shrewsbury in 1650, showing annual deaths in the parishes of St Mary and St Chad for the years 1634–55 and monthly deaths in the parish of St Chad for the years 1648 and 1650.

quinquennial average.[1] Moreover, whereas the plague-burials registered in St Chad's parish constitute practically 78 per cent of the total burials,[2] in that of St Mary's they account only for 50 per cent of the total.[3] It is evident therefore that this visitation of plague, like that of 1631, afflicted St Chad's parish more severely than St Mary's. A marginal note in St Chad's parish register reads: 'The plaige begun in Shrowsbure the 12th of June 1650 in Frankwell, at John Conie's house',[4] which was traditionally located in White

Horse Passage. On 3 July '2 boyes from the Jarsey Schoole, suspected for the plauge',[1] were buried at St Mary's Church, but the disease was not officially recognized in this parish until the 11th. Only 14 plague-burials are entered in its register, to wit, 3 in July, 1 in August, 5 in September, and 5 in October,[2] whereas the corresponding monthly figures in St Chad's register are 47, 73, 54, and 43.[3] This was the last appearance of bubonic plague in this ancient borough, whose population at this time probably did not exceed 3,000 souls. As the plague-deaths certainly exceeded 300 Shrewsbury lost at least one-tenth of its population from plague in 1650.

Some 18 miles to the north of Shrewsbury, at the divergence of the road to Chester and to Manchester, stands the market-town of Whitchurch. Here, according to a note in the parish burials register, plague appeared on 2 August 'and Immediately after in some other parts of the parish'.[4] The note adds that the plague-burials are marked thus [✓]. There are 110 of these marked burials in 1650[5] and 7 more in the first 9 or 10 weeks of 1651, possibly remote deaths from sequelae of the disease.[6] As figure 62 shows, the epidemic reached its peak towards the end of September, continued with slightly diminished activity throughout October, and then declined rapidly in November to its extinction early in January. The annual average of burials in Whitchurch during the quinquennium commencing with 1651 was 76[7] and, as figure 62 reveals, there were excessive mortalities in the town in each of the years 1648,[8] 1649,[9] and 1650. The analyses of the monthly burials show that in the last of these years, although plague did not erupt there until the beginning of August, the mortality-curve of the epidemic is indicative of that disease, for the three months August–October contributed nearly 61·0 per cent of the annual burials. By contrast the mortality-curve in each of the two preceding years excludes plague as the disease responsible for their excessive death-rolls. In 1648 for instance the peak of the mortality occurred in February and the burials registered during the autumn and winter months comprise slightly more than 71·0 per cent of the annual total, while in 1649 the burials registered in the corresponding months contributed 61·0 per cent of the annual burials. The burials register of the parish of St Chad in Shrewsbury also records an excessive mortality in 1648 (see figure 61) which, while it was less than two-thirds of the plague-toll in 1650, was more than double the average annual mortality of the 3 years immediately preceding it.[10] The peak of this mortality occurred in November and the autumn months contributed just over 52·0 per cent of the registered annual burials. It seems extremely probable that in 1650 plague spread from Shrewsbury to Whitchurch, taking about 6 weeks to cover the intervening distance—which is consistent with its spread by rat contacts—and it seems equally probable

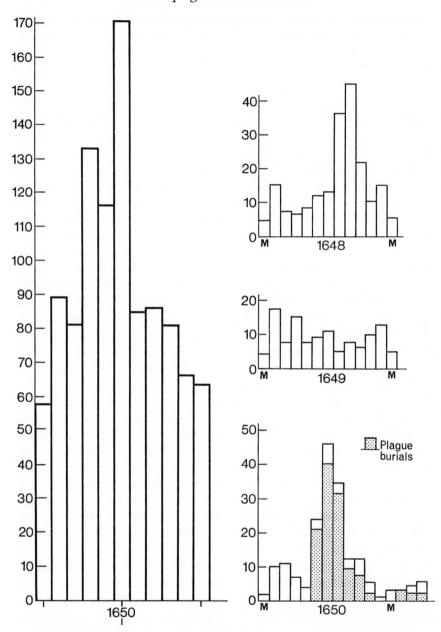

62. The epidemic of bubonic plague at Whitchurch, Shropshire, in 1650, showing annual burials for the years 1645–55 and monthly burials for the years 1648, 1649 and 1650–1.

that in 1648 the epidemic at Shrewsbury also spread to Whitchurch, on this occasion in the matter of a day or two by human contacts. The identity of this disease is obscure, but the speed of its spread is suggestive of either smallpox or influenza. The epidemic which afflicted Whitchurch in 1649 was possibly an outbreak of typhus fever, facilitated by the residual distress of the previous suffering and mortality. Whatever the nature of these successive epidemics of disease, however, it is obvious that their summation of disablement and death must have been a calamity for Whitchurch, a fact that its next local historian will perhaps consider worthy of mention.

It is significant that there is a gap of five years around 1650 in the burials register of the parish church of Wem,[1] because this town is situated almost midway along the road from Shrewsbury to Whitchurch and it is a reasonable presumption therefore that it was involved in any epidemic of disease, spreading either by human or rat contacts, travelling either from Shrewsbury to Whitchurch or in the reverse direction. The visitation of Appledore by plague this year brought a grant of £43 8s. from the citizens of Exeter for the relief of the plague-stricken at 'poore Appledore',[2] and if, as is possible, this was only one of several similar grants, Appledore may have suffered severely. Concerning Wellington, apart from a notice at the Taunton Sessions of an outbreak of plague there in 1650,[3] no information appears to be extant about the severity of its visitation unless its parish registers contain this information. With regard to the outbreak at Cockerham, Axon quotes a note in the parish register which records that 21 persons died of plague there in July 1650, including 11 members of the Braid family, which seems to have been exterminated. In August 34 died, including the vicar; in September 5, and in October 4, but not all of these are marked as plague-burials. The last marked plague-burial was on 8 October, 'and here the Plague ceased' the note ends.[4] Unfortunately Axon does not give the total number of burials registered in the parish this year and it is therefore not possible to calculate the percentage mortality-rate of the 'plague-months'.

In 1651 an epidemic of disease involved the seaside townships in Lancashire, Cheshire, and North Wales which Axon opines was an epidemic of influenza,[5] on the grounds that Creighton, citing Whitmore, remarks that 80 and 100 people were simultaneously ill in small villages like Stanney, Dunham-on-the-Hill, and Norton.[6] It may well have been influenza; but it evidently created an alarm of plague in Liverpool because at a Town Assembly on 24 October 'it was p'pounded concerning the setting at lib'tie of Mrs Chambers and Balive Sturzaker, who have been seaven weeks confyned for suspition of the sicknes'. These unfortunate suspects were granted permission 'to walk to the water syde' but also simultaneously ordered 'to

sequester themselves from companie' until 2 or 3 January, when they were to be freed from all restraint provided that they remained in good health in the meantime. Sturzaker was also given leave to visit his shop during the night time 'to use what meanes hee pleases for clensing it'. There was evidently a third suspect who was more fortunate, because he was only required 'to continue in his howse for a fortnight'.[1] Truly the fear of plague was a fearsome thing in seventeenth-century England.

By contrast with England, Wales was severely attacked by plague in 1651, Carmarthen and Haverfordwest being grievously visited by it. According to a mayoral report it erupted at Carmarthen in May, raged without abatement until December, and then smouldered on until the ensuing April. 'The town and market have been forsaken of all commerce', the mayor laments, 'and the inhabitants loathsome to their nearest friends.'[2] Spurrell is more informative than Lloyd about the mortality of this visitation. He notes that plague appeared in the town on 25 May, that the subsequent epidemic destroyed whole families, and that because of its intensity and extent the mayor was sworn in at his own residence instead of at the Town Hall 'according to ancient custom'.[3] By comparison Phillips presents a comprehensive account of the epidemic at Haverfordwest. He opines that it began late in the summer of 1651 and remarks that it subsided temporarily during the cold weather of the autumn months. He affirms that it caused at least 110 deaths before the beginning of October and he says that from then until the beginning of March 46 deaths from all causes were registered in the town. In January the mayor protested to the county justices about their prohibition of food imports into the town as only 4 plague-deaths had occurred during the month, and a report presented to them on 18 February stated that although three or four houses were segregated only one person was sick in them. Plague recrudesced in March, however, to produce a death-roll of 48 during the month, and the monthly plague-deaths from 1 April to 7 July—when the Bills of Mortality ceased to be issued—were respectively 30, 33, 45, and 11. The peak week of the epidemic was the one ending 28 June in which 15 plague-deaths were returned. 'For the remainder of the municipal year', Phillips continues, 'we have only the record of the deaths in the pest-house and in the "house of recoverie" in Cokey Street, to wit, 11 for the remainder of July, 15 for August, and 18 for September. Probably this represents a total plague mortality for the same period of 90 to 100.'[4] In February the Town Council rented two houses, the larger of which—known as 'the great house'—was used as the pest-house, while the other, described as 'Edward Lloyd's house', was reserved for the accommodation of the men who tended the sick and buried the dead.[5]

Twice a week provisions were sent to the pest-house and to the Cokey Street 'Convalescent Home'. The usual allowance for each plague-sick inmate was 1 lb. of butter, 1 quart of oatmeal, and 8*d.* in money; for each convalescent two 3*d.* loaves of bread, 2 lb. of cheese, and 1 quart of oatmeal, to which was added during the last eight weeks of convalescence 1 lb. of beef. He notes that there are also several entries of money spent on 'necessaries for the sicke'.

It is clear [he continues], that even sick-room comforts of the simplest kind were rarely seen in the pest quarters. There can be no doubt that private benevolence, from both town and country, largely supplemented the relief given by the authorities...A list of the persons in the pest-house and in Cokey Street was made on Tuesday and Saturday. Those in the pest-house were divided into three classes: (1) Sick on the town's charge; (2) Sick on other men's charge; (3) on recovery on the town's charge. The number, including those in Cokey Street, but not those— usually 5 or 6—'on other men's charge', rose from 31 on 20 May to 72 on 18 August, and a fortnight later it stood at 70, but gradually decreased to 37 on 2 October—the end of Mayor David's administration. The provision account, which extends into the next mayoralty, shows a rapidly decreasing number of inmates both in the pest-house and in Cokey Street. On 20 November the Cokey Street house was empty, and there was in the pest-house only one inmate, and that was one 'on recoverie'.[1]

Phillips adds that there was apparently a slight recurrence of plague in Haverfordwest in the autumn of 1653, but no details about it are recorded in the town's archives. It is improbable that Haverfordwest was unique among British towns either in its provision for the plague-stricken or in its classification of the inmates of its pest-house, and the details that Phillips has laudably extracted from its municipal archives epitomize in all probability measures that were commonly applied throughout the realm.

The single notice of plague in England in 1651 is supplied by Morley, who asserts that it was responsible for more than 200 deaths in Liverpool, a toll which he opines represented one-tenth of its population.[2] He notes that the Custom-house was moved early in 1652 into the country, where it remained for a whole year,[2] 'during which time none of the State's vessels came into the harbour'.[3] This quotation from the *Calendar of State Papers, Domestic Series* suggests that by this date Liverpool had drawn the Irish trade away from Chester. In all probability Bootle, where plague appeared in July 1652, was infected from Liverpool. It seems to have escaped much more lightly than its neighbour, however, as only 13 plague-deaths were recorded there in July.[4] Apparently plague smouldered in this area throughout the autumn and winter of this year, probably in an enzootic state among the house-rats, because in March its activity was officially reported to be

preventing the despatch of provisions from Liverpool to Ireland.[1] It may even have lingered into the spring of 1653, as a warning about its supposed persistence was sent to the Navy commanders in June;[2] but it had disappeared from Liverpool by September because another despatch circulated to those officers in that month speaks of 'the sickness being so lately in the town'.[3]

In 1654 plague moved southwards and struck at Chester and Tarvin. Judging by the petition which the sheriffs of Cheshire presented to the Protector on 28 April[4] the disease must have become epidemic in Chester early in the spring of that year. Parliament had ordered 'that the sheriffs should keep their courts monthly in the Common Hall of Pleas in Chester Castle', but the petition prayed that as Chester was plague-stricken and 'the sickness' was still spreading, the people could not safely attend a court held in the castle and the assizes should therefore be transferred to Nantwich or some other Cheshire town.[5] The spring was evidently unusually mild this year, so much so that the weather was 'very hott' in May over all England.[6] This contemporary weather report is significant because the early arrival of warm weather would reactivate the hibernating plague-fleas earlier than usual and an epidemic of bubonic plague would therefore erupt before its customary season. Chester's visitation on this occasion was severe enough to procure the transference of the assizes to Nantwich. Concerning Tarvin Ormerod reports that during May the parish register records the deaths from plague of five members of the Gaskin family,[7] which Axon asserts was exterminated.[8] As Ormerod adds that there is no further notice of its spread it seems evident that the visitation of Tarvin was fortunately confined to a single household on this occasion.

For the next two years England and Wales appear to have been free from bubonic plague. There was an excessive mortality in the parish of Histon in 1655 but Sweeting affirms that it was not ascribed to plague.[9] The menace of plague still hung over England, however, and the fear of its reappearance induced 'Jorge Tucke' to include in his 'physeianly receeates' prescriptions for 'the Golden Oil and the Plagge Water'.[10] The latter is a typical example of the medieval 'blunderbuss' herbal remedies—in this case containing 21 different plants—and was quite worthless as a remedy for plague. But as Kipling wrote:

Anything green that grew out of the mould
Was an excellent herb to our fathers of old.[11]

The next notice of the possible presence of bubonic plague in England is contained in the Order in Council of 10 September 1657 appointing 'a day of humiliation for all England and Wales'.[12] The incentive for this order was

presumably a major outbreak of some epidemic disease involving a large area of the country, although it is difficult to reconcile this conjecture with the apparent absence of any municipal, parochial, or personal notice of plague or other pestilence this year. On the other hand the proclamation in the ensuing spring that 5 May 1658 was to be kept as 'a day of fasting and humiliation in London' and 19 May in the country 'for plague',[1] suggests that plague was active somewhere in 1657. Moreover this later proclamation was succeeded by a similar one towards the end of September appointing 13 October as another day 'of solemn fasting and humiliation for plague'.[2] As the nation was thoroughly familiar with the clinical picture of bubonic plague by this time, the official use of 'plague' in these proclamations must have meant the bubonic disease. Buchan's assertion that a malignant type of influenza raged through the land in 1657 and recurred in April 1658, and again in August in spite of days of prayer and fasting,[3] does not exclude the co-existence of bubonic plague. Cromwell's proclamation on 13 July 1658 of a day of public thanksgiving for the relief from 'an epidemical sickness that lay sore on London'[4] may well refer to epidemic influenza; but its concluding sentence—'also the plague stayed two weeks after the fast day'— refers in all probability to the co-existence of bubonic plague. Nevertheless it was influenza not plague that may have altered the history of the British Isles at this juncture, because Buchan's account of the Protector's fatal illness is very suggestive of a virus pneumonia.[5] The relative paucity of notices of plague in England and Wales during the Commonwealth is puzzling, for there was no change in the social or sanitary state of the country to account for its seeming freedom from plague. Undoubtedly war with the Netherlands reduced the chances of its maritime importation, but there were opportunities for its importation from Baltic and Mediterranean ports. However Holland was the principal European source for the introduction of *P. pestis* to England and the denial of that source undoubtedly greatly reduced the risk of the importation of the plague bacillus, especially as bubonic plague was prevalent in the Netherlands during this period. For instance it was epidemic there in September 1655, and the Commissioners of Customs were therefore warned that they must be particularly careful to ensure that no infected refugee was allowed to land in Britain.[6] The continued apparent freedom of most of Britain from plague during the first five years of the Restoration may similarly be attributed to the lack of opportunity for the importation of *P. pestis* from the Netherlands. During this quinquennium there seem to be only two references to the presence of plague in England, namely, at Oxford in the autumn of 1660[7] and in Cheshire in the late summer of 1661,[8] and neither of them is convincing. The government was wisely doubtful about the perma-

nency of this freedom, however, and there is evidence that the authorities were convinced by this time that plague was a maritime importation and not an indigenous disease. For example the lord mayor of London's assertion that the epidemic of 1625 was imported from Holland[1] was not questioned by the Court of Aldermen, which recommended that vessels coming from infected countries should not be allowed to approach nearer the city than Gravesend.[2] It was accepted also by the Privy Council, which warned the lord mayor that plague was again prevalent in Amsterdam and Hamburg and recommended that London's lazaretto should not be closer to the city than Tilbury Hope.[3] In their reply to the Council the civic authorities reported that agreement had been reached with the Farmers of the Customs to establish the lazaretto at Moll Haven in a creek that would accommodate 100 vessels; that one or more warships should be stationed below the haven to examine *every* ship and ensure that infected vessels entered the haven; that a guard of twenty or more men should be appointed to prevent any communication between the vessels in the haven and people on shore; that on the arrival of any infected ship a list of all persons on board should be made, and that 'if any should die, the body should be searched before casting it overboard'.[4] Finally, if at the end of 40 days the surgeons appointed as plague-inspectors reported that a quarantined vessel was free from contagion —all the apparel, goods, household stuff, bedding, and such like articles on board it having been aired in the meantime on shore—it was to be allowed to trade freely.[4] The government and the civic authorities seem to have been satisfied with the efficacy of these precautions but their mutual satisfaction was destined to be short-lived, for the shadow of the great national outburst of bubonic plague of 1665-6 was already looming over the land.

Before proceeding to an account of that calamity, a note about an unknown English medical hero of plague would seem to be worthy of interpolation here. Willis wrote: 'Dr. Henry Sayer, a very learned Physician, and happy in his Practice, many others refusing this Province, boldly visited all the sick, poor, as well as rich, daily administered to them Physick, and handled with his own hands, their Buboes, and virulents Ulcers, and so cured very many sick, by his sedulous, though dangerous labour.'[5] According to Willis Sayer's prophylactic against plague was to drink a large draught of sack before he started his round of visits and another as soon as he had completed his round. Unfortunately, continues Willis, his exemption from plague seems to have made him careless because, when he was asked to attend at 'Wallingford Castle, where this Disease cruelly raged', he foolishly lay in the same bed with an intimate friend who was ill with 'plague', contracted the disease, and died.[5] It seems most probable that Dr Sayer was one of those fortunate

individuals, like the Rector of Great Hampden, who are naturally antipathetic to fleas, for this would explain his immunity to bubonic plague. As most people went to bed naked in his day, he died in all probability of the old Irish 'bed-sickness', in other words typhus fever, the most certain way of contracting which was to share a bed with a patient. Moreover typhus fever was epidemic in the Thames valley at the time and the royalist garrison of Wallingford Castle—which was the last place in Berkshire to surrender after a long siege to the parliamentary forces in July 1646[1]—was an ideal focus for typhus fever. As Sayer's treatment for plague consisted of making his patients vomit by the administration of an emetic composed of *Crocus metallorum* and either white or Roman vitriol, and then inducing them to sweat by the administration of a diaphoretic after they had ceased vomiting, it is obvious that those who recovered did so in spite of his therapy. It was probably the psychological effect of his sympathetic and courageous care and attention to which they owed their survival, for that help must have been of inestimable value to persons deserted by their kinsfolk and friends and ill with a disease which most physicians refused to treat for 'fear of the Contagion'.[2]

It is not possible to present an account of the great epidemic of bubonic plague of 1665-6 without plagiarizing to some extent Bell's erudite and comprehensive account of that calamity,[3] but it would be an inexcusable literary crime to paraphrase it as one's personal contribution to the history of plague. The student is therefore urged to read Bell's history at this juncture as much of what follows in this chapter is in effect merely a supplement to it.

Bell estimates that the population of London in 1665 'fell short' of 500,000 persons, among whom there were 97,306 registered deaths from all causes that year, of which 40,748 occurred in the out-parishes and the rest in the city and liberties, a proportion of 8 to 11.[4] The plague statistics presented in the Bills of Mortality are in his opinion largely worthless because many plague-deaths were not reported to the authorities. Only the women 'searchers' were officially required to notify these deaths, in the first instance to the parish clerks, and as the Quakers, Jews, Anabaptists and other sectaries refused to allow the plague-deaths among their members to be included in the Church returns, the plague-mortality among them mostly escaped the bills.[5] Many plague-deaths among conformists were also either deliberately hidden from the 'searchers' or those officials were bribed or intimidated to refrain from reporting them. He avers that the apportionment of the total mortality in the bills to plague is therefore 'wholly unreliable. It stretches human credulity to believe that a capital whose normal weekly

death-rate, when fully populated, had been but 350, should when plague-stricken and partly depopulated have lost in one week ending the 1st August 1,004 of its inhabitants by death other than Plague, besides 2,010 from the infection.'[1] Noorthouck—who is not included in Bell's list of authorities—had previously expressed a similar opinion about the value of the plague-mortality figures published in the bills.

At the beginning of the disorder [he remarks] there were great knavery and collusion in the reports of deaths; for while it was possible to conceal the infection, they were attributed to fevers of all kinds, which began to swell the bills; this was done to prevent their houses being shut up, and families shunned by their neighbours. Add to this that the dead carts working in the dark, no exact accounts were kept; the clerks and sextons being naturally averse to so dangerous a duty, and frequently falling sick themselves before such accounts as they had were delivered in. Quakers and Jews also who had separate burial grounds, were not mentioned in the weekly bills; nor was any register taken of those who died on board vessels of all kinds in the river. It was well known that numbers of poor despairing creatures wandered out of town into the fields, woods, and other remote places, where they died of the infection and of want...On the whole it was the opinion of eye-witnesses, that the plague destroyed 100,000 at least. The yearly bill mentions but one parish that remained quite exempt from infection, which was that of St John the Evangelist in Watling Street.[2]

Proof that some plague-mortality returns were falsified is supplied by Pepys' entry in his diary under the date of 30 August 1665, where he tells how the clerk of his parish admitted to him that he had returned only 6 plague-deaths in the parish that week though there had been 9.[3]

Bell declares that the winter of 1664 was a very severe one, and Harvey affirms that 'a very dry and violent frost from the beginning of winter 1664 froze up all things, and did not abate till the beginning of March'.[4] He asserts that the first official recognition of the presence of plague in London was the return of one plague-death within the walled city and eight in the suburbs in the weekly Bill of Mortality at the beginning of May.[5] He and Bell agree that the parish of St Giles-in-the-Fields was the first one to be attacked,[6] and the latter adds that it bore the main brunt of the epidemic up to the beginning of August, 'when Cripplegate surpassed it'.[7] Harvey then presents a most interesting account of the behaviour of plague which Bell and other writers appear to have ignored. After reiterating that it first appeared in the parish of St Giles, he writes:

And being restrained to a house or two, the seeds of it confined themselves to a hard frosty winter of near three months continuance: it lay asleep from Christmas to the middle of February, and then broke out again in the same parish; and after another long rest till April, put forth the malignant quality as soon as the warmth of spring

446

gave sufficient force, and the distemper showed itself again in the same place. At the beginning it took one here, and another half a mile off; then appeared again, where it was first: neither can it be proved that these ever met; especially after houses were shut up.[1]

This is such an acute observation upon the characteristic behaviour of bubonic plague in its English environment that it is difficult to realize that Harvey was not an eye-witness of this metropolitan epidemic. This erratic and unpredictable spread of the human disease was the reason why plague was so greatly feared. The people of seventeenth-century England could understand the mode of spread of primary human diseases like smallpox, measles, influenza, and dysentery, which were obviously transmitted by direct and indirect human contacts; but, not knowing that plague obeyed the same laws among its natural rodent hosts, they were forced to invoke the supernatural to explain its unnatural spread among their own kind. The one flaw in Harvey's account is that the apparent stirring of plague between Christmas and February was almost certainly a slight outbreak of typhus fever.

Bell provides the complementary note to Harvey's meteorological report with his note that June commenced with a 'heat-wave', with the result that 112 plague-deaths were recorded in the week ending the 13th, 68 of which occurred in the parish of St Giles in the Fields.[2]

Lying out west of the City [Bell comments] St Giles's in its populated part was essentially a town area, built about Holborn as its main street. It had in Whetstone Park the most notorious of the Restoration resorts of ill-fame; and there and elsewhere its streets were thick and foul with the filth, the profligacy and misery that then and long afterwards made the St Giles's Rookery a by-word and disgrace to London till its clearance, less than a century ago. Difficult in any case, the situation was made worse by the migration of the derelicts, the needy, and the destitute of other parishes into the slum areas of St Giles's. The poor in their foetid slums the Plague struck first and foremost and with the greatest persistence. It was to earn the ominous name of 'the poore's Plague'.[3]

In 1665 London was unusually crowded with poor people, and while there were many poor within the city itself, the majority could not find accommodation within the walls and herded together in the liberties and out-parishes.

But the Liberties [Bell continues] if stifling by the close contact of too many people, were old enough to be opened up for trade by streets. The out-parishes, where they touched the Liberties, had not this small advantage of space and air. They had no main arteries besides the country highways into London, which made one thread of communication. Left and right of these, the low overhanging wooden houses, ill-kept, dark and congested, covered the ground in seemingly impenetrable

rookeries of filthy courts and blind alleys...We have no slums like these, for in the most sordid quarters of East London today there are at least a pure water supply, and drainage, and refuse removal.[1]

It is against this background of poverty, squalor, gross overcrowding, and concomitant massive infestation with *Rattus rattus* that *The Great Plague of London* must be viewed.

Bell says that most of the doctors fled out of London early in the epidemic, especially those with wealthy practices—including Alston, the president of the College of Physicians, and Sydenham—but a few stayed to save the honour of the profession.[2] The king and the court also fled into the country in July, and with Charles's desertion London was deprived of effective central authority as the lord mayor, who controlled the city and its liberties, had no jurisdiction over the out-parishes. This legislative vacuum was quickly detected and nine Justices of the Peace were appointed with wide powers to control the out-parishes; but as the government was personally vested in the sovereign, the king's absence seriously weakened the force of any measures taken by the civic authorities to combat the epidemic. Bell opines that the king's departure was a justifiable precaution for the safety of the state—an opinion with which I emphatically disagree—'but', he continues, 'no excuse is possible for the abandonment of the stricken capital by those to whom its welfare should have been a first consideration, with a callous indifference to its fate that must for ever remain a black stain on Charles's Government.'[3] In seven months, during which he declares that 100,000 people died in London, the Privy Council only met three times, and on two of these occasions its sole concern was to keep plague away from the place where the king and court happened to be. London might well have collapsed into chaos but for the laudable efforts of three men—the Duke of Albemarle, the Earl of Craven, who kept open his house in Drury Lane to shelter numbers of distressed people, and Sir William Lawrence, the lord mayor.[4] Undoubtedly the determined efforts of the absent government to enforce the anti-plague laws of 1646—of which Bell gives a detailed and critical account[5]—contributed largely to the disruption of law and order in London. The terror excited by the barbarous regulation that when a single person fell ill of plague, every family in a crowded tenement—which commonly harboured 4 to 6 families in London's mean alleys—must be shut in and in many cases thereby condemned to death, was universal. The poor were bitterly hostile to it; the middle class evaded it whenever possible, and the upper class flouted it. It is no surprise therefore that the results of the strenuous efforts of the London magistrates to enforce it on the orders of the Privy Council were to ensure a precipitate flight from every house in which plague appeared

of every inmate who could leave it; to induce a wholesale concealment of cases of the disease and consequent falsification of the Bills of Mortality, and to augment the plague-deaths in the segregated house four- or fivefold.[1] The evasion of this regulation has been touchingly depicted in the painting entitled 'Rescued from the Plague, London 1665' (plate 4) by the English subject-painter, F. W. W. Topham, R.I., the original of which now hangs in the Art Gallery of the Guildhall. The incident which provided Topham with his subject is described by Pepys in his diary under the date of 3 September 1665.[2]

In fairness to the lay authorities it must be noted that the segregation of the sick and the sound together in plague-infected houses was advocated by the College of Physicians, the supreme medical authority in Stuart England, although the medical profession as a whole was divided upon the value and wisdom of this measure. It appears to have been divided also upon the fallacy of the mutual antagonism of bubonic plague and syphilis. 'Most unhappily a report got abroad', Bell records, 'that venereal disease gave immunity from Plague...Its results beggared in horror the worst effects of the Plague itself.'[3] This falsehood was widely circulated and there is no evidence that it was denounced by the medical profession; indeed some doctors undoubtedly believed it for Hodges mentions that in a few cases both poisons were cast off by a patient together,[4] and Boghurst, remarking about the mutual incidence of the two diseases in London, wrote: 'Of all the common hackney prostitutes of Lutener's Lane, Dog Yard, Cross Lane, Baldwin's Gardens, Hatton Garden, and other places; the common criers of oranges, oysters, fruit, etc.; all the impudent, drunken, drabbing bayles and fellows, and many others of the Rouge Rout, there are few missing.'[5]

The authorities also contributed both to the mortality of plague and the terror it excited by appointing so-called 'nurses' to attend the plague-stricken. Bell describes these 'plague-nurses' as wholly illiterate women, who had no skill or experience in nursing and in most cases no character either, who were constrained to undertake the perilous duty—as it was believed at the time—of attending the plague-sick by sheer desperation, poverty, and want. As the wage the 'nurse' was paid by the parish was insufficient for her subsistence, she was forced to rely for a livelihood on the opportunities that came her way for peculation and theft.[6] Vincent, who like Hodges stayed in London throughout the epidemic, declares that the plague-stricken were more afraid of the official plague-nurses than of the disease itself. Hodges, who was a competent physician in his day and a man of the highest character, is equally censorious of them.

449

But what greatly contributed to the loss of people thus shut up [he writes] was the wicked practices of the nurses, for they are not to be mentioned but in the most bitter terms. These wretches out of greediness to plunder the dead, would strangle their patients, and charge it to the distemper of their throats. Others would secretly convey the pestilential taint from sores of the infected to those who were well. Nothing, indeed deterred these abandoned miscreants from prosecuting their avaricious purposes by all the methods their wickedness could invent.[1]

It seems evident that the London 'plague-nurses' had little in the way of evil to learn from the Milanese *monatti* in the planning and performance of their evil deeds.

The human inhabitants of London were not the only sufferers from the misdirected efforts of the authorities to control the epidemic, for there was the customary slaughter of dogs and cats. Bell remarks that London always had a large canine population because the possession of one or more dogs was the tradesman's best protection against thieves in the absence of a police force. He affirms that the usual payment to the official slaughterers was 2*d.* a cadaver and that the city paid £36 10*s.* on this occasion for the dogs that were destroyed,[2] a sum which represents 4,380 dogs. Unlike today, labour charges rose slowly in those days for Cox affirms that the vestry of St Martin-in-the-Fields paid a dog-killer 2*d.* for every dog killed in 1593.[3]

Drawing now upon his imagination, Bell describes his impression of the state of London about the peak of the epidemic, an impression which the reader should correct by a perusal of Pepys' description of the city at this time.[4]

The sights in the streets [Bell writes] would have appalled the stoutest heart. Coffins were seen everywhere. They were brought out from the houses at all hours, now [12 August] the nights no longer sufficed for such large numbers of burials. Many corpses wrapped only in rough shrouds knotted together were carried away to the graveyards and pits. The dread of receiving infection was such that those compelled to pass through the streets moved in a corkscrew fashion, crossing from side to side to avoid contact with other pedestrians. Many would hold their noses when hastening past a door marked with the Plague cross, or on meeting a searcher, or a corpse being carried to burial.[5]

As he asserts that the sign of plague came to be marked on almost every door of the inhabited streets, Pepys and his fellows who remained in the city must have gone abroad with their mouths perpetually open like fishes out of water, though Pepys does not mention the fact. He bought some roll tobacco 'to smell and to chaw'[6] as a prophylactic, and with that safeguard he pursued his amorous adventures with scarcely diminished ardour.

In Bell's opinion 'the Great Plague had one effect made permanent in our

history, of momentous significance. We must not overlook it', he adjures, 'for it has vastly influenced English life and thought in all subsequent generations...[It] established English Nonconformity.'[1] The Nonconformist ministers did splendid work among the plague-sick in London he avers, and several of them died of plague. Prior to this epidemic they had been persecuted and had been forced to work secretly. During it they were able to work openly, and the fine spirit they showed and the noble example they set so won public approval that subsequent official attempts to suppress them were unsuccessful.[1] The immediate effect of their overt ministrations was, however, the passage by parliament of the Five Mile Act, 'as monstrous a piece of persecution', Bell exclaims, 'as ever disgraced the Statute book' and one which crowded the gaols.[1] This act merely supplemented, however, 'the code of persecution'[2] which had been embodied in the previous year in the Conventicle Act, 'which punished with fine, imprisonment, and transportation on a third offence all persons who met in greater number than five for any religious worship save that of Common Prayer; while return, or escape from banishment was punished by death'.[2] The succeeding act was designed to make it virtually impossible for Nonconformist ministers to preach and teach, as most of them belonged to the urban and trading classes and the Five Mile Act forbade them to go within 5 miles of any borough, or any place where they had been accustomed to minister. Green[2] does not attach to this epidemic of plague the religious significance that Bell accords to it; in fact he makes no mention whatever of plague in his account of the way in which English Nonconformity was established. Nevertheless there seems to be some substance in Bell's argument; perhaps some future historian will assess its value.

During this epidemic the enforcement of the Conventicle Act was responsible for an atrocity that is a blot on English justice. The London magistrates, embarrassed by their rigorous enforcement of it, decided to clear the gaols of the Quakers and Nonconformists who were overcrowding them. They accordingly transferred 55 Quakers—37 men and 18 women—in August to the ship, the *Black Eagle*, which was then lying off Greenwich. The men were confined below decks in a space which was so low that they could not stand upright, and in this space they were kept for seven weeks until plague invaded the ship. It was then moved to the Downs, where Bell says it was still lying in January, although by the end of October 19 of the Quakers (15 men and 4 women) were dead of plague. The ship arrived at Plymouth in February but the port authorities refused to allow anyone to land from it or to have any contact with it. The day after it sailed from Plymouth for the West Indies it was captured by a Dutch privateer and the

survivors were liberated in Holland; but by that time 27 of them had succumbed to plague.[1]

The peak of the metropolitan epidemic was reached in the week ending 17 September, when 7,165 plague-deaths were recorded in a total of 8,297 deaths from all causes. This was the most virulent period of the epidemic according to Bell, with a case-mortality rate of almost 100 per cent.[2] Even so, the published death-roll of plague was declared to be less than the truth by contemporary observers. Hodges reckoned that the plague-deaths exceeded 12,000[3] and Albemarle told the French ambassador that they amounted to 14,000 at least, excluding many Quakers.[4] As already noted, the plague-mortality returns of some of the London parishes were deliberately falsified. For example the clerk of St Olave's parish in Southwark, which was a poor parish and a heavily infected one, returned 171 deaths from diseases other than plague this week in a total death-roll of less than 500. Bell comments:

St Olave's average weekly mortality till the Plague had been sixteen. The dishonesty of the Bills could not be more flagrantly illustrated...For days together the deaths were so many that burial on the same day could not always be secured... The streets and fields presented some fearful sights to any wayfarer who chanced to pass. Corpses lay piled in heaps above ground, lightly covered and often naked, for some hours together before either time could be found for their removal or place to bury them in...None can tell actually how many died that week, and none will ever know.[5]

He added that from 22 August to 26 September, 38,195 deaths were recorded in London, of which 32,332 were ascribed to plague.[6] It is of interest to note the close agreement of the plague-mortality rates for the peak week (86·3 per cent) and for this period of five weeks (84·3 per cent). When allowance is made for the horrific reporting by writers afflicted with the 'Black Death' virus of plague, from which unfortunately not even Bell was immune, there can be no doubt that most distressful sights could be seen in some parts of London, especially in the slum areas, during the height of the epidemic; yet throughout the epidemic Pepys went about London on his business with the Navy and Tangier affairs, and his eye-witness contribution to Bell's account of unburied corpses cluttering the metropolitan streets and alleys is the entry in his diary on 12 August: 'The people die so, that now it seems they are fain to carry the dead to be buried by day-light, the nights not sufficing to do it in.'[7] An extract from the London Bill of Mortality for the year ending 19 December 1665 is appended, with the proviso that Bell insists that the most conservative estimate of the plague-mortality gives a figure of 100,000 deaths and that in his opinion the City's total death-roll was not less than 110,000.[8] He affirms that there was no death from plague among the

Cause of Death	Deaths
All Causes	97,306
Plague	68,596
Flox and Smallpox	655
French Pox	86
Griping in the Guts	1,288
King's Evill	86
Spotted Feaver and Purples	1,929
Ague and Feaver	5,257
Surfet	1,251
Bloudy Flux, Scowring & Flux	185

nobility, the aldermen, the magistrates, and the financiers,[1] which is not surprising as most of them fled from London as soon as the epidemic erupted. The city's high municipal officers did their duty bravely, however, and Bell remarks that he has 'but rarely found a gap in their ranks by the Plague',[2] which may mean either that few of them died of it or that few deserted their posts for fear of it. The City Coroner and the City Remembrancer died of it in September, when possibly as many as 1 in 3 of all those who remained in the city succumbed to it.[3] The decline of the epidemic in October induced many merchants and tradesmen to return, with the result that there was a sharp increase in the number of plague-deaths during the first week in November because there were 'blocked' fleas still alive and active in many of the empty houses. However the mortality fell rapidly during the week ending 21 November, and a sharp frost which commenced on the 22nd and persisted—with a short intermission—thoughout December, extinguished the epidemic.

To his credit the king returned to Whitehall on 1 February although plague was reported to have recrudesced—or more probably an outbreak of typhus fever had erupted—and was causing some 50 deaths each week. Bell gives the plague-mortality returns in the Bills for the five months of January–May as respectively, 334, 222, 107, 118, and 58.[4] These are figures that are consistent with a seasonal epidemic of typhus fever. Creighton affirms that plague lingered in London throughout 1666, 'causing 1998 deaths in all'.[5] Grave fears were entertained by the authorities of a recurrence of the previous epidemic when the hot weather arrived, and a special meeting of the Privy Council was therefore convened on 11 May to concert measures to prevent such a calamity. The Earl of Craven was co-opted for this purpose and he told the council frankly that its old policy for the control of plague had failed and that the imprisonment of entire families in their

infected houses was a disastrous and inhuman measure. He asserted that there was no effective alternative to the building of adequate pest-houses on convenient sites in the city and its suburbs in which the plague-sick could be properly accommodated. He declared that if these pest-houses had been available the recent outbreak of plague would have been arrested much earlier, because infection did not derive from the air 'but from want of conveniency and care for the timely removal of infected persons in the beginning, whereby to have hindered the spread of it'.[1] He was wrong as we know now, because the extermination of the house-rat and its fleas was the essential prerequisite for the arrest of the epidemic, but his advice was given to the best of his knowledge and it was courageous of him to deal so bluntly with the Privy Council. That august body made a partial acknowledgement that its previous policy had been a mistake by the issue in May 1666 of new *Rules and Orders*, under which every city and town was commanded to allocate forthwith an isolated site for the building of an adequate pest-house, if and when such a building should be required. If plague appeared, faithful searchers and examiners were to be appointed immediately and every case of plague was to be removed to the pest-house at once 'for the preservation of the rest of the family'. But, still imbued with the notion that somehow plague was transmitted by human contacts, it adhered to its old policy that the house was then to be marked, locked, and guarded as before. If the rest of the family remained healthy they were to be liberated after 40 days; but for an additional 20 days, during which period it was to be aired and fumed, the house was to be marked with a white cross. Until the extended period of quarantine had expired no lodgers should be allowed to reside in the house. It is extremely doubtful whether any would want to. Bell affirms that the *Rules and Orders* were ignored by local authorities, with the possible exception of those of Colchester, Ipswich, Gravesend, and Chatham, whose towns were infected from London in 1665 and experienced epidemics of plague in consequence in 1666.[2]

It is difficult to assess the remote effects of a calamity such as London sustained in 1665, with the certain loss of one-quarter of its permanent resident population and the possible loss of more than one-third of it. It is unfortunate that the mortality statistics of this visitation of bubonic plague are inaccurate; but as they are all that are now available the best use must be made of them in an attempt to assess the effects of this epidemic. Whatever may be the immediate context from which they are taken they derive from one of two sources, to wit, the London Bills of Mortality or the burials registers of the metropolitan parishes. Only about a third of these have been published, however, and some of these have an ominous gap in their records

for the years 1665 and 1666. During the Great Fire of London in the latter year a number of registers were lost in the destruction of their parish churches, and during the intervening centuries others have been lost through decay or because their parishes have disappeared by absorption into or amalgamation with contiguous parishes. Nevertheless the metropolitan parish registers appear to be the more reliable of these two contemporary sources for the mortality of 1665 for these reasons, in spite of the falsification of some of their records. They were compiled and maintained under the scrutiny of a number of independent witnesses, to wit, the incumbent, the clerk, the churchwardens, the sexton, and the constable, each of whom would be cognizant of any gross and persistent attempt to falsify their records. They were also open to inspection by the parishioners and in the smaller parishes many of these—especially the tradesmen—would be capable of forming a shrewd judgement about the true size of the parish toll of plague. Compared with this potential control of parochial mortality figures the central authority, which issued the Bills of Mortality, had no means of checking the accuracy of the returns from the different parishes, and in numerous instances the figures given in the Bills do not tally with the figures recorded in the parish registers, although the discrepancies are not as great as Bell's censure of the Bills suggests. Table 37 shows the returns published in the London Bill for 1665 as the central authority received them from the 125 parishes in London and the 5 in Westminster, with my addition of the percentage plague-mortality rates of the individual parishes. The burials registers of 16 of these parishes are now available for study in the publications of the Harleian Society, and a comparison of the plague-mortality figures of 13 of them with the figures published in the Bill is presented in table 38. Except for the parish of St Martin Orgar, the agreement between the two sets of figures is remarkably close for those parishes in which the plague-burials are marked in the register. Unfortunately in six of the parishes listed the registers do not specify which of the burials were plague-burials; but as the epidemic raged throughout August, September, and the first three weeks of October, there is no doubt that plague was responsible for 90 per cent of the total burials registered during that period, and in addition for many registered in June and July. According to Pepys, the Duke of Albemarle informed him that in the week ending 20 September there had been 7,165 deaths from plague in a total of 8,297 deaths from all causes in London,[1] a plague-mortality rate of 86·3 per cent. If these figures were correct, this must have been the peak week of the epidemic, and Pepys' comment that they were 'more in the whole by above 50, than the biggest Bill yet',[2] supports this conclusion. It is evident therefore that the figures of plague-deaths recorded in the Bill of Mortality

455

TABLE 37A–D

Burials registered in London parishes in 1665 as published by Dr N. Hodges in his Loimologia

	Total burials	Plague-burials	Percentage plague-mortality rate
A **In the 97 parishes within the walls**			
St Albans Woodstreet	200	121	60·5
St Alhallows Barkin	514	330	64·2
St Alhallows Breadstreet	35	16	45·7
St Alhallows the Great	455	426	93·6
St Alhallows Honey-lane	10	5	50·0
St Alhallows the Less	239	175	73·2
St Alhallows Lombardstreet	90	62	68·8
St Alhallows Staining	185	112	60·5
St Alhallows the Wall	500	356	71·2
St Alphage	271	115	42·4
St Andrew Hubbard	71	25	35·2
St Andrew Undershaft	274	189	65·3
St Andrew Wardrobe	476	308	64·7
St Anne Aldersgate	282	197	70·0
St Anne Black-Friers	652	467	71·6
St Antholins	58	35	60·3
St Austins	43	20	46·5
St Bartholomew Exchange	73	51	69·8
St Bennet Finch	47	22	46·8
St Bennet Grace-church	57	41	72·0
St Bennet Pauls Wharf	355	172	48·4
St Bennet Sherehog	11	1	9·0
St Botolph Billinsgate	83	50	60·2
Christ Church	653	467	71·5
St Christophers	60	47	78·3
St Clements Eastcheap	38	20	52·6
St Dionys Back-church	78	27	34·6
St Dunstans in the East	265	150	56·6
St Edmunds Lombardstreet	70	36	51·4
St Ethelborough	195	106	54·3
St Faiths	104	70	67·3
St Fosters	144	105	72·9
St Gabriel Fenchurch	69	39	56·5
St George Botolph-lane	41	27	66·0
St Gregories by Pauls	376	232	61·7
St Helens	108	75	69·4
St James Dukes-place	262	190	72·5
St James Garlickhith	189	118	62·4
St John Baptist Walbrook	138	83	60·1
St John Evangelist	9		
St John Zachary	85	54	63·5
St Katherine Coleman-street	299	213	71·2
St Katherine Cree-church	335	201	60·0

TABLE 37 A–D *cont.*

	Total burials	Plague-burials	Percentage plague-mortality rate
A *In the 97 parishes within the walls*			
St Lawrence Jewry	94	48	51·0
St Lawrence Pountney	214	140	65·4
St Leonard Eastcheap	42	27	64·3
St Leonard Foster-lane	335	255	76·1
St Magnus	103	30	29·1
St Margaret Lothbury	100	66	66·0
St Margaret Moses	38	25	65·2
St Margaret New Fishstreet	114	66	58·0
St Margaret Pattons	49	24	48·9
St Mary Abchurch	99	54	54·5
St Mary Aldermanbury	181	109	60·2
St Mary Aldermary	105	75	71·4
St Mary-le-Bow	64	36	56·2
St Mary Bothaw	55	30	54·5
St Mary Colechurch	17	6	35·3
St Mary Hill	94	64	68·0
St Mary Mounthaw	56	37	66·0
St Mary Somerset	342	262	76·6
St Mary Stainings	47	27	57·4
St Mary Woolchurch	65	33	50·7
St Mary Woolnoth	75	38	50·6
St Martins Ironmonger-lane	21	11	52·4
St Martins Ludgate	196	128	65·3
St Martin Orgars	110	71	64·5
St Martins Outwich	60	34	56·6
St Martins Vintrey	417	349	83·6
St Matthew Friday-street	24	6	25·0
St Maudlins Milk-street	44	22	50·0
St Maudlins Old Fish-street	176	121	68·7
St Michael Bassishaw	253	164	64·8
St Michael Cornhil	104	52	50·0
St Michael Crooked-lane	179	133	74·3
St Michael Queenhith	203	122	60·1
St Michael Quern	44	18	41·0
St Michael Royal	152	116	76·3
St Michael Woodstreet	122	62	50·8
St Mildred Bread-street	59	26	44·0
St Mildred Poultrey	68	46	67·6
St Nicholas Acons	46	28	60·8
St Nicholas Coleabby	125	91	72·8
St Nicholas Olaves	90	62	68·8
St Olaves Hart-street	237	160	67·5
St Olaves Jewry	54	32	59·2
St Olaves Silver-street	250	132	52·8
St Pancras Soper-lane	30	15	50·0
St Peters Cheap	61	35	57·3

TABLE 37 A–D *cont.*

	Total burials	Plague burials	Percentage plague-mortality rate
A *In the 97 parishes within the walls*			
St Peters Cornhil	136	76	55·8
St Peters Pauls Wharf	114	86	75·4
St Peters Poor	79	47	59·5
St Stephens Coleman-street	560	391	69·8
St Stephens Walbrook	34	17	50·0
St Swithins	93	56	60·2
St Thomas Apostle	163	110	67·4
Trinity Parish	115	79	68·7
ALL 97 PARISHES	15,207	9,887	65·0
B *In the 16 parishes without the walls*			
St Andrew Holborn	3,958	3,103	78·4
St Bartholomew the Great	493	344	69·7
St Bartholomew the Less	193	139	72·0
St Bridget	2,111	1,427	67·6
Bridewel Precinct	230	179	77·8
St Botolph Aldersgate	997	755	75·7
St Botolph Aldgate	4,926	4,051	82·2
St Botolph Bishopsgate	3,464	2,500	72·1
St Dunstans in the West	958	665	69·4
St George Southwark	1,613	1,260	78·1
St Giles Cripplegate	8,069	4,838	59·9
St Olaves Southwark	4,793	2,785	58·1
St Saviours Southwark	4,235	3,446	81·3
St Sepulchres	4,509	2,746	60·9
St Thomas Southwark	475	371	78·1
Trinity Minories	168	123	73·2
At the Pesthouse	159	156	98·1
ALL 16 PARISHES	41,351	28,888	69·8
C *In the 12 parishes in the outer parts*			
St Giles in the Fields	4,457	3,216	72·1
Hackney Parish	232	132	56·9
St James Clarkenwell	1,863	1,377	73·9
St Katherines Tower	956	601	62·7
Lambeth Parish	798	537	67·2
St Leonards Shoreditch	2,669	1,949	73·0
St Magdalens Bermondsey	1,943	1,363	70·1
St Mary Newington	1,272	1,004	78·9
St Mary Islington	696	593	85·2
St Mary Whitechappel	4,766	3,855	80·8
Rotherhith Parish	304	210	69·0
Stepney Parish	8,598	6,583	76·5
ALL 12 PARISHES	28,554	21,420	75·0

TABLE 37 A–D *cont.*

	Total burials	Plague-burials	Percentage plague-mortality rate
D *In the 5 parishes of the city and liberties of Westminster*			
St Clements Danes	1,969	1,319	67·0
St Paul Covent Garden	408	261	64·0
St Martins in the Fields	4,804	2,883	60·0
St Mary Savoy	303	198	65·3
St Margarets Westminster	4,710	3,742	79·4
Whereof at the Pesthouse	—	156	—
ALL 5 PARISHES	12,194	8,403	68·9
Total of the burials	97,306⎫		
Died of the plague	68,596⎭		70·4
Besides many, of which no account was given by the parish clerks, and who were privately buried.			

TABLE 38

Some London parish mortality records as registered and as returned in the Bill for 1665

	Burials registered in the parish church			Deaths returned in the Bill	
	Total	Plague	Total for August, September and October	Total	Plague
St Peeters Cornhill	123	76	58	136	76
St De'nis Backchurch	75	—	52	78	27
St Mary Aldermary	99	—	73	105	75
St Thomas the Apostle	157	—	117	163	110
St Antholin, Budge Row	47	—	41	58	35
St Ben'et, Paul's Wharf	343	—	261	355	172
Allhallows, Bread Street	28	20	17	35	16
St Mary Somerset	339	274	236	342	262
St Olave, Hart Street	223	161	155	237	160
St Mary the Virgin, Aldermanbury	169	105	99	181	109
St Martin Orgar	115	100	89	110	71
St Michael Bassishaw	246	165	112	253	164
St Lawrence Jewry	92	—	64	94	48

for the parishes of St De'nis Backchurch and St Ben'et, Paul's Wharf are much lower than the truth, and that the figure in the Bill for the parish of St Lawrence Jewry is lower than it should be. Possibly this sample of parishes is too small to be truly representative of the metropolitan parishes as a whole, especially bearing in mind the characteristic erratic distribution of plague, but it suggests nevertheless that many parishes sent returns of their plague-mortalities to the central authority which were as accurate as they could be under the circumstances. Where the bills failed to give accurate figures the explanation is to be found in the footnote supplied by Hodges to his copy of the Bill for 1665 (see table 37). The references by Bell and Harvey to the state of the parish of St Giles in the Fields are in neither case supported by the available evidence. As table 37 shows, three of the parishes in the liberties and two of those in the out-parishes had bigger death-rolls, and a comparison of the plague-mortality rates of the metropolitan parishes reveals that 12 of those within the Walls, 8 of those in the liberties, and 6 of those in the out-parishes had higher rates than that of St Giles. Admittedly, without knowing the exact size of the population in each parish, it is not possible to make an accurate comparison of their degree of affliction; but it would seem to be a reasonable assumption that in most cases the proportion of the annual total burials to the population was roughly equal. This table does confirm, however, Bell's assertion that the epidemic raged more fiercely without than within the walls,[1] and there is no doubt that his explanation of the difference is the correct one, to wit, that the human fuel for it was packed more tightly in the liberties and the out-parishes than in the walled city. In other words, outside the walls each 'blocked' flea had many more opportunities of transmitting *P. pestis* to fresh victims than its kindred within the walls. Confirmation of this distribution is implicit in Pepys' statement that plague was prevalent outside the city for three or four weeks before it appeared within the walls.[2] The first plague-burial to be recorded as such in a London parish register appears to be the one dated 27 June in that of St Michael Bassishaw.[3] The victim was a daughter of a Richard Chadburne, who had already buried another daughter on the 17th and a son on the 26th, and who buried another son on the 28th and his wife on the 29th. The last three of these burials are marked 'plague'. As it is practically certain that the first two members of his family also died of plague, the date of the appearance of the disease in this parish can reasonably be advanced to 14 or 15 June, when the house-rats in the Chadburne dwelling were infected with *P. pestis*. Several plague-deaths had been reported within the walls before this date, however, for in a news report dated 11 May one was reported in the parish of St Mary Woolchurch,[4] and we know from Pepys' entry in his diary that

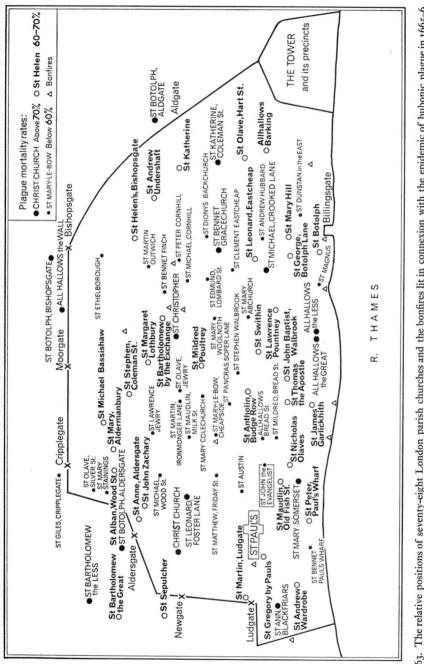

Plague mortality rates:

- ● CHRIST CHURCH Above 70%
- ○ St Helen 60–70%
- • ST MARY-LE-BOW Below 60%
- △ Bonfires

THE TOWER and its precincts

R. THAMES

63. The relative positions of seventy-eight London parish churches and the bonfires lit in connexion with the epidemic of bubonic plague in 1665–6. (Drawn from the map engraved for Noorthouck's *History of London*.) Plague mortality rates calculated from the figures published in the Bill for 1665.

461

another had been reported on 10 June in the parish of St Bennet Finch.[1] The record of a plague-burial on 12 April in the Westminster parish of St Paul, Covent Garden[2] might suggest that the epidemic erupted in the western outskirts of London; but when the positions of the London parishes are plotted according to their plague-mortality rates (see figure 63), the result suggests that from shipping in the Thames plague-infected rats probably came ashore in April and May at several places between the parishes of Stepney and St Paul's, Covent Garden. Once the disease had been brought on shore its dissemination was erratic as figure 63 reveals and as its aetiology would ensure. In all probability the density of the house-rat population varied widely in the different parishes with a consequent variation in the intensity of the human disease; but in general the house-rats would tend to congregate more densely in the riverside parishes and in the metropolitan slums than in the commercial and residential parishes. With some inevitable exceptions this postulated rodent distribution is supported by figure 63, for the highest plague-mortality rates would occur in those parishes where the house-rats were most numerous and where the rat-flea populations would therefore be the largest, with consequently increased opportunities for the transmission of *P. pestis* from rat to rat and from rat to man. The rapid, almost 'explosive' development of this epidemic, which is clearly shown below, also strongly supports the contention that it took origin from multiple

Mortality in London, June–December 1665

June	July	Aug.	Sept.	Oct.	Nov.	Dec.
590	6,137	17,036	26,230	14,375	3,449	590

(Composed from Boghurst's *Loimographia* edited by J. F. Payne, London 1894.)

riverine foci of rat-plague. The monthly total of officially recorded plague-deaths was multiplied more than 44 times in the space of three months, and this huge increase occurred in a population that had been diminished by the panic flight of possibly one-quarter of its number in the early weeks of the epidemic. As in most epidemics of bubonic plague its onset was insidious, and it seems evident that the civic authorities did not appreciate that they were faced with a formidable epidemic of it until the end of May. Even during June the curve of the metropolitan mortality-rate gave no warning of the enormous augmentation that was to occur in the succeeding three months, and it is inconceivable that this expansion took origin from a single focus of rat-plague located in a parish outside the walls. From the end of June, as figure 64 shows, the toll of plague-deaths climbed swiftly and inexorably to a peak in September, by which time much of the available rodent

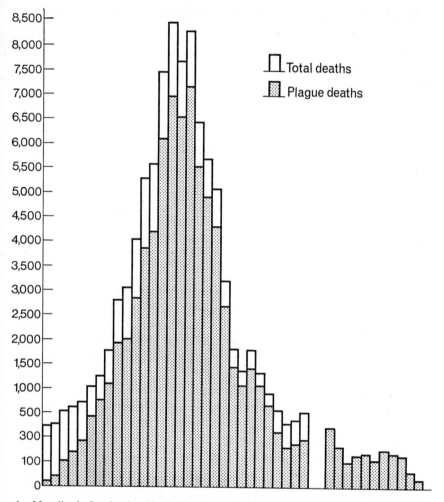

64. Mortality in London in 1665–6. Showing (left) the deaths each week from 30 May to 19 December 1665, and (right) the number of plague deaths in each month from December 1665 to November 1666.

fuel for the maintenance of the fundamental epizootic must have been exhausted. Consequently the epidemic began to decline in October as the number of 'blocked' fleas diminished by natural or violent death, and rapidly in November, on the 22nd of which Pepys noted that a marked decrease in London's death-roll had occurred, adding the comment that there were 'great hopes of further decrease, because of this day's being a very exceeding hard frost, and continues freezing'.[1]

463

Mention has been made of Pepys' prophylactic and Bell says that

for personal disinfection, nothing enjoyed such favour as tobacco... belief in it was universal, and even children were compelled to light the leaf in pipes. Thomas Hearne, the antiquary, remembered an acquaintance, one Tom Rogers, telling him that when he was a scholar at Eton in the year that the Great Plague raged, all the boys smoked in school by order, and that he was never whipped so much in his life as he was one morning for not smoking. It was long afterwards a tradition that none who kept tobacconists' shops in London had the plague.[1]

Another popular fallacy was a firm belief in the prophylactic efficacy of strong-smelling disinfectants, which were in fact recommended by the College of Physicians.

Nitre, tar, rosin, and other like substances were burnt in the rooms, often upon clear coal fires, adding oppressive heat to that of the hot summer. Fires of woods that gave out pungent odours were deemed most effective. A popular expedient was to flash gunpowder in pans... Poor folk burnt old shoes and odd scraps of leather and horn to get the smell.[2]

There seems to be little doubt that this outburst of plague was imported from Holland, but the exact date of the Dutch consignment of *P. pestis* will never be known. It was apparently not unloaded during 1664 as the London Bill of Mortality for that year records only three plague-deaths according to Vincent,[3] and these may really have been deaths from typhus fever, which was indigenous in England. The first official notice of plague in London in 1665 seems to have been the proclamation on 14 June cancelling Barnwell Fair—which was held annually on 24 June—'for fear of spreading the plague'.[4] This wording does not suggest that the authorities were seriously alarmed about the disease at this date, but the populace certainly was, as Pepys reports[5] and as Vincent confirms.

Now guilty sinners begin to look about them [he declaims with unction] and think themselves into what corner of the land they might fly to hide them... Now those who did not believe an unseen God, are afraid of unseen arrows... The Great Orbs begin first to move; the Lords and Gentry retire into their Countries; few ruffling Gallants walk the streets; few spotted Ladies to be seen at windows...[6]

Six days after his first report on the exodus, when Pepys visited the *Cross Keys* Inn at Cripplegate (see figure 63), where, in spite of the plague, he 'had some of the company of the tapster's wife a while'[7]—to what purpose the reader of his diary can guess—he found 'all the towne almost going out of towne, the coaches and waggons being all full of people going into the country'.[7] Vincent also saw the roads leading out of London thronged with fugitives and their portable possessions, and he comments: 'Now roses and

other sweet flowers wither in the Gardens, are disregarded in the Markets, and People dare not offer them to their noses, lest with their sweet savour that which is infectious should be attracted: Rue and Wormwood is taken into the hand; Myrrhe and Zedoary into the mouth; and without some antidote few stir abroad in the morning.'[1] He added that many houses were now segregated and their occupants imprisoned in them, and that the opulent tradesmen and many clergymen were deserting the city. 'I do not blame many Citizens retiring', he charitably remarks, 'when there was so little trading, and the presence of all might have helped forward the increase and spreading of the infection.'[2]

As June drew towards its close the epidemic grew in violence, 'increasing mightily' to quote Pepys,[3] but even as late as 9 July there were parishes in the walled city into which *P. pestis* had not penetrated, the parish of St Michael, Cornhill being one such.[4] It seems extremely probable, however, that Vincent was correct in his belief that by the end of July most of the metropolitan parishes, both within and without the walls, together with those in Westminster, had been invaded by plague.[5] Early in the month a royal proclamation announced that certain specific days were to be kept in London and elsewhere in England and Wales as fast days until the epidemic ceased.[6] By this time both the state and the civic authorities were aware of the calamitous scale of the epidemic, for no man in his senses could fail to appreciate the warning contained in the rise of the plague-deaths each week from 470 to 2,010,[7] or of its virulence, concerning which there is Allin's contemporary observation that 'many whole families of 7, 8, 9, 10, 18 in a family' were destroyed by it.[8]

The State reacted to the danger by proroguing Parliament and transferring the Exchequer to the royal palace of Nonsuch, which Charles II had not yet given to his mistress, the Duchess of Cleveland, who had it demolished, sold the materials, and disparked the land.[9] It also announced through the Privy Council 'where the famous remedies of James Angier, recommended by certificates from Lyons, Paris, and Toulouse, established by experiments under his own direction, and sworn to be of singular virtue by witnesses, could be had, authorised advertisements of other shops, and ordered the Middlesex justices to treat with Angier for remedies'.[10] Mullett adds that in 1670 the Treasury issued warrants for £86 to Angier 'for fumes in the late sickness time,[11] which suggests that one of his activities may have been the disinfection of infected houses and their contents by the generation of some irritant gas, possibly sulphur dioxide. Support for this supposition is supplied by Plomer's note that in the presence of several responsible officials Angier's servant entered a plague-infected house in Newton Street in the parish of

St Giles-in-the-Fields[1] and presumably disinfected it. Prior to this test four of the inmates had died of plague and at the time of the test two of the remaining eight occupants were ill with it. Some time afterwards several witnesses who were examined on oath before the Justices affirmed that no further death had occurred in this house or in several others after Angier's remedies had been used in them.[1] In the absence of knowledge of the chemical nature of the remedies it is not possible to assess the value of this sworn testimony, but the report was submitted to the Privy Council, and after several more tests the Justices were authorized to advertise publicly that Angier's remedies, with directions for their use, could be purchased at six given addresses.[1] He probably made a fortune; but his remedies had no effect on the continued progress of the epidemic and the civic authorities preferred to trust to the orthodox anti-plague measures, combined with an energetic effort to rid the atmosphere of its mythical plague-venom.

That nothing might be left to disperse the contagion [Noorthouck relates] large fires were ordered to be made in the public streets; yet the physicians were very diffident of the success of this expensive experiment, and the trial soon decided in favour of their doubts. Coals were then 4 *l.* per chauldron, and 200 chaldron were applied in making fires at the Custom-house, Billingsgate, at the Bridge-foot, Three cranes, Queenhithe, Bridewell-gate, the corner of Leadenhall and Gracechurch Streets, at the north and south gates of the Royal Exchange, Guildhall, Blackwell-hall, at the lord mayor's door in St Helen's, at Bow Church, and at the western end of St Paul's cathedral. These fires continued for three days, and were then almost extinguished by a smart rain; but the following night, from whatever cause it might proceed, was the most fatal of the whole, for more than 4000 then expired! and this unfortunate event was a discouragement to any further attempts of that nature*[2]

As is to be expected from its aetiology, plague was not evenly dispersed in the invaded parishes. Although four plague-deaths were registered in the parish of St Clement Danes during the week ending 11 May,[3] in the middle of July Lord Craven issued a warrant to permit a gentleman and his man-servant who resided in that parish 'to pass to Hampstead Marshall, near Newbury, co. Berks, as they themselves, the house from which they came, and all the persons therein are free from any infection of the plague'.

Endorsed. A passe in the plage tyme. 1665, July the 17 daye, God be praised.[4]

* Excluding the fires lit in front of the lord mayor's door and at Blackwell-hall, the positions of which have not been identified, the approximate sites of these bonfires are marked in figure 63. Their relative concentration along the river bank suggests that the authorities regarded the Thames as the most dangerous contributor to the creation of the pestilential atmosphere, although as salmon could still be caught in the river at London Bridge in 1665, the degree of its sewage and industrial pollution must have been slight.

In view of his character and his conduct throughout this visitation, no one could accuse Lord Craven of issuing such a warrant without assuring himself that it was a true one, and there is no doubt that many scores, possibly hundreds of similar and equally truthful warrants were issued at this time. The common error of depicting London, even at the peak of this epidemic, as a vast charnel-house in which every street was strewn with decomposing plague-corpses and every dwelling-house smelt of death, may make a 'best-seller'; but it is false history. It is true that Pepys declared on 20 July that plague was almost everywhere,[1] but this exaggeration was belied by his own movements about London, because it is certain that he did not knowingly go where plague was active. On 29 July he went by coach to the house of a kinswoman, Kate Joyce, to urge her husband to let her leave London for Brampton in Huntingdonshire.[2] Admittedly he added: 'So I took leave of them, believing it is great odds that we ever all see one another again; for I dare not go any more to that end of the town.'[3] The mere fact that he went, however, and by coach, indicates that the epidemic was not ubiquitous and that there was movement of men and merchandise about London. The significance of Pepys' coach journey at this time has either been overlooked or deliberately ignored by those writers whose horrific accounts convey the falsehood that no man and nothing, except the dead-carts, moved about the streets of London in the summer of 1665. Of course there was movement of men and goods, because life went on although death was widespread. Moreover, unless Edward Swan was lying when he recommended Henry Oxinden to stay at the *Red Lion* in Aldersgate Street,[4] there was at least one inn within the walls that plague never entered during this epidemic. In all probability it was one of many that escaped, possibly because they provided so much available food on their premises that their house-rats had no need to forage outside and so make contacts with infected house-rats. And it is certain that these free inns did a busy trade throughout the epidemic so long as no customer brought any 'blocked' fleas in with him. Cox may be correct in his assertion that plague spared only four sparsely populated parishes in the 130 located in and around London,[5] but he is indubitably wrong in his accompanying declaration that the epidemic 'took about six months to travel from the western suburbs of Westminster across the city to the eastern suburbs of Stepney',[6] because this declaration is contradicted by the aetiology of bubonic plague. To cross from west to east *P. pestis* would have had to move in its rodent and flea hosts across the main channels of metropolitan trade, which radiated from the wharves on the river bank along the highroads leading east, north, and west from the walled city. All the historical evidence about the spread of bubonic plague indicates that, with rare, localized

TABLE 39

Total monthly burials registered in sixteen metropolitan parishes during the summer and autumn of 1665

	July	August	September	October	November
St Peeters Cornhill	7	17	20	21	7
St De'nis Backchurch	2	8	26	18	9
St Mary Aldermary	2	17	41	15	16
St Thomas the Apostle	19	45	47	25	11
St Antholin, Budge Row	1	7	28	6	1
St Ben'et, Paul's Wharf	23	91	123	47	12
Allhallows, Bread Street	1	7	7	3	2
St Mary Somerset	4	45	115	76	29
St Olave, Hart Street	4	40	64	51	16
St Vedast, Foster Lane*	6	53	37	21	6
St Mary the Virgin, Aldermanbury	4	19	58	22	12
St Martin Orgar	1	26	46	17	3
St Michael Bassishaw	44	46	53	13	2
St Lawrence Jewry	1	27	24	13	7
St James, Clarkenwell	388	492†	139	71	7
St Paul, Covent Garden	19	44	97	42	21

exceptions, the disease invariably spreads along the trade routes with the passive transport of *R. rattus* and its fleas.

The weather in August appears to have been hotter than in July this woeful year, and with the arrival of the 'dog-days' the epidemic increased rapidly in both extent and fury. Whereas 6,137 plague-deaths had been registered in July, the toll rose to 17,036 in August according to Cox.[1] This exacerbation was not evenly distributed, however, because as table 39 shows, while the monthly mortality in some parishes hardly rose at all and in some was only doubled, others exhibited a manifold increase. It seems probable that the worst afflicted parish this month was one of the sixteen parishes without the walls, namely, St Giles Cripplegate. A contemporary report affirms that it was the most heavily infected parish in each of the last two weeks of August with death-rolls of 847 and 842 respectively, of which totals plague was credited with 572 and 605 deaths.[2] As table 37 shows, it returned the second largest plague-mortality of the metropolitan parishes and more than half that mortality appears to have occurred in August. The epidemic undoubtedly raged more fiercely among the parishes in the liberties than among

* The church of St Vedast is on the east side of Foster Lane, Cheapside, and is dedicated to St Vedast, a sixth-century bishop of Arras. It was originally known as St Fauster's or Foster's, and is so named in the Bill of Mortality. (See table 37.)

† Minimum figure; the deaths of numerous children, apparently interred with a parent or parents, should probably be added.

any other numerically equal group of metropolitan parishes this month, for their total of 5,076 plague-deaths in the second half of August was almost half of the total of plague-deaths (10,339) returned from all the London and Westminster parishes during that period.[1]

In view of the augmentation of the epidemic it is not surprising that Bartholomew and Sturbridge Fairs were cancelled on 7 August, and the proclamation announcing their cancellation carried the additional injunction that 'no citizens of London were to attend any fairs whatever'.[2] Towards the end of this month several more fairs were cancelled, to wit, Holden or Howden Fair, together with all other fairs held in Yorkshire, on the 27th;[3] Wayhill Fair in Hampshire on the 28th, 'for fear of spreading the infection to parts of the land that are still free from it',[4] and Woodbury Fair also on the 28th.[5] Two days later parliament, which had been prorogued until 3 October at Westminster, was further prorogued until the 9th at Oxford 'on account of the dreadful increase of the plague'.[6] The apprehension aroused by this increase is manifest in all the contemporary records of this epidemic. Pepys and his colleagues sat all the morning of 10 August in the Navy Office 'in great trouble to see the Bill rise so high'[7] that week, and he made a new will in the afternoon because London had become so unhealthy that he feared that no one residing in it could depend upon living more than two days.[8] He notes in his diary this day 'an odd story of Alderman Bence's stumbling at night over a dead corps in the streete, and going home and telling his wife, she at the fright, being with child, fell sick and died of the plague.'[9] More probably she had a miscarriage with a fatal post-partum haemorrhage, which under the circumstances would be recorded as a death from plague. Two days later Pepys noted that the plague-deaths had become so numerous that the authorities were forced to start burying the dead during daylight as the nights were not long enough for the task.[10] He added that the lord mayor had imposed a curfew at 9 p.m. in order that the plague-stricken families might leave their domestic prisons for air and exercise,[11] a humane relaxation of the segregation regulations. Pepys himself encountered a plague-corpse to his 'great trouble' on 15 August in Churchyard Passage,[12] a narrow alley opening off Upper Thames Street close by London Bridge, as he was returning from Greenwich after dark. However next day he was about again because he exclaims in his diary: 'But Lord! how sad a sight it is to see the streets empty of people, and very few upon the 'Change...and about us two shops in three, if not more, generally shut up.[13] Vincent was more emotionally distressed than Pepys by the desolation wrought by the epidemic in August.

Now there is a dismal solitude in London streets [he records sadly] Now shops are shut in, people rare and very few that walk about, in so much that the grass begins

to spring up in some places, and a deep silence almost in every place, especially within the walls...no *London* cries sounding in the ears. Now shutting up of visited houses (there being so many) is at an end...not one house in an hundred but is infected; and in many houses half the family is swept away; and in some the whole, from the eldest to the youngest; few escape with the death of but one or two; never did so many husbands and wives die together; never did so many parents carry their children with them to the grave.[1]

After allowing for their difference in temperament, it is evident that both Pepys and Vincent witnessed a state of affairs in London which acutely distressed and saddened them. Undoubtedly London was in a parlous state in August 1665, with its communal life nearly destroyed, its trade stagnant, its population reduced possibly to about half its normal size by death and desertion, and its civic organization disrupted. It is noteworthy, however, that Vincent—the more impressionable of the two—does not state that grass grew knee-high or even a foot high in the streets; that no man walked in those streets except the corpse-collectors; that nothing moved in them except the dead-carts, and that the streets were cluttered with decomposing corpses, the stench from which made the air almost unbreathable. He left that sort of description to later writers of the 'Black Death' fraternity. His account of the capital is grim enough to need no horrific embellishment. Towards the end of August Pepys' 'good friend and neighbour' Dr Burnett died, and Pepys ascribed his death to plague.[2] He was one of a number of physicians, surgeons, and apothecaries who attended an autopsy on a plague-corpse 'which was full of the tokens; and being in hand with the dissected body, some fell down immediately, and others did not outlive the next day at noon'.[3] Thomson, who claims that he was the instigator of this autopsy, obtained permission from a patient who recovered in spite of his therapy, to perform a post-mortem examination of the body of the patient's servant, a lad of about 15 years of age who had died of plague.

Having obtained that desire [he records] I girt myself up with all expedition, getting in readiness what instruments were fitting, with a porringer containing Sulphur to burn under the Corps, which was at that time placed in the open in a yard there adjacent...The head of the Coffin being taken off, and the linnen cleared away, I could not but admire to behold the skin so beset with spots black and blew, more remarkable for multitude and magnitude than any I have yet seen.[4]

He embellished his report with a line drawing of this autopsy (plate 3) with himself as the calm and fearless scientist receiving the prayerful admiration of an onlooker. A contributor to the *British Medical Journal* asserts that Thomson contracted bubonic plague from this autopsy, but such a sequel is most unlikely for several reasons.[5] The corpse had been enclosed in a coffin

for some time, possibly two or three days, and decomposition had obviously begun when it was examined. *P. pestis* exhibits little resistance to inimical agencies and is quickly destroyed by the conditions accompanying putrefaction. As the corpse had been stripped naked before enclosure in the coffin it is extremely improbable that even a single 'blocked' flea was immured with it in the coffin, and even if that unlikely event had happened it is most improbable that it would have been sufficiently active after its confinement in an atmosphere of putrefaction and its subsequent exposure to the fumes of burning sulphur to have attacked any of the people present. Finally, if Thomson had contracted plague and died, he could hardly have written his account of it which he published in 1666. He certainly contracted an infection from this autopsy, but his description of it is strongly suggestive of a streptococcal infection, which is most probably what also killed Dr Burnett. Thomson recovered after treating himself with heroic doses of his 'best medicaments', namely, *Tinctura polyacaea* and *Pulvis pestifugus*, which were probably herbal 'blunderbuss' remedies, and *Helmont's xenexton*, a preparation of powdered toad, which Hodges states was 'prodigiously extolled by every Body'.[1] He probably attributed his escape partly also to his foresight in equipping himself with an amulet prior to the autopsy in the shape of a large, dried toad, which he had prepared 'in as exquisite a manner as he possibly could, with his own fingers',[2] and which he hung round his neck in a linen bag. After this amulet had been resting for some hours in the region of his stomach it became, he says, 'so tumefied, distended, (as it were blown up) to that bigness, that it was an object of wonder to those that beheld it'.[3] He undoubtedly ascribed its swelling to its absorption of the plague-venom; but in that sultry August weather the physical exertion, the excitement, and the tension of the autopsy had conjoined to make him sweat so profusely that the toad was more than reconstituted and any 'blocked' flea which tried to attack him would probably have drowned before it could have driven its attack home.

August with its terrible toll of plague-deaths passed—6,102 of them in a total of 7,496 deaths in London in the week ending the 31st[4]—but the city's ordeal was not ended and September brought even more death and desolation. Pepys celebrated his survival by buying a new wig some time in August, though he did not dare to wear it until 3 September as plague was prevalent in Westminster where he bought it;[5] but his purchase shows that some shops were still open and that not all the metropolitan trade was dead. He speculated upon the possibility of a change in fashion after the epidemic ceases 'for nobody will dare to buy any haire, for fear of infection, that it had been cut off the heads of people dead of the plague'.[6] Three weeks later he wrote in his diary:

But, Lord! what a said time it is to see no boats upon the River; and grass grows all up and down White Hall court, and nobody but poor wretches in the streets! And, which is worst of all...that it [plague] is encreased about 600 more than the last, which is quite contrary to all our hopes and expectations, from the coldness of the late season.[1]

Unfortunately this September chill was neither severe enough nor sufficiently prolonged to induce the plague-fleas, ensconced in the warm burrows of the house-rats, to hibernate, and with the return of warmer weather the epidemic increased in fury. Evelyn, who had prudently sent his wife and family into the country early in August, remarks that nearly 10,000 deaths were recorded in London in the week ending 7 September, and he adds: 'I went all along the city and suburbs from Kent Street to St James's, a dismal passage, and dangerous to see so many coffins in the streets, now thin of people; the shops shut up, and all in mournful silence not knowing whose turn might be next.'[2] Those who still lived in the stricken city had good cause for apprehension this month, for the weekly Bills returned mortalities of 6,988, 6,544, 7,165, and 5,538, an increase of more than 9,000 over August's distressful death-roll. Vincent's eye was horrified by the state of the churchyards which, he says, were 'stufft so full with dead corpses, that they are in many places swell'd two or three feet higher than they were before; and new ground is broken up to bury the dead'.[3] He is possibly referring here to the mass burials in unconsecrated ground, the 'plague-pits', of which Bell, citing Defoe's *A Journal of the Plague Year*, gives what he apparently believes is a factual account.[4] It is evident from Vincent's account that until the end of August most of the victims were interred in consecrated ground, although several bodies were placed in each grave. Then when no more corpses could be packed into the existing churchyards the victims were buried in authorized ground which was either consecrated at the time or afterwards. Only when the social organization for the reverent disposal of the dead was disrupted by the great increase in mortality in September were the plague-dead tumbled indiscriminately into hastily dug pits outside the city precincts.

In spite of this great increase the epidemic was not ubiquitous throughout the metropolitan area even in September; it could not be so in the nature of bubonic plague. In general, as table 39 shows, the parishes which had been most severely attacked in August were the ones that suffered worst in September, though there were exceptions and in at least two parishes the reverse process occurred. In view of the gravity of London's state this month the indifference of the government is incomprehensible and inexcusable. Only two proclamations about plague seem to have been issued and neither is concerned with the dire strait of the capital. The first, on 21 September,

merely cancelled Wantage Fair in Berkshire;[1] the second, five days later, postponed Michaelmas Term to Martinmas and transferred it to Oxford.[2]

Despite its huge mortality, this visitation conformed to the usual behaviour of bubonic plague in England. In most of the English outbreaks in which the peak occurred in September the disease killed more slowly in that month and more patients recovered from it. In other words, although the toll of plague-deaths was highest in September, the case-fatality rate declined during that month though more people were infected than in any of the preceding months. A convincing contemporary record of this decrease in the virulence of *P. pestis* is provided by the incident which the bishop of Ely described in a letter written on 19 September.

I saw last Tuesday [he records] about 30 people in the Strand, with white sticks in their hands and the dr. of the pest house walking in his gowne before them; the first woman rid on an horse, and had a paper flag on the top of her stick with *Laus Deo* written in it. They were going to the justices, being poor people sent thither and recovered by him of the plague. He seemed to take no small content in his stately march before them;[3]

although they had recovered spontaneously and in all probability in spite of his treatment. Unfortunately the bishop does not name the pest-house from which they came; but as he met them in the Strand it seems probable that it was the pest-house for the sixteen parishes outside the walls. Now the plague-mortality rate for that pest-house, as calculated from the returns in the Bill of Mortality for 1665 (see table 37) was 98·1 per cent, so if thirty of its occupants had recovered by 19 September there must have been a considerable decline in the virulence of *P. pestis*. Hancock supplies confirmation of this decline in virulence of the plague bacillus.

About the 10th of September [he notes] the disease came to its height, at which time, according to a reasonable calculation, more than 12,000 died in a week, though at least two-thirds of the inhabitants had retired into the country. 'The city and other parts where the weight of the disease now lay was, notwithstanding, exceedingly crowded; and perhaps more so, because people had for a long time a strong belief that the Plague would not come into the City, nor into Southwark, nor Wapping, or Ratcliffe at all'.

'It now killed in two or three days, and not above one in five recovered; or four in five died.'

'But after this period, when the disease was on its decline, it did not kill under eight or ten days, and not above two in five died.' So that it was calculated by Dr Heath that there were not fewer than 60,000 people infected in the last week of September, of whom near 40,000 recovered. For the plague being come to its crisis, its fury began to assuage, and accordingly the Bill decreased almost 2000

473

that week. 'For, had the mortality been in the same proportion to the numbers infected, as at the height, 50,000 would very probably have been dead instead of 20,000, and 50,000 more would have sickened; for, in a word, the whole mass of people began to sicken, and it looked as if none would escape, as not one house in twenty was uninfected.'

'Just then, says the writer, it pleased God, by his immediate hand, to disarm this enemy. Nor was this by any new medicine, or new method of cure discovered; the disease was enervated and the contagion spent. Even the Physicians themselves were surprised: wherever they visited they found their patients better...so that in a few days, whole families that expected death every hour, were revived and healed and none died at all out of them.' Yet it appeared that more people fell sick then, when not above one thousand died in a week, than when five or six thousand died in a week.[1]

An even more valuable confirmation of this decline in virulence is supplied by Hodges who witnessed it. 'Before the Number infected decreased, its Malignity began to relax, insomuch that few died, and those chiefly such as were ill managed...The Pestilence did not however stop for Want of Subjects to act upon, (as then commonly rumoured) but from the Nature of the Distemper.'[2]

In October, as figure 64 shows, there was a welcome fall in the number of plague-deaths; but the mortality was still high, for more than 14,000 people died of plague during this month, some of them possibly from complications of the disease contracted previously. This reduction was not due to a decline in the predatory activity of the plague-fleas because there is no contemporary notice of the arrival of cold weather during the first half of October. It is not until the 22nd that Josselin notes in his diary that the weather had become dry and cold, with frost,[3] and 5 days later he records that the epidemic in London had greatly abated.[4] It is evident therefore that there must have been a progressive spontaneous decline in the virulence of *P. pestis* to account for the reduction of more than 50 per cent of the September mortality, and every English outbreak of bubonic plague in the past ended in this way. It was on 16 October that Pepys walked to the Tower and saw 'so many poor sick people in the streets full of sores',[5] a sight that he had not seen before since the epidemic started. It is not certain that these people were all convalescents from bubonic plague whose buboes had suppurated and ruptured; some may have been convalescents from smallpox and in some the sores may have been syphilitic, for both these diseases were active along with plague; but taken in conjunction with the recoveries at the pest-house it is evident that many more patients were recovering from plague in October who would have died of it in September. The last entry of a specified plague-burial in the London parish registers is dated 11 October.[6]

474

October ended in the grip of a spell of cold weather and this—with a slight intermission during the first week in November, which produced an increase of 399 plague-deaths in London during the week ending the 12th[1]—continued throughout November. Pepys notes that on the 22nd there was 'a very exceeding hard frost'[2] which would undoubtedly force the plague-fleas to hibernate and consequently the plague-deaths in November fell by nearly 11,000 from the October total. Hodges avers that as plague declined, disease which it had masked, 'Quinseys, Dysenteries, Smallpox, Measles',[3] became prominent again; but these did not arouse the terror that plague excited so that from the beginning of November the fugitives began to return to London. And in December 'they crowded back as thick as they fled',[4] although, as figure 64 shows, plague was still causing between 200 and 300 deaths a week up to the 19th, most of them, however, probably from secondary infections with pyogenic bacteria and from sequelae of plague. Hodges affirms that people were so confident that the epidemic was extinguished 'that many went into the Beds where Persons had died before they were even cold, or cleansed from the Stench of the Diseased'.[5] This confident reflux was the more remarkable because the authorities did not share the popular belief that the epidemic had ceased. On the contrary, for on 10 November the government cancelled Boston Fair with the added warning that no Londoner was 'to repair to any faire in the Kingdom on pain of contempt'.[6] Six weeks later it was still so uncertain about the extinction of the epidemic that it cancelled St Paul's Fair at Bristol[7] though that fair was not scheduled to be held until 25 January. Incidentally Hodges also was convinced that plague had been imported from Holland in 'packs of Merchandise', and he adds: 'By common Fame, it came thither from Turkey in Bails of Cotton or Silk...For that Part of the World is seldom free from such Infections, altho' it is sometimes more severe than others.'[8] A very shrewd observation which does credit to the perspicacity of our seventeenth-century ancestors who, though they were ignorant of the aetiology of bubonic plague, had a much more accurate notion of where it came from than many later writers. Hodges' list of communicable diseases that were masked by plague is incomplete, however, because in May 1666 the parish of St Clement Danes registered six deaths from *spotted fever*[9] and in August and September three more victims of typhus fever were buried at the church of St Michael Bassishaw.[10] As the mistake has been commonly made of assuming that bubonic plague was solely responsible for the huge mortality sustained by London in 1665, table 40 is presented as a corrective. Admittedly the figures given in it are only approximations to the truth, but this weakness applies equally to the plague returns and to each of the other diseases listed,

TABLE 40

Showing the numbers that died of other diseases and of plague in the latter half of 1665

Month and week	Other diseases	Consumption	Fever	Flox and Smallpox	Quinsy	Spotted Fever	Surfeit	Teeth*	Plague	Total
30 May	382	—	—	—	—	—	—	—	17	399
6 June	362								43	405
13	446	347	193	63	2	62	65	101	112	558
20	443								168	611
27	417								267	684
4 July	536								470	1,006
11	541								727	1,268
18	672	563	619	85	6	378	300	305	1,089	1,761
25	942								1,843	2,785
1 Aug.	1,004								2,010	3,014
8	1,213								2,817	4,030
15	1,439	575	1,398	37	16	686	345	447	3,880	5,319
22	1,331								4,237	5,568
29	1,394								6,102	7,496
5 Sept.	1,464								6,988	8,452
12	1,146								6,544	7,690
19	1,132	571	1,474	22	4	483	223	591	7,165	8,297
26	927								5,533	6,460
3 Oct.	791								4,929	5,720
10	741								4,327	5,068
17	554	301	451	11	2	136	90	187	2,665	3,219
24	385								1,421	1,806
31	357								1,031	1,388
7 Nov.	373								1,414	1,787
14	309	182	235	6	—	27	27	124	1,050	1,359
21	253								652	905
28	211								333	544
5 Dec.	218								210	428
12	199	158	90	6	—	14	11	54	243	442
19	244								281	525
Whole year	28,710	—	—	—	—	—	—	—	68,596	97,306

476

so the fact remains that diseases other than bubonic plague were responsible for 41·8 per cent of the total deaths recorded in London that year.

The authorities must have felt justified in December for doubting if plague was extinguished, 'notwithstanding there hath been a day or two great frosts',[1] as Pepys notes on the 13th. He adds the hope that the resurgence of 'plague' about this time was 'only the effects of the late close warm weather',[2] from which notice it may be inferred that the frost broke about the end of the first week in December, to be succeeded by some days of warm humid weather. It is possible that a few plague-fleas were still active at this date, but the bulk of them had certainly been driven to hibernate by the preceding cold weather and there seems little doubt that most of the deaths returned as 'plague' were actually deaths from typhus fever. The body-louse becomes much more active with a slight increase in the surrounding external temperature and among the citizens of London, whether crowded in their communal bedrooms or jostling one another in the shops and places of entertainment, there would therefore have been a generous exchange of *Pediculus humanus* var. *corporis*, some of which were infected with *Rickettsia prowazeki*. Fortunately, if plague was stirring again—the return of 'plague-deaths' rose from 428 in the first half of the month to 525 on the second half[3]—it was only a transient resurgence for Pepys was able to record on 31 December that 'plague' had 'abated almost to nothing'.[4] Five days later he commented that it was delightful 'to see the towne full of people again as it now is' and the shops reopening, 'though in many places seven or eight together, and more, all shut'.[5] Alas! many of them would never open again with their former owners. Typhus fever continued its activity during January, for that months' total of alleged plague-deaths was still more than half of December's total. Its activity progressively declined during the winter, as one would expect it to do, and the 'plague-deaths' fell from 382 in January to 222 in February and 107 in March, and this outbreak of plague's masquerader was only feebly active at the end of the old year of 1665. Nevertheless this activity induced the government in January to adjourn Hilary Term to Windsor Castle.[6]

It seems probable that anything like a recurrence in 1666 of the calamitous epidemic of the previous year would have been a catastrophe which might have altered the history of London and indirectly of the United Kingdom. It might have caused the permanent removal of Parliament from Westminster, because that twin city would have been involved in it as it was in the epidemic of 1665 when its recorded plague-deaths accounted for 12 per cent of the metropolitan total, while its five parishes and its pest-house con-

tributed only 1,484 fewer deaths than the number returned for the ninety-seven parishes within the walls.

One fallacy about the effect of bubonic plague upon London in particular and England in general that has been given considerable publicity is that the mortality caused by it was responsible for the slow growth of the English population in the seventeenth century. Admittedly an excess of deaths over births occurred in any year in which that disease was extensively and virulently epidemic; but the city's death-rate exceeded its birth-rate in the years when bubonic plague was either absent from the capital or was only sporadically active there, a fact that Maitland conclusively demonstrated as Brett-James emphasizes.[1] Maitland, who borrowed the figures from Graunt, states that in the twenty years 1624–43 there were 267,832 registered burials and 186,608 registered christenings in London. In the next twenty years the respective figures were 257,058 and 142,256; in the succeeding equivalent period they were 457,508 and 241,587, while in the last of these 20-year periods they were 430,349 and 299,781.[2] In each of the vicennia in which a major epidemic of plague occurred the excess of deaths over births was nearly doubled; but it is significant that in the two vicennial periods in which there was no epidemic of plague the deaths still exceeded the births by nearly 50 per cent. Obviously in the face of these figures the continuous increase in the size of the population of London which occurred cannot be ascribed to the procreative ability of its citizens—enthusiastic as it undoubtedly was—as Hodges opined. His remark that towards the end of November 1665 the people of London 'had the Courage now to marry again, and betake of the Means to repairing the past Mortality' and that the loss of life was 'after a few Months ...hardly discernable',[3] credits his fellow-citizens with a much greater reproductive activity than they possessed, however willing they were to support him. As Maitland's figures show that bubonic plague was not solely responsible for the failure of the City's indigenous population to grow, it is evident that those other diseases about which so little has been written played an important part in that restriction, especially those responsible for the high death-rolls in infancy and early childhood. The fact that the population of London did grow continuously in spite of its cumulative retardation by epidemic and endemic diseases was due to the constant influx of settlers from other parts of the United Kingdom, an influx which Graunt estimated to be 6,000 persons annually throughout this century,[4] and which has continued down to the present day.

This sketch of the course of the visitation which has since become known as the Great Plague of London has perhaps laid too much emphasis upon the lethal power of *Pasteurella pestis*. Its conclusion with the presentation of

two contemporary experiences of bubonic plague will, I hope, reduce that emphasis to its proper proportion. The first of these experiences concerns the North family; the second that of Temple. Sir Dudley North was a boy of 14 when he and his little sister, Mary, simultaneously contracted bubonic plague and

were confined in their father's house in London. His father removed because of his promiscuous converse; but his excellent mother stayed, and with her own hands nursed her two tender children. I have heard her say that once, feeling a swelling upon the little boy's head, the plague sore (as it proved to be) broke in her hand. This incomparable piety and courage in her was providentially rewarded, first by the recovery of both her children and next by her own and her family's wonderful escape, for neither she nor any one else in her house had the plague. I well know by ocular inspection, the gross scar of this sore was very manifest to be seen upon this gentleman's head all the days of his life[1]

Dudley North became an English merchant in Constantinople, and while he was living there his brother, Montagu, came from Aleppo to visit him and fell ill with plague in his house.

He lay four days in the rage of the fever without any crisis or sensible sleep, and without any physic or anything else coming between his lips except lemons; and of those they gave him one after another continually, so that he might never be without one in his hand to suck. It seems that acid is a specific against the venom of the plague; for, by the price of lemons in that city, they can tell if the plague rages or not; for if they are cheap the city is less visited; and, if dear, the disease is more frequent.[2]

Lady Temple—the Dorothy Osborne of the famous letters—had borne five children before 1663, all of whom had died at birth or in infancy, a mortality that was a commonplace in London in the absence of bubonic plague. A son, Jack, was born in the last quarter of that year and a daughter, Nan, in the autumn of 1665. The terrible summer of that year found her and her sister-in-law, Lady Giffard, alone with the little boy at Sheen, as Sir William Temple had been sent abroad on a diplomatic mission.

He was scarcely gone before the plague burst forth in all its horror. It soon spread to Sheen, and 'a servant dying of it in a house joyning theirs and one being taken ill in their own, they resolved to go to London...But they found a dismal scene there, soe many houses shut up with crosses upon the doors, as they passed into the town, the people in them crying and wringing their hands at the windows, the bells all day tolling, the streets almost empty of everything but funerals, that were perpetually passing by, the difficulty of finding a lodging from the fright everybody was in of receiving the infection with them, few going thither on any occasion but flying from it at home, people coming in like Job's messengers all day, with one

sad story before another was ended. Yt after two dayes spent in this dismal place they ventured to go home [to Sheen] and trust with God Almighty's blessing what the use of care and cordialls could do to preserve them at home.[1]

Lady Giffard ascribed their escape from plague in great measure to the use of Sir Walter Raleigh's cordial, which was alleged to be a sovereign remedy for the disease and was described in most recipe books of the time. The ladies gave a spoonful or two of this cordial to each member of the household every morning, 'burnt Burgamot Spirit, and made as many servants as they could after ye smoke was gone take tobacco for a great part of ye day, strewed rue in ye windows and held myrrh in their mouths when they came anywhere that they apprehended infection'.[2] The widespread belief in seventeenth-century England that tobacco effectively protected the individual from absorbing into his body the atmospheric plague-venom, permits of the speculation that the modern use of tobacco in Britain—with its resultant fortunes for the tobacco barons and the presentation to the State of a large part of its revenue—may have derived from its supposititious efficacy as a prophylactic against bubonic plague, for the menace of plague and the terror inspired by its rumoured approach persisted among the populace until late in the nineteenth century. Sir Walter Raleigh's cordial was merely another of the valueless 'blunderbuss' herbal remedies that have always abounded in England. A century later Oliver Goldsmith, himself a doctor, wrote: 'The English are peculiarly excellent in the art of healing. There is scarcely a disorder against which they are not possessed of an infallible antidote.'[3] The popularity of lemon juice as a cure for plague in the Near East was probably due to its efficacy as a thirst quencher, for thirst was an invariable and distressing concomitant of the hyperpyrexia of bubonic plague. It does not seem to have been used in England, although the lemon was imported from the Azores as early as 1494,[4] probably because it was too expensive for popular use in Stuart England. Strangely enough no use appears to have been made either of the orange—also a valuable thirst quencher—which was apparently in relatively plentiful supply in the days when Mistress Nell Gwynne made history.

As I have already explained, London's ordeal was terminated by a spontaneous loss of virulence by *P. pestis*, but Hancock supplies a note about a civic activity that may unwittingly have helped to expedite its termination, for he states that 'all possible endeavours were used to destroy mice and rats: multitudes of them were destroyed by ratsbane and other poisons. Dogs and cats, being domestic animals, apt to run from house to house, and capable of carrying the effluvia or infectious steams'—in modern words, 'blocked' fleas—'in their fur or hair' were slaughtered wholesale. He affirms that

TABLE 41

Plague-deaths recorded in townships within 25 miles of London in 1665*

	Deaths	Approximate distance in miles from London Bridge	
Ware	160	23½	⎫
Hertford	90	23	⎟
Hoddesdon	30	21	⎟
Enfield	32	9	⎬ North
Edmonton	19	6½	⎟
Tottenham	42	5	⎟
Stoke Newington	17	3	⎭
Waltham Abbey	23	12	North by North-east
Epping	26	15	North-east by North
Brentwood	70	18½	⎫ North-east
Romford	109	13	⎭
Barking	200	7½	East
Bromley	8	10	⎫
Greenwich	231	5½	⎬ South-east
Deptford	623	3	⎭
Croydon	61	9½	⎫
Eltham and Lewisham	82	6	⎬ South
Dulwich	35	5	⎭
Chertsey	18	20½	⎫
Staines	82	19	⎟
Kingston-on-Thames	122	12	⎬ South-west
Putney	74	7½	⎟
Wandsworth	245	7	⎭
Kensington	28	4½	⎫
Windsor	103	21½	⎬ West by South-west
Brentford	432	20½	⎭
Uxbridge	117	17	West
Watford	45	16½	North-west
St Albans	121	21	⎫
Barnet and Hadley	43	10	⎬ North-west by North
Hornsey	58	5	⎭

40,000 dogs and 200,000 cats were destroyed in London during the epidemic, 'few houses being without a cat, some having five or six'.[1]

In view of the extent and severity of the metropolitan visitation it is not surprising that many of the townships and parishes within a day's ride of London—about 25 miles—especially those in the Thames valley, were

* Rearranged from the list supplied by T. Hancock, *Researches into the Laws and Phenomena of Pestilence; including a Medical Sketch and Review of the Plague of London in 1665: and Remarks on Quarantine* (London, 1821), with my additions of distances and compass-bearings.

invaded by plague in 1665. Hancock lists a number of these[1] which are presented in table 41, and of towns farther afield which were also involved that year Bell names Poole and Sherborne, Southampton, Dover, Ipswich, and Yarmouth.[2] Robinson gives the figures for the registered burials in the parish of Stoke Newington as 27 in 1664, 15 in 1665, and 24 in 1666. He affirms that the register is defective for 1665 because it is evident from the Vestry Minutes for April 1666 that plague was 'very fatal' there in 1665, and he opines that probably many of its victims were buried in gardens and fields and their names were therefore not entered in the register.[3] Jones, after remarking that Croydon was a small market town in 1665, says that at the end of April there was 'mighty hot weather', which continued to the middle of May. He opines that the first plague-death in Croydon, that of a fugitive from London, happened on 12 June, but the first burial entry marked *pestis* in the parish register is dated 27 July. In August the number of registered burials was only slightly above the average for the month, and no plague-burial occurred during the week ending the 28th, which was a week of unseasonably cool weather. However in September 39 burials were registered compared with a monthly average of 10, and one family, which contributed 9 to the total, was apparently exterminated as two more members were buried in October and another 3 in November. The earlier part of October was warm and 27 burials were registered during the first half of the month, a six- or sevenfold increase compared with the average figure for that period. In the latter part of the month the weather was dry, cold, and frosty, but Jones says that plague-burials continued at a steady rate, 25 being registered in the second half of October. There was a sharp decline in the plague-mortality during November, the number of deaths registered being only half the total for October, and the arrival of 'a very exceeding hard frost' on the 22nd, which heralded a spell of cold weather, virtually extinguished the epidemic, although 16 plague-burials were registered during the first 17 days of December and 2 more before the month ended. (Some of these, as in London, may have been remote deaths from plague, but most of them were probably deaths from typhus fever.) He notes that in this month plague was practically confined to one household, 10 of whose members died of it, though not all of them in December. Ignoring typhus fever, he comments that plague smouldered on in this parish as it is reported to have done in London, for 8 plague-burials were registered in January, 8 in February, and 4 in March, the last one—bringing a family's total to 16—being registered on the 17th of that month. He remarks that the parish register shows a total of 141 plague-burials in 1665, of which number nearly one-quarter was contributed by 4 families, all of which seem to have been exterminated. He estimates that this

epidemic destroyed about one-twentieth of Croydon's population and he avers that the town did not recover from this calamity until the closing years of the century.[1]

Young relates that 'plague did not spare Dulwich' in 1665 'for the Register records the names of thirty-five persons buried in the church-yard who had died of it'. He notes that the names of a household of 8 fugitives, 7 of whom died of plague elsewhere, are also recorded, bringing the total of plague-deaths among Dulwich residents to 40. 'The College itself escaped', he adds, 'with the loss of two poor scholars, the kitchen boy, and the cook, all of whom died in February and March 1665/6, and were almost the last victims, there being only one more person buried whose death is attributed to plague.'[2] Hammond reports that a sum of £63 9s. 8d. was raised in the parish of Putney this year to enable the churchwardens to cope with its epidemic of plague. He does not say how the churchwardens used this money, apart from the note that they employed a man to patrol the streets to kill stray dogs, but some of it was probably expended on the excavation of a pit for the disposal of plague-corpses which, it is said, was located at the foot of Charlton Road. He adds that in this neighbourhood objects called 'plague-pipes' are sometimes unearthed. These are supposed to have been used by the buriers to protect themselves from infection and were presumably clay or earthen-ware pipes in which tobacco was smoked.[3] Another Hammond mentions, in connexion with the synchronous epidemic at Wandsworth, that many entries appear in the town archives relating to the establishment of a pest-house and to the excavation of 'plague-pits' on each of its hills.[4] The parish register of Kensington contains 28 marked plague-burials in a total of 64 burials in the parish in 1665.[5] The peak of the visitation was in September when 9 plague-burials were registered. The evidence suggests that its involvement in the metropolitan epidemic was relatively slight, for the annual average of its burials for the decennium immediately preceding 1665 was 47.[6] More-over in 1661, which was not a plague-year, there were 81 burials and in 1666 there were 74, including 15 more victims from plague. In this year the first marked plague-burial is dated 10 April, and 2 of the remaining plague-burials are noted as 'From ye Pesthouse'.[7] As there is no notice of a pest-house in the burials register for 1665, one was possibly built or requisitioned late in that year, perhaps in November, in which month 5 plague-burials were registered. As table 41 shows, Brentford was proportionately one of the worst afflicted of the towns within a day's ride of London, and Thomas Povey was not exaggerating its suffering when he reported on 5 October that more than 300 people had died of plague there. He had, he said, 'been daily providing for infected persons' there; but 'Death has become so familiar

TABLE 42

Showing the number of deaths by plague each month from 19 December 1665 to the year 1671. *

	Dec.	Jan.	Feb.	Mar.	Apr.	May	June	July	Aug.	Sep.	Oct.	Nov.
1665 and 1666	222	382	222	107	158	162	114	205	162	158	69	28
1666 and 1667	15	13	3	—	1	—	—	2	1	4	1	1
1667 and 1668	2	4	4	1	2	—	—	—	2	1	1	—
1668 and 1669	1	—	—	—	—	—	—	—	—	—	3	—
1670	—	—	—	—	—	—	—	—	—	—	—	—
1671	—	—	—	—	—	1	—	—	2	—	1	1

and the people so insensible of danger', he complains, 'that they look on those who provide for the public safety as tyrants; the richer will not contribute, nor the meaner submit, though for their own preservation.'[1] Woolwich also appears to have been seriously involved. As early as 15 August the Commissioners of the Navy were informed that plague had appeared in two houses in the town,[2] and towards the end of September they were warned that it was increasing its ravages and that many of the workmen in the naval dockyard had died of it.[3]

The year 1666 must have early brought dismay to the citizens of London because 158 plague-deaths were officially notified in April, whereas no plague-death had been recorded in the previous April. When May showed no diminution of the plague-mortality (see table 42) the menace of a repetition of the calamity of 1665 must have terrified the people, for no one could then have foreseen that 1666 would witness the final epidemic flicker of bubonic plague in London. This last occurrence of the disease, which reached its peak in July, is credited by Creighton with 1,998 deaths,[4] but the total of monthly deaths given by Hancock (table 42) amounts only to 1,087. The wide distribution of the disease undoubtedly gave additional cause for apprehension as it was reported in 104 of the parishes according to Hancock,[5] compared with the 130 which were invaded in 1665.[5] The public's anxiety was reflected in the government's prorogation of Parliament on 16 April until 18 September,[6] although it is possible that Charles II used the excuse of the prevalence of plague to free himself temporarily from the shackles of parliamentary control.

* Copied from Hancock, *op. cit.*

There is no doubt, however, that the government was afraid of this re-crudescence of plague, for that fear was manifest in the publication on 11 May of its *Rules and Orders To be observed, by all Justices of Peace, Mayors, Bayliffs, and other Officers, for prevention of the spreading of the Infection of the Plague.*[1] These comprised 16 rules which are presented in appendix I. A fortnight later another proclamation cancelled Barnwell Fair on account of the danger of the spread of plague from it to the University of Cambridge.[2] Apparently the king and court deserted London again early in June as the government seems to have shown no further interest in the efforts of the civic authorities to arrest the metropolitan epidemic until the last week in September, when it cancelled Gravesend Fair,[3] which was held annually on 13 October. In the meantime the Great Fire, which broke out in the early hours of Sunday, 2 September—in the house of the king's master-baker in Pudding Lane, according to the information given to Pepys by the Lieutenant of the Tower,[4] and finished at Pie Corner according to tradition—distracted public and municipal attention from the smouldering activity of plague, and by the time the excitement aroused by the fire had subsided the epidemic was also obviously subsiding.

As several writers, both medical and lay, have suggested that the Great Fire was responsible for the permanent disappearance of bubonic plague from London, a categorical denial is here entered that the fire exerted any such effect. In the first place it was limited to the old walled city, whereas for a century past plague had had its chief foci in the liberties and out-parishes. Secondly the house-rat was not the sort of animal to cower in its burrows in the thatched roofs and wait to be incinerated by fire that gave sufficient warning of its approach to enable adult rats to escape. Although there is no extant record that any eye-witness noticed *R. rattus* in its scores forsaking the doomed houses and workplaces, there is not the slightest doubt that such a migration occurred. Undoubtedly some plague-sick and nestling rats perished in the fire; but if all the house-rats in the old walled city had been destroyed, there was a large enough rodent population untouched in the liberties and the out-parishes to engender many more major epidemics of bubonic plague, and the Great Fire of London did nothing to reduce the proportionate populations of the house-rat in every city, town, and village in the provinces, from which the capital was certainly rapidly recolonized. Bubonic plague disappeared from London and from England because the maritime importa-tion of *Pasteurella pestis* in plague-infected ship-rats from European and Levantine ports ceased, and it was purely a coincidence that the Great Fire happened at that time. Plague disappeared from western and central Europe also during the latter half of this century for the same reason, to wit, the

development of the all-sea trade between Europe and India, which abolished the caravan route for merchandise from the East across Asia Minor and with it the 'rodent pipe-line' for the transit of *P. pestis* from its Indian homeland to the ports of the Levant. Bubonic plague lingered sporadically in London until 1679, the annual deaths returned for it in the Bills of Mortality from 1672 to 1679 inclusive being 5, 5, 3, 1, 2, 2, 5, and 2; but after 1679 it ceased to appear as a cause of death in the Bills.

It is doubtful whether the epidemic of 1665 really merits the appellation of the Great Plague of London by which it is commonly known. The name suggests that it surpassed in extent and severity all the previous visitations of the city by bubonic plague, and it is true that the officially recorded mortality from it was numerically much larger than that recorded for any of its predecessors; but this numerical superiority does not prove that proportionately it was more destructive than some of the outbreaks which preceded it. Unfortunately it is not now possible to make an exact comparison between it and its predecessors because of the lack of reliable statistics of the size of London's population at the relevant times. Numerous estimates of the size of the population of Tudor and Stuart London have been made, but they are at best only approximations as they are based upon figures that are themselves merely contemporary estimates. Nevertheless it is incumbent to examine them because no history of London—or of England for that matter —is complete without an attempted assessment of the influence which bubonic plague exerted upon the social, commercial, municipal, and political development of the capital and the country. Creighton, whose estimates are considered by Brett-James to be the most accurate,[1] concluded that London had a population of about 60,000 around 1543 and that about two-thirds of it dwelt within the city walls.[2] He estimated it to be 93,276 in 1563 and 120,000 about 1580,[3] an increase of more than 20,000 in less than twenty years, and this, comments Brett-James, 'in spite of plague and a small birth-rate', so that the increase 'must have been due in the main to immigration from the provinces or abroad'.[4] As the Massacre of St Bartholomew's Eve and the Spanish Fury at Antwerp both happened within this period, it is practically certain that London received a large influx of French and Flemish refugees. Bell opines that about the time of the alleged mayoral census in 1631—which gave a certified total of 130,280 for the city and the liberties— the population of the out-parishes was about 40,000.[5] so that the total population of the metropolitan plague-area would be about 170,000. In the course of the next thirty years the city's population must nearly have trebled itself if Graunt's estimate is correct that Greater London contained 460,000 inhabitants at the accession of Charles II.[6] Bell evidently considered this

TABLE 43

Gregory King's estimate of the population of London in 1690

	Inhabited houses	Souls per house	Number of souls
The 97 parishes within the walls	13,500	5·4	72,900
The 16 parishes without the walls	32,500	4·6	149,500
The 15 out-parishes in Middlesex and Surrey	35,000	4·4	154,000
The 7 parishes in the city and liberties of Westminster	24,000	4·3	103,200
So London and the Bills of Mortality contain	105,000	4·57	479,600

estimate to be too high as he affirms that the metropolitan population was less than half-a-million in 1665,[1] because it is certain that the first five years of the Restoration witnessed a great influx of people into the capital, perhaps the largest immigration in any quinquennium up to that time. King estimated that in 1696 the population of London, Westminster, their liberties, and out-parishes, amounted to 479,600 persons of all ages. He computed his estimate (see table 43) on the basis of 'the Number of Houses in the Kingdome, as charg'd in the Books of the Hearth Office at Lady Day 1609'. From this number he deducted divided houses, empty houses, smiths' shops, and similar buildings, and obtained the figure of 1,290,000 as 'the true Number of Inhabited Houses in England', from which he apportioned the number in London.[2] There were certainly five major epidemics of bubonic plague in Tudor and Stuart London, to wit, in 1563, 1593, 1603, 1625, and 1665. Judging from the estimates that have been noted, it would seem reasonable to assign to London and its environs at those dates populations of the order of 80,000, 120,000, 190,000, 250,000, and 400,000 respectively. Now the total deaths from plague recorded for each of those epidemics were, in round numbers, 20,000, 15,000, 36,000, 41,000, and 69,000, so that the percentage plague-mortality rate of each is 25·0, 12·5, 19·0, 16·4, and 17·25. Admittedly these percentages are conjectural, but they nevertheless present some evidence that there were at least two previous metropolitan epidemics of bubonic plague which were proportionately more destructive than that of 1665, and I believe from my study of its history that the epidemic of 1563 was the severest visitation of plague that London experienced during the sixteenth and seventeenth centuries. Why was so little fuss made about it in contemporary writings? Elizabeth I and her ministers could probably have given the answer to that question, but they have chosen to keep silent about it. One final note about epidemic disease in London by Boghurst is worthy

of inclusion here before a final goodbye is said to bubonic plague there. 'In the summer before the Plague in 1664', he writes, 'the Small Pox was so rife in our Parish that betwixt the Church and the Pound in St Giles, which is not above six score paces, about forty familyes had the Small Pox.'[1]

Although most English writers on plague in the second half of this century have concentrated their attention upon its invasion of London, that visitation was but an incident in a great national outburst of the disease, and some of the provincial towns that were involved in it suffered heavier proportionate mortalities than the capital. It is also probable that the Port of London was not the only portal through which the fresh strain of *P. pestis* entered England on this occasion. Josselin recorded in his diary under the date of 28 May 1665 that plague had 'gott into o^r land at Yarmouth and London',[2] and if that note is correct for Yarmouth, Harwich, Lowestoft, and King's Lynn may well have been other ports of entry for it. In view of its extensive dispersion, the course and behaviour of this outbreak can most conveniently be reviewed by describing its activity separately in each of these regions, to wit, the counties south of the Thames; East Anglia, including Essex; the Midlands; the counties north of the Humber–Mersey line, and Wales.

It was to be expected that many of the townships along the reaches of the Thames would be involved in this outburst, and at some time during 1665–6 Chatham, Rochester, Gravesend, Greenwich, Woolwich, and Deptford were attacked by plague. Buckland states that the register of the Chatham parish of St Mary records 534 burials between 6 March 1665 and 7 February 1666. Unfortunately he does not say how many of these, if any, were marked in the register as plague-burials, and he has not supplied the figures for the monthly burials during that period.[3] There is other evidence that the town was probably severely afflicted, perhaps more gravely in 1666 than in 1665. Towards the end of August 1665 Pepys received a report that it was feared that plague would spread in Chatham as two houses were shut up,[4] a fear which was evidently fulfilled as a week later the Commissioners of the Navy were warned that it was increasing 'very much' in both Chatham and Rochester.[5] About a month later the Commissioners for the sick and wounded seamen told the government that Chatham could no longer be used as a reception centre for those seamen on account of the prevalence of plague there.[6] Apparently the epidemic subsided in the autumn and remained quiescent during the winter, because no further official notice of its presence seems to be on record until the summer of 1666. It may have recrudesced some time in July, for on 11 August the Navy Commissioners were warned that plague was increasing in Chatham, that 30 people had died of it during the previous week, and that 100 houses were infected.[7] A simultaneous com-

plaint was made to them that no order was being maintained by the municipal authorities who were allowing the plague-sick and the healthy to mix promiscuously. Buckland is the authority also for the statement that the burials register of the parish of St Nicholas in Rochester contains a long list of plague-deaths in 1666.[1] Regrettably he did not count their number. It is to be hoped that some future local historians will rectify his omissions for both Chatham and Rochester and give complete accounts of the ravages of bubonic plague in those towns at this time. If Pepys' information was correct, some time in August 1665 Greenwich, Woolwich, and Deptford were sharply attacked by plague, because on the 29th he notes that in those towns 'it begins to grow very great'.[2] It seems probable that numerous other townships in Kent were synchronously invaded although only a few are named in contemporary records. Early in February 1666 Evelyn reported that since 18 November 1664 7,030 sick and wounded seamen had been landed at nine Kentish ports, that 84 of them had died of plague, and that 403 had died from other diseases.[3] He attributed their deaths from plague to the spread of the disease from London by fugitives who entered these Kentish ports without the knowledge of the Commissioners of the Navy.[3] Gravesend, Sittingbourne, Maidstone, Canterbury, Eastry, Westwell, Sandwich, Deal, Dover, and Sandgate are named in contemporary notices of this epidemic. Concerning Gravesend we have Pepys' note of 18 August: 'I late in the dark to Gravesend, where great is the plague. . .'[4] There is no further notice of the town's visitation until mid-December 1666, when a report from it stated that plague had 'broken out fresh' there.[5] In view of the time of year it is possible that this was an outbreak of typhus fever, although it might have been a transient recrudescence of plague due to the persistent activity of some rat-fleas in particularly sheltered circumstances. In the above report Sittingbourne was said to be free from plague at the time of its despatch, a statement that might mean either that it had been attacked and the disease had been extinguished or that it had escaped invasion. The official information about Maidstone's involvement is meagre—a single report, dated 24 October 1666, that plague had 'broken out much of late' in the town.[6] Maidstone may have escaped lightly as it was apparently not attacked until so late in the year; but a careful study of its parish registers and municipal archives is needed to discover the extent of its involvement. There is little more information about Canterbury's involvement. Early in August 1665 it was reported that four houses had been segregated there but were now open again,[7] a note which suggests that plague may have appeared there early in June as in all probability the houses would have been kept closed for forty days from the death or recovery of the last case of plague in them. The report added that only one

plague-death had occurred in Canterbury during the previous week. Five days later a report from Dover mentioned that seven houses were then segregated in Canterbury although only a few plague-deaths had been recorded there;[1] but as this report was possibly repeating a rumour its value is doubtful. The city was asserted to be free from plague on 15 October,[2] though one plague-death—possibly from some complication—occurred there between 15 October and 4 November.[3] The hamlets of Eastry and Westwell seem to have escaped lightly as only one plague-death was recorded in each of them up to 12 August,[4] and the victims may well have been fugitives from London. In this report also one plague-death is stated to have occurred 'at the Earl of Winchelsea's park'.[4] This was possibly Eastwell Park, about 1½ miles to the east of Westwell.

By 12 August one house in Sandwich was segregated[5] and by mid-September plague was evidently established in the town.[6] By mid-October it may have been in the throes of an epidemic, because a report despatched from it on the 15th reads: 'In Dover twenty-four houses are shut up, and there is an increase at Sandwich; but Canterbury is free, as also Deal, Ashford, Maidstone, and Sittingbourne.'[7] Plague was said to be still on the increase there on 12 November,[8] but as this report was apparently written from Deal its accuracy is open to doubt, especially as it was unusual for English outbreaks of bubonic plague to increase in severity during the autumn months, even when the weather was milder than usual. On the other hand plague may have smouldered in Sandwich during the autumn of 1665 as it raged there in the succeeding summer.[9] In August 1666 in one parish alone 60 houses were reported to be infected[9] and the epidemic was increasing in severity four days later.[10] It is as difficult to discover the degree of Deal's affliction by plague at this time from contemporary notices as it is to ascertain the extent of the loss that Sandwich suffered, and up to the present no local historian of either of these ancient seaports has published a critical study of their parish registers. At the end of August two houses in Deal were segregated 'on suspicion of plague',[11] but 6 weeks later it was declared to be free from the disease.[12] If that report was correct, then either plague smouldered as an unnoticed enzootic among the house-rats until the ensuing spring or Deal was invaded afresh by it then, because early in July 1666 plague was raging in the town.[13] Some three weeks later a report from Dover contained the warning that 'the sickness [was] very sad at Deal',[14] but nine days later a report from Walmer put a different complexion on the virulence of the outbreak at Deal. After asserting that 'the distemper' had much decreased at Deal, the reporter continued: 'Two hundred have sores; before few had sores, but only swelling, and then they died.'[15] This observation is of epi-

demiological interest because it indicates that in Deal, as in London, this national outburst of bubonic plague subsided as a consequence of a spontaneous loss of virulence by *P. pestis*. Nevertheless that bacterium was still dangerous as two subsequent reports reveal, for on 17 August the state of Deal was reported to be worse than that of Sandwich[1]—where 60 houses were infected—and four days later another report stated that although plague was declining at Deal 'three quarters of those who stayed in the town' had died of it.[2] The first notice of plague in Dover, early in August 1665, possibly cheered the townsfolk as the danger was asserted to be obviated with the removal of the one infected family 'to the hills'.[3] Another report five days later was equally cheering with its official assurance that Dover was free from plague,[4] though it contained the ominous news that another house in the town was segregated. Dover's freedom was in fact short-lived and by the beginning of October 20 houses were segregated and the epidemic was increasing,[5] albeit slowly as only 4 more houses were infected there during the next fortnight.[6] As there seems to be no other official notice of plague at Dover in 1665, it is a reasonable supposition that plague ran true to its English form there and became quiescent with the arrival of the autumn frosts. As at Deal, however, there was either a recrudescence of the disease in the spring or the town was reinfected in 1666, because on 18 July 'several fresh houses in Dover', were reported to be infected.[7] During the next fortnight plague spread widely in the town[8] and by mid-August it was increasing in intensity daily.[9] A 'true account of the bill of mortality' for the week ending 13 September recorded 150 plague-deaths during the week and 96 houses in the town segregated.[10] Assuming that this was the peak week of the epidemic and that there had been a progressive weekly increase in the mortality from the reappearance of the disease in July, it seems probable that between 500 and 700 of the townspeople were destroyed by plague in a population that possibly did not exceed 3,000 persons. Throughout October plague continued to afflict Dover though there is evidence that the epidemic was declining. It was still widespread in the town on the 14th, when a report stated that 46 plague-deaths had been recorded during the preceding week and that fresh deaths were occurring every day.[11] A second report five days later contained the news that 36 plague-deaths had occurred in the previous week and that many houses were closed, 'so that it is like to be a very poor town'.[12] Indeed as late as the 24th many people were still dying of plague[13]—40 or 50 a week according to one reporter[14]—apparently in consequence of an exacerbation of the epidemic. This continued into November, for a report on the 11th said that 'the sickness' had again increased, that 24 people had died of it the previous week, and that many fresh houses had recently become infected.[15] The reporter contradicted

himself in his next despatch on the 18th because, after asserting that the epidemic was abating and noting that only 18 plague-burials had been registered in the previous week, he added: 'But fresh houses break out daily, and many die'.[1] However this appears to have been the final flicker of the epidemic as a month later the fugitives were returning to their homes and only 1 plague-death had been recorded in Dover during the previous ten days.[2] The notice of an outbreak of plague 'at a village near Calais, called Sandgate',[3] seems to be a mistake of location founded on rumour, for though there is a village of Sangatte in the Pas de Calais—which was possibly anglicized as 'Sandgate' when Calais was an English possession—there does not appear to be any record of plague there in 1665. If it was active at a place called Sandgate it must have been at the Kentish township of that name.

TABLE 44

Plague-mortality at Rye, as recorded in the parish register of burials

	Plague-burials registered in				Total burials		Percentage of plague-burials
	July	August	September	October	Plague	All causes	
1544	92	128	54	—	274	462	59·3
1563	—	105	290	168	563	765	73·5
1580	592 burials registered during the year, compared with an annual average of about 80.						

The absence of official reports of the involvement of any Sussex town in this great national outburst of bubonic plague is puzzling. John Allin was in constant correspondence with friends in Rye[4] during the summer and autumn of 1665 and they would assuredly have told him if plague had appeared in that town and would probably have passed on to him any rumours they heard of its presence in neighbouring places. Cooper supplies in his presentation of that correspondence some interesting data about the visitations of Rye by plague which are shown in table 44. It is also surprising that only two towns in Surrey, Godalming and Epsom, appear to be mentioned in contemporary references to this outburst in view of the county's proximity to and ease of access from London. According to Cox Godalming was not attacked until 1666, when 32 plague-burials were registered there.[5] Some of these entries in the parish register, he comments, have the marginal note 'buried in ye garden'. On 10 November 1665 Pepys was told that his neighbour, Mr Harrington, had died of plague at Epsom,[6] but as he learnt on the 22nd that Mr Harrington was not dead,[7] the possibility that Epsom

was attacked by plague that year will not be resolved until a local historian studies its parish registers.

The contiguous county of Hampshire with a naval base at Portsmouth and an important seaport at Southampton was prone to invasion by plague, and on this occasion both towns were attacked by it, although Portsmouth was apparently not involved until 1666. At Southampton plague was prevalent early in July[1] and by the 11th it was raging there.[2] The epidemic was reported to be still increasing in violence at the beginning of September[3] and by the end of that month the town was said to be almost depopulated.[4] Some time during the epidemic, possibly in September, an English couple were married by Mgr Couraud, the pastor of the Walloon church, because all the English ministers had fled,[5] undoubtedly along with a panic exodus of all those members of their congregations who had the means to desert the stricken town. During this visitation a Colonel Slingsby, writing from the Isle of Wight at the end of October, described an incident that illustrates the insensate panic that bubonic plague excited in seventeenth-century England. 'Two young sailors', he relates, 'were hired by a mother in the island to go to Southampton, and fetch thence her daughter from a house where all but she were [dead of the plague]. They did it but were discovered; she and one of the seamen are shut up, and Sir Wm. Berkeley will try by a court martial the other, who has escaped on shipboard.'[6] The naval authorities at Portsmouth were apprehensive about the imminent introduction of plague throughout the summer and autumn of 1665 because they did not know 'how to remedy the great evil of seamen going to and from London, and their wives coming down, some with plague sores on them; nothing but a miracle', one of them wailed to Pepys, 'can prevent the infection spreading'.[7] Perhaps if he had known that the real danger was not the plague-sores which some of the women bore but the 'blocked' fleas that might be roosting in their clothing, he might have wailed even louder; for a woman with a plague-sore could be distinguished from a healthy woman, whereas there was then no means of distinguishing plague-fleas from the multitudes of innocent human fleas that swarmed in the dwellings of the poorer classes. Nevertheless the miracle happened because there was no spread of plague from London to Portsmouth this year, and when it appeared there early in 1666 it was almost certainly imported by the *Essex*, which had lost 8 of its seamen from plague when it arrived there.[8] This warship was not the only one to be infected, for in June the *Rupert*, which appears to have been at Chatham at the time, had 3 or 4 plague-deaths among its crew.[9] It is of interest in connexion with the infection of men-of-war by plague that almost a year after these English ships were attacked the disease appeared in some of the ships of the French

Channel Fleet, which seems to have suffered more severely than ours as a report from Falmouth in April affirmed that there was 'great sickness in that fleet', 300 plague-sick sailors having been removed from one ship alone out of a complement of 600.[1] The immunity which Portsmouth had enjoyed in 1665 was lost during the summer of 1666, when 7 plague-deaths were included in the 11 deaths recorded there during the last week in August.[2] Although no more mortality statistics are given in the official references to its visitation, the available evidence suggests that Portsmouth was hard hit by plague on this occasion. At any rate the disease was still prevalent in the town at the end of September[3] and early in October it was reported to be increasing in extent.[4] It is possible, however, that rumour was busy with plague in September because a despatch from Portsmouth on 7 October noted that the town had been 'in tolerable health for a good while' but plague had now reappeared 'in some fresh houses'.[4] Another report on the 11th stated that although plague persisted few patients were dying of it in spite of its extension to 3 or 4 more houses.[5] Presumably the virulence of *P. pestis* was now waning at Portsmouth as it had waned at Deal, because 'the sickness' had so much abated there by the 23rd that only 4 or 5 plague-deaths had been recorded during the previous week, 'which is a miracle', comments the reporter, 'considering the many houses shut up'.[6] But the extinction of an epidemic consequent upon a spontaneous loss of virulence by the causal agent is always a gradual process and plague was therefore slow to disappear from Portsmouth. Indeed it did not finally quit the town until the middle of December although its activity was only sporadic for several weeks before its extinction, as no plague-death was recorded in Portsmouth during the last 10 days of November.[7] Three occurred in the second week of December— possibly as remote deaths from complications[8]—but since then Portsmouth has been free from bubonic plague. Whether or no plague was re-imported into the Isle of Wight early in November 1666, as a newsletter from Portsmouth feared,[9] it was certainly present in Newport late in the previous summer, according to a report that Pepys received in September 1665. The writer, a naval commander, incriminated 'a certain knight who had an estate there and sickened and died at his lodgings; the master of the house thought it quinsey, and threatened the mayor for shutting up the house, but two women took the infection, and died from merely changing and airing the sheets of his bed'.[10] The commander added that the householder 'was obliged to bury the bodies himself in his own garden', and he concluded his report with the statement that 'sheep and goats since put in the house' had all died. Sheep and goats are difficult to infect with *P. pestis* under experimental conditions and in all probability are refractory to infection with it under

494

natural conditions. It seems very probable therefore that the commander fell for one of the multitude of rumours that abounded in England in plague-time. If it was true that the women caught the infection in the course of their household duties, it is more likely that they died from typhus fever than from bubonic plague. Two other towns in Hampshire are named in the records of this outbreak, to wit, Basingstoke and Winchester. Plague attacked the former in 1666, causing 46 plague-burials to be registered at the parish church according to Cox.[1] The visitation may have been more severe than the parish register indicates, because he remarks that in the churchwardens' accounts the death-roll for the year is stated to have been upwards of 80. Whatever may have been the true number of plague-deaths, the visitation constrained the churchwardens to expend 1s. 6½d. on the purchase of 'three chafing dishes, resin, frankincense, and tobacco sticks to burn in the church in the time of Visitation'.[2] Concerning Winchester Jacob relates that in 1666 the number of burials registered in St Michael's parish church rose from 8 to 16, and from 16 to 38 in St Maurice's register. In the latter register 12 of the entries, he notes, are marked 'with *O*, denoting death "from the spots" as plague was called. In 1666 the disease was most destructive, and the register of St Maurice, by its abrupt break in the entries (at the 20th of May) shows that the authorities were paralysed and burials unregistered.'[3] It seems probable that the break in the parish register signifies the hurried departure of the incumbent with the key to the parish chest in which the register was kept. Kitchen declares that the chapter-books show that the chapter was panic-stricken; that the midsummer chapter was not held this year, and that the prebendaries either fled into the country or isolated themselves in their houses throughout the epidemic.[4] 'In April and May', Jacob continues, 'there are fourteen deaths spot-marked, three with the word Plague; and the last entry has "She dyed of the plague, and so did several of those above".'[5] He ends his account of the city's ordeal with the assertion that 'the burials of the victims were in pits on the Downs, and thus un-recorded'.[6] Unfortunately he presents no supporting evidence from con-temporary records for this statement, which is open to the objection that in England such interment of the plague-dead was only resorted to as a rule when no more consecrated ground was available for their burial. If his state-ment is correct, then Winchester must have suffered a calamitous visitation from plague at this time. It undoubtedly suffered severely for the townsfolk formed the *Society of Natives* during the summer 'in order that the survivors might provide for the children of those citizens who had perished in the plague', and Kitchen adds that the Society 'to this day carries on its bene-ficent work of apprenticing boys and girls, with strange traditional usages'.[7]

The transference of the County Sessions in July to Basingstoke is also indicative of a serious prevalence of plague in Winchester, though it does not signify that the civic authorities had copied the ecclesiastical authorities in their desertion of the city. In the absence of a Bill of Mortality for this visitation the city's plague-toll cannot be compared with its plague-mortality on previous occasions—more particularly that of 1625 when 82 plague-deaths were registered, of which 25 were in August, 27 in September, and 10 in October. Jacob, who supplies these figures and others for prior outbreaks,[1] relates three incidents which illustrate the panic fear that plague generated in Winchester. In 1593, when an alarm of plague made the civic authorities place a continuous guard on each of the city's six gates to keep all persons from infected places from entering the city, 'Christian Wilson, wife of James Wilson of Kingston-on-Thames or Guildford, infected places, came to the citie with her two children, to her mother's house, and she is expelled with a passport to return to her husband, with the citie charitie of 2 shillings'.[2] It is to their credit that the Winchester magistrates were so humane, for many towns would have expelled the woman and her children without either passport or charity. Simultaneously with or shortly after this ordinance the magistrates prohibited until Michaelmas all trade with London, Farnham, and Alton, which they branded as infected places. In defiance of this prohibition one of the aldermen went to London and bought unspecified wares there, whereupon the magistrates decreed that when he returned he was 'to be imprisoned fourteen days in St John's House, or else to have his shoppe shutt for a month'.[3] St John's House was possibly the pest-house. The third incident occurred in December 1594 after two houses had been pronounced to be plague-infected and had been accordingly segregated. 'One Pearce the bagman's wife repayred' to one of the houses 'and weaved yarne, to her own danger and the inhabitants. She shalbe com'itted to the caidge, and there remayne till further order be taken, and on the door a writinge expressinge her contempte and disobedience.'[4] Jacob concludes his notes with the statement that Petersfield, Andover, and Basingstoke were synchronously involved with Winchester in the epidemic of 1666—although if Basingstoke was then attacked by plague the County Sessions would certainly not have been transferred there—and that the last record of plague in Winchester is the entry in the burials register of St Peter Cheeshill of two victims, a man and his wife, in 1677.[5]

A report that plague was prevalent in Wiltshire reached London early in October 1665;[6] but a month earlier a letter from a Londoner who was 'well acquainted att the' court at Salisbury contained the news that plague had appeared in that city.[7] Salisbury was in fact invaded early in the summer,

possibly about the middle of July, for in the second week of August Sir Thomas Ogle explained that he dared not visit the city as 'the sickness' was prevalent there.[1] Then a day or two later Sir William Coventry commiserated with Lord Arlington upon the outbreak of plague there, adding the cold comfort that the disease was more dangerous in little towns where there were less means of avoiding it than in London.[2] Arlington was presumably in attendance upon the king, who left Salisbury precipitately as soon as plague appeared there. It seems evident that the arrival of the autumn frosts caused plague to become quiescent as there is no more news of its activity in Salisbury in 1665 after 5 September; but it was only slumbering and in the spring of 1666 it recrudesced with augmented violence, so much so that in July 1666, in response to a letter from the mayor, the Quarter Sessions rated the whole county at £100 for 20 weeks for the relief of Salisbury. In his letter he affirmed that there were then 52 houses segregated, the 196 inmates of which were costing the city in maintenance £22 15s. a week; 23 families comprising 58 persons were in the pest-house costing £6 15s. 4d. a week, and 553 families comprising 1,885 persons were in receipt of domiciliary relief costing £108 4s. 2d.[3] These charges amount to £137 14s. 6d., but the mayor asserted that the city was spending £154 7s. 6d.[3] The discrepancy possibly represents payments to guards at the pest-house, to searchers and to nurses. On 8 January 1666/7 the mayor wrote a second letter to the County Quarter Sessions in which he reported that the city was now free from plague but only £990 15s. 7d. had been received for plague-relief; that there were still 692 families comprising 2,192 persons receiving relief, and that the city was £700 in debt.[4] Plague troubled Salisbury throughout the summer—24 plague-deaths were notified there during the last week in August—[5] and even at the end of September its activity caused the election of the mayor and other officers to be held by royal licence 'in the Close of the Cathedral as less infected with the plague'.[6] However in the closing fortnight of that month the epidemic began to subside and the registered weekly plague-deaths fell to 15 and then to 14.[7] Nevertheless plague was still active there in October as was manifest by the 8 deaths attributed to it in the Bill of Mortality for the third week of the month.[8] Indeed it did not finally disappear from the city until the end of November, as 6 deaths from it were recorded in that month,[9] though these were possibly remote deaths from sequelae of the disease. It is regrettable that no information about the mortality of this visitation appears to have been published, although there is surely some record of it in the diocesan and parochial burials registers. The mayoral letter suggests that the epidemic inflicted a grave hurt on the city and it is possible that it destroyed upwards of 500 people in a population

that cannot have exceeded 5,000 persons of all ages. This is a large urban aggregate for Stuart England, and it may appear to be an over-estimate for a town whose population at the 1901 census was only slightly in excess of 17,000; but Salisbury was relatively a much more important place in 1666 than it is today. Then it was a comparatively large industrial centre, a busy market town, and an important trade and traffic centre. If it lost no more than one-tenth of its population from bubonic plague in 1665–6, that loss may perhaps partly explain why it lapsed for so long into a somnolent episcopal borough. In addition to Salisbury plague attacked the Wiltshire localities of Donhead St Mary, Mildenhall, Ogbourne St Andrew, and Fisherton during the course of this national outburst. At the County Quarter Sessions in January 1665 an order was made for the levy of a tax for the relief of the plague-stricken at Donhead St Mary,[1] but no information is given about its scale. A year later the churchwardens and Overseers of the Poor at Mildenhall lodged a complaint at the Sessions against '"a gentleman of a good and plentiful estate", for abandoning his house with the greater part of his family, upon its being visited with the Plague, and taking no care of the sick people therein, but leaving them wholly to be the charge of the parish at a cost of £5'.[2] Some gentleman! But one is forced to the regretful conclusion from the wording of this complaint that the parochial authorities were more concerned with the expense incurred than with humanitarian feeling for the plight of the sick people he deserted. Apart from a laconic note in the minutes of the Sessions that Ogbourne St Andrew was 'visited by the Plague' in 1666[3] nothing is known about the degree and duration of its affliction as no one has yet studied its parish registers. At Fisherton a suspected death from plague early in September 1665 was sufficient for the king and his court to discuss the advisability of an early departure from Salisbury.[4] As plague had appeared in Salisbury a month before this suspect death occurred, it seems evident that Charles II was not residing in the city itself at this time but in one of the large country houses nearby, possibly in one situated in or near the parish of Fisherton.

The invasion of Sherborne may represent the terminal of the westward overland spread of this outburst. Further west Plymouth was attacked in the summer of 1666, but in all probability its infection resulted from the importation of *P. pestis* either by coastal shipping or by naval vessels. Sherborne appears to have been visited in the autumn of 1665, because early in November it was reported from the town that plague was spreading 'apace; two have died and six or eight are ill; two houses are shut up'.[5] Presumably the autumn frosts were late in coming to Sherborne that year because on the 13th another report stated that plague was still active in the town, that 10

or 11 plague-deaths had occurred, and that 4 houses were segregated.[1] However, as there is no further official notice of the disease there, plague was presumably extinguished with the arrival of cold weather.

The official notice of Plymouth's visitation is confined to a report, dated 27 October 1666, that 8 plague-deaths had been recorded there.[2] If these were in truth the full extent of Plymouth's experience of plague this year it was very fortunate to escape so lightly. It may even have escaped altogether—it was certainly free in August[3]—as these victims may have been seamen brought ashore from an infected ship. On the other hand the precautions taken by the civic authorities of Exeter to protect that city from infection indicate that they were much alarmed about the danger of plague reaching them from London, and its maritime importation through Plymouth was much more likely to involve Exeter than an overland transport of the disease, a fact that they had undoubtedly learnt from past experience. Pickard records that the Exeter magistrates prohibited the entrance of both persons and goods from London; cancelled Magdalen and Lammas Fairs; petitioned the king to postpone the Assizes; desired Mr Receiver to complete the pesthouse, and decreed that persons and goods coming to St Nicholas Fair were not to be lodged in the city.[4] He notes that there were three pest-houses in the city at this time, all of them in St Sidwell's parish, and he adds that an order was made on 16 October 1677 for the disposal of the pest-house acquired in 1665.[5] As he does not report any outbreak of plague in Exeter in 1665 or 1666, the civic authorities probably congratulated themselves on the efficiency of their precautions.

There can be no doubt that East Anglia was invaded synchronously by a landward extension of plague from London and by its seaborne importation through one or more of its busy sea- and river-ports. The dates on which the disease is stated in contemporary reports to have made its appearance in East Anglian towns support the presumption that plague invaded that region both by sea and land, because Yarmouth was attacked on 28 May 1665;[6] Colchester early in August;[7] Harwich at the beginning of September;[8] Ipswich on the 13th,[9] and Norwich in the first days of October.[10] It seems practically certain that Colchester and Braintree were the hardest-hit towns in Essex; indeed proportionately the former suffered more grievously than London, for between the beginning of August 1665 and 25 November 1666 at least 1,655 of its inhabitants died of plague according to the incomplete mortality figures supplied by Josselin.[11] Figure 65 depicts a partial record of the mortality and duration of this visitation. The exact size of Colchester's population at this time is unknown, but it was relatively more populous then than it is today and it may possibly have had around 7,000 inhabitants at the

499

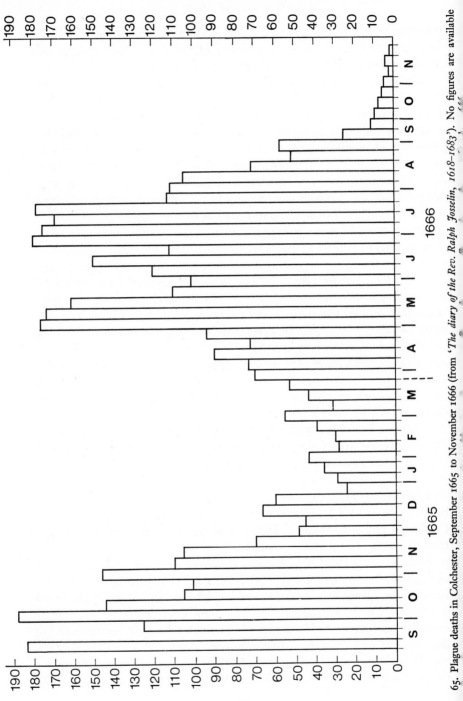

65. Plague deaths in Colchester, September 1665 to November 1666 (from 'The diary of the Rev. Ralph Josselin, 1618–1683'). No figures are available

time of this calamity. It seems very probable that it lost at least one-quarter of its population—it may have lost as much as one-third—from this epidemic of plague, and as the bulk of the loss would fall upon the labourers, the artisans, and the small craftsmen who lacked the means to flee from the town, this epidemic may have changed Colchester from a thriving industrial town of Stuart England to the stagnant market-town of the eighteenth century. Josselin's entries in his diary reveal the progress and destructiveness of the epidemic. He notes on 16 September that plague was spread over the whole town;[1] that 188 victims had been buried in the week ending 8 October,[2] and that as late as 12 November 110 plague-deaths were registered.[3] The arrival of frosty weather on 24 December brought about a great abatement of the epidemic during the remainder of that month;[4] but a spell of 'open and warm' weather during the first half of January resuscitated it.[5] From the end of January until 1 April 1666 it was relatively dormant;[6] then, with the return of warmer weather in April, it recrudesced and 177 plague-deaths were recorded in Colchester on 6 May.[7] During May 622 plague-deaths were registered there.[8] In July, which was 'a very hot season', it raged in both Braintree and Colchester, '40, 50 or more dying in a weeke' in the former town and 113 in the latter.[9] Not until 16 September could he record: 'Plague abated at Colchester to 25' deaths and then it was 'sad at Cogshall and other places'.[10] It was extinguished at Colchester by the end of November. From the behaviour of plague in this and other urban outbreaks it would seem to be a reasonable supposition that the autumn and winter of 1665-6 were milder than usual over a large part of England and Wales and certainly in East Anglia. Consequently the rat-fleas remained active in many places throughout the greater part of the autumn; *P. pestis* was kept viable and virulent by a smouldering enzootic of rat-plague in many colonies of house-rats throughout the winter, and there was therefore a vigorous recrudescence of epizootic and epidemic plague in the ensuing spring. Figure 65 shows that Colchester's visitation conformed to this pattern. There were two peaks of plague-mortality separated by an interval of about eight months, during which period the town's weekly mortality was above the average for the particular time of the year. As smallpox was active at Colne, in October 1665[11] and Halstead was 'much struck' by it in December,[12] it is probable that it was responsible for the excessive mortality at Colchester in the interval between the plague-peaks. The second of these is itself a compound of two peaks separated by several weeks of excessive mortality for which smallpox might also be responsible. Each of these secondary peaks appears to have coincided with a spell of hot weather. The unusual shapes of the mortality-curves of this protracted visitation are due to the deficiencies in Josselin's statistics.

Bubonic plague in the British Isles

According to Cutts Colchester lost more than 4,000 of its townsfolk during this epidemic of plague,[1] a figure which he probably borrowed from Morant, who affirms that 4,731 plague-deaths were recorded there between 14 August 1665 and 7 December 1666.[2] Josselin's figures suggest, however, that Colchester's plague death-roll was of the order of 2,000, a loss which must have been a catastrophic one for the seventeenth-century town. Perhaps some future local historian of that ancient borough will improve English social history with a comprehensive study of Colchester's calamity.

Other Essex townships named as places involved in this outburst are Burntwood (Brentwood), Coggeshall, Colne, Colnford Hill, Dedham, Harwich, and Kelvedon. Josselin, who was seemingly the vicar of Earls Colne, a parish 2½ miles south of Halstead, is the authority for the inclusion of all in this list except Brentwood;[3] but, except for Braintree and Colnford Hill, he gives no mortality figures for them. He notes on 1 October that plague-deaths had occurred at 'Colnhill'[4] and a week later he records that the disease had erupted at Braintree and Kelvedon.[5] 'And yett', he exclaims, 'Colne, sinfull Colne, spared!'.[6] To his obvious perplexity a punitive God continued to spare sinful Colne, although at Colnford Hill—which seems to have been less sinful in his estimation—7 people died of plague during the third week in October and 3 more developed suspect plague-sores.[7] His perplexity was justly intensified by the fact that the weather at this time was dry, cold, and frosty, and should therefore in his experience have caused an abatement of plague. It probably did, but smallpox and typhus fever would find such weather favourable to assume the lethal mantle of bubonic plague. Braintree may not have been seriously afflicted in 1665 because of the later arrival of *P. pestis* in October, but the recrudescence of or reinfection with the disease in July 1666 produced a calamitous epidemic in the summer and early autumn of that year. Cunnington refers to the existence of a document —which was compiled by a Braintree man who was a barrister of the Inner Temple—that records that 665 of the inhabitants died during the epidemic. It must have been one of the most malignant experienced by any English town during this last great invasion of the country by bubonic plague, for the case-mortality rate in Braintree was nearly 97 per cent, only 22 patients recovering from the disease.[8] Cunnington explains that the document lists the charitable donations which were collected for the relief of the plague-stricken families, and he gives a list of their names which appears to comprise 251 families. Unfortunately in many cases the number of victims in a family is now illegible, but I am indebted to the County Archivist for the information that the total is legible and is as transcribed on the document.[9] As it seems unlikely that the population of Braintree exceeded 1,500 souls in

1666, and may have been considerably less, plague may have destroyed one-half or more of its population, as great a proportionate loss as that sustained by any township in the British Isles between 1348 and 1667. The evaluation of the effect of this catastrophic mortality upon the subsequent history of Braintree is a matter for the professional social historian; but it is noteworthy that in spite of it Braintree was not abandoned by its townsfolk to become one of the so-called and fictitious 'lost plague-villages' of England. Apparently Dedham and Coggeshall were not attacked until 1666, the former early in April,[1] the latter not until 26 August.[2] Other places that are named in Josselin's diary as having been involved in this outburst are Cambridge, Royston, Oxford,[3] Bocking, and Oundle.[4] The 'Burntwood' of Lady Gauden's letter[5] is presumably the modern town of Brentwood. There plague was 'in divers places in the towne' at the beginning of October 1665 and one death from it had already occurred in the pest-house.[5] To her obvious relief the pest-house was thereupon promptly moved to a safer place in the town. As there is no further notice of plague in Brentwood in this correspondence, and as no one appears to have published a study of its parish registers, its fate on this occasion remains unknown.

The exact date of the invasion of Harwich by *P. pestis* in 1665 is not known, but it may have occurred either shortly before or shortly after Yarmouth was attacked, that is to say towards the end of May or early in June. Its presence was not officially recognized until much later in the year when the Navy Commissioners were notified on 2 September that it was active in the town.[6] By that date it must have been well established because towards the end of September 'the sickness' was reported to be hot at Harwich,[7] and a month later Josselin noted that 100 plague-deaths had been notified there in three weeks.[8] Although the Navy Commissioners warned the government in October that sick and wounded seamen could not be received at the port on account of plague,[9] the epidemic seems to have declined during this month as Josselin reported on 11 November that plague had abated there though the town was not yet free from it.[10] Harwich was subjected either to a recrudescence or a return of plague in 1666, for 'the sickness' was reported to be increasing there towards the end of June.[11] It seems probable that *P. pestis* had now lost some of its virulence, however, as only three or four houses had been infected by the end of the month.[12] Nevertheless it was still virulent enough to inflict considerable loss of life and it flared up again at the beginning of September.[13] Indeed it was prevalent as late as the middle of October,[14] but it was evidently extinguished in November as there is no further reference to it at Harwich after 16 October 1666.

Ipswich was a busy port in 1665, which probably explains the severity of

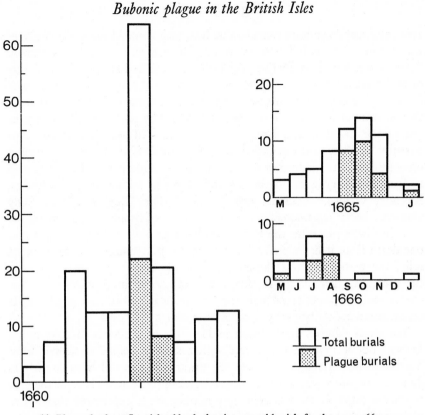

66. Plague deaths at Ipswich 1665–6, showing annual burials for the years 1660–9 and monthly burials for May to January of the years 1665 and 1666.

its invasion by plague. The burials register of the parish church of St Nicholas records a plague-burial on 13 September, the first of 23 such burials between that date and the end of the year.[1] Figure 66 depicts the plague-mortality curve in this parish in 1665–6. It is noteworthy that October was the peak month of the visitation in 1665 and that the disease became quiescent in November. In May 1666 it recrudesced, but fortunately for Ipswich this recrudescence was feeble and transient. The last plague-burial in the parish of St Nicholas was registered on 26 August 1666.[2] It may not represent the last plague-death in the town, however, as there were 5 more parishes in Ipswich and until their registers have been critically studied the full extent of the borough's affliction will not be known. Jones declares that between 1,000 and 1,200 persons died in Ipswich during this epidemic; but as he presents no evidence from either the borough archives or the parish registers to support his declaration it would appear to be no more than a guess. He

says that plague appeared in the parish of St Mary Key (or Quay) in May 1665, that it persisted there through 1665 and 1666, and that it 'was particularly severe in St Margaret's parish'.[1] He relates that from Ipswich 'the plague spread to Needham Market, which town dwindled and lost its importance...Stowmarket was free of the plague. The inhabitants brought their goods to a point halfway between the towns and left their money in a vessel filled with vinegar and water.'[2] Josselin notes that plague was 'hott at Ipswich' in the early part of October 1665[3] and that Needham Market was sadly scourged by it in July 1666.[4] The Commissioners for the sick and wounded seamen warned the government on 10 October that Ipswich could not be used for their reception because of the prevalence of plague.[5] The absence of any further official notice of the disease there during the remainder of 1665 suggests that its behaviour in the parish of St Nicholas (see figure 66) was representative of its behaviour in the borough. A report on 16 February that 11 plague-deaths had been recorded in Ipswich that month in a total of 19 registered deaths[6] is more likely to signify an outbreak of typhus fever than a winter resurgence of bubonic plague. The recrudescence of plague in the spring of 1666 provoked an alarmist report to the Navy Commissioners in June that plague was spreading rapidly in Ipswich,[7] but the register of St Nicholas has no entry of a plague-burial this month. The disease may have been active in other parts of the borough, however, as a newsletter dated 27 July tells of 15 plague-deaths in a total of 19 deaths registered in Ipswich during the previous week.[8] This recurrence of plague seems to have increased slowly in severity during July to reach a low peak about the middle of August, after which it gradually subsided although it was still feebly active in October. During the last week of August 8 plague-deaths were said to have been notified in Ipswich,[9] and 2 or 3 more were recorded there during October.[10] At Woodbridge, some 7 miles north-east of Ipswich, plague appeared early in July 1666;[11] but as there is no further notice of it there in contemporary records it may have been confined to a single household. 'A village near Theberton', the name of which Jones either did not know or did not consider worthy of mention, was apparently attacked that year because 'Theberton bought "A Book and Proclamation to keep a fast to stay the Plague"'.[12] Tymms notes that in 1665, in anticipation of its visitation by plague, the corporation of Bury St Edmunds decreed in August that 'the greate Barne, called Almoner's Barne', was to be used as a pest-house.[13] Regrettably he supplies no information about Bury's fate at this time and Jones merely copies his note.[14] Perhaps some future historian of Bury will be more painstaking and consult its parish registers.

Bubonic plague disappeared from Ipswich for good in 1666, but the terror

it excited persisted undiminished by oral tradition for nearly 2½ centuries, to create the 'plague-scares' in East Suffolk in the years between 1905 and 1911. There is no doubt that *P. pestis* sneaked up the estuary of the river Orwell once again in 1910 on board a grainship from Rosario in the Argentine province of Santa Fé, and that its disembarkation produced an extensive epizootic of rat-plague in East Suffolk. But in the intervening centuries a profound ecological change had occurred in the rodent population of the British Isles; a change of decisive importance with respect to human plague, for *Rattus Norvegicus*, the field-rat, had replaced *Rattus rattus*, the house-rat, as 'the rat' of the islands almost everywhere in country, village, town, seaport, and even on board ship. Mercifully the most extensive and virulent epizootic of plague among field-rats is of little danger to human beings in temperate climates because, owing to its living and breeding habits, the fleas harboured by the field-rat have few opportunities to attack human beings, and it rarely if ever in temperate climates harbours *Xenopsylla cheopis*, the chief transmitter of *Pasteurella pestis* from rat to man. This profound and decisive change in the conditions governing the transmission of bubonic plague from rat to man had not been accompanied, however, by any lessening of the panic aroused by the mere rumour of plague, and *The Lancet*, commenting upon 'the mysterious disease in Suffolk', felt it necessary to write: 'We were glad to observe that the occurrence of these deaths caused little comment at the time, as undoubtedly considerable public apprehension, and much of it of a needless kind, would have been aroused by the belief that plague had established a foothold in this country.'[1] It is indeed a remarkable testimony to the terror that the name 'plague' still excited in the public mind that the rapid deaths of four persons in the hamlet of Freeston should have been deemed of sufficient importance to warrant this notice. The reason why no public apprehension, 'much of it of a needless kind', was aroused by these deaths was simply that for some unknown reason no newspaper reported them under a banner headline, '*The Black Death threatens England*'. Possibly the government of the day may have had something to do with this remarkable abstention on the part of the Press. It was in December 1906 that a family of 8 persons, living in great poverty and under conditions of gross overcrowding in a cottage in the hamlet of Shotley (see figure 67), was suddenly seized with an acute infectious illness from which 6 of them died, and which their medical practitioner—almost certainly correctly—diagnosed as acute pneumonia superposed on influenza, which was then epidemic in the district. In December 1909 and January 1910 a family of 7 people, and the child of a neighbour, living in the hamlet of Trimley (see table 45) was successively taken ill with a communicable disease from which 5 of them died.

TABLE 45

The outbreak at Trimley, most probably of typhus fever, 1910–11

Family	Sex	Age	Relation	Onset of illness	Result
1	M	50	Father	9 January 1910	Recovered
	F	46	Mother	19 December 1909	Found dead in bed 23 December
	F	14	Daughter	26 December 1909	Died 5 January 1910
	F	9	Daughter	8 January 1910	Died 10 January 1910
	M	12	Son	15 January 1910	Died 17 January 1910
	M	6	Son	18 January 1910	Recovered
	F	18	Daughter	20 January 1910	Recovered
2	F	7	Child of neighbour	3 February 1910	Died 6 February 1910

The family was living in very poor and overcrowded circumstances in a dwelling which was said to be swarming with fleas, most of which were presumably *Pulex irritans*. The first case in chronological order, the mother, was reported by a daughter and by neighbours to have had red spots on her face, hands, and legs, and on the last day of her fatal illness a swelling the size of a hen's egg at the angle of her lower jaw. The verdict at the inquest was 'Death due to exhaustion, the result of a weak heart'. Each of the next two cases, girls of 14 and 9 years respectively, also had a swelling of similar size in an identical situation. The viscera of the second girl were sent to the county analyst for examination. He opined that she died of a disease of bacterial origin; the inquest verdict was 'Cause unknown'. The father had an enlarged inguinal gland which was incised in hospital, where apparently no examination of it was made, and which eventually sloughed away. The two boys were seemingly in good health when they were taken to Barham workhouse. No information is available about the cause of death of the elder boy. The eldest daughter was admitted to hospital with a swelling in her groin which burst spontaneously; no attempt was made to examine the morbid material bacteriologically. The neighbour's child was admitted to hospital for an emergency operation for acute abdominal trouble. The surgeon who operated found that 'the omentum and mesentery were full of enlarged glands, varying in size from a pea to a marble; the intestines were inflamed'. At the subsequent autopsy nothing to explain the condition was found and the inquest verdict was 'Peritonitis'. If anyone had taken the trouble to examine the swollen glands microscopically it is very probable that he would have found the bovine type of *Mycobacterium tuberculosis*. As a consequence

of subsequent official enquiries the surgeon expressed the belated opinion that the child died of bubonic plague.[1] This outbreak of communicable disease has been described in some detail because it is extremely doubtful whether—even during the height of the 'plague-terror' in the seventeenth century—any such outbreak has been identified in England as one of bubonic

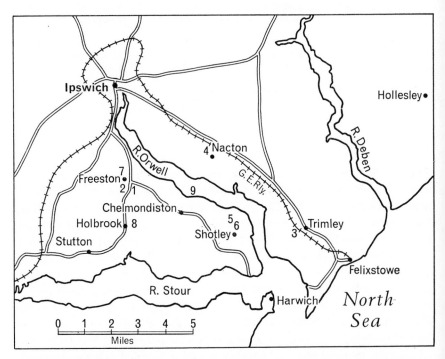

67. The epizootic of bubonic plague among field-rats and other rodents in 1906–7 and 1909–10. 1. Primary cases of human illness at Freeston. 2. Secondary case at Freeston. 3. Primary cases of human illness at Trimley. 4. Secondary case at Nacton. 5. Primary cases of human illness at Shotley. 6. Secondary cases at Shotley. 7. Wood at Freeston in which the first rat dead of plague was found. 8. Wood at Holbrook in which the first hare dead of plague was found. 9. Butterman's Bay, where large grain ships lighten before proceeding to the Ipswich Docks.

plague on flimsier evidence. It should be noted that *R. Norvegicus* is a natural carrier of the causal agent of typhus fever and that initially that agent is transmitted from the rat to man through the agency of a rat-flea, thereafter being transmitted from man to man by the body-louse. In a poverty-stricken, overcrowded dwelling swarming with fleas, it is practically certain that in 1910 the body-louse would also have been abundant. Moreover the history of bubonic plague in England almost conclusively excludes an outbreak of the disease in January, whereas that month was the preferential one for

typhus fever. Unfortunately medical history is not included in the medical curriculum in England; if it were some egregious diagnostic errors with respect to epidemic disease would be obviated.

It was in September 1910 that the deaths of 4 people from an acute pulmonary infection in the hamlet of Freeston (see figure 67) apparently first attracted the attention of the Health Department of the Local Government Board to East Suffolk and the consequent despatch of an official investigator to Freeston. The local medical practitioners diagnosed the outbreak as one of pneumonia secondary to some underlying and undiscovered primary infection, and bacteriological examination of specimens of sputum and blood failed to reveal the presence of *P. pestis*, which is easily cultivable and can be recognized under the microscope. However an official diagnosis of pneumonic plague was made by the investigator because there happened to be a concurrent epizootic of rat-plague among the field-rats in the district, although he expressed his amazement that pneumonic plague—the most highly infectious of all the *bacterial* diseases of man—had been confined to 4 persons, and that no case of bubonic plague had occurred among the individuals who had handled the many thousands of rats destroyed in the district without taking any precautions to protect themselves from plague.[1] The explanation of this immunity—and the utter nonsense of the diagnosis of pneumonic plague—was provided by the investigation of the epizootic by Martin and Rowland. They found that with the exception of a few water-rats (*Arvicola amphibius*), all the animals they examined were *R. Norvegicus*, and exhaustive enquiries among ratcatchers and gamekeepers disclosed that *R. rattus* was unknown to them. Moreover their examination of 1,065 fleas, collected from rats and rats' nests in the area, failed to yield a single specimen of *X. cheopis*; the commonest flea infesting the rats was *Ctenophthalmus agyrtes*, the natural host of which is the field-mouse and which does not bite man.[2] It seems probable that the Freeston outbreak was one of virus pneumonia complicated by a secondary bacterial infection of the damaged lung tissue; but if, as is quite possible under the circumstances, the family had been sleeping on straw contaminated with the spores of *Bacillus anthracis*, this fatal incident may have been an outbreak of pulmonary anthrax. This postulated diagnosis would explain its confinement to the family, and *B. anthracis* would almost certainly be overlooked by a laboratory technician in 1910 who was instructed to concentrate on finding *P. pestis*. Nevertheless the word 'plague' had been rumoured in connexion with human deaths, so when the Samford Rural District Council met on 13 October 1910, the clerk of the Board of Guardians 'reported that the medical superintendent of the county asylum at Melton had declined to take any pauper lunatic into the

asylum until he or she had been in quarantine for ten days. The guardians decided that it would be advisable to leave lunatics on the doorsteps of the asylum after the proper formalities had been gone through.'[1] Only bubonic plague could resurrect the mentality of the middle ages in twentieth-century England! Furthermore the word 'plague' had reached London in connexion with the deaths at Freeston, so understandably(?) the London merchants cancelled all their orders placed with the vegetable growers and nursery gardeners in Suffolk.[2] And these were not the only residents in that county who suffered severe financial losses, for the game and rabbit dealers, the poulterers, and the dairy farmers also found their metropolitan markets closed to them.[3]

As we are now obviously back in the seventeenth century, it is no surprise to find contemporary records of the grievous involvement of Norfolk in this last great English outbreak of bubonic plague. Yarmouth was one of the first places in England to be attacked on this occasion as plague is reported to have erupted there on 28 May 1665.[4] Contemporary records appear to be silent then about its visitation until mid-August, when plague was reported to be on the increase there.[5] It was evidently epidemic then as 96 plague-deaths were registered in a total of 117 deaths from all causes during the last week of August.[6] The next week 100 deaths were ascribed to plague in a total of 110,[7] a proportionate mortality which suggests that the epidemic reached its peak some time in September. The disease was still active in November as 22 plague-deaths were recorded on the 9th,[8] and 5 'plague-deaths' are said to have been notified there as late as 16 February.[9] These were either remote deaths from sequelae of the disease or more probably deaths from typhus fever; but whichever they were they signified the last flicker of bubonic plague in Yarmouth as the town was officially affirmed to be free from plague in March[10] and has remained so ever since. Cooper declares that 2,500 people died there in this epidemic, but he supplies no contemporary evidence to substantiate this figure.[11] Norwich seems to have escaped attack until the end of the summer of 1665, for there is a civic Bill of Mortality extant which dates its visitation to the twelve months from 3 October 1665 to 3 October 1666. During that period plague was officially credited with 2,251 deaths in a total mortality of 3,012,[12] a mortality-rate of 74·7 per cent. Owing to its introduction so late in the year it is unlikely that plague attained epidemic proportions in Norwich in 1665. A memorandum dated 9 November states that 19 plague-deaths had been registered in the city during the previous week,[13] and it is probable that December's toll was considerably smaller. Plague possibly maintained a sporadic activity in the

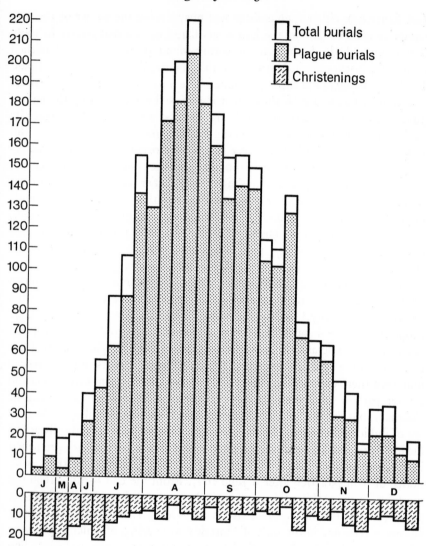

68. Plague deaths at Norwich, 1665–6. (Compiled from Bills of Mortality preserved in the *Calendar of State Papers Domestic, 1666–7*, CLXXXV, no. 5).

city during the succeeding winter months as figure 68 shows, for there were at least 13 alleged plague-deaths registered during January, and there is a report that 4 'plague-deaths' occurred in the city during the second half of February.[1] As 4 more were recorded in the first week of March and another 8 during the last three days of that month and the first four days of April

(see figure 68), either typhus fever was busy during the winter or the presumptive enzootic among the house-rats flared up unusually early in 1666. There seems little doubt that the spring found plague widely established among the house-rats in Norwich, so that the requisite foundation was laid for the epidemic in the ensuing summer. The initial speed of this epidemic is not known, but figure 68 shows that it was well established by the end of June, and that it raged through July and the first week of August to reach its peak in the third week of that month. During the peak week the civic Bill returned a plague death-roll of 203 in a total mortality of 220, a mortality-rate of practically 92·3 per cent. From this peak the epidemic declined slowly, manifesting, however, fluctuations in intensity that are not prominently shown in the mortality-curve. For instance one report from Norwich in mid-September reads: 'The sickness has been decreasing, but is increasing again, and there are thirty new houses.'[1] Three weeks later this reporter affirmed that plague was spreading rapidly again and invading many fresh houses,[2] and in the last week of October 58 plague-deaths were registered in the city.[3] During the first week in November its daily appearance in fresh houses aroused great alarm;[4] the next week it was responsible for 31 of the 46 deaths recorded in the city,[5] and in the week ending 24 November it killed 31 people.[6] Blomefield states that 699 plague-deaths occurred in Norwich this year, that the civic authorities expended £200 a week in relief, and that the total cost of the epidemic exceeded £8,000.[7] Plague appears to have become quiescent there early in December and to have lain dormant throughout the greater part of the winter. It may have stirred again towards the end of February, but the two 'plague-deaths' notified in the week ending 20 March[8] are of dubious accuracy. The disease seems to have been sporadically active during April and May as it was credited with 4 deaths in a total of 14 returned in the first week of June.[9] This was its last effort, however, for there is no notice of it in Norwich after 8 June 1667. From the end of June 1666 the mortality-curve of this epidemic is typical of an English epidemic of bubonic plague, except for the transient rise in mid-October. The total deaths from all causes returned in the Bills of Mortality were 2,895, of which 2,483 were officially ascribed to plague, giving a mortality-rate of 85·7 per cent. The rate for the four 'plague-months' of July–October was 75·5 per cent and the plague-burials in those months accounted for 88·0 per cent of the annual burials ascribed to the disease. It is evident from these figures that this epidemic was one of sustained virulence and probably one of the most destructive epidemics of disease ever experienced by the citizens of Norwich. The registered weekly christenings (see figure 68) outnumbered the burials on only two occasions during the twelve months of the epidemic. Neverthe-

less the epidemic did not extinguish human reproductivity in Norwich even at its peak, and there is not the slightest doubt that human reproduction was similarly maintained in every community in the British Isles however grievously the particular community was ravaged by bubonic plague. Undoubtedly the loss of life resulting from a severe visitation of plague was in some communities only repaired by a natural increase of population after many years; but in the worst hit life went on under the urge of biological forces that were stronger than the worst scourge of plague, and no community larger than a family was ever exterminated by the disease in the British Isles. Elsewhere in Norfolk King's Lynn was apparently invaded by plague towards the end of August 1665, because early in November a report stated that it had been present in the town for eight weeks and that 22 persons had died of it, though no plague death had been recorded there in the week ending 6 November.[1] If these were the only plague-deaths that happened there King's Lynn was fortunate to escape so lightly, but a comprehensive study of its parish registers might reveal a much more serious affliction.

The list of places in the Midlands named in contemporary records suggests that plague spread northwards from London along the main highways of traffic in seventeenth-century England. Although it is practically certain that Woburn was not the only place in Bedfordshire to be involved in this radial spread from London, no other place in the county appears to be mentioned in contemporary records. Thomson affirms that there were 40 plague-deaths at Woburn in two months in 1665 and that a number of the ducal retainers died of it. She quotes an entry in the ducal accounts relating to this visitation.

1665.—To nurses for their attendance on sundry of his lordship's servants in the time of their sickness and for the burials of some of them viz. of Thomas Bell, sickness, £5. 17. 6.; of John Harris and for his burial, 19.4,; and of Robert Scarborow and for his burial, 16s. 10d. In all, with 7s. 6d. for looking to John Keeper and Thomas Cole in their weakness, £8. 1. 2.[2]

If the inference to be drawn from these accounts is that 3 out of 5 of the Duke of Bedford's servants recovered from their attack of plague, either the strain of *P. pestis* which infected them was of subnormal virulence or the survivors were the fortunate possessors of remarkably robust constitutions.

In Hertfordshire Wheathampstead is said to have been attacked by plague in 1667 but no information is given about the severity of its visitation.[3] Farther north Ramsey in Huntingdonshire was attacked in 1666. Sweeting cites Burn 'as his authority for the statements that plague was imported in February in a parcel of cloth from London. He affirms that the tailor who made up the cloth and all his family died of the disease and that the subsequent epidemic destroyed more than 400 of the townsfolk.[4] If the disease

really invaded Ramsey in February it must have been confined to the tailor's household for many weeks, because the first plague-burial noted in the parish register was that of a woman who 'was buried in her own Garden' on 16 July.[1] It is much more probable that the parcel of cloth had nothing to do with the introduction of *P. pestis* to the tailor's household but was incriminated as an afterthought when that household was exterminated during the epidemic in the summer. Cox asserts that the parish register states that 400 of the townsfolk died of plague,[2] so presumably Sweeting added the adjective to cover an unspecified number of burials which he assumed were made in unconsecrated ground. Page comments that though Ramsey was heavily visited Huntingdon—18 miles to the south—seems to have escaped.[3] Huntingdon figures, however, in an interesting reference to the disinfection of mail in plague-time. On 14 August 1665 the postmaster there was instructed to forward certain letters after 'airing them over vinegar'. The instruction emanated from the man who at the time was apparently the equivalent of our modern Postmaster-General, because he remarked that the post office in London was 'so fumed morning and night' that the people in it could hardly see each other. 'But had the contagion been catching by letters', he added, 'they had been dead long ago...'[4] The practice of disinfecting mail in plague-time originated on the Continent. The date of its introduction to England is uncertain, but it was evidently well established here by 1665 as in that year the corporation of Cambridge ordered its post-boy 'to fume his letters' and then hand them to another official for delivery to their addressees.[5] The Bishop of Ely was evidently aware of the practice when he wrote to a friend in August 1665: 'If you think there is any danger from these papers, which you receive, the fire, I suppose, will expel it, if you let them see it before they come to your hands.'[6] Mail was not the only matter that was subjected to disinfection by fumigation, for houses and even persons were fumigated in plague-time. In the *Directions for the Cure of the Plague* issued by the College of Physicians in 1665, brimstone burnt plentifully in any room or workplace was recommended as 'effectually correcting the air',[7] and Worthington declared that this fumigation preserved his household in London from plague. 'To your enquiry about what outward means he used', he wrote to an acquaintance, 'this was all:—a little conserve of wood sorrel and London treacle, mixed together upon the point of a knife, we took first in the mornings, and twice a day we fumed the house with brimstone.'[8]

Still moving northwards, plague attacked Cambridge, Thorney, Ely, Peterborough, and Oundle in the east Midlands. Cambridge was scourged by it in 1665, as its toll of 413 burials (excluding those in St Giles's parish),[9] indicates. It was even more grievously afflicted in 1666, when 797 burials were regis-

tered in its parishes, not counting a number that occurred in St Giles's parish.[1] Cooper's statement that plague was prevalent there in August 1665 suggests that the disease probably appeared in the town some time in June, and on 1 September Sturbridge Fair was cancelled.[2] Eleven days later the corporation cancelled the public dinner held annually on Michaelmas Day,[2] and early in October the university passed a grace for its closure.[2] About the middle of the month the epidemic began to decline, for Josselin noted in his diary on the 27th that plague had 'much abated in Cambridge, Royston, and many other places'[3] in consequence of the arrival of cold weather on the 22nd.[4] Unfortunately this cold spell was neither sufficiently intense nor prolonged to force all the plague-fleas to hibernate and the disease accordingly continued to manifest a desultory activity for several more weeks. A Bill of Mortality for the fortnight 2–16 November records 19 plague-deaths—of which 4 occurred at the pest-house—in a total of 26 deaths from all causes.[5] In all probability the onset of persistent cold weather later in the month forced all the rat-fleas to hibernate, because there is no further notice of plague in Cambridge until the summer of 1666, and the announcement on 15 March that the university would reassemble, as there has been no plague death in the town during the preceding six weeks,[6] indicates that plague was quiescent during the winter. The visitation appears to have been confined to the town in 1665 because a note prefixed to the Bill of Mortality reads: 'All the Colleges (God be praised) are and have continued without any infection of the plague.'[7] Cooper remarks that 'amongst those who left the University on this occasion was the great Newton, who retired to his estate at Woolsthorpe, and there the fall of an apple from a tree suggested to him the principal of universal gravitation'.[8] Thomas Tusser could not have foreseen that an epidemic of bubonic plague would provide the stimulus for the enunciation of the Law of Gravitation when he wrote in his *Five Hundred Points of Good Husbandry*: 'It is an ill wind turns none to good.'[9]

Some time in the spring of 1666 the dormant disease recrudesced with augmented violence in Cambridge. During June two presumptive plague-burials were registered in St Michael's parish[10] and by mid-July plague had become so destructive that on the 18th 'Thomas Warren, the apothecary, living at the Golden Anchor and Hart in Basing Lane, was appointed by the University of Cambridge to receive contributions from Londoners for the relief of the plague-poor of Cambridge'.[11] By the end of the month there seems little doubt that plague was raging in Cambridge and on 3 August Sturbridge Fair was cancelled.[12] Simultaneously all public meetings in both university and town were prohibited and the Bishop of Ely cancelled all the fairs in his

diocese because of the involvement of Peterborough and Ely in this epidemic.[1] About this time also the corporation petitioned for an Act of Parliament authorizing it to enclose 40 acres of land in Coldham's Common in order 'there to erect such pest-houses as shall be thought fit, that place being most advantageous for water and other necessaries'.[2] The peak of this recurrent epidemic was probably reached towards the end of August as the register of St Michael's parish records 12 burials that month compared with 5 in September.[3] Venn says that one more burial was registered in that parish in February, making an annual total of 20, of which 85·0 per cent was contributed by the months of August and September.[3] Additional evidence of the severity of the epidemic in August is contained in a report on the 20th that plague was 'so sore at Cambridge' that the harvest could hardly be gathered, although labourers were being offered a weekly wage of 7*s.*, a rate that was at least double and possibly nearly treble the usual rate.[4] The registers of four of the Cambridge parishes also testify to the gravity of the epidemic. Sweeting reports that the register of All Saints contains a great number of entries of plague-burials between 20 July and 26 November; that there was an excessive mortality in St Benedict's parish—in the register of which many of the burials are marked ' + plauge'—and that the register of St Giles's parish includes 'The Burialls of the visited att the Green and att Ham from 23 June to 28 Nov.'.[5] This note evidently refers to deaths in the pest-houses, which Sweeting says amounted to between 30 and 40. The register of St Clement's parish records its first plague-burial on 31 July and this was succeeded by many more such burials between that date and October.[6] Most regrettably Sweeting did not consider it necessary to count the numbers of the total and the plague-burials in these registers, to which he evidently had access, because those figures would have been of much greater historical value than his general statements. Nevertheless his notes and other contemporary references leave no doubt that this protracted visitation was a calamity from which the town of Cambridge might never have fully recovered if it had not been the seat of a university. A loss of upwards of 1,200 inhabitants in two years from a population that cannot have exceeded 4,000 persons of all ages in 1665 would have permanently crippled many towns. 'It was January, 1667, before the Vice-Chancellor and the Heads of Houses notified that the scholars might return to the colleges.'[7]

Sweeting affirms that the mortality from plague at Thorney in 1666 was so great that no attempt was made to record the names of the dead in the parish register;[8] but unless the register contains specific contemporary notice to that effect, which he did not trouble to quote, his statement is of questionable value. The only reference to Ely's visitation is the note that has been quoted

of the bishop's cancellation of the fairs.[1] A report sent from the contiguous county on 20 August 1666 reads: 'In Northamptonshire the sickness rages extremely, especially in Peterborough, Oundle, and Newport Pagnell, in which last, though a market town, only 700 or 800 people are left.'[2] That market town certainly appears to have experienced a calamitous visitation because Cox states that its registered burials rose from 37 in 1665—apparently its annual average number of burials—to the appalling total of 697 in 1666.[3] The peak of the epidemic was reached in July, in which month 257 burials were registered.[3] According to Sweeting Peterborough suffered on this occasion the most destructive epidemic of disease in its history, with plague raging there intermittently for 20 months from the summer of 1665 to the spring of 1667. He remarks that there is a note in the cathedral register to the effect that the disease was supposed to have been brought from London by a woman and that the plague-burials are marked in the register with a cross. The first of these is dated 22 September 1665; the last is entered on 9 May 1667. 'As nearly as I can tabulate the deaths', he continues, 'I make out that there are no less than 462, besides some seven or eight victims buried in Dosthorpe not registered.'[4] For the first nine months of the visitation—until May 1666—there were comparatively few plague-burials (the maximum number in any one of those months was 11), but in June there were 57, in July 121, in August 97, in September 70, and in October 49. Although most of the plague-dead (351) were buried at the pest-house, 47 were buried in the yard, close, orchard, or garden attached to their homes, and others were interred in other situations. Only 12 were buried in the churchyard.[5]

Early in October 1665 a report from Buckinghamshire asserted that plague was active in 20 parishes in the county,[6] but unfortunately the parishes were not named. Parishes named as involved in this outburst of plague are High Wycombe, Great Hampden, Great and Little Marlow, Bletchley, Fenny Stratford, and Lavendon; but it seems probable that a comprehensive study of the registers of the county's parishes would disclose that other places in it were attacked in 1665 and 1666. Plague threatened Chalfont St Giles also, for the parish register records the burials of two supposed victims of the disease.[7] Fortunately the threat did not materialize, because it was to the presumptive safety of this rural parish that the blind Milton fled from the epidemic that was raging in London, and there that he wrote *Paradise Regained* and *Samson Agonistes*. Chalfont was indeed fortunate for 6 miles to the west High Wycombe was hard hit by plague. Jenkinson affirms that in 1665 plague was responsible for 96 of the 149 burials entered in the parish register of High Wycombe, and for 101 of the 144 burials in 1666;[8] but Downs quotes a note in the register which records only 68 plague-burials in

1665.[1] He asserts that the town had previously experienced severe outbreaks of plague in 1617, 1624, 1625, 1631, and 1632, when 'in every instance it was during the autumn that the plague raged so fearfully'.[1] The visitation in 1665 ran true to form, for he notes that the register specifically states that there was no burial in June that year. Plague erupted in the town in July and increased very rapidly in August to reach a peak in September. In all probability the disease lay dormant during the winter to recrudesce with increased violence in the spring of 1666. Downs reports that a note in the parish register of Little Marlow records that 50 victims of plague were buried in the parish in 1665, in which year Great Hampden and Great Marlow were also visited.[1] Bradbrook remarks that the annual burials registered in the parish of Bletchley up to 1732 usually numbered less than 20, and he estimates that its population in 1650 was about 900 and in 1680 about 780. In 1665 the registered burials numbered 126, a six-fold increase on the annual average. He notes that Watling Street, 'the great highway from London to Chester', ran through the Fenny Stratford end of the parish,[2] and there is little doubt that it was along this highway that *P. pestis* was carried from London to Bletchley. Undoubtedly there was frequent passage of bulky merchandise through the parish suitable for the hidden transport of *Rattus rattus* and its fleas, and it is probable that Bletchley was one of the recognized night halting-places for this traffic. Spilman states that the highway was temporarily diverted during Bletchley's visitation, that the inns of the parish were closed, and that the market was not held again for many years afterwards. She comments: 'The town has never recovered its former status.'[3] Lavendon possibly suffered proportionately more severely than Bletchley, for it was a sparsely populated rural parish in 1665 and either 66[4] or 76[5] burials were registered in it that year compared with an annual average of 10.[4] Bradbrook mentions that in the neighbouring and similar parish of Clifton Reynes two collections were made for the relief of the plague-stricken in Lavendon and that each realized 7s.[5] Continuing its travel along Watling Street, *P. pestis* called at the hamlet of Barton Segrave on its way across Northamptonshire, to effect one of those family tragedies of which it was a pastmaster by exterminating a household of 7 persons.[6] As Cox says nothing about an excessive number of burial entries in the parish register it seems probable that plague was restricted to this household.

In Warwickshire Warmington, Burton Dassett, and Wilnecote are reported to have been visited, and Hutton alleges that Birmingham was depopulated by an epidemic of plague in 1666.[7] Another local historian added the all too common horrific exaggerations to his imaginary account of this hypothetical epidemic.

The infection is said to have been brought to the town in a box of clothes by a carrier [he writes] and lodged at an inn called the White Hart. Thereupon followed the usual melancholy scenes which always attended the ravages of this terrible scourge. Houses were desolate; silence reigned in the streets; and on many doors appeared the fatal sign of the presence of the plague—a large red cross, and the words 'Lord have mercy upon this House'. The number of victims was so great that the churchyard was insufficient to contain them, and a large pit was dug on Lady-wood Green, an acre of waste land near the present church (St John's), which has since borne the name of 'The Pest Ground'.[1]

It is regrettable that neither of these local historians considered it necessary to examine the registers of Birmingham's parish church of St Martin before writing their fictitious and misleading accounts because, as figure 69 shows, there was no excessive mortality, commensurate with a depopulating epidemic of bubonic plague, in Birmingham in either 1665 or 1666. It is true that in the former year the registered burials were 75 per cent more numerous than the annual average (70) of the preceding decennium;[2] but an analysis of the monthly burials reveals no significant increase in mortality during the 'plague-months'. On the contrary the burials registered during the five months June–October constitute only 32·0 per cent of the annual total, whereas those registered in December and the three winter months comprise 53·0 per cent of that total. The cause of this excessive seasonal mortality is obscure. It could have been caused by an epidemic of typhus fever, which at that time would have been called 'plague', or by one of smallpox. As there is no entry in the burials register in June 1666, only the figures of the burials in the next four 'plague-months'[3] are available for analysis. Their total of registered burials constitutes 38·0 per cent of the annual total, and more than 43·0 per cent of their total of 46 burials were 'child' burials—a fact recorded in the register. As plague exhibits no selective age incidence for children, it was not responsible for this 'summer mortality' of children in Birmingham in 1666. The diseases most likely to have caused it are scarlet fever—if the summer was dry and dusty—or one of the enteric fevers in view of the abundance of carrion flies that would certainly be present. A contributor to the local newspaper who examined the parish burials register and realized that its record debunked the legend of a depopulating epidemic of plague in 1666, asserted that the churchyard was not used for the interment of the plague-dead. 'Neither could burials have taken place [in the churchyard] without being recorded,' he argues, 'as in that case a *hiatus* would have occurred [in the register] which does not exist. Those who died of ordinary diseases, then, would be buried in the Churchyard, and the victims of plague in the pest ground.'[4] I have been unable to find any evidence to support this hypothesis. The district of the alleged pest-ground has been extensively built-over—the

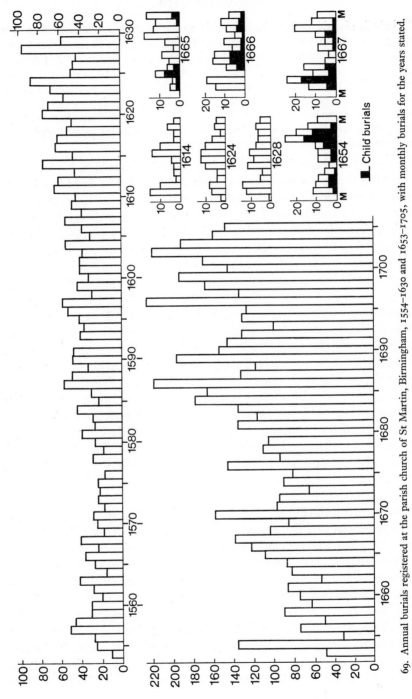

69. Annual burials registered at the parish church of St Martin, Birmingham, 1554–1630 and 1653–1705, with monthly burials for the years stated.

520

Children's Hospital most probably covers part of the supposed pest-ground —and many excavations have been made over the whole area in the course of erecting the buildings that now cover it, and by German bombs in the last war, without discovering to my knowledge any reported dump of human skeletons. It is possible that plague paid a visit to the *White Hart* in Birmingham in the summer of 1666 and that the terror its appearance there excited, assisted by rumour, and exaggerated by the 'Black Death' mentality of so many writers about bubonic plague, magnified the hostelry visitation into the tradition of a depopulating epidemic. No doubt there was a pest-house at Ladywood Green and that the corpses of those who died of plague there were buried in its vicinity; but there is no convincing evidence that it was used at all in either 1665 or 1666, at any rate for the reception of the plague-stricken. During the First World War the Germans dropped a few small high-explosive bombs from their Zeppelins one night upon the town of Hull. The morning after the raid, the newsboy who delivered our papers greeted my mother as she opened the door to him with the exclamation: 'They've flattened 'Ull, missus!' Birmingham is not the only English town to have been 'flattened' by bubonic plague in the pages of local historians whose imaginations excel their knowledge of its limitations.

The parishes of Warmington and Burton Dassett were as fortunate as Birmingham, for each appears to have had a near-escape from plague at this time. At the Warwickshire Epiphany Sessions in 1666 a resident of Arlescott in the parish of Warmington was granted a refund of the £5 which he had been compelled to pay 'for the burying of a person that was found dead of plague in the said parish'.[1] It seems evident that the victim was a stranger, possibly a fugitive from Bletchley. At these Sessions also, a parishioner of Burton Dassett was ordered to pay £6 to the parish constable, who had promised that sum to a gravedigger for burying the parishioner's mother and 2 of his children who had died of plague(?) in his house. As there is no further notice of plague—if indeed the disease was plague—in this parish, it is a reasonable supposition that it was confined to this one house. It could have been diphtheria. Also at this Sessions authority was given to levy a rate for the plague-stricken inhabitants of Wilnecote,[2] a village on Watling Street some 2¼ miles south of Tamworth and 3 miles north of Kingsbury. Wilnecote may have experienced a widespread outbreak on this occasion because a man who was lodging in a house there was, on his return to his home parish of Kingsbury, shut up 'with his wife and two children for the space of a month' by the parish constable 'by consent to most of the parish'.[3] The parishioners of Kingsbury were evidently not as willing to pay the bill for the segregation of this family as they were to agree to its segregation, and the question of who

was responsible for the expense was referred to the Michaelmas Sessions, at which the ruling was made that it must be shared by the parishioners.[1] Walsall was another fortunate place in 1665 as Willmore reports that the register of St Matthew's parish church records only one entry of a plague-burial this year,[2] that of a man who was most probably a fugitive from a plague-area.

Cooper quotes a report that Newark lost one-third of its inhabitants from an epidemic of plague that afflicted it in either 1665 or 1666;[3] but unless the report is confirmed by some future examination of its parish registers it may be only another of the legion of rumours that circulated in plague-time. Bell affirms that Derby suffered severely in 1666. 'The residents, with Eyam's example before them, mostly fled. Those who remained erected at Nun's Green, outside the town, a market stone or headless cross, whereon the market people from the country, coming with their mouths primed with tobacco as a disinfectant, left provisions.'[4] Incidentally he also reports that 'plague was in Bristol from the middle of April 1666, to September, when seventy-two persons died of it'.[5] The visitation of Derby has, however, been completely overshadowed in the English literature of plague by the calamity which the disease inflicted upon the little village of Eyam, some 27 miles north of the county town, which had a population of some 350 people in 1665 according to Wood,[6] who published a detailed account of the tragedy. He opines, and justifiably, that the visitation of Eyam was proportionately more destructive and desolating than that of any previously recorded epidemic of bubonic plague in England—and yet Eyam was not deserted by the survivors of the epidemic. He estimates that from the end of 1664 to December 1665 about one-sixth of the population of London was destroyed by plague, whereas at Eyam five-sixths of the population perished.[7] He expresses his justifiable surprise that this secluded village, tucked away from traffic among the foothills of the Peak District, should have been involved in the outburst of plague that originated in London 150 miles away. 'It is, however, most positively stated', he remarks, 'that this terrible disease was brought from London to Eyam in a box of old clothes, and some tailor's patterns in cloth, or other materials belonging to a tailor.'[8] Mead, the famous physician of the first half of the eighteenth century, who was supplied with an account of the visitation by George Mompesson, the son of the rector of Eyam, averred that the outbreak began in the house to which the box of tailor's materials was delivered and that the entire household died of plague with the exception of the mother.[9] There does seem to be a strong probability that in this instance. *P. pestis* was introduced to the house-rats of Eyam by 'blocked' fleas roosting in the box of tailor's materials because, as figure 70

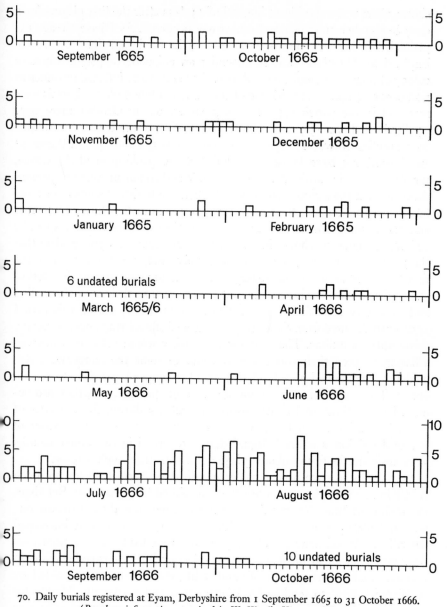

70. Daily burials registered at Eyam, Derbyshire from 1 September 1665 to 31 October 1666.
(*Based on information contained in W. Wood's History of Eyam.*)

shows, there was a significant interval of 14 days after the first plague-death on 7 September 1665 before the next one occurred. As I have already explained, this interval appears to have been the minimum time required in England for 'blocked' fleas to engender an epizootic of plague among a colony of house-rats, and for the fleas of those rats to be infected in sufficient numbers to generate an epidemic of the disease. Only 6 plague-burials were recorded in the parish register in September, but in October there were 29 distributed among 7 households. Twenty-four of these were contributed by 5 families, to wit, Thorpe 6, Sydall 6, Torre 5, Bands 4, and Ragge 3.[1] In November 5 fresh houses were infected and panic gripped the village, for plague usually subsided in the autumn. Wood comments that few persons dared to visit the stricken families and when the healthy members of those families ventured out of their houses they were shunned.[2] During December and the ensuing winter months plague continued to manifest a sporadic activity, as figure 70 shows, instead of lying dormant. It seems evident that though the autumn may have been unusually mild, the weather during the first two months of the succeeding spring was too cold among the Derbyshire hills to allow the hibernating rat-fleas to resume their normal breeding and predatory activities. The small number of deaths during this period apparently resulted from the activity of 'blocked' fleas living under especially favourable conditions. The cold spring weather would naturally cause the villagers to keep their cottages warm, and in some the temperature was evidently maintained at a level that enabled some plague-fleas to remain active. These conditions were not of course unique to Eyam; they had occurred many times in English towns and villages during the centuries of plague's activity in England, so that in many instances it is a matter of personal opinion whether 'plague' deaths recorded in the winter months were truly deaths from bubonic plague or deaths from typhus fever.

May seems to have been a colder month than April in Eyam, so much colder in fact that plague was nearly extinguished (see figure 70). But about the middle of June the arrival of warmer weather roused the lethargic rat-fleas and plague consequently recrudesced. 'Horror and dismay enveloped the village', Wood writes, 'and many persons were led to practise numerous weak and absurd expedients to prevent infection.'[3] These expedients would probably include the wearing of amulets like those 'it pleased a noble lady of Warwickshire' to send to Dr Worthington and his family. The doctor wrote in his diary: 'They were prepared and brought to me by a chemist near London, commended for a knowing and honest person (and he seemed to me to answer his character). His father and family in Germany were more than once preserved by these, under God's blessing, he said. They were done

up in little silk bags to a string, and so to fall as to be under the left pap.'[1] In other words to rest over the heart. They were designed to be worn so because the heart was believed to be the organ that was principally affected by plague. The doctor was chary of using the amulets, however, until the chemist revealed their nature to him—a dried toad. To his credit Worthington comments that he had 'no persuasion of any great good to come thereby[2].'

Up to the beginning of June 1666 the registered plague-deaths in Eyam totalled 77; during that month 19 were added.

It was at this period of the calamity [Wood notes] that the inhabitants began to think of escaping death by flight. Indeed, the most wealthy of them, who were but few in number, fled early in the spring with the greatest precipitation. Some few others, having means, fled to the neighbouring hills and dales, and there erected huts, where they remained until the approach of winter. But it was the visible manifestation of a determination in the whole mass to flee, that aroused Mompesson.[3]

The Rev. W. Mompesson, Rector of Eyam, was a man of high resolve and great moral and physical courage. Unfortunately he was completely ignorant of the nature of bubonic plague, so when he persuaded the villagers of Eyam to segregate themselves strictly in their village, he ensured that unique and optimal conditions were provided for the wellnigh ubiquitous dissemination of *P. pestis* in the village. If the villagers had evacuated Eyam at the end of June, when plague was manifesting rapidly increasing epidemic activity, it is certain that only a few more plague-deaths would have happened among them, due to the transport of some 'blocked' fleas in the clothes of some of the fugitives; and in the temporarily deserted village plague would have spontaneously died out with the extermination of the house-rat population and the death from starvation of their fleas. As it was, the rector's action was unwittingly responsible for the terrible mortality of the summer months. During those months 'every family, while any survived', Wood relates, 'buried its own dead; and one hapless woman, in the space of a few days... dug the graves for, and buried with her own hands, her husband and six children'.[4] Towards the end of June or early in July the rector closed the church for public worship and the churchyard for the reception of the plague-dead. Thereafter he conducted religious worship in the open air, using as a pulpit 'the Natural Rock, called "The Cucklett Church"',[5] while the victims of the epidemic were buried in the gardens and fields around the homes and in the soil they had known and loved in life. It is noteworthy that Wood makes no mention of the use of a communal pit for the disposal of the dead, because there is not the slightest doubt that such a method of indiscriminate interment of the corpses of kinsfolk and neighbours was abhorrent to the bulk of the people of seventeenth-century England. In all probability

plague-pits were only rarely dug in London and a few of the largest towns when the mortality was so great that the customary reverent method of individual burial could not cope with the rapid accumulation of corpses. A lot of nonsense has been written about alleged 'plague-pits' and traditional references to their existence should be treated with polite scepticism in connexion with epidemics of plague in small towns and villages. Wood avers that by the end of August nearly four-fifths of the population of Eyam had perished,[1] and one of the victims in this, the peak month of the epidemic, was Mrs Mompesson, the devoted wife of the rector. 'The sixth, twenty-sixth, and the last day of August, were the only days in that awful month', Wood laments, 'on which no one died, while the whole number who perished in the other twenty-eight days [was] seventy-seven. This number of deaths must be considered really appalling', he continues, 'especially when it is taken into estimation that the population of the village on the 1st of August was considerably under two hundred.'[2] As figure 70 shows, however, there was a fourth free day in August, the 29th, which he evidently overlooked when he extracted the daily record of burials from the parish register. He affirms that by the end of August the houses situated to the east of the middle of the village were nearly all empty.

The inhabitants of the extreme western part of the village, who were at that time very few, shut themselves close up in their houses, nor would they, on any occasion whatever, cross a small rivulet eastward, which runs under the street in that part of Eyam. That portion of the street which crosses this small stream is called to this day 'Fiddler's Bridge'; and it is very commonly asserted that plague never crossed it westward.[3]

He declares, however, that this tradition is not true; 'but as there were but few inhabitants in that direction, not many deaths could occur'.[4]

In September the epidemic began to decline, probably because the available rodent fuel was nearing exhaustion and the number of 'blocked' fleas was consequently growing smaller. Nevertheless a sufficient number remained alive and active at the end of the month to account for 14 deaths in the first ten days of October; but plague was extinguished during the second half of the month by a combination probably of cold weather and an insufficiency of both human and rodent material to sustain the predatory activities of the rat-fleas. In a letter dated 20 November the rector wrote:

There have been 76 families visited within my parish, out of which 259 persons died. Now (blessed be God) all our fears are over, for none have died of the plague since the eleventh of October, and the pest houses have been long empty...During this dreadful visitation, I have not had the least symptom of disease, nor had I ever

TABLE 46

Plague at Eyam in 1666: mortality records of eleven families

	Talbot	Buxton	Thorpe	Thornley	Lowe	Torre	Naylor	Neator	Mortin	Hancock	Frith
March	1	1									
April			1								
May			2								
June		1		6	1						
July	10		3	4	4	3	1	2	1		
August	2	2	1			1	3	3	5	7	8
September									2		3
October							1		3		

better health. My man had the distemper, and upon the appearance of a tumour I gave him some chemical antidotes, which operated, and after the rising broke he was very well.[1]

After stating that 'some few' of those who contracted plague recovered, he added: 'The winter which succeeded the cessation of the pestilence was, by the very few who were left, wholly spent in burning the furniture of the pest houses, and likewise nearly all the bedding and clothing found in the village: reserving scarcely anything to cover their nakedness.'[2] There is a slight discrepancy between the mortality figure given by the rector in his letter and that published by Wood in his history; but the rector was probably writing from memory, whereas Wood supplies the name of every victim and the date of burial. His total of plague deaths was composed of 137 males, 126 females, and 4 children whose sex is not specified.[3] This equalization of the sexes confirms the indiscriminatory sex incidence of bubonic plague; the preponderance of female victims in numerous English epidemics was simply due to the fact that the menfolk were frequently away from home by reason of their occupation. Thus in seaports, fishing-ports, and to a lesser extent in some agricultural communities, the women were more exposed to the attacks of 'blocked' fleas. Moreover *X. cheopis* is not a nocturnal predator like the bed-bug; it will bite at any time during the 24 hours, especially when it is hungry.

Accepting for the purpose the rector's mortality figure, each of the families attacked suffered an average loss of 3·4 members if *P. pestis* was evenly distributed among them; but its distribution was uneven, as the aetiology of the disease ensures, and therefore, as table 46 shows, 11 families supplied one-third of the deaths. It seems practically certain that 9 of these families were exterminated. The rector's statement that a few cases recovered, and his own exemption from plague, are observations of particular importance because they give the lie to assertions that bubonic plague depopulated English towns and villages. In this epidemic at Eyam bubonic plague was provided with a unique opportunity to depopulate a village, and the fact that at least one-quarter of the population of Eyam survived means that at least that proportion also survived the most malignant epidemic of the disease experienced by any English town, village, or hamlet. It is a cardinal mistake to regard this epidemic at Eyam as representative of local English epidemics of bubonic plague, for it is on the contrary unique in the English annals of the disease. Eyam was in fact for all practical purposes a segregated household in the summer of 1666 as far as plague was concerned, and the marvel is not that that household lost three-quarters of its members but that one-quarter survived. It is noteworthy that the rector was not the sole person to pass through the visitation unscathed, because it is a reasonable assump-

tion that the larger the population of the particular community attacked, the greater will be the number of individuals who are naturally antipathetic to *X. cheopis*. The historical lesson that Eyam's calamity teaches is that the popular instinct to flee from a plague-area offered the only effective individual protection against bubonic plague in seventeenth-century England, and there is no doubt that it was the free expression of the instinct that saved other places from sharing Eyam's fate. It is worthy of repeated emphasis that Eyam was not abandoned by its survivors because its continued habitation, after the most desolating visitation by plague in English history, makes the repeated allegations in historical writings that plague was responsible for the permanent abandonment of English villages an absurdity. With rare exceptions the ties that bound an Englishman to his home in rural areas were too strong to be broken by bubonic plague or any other epidemic disease in the days before the Industrial Revolution produced a population of urban dwellers with no stake or interest in their native soil. There is convincing evidence, however, that though plague was incapable of exterminating a village community, the panic terror it excited exerted an enduring psychological effect upon the survivors, their descendants, and even people not remotely connected to them. The name of Eyam is still used by writers of historical fiction to thrill their readers with horror, and after 300 years the tradition of its calamity is still preserved—mainly now for pecuniary purposes—in the village. When I visited Eyam some years ago several of the villagers independently pointed out to me the different cottages in which they assured me the visitation of 1665–6 started, and the visitor to Derbyshire is officially enjoined and expected to make a pilgrimage to its 'plague-village'. Incidentally it seems a pity that for the benefit of foreign visitors the villagers cannot agree upon 'the cottage' in which the visitation began. The rector's arm-chair is also carefully preserved in the parish church, and his name is justifiably remembered with pride, for though it is now known that he made a tragic mistake, he acted in good faith and with a noble purpose and set an example of faith and courageous devotion to duty of which the Church he served so well may rightly be proud. Moreover he was not wholly responsible for the disastrous decision to pen the villagers in the company of *P. pestis*. After plague recrudesced in the spring of 1666 he appealed for relief to the Earl of Devonshire at Chatsworth. That nobleman promised to do all in his power to help the villagers—'provided they kept themselves within a specified bound'.[1]

Travelling westwards along the Thames valley—probably by riverine portage—*P. pestis* approached Oxford towards the end of the summer of 1666. The city had evidently escaped involvement up to 16 October, because

on that date the Earl of Clarendon complained of the danger to Oxford of the unchecked spread of plague from London. 'Wee have reason to complayne of the ill government of the citty of London', he wrote to the Master of the Rolls, 'which, for want of shuttinge up infected houses, hath skattered the contagion over the kingdom... God knowes how longer we shall continue free, many villages aboute us beinge infected.'[1] As there is no contemporary notice of the presence of plague in Oxford this year, the city was presumably saved by the arrival of the autumn frosts and the consequent extinction of the disease in the neighbouring villages. Farther west Upton-on-Severn was attacked, apparently either in the late summer or early autumn of 1665, as a local diarist recorded that plague appeared that year in a household of which many members were destroyed by it and that it spread to 'divers others houses' in the town.[2] As Upton was a river-port at this time and the site of an important ferry, it seems likely that it was infected by a riverine importation of *P. pestis.*

Among the northern counties those on the east side of the Pennines seem to have been more extensively involved than those on the west side of that mountain range. Only three places on the west side—Chester, Liverpool, and Thursby—are mentioned in connexion with this national epidemic, whereas on the east side Beverley, North Frodingham, Bradford, Marske, Forcett, Sunderland, Monkwearmouth, Gateshead, Newcastle-upon-Tyne, and Tynemouth are reported to have been involved. Bell's assertion that 'the North of England generally save for a mild outbreak in Durham and Northumberland, escaped Plague. Lancashire was wholly free, and it is scarcely traceable in Yorkshire',[3] is not correct, especially as a study of the relevant parish registers may well reveal that more places were involved than those named in contemporary records; but it is one of the few mistakes he made in his masterly account of the last great visitation of bubonic plague in England. No record of Chester's mortality on this occasion appears to have been published, but a note in the register of the parish church of St Mary-on-the-Hill, which may have been made by an eye-witness, suggests that the city may have experienced a sharp outbreak of plague some time in 1665. This note reads: 'The plague takes them very strangely, strikes them black on the one side & then they run mad, some drown themselves, others would kill themselves, they dye within few hours, some run up & down in the streets in their shirts to the great horrour of those in the city.'[4] Moreover there is evidence provided by the public meeting of the burgesses of Liverpool that plague was active in Chester and other places in the county. At this meeting on 2 November the burgesses 'upon consideration and apprehension of the spreading contagion of the plague in divers neighbouring towns in

Cheshire and other parts', resolved to cancel the fair annually held in Liverpool on St Martin's Day (11 November) in order to prevent the customary influx of visitors.[1] Morley says nothing about an outbreak of plague in Liverpool on this occasion[2] and Axon affirms that the town escaped;[3] but until some local historian has confirmed its escape by a careful study of its parish registers the possibility remains that it was invaded some time in either 1665 or 1666 from one of the neighbouring infected townships. Wilmslow had in 1894 a solitary gravestone in a field as a memento of its fortunate escape from an outbreak of plague in 1665. Axon remarks that its presence is explained by this entry in the parish register: '1665, July. The 17th day was buried E...Stonaw, at her owne house, shee beinge suspected to dye of the plague, she but comeing home the day before.'[4] If Liverpool escaped on this occasion it was less fortunate in September 1901 when a young man was admitted to the Liverpool workhouse suffering with fever and buboes, and with a history of recent injury on the football field. The swollen glands were excised on 2 October and he died 24 hours later from 'septicaemia'. A post-mortem examination was made but 'no gross changes in any of the internal organs' were discovered. There was no suspicion of bubonic plague when the glands were sent for examination to a medical worker in University College, and it must have been an unpleasant shock to the workhouse surgeon when he was informed on 18 October that the glands were most probably plague-glands. Eight days later two certain cases of bubonic plague were notified to the public health authorities. The enquiries that were immediately instituted revealed that there had been several suspicious deaths in Liverpool about the end of September and early in October, although no connexion could be traced between them and that of the young man. 'Subsequent careful investigation, however, revealed the fact that four families living in the same locality, and having somewhat intimate relations with one another, had been invaded by illness.'[5] Bruce Low opines from their case histories and their associations that all these sick people were cases of bubonic plague, so that between 29 September and the end of October there were 11 cases of plague in Liverpool with 8 deaths,[6] a case-mortality rate of 72·7 per cent. Evidently *P. pestis* had lost none of its virulence after an absence of more than two centuries. The port and city were officially declared to be free from plague on 18 November. As an illustration of the care and attention which Bruce Low—a historian of epidemic diseases who has never been given the acclaim he merits—gave to the compilation of his reports, it is instructive to compare his account of this Liverpool visitation with the garbled and defective account of it published in *The Lancet*.[7] No evidence was obtained by the health authorities of the existence of plague among the local rats 'though

careful search was made not only in the invaded houses but throughout the city'.[1] The control measures, which have a certain savour of the seventeenth century, included the removal of the sick to the isolation hospital and the segregation of their contacts, who were, however, compensated for the loss of their personal effects and their absence from work. The infected houses were thoroughly disinfected, the paper stripped from the walls, and the bedding and clothing of the patients burnt. All the ashpits in the streets containing the infected houses were cleansed and disinfected and the drains and sewers were thoroughly flushed with powerful disinfectants. Destruction of rats everywhere in the city was energetically prosecuted. The day and Sunday schools in the affected area were closed for about three weeks.[2] As far as bubonic plague was concerned much of this activity was a waste of civic effort and public money, though it undoubtedly improved—temporarily at any rate—the sanitary state of that particular area of Liverpool. The stripping of the wallpaper for instance very probably resulted in the discovery and destruction of bed-bugs, and the cleansing of the ash-pits undoubtedly rendered the circumambient air less malodorous. The port authorities also acted with equal zeal and misguided vigour to abolish plague, and Bruce Low describes in detail the methods they employed.[3]

Why did Liverpool escape so lightly on this occasion? Simply because *R. Norvegicus* was the predominant rat in both port and city. Bruce Low records that of the rats caught and examined in the Port of London from 1901 to 1912 inclusive, a number in excess of 794,000, about 20 per cent were *R. rattus*, about 75 per cent were *R. Norvegicus*, and the remainder were *R. alexandrinus*.[4] A similar, possibly greater preponderance of the field-rat occurred in Liverpool for, as a young bacteriologist on the staff of the Public Health Bacteriological Department of the city, my first duty each morning was to examine for plague the carcases of several hundred rats that had been caught the day before by the city rat-catchers, and in the two years 1923–5 I never encountered a specimen of *R. rattus*.

Nothing was seen of the human disease in Liverpool after its disappearance in October 1901 until it reappeared in a characteristic household outbreak in July 1914, during which month 10 cases were notified, 4 of which were fatal. Nine of the cases were members of one family, while the tenth was a little boy who frequently visited the house to play with the children there. Bruce Low reports that no infected rats were found in the house, but it was swarming with fleas and all the surviving members of the household showed extensive signs of recent flea attacks. He notes that during the year 13,868 rats were destroyed in the city and 77,460 in the port. No plague-infected animal was found among 3,430 which were examined bacteriologically.[5]

The parish of Thursby, some 4 miles south-west of Carlisle, was undoubtedly invaded by plague in the summer of 1665 because its register
contains the appended record of collections that were made for the relief of
its plague-stricken people:

> Aug: 3 Collected yis day for ye people visit wt pest 5s.
> Aug: 6 Collected for floohbing 8 grots.
> Sept 6 Collected for ye people visit wt ye pest 5s.[1]

The meaning of 'floohbing' is obscure. An editorial note suggests that it is
a misspelling of Flookburgh, a hamlet some 2 miles south of Cartmel in
Furness.

Beverley was apparently one of those fortunate places where plague was
confined to a single household, for although the disease was reported to have
appeared there in August, 1665[2] there is no record of its epidemic activity
in the town either in 1665 or 1666. A certificate that North Frodingham was
free from plague was issued by the mayor of Beverley on 10 March 1665.[2]
Some time prior to the issue of this certificate a Holderness man reported to
the chief constable of the bailiwick, who resided in Beverley, that 14 persons
had recently died of plague at North Frodingham within 10 days. 'Whereupon', records the mayor,

> I gave order [to] the watch that none of that place might have entrance within us;
> yesterday came a young man from thence with a sickman's water to one James
> Bowman a Chirurgeon [of] our towne; but was denied entrance by the watch not-
> withstanding Bowman [having] intelligence the young man was at the townes end,
> ordered his servant to take the water of him and bring it to him which was donn—
> as soone as I had intelligence thereof [I] went down to Bowman's house and
> appointed him to keepe [his house] and that none of his family should come forth
> nor receive any into his house upon any occasion whatsoever untill further order
> which he promised he would observe, but he forgetting or sleighting his promise he
> presently opened his doore which was before shut up and permitted some to goe
> into his house upon which immediately I set a watch on the foreside and back side
> of the house.[3]

Evidently Lilly was not the only practitioner of urinoscopy in the England
of Charles II. No information is available about the length of time the surgeon
and his family were imprisoned in their house because he was dutiful enough
to agree to examine a sample of urine from a sick man, who was living some
9 miles away, and who may have been suffering from any disease other than
bubonic plague; but it is quite likely that they were imprisoned for 40 days.
The moral of this record seems to be that it was dangerous to make water
in plague-time.

If both Marske and Forcett escaped a visitation from plague at this time the North Riding magistrates doubtless congratulated themselves on the prompt and effective action they took to protect those hamlets. At the Sessions held at Richmond on 8 August 1665 they made an order 'that six men of Marske do diligently from time to time, day and night, at, namely, two of the night and one of the day, for forty days now next coming, at the proper charge of Geo. Mason of Marske, and after the direction of the Constable, keep a strict and careful watch at the door and house of the said Geo. Mason to the end that none of his present family mix themselves or have any society with any other family or families or people during the aforesaid forty days, by reason of the great fear of the persons received by the said Geo. Mason lately come from the city of London'.[1] Eight Forcett men were similarly ordered to watch the houses of Ann Firbancke and Timothy Iveson, who had each given shelter to fugitives from London. One feels that it was adding insult to injury to charge Geo. Mason with the expense of having his house segregated and watched for the public safety; but equity, liberty, and common sense ceased to exist in the presence of the merest threat of plague in Stuart England.

About the middle of July 1665 a report from Durham stated that there were then 7 plague-infected houses in Sunderland, 1 in Monkwearmouth, and 1 in Durham City, 'where', added the reporter, 'there is great fear because of the resort of persons from London'.[2] Surtees is almost certainly correct in his assertion that plague was imported into the county by shipping, especially if his additional note is correct that it was 'providentially confined to a very few individuals in the Port of Sunderland'.[3] It is probable that this port was infected by coastal shipping coming from one of the East Anglian ports rather than directly from London. He states that the parish register of Gateshead records a number of plague-burials in 1665 and that some of the victims were buried in the churchyard. Unfortunately he did not count the number of these burials, but as the first occurred on 31 July and the last on 21 September[4] they may not have exceeded 50. The report at the end of January that two houses were segregated in Gateshead[5] represents more probably a slight activity of typhus fever rather than a persistence of bubonic plague in the town. Newcastle seems to have escaped lightly from the plague's northward travel. Early in November Durham City was asserted to be healthy although another house had been infected[6] since the previous report,[7] which had included the news that two houses were then segregated in Newcastle. As there do not appear to be any more notices of plague in either Durham or Newcastle it seems reasonable to assume that neither experienced an epidemic of plague in either 1665 or 1666. According to the parish register of

Tynemouth 2 unrelated victims of plague were buried simultaneously on 4 February 1665, and Adamson also quotes a marginal note in the register which reads: 'The sickness was discovered ye 4th of ffebr., only 14 psons yt died of it from yt time untill & with March ye 4th.'[1] It seems most probable, in view of its seasonal incidence and the latitude of Tynemouth, that this was an outbreak of typhus fever.

There is a reference to the activity of bubonic plague in Wales at this time in the *Bronwydd Documents*. It reads: 'The said markett was discontinued at Newport for and by meanes of the sickness in or about ye year 1665, for that the said sickness being at yt time by reason of the many inhabitants at Newport very contagious and fatall there, the markett was...removed into Fishguard and has ever since been kept at Fishguard...'[2] It is evident from this record that Newport was involved in this last national outburst of bubonic plague and it seems probable that it sustained a heavy mortality. Possibly the borough archives or the parish register will provide some future local historian of Newport with information about the town's death-roll on this occasion and enable him to assess its effect upon the social and economic life of the town. Bubonic plague visited Wales once again at Cardiff in 1900. The chain of events that culminated in its eruption there explains the ancient terror of a disease which did not obey the laws governing the spread of other communicable diseases with which the peoples of the British Isles were familiar. On 22 September 1900 the S.S. *South Garth* arrived at South Shields from Rosario with a cargo of grain, having called on the way at King's Lynn, where some of the cargo was presumably landed as the ship remained 8 days in that port. The crew were paid off at South Shields on the 24th and one of its members—who had been taken ill on the 20th, the day the ship sailed from King's Lynn—consulted next day a medical practitioner in South Shields who diagnosed 'malaria'. Probably reassured by this diagnosis the man travelled by train to his home in Llandaff. There he consulted another doctor who suspected plague and sent him on 2 October into hospital in Cardiff, where he died on the 4th. At the subsequent autopsy an inguinal bubo was discovered. Bruce Low comments that there was no history of dead rats having been found on board the *South Garth* throughout the voyage. On 27 January 1901 a workman in a flour mill adjoining the docks in Cardiff developed plague and died on the 31st. About a fortnight before he was taken ill 'it was noted that rats had been dying in some numbers in and around the mill, and deceased had handled some of the dead animals, conveying them to be destroyed in the mill's boiler furnace'.[3] An unusual rat-mortality was also noticed about this time at another flour mill and granary in the same dock. *P. pestis* was isolated from the carcase of a dead rat from the

first mill, the owners of which counted 49 dead rats in it in a fortnight. Also 'fleas were observed in considerable numbers on the white flour sacks in the warehouse'.[1] The corporation of Cardiff reacted promptly and sensibly to the threat revealed by these findings. It doubled its staff of official rat-catchers from 3 to 6 and advertised publicly that it would pay a fee of 4*d.* 'for every rat guaranteed to have been caught within the borough or port sanitary district and delivered at the corporation depot'.[1] The Port Sanitary Authority added a regulation making it obligatory for every ship arriving from a plague-infected or suspect place to keep an experienced rat-catcher on board while it was in the port.[1] If the rats in Cardiff in 1900 had been predominantly *R. rattus* there would have been an outbreak of bubonic plague in the city in spite of the efforts of the municipal authorities. Fortunately the predominant rat there then, as in Glasgow and Liverpool, was *R. Norvegicus* which, though it is rightly regarded as a most destructive and dangerous pest, yet has a slender claim upon our gratitude for the part it has played and still plays in keeping twentieth-century England free from epidemic bubonic plague.

There are a few notices of plague in England after 1666, but in each case the activity of the disease appears to have been feeble and short-lived, most probably because the existing strain of *P. pestis* had lost most of its pristine virulence, and there are no records of the 'trailer' outbreaks that had previously followed a major outburst of the disease. Creighton remarks that 'the history of plague in England must be made to end with a solitary epidemic at Nottingham in 1667, but not without some misgivings as to the date'.[2] Time has shown that this affirmation is not strictly accurate, and John Allin is more explicit about the last flicker of the disease at Nottingham. He affirms that Nottingham was free from plague in 1665, when 149 burials were registered there. There were 180 in 1666 and in 1667, with a visitation of plague which was 'not heavy', the number rose to 219, most of the deaths occurring in August.[3] In March 1667 it was reported that 'the sickness' had broken out at Burlington, a hamlet in east Shropshire 3 miles north-east of Shifnal;[4] but as there is no further notice of this outbreak it was probably confined to a single household or, as it occurred in March, it may have been a domiciliary spark of typhus fever. About a month after this report one from Norwich mentioned that 'only two' persons had died of plague in that city during the third week in March.[5] A reasonable inference from the wording of this report would seem to be that there had been a heavier mortality from plague—or from the disease confused with it, typhus fever—earlier in the winter. However, as a second report early in July stated that 4 plague-deaths were included in the 14 deaths from all causes returned in the Norwich

Bill of Mortality for that week,[1] it may be that plague maintained an intermittent, sporadic activity there from the subsidence of the epidemic of 1666 until the autumn of 1667. Plague may have lingered in some places in the fen country—emulating the legendary exploits of Hereward the Wake—for some time after it disappeared from the rest of England. It certainly seems to have recrudesced feebly at Peterborough in April 1667.[2] The corporation of Salisbury was apparently satisfied in 1668 that that city need fear no more visitations of plague, for on 16 May it ordered 'the pesthouse to be taken downe and the brick and materials, or the house itselfe as it stands, to be solde'.[3] It would possibly have postponed that order if it had known that in Pembury St Peter, in the diocese of Rochester, there died of 'ye sickness Benge and his wife and two daughters, John Sisby and his wife of Yalden, buried in the backsides'.[4] The last deaths from bubonic plague in seventeenth-century England of which I have knowledge occurred in August 1671, when two plague-deaths were registered in the parish of Redriff (Redruth) in Cornwall.[5]

As a medical graduate I may perhaps be excused by professional historians for ending this history of bubonic plague in the British Isles with the petition of Nicholas Butler to Charles II on 21 February 1670 'for a *mandamus* to Cambridge University for the Degree of Doctor of Physic'.[6] In support of his plea Butler stated that he had been engaged in medical practice for some years, having received his licence to practise from the Archbishop of Canterbury. During the epidemic of 1665 he had remained constantly in London and, in addition to treating patients of better quality, he had supplied medicines free to 200 or 300 of the meaner sort daily, very few of whom had 'miscarried' under his care. He presented in confirmation of his statement a certificate signed by John Jollife and seven other citizens of London to the effect that he had continued to reside in the parish of St Helen when almost all the other physicians in the city had retired into the country, and that during the epidemic he freely administered medicines which restored great numbers of people. He added a second certificate signed by Sir John Laurence, in which the lord mayor affirmed that during his mayoralty 'the above matter was reported to him for truth by some of the persons named, and he then gave, and still gives, credit to it'.[7]

It is pleasant to be able to record that a month later the king recommended to the Vice-Chancellor and Convocation of Cambridge University that Nicholas Butler should be given the degree of M.D. without being required to perform the customary exercises.[8] It is to be hoped that the university implemented the royal recommendation, for Nicholas Butler appears to have been one of that noble band, who

when the sickness was sore in the land,
    And neither planet nor herb assuaged,
They took their lives in their lancet-hand
    And, oh, what a wonderful war they waged!
Yes, when the crosses were chalked on the door—
    Yes, when the terrible dead-cart rolled,
Excellent courage our fathers bore—
    Excellent heart had our fathers of old.
        None too learned, but nobly bold,
        Into the fight went our fathers of old.[1]

RULES AND ORDERS, 1666 (see above p. 485)

1 No stranger was to be allowed to enter a town unless he was provided with a certificate of health.
2 No furniture was to be removed from any infected house.
3 No public gatherings (Funerals, Wakes, or Revels), were to be permitted.
4 No beggars were to be tolerated, and all public places must be kept clean.
5 All houses were to be cleaned.
6 Fires must be kept burning in all houses.
7 Unwholesome food must be destroyed.
8 Animals [presumably including the domestic animals as well as pets], were to be excluded from infected streets.
9 A strict limitation of ale-houses and similar places was to be enforced.
10 A pest-house was to be erected in readiness in every town, and sworn searchers were to be appointed.
11 Every infected house was to be marked with a red cross and an inscription, and must be segregated for 40 days.
12 A white cross was to be placed on each house at the expiration of its period of segregation, and retained in position for 20 days.
13 Plague-pits were to be boarded to a height of 10 feet, and unslaked lime was to be put into them. Graves [presumably only those containing plague-corpses] were not to be opened for one year.
14 Rates were to be levied for plague-relief.
15 An account of every measure executed by a local authority must be kept.
16 Monthly fasts and prayers on Wednesday and Friday were to be maintained, as enjoined in the proclamation of 6 July 1665.

Rules and Orders To be observed, by all Justices of Peace, Mayors, Bayliffs, and other Officers, for prevention of the spreading of the Infection of the Plague. Published by Proclamation by Order of the Government, May 11, 1665.

APPENDIX II (see above p. 393)

Bubonic plague is the deadliest of all *bacterial* diseases to the expectant mother and her unborn child. In 1665 'one of the most deplorable cases in the calamity [in London] was that of women with child, whom, when their pains came on, could neither have help of one kind or another; neither midwife nor neighbouring women to come near them; most of the midwives, especially those who served the poor, were dead, all those of note were fled; so that a woman who could not pay an immoderate price could get no midwife; those who were to be had were generally

unskilful, ignorant pretenders; the consequence of which was, that a most unusual and incredible number of women were reduced to the utmost distress. Some were delivered and spoiled by rashness and ignorance: children without number were murdered, by pretending to save the mother, when frequently both were lost. Where the mother had the distemper, nobody would come near them, and both most commonly perished: sometimes the mother died of the plague, and the infant half born, or born, but not parted from the mother; some died in the pangs of travail, not delivered at all.'

'The unusual number in the weekly bill (though far from exact) under the articles of childbed, abortive, and still-born, will evidence the distress:

In the year 1664, there were buried,

Abortive and still-born	458
Childbed	189
	647

In the year 1665, there were buried,

Abortive and still-born	617
Childbed	625
	1242

The inequality is exceedingly augmented when the disparity of the numbers of the people are considered.'

An Historical Narrative of the Great Plague at London, 1665, Anonymous (London, 1769), pages 395–6.

APPENDIX III (*see above p. 532*)

In 1902, more than two centuries after the *Rules and Orders* in Appendix I were promulgated, the Local Government Board, acting for the British government, issued the appended anti-plague measures for adoption by local authorities. It is a noteworthy achievement on the part of bubonic plague and its 'Black Death' halo that the essence of the earlier orders still clings to these.

1. Notification of all cases of plague or suspected plague to the Local Authority, and to the Local Government Board.

2. Verification of the diagnosis by an expert bacteriologist, if a sample of material from the patient is forwarded by the Medical Officer of Health to the Board.

3. Isolation of cases in hospital to be provided by the Local Authority.

4. Segregation of contacts in 'shelters' to be provided by the Local Authority, where observation for 10 days can be carried out.

5. Disinfection of infected clothing, bedding, and effects to be carried out by the Local Authority, as well as disinfection of infected houses.

6. Inoculation by Haffkine's prophylactic fluid to be offered to all whose duty has brought them into personal relations with actual plague.

7. Special inspection of Common Lodging-Houses; to observe the health of the inmates, and to detect any cases of suspicious illness among tramps and others, and to secure the removal of overcrowding, and other unhealthy conditions.

8. Warning of all local medical men, and especially medical officers of hospitals and Poor Law Infirmaries, as to the possibility of mild plague cases applying for treatment.

9. Destruction of rats to be carried out, and careful watch to be kept for evidence of unusual mortality among those animals.

10. Increased efforts for removal of nuisances of all kinds, and for the amelioration of all unwholesome conditions likely to foster the spread of infection, such as overcrowding, deficient ventilation, dirt, and squalor.

11. Should actual plague occur, a house to house visitation of the immediate neighbourhood to be carried out.

Reports and Papers on Bubonic Plague, with an Introduction by the Medical Officer of the Local Government Board, by R. Bruce Low, Local Government Board (London, 1902), pp. 37–8.

ABBREVIATIONS

APC	*Acts of the Privy Council of England*
Bell	Bell, W. G., *The great plague in London in 1665*, London, 1924
Birch	Birch, T., *The court and times of Charles I*, London, 1849
Blomefield	Blomefield, F., *The history of the city and county of Norwich*, Fersfield, 1741
CARD	*Calendar of the Ancient Records of Dublin*, ed. J. T. Gilbert, Dublin, 1891–4
CCR	*Calendar of the Close Rolls*
Cooper	Cooper, C. H., *Annals of Cambridge*, Cambridge, 1842
Cox	Cox, J. C., *The Parish Registers of England*, London, 1910
CPR	*Calendar of the Patent Rolls*
Creighton,	Creighton, C., *A History of Epidemics in Britain*, Cambridge, 1894
ERBE	*Extracts from the Records of the Burgh of Edinburgh*
Fabyan	Fabyan, R., *The New Chronicles of England and France, in Two Parts*, reprinted from Pynson's Edition of 1516, ed. H. Ellis, London, 1811
FM	*Annals of the kingdom of Ireland by the Four Masters*, translated J. O'Donovan, Dublin, 1856
Grafton	Grafton, R., *A Chronicle at Large, and meere History of the Affayres of England, and Kings of the same*, London, 1569
HLP	Hand-list of Proclamations, Crawford, *Bibliotheca Lindesiana*, I, Aberdeen University Press, 1893
HMC	Historical Manuscripts Commission
Kelly	Kelly, W., 'Visitations of the Plague at Leicester', *Transactions of of the Royal Historical Society*, VI, London, 1877
LPH	*Letters and Papers, Foreign and Domestic, of the Reign of Henry VIII*
Lunn	Lunn, J., *The Black Death in the Bishops' Registers* (References to this work cannot be paginated because the author is unable to supply the version which he kindly lent to me originally)
NQ	*Notes and Queries*
PCS	*Register of the Privy Council of Scotland*
Pickard	Pickard, R., *The Population and Epidemics of Exeter in Pre-Census Times*, Exeter, 1947
PMV	*Calendar of the State Papers and Manuscripts, relating to English Affairs, existing in the Archives and Collections of Venice, and other Libraries in Northern Italy*
Remenbrancia	*Analytical Index to the Series of Records known as the Remenbrancia. Preserved among the Archives of the City of London*

Abbreviations

SHH	*Calendar of the Manuscripts of the Most Honourable the Marquis of Salisbury, K.G., preserved at Hatfield House, Hertfordshire*, ed. M. S. Guiseppi, published by the Historical Manuscripts Commission.
Short	Short, T., *A General Chronological History of the Air, Weather, Seasons, Meteors, Etc.*, London, 1749
SPD	*Calendar of State Papers, Domestic Series*
Stow	Stow, J. and Howes, E., *The Annals, or Generall Chronicle of England*, London, 1631
TSP	A Bibliography of the Royal Proclamations of the Tudor and Stuart Sovereigns, *Bibliotheca Lindesiana*, v, Oxford, 1910
VCH	*The Victoria History of England*
Ware	Ware, Sir J., *The History and Antiquities of Ireland*, London, 1705
Wilson	Wilson, F. P., *The Plague in Shakepeares' London*, Oxford, 1963

REFERENCES

PAGE 4
1 L. F. Hirst, *Brit. Encycl. Med. Pract.* IX, 678–9.

PAGE 7
1 R. A. Donaldson, *The Rat*, p. 4.
2 T. Wright, *Anglo-Saxon and Old English vocabularies*, 2nd ed., R. P. Wulcker, I, 119.
3 M. A. C. Hinton, *Rats and mice as enemies of mankind*, especially pp. 3–8.

PAGE 9
1 P. S. Pallas, *Voyages de M.P.S. Pallas, en différente Provinces de l'Empire de Russie, et dans l'Asie septentrionale: traduits de l'Allemand par M. Gaulthier de la Peyronie*, I, 481.
2 P. S. Pallas, *Travels through the Southern Provinces of the Russian Empire in the years 1793 and 1795*, trans. from the German, I, 48.
3 *Ibid.* I, 105.
4 Donaldson, *The rat*, pp. 7–10.

PAGE 10
1 Rev. J. G. Wood, *Bible animals*, 311.
2 Sir G. De Beer, *Alps and elephants*, p. 93.
3 C. P. Bryan, *The Papyrus Ebers*, pp. 163–6.
4 E. Robertson, 'Early navigation: its extent and importance', *Bull. John Rylands Library*, XXIV, 296.
5 Wood, *Bible animals*, 94–6.

PAGE 11
1 L. F. Hirst, *The conquest of plague*, p. 10.
2 Sir J. Arthur Thomson, *The outline of natural history*, p. 75.
3 Hinton, *Rats and mice as enemies of mankind*, p. 4.
4 Sir E. Sullivan, 'The Book of Kells', *The Studio* (1914), pp. 11 ff.
5 J. Hooper, 'Host eaten by mice', *NQ*, XII, 263.

PAGE 12
1 J. W. Holmes, *Bacillary and rickettsial infections*, p. 13.
2 R. S. R. Fitter, *London's natural history*, p. 59.
3 'The Pardoner's Tale', *The Canterbury Tales*, trans. Nevill Coghill, p. 279.
4 G. de Barry, 'Typographia Hibernica, et Expugnatio Hibernica', ed. J. F. Dimock, in *Giraldi Cambrensis Opera*, ed. J. S. Brewer, V, 61.
5 *Idem*, 'Distinctio Secundo de Mirabilibus Hiberniae et Miraculis', *ibid.* V. 120.
6 *Idem*, 'Itinerarium Kambriae', *ibid.* VI, 110.

References

PAGE 13

1 C. B. Moffat, 'The mammals of Ireland', *Proc. Roy. Irish Acad.* XLIV (1938), 94.
2 H. D. Traill and J. S. Mann, *Social England*, II, xlviii.
3 'The vision of the field full of folk', *Piers Plowman*, ed. A. Burrell, p. 9.
4 R. Higden, *Polychronicon Ranulphi Higden Monachi Cestrensis*, ed. C. A. Babington, V, 119.
5 *Ecclesiastical history of England*, trans. J. A. Giles, p. 185.
6 J. F. Olliffe, 'Reflections on the treatment of variola by the "Ectrotic method"', *The Lancet*, i (1840–1), 676.

PAGE 14

1 A. Boorde, *A Compendyous Regyment or a Dyetary of Helth made in Mountpyllier by Andrewe Boorde of Physycke Doctor*, ed. F. J. Turnivall, p. 249.
2 W. G. Bell, *The great plague of London in 1665*, p. 10.
3 J. C. Cox, *Churchwardens' accounts from the fourteenth century to the close of the seventeenth century*, p. 307.

PAGE 15

1 'Franciscus', 'Payments for the destruction of vermin', *NQ*, I, 447–8.
2 Cox, *Churchwardens' accounts*, p. 298.
3 R. Crawfurd, *Plague and pestilence in literature and art*, p. 13.
4 Wu Lien-Teh *et al. Plague*, p. 223.
5 D. Zabolotny, 'Études épidémiologiques: 1. l'origine de la peste endémique', *Ann. Inst. Pasteur*, XXXVII, 624.

PAGE 16

1 R. Bruce Low, 'The progress and diffusion of plague, cholera and yellow fever throughout the world, 1914–17', *Rep. Pub. Health and Med. Subjects*, p. 96.

PAGE 17

1 Rufus of Ephesus, *Œuvres d'Oribase*, French trans. Bussemaker and Daremberg, III, 607–8.
2 F. H. Garrison, *An introduction to the history of medicine*, p. 100.

PAGE 18

1 E. Gibbon, *The decline and fall of the Roman Empire*, I, 55.
2 W. J. Simpson, *A treatise of plague*, p. 3.
3 Procopius, *History of the wars*, trans. H. B. Dewing, I, 457–67.
4 Evagrius, *The history of the church*, trans. from the edition of Valesius, pp. 490–1.
5 F. G. Clemow, *The geography of disease*, p. 315.
6 H. Pirenne, *Mohammed and Charlemagne*, p. 95.

PAGE 19

1 Gregory of Tours, *The history of the Franks*, trans. O. M. Dalton, II, 119.
2 Simpson, *A treatise of plague*, p. 12.

3 Paul the Deacon, *History of the Langobards*, trans. W. D. Foulke, pp. 56–7.
4 Gregory of Tours, II, 600. 5 *Ibid.* 516.
6 *Ibid.* 141. 7 *Ibid.* 395.
8 Procopius, p. 57. 9 Simpson, footnote 17.
10 H. E. Sigerist, 'Problems of historical-geographical pathology', *Bull. Inst. Hist. Med.* I (1933), 17.

PAGE 20

1 W. Bonser, *The medical background of Anglo-Saxon England*, p. 59.
2 *Annals of Ulster*, ed. W. M. Hennessy, I, 49.
3 Sir W. Wilde, *The census of Ireland for the year 1851*, I, 416.
4 *Annals of Clonmacnoise*, ed. Rev. D. Murphy, p. 84.
5 *Annals of Ulster*, I, 55. 6 *Annals of Clonmacnoise*, p. 89.
7 *Annals of Ulster*, I, 65. 8 Bonser, p. 60.
9 *Annals of Clonmacnoise*, p. 109. 10 *Annals of Ulster*, I, 133.
11 *Opera Historica*, trans. J. E. King, I, 485.
12 *Ibid.* I, 485. 13 Bonser, p. 60.

PAGE 21

1 Simpson, *A treatise on plague*, p. 17.
2 Bonser, *The medical background of Anglo-Saxon England*, p. 67.
3 J. F. D. Shrewsbury, 'The yellow plague', *J. Hist Med.* (1949), I, 24–36.
4 L. F. Hirst, 'Plague', *Brit. Encycl. Med. Pract.* IX, 682.

PAGE 22

1 L. F. Hirst, 'Plague', *Brit. Encycl. Med. Pract.* IX, 685.
2 Gregory of Tours, *The history of the Franks*, II, 395.
3 D. and S. Lysons, *Magna Britannia*, I, 419.
4 *The Paston Letters*, ed. J. Gairdner, II–VI.
5 *Ibid.* II, 182.

PAGE 23

1 R. A. Pelham, *An historical geography of England*, ed. H. C. Darby, p. 233.
2 G. G. Coulton, *Medieval panorama*, p. 68.
3 H. S. Bennett, *Life on the English manor. A study of peasant conditions, 1150–1400*, p. 239.
4 Maud Sellers, *York Memorandum Book*, pt. 2, p. ii.
5 J. C. Russell, *British medieval population*, p. 146.
6 *Ibid.* p. 258.

PAGE 24

1 Russell, *British medieval population*, p. 142.
2 Coulton, *Medieval panorama*, p. 103.

References

PAGE 26

1 Pelham, *An historical geography of England*, p. 231, also the South Sheet of the Ordnance Survey Map of *Monastic Britain*.

PAGE 27

1 Russell, *British medieval population*, pp. 132–3.

PAGE 28

1 Pelham, pp. 260–5.
2 C. L. Kingsford, *The Stonor letters and papers, 1290–1483*, I, p. xlvi.
3 L. F. Salzman, *English life in the Middle Ages*, pp. 266–9.
4 Kingsford, *The Stonor letters and papers*, I, p. xlvi.
5 Coulton, *Medieval Panorama*, pp. 323–4.
6 *The Paston Letters*, II–VI.   7 J. Lunn.

PAGE 29

1 Pelham, *An historical geography of England*, p. 261.
2 L. F. Hirst, *The conquest of plague*, p. 308.
3 Pelham, p. 239.

PAGE 30

1 Sir J. Clapham, *A concise economic history of Britain*, p. 105.
2 Pelham, *An historical geography of England*, pp. 241–2.
3 R. S. R. Fitter, *London's natural history*, p. 40.
4 A. W. Andrews, *A text-book of geography*, p. 136.
5 A. G. Tansley, *The British Islands and their vegetation*, p. 75.
6 *Ibid.* 76.

PAGE 31

1 G. M. Trevelyan, *English social history*, p. 144.
2 G. Chaucer, *The Canterbury Tales*, trans. Nevill Coghill, p. 239.
3 W. Langland, *Piers Plowman*, ed. A. Burrell, p. 116.
4 Trevelyan, p. 21.
5 C. Walford, *Fairs past and present: a chapter in the history of commerce*, pp. 54–243.

PAGE 32

1 K.P.D.E., 'Provincial Fairs', *NQ*, VIII, 270.
2 Helen M. Cam, VCH, *Northamptonshire*, III, p. 24.
3 A. Burrell (ed.), *Piers Plowman*, p. 183.
4 C. Walford, *Fairs past and present*, p. 161.
5 G. G. Coulton, *Chaucer and his England*, p. 86.
6 G. de Barry, 'Itinerarium Kambriae', ed. J. F. Dimock, in *Giraldi Cambrensis Opera*, ed. J. S. Brewer, VI, 36.
7 *The Canterbury Tales*, trans. N. Coghill, pp. 25 ff.

References

PAGE 34

1 A. W. Andrews, *A text-book of geography*, p. 131.
2 H. S. Bennett, *Life on the English manor*, p. 225.
3 L. F. Hirst, *The conquest of plague*, p. 303.
4 *Life on the English manor*, p. 227.
5 G. G. Coulton, *Medieval panorama*, p. 311.

PAGE 35

1 G. G. Coulton, *Chaucer and his England*, p. 86.
2 G. M. Trevelyan, *English social history*, p. 20.

PAGE 37

1 'Black Death', *O.E.D.* III, 73
2 'Smallpox at Milan, *The Lancet*, ii (1888), 89.
3 C. F. Mullett, *The bubonic plague and England*, p. 4.

PAGE 38

1 H. B. Allyn, 'The Black Death', *Ann. Med. Hist.* VIII (1925), 232.
2 *Calendar of the Fine Rolls*, Edward III, VI, 214, membrane 49.
3 *The Diary of Fr. W. Herle*, ed. G. J. Symons.
4 *Knighton's Chronicle*, II, 2599–601.
5 J. Rymer, *Foedera*, V, 655.
6 J. C. Cox, VCH, *Berkshire*, II, 13.
7 *Knighton's Chronicle*, II, 2599–601.

PAGE 39

1 *Adam of Murimuth's Chronicle*, p. 178.
2 *Robert of Avesbury's Chronicle*, pp. 406–7.
3 *Le Baker's Chronicle*, pp. 98–100.

PAGE 40

1 *Knighton's Chronicle*, II, 2599–601.
2 *Ibid.*

PAGE 41

1 *Knighton's Chronicle*, II, 2599–601.
2 *Ibid.*
3 A. Jessopp. *The coming of the friars and other historic essays*, p. 243.

PAGE 42

1 H. C. Gillies, *Caledon. Med. J.* III, 193.
2 *The Canterbury Tales*, trans. N. Coghill, p. 41.
3 *Piers Plowman* (ed. London, 1919), pp. 171–2.
4 *Ibid.* 118.
5 C. F. Mullett, *The bubonic plague and England*, p. 4.

References

PAGE 43

1 A. C. Klebs, *VIme Congrès Internationale d'Histoire de la Médecine 1927*, p. 230.

PAGE 44

1 *Le Baker's Chronicle*, pp. 98–100.
2 L. F. Hirst, *Brit. Encycl. Med. Pract.* IX, 676.

PAGE 45

1 *Knighton's Chronicle*, II, 2599–601.
2 J. Barnes, *The history of that most victorious monarch Edward III*, p. 440.
3 *Le Baker's Chronicle*, pp. 98–100.
4 Fordun's Chronicle, *The Historians of Scotland*, IV, 359.
5 L. A. Barbé, *Chambers' Journal*, seventh series, IV, 234–7.

PAGE 46

1 W. Rees, *Proc. R. Soc. Med.* XVI, 33.
2 W. J. Simpson, *A treatise of plague*, p. 24.
3 Clynn and Dowling, *Annals of Ireland* (ed. Dublin, 1849), p. 35.
4 *Ibid.*

PAGE 47

1 H. D. Traill and J. S. Mann, *Social England*, I, 193.

PAGE 48

1 *Annals of the Kingdom of Ireland by the four masters*, III, 617.
2 A. Gwynn, *Studies*, XXIV, 25–42.
3 *Ibid.*   4 *Ibid.*
5 *Annals of Ulster*, II, 491.   6 *Annals of Clonmacnoise*, p. 297.
7 J. Barnes, *The history of that most victorious monarch Edward III*, p. 440.

PAGE 49

1 F. W. Joyce, *A social history of ancient Ireland*, I, 25.

PAGE 50

1 *CCR*, Edward III, IX, 376.
2 A. H. Thompson, *The Archaeological Journal*, LXVIII (1911), 301–38.
3 J. Lunn.
4 J. C. Russell, *British medieval population*, pp. 220–1.
5 J. C. Cox, VCH, *Hampshire and the Isle of Wight*, II, 36.

PAGE 51

1 J. C. Russell, *British medieval population*, p. 218.
2 J. Lunn.   3 *Ibid.*
4 A. H. Thompson, *The Archaeological Journal*, LXVIII (1911), 301–38, and LXXI (1914), pp. 97–127.

References

PAGE 52

1 J. Lunn.
2 J. C. Russell, *British medieval population*, p. 221.
3 *Ibid.* pp. 132–3.

PAGE 57

1 *CPR*, Edward III, IX, 323 membrane 5.
2 M. C. Fripp and P. Wragge, VCH, *Dorset*, II, 239.
3 *Calendar of the Fine Rolls, 1347–56*, VI, 182, membrane 18.
4 Richenda Scott, VCH, *Wiltshire*, IV, 39.
5 W. Rees, *Proc. R. Soc. Med.* XVI, 29.
6 Richenda Scott, VCH, *Wiltshire*, IV, 39.

PAGE 58

1 J. C. Cox, VCH, *Berkshire*, II, 13.
2 E. C. Lodge, VCH, *Berkshire*, II, 185–6.
3 Catherine Jamison and Marjory Hollings, VCH, *Berkshire*, III, 315 and 413.
4 W. Rees, *Proc. R. Soc. Med.* XVI, 29.

PAGE 60

1 J. Lunn.
2 J. C. Russell, *British medieval population*, p. 223.
3 D. and S. Lysons, *Magna Britannia*, III, 33.

PAGE 62

1 F. A. Gasquet, *The Black Death of 1348 and 1349*, p. 101.
2 R. Pickard, *The population and epidemics of Exeter in pre-census times*, p. 26.
3 Gladys Bradford, VCH, *Somerset*, II, 290.
4 T. Scott Holmes, VCH, *Somerset*, II, 25–6.
5 W. Rees, *Proc. R. Soc. Med.* XVI, 29.

PAGE 63

1 *CPR*, Edward III, VIII, 441, membrane 5.
2 *CPR*, Edward III, X, 16–17, membrane 20.
3 J. Lunn.

PAGE 64

1 'Andrew Boorde', *DNB*, V, 371.
2 J. Lunn.

PAGE 65

1 J. Lunn.
2 Rose Graham, VCH, *Gloucester*, II, 19–20.

References

PAGE 67

1 Ruth F. Butler, VCH, *Gloucester*, II, 145.
2 J. C. Russell, *British medieval population*, p. 223.
3 J. W. Willis-Bund, VCH, *Worcester*, II, 32.
4 A. A. Locke, VCH, *Worcester*, IV, 448.
5 *Ibid.* II, 124.
6 W. Rees, *Proc. R. Soc. Med.* XVI, 30.
7 J. C. Cox, VCH, *Warwick*, II, 18.
8 *Ibid.* II, 67.
9 Mary Dormer-Harris, VCH, *Warwick*, II, 145.
10 P. Styles, VCH, *Warwick*, III, 14.

PAGE 68

1 W. Rees, *Proc. R. Soc. Med.* XVI, 30.
2 J. W. Willis-Bund, VCH, *Worcester*, II, 32.
3 J. Lunn.   4 *Ibid.*
4 *Ibid.*

PAGE 69

1 J. Lunn.
2 *CCR*, Edward III, IX, 376.   3 *CPR*, Edward III, VIII, 428.

PAGE 71

1 J. Lunn.
2 J. Lunn.
3 J. Lunn.
4 'Shropshire', *Chambers' Encyclopaedia*, XII, 515.
5 H. M. Auden, *Church Stretton*, II, 163-79.

PAGE 72

1 G. Bellett, *The Antiquities of Bridgnorth*, 107.
2 H. Owen and T. B. Blakeway, *A History of Shrewsbury*.
3 T. Wright, *The History of Ludlow and its Neighbourhood*.
4 W. Watkins-Pitchford, 'The history of Morville', p. 9, *Bridgnorth Pamphlets*.
5 J. Peake, *Ellesmere, Shropshire*, 21.
6 H. M. Auden, *The Register of Montford*, p. iv.
7 C. C. Walker, *A Brief History of Lilleshall*, pp. 23-4.
8 *Ibid.* p. 25.
9 S. F. F. Auchmuty, *History of the Parish of Cleobury Mortimer, Salop*, p. 41.
10 W. Rees, *Proc. R. Soc. Med.* XVI, 38, appendix II.

PAGE 73

1 J. Lunn.   2 W. Rees, *Proc. R. Soc. Med.* XVI, 29.
3 *CPR*, Edward III, IX, 105.   4 J. Lunn.
5 J. C. Cox, VCH, *Derby*, II, 12.

References

PAGE 74

1 J. H. Lander, VCH, *Derby*, II, 167.
2 J. Lunn.   3 *Ibid.*

PAGE 75

1 J. Lunn.
2 W. Rees, *Proc. R. Soc. Med.* XVI, 38–9, appendix III.
3 W. E. A. Axon, *Bygone Cheshire*, pp. 123–8.
4 W. Tait, VCH, *Lancaster*, II, 29–30.
5 *Ibid.*
6 Alice Law, VCH, *Lancaster*, II, 285.
7 *Ibid.* p. 285, footnote. The manuscript is in the Public Record Office.
8 W. Tait, VCH, *Lancaster*, II, 30.

PAGE 76

1 J. Lunn.

PAGE 77

1 J. Lunn.   2 *Ibid.*

PAGE 79

1 J. Lunn.
2 H. E. Salter, VCH, *Oxford*, II, 17.
3 Beatrice A. Lees, VCH, *Oxford*, II, 178.
4 Mary D. Lobel, VCH, *Oxford*, V, 226.

PAGE 81

1 W. Rees, *Proc. R. Soc. Med.* XVI, 29.
2 E. P. Baker, Moira Long *et al.* VCH, *Oxford*, VI, 199.
3 Barbara Harvey, VCH, *Oxford*, VI, 215.
4 H. M. Colvin, VCH, *Oxford*, VI, 247.
5 Marjorie Jones *et al.* VCH, *Oxford*, VII, 153.
6 Sir E. Craster, VCH, *Oxford*, VIII, 159.
7 H. B. Allyn, *Ann. Med. Hist.* 232–5.
8 Strickland Gibson, VCH, *Oxford*, III, 9.
9 *CPR*, Edward III, VIII, 488.

PAGE 82

1 A. H. Thompson, *The Archaeological Journal*, LXVIII, 301–38.
2 *CPR*, Edward III, XI, 4
3 Margaret Toynbee *et al.* VCH, *Oxford*, VI, 393.
4 W. L. Langer, *Scientific American*, February, 1964, p. 6.
5 Creighton, I, 201.
6 *Ibid.* p. 127.
7 *Le Baker's Chronicle*, pp. 98–100.

References

PAGE 83

1 *CCR*, Edward III, IX, 28, membrane 14.
2 *Ibid.* IX, 1, membrane 28.
3 *Ibid.* VIII, 563.
4 *Robert of Avesbury's Chronicle*, pp. 406–7. J. Stow, *A survay of London*, p. 391.
5 J. Noorthouck, *A new history of London*, p. 70.
6 Creighton, I, 128.
7 *The Book of Common Prayer*, pp. lvii–lviii.

PAGE 84

1 Phyllis Wragge, VCH, *London*, I, 443.
2 Joyce J. Davis, E. J. Davis and M. E. Canford, VCH, *London*, I, 208.
3 *CPR*, Edward III, VIII, 459.
4 R. Fowler, *The Lancet*, ii, 908–9.
5 H. T. Riley, *NQ*, second series, II, 309.

PAGE 85

1 G. S. Minchin, VCH, *Middlesex*, II, 78–80.
2 *Ibid.*
3 C. F. Mullett, *The bubonic plague and England*, p. 21.
4 Rev. J. C. Cox, VCH, *Essex*, II, 16.

PAGE 86

1 P. Morant, *The history and antiquities of the county of Essex*, I, 48.
2 Nora E. MacMunn, VCH, *Essex*, II, 317.
3 J. E. Cussans, *History of Hertford*, I, 37–38

PAGE 87

1 C. Johnson, *Trans. St Albans & Herts. Archit. & Archaeol. Soc.* n.s. I (1895–6), 277–8.
2 A. F. H. Niemeyer, VCH, *Hertford*, IV, 192–3.
3 *Ibid.*   4 *Ibid.* p. 195.
5 J. T. Knight, *Trans. St Albans & Herts. Archit. & Archaeol. Soc.* n.s. I (1895–6), 262–76.

PAGE 88

1 J. Lunn.
2 J. C. Cox, VCH, *Hampshire and the Isle of Wight*, II, 33–4.
3 A. F. Leach, VCH, *Hampshire and the Isle of Wight*, II, 264.
4 J. C. Cox, VCH, *Hampshire and the Isle of Wight*, II, 35.
5 Violet M. Shillington, VCH, *Hampshire and the Isle of Wight*, V, 419–20.

PAGE 89

1 *CPR* Edward III, IX, 56.
2 *CCR*, Edward III, IX, 432, membrane 19.

3 W. Rees, *Proc. R. Soc. Med.* XVI, 31.
4 A. R. Branston and A. C. Leroy, *Historic Winchester*, 149.
5 *CPR*, Edward III, IX, 223.   6 H. E. Malden, VCH, *Surrey*, I, 361.
7 J. Lunn.

PAGE 90

1 J. Lunn.
2 J. C. Cox, VCH, *Surrey*, I, 119.   3 J. Lunn.
4 L. F. Salzman, VCH, *Sussex*, II, 14.
5 Phyllis Wragge, *Sussex*, II, 182.

PAGE 91

1 W. Page and W. D. Peckham, *Sussex*, III, 86.
1 *CPR*, Edward III, VIII, 482.

PAGE 92

1 *CCR* Edward III, X, 268–9.   2 J. Lunn.
3 M. E. Simkins, VCH, *Kent*, II, 53.   4 *Ibid.*
5 J. Lunn.

PAGE 93

1 G. Slater, VCH, *Kent*, III, 346.   2 J. Lunn.
3 J. C. Russell, *British medieval population*, p. 223.
4 C. F. Mullett, *The bubonic plague and England*, p. 21.
5 M. E. Simkins, VCH, *Kent*, II, 54.

PAGE 94

1 J. Lunn.
2 A. Jessopp, *The coming of the friars and other historic essays*, p. 206.
3 M. E. Simkins, VCH, *Norfolk*, II, 241.

PAGE 95

1 M. E. Simkins, VCH, *Norfolk*, II, 241, footnote.
2 *Ibid.* II, 241.   3 J. Lunn.
4 A. Jessopp, *The coming of the friars and other historic essays*, p. 236.
5 *Ibid.* p. 202.   6 *Ibid.* pp. 203–4.
7 *Ibid.* p. 204.   8 *Ibid.* p. 198.

PAGE 96

1 A. Jessopp, *The coming of the friars and other historic essays*, p. 204.
2 *Ibid.* p. 205.   3 *Ibid.* pp. 229–30.
4 *Ibid.* p. 205.   5 J. Lunn.
6 J. Stow and E. Howes. *The Annales, or Generall Chronicle of England*, p. 246
7 J. Blomefield, *The history of the city and county of Norwich*, II, 68.
8 Creighton, I, 129.
9 'Norwich', *Everyman's Encyclopaedia*, IX, 310.

References

PAGE 97

1 Creighton, I, 131.
2 J. C. Cox, VCH, *Suffolk*, II, 19.
3 A. Jessopp, *The coming of the friars and other historic essays*, p. 200.
4 *Ibid.* p. 201.   5 J. Lunn.

PAGE 98

1 *CCR*, Edward III, IX, 620.   2 J. Lunn.
3 *Ibid.*   4 G. Unwin, VCH, *Suffolk*, I, 647.

PAGE 99

1 J. Lunn.   2 *Ibid.*
3 M. M. C. Calthrop, VCH, *Lincoln*, II, 38

PAGE 100

1 M. M. C. Calthrop, VCH, *Lincoln*, II footnote.
2 *Ibid.*
3 Rose Graham, VCH, *Lincoln*, II, 112
4 A. H. Thompson, *The Archaeological Journal*, LXVIII, 301–38.
5 *Ibid.*

PAGE 101

1 Sister Elspeth, VCH, *Leicester*, I, 362.
2 *Ibid.* I, 362, footnote 60.   3 Creighton, I, 124.
4 Sister Elspeth, VCH, *Leicester*, I, 362.
5 *CCR*, Edward III, X, 605.
6 R. M. Serjeantson and R. W. Adkins, VCH, *Northamptonshire*, II, 26.

PAGE 102

1 W. Rees, *Proc. R. Soc. Med.* XVI, 29.
2 Sister Elspeth, VCH, *Rutland*, I, 145
3 W. Rees, *Proc. R. Soc. Med.* XVI, 29.
4 Sister Elspeth, VCH, *Bedford*, I, 328.
5 *Ibid.* I, 328, footnote.
6 A. Ransom, VCH, *Bedford*, II, 88.
7 Violet Rickards, VCH, *Bedford*, III, 78.
8 *Ibid.* p. 100.
9 H. S. F. Lea, VCH, *Bedford*, III, 158.

PAGE 103

1 Muriel R. Manfield, VCH, *Bedford*, III, 299.
2 J. H. Cope, VCH, *Bedford*, III, 304.
3 W. Rees, *Proc. R. Soc. Med.* XVI, 29.
4 Sister Elspeth, VCH, *Buckingham*, I, 291.
5 Sir W. Besant, *Medieval London*, I, 345.

References

6 C. Jamison, VCH, *Buckingham*, II, 54.
7 W. Rees, *Proc. R. Soc. Med.* XVI, 29.

PAGE 104

1 Alice V. Jenkinson, VCH, *Buckingham*, III, 113, 137.
2 J. T. Knight, *Trans. St Albans & Herts. Antiq. & Archaeol. Soc.* I, 262–76.
3 A. H. Thompson, *The Archaeological Journal*, LXVIII, 301–38.

PAGE 106

1 J. Lunn.
2 Ethel M. Hampson, VCH, *Cambridge and the Isle of Ely*, IV, 34.
3 *Ibid.* footnote 81.   4 *Ibid.* footnote, 82.
5 Kathleen L. Wood-Legh, VCH, *Cambridge and the Isle of Ely*, II, 158.
6 Helen M. Cam, VCH, *Cambridge, etc.* III, 93.
7 P. A. Bezodis, VCH, *Cambridge, etc.* III, 458.
8 C. F. Mullett, *The bubonic plague and England*, p. 21.
9 J. Lunn.
10 L. F. Salzman, VCH, *Cambridge, etc.* II, 71–2.

PAGE 107

1 J. Lunn.
2 W. K. Clay, *A history of the parish of Waterbeach in the county of Cambridge*, p. 57.
3 C. F. Mullett, *The bubonic plague and England*, p. 21.
4 J. C. Cox, VCH, *Nottingham*, II, 57.

PAGE 108

1 A. B. Wallis-Chapman, VCH, *Nottingham*, II, 274.
2 A. H. Thompson, *The Archaeological Journal*, LXXI, 97–127.

PAGE 109

1 *CPR*, Edward III, VIII, 579.
2 E. Miller, VCH, *The City of York*, pp. 84–5.
3 *Ibid.*   4 L. F. Salzman, VCH, *York*, III, 39.
5 T. M. Fallow, VCH, *York*, III, 241.
6 Maud Sellers, VCH, *York*, III, 440–1.

PAGE 110

1 Maud Sellers, VCH, *York*, III, 442.
2 *Jeremiah*, xiii, 23.   3 J. Lunn.
4 Maud Sellers, VCH, *York*, III, 441.
5 J. Lunn.   6 *Ibid.*

PAGE 111

1 W. Rees, *Proc. R. Soc. Med.* XVI, 29.   2 *Ibid.* pp. 29–30.
3 A. H. Thompson, *The Archaeological Journal*, LXXI, 109.
4 *Ibid.* p. 113.   5 Maud Sellers, VCH, *York*, III, 442.

References

PAGE 112

1 *Oxford travel atlas of Britain*, p. cxciii.
2 *CPR*, Edward III, IX, 417.
3 A. H. Thompson, *The Archaeological Journal*, LXXI, 97–127.
4 W. Nicholls, *The history and traditions of Ravenstondale, Westmorland*, II, 55.
5 A. H. Thompson, *The Archaeological Journal*, LXXI, 97–127.

PAGE 114

1 H. Gee, VCH, *Durham*, II, 19 and footnote 131.
2 Margaret E. Comford, VCH, *Durham*, II, 99.
3 F. Bradshaw, VCH, *Durham*, II, 210.
4 *Ibid.* footnote 1.

PAGE 116

1 F. Bradshaw, VCH, *Durham*, II, 210.
2 *Ibid.* p. 211.   3 *Ibid.* p. 212.
4 H. Gee, VCH, *Durham*, II, 19.

PAGE 117

1 *CPR*, Edward III, IX, 15.   2 *Ibid.* p. 258.
3 *Ibid.* p. 353.

PAGE 118

1 J. Wilson, VCH, *Cumberland*, II, 36, footnote 2.
2 *CPR*, Edward, III IX, 233.   3 J. Lunn.
4 *CCR*, Edward III, IX, 206.

PAGE 119

1 W. Rees, *Proc. R. Soc. Med.* XVI, 27–45.
2 *Ibid.*

PAGE 122

1 *Calendar of the Fine Rolls*, Edward III, VI, 240.
2 Sir J. Clapham, *A concise economic history of Britain*, p. 117.
3 A. E. Levett, *The black death on the estates of the see of Winchester* (1916), 72.
4 *Ibid.* p. 142.
5 G. M. Trevelyan, *English social history*, p. 8.

PAGE 124

1 *Pepys' Diary*, I, 307.   2 *Ibid.* II, 161.
3 *Ibid.* p. 377.
4 Sir J. Megaw, *Brit. Encycl. Med. Pract.* IX, 329.
5 W. W. Topley and G. S. Wilson, *Principles of bacteriology and immunology*, II, 1842.

References

PAGE 125

1 W. W. Topley and G. S. Wilson, *Principles of bacteriology and immunology*, II, 1842.
2 J. C. Snyder, *Viral and rickettsial diseases of man*, p. 479.
3 W. Langland, *Piers Plowman*, p. 80.
4 H. Zinsser, *Rats, lice and history*, p. 185.
5 *Pepys' Diary*, III, 240.
6 Sir J. Megaw, *Brit. Encycl. Med. Pract.* IX, 329.

PAGE 126

1 *CPR*, Edward III, X, 27.
2 *Ibid.* p. 91.
3 *Ibid.* p. 279
4 *Ibid.* p. 282
5 T. H. B. Graham, *Trans. Cumber. & Westmor. Antiq. & Archaeol. Soc.*, New Series, XXV, 105.

PAGE 127

1 F. H. Garrison, *An Introduction to the History of Medicine*, p. 290
2 Sir W. Wilde, *Census of Ireland for the year* 1851, V, 431.
3 J. Noorthouck, *A new history of London*, p. 71
4 *The British Medical Journal* (1900), ii, 1248–9.
5 Creighton, I, 207.

PAGE 128

1 *Adam of Murimuth's Chronicle*, p. 178
2 *Knighton's Chronicle*, II, 2599–601.
3 *The Brut*, p. 314
4 *Anonimalle Chronicle*, p. 50.
5 V. H. Galbraith, *Anonimalle Chronicle*, p. 169.
6 *CCR*, Edward III, XI, 182.
7 Sir H. Tidy, *A synopsis of medicine*, p. 81.
8 *CCR*, Edward III, XI, 197–8.

PAGE 129

1 J. Barnes, *The history of Edward III*, p. 616.
2 R. Pickard, *The population and epidemics of Exeter in pre-census times*, p. 26.
3 *CCR*, Edward III, X, 220.   4 *Ibid.* XI, 336.
5 *Calendar of the Fine Rolls*, Edward III, VII, 341.
6 Sister Elspeth, VCH, *Leicester*, I, 362.
7 Sister Elspeth, VCH, *Rutland*, I, 145.
8 W. Kelly, *Trans. R. Hist. Soc.* VI, 398–9.
9 Stow, p. 255.
10 L. F. Salzman, VCH, *Cambridge and the Isle of Ely*, II, 71.
11 P. Bezodis, VCH, *Cambridge, etc.* III, 458.
12 W. Massingberd, VCH, *Lincoln*, II, 315.

References

PAGE 130

1 J. C. Cox, VCH, *Warwick*, II, 76.
2 Mary Dormer-Harris, VCH, *Warwick*, II, 146.
3 Barbara Harvey, VCH, *Oxford*, VI, 215.
4 D. and S. Lysons, *Magna Britannia*, I, 419.
5 *Collections for a History of Staffordshire, Sir William Salt Archaeol. Soc.* n.s. VIII, 99.
6 Ramsay Muir, VCH, *Lancaster*, IV, 43.
7 E. Miller, VCH, *York*, p. 85.

PAGE 131

1 W. Rees, *Proc. R. Soc. Med.* XVI, 32.
2 *Ibid.* p. 31.   3 *CPR*, Edward III, XIII, 21.

PAGE 132

1 Fordun's Chronicle, p. 369.
2 W. K. Skene, Introduction to Fordun's Chronicle, pp. lxxii–lxxiv.
3 *CPR*, Edward III, IX, 117–18.
4 *FM*, III, 621.
5 *Ibid.* V, 1273.
6 J. O'Donovan, *FM*, III, 621, footnote.
7 W. Farrer and J. Brownbill, VCH, *Lancaster*, II, 155.

PAGE 133

1 T. H. B. Graham, *Trans. Cumb. & Westm. Antiq. & Archaeol. Soc.* n.s. XXV, 96–113.
2 J. Wilson, VCH, *Cumberland*, II, 36, footnote 2.
3 Blomefield, p. 70.
4 *A chronicle of London from 1089 to 1483*, p. 67.
5 *FM*, III, 537.
6 J. O'Donovan, *FM*, III, 537, footnote.
7 R. Flenley, *Six town chronicles of England*, p. 188.
8 *Ibid.* p. 188, footnote 3.
9 *Early chronicles of Shrewsbury*, p. 12.
10 Creighton, I, 451–5.

PAGE 134

1 *CCR*, Edward III, XII, 426.
2 *The Brut*, p. 316.   3 *Adam of Murimuth's Chronicle*, p. 178.
4 *The Brut*, p. 321.   5 *Anonimalle Chronicle*, p. 58.
6 *Ibid.* p. 173.   7 Creighton, I, 215.
8 *FM*, III, 641.
9 Sir W. Wilde, *Census of Ireland for the year 1851*, V, 89.
10 *Annals of Ulster*, II, 545.
11 T. Short, *A general chronological history of the air, etc.* I, 180.

References

PAGE 135

1 *A chronicle of London from 1089 to 1483*, p. 67.
2 *Anonimalle Chronicle*, p. 77.   3 *Ibid.*
4 Creighton, I, 217–18.   5 *The Brut*, p. 328.
6 D. and S. Lysons, *Magna Britannia*, VI, 198–9.
7 *Ibid.* VI, xxxviii.
8 R. Pickard, *The population and epidemics of Exeter*, p. 28.
9 *CCR*, Richard II, I, 54–5.   10 Fabyan, pp. 485–6.
11 *The Brut*, p. 328.

PAGE 136

1 Fabyan, pp. 485–6.   2 *Anonimalle Chronicle*, p. 79.
3 *Ibid.* p. 124.   4 Stow, p. 282.
5 Creighton, I, 218.
6 W. Furness, *History of Penrith from the Earliest Record to the Present Time*, p. 111.
7 Creighton, I, 234.
8 L. A. Barbé, *Chambers' Journal*, seventh series, IV, 234–7.
9 *CPR*, Richard II, I, 520.
10 Sir R. Baker, *A chronicle of the kings of England*, p. 198.
11 Blomefield, p. 81.   12 Creighton, I, 219.

PAGE 137

1 Creighton, I, 219.   2 *Ibid.*
3 *FM*, IV, 691.   4 *Annals of Clonmacnoise*, p. 308.
5 *FM*, IV, 693.
6 *Ibid.* IV, 697.
7 A. Boorde, *The fyrst boke of the introduction of knowledge*, p. 131.
8 Personal communication to the author from Professor Eleanor Knott, Professor of Ancient Irish, University of Dublin.
9 Helen M. Cam, VCH, *Cambridge and the Isle of Ely*, III, 13.
10 *The customs of London, otherwise called Arnold's Chronicle*, p. xxix.
11 Creighton, I, 219.

PAGE 138

1 Creighton, I, 219.
2 *Ibid.*   3 *Ibid.*
4 Stow, p. 305.   5 Blomefield, p. 82.
6 Creighton, I, 220.
7 *Ibid.*
8 *Ibid.*
9 Maud Sellers, VCH, *York*, III, 442.
10 L. F. Salzman, VCH, *York*, III, 407.
11 Creighton, I, 220.
12 *The Chronicle of Adam of Usk*, p. 207.
13 *FM*, IV, 763.   14 *Ibid.* IV, 765.

References

PAGE 139

1 G. Sarton, *Introduction to the history of science*, III, ii, 1669–1737.
2 Dorothea W. Singer, *Proc. R. Soc. Med.* IX, ii, 173.

PAGE 140

1 *Joannis de Burgundia de pestilentia liber*, British Museum Sloane MS. 3449, fos. 8a–9a. 2 *Ibid.* fos. 5b–12b.

PAGE 141

1 J. T. C. Nash, *Evolution and disease*, p. 10.
2 Stow, p. 334.   3 Creighton, I, 221.
4 Stow, p. 334.   5 Creighton, I, 201.

PAGE 142

1 *CCR*, Henry IV, III, 297.
2 *William Gregory's chronicle of London*, p. 87.
3 *Ibid.*
4 G. M. Trevelyan, *English social history*, p. 63.
5 J. R. Green, *A short history of the English people*, pp. 273–4.
6 G. M. Trevelyan, *English social history*, p. 58.
7 A. H. Burne, *The battlefields of England*, p. 104.

PAGE 143

1 T. Short, *A general chronological history of the air, etc.*, I, 185.
2 J. Noorthouck, *A new history of London*, p. 87.
3 Creighton, I, 220. G. Vine, *A litil boke for the Pestilence*, p. xi.
4 Grafton, p. 431.
5 J. Paterson, *A warning to Great-Britain in a sermon*, p. 66.
6 C. A. Gordon, *An epitome of the reports of the medical officers to the Chinese Imperial Customs Service from 1871 to 1882*, p. 344.
7 Creighton, I, 221.
8 *Ibid.* footnote 2.
9 Maud Sellers, VCH, *York*, III, 442.
10 D. and S. Lysons, *Magna Britannia*, IV, xxxiv.
11 Creighton, I, 227.   12 *Arnold's Chronicle*, p. xxxii.

PAGE 144

1 *The Brut*, II, 467.   2 Creighton, I, 228.
3 *Arnold's Chronicle*, pp. 90–2.   4 *Ibid.* p. 91.
5 Fabyan, pp. 608–9.   6 Creighton, I, 228.
7 *A chronicle of London from 1089 to 1483*, p. 124.
8 *The Brut*, pp. 472–3.

PAGE 145

1 Creighton, I, 223.   2 Fabyan, p. 612.
3 Creighton, I, 228.   4 *Ibid.* p. 225.

References

5 *Ibid.* p. 226.
6 G. Vine, *A litil boke for the Pestilence*, p. xi.
7 Creighton, I, 228.
8 *Lincoln Corporation MSS*, HMC Fourteenth report, part 8, 10–11.
9 Creighton, I, 228.   10 *Ibid.* p. 229.
11 *Ibid.*   12 *Ibid.*

PAGE 146

1 *The Paston letters*, III, 2.
2 *Early chronicles of Shrewsbury*, p. 9.
3 Fabyan, p. 653.   4 Creighton, I, 229.
5 *Ibid.* I, 130.
6 *The Paston letters*, IV, 106.   7 Wilson, pp. 10–12.
8 F.J.F., 'Recipe for Edward IV's Plague Medicine', *NQ*, fifth series, IX, 343.

PAGE 147

1 Creighton, I, 230.
2 *The Paston letters*, IV, 180.   3 Creighton, I, 230.
4 *Ingulph's Chronicle of Croyland*, p. 443.
5 Creighton, I, 230.
6 C. F. Mullett, *The bubonic plague and England*, p. 40, footnote 35.
7 J. N. Radcliffe, *The pestilence in England: an historical sketch*, p. 28.
8 Maud Sellers, VCH, *York*, III, 442.
9 Creighton, I, 231.

PAGE 148

1 *The Brut*, p. 604.
2 W. W. Skeat, *A concise etymological dictionary of the English language*, p. 520.
3 R. Holinshed, *The chronicles of England, Scotland, and Ireland*, p. 1350.
4 Creighton, I, 231.
5 Warkworth, *A Chronicle*, p. 23.   6 Creighton, I, 231.

PAGE 149

1 *Arnold's Chronicle*, p. xxxvii.   2 Fabyan, p. 666.
3 *FM*, IV, 1107.   4 *The Cely Papers*, pp. 16–19.
5 J. T. C. Nash, *Evolution and disease*, p. 10.
6 Creighton, I, 134.   7 *Ibid.*
8 *FM*, IV, 1107, footnote.

PAGE 150

1 J. D. Comrie, *History of Scottish medicine*, I, 203.
2 *Ibid.*
3 Creighton, I, 234.   4 *Ibid.* p. 235.
5 *Ibid.*
6 Sir H. L. Tidy, *A synopsis of medicine*, p. 111.
7 *Ibid.* p. 107.

References

PAGE 151

1 Creighton, I, 235. 2 *Ibid.*
3 ERBE, I, 72. 4 *Ibid.* pp. 74–5.
5 *Ibid.* p. 76. 6 *Ibid.* pp. 76–7.
7 *Ibid.* pp. 77–8. 8 Creighton, I, 236.

PAGE 152

1 *FM*, IV, 775. 2 *Ibid.* p. 827.
3 *Ibid.* p. 841. 4 *Ibid.* p. 861.
5 *Ibid.* 863 6 *Annals of Ulster*, III, 97.
7 *FM*, IV, 871. 8 *Annals of Ulster*, III, 117.
9 *FM*, IV, 897. 10 *Ibid.* p. 901.
11 *Ibid.* 12 *Ibid.* p. 913.
13 *Ibid.* p. 917. 14 *Annals of Ulster*, III, 145.
15 Topley and Wilson's *Principles of Bacteriology and Immunity*, II, 1803.

PAGE 153

1 *Annals of Ulster*, III, 161 2 *FM*, IV, 951–3.
3 *Ibid.* pp. 951–2, footnote. 4 *Ibid.* p. 953.
5 *Ibid.* 6 *Ibid.* p. 985.
7 *Ibid.* p. 1029. 8 *Ibid.*
9 *FM*, IV, 1029. 10 *Ibid.* p. 1055.

PAGE 154

1 *Annals of Ulster*, III, 229. 2 *Ibid.* p. 229, footnote.
3 *FM*, IV, 1071. 4 *Ibid.* p. 1107.
5 *Annals of Ulster*, III, 293. 6 *FM*, IV, 1157.
7 *Ibid.* p. 1157. 8 *Ibid.*
9 *Ibid.* p. 1167. 10 *Annals of Ulster*, III, 331.
11 *FM*, IV, 1195. 12 *Annals of Ulster*, III, 359.

PAGE 155

1 *FM*, IV, 1239. 2 *Annals of Ulster*, III, 427.
3 *Ibid.* p. 419. 4 *Ibid.* p. 431.
5 *FM*, IV, 1247.

PAGE 156

1 C. L. Kingsford, *The Stonor letters and papers*, I, xlvi.

PAGE 159

1 C. Wriothesley, *A chronicle of England*, I, 4.
2 R. Holinshed, *The chronicles of England, Scotland, and Ireland*, II, 1454.
3 Fabyan, p. 687.
4 Creighton, I, 287.
5 *Calendar of State Papers Spanish*, I, 238.
6 Creighton, I, 287.

References

7 *Early chronicles of Shrewsbury*, p. 13. 8 Stow, p. 481.
9 *Calendar of State Papers Spanish*, I, 253.
10 Creighton, I, 287.   11 *Ibid.* p. 288.
12 Pickard, p. 29.

PAGE 160

1 F. H. Gervis, *On the sweating sickness*, p. 13.
2 Creighton, I, 288.   3 Short, I, 203–4.
4 *LPH*, I, i, 469 (no. 905).   5 *Ibid.* I, i, 484 (no. 964).
6 Creighton, I, 288.   7 Cooper, I, 295.
8 *LPH*, I, ii, 1014 (no. 2260).   9 *Ibid.* I, ii, 1000 (no. 2229).
10 *Ibid.* I, ii, 1019 (no. 2278).   11 *Ibid.* I, ii, 1070 (no. 2412).
12 Short, I, 204–5.   13 *LPH*, I, ii, 1076 (no. 2424).
14 Fabyan, p. 689.   15 *LPH*, I, ii, 1103 (no. 2493).
16 Stow, p. 481.

PAGE 161

1 *Chronicle of the Grey Friars of London*, p. 29.
2 Creighton, I, 289.
3 *LPH*, I, ii, 1266 (no. 2929).   4 Creighton, I, 289.
5 *Ibid.*   6 Short, I, 206.
7 G. Ormerod, *The history of the County Palatine and city of Chester*, p. 234.
8 Creighton, I, 290.   9 *LPH*, II, ii, 1160 (no. 3675).
10 *Ibid.* II, ii, 1175 (no. 3723). 11 *Ibid.* II, ii, 1179 (no. 3747).
12 F. H. Gervis, *On the sweating sickness*, p. 14.
13 *LPH*, II, i, 522 (no. 1832).   14 *PMV*, II, 62 (no. 944).
15 C. A. Gordon, *An epitome of the reports of the Medical Officers to the Chinese Imperial Customs Service from 1871 to 1884*, p. 349.
16 F. H. Gervis, p. 14.   17 *Ibid.* p. 15.

PAGE 162

1 *LPH*, II, ii, 1188 (no. 3788).   2 Creighton, I, 251.
3 *LPH*, II, ii, 1242 (no. 4009).   4 *Ibid.* II, ii, 1331 (no. 4308).
5 *LPH*, II, ii, 1333 (no. 4320).   6 Creighton, I, 456–7.
7 *LPH*, II, ii, 1334 (no. 4326).   8 *Ibid.* II, ii, 1335 (no. 4332).
9 Stow, pp. 506–7.   10 Creighton, I, 290–1.
11 *LPH*, II, ii, 1276 (no. 4125).

PAGE 163

1 *LPH*, II, ii, 1276 (no. 4125)   2 *Ibid.* II, ii, 1546 (appendix, no. 56).
3 Creighton, I, 292.   4 *LPH*, III, i, 348 (no. 942).
5 HMC, *Corporation of Beverley MSS.* p. 173.
6 *Ibid.* p. 174.   7 *Early chronicles of Shrewsbury*, p. 16.
8 Grafton, p. 1051.   9 Stow, p. 514.
10 *LPH*, III, ii, 1581 (appendix, no. 31).
11 *SPD*, I, 71 (no. 42).   12 Creighton, I, 292.

References

13 Cooper, I, 304.   14 Short, I, 210.
15 Cooper, I, 310.

PAGE 164

1 Grafton, pp. 1140–1.
2 Sir R. Baker, *The chronicles of the kings of England*, p. 274.
3 Creighton, I, 284.
4 J. Ritchie, *Edinburgh Medical Journal*, LV, 691.
5 Creighton, I, 361.   6 ERBE, I, 84–5.
7 *Ibid.* pp. 100–1.   8 J. Ritchie, p. 692.
9 Ware, p. 50.

PAGE 165

1 *Annals of Ulster*, III, 476–7, footnote.   2 Ware, p. 51.
3 *Accounts of the Lord High Treasurer of Scotland*, II, 463.
4 ERBE, I, 100–1.
5 *Ibid.* p. 105.   6 *Ibid.* p. 106.
7 *Ibid.* pp. 124–5.   8 'State of Ireland', *LPH*, III, ii, 11–21
9 ERBE, I, 136–8.

PAGE 166

1 ERBE, I, 139–41.
2 J. D. Comrie, *History of Scottish medicine*, I, 207.
3 ERBE, I, 141.   4 Creighton, I, 362.
5 *Annals of Loch Cé*, II, 229.   6 *LPH*, III, ii, 1570.
7 *FM*, V, 1349.   8 *Annals of Ulster*, III, 535.
9 *LPH*, III, i, 339.   10 *SPD*, II, iii, 38–9.
11 *LPH*, III, i, 357.   12 *SPD*, II, iii, 84.
13 Ware, p. 75.

PAGE 167

1 Creighton, I, 371.   2 Ware, p. 78.
3 *LPH*, III, i, 168.   4 ERBE, I, 196.
5 J. D. Comrie, *History of Scottish medicine*, I, 208–9.
6 ERBE, I, 196.   7 *Ibid.* p. 204.
8 *PMV*, III, 551.   9 *Ibid.* p. 558.
10 *LPH*, IV, i, 1048.   11 *Ibid.*
12 *Ibid.*   13 Cooper, I, 324.
14 Creighton, I, 292.   15 Cooper, I, 330.

PAGE 168

1 *Early chronicles of Shrewsbury*, p. 16.
2 *LPH*, IV, ii, 1903.   3 Creighton, I, 292.
4 *Ibid.* p. 293.   5 *LPH*, IV, iii, 2855.
6 *Calendar of State Papers Spanish*, IV, i, 707.
7 Creighton, I, 293.

8 *PMV*, IV, 305.
9 Creighton, I, 293.
10 *Ibid.*
11 *PMV*, IV, 353.
12 *Ibid.* p. 358.
13 *LPH*, V, 584.
14 *Ibid.* pp. 609–10.
15 *Ibid.* p. 613.

PAGE 169

1 *LPH*, V, 615.
2 *Ibid.* p. 626.
3 *Ibid.* p. 644.
4 Cooper, I, 346.
5 *Ibid.* p. 354.
6 *Shropshire Archaeol. and Nat. Hist. Soc.* VI, 102–3.
7 *LPH*, V, 591.
8 *Ibid.* p. 563.
9 Creighton, I, 297.
10 *LPH*, IX, 13.
11 *Ibid.* p. 30.
12 *Ibid.* p. 34.
13 *Ibid.* p. 39.
14 *Ibid.* p. 44.
15 *Ibid.* p. 115.
16 *Ibid.* p. 124.
17 *Ibid.* p. 159.
18 *Ibid.* p. 235.

PAGE 170

1 Creighton, I, 301.
2 *LPH*, XI, 169.
3 *Ibid.* p. 202.
4 *Ibid.* XII, ii, 45.
5 *Ibid.* ii, 58.
6 *Ibid.* ii, 121.
7 *Ibid.* ii, 123.
8 *Ibid.* ii, 275.
9 *Ibid.* ii, 287.
10 *Ibid.* ii, 311.
11 *Ibid.* ii, 296.
12 *Ibid.* ii, 311.
13 *Ibid.* ii, 346.
14 *Early chronicles of Shrewsbury*, p. 18.
15 *LPH*, X, 439.
16 Creighton, I, 302.
17 *Ibid.* p. 301.
18 *LPH*, XI, 166.

PAGE 171

1 *LPH*, XI, 337.
2 *Ibid.* pp. 360–1.
3 *LPH*, XIII, i, 117.
4 *LPH*, XII, ii, 60.
5 *Ibid.* ii, 87.
6 *Ibid.* ii, 115.
7 *Ibid.* ii, 220.
8 *Ibid.* ii, 275.

PAGE 172

1 *LPH*, XII, ii, 280.
2 *Ibid.* ii, 288.
3 Cooper, I, 386.
4 *LPH*, XIII, i, 151.
5 *Ibid.* i, 163.
6 *Ibid.* i, 80.
7 *Ibid.* i, 101.
8 *Ibid.* i, 193.
9 *Ibid.* i, 255.
10 *Ibid.* i, 16.
11 *Ibid.* i, 189.
12 *Ibid.* i, 220.
13 *Ibid.* i, 262–3.
14 Cooper, I, 391.

PAGE 173

1 *LPH*, XIII, i, 303. 2 *York Civic Records*, V, 29.
3 *LPH*, XIII, ii, 60. 4 *Ibid.* ii, 431.
5 C. Wriothesley, *A chronicle of England*, I, 123.
6 *Ibid.*
7 Fabyan, p. 701. 8 Stow, p. 581.
9 *LPH*, XV, 150. 10 *LPH*, XVI, 64.
11 J. C. Morley, *Bygone Lancashire*, p. 106.
12 Creighton, I, 302.

PAGE 174

1 *LPH*, XIII, 117.
2 *Yorkshire Archaeol. and Topogr. Journ.* XII, 310.

PAGE 175

1 *Publ. Harl. Soc.* XLIV, 258–64.

PAGE 176

1 *Publ. Harl. Soc.* XLIV, 284–92.

PAGE 177

1 *Ludlow*, Shropshire Parish Register Soc. XIII, i, 250–5.
2 *Early Chronicles of Shrewsbury*, p. 73.
3 *Ludlow*, pp. 274–7.
4 Colyton, *Publ. Devon & Cornwall Rec. Soc.* II, 569–604.

PAGE 178

1 Colyton, *Publ. Devon & Cornwall Rec. Soc.* II, 576–7.
2 *Ibid.* pp. 577–8. 3 *Ibid.* 597–8.
4 *Publ. Harl. Soc.* XLIV, 285. 5 *LPH*, XVIII, ii, 32.
6 *Ibid.* 178.
7 C. Wriothesley, *A chronicle of England*, I, 145.
8 *LPH*, XVIII, ii, 267. 9 *Ibid.* p. 257.
10 A. Vallance, *Archaeologia Cantiana*, XLIII, 13.
11 *Trans. Bristol and Glos. Archaeol. Soc.* XIX, 105–41.
12 *LPH*, XVIII, ii, 257.

PAGE 179

1 Creighton, I, 303. 2 *LPH*, XIX, ii, 405–6.
3 *Ibid.* ii, 39. 4 *Ibid.* ii, 202.
5 *Publ. Harl. Soc.* LXII, i, 133.

PAGE 180

1 Grafton, p. 1291. 2 *Publ. Harl. Soc.* XLIV, 285.
3 *Strype's ecclesiastical memorials*, II, i, 95.
4 Creighton, I, 314. 5 *Publ. Harl. Soc.* XLIV, 285–6.

6 *Ibid.* VII, 177–8.   7 *Ibid.* VIII, 6–7.
8 *Ibid.* XLIII, 157.

PAGE 180

9 *Publ. Harl. Soc.* XLIV, i, 171.
10 C. Wriothesley, *A chronicle of England*, II, 5.
11 *Strype's ecclesiastical memorials*, II, i, 185.
12 *Publ. Harl. Soc.* XLIV, 286.   13 *Ibid.* III, 183.
14 *LPH*, XX, i, 262.   15 *Ibid.* i, 363.
16 *Ibid.* ii, 242.

PAGE 181

1 *LPH*, XX, ii, 242.   2 *Ibid.* ii, 154.
3 *Ibid.* ii, 203.   4 *Ibid.* ii, 295.
5 *Ibid.* ii, 416.   6 Cooper, I, 429.
7 *LPH*, XX, ii, 154.   8 Cooper, I, 440.
9 *LPH*, XXI, ii, 116.

PAGE 182

1 Creighton, I, 303.   2 *LPH*, XXI, i, 746.
3 *Magna Britannia*, III, 297.
4 Camborne, *Publ. Devon & Cornwall Rec. Soc.* I, 78–81.

PAGE 183

1 *The registers of Banstead*, The Parish Reg. Soc. pp. 22–3.
2 *Ibid.* p. 22.   3 Creighton, I, 304.
4 HMC, Fourteenth Report, part X, 42–3.
5 *York Civic Records*, V, 29.

PAGE 184

1 *York Civic Records*, V, 30.   2 *Ibid.* p. 33.
3 *Ibid.* p. 36.   4 *Ibid.* p. 37.
5 *Ibid.*
6 T. Laycock, *Report on the State of York*, p. 58.
7 *Ibid.* p. 59.   8 *Middlesex County Records*, I, 3.
9 *Publ. Harl. Soc.* XLIV, 286.
10 E. A. B. Barnard, *Worcester Diocesan Magazine*, XXVI, 146.
11 Cox, p. 144.   12 *Publ. Harl. Soc.* XXV, 103.

PAGE 185

1 *Trans. Bristol and Glos. Archaeol. Soc.* XIX, 105–41.
2 HMC, *MSS. in various collections*, VII, 58.
3 Cooper, II, 58–9.
4 W. E. A. Axon, *Trans. Lancs. and Cheshire Antiq. Soc.* XII, 58.
5 ERBE, II, 5.   6 *Ibid.* p. 16.
7 *Ibid.* p. 19

8 R. E. C. Waters, *Parish registers in England*, p. 72.
9 R. Hancock, *Narratives of the Reformation*, p. 82.
10 Waters, p. 72.

PAGE 186

1 ERBE, II, 10.
2 *Ibid.* pp. 28–30.
3 *Ibid.* pp. 35–7.
4 *Ibid.*
5 *Ibid.* p. 42.
6 *Ibid.*
7 *Ibid.* p. 43.
8 *Ibid.*
9 *Aberdeen Records*, I, 130.
10 *Ibid.* I, 130.

PAGE 187

1 Ware, p. 93.
2 *LPH*, IX, 33.
3 *Calendar of State Papers Carew* (1515–74), p. 71.
4 *SPD*, II, iii, 280.
5 Creighton, I, 371.
6 *Annals of Ulster*, III, 604.
7 *FM*, V, 1425.
8 *Annals of Ulster*, III, 631.
9 *FM*, V, 1493.
10 *The chronicle of Perth*, p. 2.
11 ERBE, II, 91.
12 *Aberdeen Records*, I, 165.
13 Creighton, I, 362.
14 *A concise etymological dictionary of the English language*, p. 57.
15 G. Henslow, *Medical works of the fifteenth century*, p. 35.

PAGE 188

1 G. Harvey, *Little Venus unmask'd*, pp. 27 ff.
2 *Ayr Burgh Accounts*, p. c.
3 *Ibid.* p. c.
4 *Ibid.* p. ci.
5 *LPH*, XX, i, 616.
6 *Ibid.* ii, 242.
7 *Ibid.* i, 496.
8 *Aberdeen Records*, I, 222.
9 *Ibid.*
10 *Ibid.* p. 246.
11 ERBE, II, 126.
12 Creighton, I, 363.

PAGE 189

1 J. Ritchie, *Edinburgh Medical Journal*, LV, 691–701.
2 *Rutland MSS.*, HMC, Twelfth Report, appendix, part 4, II, 42.
3 *Aberdeen Records*, I, 244.
4 *Ibid.* I, 273.
5 Creighton, I, 304.
6 *Publ. Harl. Soc.* XXV, i, 107–8.
7 *Ibid.* pp. 106–7.
8 *Ibid.* VII, 184.
9 *The diary of Henry Machyn*, p. 310.

PAGE 190

1 P. Furnivall, *NQ*, V, 361.
2 *The diary of Henry Machyn*, p. 310.
3 Creighton, I, 308.
4 T. Wright, *Queen Elizabeth and her times*, I, 138.
5 'Historical memoranda in the handwriting of John Snow', *Three fifteenth-century Chronicles*, pp. 126–7.
6 Cox, p. 144.

7 *Ibid.*   8 *Publ. Harl. Soc.* LXI, 23–5.
9 *Ibid.* p. 24.   10 *Ibid.* pp. 24–5.

PAGE 192

1 T. Wright, *Queen Elizabeth and her times*, I, 152.
2 Stow, pp. 656–7.   3 *Publ. Harl. Soc.* XXV, i, 110–12.
4 Stow, p. 657.
5 J. Jones, *A dial for all agues*, cap. 8, aph. 9, sectio 3.
6 *Ibid.*

PAGE 194

1 T. Wright, *Queen Elizabeth and her times*, I, 138, footnote.
2 *Publ. Harl. Soc.* XXV, i, 112.   3 C.J.R., *NQ*, XI, 100.
4 E. A. B. Barnard, *Worcester Diocesan Magazine*, XXVI, 146.
5 W. Furness, *History of Penrith*, p. 112.
6 Cooper, II, 105.   7 *Ibid.* p. 110.

PAGE 195

1 Cooper, II, 105.
2 HMC, Fourteenth report, parts, 8, 9 and 10, XIV, viii, 49.
3 Colyton, *Publ. Devon & Cornwall Rec. Soc.* pp. 576–7.
4 E. A. B. Barnard, p. 147.   5 Colyton, pp. 577–8.
6 *Solihull parish register*, The Parish Reg. Soc. LIII, 164–7.
7 R. Pemberton, *Solihull and its church*, p. 131.
8 Cox, p. 159.

PAGE 196

1 Ormerod, *Chester*, p. 235.
2 J. C. Morley, *Bygone Lancashire*, p. 107.
3 VCH, *Lancaster*, IV, 16.   4 Creighton, I, 304.
5 *The Registers of Stratford-on-Avon*, The Parish Reg. Soc. VI, 1–4.

PAGE 198

1 Kelly, p. 399.
2 A. L. Rowse, *The England of Elizabeth*, p. 220.
3 'The parish registers of Halifax', *Publ. Yorks. Par. Reg. Soc.* pp. 310–14.
4 *Ibid.* pp. 314–29.   5 Short, p. 271.
6 *Oswestry*, Shropshire Par. Reg. Soc., St Asaph Diocese, IV–VII, 4–16.
7 *Ibid.* p. 5.

PAGE 199

1 *Oswestry*, Shropshire Par. Reg. Soc., St Asaph Diocese, IV–VII, 14–16.

PAGE 200

1 *SPD*, XI, 122 (no. 38).   2 *Ibid.* (no. 42).
3 *Ibid.* (no. 45).   4 Stow, pp. 656–7.
5 SHH, I, 274.   6 *Ibid.* p. 277.

References

7 W. A. Greenhill, 'Registers of the Hastings parishes', *Sussex Archaeol. Collections*, XIV, 195–6.   8 Creighton, I, 309 and footnote.
9 Creighton, I, 309.   10 Kelly, pp. 399–400.

PAGE 201

1 Kelly, p. 400.   2 *Ibid.* p. 401.
3 J. T. C. Nash, *Evolution and disease*, pp. 11–13.
4 SHH, I, 281.   5 'Juxta Turrim', *NQ*, XI, 326.
6 W. Robinson, *The history and antiquities of Stoke Newington*, p. 183.
7 *Publ. Harl. Soc.* XVI, 85.   8 Cooper, II, 178.
9 *Ibid.* p. 187.   10 *Ibid.* p. 205.
11 HMC, Fifteenth Report, appendix, XV, x, 15.
12 *York Civic Records*, VI, 70.   13 *NQ*, XI, 69.

PAGE 202

1 *York Civic Records*, VI, 83.   2 *Ibid.* p. 84.
3 *Magna Britannia*, III, 73.   4 Kelly, p. 401.
5 *The Registers of Stratford-on-Avon*, The Parish Reg. Soc. pp. 9–15.
6 *Ibid.* p. 9.   7 *Ibid.*
8 'Mary Arden's House', now in the possession of the Shakespeare Trust.

PAGE 203

1 *Trans. Bristol and Glos. Archaeol. Soc.* XIX, 105–41.
2 *Archaeologia*, XLI, 363.   3 *Magna Britannia*, VI, 199.
4 Pickard, p. 30.   5 *Publ. Harl. Soc.* XLIV, 289.
6 *Ibid.* VII, 190–1.   7 *Ibid.* XLIII, 162.
8 *Ibid.* XLIV, 175.   9 *Ibid.* p. 260.
10 *Ibid.* XLVI, 109.
11 *Calendar of State Papers Spanish*, II, 193.
12 Stow, p. 663.   13 *Publ. Harl. Soc.* VII, 191.
14 *Ibid.* XLVI, 109–10.
15 SHH, I, 476.

PAGE 204

1 *Calendar of State Papers Spanish*, II, 262.
2 *Ibid.* p. 270.   3 Pickard, p. 30.
4 *Ibid.* p. 31.   5 *Publ. Harl. Soc.* XLVI, 111.
6 Creighton, I, 339.
7 J. C. Cox, *Churchwardens' accounts from the fourteenth century to the close of the seventeenth century*, p. 317.

PAGE 205

1 *Publ. Harl. Soc.* XLVI, 112.   2 *SPD*, XCV, 477.
3 Creighton, I, 339.   4 *Publ. Harl. Soc.* XLVI, 113.
5 *Ibid.* XLIV, 261.   6 *Ibid.* XXV, i, 118–20.
7 SHH, II, 107.

References

PAGE 206

1 Creighton, I, 340 and footnote.
2 *Calendar of State Papers Rome*, II, 231.
3 ERBE, III, 184.   4 *PCS*, I, 279.
5 ERBE, III, 185.   6 *PCS*, I, 279.
7 *Ibid.* p. 281.   8 *Ibid.*
9 *Ibid.*
10 *PCS*, I, 281
11 R. Chambers, *Domestic annals of Scotland*, I, 52.

PAGE 208

1 ERBE, III, 253.   2 *Ibid.*
3 ERBE, III, 253–6.   4 *Ibid.* 257.
5 J. D. Comrie, *History of Scottish Medicine*, p. 212, footnote.

PAGE 209

1 SHH, I, 372.   2 ERBE, III, 259.
3 *Ibid.* p. 261.   4 *Ibid.* p. 269.
5 *Ibid.* p. 267.   6 Creighton, I, 365–6.
7 R. Chambers, *Domestic annals of Scotland*, I, 55.
8 *Ibid.* I, 53.   9 *Ibid.* pp. 53–4.
10 ERBE, IV, 29–30.
11 J. D. Comrie, *History of Scottish medicine*, I, 219.

PAGE 210

1 ERBE, IV, 28–9.   2 *Ibid.* pp. 29–30.
3 *PCS*, II, 419–20.   4 *Ibid.* p. 415.
5 ERBE, IV, 35.   6 *Ibid.* p. 36.
7 *Ibid.* p. 31.   8 *Ibid.* p. 36.
9 *FM*, V, 1663.   10 Ware, p. 17.
11 *Ibid.*
12 *Calendar of State Papers Carew* (1575–88), p. 99.
13 SHH, II, 104.
14 R. Holinshed, *The chronicles of England, Scotland, and Ireland*, VI, 374.
15 *O.E.D.* II, 238–9.

PAGE 211

1 R. Holinshed, *The chronicles of England, Scotland and Ireland*, VI, 374
2 T. Wright, *Queen Elizabeth and her times*, II, 27.
3 *FM*, V, 1681.   4 Creighton, I, 372.
5 CARD, II, 100.

PAGE 212

1 CARD, II, 103–4.   2 *Ibid.* p. 111.
3 *Ibid.* p. 102.

References

PAGE 215

1 *Publ. Harl. Soc.* XLVI, 114–16.
2 *Rutland MSS.* II, 115, HMC, Fifteenth Report, appendix, part 10.
3 T. Wright, *Queen Elizabeth and her times*, II, 66–7.
4 SHH, II, 222, HMC.
5 HMC, Twelfth Report, appendix, part 4, XII, iv, 114.
6 *Ibid.* XII, iv, 115.   7 *APC*, IX, 388.

PAGE 216

1 *APC*, X, 22.   2 *Ibid.* p. 35.
3 *Ibid.* p. 36.   4 *Ibid.* p. 86.
5 Creighton, I, 341–4.   6 *Ibid.* p. 345.

PAGE 217

1 *APC*, X, 321–2.   2 *Ibid.* p. 326.
3 *Ibid.* p. 362.   4 *Ibid.* p. 381.
5 *Ibid.* p. 339.   6 *Ibid.* p. 386.
7 *Ibid.* p. 388.

PAGE 218

1 *APC*, XXIII, 204.   2 *Ibid.* X, 392.
3 *Ibid.* p. 413.   4 *Ibid.* 435.
5 *SPD*, LXXIII, 388.   6 *Ibid.* p. 389.
7 Cox, p. 155.   8 *York Civic Records*, VII, 11.
9 SHH, XIII, 99.
10 H. S. Cowper, *The oldest register book of the parish of Hawkshead in Lancashire*,
   p. lxxi.   11 Creighton, I, 338.
12 Cooper, II, 270–9.   13 *Ibid.* p. 278.
14 *Ibid.* p. 279.

PAGE 219

1 J. S. Attwood, *NQ*, III, 17.   2 Ormerod, *Chester*, p. 236.
3 Cooper, II, 321.   4 *Ibid.* footnote 2.
5 *Ibid.* p. 322.   6 *Ibid.* p. 324.
7 *SPD*, CIII, 493.   8 Cox, p. 171.

PAGE 220

1 SHH, II, 106.   2 *Early chronicles of Shrewsbury*, p. 37.
3 *APC*, IX, 14.   4 *Ibid.*
5 J. Sykes, *Yorkshire Archaeol. J.* IX, 196
6 *Early chronicles of Shrewsbury*, p. 39.   7 *SPD*, CXLIII, 269.

PAGE 221

1 *York Civic Records*, VII, 125.
2 H. S. Cowper, *The oldest register book of the parish of Hawkshead in Lancashire*,
   p. lxxi.   3 *Ibid.* pp. lxxi–lxxii.

4 *Publ. Harl. Soc.* XLVI, 116.   5 *APC*, XI, 249.
6 *Ibid.* p. 211.   7 *Middlesex County Records*, I, 116.
8 *APC*, XI, 165.   9 *Ibid.* p. 437.
10 *Ibid.* XII, 109.   11 *Ibid.* XIII, 128.
12 HMC, Fifteenth Report, XV, x, 127.
13 *APC*, XIII, 224.   14 *Publ. Harl. Soc.* XXI, 277.

PAGE 222

1 *SPD*, CLV, 70.   2 HMC, Fifteenth Report, XV, x, 142.
3 SHH, XIII, 212.
4 W. Maitland *et al.*, *The history and survey of London*, I, 268.
5 Creighton, I, 344.   6 *British Medical Journal*, ii, 1300.
7 T. Wright, *Queen Elizabeth and her times*, II, 187.
8 *Middlesex County Records*, I, 136–7.   9 *APC*, XXIII, 118.
10 *Ibid.* p. 182.   11 *Publ. Harl. Soc.* XXV, 135–7.
12 *Ibid.* VII, 204.
13 J. C. Cox, *Churchwardens' accounts from the fourteenth century to the close of the seventeenth century*, p. 317.

PAGE 224

1 *APC*, XXIII, 195.   2 *Ibid.* p. 232.
3 Creighton, I, 352.   4 *APC*, XXIV, 22.
5 *Ibid.* pp. 31–2.   6 *Publ. Harl. Soc.* XLVI, 125–7.
7 *SPD*, CCXLV, 353.

PAGE 226

1 *APC*, XXIV, 347–8.   2 *Ibid.* p. 374.
3 *Ibid.* p. 400.   4 *Ibid.* p. 405.
5 *Ibid.* p. 429.   6 *Ibid.* p. 443.
7 *Ibid.* pp. 422–443.   8 Stow, p. 766.
9 Creighton, I, 353.   10 *Publ. Harl. Soc.* I, 143.

PAGE 227

1 Anonymous, *A collection [of very valuable and scarce pieces] relating to the [last] plague [in the year 1665]*, p. 53.
2 *Publ. Harl. Soc.* I, 140–3.
3 Anonymous, *A collection relating to the plague*, p. 53.

PAGE 228

1 Creighton, I, 352.   2 *SPD*, Elizabeth, 1595–7, p. 45.
3 *Publ. Harl. Soc.* LXXV, 11–12.   4 E. Freshfield, *Archaeologia*, XLV, 66.

PAGE 229

1 *Publ. Harl. Soc.* XLIV, 291.
2 J. Jewers, *The Home Counties Magazine*, III, 109–10.

References

PAGE 230

1 SHH, IV, 382. 2 *APC*, XXIII, 203.
3 Creighton, I, 356. 4 *Ibid.* p. 354.
5 *Ibid.* 6 F. C. B. Terry, *NQ*, I, 252.
7 A. L. Rowse, *The England of Elizabeth*, p. 221, footnote 1

PAGE 232

1 *The parish registers of S. Breward in Cornwall*, pp. 111–12.
2 H. Barnes, *Trans. Cumb. and Westm. Antiq. and Archaeol. Soc.* X, 158–85.
3 J. Allen, *ibid.* IV, 33–40. 4 M. L. Armitt, *ibid.* VIII, 136–99.
5 H. S. Cowper, *The oldest register book of the parish of Hawkshead in Lancashire*, p. lxv.
6 M. L. Armitt, *ibid.* VIII, 136–99.
7 Cooper, II, 357.
8 S. Tymms, *Proc. Bury and West Suffolk Archaeol. Soc.* I, 40.
9 *SPD*, CXVII, 560.
10 E. P. Brown, *Trans. Cumb. and Westm. Antiq. and Archaeol. Soc.* XXIV, 123–48.
11 Blomefield, p. 248. 12 Cooper, II, 273.
13 SHH, XIV, ii, 215. 14 *Ibid.* XIV, ii, 214.
15 *Ibid.* p. 201.

PAGE 233

1 Creighton, I, 347. 2 *Ibid.*
3 P. Morant, *The history and antiquities of the county of Essex*, pp. 50–1.
4 Cox, p. 156.
5 E. A. B. Barnard, *Worcester Diocesan Magazine*, XXVI, 147.
6 *The registers of Stratford-on-Avon*, The Parish Reg. Soc. VI, 27–8.
7 W. Dyde, *The history and antiquities of Tewkesbury*, p. 109.

PAGE 234

1 Dyde, *Tewkesbury*, p. 109. 2 *SPD*, CXXIII, 587.
3 G. R. Corner, *Archaeologia*, XXXIV, 61.
4 HMC, *MSS. in various collections*, IV, 229.
5 Creighton, I, 348. 6 *APC*, XI, 437.
7 Cox, p. 166. 8 *APC*, XI, 211.
9 Cox, pp. 169–70.
10 E. A. B. Barnard, *Worcs. Dioc. Mag.* XXVI, 147.
11 *Wolverhampton*, Staffs Parish Reg. Soc. p. 2.
12 C. H. Mayo, *Notes and Queries for Somerset and Dorset*, II, 179.

PAGE 235

1 *SPD* Elizabeth, 1547–80, CXXXVII, 652.
2 *Ibid.* p. 681. 3 *Ibid.* p. 679.
4 Dyde, *Tewkesbury*, p. 109. 5 *SPD*, CXXXVII, 652.

References

6 HMC, Thirteenth Report, XIII, IV, 71.
7 Creighton, I, 348.
8 *APC*, XIII, 44.
9 W. D. Sweeting, *Fenland Notes and Queries*, II, 156.
10 J. Sykes, *Yorks. Archaeol. J.* IX, 196.
11 Creighton, I, 348.   12 Blomefield, p. 249.
13 J. Sykes, *Yorks. Archaeol. J.* IX, 475.
14 L. F. Salzman, *The history of the parish of Hailsham*, p. 55.
15 F. D. Wardle, *Somerset Record Soc.* XXXVIII, 71.
16 F. W. De Grave, *Proc. Huguenot Soc. London*, V, 131.

PAGE 236

1 Creighton, I, 349.   2 *Ibid.* p. 348.
3 *Early chronicles of Shrewsbury*, p. 64.
4 *Oswestry*, Shropshire Parish Reg. Soc. St Asaph Diocese, VI, 97–104.
5 *Ibid.* p. 107.
6 *Early chronicles of Shrewsbury*, p. 65.
7 *Shrewsbury St Mary*, Shropshire Parish Reg. Soc. Lichfield Diocese, XII, 2–3.
8 *Early chronicles of Shrewsbury*, p. 65. 9 *Oswestry*, pp. 104–25.
10 *The registers of Stratford-on-Avon*, The Parish Reg. Soc. VI, 40–42.
11 *Shrewsbury St Mary*, pp. 7–9.

PAGE 237

1 *Early chronicles of Shrewsbury*, p. 73.
2 Anonymous, *The history of the county of Lincoln*, I, 228.
3 Creighton, I, 349.   4 HMC, Eleventh Report, XI, iii, 31.
5 *APC*, XIV, 220.   6 Cooper, II, 426.
7 *Archaeologia*, VI, 79–86.

PAGE 238

1 W. E. Godfrey, *J. Derby. Archaeol. & Nat. Hist. Soc.* LXXIV, 32–42.

PAGE 239

1 W. E. Godfrey, *J. Derby. Archaeol. & Nat. Hist. Soc.* LXXIV, 32–42.
2 HMC, Twelfth Report, XII, iv, 210.

PAGE 240

1 *APC*, XIV, 220.   2 *Magna Britannia*, V, 104.
3 Creighton, I, 349.
4 Personal communication to the author from the town clerk of the city of Lincoln, 25 August 1948.
5 T. Richmond, *The local records of Stockton and the neighbourhood*, p. 26.
6 H. Barnes, *Trans. Cumb. & Westm. Antiq. & Archaeol. Soc.* XI, 158–85.
7 Cox, p. 169.
8 HMC, Twelfth Report, XII, iv, 217. 9 *NQ*, XI, 385.

References

PAGE 241

1 S. Tymms, *Proc. Bury and West Suffolk Archaeol. Soc.* I, 40.
2 Creighton, I, 350.
3 G. M. Trevelyan, *English social history*, p. 196.
4 Blomefield, p. 250.
5 Creighton, I, 349.
6 H. Barnes, *Trans. Cumb. & Westm. Antiq. & Archaeol. Soc.* XI, 158–85.
7 Cox, p. 166.

PAGE 242

1 R. E. C. Walters, *Parish registers in England, their history and contents*, p. 64.
2 Cox, pp. 167–8.
3 Creighton, I, 350.
4 *APC*, XIX, 449.
5 HMC, Tenth Report, X, iv, 539.
6 Pickard, pp. 31–2.
7 *Ibid.* p. 33.

PAGE 243

1 Pickard, p. 33.
2 *Ibid.* p. 34.
3 Allhallowes, Goldsmith Street, City of Exeter, *Publ. Devon & Cornwall Rec. Soc.* I, 65–66.
4 Widecombe-in-the-Moor, *ibid.* p. vii.
5 Cox, pp. 173–4.
6 Creighton, I, 351.
7 Harding, *History of Tiverton*, I, 36.

PAGE 244

1 Harding, *History of Tiverton*, I, 36.
2 *Everyman's Encyclopaedia*, VII, 687.

PAGE 245

1 *Magna Britannia*, VI, 527.
2 Cox, p. 174.
3 F. C. Peter, *NQ*, IV, 448.
4 HMC, *MSS. in various collections*, I, 2.
5 Blomefield, II, 250.
6 P. Thomson, *NQ*, XI, 497.
7 *Early chronicles of Shrewsbury*, p. 88.
8 *Wem*, Shropshire Parish Reg. Soc. Lichfield Diocese, X, 108–15.
9 Dyde, *Tewkesbury*, p. 110.
10 Cox, p. 171.
11 S. Tymms, *Proc. Bury and West Suffolk Archaeol. Soc.* I, 41.

PAGE 246

1 Creighton, I, 357.
2 Dyde, *Tewkesbury*, p. 110.
3 Creighton, I, 357.
4 W. Robinson, *Stoke Newington*, p. 183.
5 HMC, *MSS. in various collections*, I, 60.
6 Cooper, II, 520.
7 *Ibid.* p. 522.
8 *Ibid.* p. 523.

References

PAGE 247

1 Kelly, p. 402.   2 *Ibid*. pp. 402–7.
3 *Ibid*. p. 412.   4 *Ibid*. pp. 411–12.
5 *Magna Britannia*, V, 104, footnote *h*.
6 Walters, *Parish registers in England*, p. 73.

PAGE 248

1 *Magna Britannia*, V, 104, footnote *h*.   2 Cox, p. 160.
3 C. S. B. Buckland, VCH, *Huntingdon*, II, 89.
4 Creighton, I, 357.
5 *Bishops Castle*, transcript of the Bishop's register, Public Library, Shrewsbury,
pp. 93–103.

PAGE 250

1 *Bishops Castle*, transcript of the Bishop's register, Public Library, Shrewsbury, pp. 93–103.
2 *Everyman's Encyclopaedia*, II, 273.
3 E. Southall, *Trans. Woolhope Nat. Field Club for 1890–2*, p. 5.
4 E. A. B. Barnard, *Worcs. Dioc. Mag.* XXVI, 148.
5 C. H. Medland, *Trans. Bristol and Glos. Archaeol. Soc.* XXIII, 128.
6 *SPD*, Elizabeth, 1591–4, CCXLIV, 312.
7 SHH, IV, 609.   8 Creighton, I, 365.

PAGE 251

1 *The Lancet*, 18 May 1839.   2 Creighton, I, 357–8.
3 J. Phillips, *Archaeol. Cambrensis*, II, 115–27.
4 W. Jackson, *Trans. Cumb. & Westm. Antiq & Archaeol. Soc.* pp. 287–99.
5 T. Lees, *ibid*. pp. 336–46.

PAGE 252

1 H. Barnes, *ibid*. XI, 158–85.   2 C. A. Parker, *ibid*. VIII, 70–9.
3 W. Nicholls, *The history and traditions of Ravenstonedale, Westmorland*,
II, 55.
4 W. F. Gillbanks, *Trans. Cumb. & Westm. Antiq. & Archaeol. Soc.* VIII,
245–56.   5 H. Barnes, *ibid*. XI, 158–85.

PAGE 253

1 H. Barnes, *ibid*. XI, 158–85.   2 Cox, pp. 168–9.
3 H. Barnes, *Trans. Cumb. & Westm. Antiq. & Archaeol. Soc.* XI, 158–85.
4 T. Lees, *ibid*. pp. 336–46.   5 Creighton, I, 359.

PAGE 254

1 J. Walker, *The history of Penrith from the earliest period to the present time*, p. 54.
2 Creighton, I, 358.   3 *Ibid*. p. 359.
4 *Ludlow*, Shropshire Parish Reg. Soc. Hereford Diocese, XIII, 274–7.

References

PAGE 255

1 *Wem, ibid.* Lichfield Diocese, X, 119–20.
2 *Newport*, transcript of Bishop's register, Public Library, Shrewsbury, 8–10.
3 *Oswestry*, Shropshire Parish Reg. Soc. St Asaph Diocese, VI, 188–205.
4 *Ludlow*, Shropshire Parish Reg. Soc. Hereford Diocese, XIII, viii.
5 'Leominster Burials in 1587 and '97', *NQ*, XI, 385.
6 Dyde, *Tewkesbury*, p. 111.
7 W. A. Greenhill, *Sussex Archaeol. Collections*, XIV, 196.
8 *Ibid.*

PAGE 256

1 *PCS*, III, 229.
2 J. Ritchie, 'Quarantine for Plague in Scotland', *Edinburgh Med. J.* LV, 691–700.
3 *PCS*, III, 313–14.
4 J. Ritchie, *Edinburgh Med. J.* LV, 691–700.
5 Creighton, I, 367
6 *The chronicle of Perth*, pp. 2–4.
7 R. Chambers, *Domestic Annals of Scotland*, I, 155.
8 ERBE, IV, 344–5.
9 R. Chambers, *Domestic Annals of Scotland*, I, 155.
10 *The chronicle of Perth*, p. 4.
11 R. Chambers, *The Domestic Annals of Scotland*, I, 158.
12 *Extracts from the Kirk Sessions Records of Perth*, p. 55.

PAGE 257

1 *Extracts from the Kirk Sessions Records of Perth*, p. 56.
2 *PCS*, III, 695.   3 ERBE, IV, 344–5.
4 *Extracts from the council register of Aberdeen*, II, 52–4.
5 *Ibid.*   6 *Ibid.* II, 56
7 *Ibid.* II, 57.   8 *PCS*, III, 744, footnote.
9 ERBE, IV, 413–14.

PAGE 259

1 ERBE, IV, 414–16.
2 R. Chambers, *Domestic Annals of Scotland*, I, 158.
3 'The Diarey of Robert Birrel, Burges of Edinburghe', *Fragments of Scottish History*, Dalyell, p. 23.   4 ERBE, IV, 419.
5 *Ibid.* p. 436.   6 *Ibid.* p. 419.
7 *Ibid.* pp. 430–44.

PAGE 260

1 T. Wright, *Queen Elizabeth and her times*, II, 265.
2 *PCS*, IV, 1.   3 *Ibid.* III, 752–3.
4 *Ibid.* IV, 6–7.
5 R. Chambers, *Domestic Annals of Scotland*, I, 158.

6 Creighton, I, 368–9.
7 L. A. Barbé, *Chambers' Journal*, IV, 234–7.
8 ERBE, IV, 463. 9 *Ibid*. 462–3.
10 SHH, III, 298. 11 ERBE, VI, 504.

PAGE 261

1 R. Chambers, *Domestic Annals of Scotland*, I, 182.
2 *Ayr burgh accounts*, p. 159. 3 Creighton, I, 369.
4 ERBE, V, 92. 5 *Ibid*. p. 93.
6 *Ibid*. p. 192. 7 *Ibid*. p. 193.
8 *Ibid*. p. 194. 9 *Ibid*.
10 *Ibid*. 11 *Ibid*. pp. 194–5.

PAGE 262

1 ERBE, V, 195–6. 2 *Ibid*. pp. 196 ff.

PAGE 263

1 *The chronicle of Perth*, p. 7. 2 Creighton, I, 370.

PAGE 264

1 R. Chambers, *Domestic Annals of Scotland, from the reformation to the revolution*,
I, 318. 2 *TSP*, II, ii, 268.

PAGE 265

1 Chronicles of the Frasers (the Wardlaw MS.), ed. W. Mackay, *Publ. Scot. Hist.
Soc.* XLVII, 236.
2 R. Chambers, *Domestic Annals of Scotland*, I, 357.
3 *TSP*, II, ii, 270.
4 R. Chambers, *Domestic Annals of Scotland*, I, 357.
5 *Ibid*.
6 J. D. Comrie, *History of Scottish medicine*, I, 219.
7 ERBE, V, 298.
8 D. C. Herries, 'An Annandale minister in the seventeenth century', *Dumfries
& Galloway Nat. Hist. & Antiq. Soc.* V, 32.
9 *TSP*, II, ii, 270. 10 ERBE, V, 301.
11 *Ibid*. p. 302.
12 'The Diarey of Robert Birrel, Burges of Edinburghe', p. 56.
13 ERBE, V, 306. 14 *The chronicle of Perth*, p. 9.
15 SHH, XV, 274.

PAGE 266

1 ERBE, V, 321. 2 *Ayr burgh accounts*, p. 219.
3 Wilson, p. 86. 4 *Ibid*. p. 87.
5 *Ibid*. p. 85. 6 Wilson, p. 85.
7 *Ibid*. pp. 85–6.

References

8 *Henslowe Papers*, ed. W. W. Greg, p. 35.
9 Wilson, p. 86.   10 *Ibid.* p. 87.
11 *Ibid.*   12 *Ibid.* p. 88.
13 Register of St Mary Magdalen, Milk Street, *Publ. Harl. Soc.*
LXII, 43.   14 *PMV*, X, 33.
15 *Ibid.* p. 42.   16 *TSP*, I, 108.
17 *Ibid.* p. 109.   18 *Ibid.* p. 110.
19 *Ibid.*   20 *Ibid.* p. 111.

PAGE 267

1 *PMV*, X, 92.   2 *Ibid.* p. 90.
3 *Ibid.* p. 92.   4 *TSP*, I, 112.
5 *PMV*, X, 120.   6 Creighton, I, 477, footnote.
7 Stow, p. 857.
8 'Reflections on the weekly bills of mortality', *A collection of very Valuable and Scarce Pieces*, p. 53.

PAGE 268

1 Register of St Peeters upon Cornhill, *Publ. Harl. Soc.* I, 159.
2 Register of St Mary Magdalen, Milk Street, *Publ. Harl. Soc.* LXXII, 43.
3 Register of St Michael, Cornhill, *Publ. Harl. Soc.* VII, 211–13.
4 Register of St Antholin, Budge Row, *Publ. Harl. Soc.* VIII, 41–2.
5 Register of St Pancras, Soper Lane, *Publ. Harl. Soc.* XLIV, 294.

PAGE 269

1 SHH, XV, 189.   2 J. C. Cox, *Churchwarden's accounts*, p. 148.
3 *Ibid.* p. 318.   4 Creighton, I, 477, footnote.
5 Register of St James, Clerkenwell, *Publ. Harl. Soc.* XVII, iv, 72–86.
6 Register of St Martin-in-the-Fields, *Publ. Harl. Soc.* XXV, 148–53.
7 Register of St James, Clerkenwell, *Publ. Harl. Soc.* XVII, iv, 66–72 and 86–96.
8 Register of St Martin-in-the-Fields, *Publ. Harl. Soc.* I, 145–8 and 153–7.
9 Register of Kensington, *Publ. Harl. Soc.* XVI, 96–7.
10 Robinson, *Stoke Newington*, p. 184.
11 W. Robinson, *The history and antiquities of the parish of Tottenham in the county of Middlesex*, II, 178.
12 E. Hammond, *Bygone Wandsworth*, p. 11.
13 J. Hargrove, 'The plague at Datchet', *NQ*, VI, 90.
14 *The diary of Lady Anne Clifford*, p. 11.
15 P. Morant, *The history and antiquities of the county of Essex*, p. 52.
16 HMC, Tenth Report, part 4, p. 5.

PAGE 270

1 Cox, pp. 172–3.   2 *Ibid.* p. 173.
3 HMC, Twelfth Report, appendix, part 1, p. 45.
4 Cox, p. 173.

References

5 R. W. Blencowe, 'Extracts from the parish registers and other parochial documents of East Sussex', *Sussex Archaeol. Collect.* IV, 243–90.
6 C. W. Boase, *Historic towns: Oxford*, p. 135.
7 HMC, *Manuscripts in various collections*, I, 74.
8 *Ibid.*   9 *Ibid.* p. 73.

PAGE 271

1 HMC, *Manuscripts in various collections*, I, 74.
2 A. E. Hudd, *Trans. Bristol. and Glos. Archaeol. Soc.* XIX, 105–41.
3 *Ibid.*   4 Dyde, *Tewkesbury*, p. 112.
5 Cox, p. 164.
6 D. Sweeting, *Fenland Notes and Queries*, II, 154.
7 Cox, *Churchwardens' accounts*, p. 318.
8 Creighton, I, 360.   9 SHH, XV, 264.
10 Cooper, III, 3.
11 A. G. E. Jones, 'Plagues in Suffolk in the seventeenth century', *NQ*, CXCVIII, 384–6.

PAGE 272

1 A. G. E. Jones, 'Plagues in Suffolk in the seventeenth century', *NQ*, CXCVIII, 384–6.
2 *The Registers of St Nicholas, Ipswich*, The Parish Register Soc. VII, 128–9.
3 Jones, *loc. cit.*   4 Blomefield, p. 253.
5 HMC, Tenth Report, part 5, 89 (no. 568).
6 Cox, p. 155.   7 *Ibid.*
8 *Ibid.*
9 T. Allen, *The history of the county of Lincoln, from the earliest period to the present time*, I, 228.   10 Creighton, II, 40
11 *Ibid.* I, 498.

PAGE 273

1 Ormerod, *Chester*, I, 238.
2 D. and S. Lysons, *Magna Britannia*, II, ii, 602–3.
3 Creighton, I, 498.   4 Ormerod, I, 238.
5 *Ibid.* p. 239.   6 *Ibid.*
7 Cox, p. 161.   8 Creighton, I, 498
9 Kelly, pp. 413–14.   10 *Ibid.* p. 414.

PAGE 274

1 L. M. Stanewell, *Calendar of the ancient deeds, letters, etc., in the archives of the corporation of Kingston-upon-Hull* (M. 113), p. 325.
2 *Ibid.*   3 *Ibid.*
4 Maud Sellers, VCH, *York*, III, 455.
5 *Ibid.*
6 R. N. Scaife, 'Extracts from the registers of the church of St Mary, Castlegate, York', *Yorks. Archaeol. J.* XV, 157.

References

1 T. Laycock, *Report on the state of York*, p. 60.
2 *Ibid.* p. 60. 3 SHH, XVI, 327.
4 Creighton, I, 496–9.
5 C. F. Mullett, *The bubonic plague in England*, p. 109.
6 Creighton, I, 499.
7 R. Surtees, *The history and antiquities of the county Palatine of Durham*, IV, 7.
8 T. F. Thistleton-Dyer, *Old English social life as told by the parish registers*, p. 86.
9 *Monk Fryston, 1536–1678*, The Parish Register Soc. V, 48–55.

1 Thistleton-Dyer, *op. cit.* p. 86. 2 Ormerod, *Chester*, II, 597.
3 SHH, XVI, 459.
4 *The register of Shrewsbury St Mary*, Shropshire Parish Reg. Soc. Lichfield Diocese, XII, 32–5.
5 *Ibid.* pp. 17–32. 6 *Ibid.* pp. 37–50.
7 *The register of Myddle*, Shropshire Parish Reg. Soc. Lichfield Diocese, XIX, i, 55–61.
8 *The register of Condover*, Shropshire Parish Reg. Soc. Lichfield Diocese, VI, i, 43.
9 *Ibid.* pp. 30–43. 10 *Ibid.* pp. 45–56.
11 *Ibid.* pp. 43–5. 12 *Ibid.* pp. 45–6.
13 *Mucklestone, 1555–1701*, Staffs. Parish Reg. Soc. I, 63.
14 SHH, XVI, 111.

1 *The registers of Stratford-on-Avon in the county of Warwick*, The Parish Reg. Soc. LV, 69–71.

1 *The registers of Stratford-on-Avon in the county of Warwick*, The Parish Reg. Soc. LV, 75–7.
2 W. H. Medland, 'St Nicholas Church, Gloucester', *Trans. Bristol and Glos. Archaeol. Soc.* XXIII, 109–8. 3 SHH, XVI, 179.
4 J. R. Burton, *A history of Kidderminster, with short accounts of some neighbouring parishes*, p. 71.
5 SHH, XVI, 274. 6 *Ibid.* XVI, 310–12.
7 The registers of the Abbey Church of SS. Peter and Paul, Bath, *Publ. Harl. Soc.* XXVIII, ii, 339–40. 8 *TSP*, I, 114.
9 E. Giles and R. W. Thrale, *Historic Sandridge. The story of a Hertfordshire parish*, p. 22.
10 W. D. Sweeting, 'The plagues of 1605 and 1625', *NQ*, II, 390–1.
11 W. G. D. Fletcher, *A short history of Shelton and Oxon*, p. 20.
12 Cox, p. 156.
13 C. W. Boase, *Historic towns: Oxford*, p. 135.
14 *SPD, 1603–10*, IX, 141 (no. 9).

PAGE 279

1 *The parish registers of Horsham in the county of Sussex, 1541–1635*, Sussex Record Soc. XXI, 364.
2 Violet M. Shillington, VCH, *Hampshire and the Isle of Wight*, V, 426.
3 T. W. W. Smart, 'The plagues of 1605 and 1625', *NQ*, II, 390.
4 *Ibid.* II, 390.
5 R. W. Merriman, 'Extracts from the records of the Wiltshire Quarter Sessions', *Wilts. Archaeol. and Nat. Hist. Mag.* XXII, 12–13.
6 Pickard, p. 34.   7 *Ibid.* pp. 34–5.

PAGE 280

1 *PMV*, X, 130 (no. 186).

PAGE 281

1 *PMV*, X, 120, 125, and 126 (nos. 167, 172, and 175).
2 *Ibid.* pp. 130 (no. 186).
3 *Ibid.* pp. 132–47 (nos. 188, 190, 199, 201, 204, 207, and 213).
4 *Ibid.* pp. 150–5 (nos. 217, 220, 223, and 227).
5 *Ibid.* pp. 163–75 (nos. 233, 236, 242, 248, 251, and 259).
6 Register of St Michael, Cornhill, *Publ. Harl. Soc.* VII, 213.
7 SHH XVI, 77.   8 *Ibid.* p. 387.
9 W. Spurrell, *Carmarthen and its neighbourhood*, p. 5.
10 J. Phillips, 'The oldest parish registers in Pembrokeshire', *Archaeol. Cambrensis*, II, 115–27.
11 Register of St Lawrence Jewry, *Publ. Harl. Soc.* LXX, 134.
12 Register of St Antholin, Budge Row, *Publ. Harl. Soc.* VIII, 43–4.
13 Register of All Hallows, Bread Street, *Publ. Harl. Soc.* XLIII, 171–2.
14 J. C. Cox, *Churchwardens' accounts*, p. 317.
15 SHH, XVII, 307.

PAGE 282

1 *SPD, 1603–1610*, CCXLV, 213 (no. 83).
2 SHH, XVII, 206.   3 Cox, p. 155.
4 C. W. Boase, *Historic towns: Oxford*, p. 135.
5 C. S. B. Buckland, VCH, *Huntingdon*, II, 89.
6 Cox, p. 156.   7 Cooper, III, 19.
8 D. G. Lumb, 'The registers of the parish church of Methley in the county of York, from 1560 to 1812', *Publ. Thoresby Soc.* XII, 69–70.
9 *Monk Fryston 1536–1678*, The Parish Reg. Soc. V, 52–5.

PAGE 283

1 W. E. A. Axon, 'Chronological notes on the visitations of plague in Lancashire and Cheshire', *Trans. Lancs. and Ches. Antiq. Soc.* XII, 68.
2 *Ibid.* p. 69.
3 C. H. Mullett, *The bubonic plague and England*, p. 109.

References

4 Axon, *Trans. Lancs. and Ches. Antiq. Soc.* XII, 69–70.
5 HMC, XIV, appendix, part 4, 14.
6 T. Phillips, *The history and antiquities of Shrewsbury*, p. 17.
7 *The register of Condover*, Shropshire Parish Reg. Soc. VI, i, 43–6.
8 SHH, XVII, 307.

PAGE 284

1 W. P. Barrett, *Present remedies against the plague*, Shakespeare Association Facsimiles, no. 17, p. xvi.
2 Register of St Peeters upon Cornhill, *Publ. Harl. Soc.* I, 159.
3 J. Bell, *London's Remembrancer*, A4 (verso).
4 T. Dekker, 'The Wonderfull yeare', *The Plague Pamphlets of Thomas Dekker*, ed. F. P. Wilson, p. 26.
5 *Idem*, 'A Rod for Run-awayes', *ibid.* p. 143.
6 Wilson, p. 114.　　　　　7 *Ibid.* p. 114, footnote 3.
8 *Ibid.* p. 114.

PAGE 285

1 *TSP*, I, 112.　　　　　　2 *Ibid.*
3 *Ibid.* p. 114.　　　　　　4 *Ibid.* p. 115.
5 *PCS*, VI, 164.

PAGE 286

1 *PCS*, VI, 269.　　　　　　2 *Ibid.* p. 311.
3 *Ibid.* p. 313.　　　　　　4 *Ibid.* p. 337.
5 *Ibid.* pp. 337–8.　　　　　6 *Ibid.* p. 223.
7 *Ibid.* p. 338.　　　　　　8 *Ibid.* p. 345.
9 *Ibid.* p. 354.　　　　　10 *Ibid.* p. 376.
11 *Ibid.* p. 379.　　　　　12 *Ibid.* VII, 4.
13 ERBE, VI, 3.　　　　　　14 *Ibid.* p. 4.
15 *Ibid.* pp. 4–5.　　　　　16 *Ibid.* pp. 5–6.

PAGE 287

1 'The Diarey of Robert Birrel', p. 62.
2 Comrie, *History of Scottish medicine*, p. 221.
3 *Ibid.*
4 R. Chambers, *Domestic Annals of Scotland*, I, 381.
5 ERBE, VI, 323.　　　　　6 CARD, II, 419–20.
7 *Ibid.* p. 424.　　　　　8 *Ibid.* III, appendix 3, 536.
9 *Ibid.* iii, 536.　　　　10 *Ibid.* iii, 537.

PAGE 288

1 *Ibid.* iii, 538.
2 N. Hodges, *Loimologia: or, an historical account of the great plague in London in 1665*, ed. J. Quincy, p. 96.

3 Anonymous, *An historical narrative of the great plague at London, 1665: etc.*
pp. 387–8.   4 CARD, III, iii, 537.
5 *PCS*, VII, 140   6 *Ibid.* pp. 123–5.
7 *Ibid.* p. 140.   8 *Ibid.* p. 51.
9 *SPD, 1603–1610*, XV, 235.   10 *PCS*, XIV, 421.
11 *Ibid.*

PAGE 289

1 Comrie, *History of Scottish medicine*, pp. 219–20.
2 Creighton, I, 503.
3 *The Egerton Papers*, pp. 406–7.
4 R. Chambers, *Domestic Annals of Scotland*, I, 395.
5 *PCS*, VII, 214.   6 *TSP*, II, ii, 276.
7 *PCS*, VII, 235.   8 *Ibid.*

PAGE 290

1 Comrie, *History of Scottish medicine*, p. 220.
2 *PCS*, VII, 248.

PAGE 291

1 *Ayr burgh accounts*, G. S. Pryde, pp. cii–ciii.
2 *Ibid.* p. ciii.
3 *Extracts from the burgh records of Dunfermline in the sixteenth and seventeenth
centuries*, ed. A. Shearer, pp. 21, 23, 43.
4 *The chronicle of Perth*, p. 11.
5 R. Chambers, *Domestic Annals of Scotland*, I, 405.
6 CARD, III, appendix, 3, p. 538.   7 Creighton, I, 502.

PAGE 292

1 *PCS*, VII, 449.   2 *TSP*, II, ii, 277.
3 *Ibid.*   4 *PCS*, VIII, 20.
5 *Ibid.* VII, 299–302.   6 *Ibid.* p. 357.
7 J. Ritchie, 'Quarantine for plague in Scotland during the sixteenth and seventeenth centuries', *Edinb. med. J.* pp. 691–701.
8 *Extracts from the burgh records of Dunfermline*, p. 28.
9 R. Chambers, *Domestic Annals of Scotland*, I, 400.
10 *Ibid.* I, 410.   11 *PCS*, VIII, 159.
12 R. Chambers, *Domestic Annals of Scotland*, I, 413.
13 *PCS*, VIII, 159.
14 *Extracts from the burgh records of Dunfermline*, p. 49.

PAGE 293

1 *Extracts from the burgh records of Dunfermline*, p. 49.
2 *Ibid.* p. 51.   3 *PCS*, VIII, 359.
4 'The plague plots of Geneva', Nova et Vetera, *Brit. Med. Jour.* (1907), ii, 99–100.

5 R. Fletcher, 'A tragedy of the great plague of Milan in 1630', *Bull. Johns Hopkins Hosp.* IX, 175–80.
6 *Extracts from the burgh records of Dunfermline*, p. 53.
7 *Ayr burgh accounts*, Scottish Hist. Soc. p. 240

PAGE 294

1 *PMV*, X, 384.   2 *Ibid.* p. 385.
3 SHH, XVIII, 273.   4 Wilson, p. 64.
5 *SPD, 1603–1610*, XXIII, 332 (no. 33).
6 *Remenbrancia*, II, 337.
7 *HLP*, 4 James I, 23 September, 1606.
8 *SPD, 1603–1610*, XXIII, 332 (no. 34).
9 Creighton, I, 494

PAGE 295

1 SHH, XVIII, 274.   2 *Ibid.* p. 279.
3 'Etonensis', 'The plagues of 1605 and 1625', *NQ*, II, 391.
4 L. W. Clarke, 'The plague in Birmingham', Birmingham Notes and Queries, *The Birmingham Journal and Daily Post*, 30 July 1863, p. 6.
5 W. D. Sweeting, 'The plagues of 1605 and 1625', *NQ*, II, 390–1.
6 Axon, *Trans. Lancs. and Ches. Antiq. Soc.* XII, 52–99.

PAGE 296

1 W. E. A. Axon, 'Documents relating to the Plague in Manchester in 1605', *Cheetham Miscellany*, III, 17–24.
2 *SPD, Addenda 1580–1625*, XXXVIII, 477 (nos. 23–33).
3 *Ibid.* p. 478 (no. 41).

PAGE 297

1 W. Spurrell, *Carmarthen and its neighbourhood*, p. 5.
2 Creighton, I, 494.   3 Kelly, p. 415.
4 *Ibid.* pp. 415–6.   5 *Ibid.* p. 417.

PAGE 298

1 Kelly, pp. 417–28.   2 *Ibid.* p. 428.
3 *Ibid.* p. 430.
4 *The register of Ludlow*, Shropshire Parish Reg. Soc. Hereford Diocese, XIII, i, 295 (footnote).
5 *The court and times of James I*, ed. R. F. Williams, I, 76.
6 *Ibid.*   7 *Ibid.*
8 *TSP*, I, 125.   9 Creighton, I, 494.
10 HMC, *Report on the manuscripts of Lord De L'Isle and Dudley*, III, 412.
11 *Ibid.*
12 *The parish register of Horsham in the county of Sussex*, Sussex Record Soc. XXI, 368–70.

13 *The register of Ludlow*, Shropshire Parish Reg. Soc. Hereford Diocese, XIII, i, 294–9.
14 Ormerod, *Chester*, I, 239.
15 Axon, *Trans. Lancs. and Ches. Antiq. Soc.* XII, 52–9.

PAGE 299

1 Cooper, III, 30.
3 *The court and times of James I*, ed. R. F. Williams, I, 96.
4 Wilson, p. 120.
6 *Ibid.* p. 325 (no. 444).
8 Creighton, I, 494.

2 Creighton, I, 494.
5 *PMV*, XI, 232 (no. 439).
7 *Ibid.*
9 Wilson, p. 121.

PAGE 300

1 Wilson, p. 121.
3 Wilson, p. 121.
5 Cox, p. 148.
7 *Ibid.* p. 373 (no. 678).
8 HMC, *Report on the manuscripts of the Marquess of Downshire*, II, 158.
9 *The court and times of James I*, ed. R. F. Williams, I, 100.
10 *Ibid.*
11 Cox, p. 173.
12 Dorothy Gardiner, 'A mayor of Canterbury: William Watmer, the children's friend', *Archaeol. Cantiana*, LXI, 98–105.

2 *PMV*, XI, 326 (no. 599).
4 *TSP*, I, 128.
6 *PMV*, XI, 365 (no. 658).

PAGE 301

1 Dorothy Gardiner, 'A mayor of Canterbury: William Watmer, the children's friend', *Archaeol. Cantiana*, LXI, 98–105.
2 *Parish register of Horsham*, Sussex Record Soc. XXI, 370–2.
3 Sir H. L. Tidy, *A synopsis of medicine*, p. 273.
4 J. H. Sperling, 'The parochial history of Westbourne', *Sussex Archaeol. Coll.* XXII, 87.
5 HMC, *Manuscripts in various collections*, I, 81.
6 E. Sinker, *Salwarpe*, pp. 54–5.
7 HMC, *Manuscripts in various collections*, I, 287–8.
8 *Ibid.* p. 288.
9 *The register of Ludlow*, Shropshire Parish Reg. Soc. Hereford Diocese, XIII, i, 296–9.

PAGE 302

1 *The register of Ludlow*, XIII, i, 287–96.
2 *Ibid.* pp. 299–309.
3 H. T. Weyman, *The register of Ludlow*, pp. viii–xiii.
4 Cox, p. 161.
5 Cox, p. 162.

PAGE 303

1 HMC, Fourteenth Report, appendix, part 8, 49.
2 Blomefield, II, 255.
3 Cox, p. 171.

References

4 'Moore MS.', *Lancs. and Ches. Record Soc.* LXVII, 47.
5 G. D. Lumb, 'The parish register of Aberford, co. York', *Publ. Thoresby Soc.*
XXXVI, 62.   6 Cox, p. 167.

PAGE 304

1 *Middlesex County Records*, II, 50.   2 Creighton, I, 494.
3 T. E. Keys, 'The plague in literature', *Bull. Med. Libr. Assoc.* XXXII, 51.
4 *D.N.B.* X, 1069–70.
5 Cox, *Churchwardens' accounts*, p. 321.
6 Coulton, *The Medieval Village*, p. 258.
7 Register of St Helen's, Bishopsgate, *Publ. Harl. Soc.* XXXI, 273.
8 Register of St Mary Somerset, *Publ. Harl. Soc.* LX, ii, 33–5.
9 Register of St Michael Bassishaw, *Publ. Harl. Soc.* LXXII, i, 174–5.
10 *Encyclopaedia Britannica* (11th ed.), XX, 330.

PAGE 306

1 Cox, *Churchwardens' accounts*, p. 321.
2 Register of St Michael Bassishaw, *Publ. Harl. Soc.* LXXII, i, 175.
3 *TSP*, I, 138.
4 *Ibid.* p. 144.
5 *Parish Register of Horsham*, Sussex Record Soc. XXI, 372–4.
6 J. Maclean, 'The plague at Tredington, 1610–1611', *Gloucestershire Notes and
Queries*, II, 71–2.
7 HMC, *Manuscripts in various collections*, I, 289.
8 Rev. E. Sinker, *Salwarpe*, pp. 54–5.

PAGE 307

1 E. A. B. Barnard, 'In the time of pestilence', *Worcs. Dioc. Mag.* XXVI, 148.
2 H. Southall, 'Retiring address of the president', *Trans. Woolhope Naturalists'
Field Club*, p. 5.   3 Cooper, III, 41.
4 *Calendar of Wynn (of Gwydir) Papers*, p. 87.
5 Ormerod, *Chester*, I, 239.
6 J. C. Morley, 'The plague of Liverpool,' *Bygone Lancashire*, p. 107.
7 J. N. Radcliffe, *The pestilence in England: an historical sketch*, p. 41.
8 R. Surtees, *The history and antiquities of the County Palatine of Durham*, II, 207.
9 *Ibid.* p. 242.

PAGE 308

1 J. Maclean, 'The plague at Tredington, 1610–1611', *loc. cit.*
2 HMC, *Rutland MSS.* IV, 476.   3 *Worcestershire county records*, I, cli.
4 HMC, *Manuscripts in various collections*, I, 84.
5 'D.O.', 'Population of Sheffield in 1615', *The Gentleman's Mag.* LXXXI, ii, 603–4.
6 HMC, *Manuscripts in various collections*, I, 298.
7 Cox, p. 155.
8 R. S. Downs, 'The parish church of High Wycombe', *Records of Bucks.* VIII,
55–87.

PAGE 309

1 *Worcestershire county records*, I, 229.
2 'Quarter Sessions records for the county of Somerset', *Somerset Record Soc.* XXIII, 238. 3 Cox, p. 165.
4 Downs, *Records of Bucks*. VIII, 264, footnote 3.
5 Kelly, p. 431.
6 H. S. Cowper, *The oldest register book in the Parish of Hawkshead in Lancashire*, p. lxxiv.
7 J. R. Stockdale, *Annals Caermoelenses: or Annals of Cartmel*, p. 568.

PAGE 310

1 J. R. Stockdale, *Annals Caermoelenses: or Annals of Cartmel*, p. 568.

PAGE 311

1 H. Barnes, 'Visitations of the plague in Cumberland and Westmorland', *Trans. Cumb. and Westm. Antiq. and Archaeol. Soc.* XI, 158–85.
2 Cowper, *Register book of Hawkshead*, p. lxxiv.
3 J. H. Nicholson, 'The parish registers of Orton, Westmorland', *Trans. Cumb. and Westm. Antiq. and Archaeol. Soc.* XI, 250–65.
4 Axon, *Trans. Lancs. and Ches. Antiq. Soc.* XII, 52–99.

PAGE 313

1 Axon, *Trans. Lancs. and Ches. Antiq. Soc.* XII, 52–99.
2 *Quarter Sessions records*, North Riding Rec. Soc. III, 214.
3 *APC, 1623–1625*, p. 457.
4 *Warwick county records*, I, 43.
5 Dyde, *Tewkesbury*, p. 113.
6 Downs, 'The parish church of High Wycombe', *Records of Bucks*, VIII, 55–87.
7 Creighton, I, 507. 8 *PCS*, XI, 410.

PAGE 314

1 *PCS*, XII, 62–3. 2 *Ibid.* p. 334.
3 R. Chambers, *Domestic Annals of Scotland*, I, 483.
4 'A modern account of Scotland by an English gentleman, 1670', *Harleian Miscellany*, VII, 438. 5 *PCS*, XIII, 622–3.

PAGE 315

1 *PCS*, XIII, 652, footnote. 2 *Ibid.* p. 652.
3 *PCS*, XIII, 663. 4 Creighton, I, 506–7.
5 *The court and times of James I*, I, 439.

PAGE 316

1 *The court and times of James I*, I, 470–1.
2 *Ibid.* p. 473. 3 Wilson, p. 129.
4 *Ibid.*

5 Sir H. L. Tidy, *A synopsis of medicine*, p. 308.
6 Register of St Michael Bassishaw, *Publ. Harl. Soc.* LXXII, 183–6.
7 *The court and times of James I*, I, 209.

PAGE 318

1 R. L. Huckstep, *Typhoid fever and other Salmonella infections*, p. 252.
2 Creighton, I, 507–8.   3 *Ibid.* p. 508.

PAGE 319

1 *APC, 1623–1625*, p. 505.   2 *Ibid.* p. 457.
3 *The Knyvett Letters, 1620–1644*, Norfolk Record Soc. p. 67.
4 Birch I, 11–16.   5 *Ibid.* p. 11.
6 *Ibid.* p. 15.   7 *Ibid.*
8 Wilson, p. 134.

PAGE 321

1 *SPD, 1625–1626*, IV, 61 (no. 61).   2 Birch, I, 28.
3 *TSP*, v, i, 168.
4 *APC, 1625–1626*, p. 98.
5 Wilson, p. 136.
6 *SPD, 1625–1626*, IV, 61 (no. 61).
7 *Calendar of Wynn (of Gwydir) Papers*, p. 217.

PAGE 322

1 Birch, I, 39.
2 *Pepys' Diary*, ed. H. B. Wheatley, v, 57.
3 Birch, I, 40–1.   4 *Ibid.* p. 41.
5 *Ibid.* p. 39, footnote 1.   6 *APC, 1625–1626*, pp. 122–3.
7 *SPD, 1625–1626*, IV, 76 (no. 76).   8 Birch, I, 43.
9 E. C. Brewer, *The reader's handbook of famous names in fiction, etc.*, p. 495.

PAGE 323

1 Birch, I, 43.   2 *Ibid.* p. 44.
3 *Skrine MSS.*, HMC, Eleventh Report, appendix, part 1, p. 21.
4 *Ibid.* p. 18.   5 *Skrine MSS.* p. 24.
6 *Ibid.* pp. 26–7.   7 *TSP*, v, i, 169.
8 *Ibid.* pp. 169–70.   9 *APC, 1625–1626*, p. 127.
10 Wilson, p. 138.

PAGE 324

1 Wilson, p. 138.   2 *Ibid.* footnote 2.
3 *Ibid.* p. 140.   4 *Skrine MSS.* p. 28.
5 *Skrine MSS.*, p. 28.
6 Birch, I, 46.   7 *APC, 1625–1626*, p. 134.
8 *SPD, 1625–1626*, p. 84 (no. 45).

PAGE 325

1 *SPD, 1625–1626*, p. 84 (no. 45).   2 *APC, 1625–1626*, pp. 142–3.
3 *SPD, 1625–1626*, p. 90 (no. 89).   4 Birch, I, 45.
5 *Ibid.*
6 *Calendar of Wynn (of Gwydir) Papers*, p. 218.
7 Birch, I, 45.   8 *Ibid.* pp. 45–6.

PAGE 326

1 Birch, p. 48.   2 *Ibid.*
3 *Ibid.*

PAGE 327

1 The life of William Lilly, student in astrology, *Autobiography*, pp. 23–4.
2 Wilson, pp. 100 and 155–6.   3 Wilson, p. 155.
4 *Skrine MSS.* HMC, Eleventh Report, appendix, part 1, p. 32.
5 *Skrine MSS.* p. 33.   6 Birch, I, 54.

PAGE 330

1 *TSP*, I, 171.   2 Birch, I, 56–7.
3 *APC, 1625–1626*, p. 194.   4 *Ibid.* p. 198.
5 *Ibid.* p. 204.
6 *Coke MSS.* HMC, Twelfth Report, appendix, part 1, p. 218.

PAGE 331

1 Birch, I, 63.
2 *Skrine MSS.* HMC, Eleventh Report, appendix, part 1, p. 36.
3 *SPD, 1625–1626*, p. 158 (no. 28).

PAGE 332

1 *APC, 1625–1626*, p. 258.   2 *PCS, 1625*, I, 209–10, footnote.
3 Birch, I, 50.   4 *APC, 1625–1626*, p. 279.

PAGE 333

1 *TSP*, I, 172.   2 Birch, I, 74–85.
3 *Ibid.* p. 90.
4 Creighton, I, 511.
5 *Skrine MSS.* HMC, Eleventh Report, appendix, part 1, p. 44.
6 *Remenbrancia*, VI, 63.   7 *SPD, 1625–1626*, XI, 177 (no. 70).
8 *Ibid.* XII, 184 (no. 39).   9 Birch, I, 48.

PAGE 334

1 Cox, *Churchwardens' Accounts*, p. 317.
2 *Ibid.* p. 318.
3 Wilson, p. 156.
4 Register of St Martin-in-the-Fields, *Publ. Harl. Soc.* XXV, 222.

References

PAGE 335

1 E. Freshfield, *Archaeologia*, XLV, 57–110.
2 F. W. Alington, 'The plague of London in 1625', *NQ*, VI, 453.
3 W. Underhill, 'The plague of London in 1625', *NQ*, VI, 324–5.

PAGE 337

1 Robinson, *Stoke Newington*, pp. 183–4.
2 Robinson, *The history and antiquities of the parish of Tottenham in the county of Middlesex*, II, 178.   3 *APC, 1625–1626*, p. 357.
4 Pegge, *Archaeologia*, VI, 78–86.
5 *Skrine MSS*. HMC, Eleventh Report, appendix, part I, p. 28.
6 Gladys Scott Thomson, *Life in a noble household, 1641–1700*, pp. 16–18.
7 *SPD, 1625–1626*, IV, 67 (no. 94).   8 Birch, I, 41–4.
9 'Etonensis', 'The plagues of 1605 and 1625', *NQ*, II, 391.
10 Wilson, p. 160.

PAGE 338

1 J. Noorthouck, *A new history of London, etc.* p. 154.
2 Wilson, p. 160.
3 *Skrine MSS*. HMC, Eleventh Report, appendix, part I, p. 8.
4 *SPD, 1625–1626*, IV, 71 (no. 111).
5 W. A. Greenhill, 'Registers of the Hastings parishes', *Sussex Archaeol. Collect.* XIV, 197.   6 *SPD, 1625–1626*, VI, 112 (no. 114).
7 *Ibid.* V, 90 (no. 89).   8 *Ibid.* IV, 71 (no. 111).
9 'The register of the Wallon or Strangers' Church in Canterbury', *Publ. Huguenot Soc.* VI, iii, 578–80.
10 W. A. Greenhill, 'Registers of the Hastings parishes', *Sussex Archaeol. Collect.* XIV, 197.

PAGE 339

1 *SPD, 1625–1626*, VI, 112 (no. 114).   2 *APC, 1625–1626*, p. 244.
3 *SPD, 1625–1626*, V, 90 (no. 89).
4 The registers of the Abbey Church of SS. Peter and Paul, Bath, *Publ. Harl. Soc.* XXVIII, ii, 351.   5 *Ibid.* pp. 345–51.
6 *Ibid.* pp. 351–7.   7 Pickard, pp. 36–7.
8 Birch, I, 60.
9 A. H. A. Hamilton, *Quarter Sessions records from Queen Elizabeth to Queen Anne*, pp. 90–1.

PAGE 340

1 Hamilton, *Quarter Sessions records*, pp. 105–6.
2 *APC, 1625–1626*, p. 56.
3 *Coke MSS*. HMC, Twelfth Report, appendix, part I, XII, i, 213.
4 *Borough of Plymouth MSS*. HMC, X, iv, 547.
5 *Ibid.*   6 Cox, p. 174.
7 Hamilton, *Quarter Sessions records*, pp. 105–6.

References

PAGE 341

1 'Quarter Sessions records for the county of Somerset', II, *Somerset Record Soc.*
XXIV, xxi–xxii.
2 *Ibid.* p. 13.   3 *Ibid.* p. 10.
4 *Ibid.* pp. 6–7.   5 *Ibid.* p. xxii.
6 *APC, 1625–1626*, p. 127.

PAGE 342

1 *APC, 1625–1626*, p. 178.
2 W. H. Jacob, 'Some notes on the plague in Winchester', *J. Br. Archaeol. Ass.*
L, 268.   3 *Ibid.* p. 272.
4 *TSP*, I, 169.
5 *SPD, 1625–1626*, IV, 74.
6 Mar and Kellie MSS. HMC, Supplementary Report, p. 231.
7 *Calendar of Wynn (of Gwydir) Papers*, p. 218.
8 Rudyard Kipling, *Rewards and Fairies*, p. 275.
9 Cooper, III, 179.   10 *Ibid.* 180–1.
11 Birch, I, 51.   12 *Ibid.* p. 80.

PAGE 343

1 L. W. Clarke, 'The plague in Birmingham', Birmingham Notes and Queries,
no. 52. *The Birmingham Journal and Daily Post*, p. 6.
2 'The records of the county of Worcester', HMC, *Manuscripts in various collections*, I, 304.
3 'The plague at Redditch (1625)', XXVII Old Bromsgrove paragraphs, *Notes and
Queries for Bromsgrove and the district of central Worcestershire*, p. 63.
4 W. Wood, *The history and Antiquities of Eyam, etc.* pp. 57–9.
5 Ormerod, *Chester*, II, 597–8.

PAGE 344

1 Cox, *Churchwardens' Accounts*, p. 318.
2 Kelly, p. 433.   3 *Ibid.* pp. 434–5.
4 *Ibid.* p. 436.   5 *Ibid.* p. 434.
6 Birch, I, 80.   7 Blomefield, p. 261.
8 Birch, I, 45.

PAGE 345

1 Blomefield, p. 261.
2 *Ibid.* p. 262.
3 C. H. Mullett, *The bubonic plague and England*, p. 145.
4 *Quarter Sessions records*, North Riding Record Soc. III, 214.
5 *Ibid.* III, 255.
6 Cox, p. 167.
7 H. Barnes, *Archaeol. Æliana*, XV, 21.
8 R. Surtees, *The history and antiquities of the County Palatine of Durham*, II, 122.

References

PAGE 346

1 Creighton, I, 511.   2 *Ibid.* p. 514.
3 Wilson, pp. 143–51.   4 *Ibid.* pp. 164–5.
5 *Ibid.* p. 170.

PAGE 348

1 Creighton, I, 521.   2 Birch, I, 92.
3 *Ibid.* p. 155.   4 J. Rymer, *Foedera*, II, 30 June 1626.
5 Blomefield, II, 262.   6 *APC, 1626*, June–December, p. 267.
7 *Ibid.* pp. 103–4.
8 R. Hoveden, *Publ. Huguenot Soc.* V, iii, 580.
9 *APC, 1626*, June–December, p. 33.   10 *Ibid.* p. 67.

PAGE 349

1 *APC, 1626*, June–December, pp. 83–4.
2 Creighton, I, 523.   3 *SPD, 1625–1626*, p. 419 (no. 7).
4 *APC, 1626*, June–December, p. 261.   5 *Ibid.* p. 188.
6 *SPD, 1625–1626*, p. 483 (no. 57).   7 *Ibid.*
8 'J.S.A.' *NQ*, III, 477–81.   9 *Ibid.*
10 *Devon and Cornwall Notes and Queries*, VI, 198.
11 *SPD, 1625–1626*, p. 350 (no. 47).   12 *Ibid.* p. 307 (no. 61).

PAGE 350

1 *SPD, 1625–1626*, p. 287 (no. 24).   2 HMC, City of Exeter MSS. p. 176.

PAGE 351

1 D. and S. Lysons, *Magna Britannia*, VI, ii, 508.
2 *SPD, 1625–1626*, p. 387 (no. 59).
3 Pickard, p. 38.   4 *SPD, 1627–1628*, p. 388 (no. 48).
5 'Quarter Sessions records', *Somerset Rec. Soc.* XXIV, 19.
6 *Warwick County Records*, I, 35.   7 *Ibid.* I, 19.
8 Grace A. Ellis, VCH, *Buckingham*, III, 282.
9 *APC, 1625–1626*, p. 478.   10 *Ibid.*

PAGE 352

1 *APC, 1625–1621*, p. 478.
2 *SPD, 1625–1626*, p. 244 (no. 17).   3 *Ibid.*
4 R. Surtees, *History of Durham*, II, 242.
5 *Quarter Sessions records*, North Riding Record Soc. III, 264.
6 *Ibid.* p. 275.   7 *Ibid.* p. 214.
8 Register of St Bene't, Paul's Wharf, *Publ. Harl. Soc.* p. 12.
9 *APC, 1627–1628*, p. 180.   10 *APC, 1627*, January–August, p. 390.
11 *APC, 1627–1628*, p. 83.
12 HMC, *Manuscripts in various collections*, I, 97.
13 *Ibid.*   14 *Ibid.*   15 *APC, 1627–1628*, p. 155.

References

1 HMC, Tenth Report, appendix, part IV, p. 548.
2 *Ibid.*
3 *SPD, 1627–1628*, p. 233 (no. 23).
4 *Ibid.* p. 261 (no. 40).
5 *APC, 1627–1628*, p. 42.
6 *Somerset Record Soc.* XXIV, 19.
7 *SPD, 1627–1628*, p. 532 (no. 67).
8 *APC, 1629–1630*, p. 306.
9 *Ibid.* p. 310.
10 *Ibid.* p. 312.

PAGE 354

1 *APC, 1629–1630*, p. 313.
2 *Ibid.* p. 317.
3 HMC, Fourteenth Report, appendix, parts I, II, and III, p. 26.
4 S. Purchas, *Hakluytus Posthumus or Purchas His Pilgrimes*, IX, 24.
5 *The Oxinden and Peyton Letters*, pp. 57–8.
6 *Ibid.* p. 60.
7 HMC, *City of Exeter manuscripts*, pp. 176–7.
8 Cooper, III, 213–22.
9 Creighton, I, 527.
10 *Remenbrancia*, VII, 340.

PAGE 355

1 *Remenbrancia*, VII, 341.
2 *Ibid.*
3 *Ibid.*
4 *Ibid.*
5 *Ibid.* p. 342.
6 Birch, II, 70.
7 *Ibid.* p. 72.

PAGE 356

1 Birch, II, 76.
2 *Ibid.* pp. 77–8.
3 *Ibid.* p. 78.
4 *TSP*, I, 189.
5 Register of St Vedast, Foster Lane, *Publ. Harl. Soc.* pp. 164–5.
6 Register of St Olave, Hart Street, *Publ. Harl. Soc.* pp. 163–4.
7 Register of St Martin-in-the-Fields, *Publ. Harl. Soc.* pp. 250–9.
8 *SPD, 1629–1631*, p. 254 (no. 45).
9 *HLP, 1630*, 6 Charles I, 1 August.
10 *TSP*, I, 191.
11 HMC, *Manuscripts in various collections*, VII, 398.
12 Birch, II, 95–104.

PAGE 357

1 Creighton, I, 527.
2 Birch, II, 72–9.
3 *Ibid.* p. 72.
4 Cooper, III, 222.
5 Birch, II, 72.
6 *Ibid.*
7 *Ibid.* pp. 72–9.
8 *Ibid.* p. 78.

PAGE 358

1 Birch, II, 78.
2 Cooper, III, 223.
3 *Ibid.*
4 Birch, II, 81.
5 *Ibid.*
6 *Ibid.* (footnote).
7 Cooper, III, 227–8.
8 *Ibid.* p. 228

596

References

PAGE 359

1 Cooper, III, 228.   2 *Ibid.*
3 *Ibid.* p. 229.   4 *Ibid.* p. 223.
5 *Ibid.* p. 224.   6 *Ibid.* p. 225.
7 *Ibid.* p. 227.
8 G. E. Hubbard, *The old book of Wye*, p. 135.
9 Cooper, III, 226.
10 *SPD, 1629–1631*, p. 309 (no. 12).   11 *Ibid.* p. 258 (no. 69).

PAGE 360

1 *SPD, 1629–1631*, p. 368 (no. 95).   2 *Ibid.* p. 414 (no. 27).
3 R. Hoveden, *Publ. Huguenot Soc.* V, iii, 580.
4 *SPD, 1629–1631*, p. 274 (no. 8).   5 Blomefield, II, 264.
6 *SPD, 1629–1631*, p. 275 (no. 15).
7 HMC, Tenth Report, appendix, part IV, p. 376.
8 H. A. Lewis, *St Martin's, St Helen's and Tean* (*Isles of Scilly*) *in legend and history*, p. 23.

PAGE 362

1 *Register of Shrewsbury St Chad*, Shropshire Parish Reg. Soc. part 3, pp. 58–65.
2 *Ibid.* pp. 76–84.   3 *Ibid.* p. 78.
4 *Register of Shrewsbury St Mary*, Shropshire Parish Reg. Soc. p. 80.
5 HMC, Tenth Report, appendix, part IV, p. 405.
6 *Register of Shrewsbury St Chad*, pp. 58–65.
7 E. B. Leech, *Trans. Lancs. and Ches. Antiq. Soc.* LVII, 155.
8 HMC, Fourteenth Report, appendix, part IV, p. 41.

PAGE 363

1 *SPD, 1631–1633*, pp. 150–1 (no. 14).
2 E. B. Leech, *Trans. Lancs. and Ches. Antiq. Soc.* LVII, 155.
3 HMC, Kenyon MSS. p. 44.   4 *Ibid.* p. 46.
5 Cox, *Churchwardens' accounts*, p. 318.
6 Register of St Martin-in-the-Fields, *Publ. Harl. Soc.* pp. 259–61.
7 Birch, II, 79.   8 *Ibid.* p. 107.

PAGE 364

1 *SPD, 1629–1631*, p. 501 (no. 32).
2 Downs, *Records of Bucks.* VII, 262–5.

PAGE 365

1 *Register of Condover*, Shropshire Parish Reg. Soc. pp. 81–2.
2 'Birmingham Notes and Queries, no. 27', *The Birmingham Journal and Daily Post*, 18 March 1911.
3 'Birmingham in 1662' in the 'Hundred of Hemlingford', *The Birmingham Post*, 16 February 1954.

4 C. Gill, *History of Birmingham*, I, 49.
5 *Transcript of the first register book of the parish church of St Martin, Birmingham, 1554–1656*, I, 82–II, 219.
6 *SPD, 1631–1633*, p. 161 (no. 26).   7 *Ibid.* p. 161 (no. 27).
8 Kelly, p. 438.   9 Cox, *Churchwardens' accounts*, p. 319.
10 W. D. Sweeting, *Fenland Notes and Queries*, II, 154.

PAGE 366

1 *The Knyvett Letters, 1620–1644*, Norfolk Rec. Soc. p. 77.
2 Blomefield, II, 265.   3 Creighton, I, 527.
4 *PCS*, IV, 264–5.
5 Axon, *Trans. Lancs. and Ches. Antiq. Soc.* XII, 79.
6 *Ibid.* p. 81.   7 *SPD, 1631–1633*, pp. 150–1 (no. 14).
8 Maud Sellers, VCH, *York*, III, 456–8.

PAGE 367

1 Maud Sellers, VCH, *York*, III, 456–8.
2 J. N. Radcliffe, *The pestilence in England: an historical sketch*, p. 43.
3 S. J. Chadwick, *Yorks. Archaeol. and Topog. Jour.* XV, 434–43.
4 *PCS*, IV, 310.
5 A. D. H. Leadman, *Yorks. Archaeol. Jour.* XIV, 115.
6 HMC, *Kenyon MSS*, p. 118.   7 *PCS*, VI, p. xiv.
8 HMC, *Marchmont MSS*. iii, 108.   9 *Ibid.*
10 *PCS*, VI, xii–xiii.

PAGE 368

1 *PCS*, VI, xii–xiii.   2 J. Buchan, *Montrose*, p. 67.
3 *TSP*, II, ii, 307.   4 *PCS, 1635–1637*, VI, 246–7.
5 *Ibid.* VI, 303.   6 *Ibid.* p. 310.
7 *Ibid.* p. 326.

PAGE 369

1 *PCS, 1635–1637*, VI, xiv.   2 *Ibid.* p. 269.
3 *Ibid.* pp. 330–1.   4 *Ibid.* pp. 353–4.
5 *Ibid.* p. xiii.   6 *Ibid.* p. 431.
7 *Ibid.* p. xiv.

PAGE 370

1 *PCS, 1635–1637*, VI, p. xiv.   2 *Ibid.* pp. xiv–xv.
3 *Ibid.* p. 681.   4 *Ibid.* p. 682.
5 *Ibid.* p. 437.   6 *Ibid.* p. 438.
7 *Ibid.* pp. 454–5.   8 *Ibid.* p. 431.
9 *Ibid.* p. 473.   10 *Ibid.* pp. 490–1.
11 *PCS, 1638–1643*, VII, 1.
12 W. Wood, *The history and antiquities of Eyam, etc.* p. 59.

References

PAGE 371

1 *SPD, 1631–1633*, p. 387 (no. 16). 2 *Ibid.* p. 419 (no. 54).
3 HMC, *Municipal Records of Shrewsbury*, p. 64.
4 P. Barrough, *The method of physick*, pp. 247–9.
5 J. N. Radcliffe, *The pestilence in England, etc.*, pp. 43–4.

PAGE 372

1 *SPD, 1635–1636*, p. 329. 2 Jones, *NQ*, CXCVIII, 384–6.
3 J. R. Green, *A short history of the English people*, p. 548.
4 Register of St Peeters upon Cornhill, *Publ. Harl. Soc.* I, 196.
5 Register of St Martin Orgar, *ibid.* LXVII, 110.

PAGE 373

1 Creighton, I, 530.
2 Elizabeth Godfrey, *Social life under the Stuarts*, p. 18.
3 J. Noorthouck, *A new history of London, etc.*, p. 162 and footnote.
4 Wilson, p. 214. 5 Birch, p. 242.
6 *HLP*, 1636, 12 Charles I, 22 April. 7 Birch, p. 244.
8 *Ibid.*

PAGE 374

1 HMC, *Egmont MSS.* p. 87.

PAGE 375

1 Register of St Antholin, Budge Row, *Publ. Harl. Soc.* VIII, 70.
2 Register of St Michael Bassishaw, *ibid.* LXXIII, 94.
3 *Remenbrancia*, VII, 346.
4 *Ibid.* pp. 346–7.
5 *HLP*, 1636, 12 Charles I, 27 May.
6 *Remenbrancia*, VII, 347. 7 *HLP*, 1636, 12 Charles I, 18 July.
8 *Ibid.* 26 July. 9 *Ibid.* 20 August.
10 *Ibid.* 6 September 11 *Ibid.* 2 October.
12 *Ibid.* 18 October. 13 *PMV*, XXIV, 6 (no. 6).
14 *Ibid.* p. 53 (no. 54). 15 *Ibid.* p. 88 (no. 93).

PAGE 376

1 *PMV*, XXIV, 116 (no. 127). 2 HMC, *Gawdy MSS.* pp. 167–170.
3 *Ibid.* 4 *Ibid.*
5 *Ibid.* 6 *Ibid.*
7 W. J. Simpson, *A treatise on plague*, p. 194.
8 A. M. Burke, *Key to the ancient parish registers of England and Wales*, p. 27.
9 *SPD, 1635–1636*, p. 385 (no. 51).
10 *Ibid.* p. 423 (no. 2). 11 *Ibid.* p. 453 (no. 12).
12 *Ibid.* p. 460 (no. 33).
13 *Middlesex County Records*, III, 62.

References

PAGE 377

1 *SPD, 1635–1636*, p. 523 (no. 7).   2 *Middlesex County Records*, III, 62.
3 *SPD, 1635–1636*, p. 544 (no. 76).   4 *Ibid.* p. 553 (no. 9).
5 F. F. Giraud, *Archaeol. Cantiana*, XXIV, 242.

PAGE 378

1 F. F. Giraud, *Archaeol. Cantiana*, XXIV, 242.

PAGE 379

1 R. W. Blencowe, *Sussex Archaeol. Collect.* XII, 46–7.

PAGE 380

1 *SPD, 1635–1636*, p. 544 (no. 88).
2 T. Hannan-Clarke, *Drama in Gloucestershire*, p. 46.
3 HMC, *Corporation of Bishop's Castle, MSS.* p. 403.
4 HMC, *Portland MSS.* III, p. 40.   5 Kelly, pp. 438–9.
6 Cooper, III, 275.   7 *Ibid.* p. 279.
8 *The Annals of Gonville and Caius College*, p. 397.

PAGE 381

1 *The diary and correspondence of Dr John Worthington*, I, 4.
2 Sweeting, *Fenland Notes and Queries*, II, 154.
3 *Ibid.*   4 HMC, *Gawdy MSS.* p. 160.
5 *Ibid.*   6 *Ibid.* p. 161.
7 Blomefield, II, 266.
8 S. Tymms, *Proc. Bury & West Suffolk Archaeol. Inst.* I, 41.

PAGE 382

1 Tymms, *loc. cit.*
2 L. M. Stanewell, *Calendar of the ancient deeds, letters, etc., of Kingston-upon-Hull*, p. 191.
3 T. Richmond, *The local records of Stockton and its neighbourhood*, pp. 26–7.
4 Surtees, *Durham*, II, 122.   5 *Ibid.* IV, 9.
6 Creighton, I, 529.

PAGE 384

1 F. W. Dendy, *Proc. Soc. Antiq. Newcastle-upon-Tyne*, I, 48.
2 Cox, p. 167.
3 J. Clepham, *Archaeol. Æliana*, VIII, 230–1.
4 *PCS*, VI, 268.

PAGE 385

1 *Quarter Sessions records*, North Riding Rec. Soc. IV, 69.
2 Creighton, I, 532.
3 Register of St Martin Orgar, *Publ. Harl. Soc.* LXVII, 110.

References

4 Register of St Peeters upon Cornhill, *Publ. Harl. Soc.* I, 196–7.
5 Register of St Bene't, Paul's Wharf, *Publ. Harl. Soc.* XLI, 23.
6 Register of St Peeters upon Cornhill, pp. 196–7.
7 HMC, *Gawdy MSS.* p. 163.   8 *TSP,* I, 211.
9 *Ibid.*   10 *SPD, 1637,* p. 57 (no. 33).

PAGE 387

1 *SPD, 1637,* p. 57 (no. 34)   2 Creighton, I, 533.
3 *Ibid.* p. 534.   4 *TSP,* I, 215.
5 F. H. Garrison, *An introduction to the history of medicine,* p. 290.

PAGE 388

1 *Middlesex county records,* III, 60.
2 Cox, *Churchwardens' accounts,* p. 318.
3 *SPD, 1640–1641,* p. 46.   4 *Ibid.* p. 333.
5 *HLP, 1641,* 17 Charles I, 21 October.
6 *Ibid. 1641–1642,* 16 March.   7 *TSP,* I, 230.
8 Register of St Michael, Cornhill, *Publ. Harl. Soc.* VII, 237–8.
9 Register of St Bene't, Paul's Wharf, *ibid.* XLI, 27–8.
10 E. Freshfield, *Archaeologia,* XLV, 79.

PAGE 389

1 HMC, *Coke MSS.* II, 291.   2 *PMV,* XXV, 207.
3 HMC, *Coke MSS.* II, 292.   4 *Ibid.* p. 294.
5 *Calendar of Wynn (of Gwydir) Papers,* p. 274.
6 *Letters of Lady Brilliana Harley,* p. 130.
7 *Ibid.* p. 143.
8 Creighton, I, 533.
9 Register of St Michael, Cornhill, *Publ. Harl. Soc.* VII, 238.
10 Register of St Mary Somerset, *ibid.* LX, 76.
11 Violet M. Shillington, VCH, *Hampshire and the Isle of Wight,* V, 426.

PAGE 390

1 HMC, *The records of Quarter Sessions in the county of Wilts,* p. 103.
2 Author's personal observation.
3 A. A. Wood, *Athenae Oxoniensis,* III, 735.
4 *The diary of Henry Townshend of Elmley Lovett,* p. vi.
5 *The register of St Alban's, in the city of Worcester,* The Parish Reg. Soc. II, 5–6.
6 *Ibid.* pp. 3–7.

PAGE 391

1 *The register of St Alban's, in the city of Worcester,* The Parish Reg. Soc. II, 6.
2 *The parish book of St Helen's Church in Worcester, ibid.* II, 121–35.
3 *Ibid.* pp. 128–9.
4 *Worcestershire County records,* I, cliv.

References

PAGE 392

1 *Worcestershire County records*, I, cliv.
2 J. R. Burton, *A history of Kidderminster*, p. 71.
3 *Warwick County records*, II, 4.   4 *Ibid.*
5 F. W. Willmore, *A history of Walsall and its neighbourhood*, pp. 277–8.

PAGE 393

1 F. W. Wilmore, *A history of Walsall and its neighbourhood*, pp. 277–8.
2 *SPD, 1637*, p. 161 (no. 119).   3 *Ibid.* pp. 282–3 (no. 25).
4 Hirst, *Brit. Encycl. Med. Pract.* IX, 694.
5 Blomefield, II, 266.   6 HMC, *Gawdy MSS.* p. 164.
7 *Ibid.* p. 167.   8 Cooper, III, 286–7.
9 *Ibid.* p. 287.   10 Cox, p. 160.
11 H. Southall, *Trans. Woolhope Naturalists' Field Club*, p. 5.

PAGE 394

1 *SPD, 1637*, p. 439 (no. 41).   2 *Ibid.* p. 409 (no. 42).
3 *Quarter Sessions records*, North Riding Rec. Soc. IV, 69.
4 *Calendar of the ancient deeds, letters, etc. of Kingston-upon-Hull*, p. 325.
5 Cox, p. 170.   6 *PCS, 1635–1637*, VI, 246–7.
7 H. Southall, p. 5.
8 HMC, *The records of the county of Worcester*, p. 313.
9 *SPD, 1637–1638*, p. 102 (no. 72).

PAGE 395

1 *SPD, 1638–1639*, pp. 26–7 (no. 139). 2 *Ibid.*
3 N. G. Brett-James, *The growth of Stuart London*, p. 139.
4 *Ibid.* p. 143.   5 *Ibid.* p. 144.
6 *Ibid.* pp. 144–253.
7 A. M. Burke, *Key to the ancient parish registers of England and Wales*, pp. 26 ff.
8 HMC, *Gawdy MSS.* p. 167.   9 *Ibid.* pp. 168–70.
10 *Ibid.*   11 *Ibid.*
12 *Ibid.*   13 *Ibid.*
14 *Ibid.*   15 Jones, *NQ*, CXCVIII, 384–6.
16 *Remenbrancia*, II, 348.   17 Cooper, III, 290.

PAGE 397

1 Cooper, III, 290.   2 *Ibid.*
3 *Ibid.*   4 *Ibid.* p. 291.
5 Sweeting, *Fenland Notes and Queries*, II, 154.
6 Cox, p. 155.   7 *SPD, 1638–1639*, pp. 394–5 (no. 7).
8 *Ibid.* p. 395 (no. 8).   9 *Ibid.* p. 10 (no. 51).

PAGE 398

1 Cox, p. 157.   2 *Ibid.*

References

3 *SPD, 1638–1639*, p. 70 (no. 84).   4 Kelly, p. 439.
5 *SPD, 1638–1639*, p. 10 (no. 51).
6 *Quarter Sessions records*, North Riding Rec. Soc. IV, 99.
7 *SPD, 1638–1639*, p. 74 (no. 94).   8 *Warwick County Records*, II, 34.
9 Kelly, p. 441.
10 Radcliffe, *The pestilence in England*, p. 44.
11 HMC, *City of Exeter MSS.* p. 177.   12 Pickard, p. 38.

PAGE 399

1 Pickard, p. 38.   2 *SPD, 1639*, p. 70 (no. 39).
3 Creighton, I, 533.   4 *SPD, 1641–1643*, p. 105 (no. 91).
5 *Ibid.* p. 115 (no. 2).   6 *Ibid.* p. 114 (no. 115).
7 Creighton, I, 545.   8 Kelly, p. 441.

PAGE 400

1 J. Simpson, *NQ*, II, 524.   2 J. Pickford, *NQ*, IV, 199.
3 *SPD, 1641–1643*, p. 66 (no. 110).
4 P. F. A. Morrell, *J. Archit., Archaeol. and Hist. Soc. Chester and North Wales*,
XV, 97.   5 *SPD, 1641–1643*, p. 118 (no. 12).
6 Pickard, p. 39.
7 HMC, *The records of Quarter Sessions in the county of Wilts*, p. 110.
8 Joanna Cannon, *Oxfordshire*, pp. 83–4.

PAGE 401

1 Cox, p. 156.   2 Cooper, III, 325.
3 Cox, p. 318.   4 Creighton, I, 559.
5 *Ibid.* pp. 549–51.
6 Earl of Clarendon, *History of the great rebellion*, III, 53.
7 J. R. Gardiner, *History of the great civil war, 1642–1649*, I, 154.
8 W. Godwin, *History of the commonwealth of England to the restoration of Charles II*,
I, 137.

PAGE 402

1 W. Godwin, *History of the commonwealth of England to the restoration of Charles II*,
I, 137.   2 Creighton, I, 549.
3 Cox, *Churchwardens' accounts*, p. 318.   4 HMC, *Captain Stewart's MSS.* p. 98.

PAGE 403

1 Cox, *Churchwardens' accounts*, p. 318.
2 *Ibid.*   3 *Ibid.*
4 Radcliffe, *The pestilence in England*, p. 45.
5 *SPD, 1645–1647*, p. 601 (no. 39).
6 *The diary of the Rev. Ralph Josselin*, p. 45.

References

1 Cooper, III, 354.
2 Register of the Abbey Church of SS. Peter and Paul, Bath, *Publ. Harl. Soc.* XXVIII, 361–3.
3 H. A. Adamson, *Archaeol. Æliana*, XV, 218–24.
4 C. S. Terry, *Archaeol. Æliana*, XXI, 180–258.
5 *Ibid.* p. 224.   6 Cox, p. 168.

1 Surtees, *Durham*, IV, 10.   2 *Ibid.* II, 242.
3 G. D. Lumb, 'The registers of the parish church of Leeds', *Publ. Thoresby Soc.* VII, 177–94.
4 *Ibid.* p. 193.   5 *Ibid.* pp. 191–4.
6 *Ibid.* p. 194.
7 T. D. Whitaker, *Loidis and Elmete*, p. 77.

1 T. D. Whitaker, *Loidis and Elmete*, p. 76.

1 Creighton, I, 556.   2 *TSP*, I, 311.
3 *Ibid.*
4 *The diary of the Rev. Ralph Josselin*, p. 16.
5 *Ibid.*   6 *The Oxinden and Peyton letters*, p. 66.
7 Harding, *History of Tiverton*, I, 60.
8 H. Southall, *Trans. Woolhope Naturalists' Field Club*, p. 5.

1 L. W. Clarke, 'Birmingham Notes and Queries, no. 52', *The Birmingham Journal and Daily Post*, p. 6.
2 'Quarter Sessions records for the county of Somerset', III, *Somerset Rec. Soc.*, XXVIII, lii.
3 HMC, *The records of Quarter Sessions in the county of Wilts*, p. 114.
4 J. H. Ward, *Notes and Queries for Somerset and Dorset*, III, 63.
5 HMC, *Portland MSS.* I, 279.
6 Register of Ottery St Mary, *Publ. Devon & Cornwall Rec. Soc.* II, 842–5.

1 'Quarter Sessions records for the county of Somerset', III, *Somerset Rec. Soc.* XXVIII, lii.   2 *Ibid.* p. liii.
3 *Ibid.*   4 *Ibid.* pp. liii–liv.

1 *The whole works of that excellent practical physician, Dr Thomas Sydenham,* trans. T. Peachey, p. 68.

2 Rudyard Kipling, *Rewards and Fairies*, pp. 275–6.
3 Cox, p. 173. 4 *Ibid.*
5 *Ibid.*

PAGE 411

1 Register of Colyton, Devon, *Publ. Devon & Cornwall Rec. Soc.* pp. 647–55.
2 *Ibid.* II, 634–47.

PAGE 413

1 HMC, *City of Exeter MSS.* p. 325.
2 *The life and times of Anthony Wood, antiquary of Oxford*, I, 127.
3 Cox, p. 160.
4 *The diary of the Rev. Ralph Josselin*, p. 30.
5 L.M. Stanewell, *Calendar of the ancient deeds, letters, etc. of Kingston-upon-Hull*,
   p. 206. 6 *Ibid.*

PAGE 414

1 Stanewell, *Calendar of the ancient deeds, letters, etc. of Kingston-upon-Hull*,
   p. 206.
2 Axon, *Trans. Lancs. and Ches. Antiq. Soc.* XII, 79.
3 *Ibid.* p. 80. 4 *Ibid.* p. 81.
5 *Ibid.* p. 83. 6 *Ibid.*
7 *Ibid.* pp. 83–5.

PAGE 415

1 Axon, *Trans. Lancs. and Ches. Antiq. Soc.* XII, 85.
2 *Ibid.* p. 86. 3 *Ibid.*
4 *Ibid.* p. 87. 5 *Ibid.*

PAGE 416

1 Axon, *Trans. Lancs. and Ches. Antiq. Soc.* XII, 88.
2 *Ibid.* p. 89. 3 *Ibid.*
4 Stanewell, *Calendar of the ancient deeds, letters, etc. of Kingston-upon-Hull*,
   p. 211.
5 Lumb, 'The registers of the parish church of Leeds', *Publ. Thoresby Soc.* VII,
   191–4.
6 Stanewell, *Calendar of the ancient deeds, letters, etc. of Kingston-upon-Hull*, p.
   210.

PAGE 418

1 Stanewell, *Calendar of the ancient deeds, letters, etc. of Kingston-upon-Hull*, p.
   210.
2 S. J. Chadwick, *The Yorks. Archaeol. and Topog. Jour.* XV, 434–43.
3 *Ibid.*
4 Stanewell, *Calendar of the ancient deeds, letters, etc. of Kingston-upon-Hull*, p. 211.
5 Surtees, *Durham*, II, 122. 6 *Ibid.* III, 257.

References

PAGE 419

1 HMC, *The records of Quarter Sessions in the County of Wilts*, p. 110.

PAGE 420

1 HMC, *The records of Quarter Sessions in the county of Wilts*, p. 111.
2 *Ibid.* pp. 111–12.   3 *Ibid.* p. 113.
4 'Quarter Sessions records for the county of Somerset', III, *Somerset Rec. Soc.* XXVIII, lii.   5 *Ibid.* pp. liii–liv.
6 W. H. Thornton, *Devon and Cornwall Notes and Queries*, VI, 198–9.

PAGE 421

1 W. H. Thornton, *Devon and Cornwall Notes and Queries*, VI, 198–9.
2 Register of Hemyock, Devon, *Publ. Devon & Cornwall Rec. Soc.* pp. 169–70.
3 'J.S.A.', *NQ*, III, 477–8.
4 W. Heberden, *Observations on the increase and decrease of different diseases, and particularly of the plague*, p. 75.
5 F. W. Willmore, *A history of Walsall and its neighbourhood*, pp. 277–8.
6 T. Middleton, *Trans. Lancs and Ches. Antiq. Soc.* LIII, 10–11.

PAGE 422

1 Cox, p. 164.
2 Axon, *Trans. Lancs. and Ches. Antiq. Soc.* XII, 92.
3 Blomefield, p. 267.
4 Sweeting, *Fenland Notes and Queries*, II, 346.
5 Cooper, III, 400.
6 *The diary and correspondence of Dr John Worthington*, Cheetham Society Publications, XIII, 23.
7 Surtees, *Durham*, II, 242.
8 C. S. Terry, *Archaeol. Æliana*, XXI, 180–258.
9 Pickard, p. 39.
10 D. and S. Lysons, *Magna Britannia*, III, 151.

PAGE 423

1 Canon R. H. Morris, *J. Archit. Archaeol. and Hist. Soc. Chester and North Wales*, XXV, 210.
2 D. and S. Lysons, *Magna Britannia*, II, ii, 602–3.
3 Ormerod, *Chester*, I, 247.
4 J. C. Morley, 'The plague in Liverpool', *Bygone Lancashire*, p. 108.
5 *The life and times of Anthony Wood, antiquary of Oxford*, I, 132.
6 Cox, p. 156.
7 Cox, *Churchwardens' accounts*, p. 343.
8 *Ibid.* pp. 342–3.   9 Kelly, p. 442.
10 Cooper, III, 415.

References

PAGE 424

1 *The diary and correspondence of Dr John Worthington*, Cheetham Society Publications, XIII, 29.
2 R. S. Downs, *Records of Bucks.* VIII, 262–3, footnote 1.

PAGE 425

1 W. Browne, *Trans. Cumb. and Westm. Antiq. and Archaeol. Soc.* IV, 257–71.
2 Cox, p. 150.
3 HMC, *The records of Quarter Sessions in the county of Wilts*, p. 117.
4 Kelly, p. 442.
5 HMC, *Portland MSS*, III, p. 465.

PAGE 426

1 J. C. Morley, 'The plague in Liverpool', *Bygone Lancashire*, pp. 109–10.
2 HMC, *Stanley Leighton's MSS.* p. 376.
3 Chambers, II, 156.   4 *Ibid.* footnote 2.
5 *TSP*, II, ii, 326.   6 *Ibid.*

PAGE 427

1 ERBE, 1642–1655, p. lvi.   2 Chambers, II, 163.
3 ERBE, 1642–1655, pp. lvi–lvii.   4 *Ibid.* appendix, 9, 418.
5 *Ibid.* p. 419.   6 *Ibid.* p. 70.
7 ERBE, 1655–1665, p. 254.   8 ERBE, 1642–1655, p. 89.

PAGE 428

1 J. Buchan, *Montrose*, p. 272.   2 Chambers, II, 164.
3 J. Buchan, *Montrose*, p. 276.
4 Comrie, *History of Scottish medicine*, I, 221.
5 A. K. Chalmers, *Report on certain cases of plague occurring in Glasgow in 1900 by the Medical Officer of Health*, p. v.
6 Comrie, *History of Scottish medicine*, I, 220.
7 W. M. Kelso, *Sanitation in Paisley*, p. 4.

PAGE 429

1 W. M. Kelso, *Sanitation in Paisley*, pp. 4–5.
2 Comrie, *History of Scottish medicine*, I, 221.
3 J. Ritchie, *Trans. Dumfries. & Galloway Nat. Hist. and Antiq. Soc.* XXI, 90–105.

PAGE 430

1 'Perth', *The new statistical account of Scotland*, X, 37, footnote.
2 Chambers, II, 166.
3 'Falkirk', *The new statistical account of Scotland*, VIII, 6.
4 'Dunfermline', *ibid.* IX, 865.
5 'Falkirk', *ibid.* VIII, 6.
6 HMC, *Portland MSS.* I, 271.

References

PAGE 431

1 Chambers, II, 164.   2 *Ibid.* p. 168.
3 J. Ritchie, *Trans. Dumfries. & Galloway Nat. Hist. and Antiq. Soc.* XXI, 90–105.
4 *PCS*, 1554–1660, VIII, 165–6.   5 ERBE, 1642–1655, p. 69.
6 *Ibid.* p. 106.
7 Sir J. Sinclair, 'Brechin', *The statistical account of Scotland*, XXI, 127.
8 Comrie, *History of Scottish medicine*, I, 218–21.

PAGE 432

1 'Largs', *The new statistical account of Scotland*, V, 796–7.
2 ERBE, 1642–1655, p. 124.
3 'Menmuir', *The new statistical account of Scotland*, XI, 656.
4 'Aberdeen', *ibid.* XII, 20.   5 'Montrose', *ibid.* XI, 277.
6 Chambers, II, 167–8, footnote 3.

PAGE 433

1 W. Heberden, *On the increase and decrease of different diseases, etc.* p. 75.
2 Sir W. Wilde, *Census of Ireland for the year 1851*, part V, 108.
3 *Ibid.* p. 109.
4 *Ibid.* p. 108.   5 *Ibid.*
6 CARD, III, 501.

PAGE 434

1 CARD, III, 501–2, and IV, 1–2.   2 *Ibid.* IV, 3–4.
3 *Ibid.* pp. 15–16.   4 *Ibid.* pp. 118–19.
5 *TSP*, II, i, 64.   6 *Ibid.*
7 *Ibid.*

PAGE 435

1 CARD, IV, appendix 4, p. xiv.
2 Sir W. Wilde, *Census of Ireland for the year 1851*, part V, 110.
3 J. Phillips, *Archaeol. Cambrensis*, II, 122–7.
4 *Register of Shrewsbury St Chad*, Shropshire Par. Reg. Soc. XV, i, 208–23.

PAGE 436

1 *Register of Shrewsbury St Mary*, Shropshire Par. Reg. Soc. XII, 110–11.
2 *Register of Shrewsbury St Chad*, pp. 208–23.
3 *Register of Shrewsbury St Mary*, pp. 110–11.
4 *Register of Shrewsbury St Chad*, p. iii.

PAGE 437

1 *Register of Shrewsbury St Mary*, 110.
2 *Ibid.* pp. 110–11.
3 *Register of Shrewsbury St Chad*, pp. 208–23.
4 *Whitchurch*, transcript of Bishop's register, Public Library, Shrewsbury, p. 173.

References

5 *Ibid.* pp. 171–9. 6 *Ibid.* pp. 179–80.
7 *Ibid.* pp. 179–96. 8 *Ibid.* pp. 159–65.
9 *Ibid.* pp. 166–71.
10 *Register of Shrewsbury St Chad*, Shropshire Par. Reg. Soc. XV, iii, 190–201.

PAGE 439

1 *Register of Wem*, Shropshire Par. Reg. Soc. X, 171.
2 HMC, *City of Exeter MSS*, p. 177.
3 'Quarter Sessions Records', *Somerset Record Soc.* XXVIII, 125.
4 Axon, *Trans. Lancs. and Ches. Antiq. Soc.* XII, 93.
5 *Ibid.* p. 94.
6 Creighton, I, 567.

PAGE 440

1 Axon, *Trans. Lancs. and Ches. Antiq. Soc.* XII, 94.
2 Sir J. E. Lloyd, *A history of Carmarthenshire*, II, 29.
3 W. Spurrell, *Carmarthen and its neighbourhood*, p. 5.
4 J. Phillips, *Archaeol. Cambrensis*, II, 122–7.
5 *Ibid.*

PAGE 441

1 J. Phillips, *Archaeol. Cambrensis*, II, 122–7.
2 J. C. Morley, *Bygone Lancashire*, p. 110.
3 *SPD, 1651–1652*, p. 182 (no. 26).
4 Axon, *Trans. Lancs. and Ches. Antiq. Soc.* XII, 94–5.

PAGE 442

1 *SPD, 1651–1652*, p. 182. 2 *Ibid.* p. 525.
3 *Ibid.* p. 527. 4 *SPD, 1653–1654*, p. 132 (no. 86).
5 *Ibid.*
6 *The diary of the Rev. Ralph Josselin*, p. 107.
7 Ormerod, *Chester*, II, 314.
8 Axon, *Trans. Lancs. and Ches. Antiq. Soc.* XII, 96.
9 Sweeting, *Fenland Notes and Queries*, II, 154.
10 HMC, *Hastings (Ashby de la Zouche) MSS.* IV, 346.
11 Rudyard Kipling, *Rewards and Fairies*, p. 275.
12 *TSP*, I, 372.

PAGE 443

1 *TSP*, I, 373. 2 *Ibid.* p. 374.
3 J. Buchan, *Oliver Cromwell*, p. 532. 4 *SPD, 1658–1659*, p. 82.
5 J. Buchan, *Oliver Cromwell*, pp. 533–8.
6 *SPD, 1655*, p. 323 (no. 96).
7 *SPD, 1660–1661*, p. 424 (no. 43).
8 D. and S. Lysons, *Magna Britannia*, II, ii, 603.

References

PAGE 444

1 *Remenbrancia*, II, 348. 2 *Ibid.*
3 *Ibid.* p. 349. 4 *Ibid.*
5 *Dr Willis's practice of Physick, etc.* p. III.

PAGE 445

1 C. Oman, *Castles*, p. 37.
2 *Dr Willis's practice of physick, etc.* p. III.
3 Bell, pp. 1–331. 4 *Ibid.* p. 13.
5 *Ibid.* pp. 17–18.

PAGE 446

1 Bell, p. 92.
2 J. Noorthouck, *A new history of London, etc.* pp. 224–5.
3 *Pepys' Diary*, V, 57.
4 G. Harvey, jun. *The city remembrancer, etc.* I, 304.
5 *Ibid.* p. 305. 6 *Ibid.*
7 Bell, p. 27.

PAGE 447

1 Harvey, *City remembrancer*, pp. 305–6.
2 Bell, p. 27. 3 Bell, p. 28.

PAGE 448

1 Bell, pp. 32–3. 2 *Ibid.* p. 62.
3 *Ibid.* pp. 66–8. 4 *Ibid.* pp. 68–70.
5 *Ibid.* pp. 75 and 84–6.

PAGE 449

1 Bell, p. 115. 2 *Pepys' Diary*, V, 61.
3 Bell, p. 99.
4 N. Hodges, *Loimologia, etc.* p. 78.
5 W. Boghurst, *Loimographia, etc.* p. 96.
6 Bell, pp. 108–9.
7 T. Vincent, *God's terrible voice in the city*, p. 35.

PAGE 450

1 N. Hodges, *Loimologia, etc.* p. 8. 2 Bell, p. 102.
3 Cox, *Churchwardens' accounts*, p. 317. 4 *Pepys' Diary*, IV, 401–24; V, 1–173.
5 Bell, p. 212.
6 *Pepys' Diary*, IV, 401.

PAGE 451

1 Bell, pp. 227–8.
2 J. R. Green, *A short history of the English people*, pp. 624–5.

PAGE 452

1 Bell, pp. 217–18.
2 *Ibid.* p. 243.
3 N. Hodges, *Loimologia, etc.* p. 19.
4 Bell, p. 244.
5 *Ibid.* pp. 242 and 244.
6 *Ibid.* p. 245.
7 *Pepys' Diary*, V, 41.
8 Bell, p. 312.

PAGE 453

1 Bell, p. 312.
2 *Ibid.* pp. 312–13.
3 *Ibid.* pp. 244–5.
4 *Ibid.* 317.
5 Creighton, I, 679.

PAGE 454

1 Bell, pp. 317–18.
2 *Ibid.* pp. 318–19.

PAGE 455

1 *Pepys' Diary*, V, 81.
2 *Ibid.*

PAGE 460

1 Bell, pp. 30–3.
2 *Pepys' Diary*, IV, 407.
3 Register of St Michael, Bassishaw, *Publ. Harl. Soc.* LXXIII, ii, 118–23.
4 HMC, *Heathcote MSS*, p. 192.

PAGE 462

1 *Pepys' Diary*, IV, 207.
2 Register of St Paul's, Covent Garden, *Publ. Harl. Soc.* XXXVI, 32.

PAGE 463

1 *Pepys' Diary*, V, 142.

PAGE 464

1 Bell, pp. 155–6.
2 *Ibid.* p. 155.
3 Vincent, *God's terrible voice in the city*, p. 30.
4 *TSP*, I, 413.
5 *Pepys' Diary*, IV, 410.
6 Vincent, p. 31.
7 *Pepys' Diary*, V, 415.

PAGE 465

1 Vincent, p. 32.
2 *Ibid.* p. 33.
3 *Pepys' Diary*, IV, 421.
4 Register of St Michael, Cornhill, *Publ. Harl. Soc.* VII, 254–6.
5 Vincent, p. 34.
6 W. D. Cooper, *Archaeologia*, XXXVII, 6.
7 Bell, p. 92.
8 W. D. Cooper, p. 7.
9 J. Timbs and A. Gunn, *Abbeys, castles and ancient halls of England and Wales, South*, pp. 145–6.
10 C. F. Mullett, *The bubonic plague and England*, p. 200.
11 *Ibid.*

PAGE 466

1 R. H. Plomer, *NQ*, III, 493.
2 J. Noorthouck, *A new history of London, etc.* pp. 223–4.
3 HMC, *Heathcote MSS.* p. 192.
4 HMC, *Montague of Beaulieu MSS.* p. 167.

PAGE 467

1 *Pepys' Diary*, V, 19.
2 *Ibid.* V, 28.
3 *Ibid.* V, 29.
4 *The Oxinden Letters*, p. 310.
5 Cox, p. 154.
6 *Ibid.* pp. 150–2.

PAGE 468

1 Cox, p. 152.
2 'The diary of Henry Newton, etc.', *Proc. Camb. Antiq. Soc.* pp. 14–15.

PAGE 469

1 'The diary of Henry Newton, etc.', *Proc. Camb. Antiq. Soc.* pp. 14–15.
2 *TSP*, I, 414.
3 *Ibid.*
4 *Ibid.*
5 *Ibid.*
6 *Ibid.*
7 *Pepys' Diary*, V, 39.
8 *Ibid.* p. 40.
9 *Ibid.* pp. 39–40.
10 *Ibid.* p. 41.
11 *Ibid.*
12 *Ibid.* p. 44.
13 *Ibid.*

PAGE 470

1 Vincent, pp. 37–8.
2 *Pepys' Diary*, V, 54.
3 Ellis's 'Original letters' quoted by H. B. Wheatley, in *Pepys' Diary*, V, 54, foonote 1.
4 G. Thomson, *Loimotomia: or the pest anatomised*, pp. 70–1.
5 *British Med. Jour.* ii, 622–3.

PAGE 471

1 N. Hodges, *Loimologia*, p. 171.
2 G. Thomson, *Loimotomia: or the pest anatomised*, p. 86.
3 *Ibid.*
4 *Pepys' Diary*, V, 58.
5 *Ibid.* p. 60.
6 *Ibid.*

PAGE 472

1 *Pepys' Diary*, V, 80–1.
2 *The diary of John Evelyn*, II, 232–6.
3 Vincent, pp. 281–3.
4 Bell, pp. 282–3.

PAGE 473

1 *TSP*, I, 414.
2 *Ibid.* p. 415.
3 *The works of Simon Patrick, D.D., etc.* IX, 518.

References

PAGE 474

1 T. Hancock, *Researches into the laws and phenomena of pestilence, etc.* pp. 56–7.
2 N. Hodges, *Loimologia*, pp. 25–6.
3 *The diary of the Rev. Ralph Josselin*, pp. 149–50.
4 *Ibid.* p. 150.   5 *Pepys' Diary*, V, 111.
6 Register of St Martin Orgar, *Publ. Harl. Soc.* LXVII, 123–5.

PAGE 475

1 *The diary of the Rev. Ralph Josselin*, p. 150.
2 *Pepys' Diary*, V, 142.   3 Hodges, *Loimologia*, p. 26.
4 *Ibid.* p. 27.   5 *Ibid.*
6 *TSP*, I, 415.   7 *Ibid.*
8 Hodges, *Loimologia*, p. 30.   9 HMC, *Heathcote MSS.* p. 247.
10 Register of St Michael Bassishaw, *Publ. Harl. Soc.* LXXIII, ii, 123.

PAGE 477

1 *Pepys' Diary*, V, 162.   2 *Ibid.*
3 Creighton, I, 662.   4 *Pepys' Diary*, V, 173.
5 *Ibid.* p. 177.   6 *TSP*, I, 416.

PAGE 478

1 N. G. Brett-James, *The growth of Stuart London*, p. 507.
2 *Ibid.*   3 Hodges, *Loimologia*, pp. 27–8.
4 N. G. Brett-James, p. 498.

PAGE 479

1 *The lives of the Norths*, II, 2.   2 *Ibid.* p. 142.

PAGE 480

1 *Martha, Lady Giffard: her life and correspondence*, pp. 49–51.
2 *Ibid.*
3 O. Goldsmith, *The bee and other essays, etc.* p. 205.
4 'Lemon', *Encyclopaedia Britannica* (11th ed.), XVI, 413–15.

PAGE 481

1 T. Hancock, *Researches into the laws and phenomena of pestilence, etc.* p. 313.

PAGE 482

1 T. Hancock, *Researches into the laws and phenomena of pestilence, etc.* p. 85.
2 Bell, pp. 140–2.   3 Robinson, *Stoke Newington*, p. 184.

PAGE 483

1 Jones, *NQ*, III, 332–4.
2 W. Young, *The history of Dulwich College*, pp. 147–8.
3 G. Hammond, *Bygone Putney*, p. 40.

4 E. Hammond, *Bygone Wandsworth*, p. 11.
5 Register of Kensington, *Publ. Harl. Soc.* XVI, 133–5.
6 *Ibid.* pp. 124–33.   7 *Ibid.* p. 135.

PAGE 484

1 *SPD, 1665–1666*, p. 5 (no. 31).   2 *SPD, 1664–1665*, p. 519 (no. 35).
3 *Ibid.* p. 576 (no. 57).   4 Creighton, I, 533
5 Hancock, *Researches*, p. 75.   6 *TSP*, I, 416.

PAGE 485

1 *TSP*, I, 417.   2 *Ibid.*
3 *Ibid.* I, 419.   4 *Pepys' Diary*, V, 393.

PAGE 486

1 N. G. Brett-James, *The growth of Stuart London*, p. 496
2 Creighton, I, 472.   3 *Ibid.*
4 Brett-James, p. 496.   5 Bell, p. 12.
6 J. Graunt, *Observations on the bills of mortality*, p. 124.

PAGE 487

1 Bell, p. 13.
2 *Two tracts of Gregory King*, pp. 16–17.

PAGE 488

1 W. Boghurst, *Loimographia*, etc. p. 26.
2 *The diary of the Rev. Ralph Josselin*, p. 147.
3 W. E. Buckland, *Kent Records*, p. 57. 4 *SPD, 1664–1665*, p. 531 (no. 7).
5 *Ibid.* p. 546 (no. 5).   6 *SPD, 1665–1666*, p. 10 (no. 66).
7 *Ibid.* p. 31 (no. 71).

PAGE 489

1 *Kent Records*, p. 19.   2 *Pepys' Diary*, V, 57.
3 *The diary of John Evelyn*, p. 243.   4 *Pepys' Diary*, V, 47.
5 *SPD, 1666–1667*, pp. 359–60 (no. 56).   •
6 *Ibid.* p. 217 (no. 18).   7 *SPD, 1664–1665*, pp. 504–5 (no. 47).

PAGE 490

1 *SPD, 1664–1665*, p. 515 (no. 14).   2 *SPD, 1665–1666*, p. 15 (no. 102).
3 *Ibid.* p. 42 (no. 34).   4 *SPD, 1664–1665*, p. 515 (no. 14).
5 *Ibid.*   6 *Ibid.* p. 568 (no. 16).
7 *SPD, 1665–1666*, p. 230 (no. 18).   8 *Ibid.*
9 *SPD, 1666–1667*, p. 47 (no. 9).   10 *Ibid.* p. 56 (no. 84).
11 *SPD, 1664–1665*, p. 543 (no. 79).   12 *SPD, 1665–1666*, p. 230 (no. 18).
13 *Ibid.* p. 491 (no. 38).   14 *Ibid.* p. 2 (no. 11).
15 *Ibid.* p. 26 (no. 37).

References

PAGE 491

1 *SPD, 1665–1666*, p. 47 (no. 9). 2 *Ibid.* p. 56 (no. 84).
3 *SPD, 1664–1665*, pp. 504–5 (no. 47). 4 *Ibid.* p. 515 (no. 14).
5 *SPD, 1666–1667*, p. 2 (no. 11). 6 *Ibid.* p. 15 (no. 102).
7 *Ibid.* p. 549 (no. 75). 8 *Ibid.* p. 36 (no. 104).
9 *Ibid.* p. 2 (no. 11). 10 *Ibid.* p. 125 (no. 115).
11 *Ibid.* p. 196 (no. 17). 12 *Ibid.* p. 208 (no. 98).
13 *Ibid.* p. 232 (no. 6). 14 *Ibid.*
15 *Ibid.* p. 252 (no. 160).

PAGE 492

1 *SPD, 1666–1667*, p. 271 (no. 121).
2 *Ibid.* p. 359 (no. 56). 3 *SPD, 1665–1666*, p. 549 (no. 75).
4 W. D. Cooper, *Archaeologia*, XXXVII, 1–22.
5 Cox, p. 174.
6 *Pepys' Diary*, V, 134. 7 *Ibid.* p. 142.

PAGE 493

1 *SPD, 1664–1665*, p. 465 (no. 41).
2 HMC, *Town of Southampton MSS.* XI, iii, 31.
3 *SPD, 1664–1665*, p. 548 (no. 14).
4 Cooper, *Archaeologia*, XXXVIII, 1–22.
5 J. W. De Grave, *Proc. Huguenot Soc. London*, V, 131.
6 *SPD, 1665–1666*, p. 35 (no. 109). 7 *Ibid.* p. 24 (no. 32).
8 *Ibid.* p. 217 (no. 12). 9 *SPD, 1666–1667*, p. 437 (no. 88).

PAGE 494

1 *SPD, 1667*, p. 32 (no. 65). 2 *SPD, 1666–1667*, p. 79 (no. 96).
3 *Ibid.* p. 159 (no. 18). 4 *Ibid.* p. 177 (no. 17).
5 *Ibid.* p. 192 (no. 141). 6 *Ibid.* p. 215 (no. 9).
7 *Ibid.* p. 310 (no. 27). 8 *Ibid.* p. 351 (no. 5).
9 *Ibid.* p. 242 (no. 80). 10 *SPD, 1664–1665*, p. 548.

PAGE 495

1 Cox, p. 174. 2 Cox, *Churchwardens' accounts*, p. 319.
3 W. H. Jacob, *J. Br. Archaeol. Ass.* L, 273–4.
4 G. W. Kitchen, *Winchester*, p. 203. 5 W. H. Jacob, p. 274.
6 *Ibid.* 7 G. W. Kitchen, p. 203.

PAGE 496

1 W. H. Jacob, *J. Br. Archaeol. Ass.* L, 272.
2 *Ibid.* pp. 269–70. 3 *Ibid.* p. 270.
4 *Ibid.* 5 *Ibid.* pp. 274–5.
6 *The works of Simon Patrick, D.D., etc.* IX, 587.
7 *Ibid.* IX, 578.

PAGE 497

1 *SPD, 1664–1665*, p. 515 (no. 17).   2 *Ibid.* p. 517 (no. 26).
3 HMC, *The records of Quarter Sessions in the County of Wilts*, p. 148.
4 *Ibid.*
5 *SPD, 1666–1667*, p. 79 (no. 96).
6 HMC, *City of Salisbury MSS.* IV, 245.
7 *SPD, 1666–1667*, p. 167 (no. 28).   8 *Ibid.* p. 222 (no. 62).
9 *Ibid.* p. 284 (no. 41).

PAGE 498

1 HMC, *The records of Quarter Sessions in the County of Wilts*, p. 147.
2 *Ibid.* p. 148.
3 *Ibid.*
4 *SPD, 1664–1665*, p. 550 (no. 28).
5 *SPD, 1665–1666*, p. 42 (no. 36).

PAGE 499

1 *SPD, 1665–1666*, p. 54 (no. 118).
2 *SPD, 1666–1667*, p. 222 (no. 62).
3 *Ibid.* p. 47 (no. 6)
4 Pickard, p. 40.
5 *Ibid.* p. 41.
6 *The diary of the Rev. Ralph Josselin*, p. 147.
7 *Ibid.* p. 148.   8 *SPD, 1664–1665*, p. 546 (no. 9).
9 Jones, *NQ*, CXCVIII, 384–6.   10 Blomefield, II, 288.
11 *The diary of the Rev. Ralph Josselin*, pp. 148–56.

PAGE 501

1 *The diary of the Rev. Ralph Josselin*, p. 148.
2 *Ibid.* p. 149.   3 *Ibid.* p. 150.
4 *Ibid.* pp. 150–1.   5 *Ibid.* p. 151.
6 *Ibid.* p. 152.   7 *Ibid.* p. 153.
8 *Ibid.*   9 *Ibid.* p. 154.
10 *Ibid.* p. 155.   11 *Ibid.* p. 149.
12 *Ibid.* p. 150.

PAGE 502

1 E. L. Cutts, *Colchester*, p. 205.
2 P. Morant, *The history and antiquities of the county of Essex*, p. 74.
3 *The diary of the Rev. Ralph Josselin*, pp. 148–155.
4 *Ibid.* p. 149.   5 *Ibid.*
6 *Ibid.*   7 *Ibid.*
8 H. J. Cunnington, *An account of the charities and charitable benefactions of Braintree*, pp. 60–4.
9 F. G. Emmison, personal communication to the author, 1 November 1957.

References

PAGE 503

1 *The diary of the Rev. Ralph Josselin*, p. 152.
2 *Ibid.* p. 154.   3 *Ibid.* p. 150.
4 *Ibid.* p. 153.
5 *The works of Simon Patrick, D.D.*, etc. IX, 586.
6 *SPD, 1664–1665*, p. 546 (no. 9).   7 *Ibid.* p. 573 (no. 45).
8 *The diary of the Rev. Ralph Josselin*, p. 149.
9 *SPD, 1665–1666*, p. 10 (no. 66).
10 *The diary of the Rev. Ralph Josselin*, p. 150.
11 *SPD, 1665–1666*, p. 456 (no. 104).   12 *Ibid.* p. 479 (no. 112).
13 *SPD, 1666–1667*, p. 85 (no. 3).   14 *Ibid.* p. 203 (no. 63).

PAGE 504

1 *Registers of St Nicholas, Ipswich*, The Parish Reg. Soc. VII, 151–3.
2 *Ibid.*

PAGE 505

1 Jones, *NQ*, CXCVIII, 384–6.   2 *Ibid.*
3 *The diary of the Rev. Ralph Josselin*, p. 149.
4 *Ibid.* p. 153.   5 *SPD, 1665–1666*, p. 10 (no. 66).
6 *Ibid.* p. 252 (no. 38).   7 *Ibid.*
8 *Ibid.* p. 581 (no. 12).   9 *SPD, 1666–1667*, p. 79 (no. 96).
10 *Ibid.* p. 222 (no. 62).   11 *SPD, 1665–1666*, p. 520 (no. 60).
12 Jones, *NQ*, CXCVIII, 484–6.
13 Tymms, *Proc. Bury & West Suffolk Archaeol. Inst.* I, 42.
14 Jones, *NQ*, CXCVIII, 384–6.

PAGE 506

1 *The Lancet*, ii, 1295.

PAGE 508

1 H. C. Bulstrode, *Fortieth annual report of the local government board*, supplement,
   appendix A, no. 3, pp. 36–75.

PAGE 509

1 H. C. Bulstrode, *Fortieth annual report of the local government board*, supplement,
   appendix A, no. 3, pp. 36–75.
2 C. J. Martin and S. Rowland, *ibid.* pp. 76–90.

PAGE 510

1 'The plague in Suffolk', *The Times*, 14 November 1910.
2 *Ibid.* 4 November 1910.
3 'Suffolk game dealers and the plague', *The Times*, 5 November 1910.
4 *The diary of the Rev. Ralph Josselin*, p. 147.
5 *SPD, 1664–1665*, p. 512.   6 *Ibid.* pp. 542–3 (no. 77).
7 *Ibid.* p. 551 (no. 28).   8 *SPD, 1665–1666*, p. 47 (no. 71).

9 *Ibid.* p. 252 (no. 38).
10 *The diary of the Rev. Ralph Josselin*, p. 152.
11 W. D. Cooper, *Archaeologia*, XXXVII, 1–22.
12 *SPD, 1666–1667*, p. 188 (no. 108).   13 *SPD, 1665–1666*, p. 47 (no. 71).

PAGE 511

1 *SPD, 1665–1666*, p. 252 (no. 38).

PAGE 512

1 *SPD, 1666–1667*, p. 141 (no. 52).   2 *Ibid.* p. 191 (no. 129).
3 *Ibid.* p. 227 (no. 105).   4 *Ibid.* p. 245 (no. 100).
5 *Ibid.* p. 265 (no. 80).   6 *Ibid.* p. 284 (no. 41).
7 Blomefield, II, 289.   8 *SPD, 1666–1667*, p. 574 (no. 81).
9 *SPD, 1667*, p. 163 (no. 149).

PAGE 513

1 *SPD, 1665–1666*, p. 44 (no. 49).
2 Gladys Scott Thomson, *Life in a Noble Household, 1641–1700*, pp. 1–2.
3 W. Page, O. M. Moger and H. Douglas-Irvine, VCH, *Hertford*, II 297.
4 Sweeting, *Fenland Notes and Queries*, II, 155.

PAGE 514

1 Sweeting, *Fenland Notes and Queries*, II, p. 154.
2 Cox, p. 165.
3 W. Page, VCH, *Huntingdon*, II, 124.   4 *SPD, 1664–1665*, p. 517 (no. 27).
5 W. M. Palmer, *Proc. Camb. Antiq. Soc.* XVII, 98.
6 *SPD, 1664–1665*, p. 531 (no. 7).
7 *The diary and correspondence of Dr John Worthington*, II, i, 182.
8 *Ibid.* pp. 181–2.   9 Cooper, III, 518.

PAGE 515

1 Cooper, III, 521.   2 *Ibid.* p. 517.
3 *The diary of the Rev. Ralph Josselin*, p. 150.
4 *Ibid.* p. 149.   5 Cooper, III, 518.
6 *Ibid.*   7 *Ibid.*
8 *Ibid.*
9 *The Oxford Dictionary of Quotations*, p. 446a.
10 *Registers of St Michael's Parish, Cambridge*, Camb. Antiq. Soc. pp. 121–2.
11 Cooper, III, 520.   12 *Ibid.*

PAGE 516

1 Cooper, III, 520.   2 *Ibid.* p. 521.
3 *Registers of St Michael's Parish, Cambridge*, pp. 121–2.
4 *SPD, 1666–1667*, p. 53 (no. 57).

References

5 Sweeting, *Fenland Notes and Queries*, II, 154.
6 *Ibid.*   7 Bell, p. 324.
8 Sweeting, p. 155.

PAGE 517

1 Cooper, III, 520.   2 *SPD, 1666–1667*, p. 53 (no. 57).
3 Cox, p. 165.   4 Sweeting, II, 155.
5 *Ibid.*   6 *SPD, 1665–1666*, p. 5 (no. 34).
7 P. W. Phipps, *Records of Bucks.* VI, 262–5.
8 Alice V. Jenkinson, VCH, *Buckingham*, III, 113–14.

PAGE 518

1 R. S. Downs, *Records of Bucks*, VIII, 55–87.
2 W. Bradbrook, *Records of Bucks*, VIII, 234–8.
3 Nancy Spilman, VCH, *Buckingham*, IV, 276.
4 Cox, p. 165.
5 W. Bradbrook, *Records of Bucks.* XI, 91–102.
6 Cox, p. 157.
7 W. Hutton, *An history of Birmingham*, p. 38.

PAGE 519

1 R. K. Dent, *Old and new Birmingham*, p. 45.
2 *Transcript of the first register book of the Parish Church of St Martin, Birmingham*, pp. 237–42.
3 *Ibid.* pp. 239–42.
4 'A.D.', 'The Pest Field', *The Birmingham Journal and Daily Post*, 24 March 1856.

PAGE 521

1 *Warwick County Records*, V, 23.   2 *Ibid.* p. 25.
3 *Ibid.* p. 28.

PAGE 522

1 *Warwick County Records*, V, 55.
2 F. W. Willmore, *A history of Walsall and its neighbourhood*, pp. 277–8.
3 W. D. Cooper, *Archaeologia*, XXXVII, 1–22.
4 Bell, p. 323.   5 Bell, p. 322.
6 W. Wood, *The history and antiquities of Eyam, etc.* pp. 60–1.
7 *Ibid.* p. 60.   8 *Ibid.* p. 61.
9 R. Mead, *A discourse on the plague*, pp. 149–50.

PAGE 524

1 Wood, p. 74.   2 *Ibid.*
3 W. Wood, *The history and antiquities of Eyam, etc.* p. 79.

PAGE 525

1 *The diary and correspondence of Dr John Worthington*, II, i, 182–3.
2 *Ibid.*   3 W. Wood, p. 83.
4 *Ibid.* pp. 88–9.
5 J. M. J. Fletcher, *The plague-stricken Derbyshire village, etc.* p. 13.

PAGE 526

1 W. Wood, *The history and antiquities of Eyam, etc.* p. 95.
2 *Ibid.* p. 106.   3 *Ibid.*
4 *Ibid.*

PAGE 528

1 W. Wood, *The history and antiquities of Eyam, etc.* pp. 110–11.
2 *Ibid.* p. 116.   3 *Ibid.* p. 111.

PAGE 529

1 W. Wood, *The history and antiquities of Eyam, etc.* pp. 83–4.

PAGE 530

1 HMC, *Verulam (Gorhambury) MSS.* p. 67.
2 Emily M. Lawson, *The nation in the parish, etc.*, p. 85.
3 Bell, p. 323.
4 T. F. Thistleton-Dyer, *Old English social life as told by the parish registers*, p. 92.

PAGE 531

1 J. C. Morley, *Bygone Lancashire*, p. 112.
2 *Ibid.*
3 Axon, *Trans. Lancs. and Ches. Antiq. Soc.* XII, 97.
4 *Ibid.* p. 98.
5 R. Bruce Low, *Thirty-first annual report of the local government board*, supplement, appendix A, no. 19, pp. 337–8.
6 *Ibid.*   7 *The Lancet*, ii, 1222.

PAGE 532

1 R. Bruce Low, pp. 337–8.
2 R. Bruce Low, *Thirty-first annual report of the local government board*, supplement, appendix A, no. 19, pp. 337–8. 3 *Ibid.*
4 R. Bruce Low, *Forty-second annual report of the local government board*, supplement, appendix A, no. 1, p. 66.
5 R. Bruce Low, *Health and medical subjects, no. 3, Ministry of Health*, p. 141.

PAGE 533

1 J. Wilson, *Trans. Cumb. and Westm. Antiq. and Archaeol. Soc.* XIV, 133.
2 *SPD, 1664–1665*, p. 517 (no. 26).
3 *Calendar of the ancient deeds, Letters, etc....of Kingston-upon-Hull*, p. 245.

References

PAGE 534

1 *North Riding Record Soc. Publications*, VI, 90–3.
2 *SPD, 1664–1665*, p. 482 (no. 33).   3 Surtees, *Durham*, I, cxiv.
4 *Ibid.* II, 122.   5 *SPD, 1665–1666*, p. 224 (no. 66).
6 *Ibid.* p. 44 (no. 55).   7 *SPD, 1664–1665*, p. 482 (no. 33).

PAGE 535

1 H. A. Adamson, *Archaeol. Æliana*, XV, 218–24.
2 *Bronwydd Documents*, l. 5329.
3 R. Bruce Low, *Reports and papers on bubonic plague, with an introduction by the medical officer of the local government board*, Local Government Board, pp. 11 and 29–31.

PAGE 536

1 R. Bruce Low, *Reports and papers on bubonic plague, with an introduction by the medical officer of the local government board*, Local Government Board, pp. 11 and 29–31.
2 Creighton, I, 691.
3 W. D. Cooper, *Archaeologia*, XXXVII, 1–22.
4 *SPD, 1666–1667*, p. 560 (no. 113).   5 *SPD, 1667*, p. 59 (no. 86).

PAGE 537

1 *SPD, 1667*, p. 163 (no. 149).   2 *Ibid.* p. 59 (no. 86).
3 HMC, *City of Salisbury MSS*. IV, 245.
4 W. E. Buckland, *Kent Records*, p. 101.
5 *SPD, 1671*, 'News Letter from Falmouth', p. 446.
6 *SPD, 1670, with Addenda 1660–1670*, pp. 78–9.
7 *Ibid.*   8 *Ibid.* p. 117.

PAGE 538

1 Rudyard Kipling, *Rewards and Fairies*, p. 276.

BIBLIOGRAPHY

ABRAM, A., *Social England in the fifteenth century*, London, 1909,
Accounts of the Lord High Treasurer of Scotland, ed Sir J. B. Paul, II, Edinburgh, 1900.
Acts of the Privy Council of England, I, III, IX, X, XI, XII, XIII, XIV, XIX, XXIII, XXIV, XXVI, ed. J. R. Dasent, London, 1890–1902.
Acts of the Privy Council of England, 1623–1625 and 1625–1626, ed. A. E. Stamp, London, 1933 and 1934.
Acts of the Privy Council of England, 1626, June–December, ed. J. R. Dasent, London, 1938; 1627, January–August, ed. J. R. Dasent, London, 1938; 1627, September–1628, June, ed. J. R. Dasent; 1629, May–1630, May, ed. R. F. Monger and P. A. Penfold, London, 1960.
A.D., 'The Pest Field,' Birmingham Notes and Queries, No. 77, *The Birmingham Journal and Daily Post*, 24 March 1856.
ADAMSON, H. A., 'Tynemouth Castle: the eve of the commonwealth', *Archaeologia Æliana*, XV, Newcastle-upon-Tyne, 1892.
ALLEN, J., 'The earlier registers and parish accounts of Hawkshead', *Transactions of the Cumberland and Westmorland Antiquarian and Archaeological Society*, IV, Kendal, 1880.
ALLEN, T., *The history of the county of Lincoln, from the Earliest Period to the Present Time*, London, 1834.
ALLYN, H. B., 'The Black Death', *Annals of Medical History*, VII, London, 1925.
ANDREWS, A. W., *A text-book of geography*, London, 1913.
Annals of Clonmacnoise, being Annals of Ireland from the earliest period to A.D. 1408, trans. into English by Conell Mageoghan, A.D. 1627, ed. Rev. D. Murphy, Dublin, 1896.
Annals of Gonville and Caius College by John Caius M.D. Master of the College, ed. J. Venn, Cambridge, 1904.
Annals of Ireland by Friar John Clyn and Thady Dowling, together with the Annals of Ross, ed. R. Butler, Irish Archaeological Society, Dublin, 1849.
Annals of the Kingdom of Ireland by the four masters, trans. J. O'Donovan, III, Dublin, 1856.
Annals of Loch Cé, ed. W. M. Hennessy, London (Rolls Series), 1871.
Annals of Ulster, ed. W. M. Hennessy, Dublin, 1887.
Annals of Ulster, II, ed. B. MacCarthy, Dublin, 1893.
APC, see *Acts of the Privy Council of England*.
ARMITT, M. L., 'Fullers and freeholders of the parish of Grasmere', *Transactions of the Cumberland and Westmorland Antiquarian and Archaeological Society*, VIII, Kendal, 1908.
AUCHMUTY, REV. S. F. F., *History of the parish of Cleobury Mortimer, Salop*, Hereford, 1911.

Bibliography

AUDEN, H. M. 'Parochial History', *Church Stretton. Some results of local scientific research*, ed. C. W. Campbell-Hyslop and E. S. Cobbold, II, Shrewsbury, 1904.

AXON, W. E. A., 'Chronological notes on the visitation of plague in Lancashire and Cheshire', *Transactions of the Lancashire and Cheshire Antiquarian Society*, XII, Manchester, 1895.

'Documents relating to the plague in Manchester in 1605', *Remains Historical and Literary connected with the Palatine Counties of Lancashire and Cheshire*, LXXIII, Manchester, 1915.

'The plague in Cheshire', *Bygone Cheshire*, ed. W. Andrews, London, 1895.

Ayr Burgh Accounts, 1534–1624, transcr. and ed. G. S. Pryde, Publications of the Scottish History Society, XXVIII, Edinburgh, 1937.

BAKER, SIR R., *A Chronicle of the Kings of England from the Time of the Romans Government unto the Death of King James*, (*London, 1674*), *with continuations to 1660 by E. Phillips, and the reign of George I by an 'Impartial Hand'*, London, 1733.

BARBÉ, L. A., 'The plague in Scotland', *Chambers' Journal*, 7th Series, IV, London, 1914.

BARNARD, E. A. B., 'In the time of pestilence', *Worcester Diocesan Magazine*, XXVI, Worcester, 1919.

BARNES, H., 'Visitations of the plague in Cumberland and Westmorland', *Transactions of the Cumberland and Westmorland Antiquarian and Archaeological Society*, X and XI, Kendal, 1891.

BARNES, J., *The history of that most victorious monarch Edward III*, Cambridge, 1688.

BARRETT, W. P., *Present remedies against the plague*, Shakespeare Association Facsimiles, No. 17, London, 1933.

BARROUGH, P., *The method of physick*, London, 1634.

BARTHOLOMEW, J., *The survey gazetteer of the British Isles*, Ninth Edition, Edinburgh, undated.

BEDE, the Venerable, *Ecclesiastical history of England*, ed. J. A. Brewer, London, 1849.

BELL, J., *London's Remembrancer*, London, 1665.

BELL, W. J., *The great plague in London in 1665*, London, 1924.

BELLETT, REV. G., *The antiquities of Bridgnorth*, Bridgnorth, 1856.

BENNETT, H. S., *Life on the English manor. A study of peasant conditions, 1150–1400*, Cambridge, 1937.

BESANT, SIR W., *London in the time of the Stuarts*, London, 1903.

Medieval London, I, London, 1906.

Bibliography of Royal Proclamations of the Tudor and Stuart sovereigns, and of others published under authority, 1485–1714, Bibliotheca Lindesiana, V, ed. R. Steele, I, England and Wales; II, part 1, Ireland; part 2, Scotland, Oxford, 1910.

BIRCH, T., *The court and times of Charles I*, London, 1849.

'Birmingham in 1662', in 'Hundred of Hemlingford', *The Birmingham Post*, 16 February, 1954.

623

Bibliography

Birmingham Notes and Queries, No. 27, *The Birmingham Journal and Daily Post*, 18 March 1911.

Bishops Castle, transcript of the Bishop's Register of the Parish, J. E. Norton, kept in the Borough of Shrewsbury Public Library.

BLENCOWE, R. W., 'Extracts from the memoirs of the Gale family', *Sussex Archaeological Collections*, XII, Lewes, 1860.

'Extracts from the parish registers and other parochial documents of East Sussex', *Sussex Archaeological Collections*, IV, Lewes, 1851.

BLOMEFIELD, F. *The history of the city and county of Norwich*, Fersfield, 1741.

BOASE, C. W., *Historic Towns: Oxford*, London, 1887.

BOGHURST, W., *Loimographia: an account of the great plague of London in the year 1665*, Introd. and ed. J. F. Payne, London, 1894.

BONSER, W. *The medical background of Anglo-Saxon England*, The Wellcome Historical Medical Library, London, 1963.

BOORDE, A., *A Compendyous Regyment or a Dyetary of Helth made in Mountpyllier by Andrewe Boorde of Physycke Doctor*, ed. F. J. Furnivall, Early English Text Society, Extra Series, No. 10, London, 1870.

The Fyrst Boke of the Introduction of Knowledge made by Andrew Borde of Physycke Doctor, ed. F. J. Furnivall, London (Early English Text Society), 1870.

BRADBROOK, W., 'Bletchley Register', *Records of Buckinghamshire*, VIII, Aylesbury, 1903.

'Clifton Reynes Parish Account Book', *Records of Buckinghamshire*, XI, Aylesbury, 1906.

BRANSTON, A. R., and LEROY, A. C., *Historic Winchester*, London, 1884.

BRETT-JAMES, N. G., *The growth of Stuart London*, London, 1935.

BREWER, E. C., *The readers handbook of famous names in fiction, allusions, references, proverbs, plots, stories, and poems*, London, 1919.

British Medical Journal, ii, London, 1902.

Bronwydd Document, 5329, The National Library of Wales, Aberystwyth.

BROWN, REV. R. P., 'Bainbrig of Hawkin in Middleton, Westmorland', *Transactions of the Cumberland and Westmorland Antiquarian and Archaeological Society*, XXIV, Kendal, 1924.

BROWNE, W., 'Bridekirk and its registers', *Transactions of the Cumberland and Westmorland Antiquarian and Archaeological Society*, IV, Kendal, 1880.

BRUCE, LOW, R., 'Plague and suspected plague in England and Wales during 1901', Supplement containing the Report of the Medical Officer of Health, Appendix A, no. 19, *Thirty-first Annual Report of the Local Government Board*, London, 1903.

'Report on the progress and diffusion of bubonic plague throughout the world during the two years 1911 and 1912', Supplement containing the Report of the Medical Officer of Health, Appendix A, no. 1, *Forty-second Annual Report of the Local Government Board*, London, 1914.

'Reports and papers on bubonic plague,' *Parliamentary Reports*, London, 1902.

'The progress and diffusion of — 1. Plague, 2. Cholera, 3. Yellow Fever through-

out the world, 1914–17', *Reports on Public Health and Medical Subjects*, no. 3, Ministry of Health, London, 1920.

BRYAN, C. P., *The Papyrus Ebers*, London, 1930.

BUCHAN, J., *Montrose*, London, 1947.

Oliver Cromwell, London, 1940.

BUCKLAND, W. E., 'The parish registers and records in the diocese of Rochester', *Kent Records*, London, 1912.

BULSTRODE, H. C., 'Report on suspected pneumonic and bubonic plague in East Suffolk and on the prevalence of plague in rodents in Suffolk and Essex', Supplement containing the Report of the Medical Officer for 1910–11, Appendix A, No. 3, *Fortieth Annual Report of the Local Government Board*, London, 1911.

BURKE, A. M., *Key to the ancient parish registers of England and Wales*. Baltimore, 1962.

BURNE, A. H., *The battlefields of England*, London, 1950.

BURTON, REV. J. R., *A History of Kidderminster, with short accounts of the neighbouring parishes*, London, 1890.

Calendar of the ancient deeds, letters, etc., in the archives of the Corporation of Kingston-upon-Hull, ed. L. M. Stanewell, Hull, 1951.

Calendar of the ancient records of Dublin, ed. J. T. Gilbert, II, III and IV, Dublin, 1891–4.

Calendar of the Carew Manuscripts preserved in the Archiepiscopal Library at Lambeth, 1515–1574 and 1575–1588, ed. J. S. Brewer and J. Bullen, London, 1867 and 1868.

Calendar of the Close Rolls, Edward III, IX, London, 1906.

Calendar of the Close Rolls, Edward III, X, London, 1908.

Calendar of the Close Rolls, Edward III, X, XI, and XII; Richard II, I, Henry IV, III, London, 1909–31.

Calendar of the Fine Rolls, Edward III, VI, London, 1921.

Calendar of letters, despatches, and state papers relating to the negotiations between England and Spain, preserved in the archives at Simancas and elsewhere, I, ed. G. A. Bergenroth, London, 1862; IV, ed. Pascual de Gayangos, London, 1879.

Calendar of the Patent Rolls, Edward III, VIII, London, 1907.

Calendar of the Patent Rolls, Edward III, IX, London, 1907.

Calendar of the Patent Rolls, Edward III, X, London, 1908.

Calendar of the Patent Rolls, Edward III, XI, London, 1911.

Calendar of State Papers Carew, see under *Calendar of the Carew Manuscripts*.

Calendar of State Papers, Domestic Series

I, II, ed. J. S. Brewer, London, 1830–1834; 1547–1580, 1581–1590, ed. R. Lemon, London, 1856; 1591–1594, 1595–1601, Addenda 1580–1625, ed. Mary A. E. Greene, London, 1867, 1869, 1872.

1603–1610 and Addenda 1580–1625, ed. Mary A. E. Greene, London, 1857 and 1872.

Calendar of State Papers, Domestic Series (cont.)
1625–1626 and 1627–1628, ed. J. Bruce, London, 1858; 1629–1631, ed. J. Bruce, London, 1860; 1631–1633, ed. J. Bruce, London, 1862; 1635–1636, ed. J. Bruce, London, 1866; 1637, ed. J. Bruce, London, 1868; 1637–1638, ed. J. Bruce, London, 1869; 1638–1639, ed. J. Bruce and W. D. Hamilton, London, 1871; 1639, ed. W. D. Hamilton, London, 1873; 1640–1641, ed. W. D. Hamilton, London, 1882; 1641–1643, ed. W. D. Hamilton, London, 1887; 1645–1647, ed. W. D. Hamilton, London, 1891.

1651–1652, London, 1877; 1652–1653, London, 1878; 1653–1654, London, 1879; 1654, London, 1880; 1655, London, 1881; 1658–1659, London, 1881; 1660–1661, London 1860; 1664–1665, London, 1863; 1665–1666, London, 1864; 1666–1667, London, 1864; 1667, London, 1866; 1670, with Addenda 1660–1670, London, 1895—all these volumes ed. Mary A. E. Greene.

1671, ed. F. H. B. Daniell, London, 1895.

Calendar of state papers and manuscripts, relating to English affairs, existing in the archives and collections of Venice and in other libraries of Northern Italy, IV, ed. Rawdon Brown, London, 1867; X and XI, ed. E. Rawdon Brown, London; 1636–1639, XXIV, ed. A. B. Hinds, London, 1923.

Calendar of State Papers, relating to the English affairs. Preserved principally at Rome, in the Vatican archives and library, ed. J. M. Rigg, London, 1926.

Calendar of Wynn (of Gwydir) Papers, 1515–1590, Aberystwyth, 1926.

CANNON, J. *Oxfordshire* (The County Books), London, undated.

CARD, see *Calendar of the ancient records of Dublin*.

CCR, see *Calendar of the Close Rolls*.

Cely Papers, selections from the correspondence and memoranda of the Cely family, merchants of the staple, A.D. 1475–1488, edited for the Royal Historical Society by H. E. Malden, London, 1900.

CHADWICK, S. J., 'Some papers relating to the plague in Yorkshire', *The Yorkshire Archaeological and Topographical Journal*, XV, London, 1900.

CHALMERS, A. K., *Report on certain cases of plague occurring in Glasgow in 1900, by the Medical Officer of Health*, Glasgow, 1901.

CHAMBERS, R., *Domestic Annals of Scotland from the Reformation to the Revolution*, Edinburgh, 1859.

CHAUCER, G., *The Canterbury Tales*, trans. Nevill Coghill, Penguin Classics, Harmondsworth, 1951.

Chronicles

Chronicle of Adam of Usk, ed. with translation, Sir E. M. Thompson, London, 1904.

Adami Murimuthensis Chronica Etc., ed. T. Hog, London, 1846.

Anonimalle Chronicle 1333 to 1381, from a MS. written at St Mary's Abbey, York, ed. V. H. Galbraith, Manchester, 1927.

Customs of London otherwise called Arnold's Chronicle: containing, among divers other matters, the original of the celebrated poem of The Nut-Brown Maid, London, 1811.

Bibliography

Brut, the, or the Chronicles of England, ed. from MS. Rawl. B.171, Bodleian Library, etc., ed. F. W. D. Brie, London, 1906.

John of Fordun's Chronicle of the Scottish Nation, trans. F. J. H. Skene, ed. W. F. Skene, *The Historians of Scotland*, IV, Edinburgh, 1872.

Chronicles of the Frasers (The Wardlaw MS.), ed. W. Mackay, *Publications of the Scottish History Society*, XLVII, Edinburgh, 1905.

Historical Collections of a Citizen of London in the Fifteenth Century (William Gregory's Chronicle), ed. J. Gairdner, London (Camden Society), 1876.

Chronicle of the Grey Friars of London, ed. J. G. Nichols, London (Camden Society), 1852.

Ingulph's Chronicle of the Abbey of Croyland, with the continuation by Peter of Blois and anonymous writers, trans. from the Latin, H. T. Riley, London, 1908.

Henrici Knighton, Canonici Leycestrensis, Chronica de Eventibus Angliae a Tempore Regis Edgari usque mortem Regis Reicardi Secundi, Historiae Anglicanae Scriptores, II, ed. Sir R. Twysden, London, 1652.

Chronicon Galfridi le Baker de Swynebroke, ed. E. M. Thompson, Oxford, 1889.

A Chronicle of London from 1089 to 1483; etc., ed. Tyrell, London, 1827.

Chronicle of Perth; a register of Remarkable Occurrences, chiefly connected with that City, from the year 1210 to 1668 (The Maitland Club), Edinburgh, 1831.

Robertus de Avesbury de Gestis Mirabilibus Regis Edwardii Tertii, ed. E. M. Thompson, London (Rolls Series,) 1889.

CLAPHAM, SIR J. *A concise economic history of Britain*, Cambridge, 1949.

CLARENDON, EARL OF, *History of the great rebellion*, ed. W. D. Macray, London, 1888.

CLARKE, L. W., 'The plague in Birmingham', *Birmingham Notes and Queries*, No. 52, *The Birmingham Journal and Daily Post*, 30 July 1863.

CLAY, W. K., *A history of the parish of Waterbeach in the county of Cambridge*, Cambridge, 1859.

CLEMOW, F. G. *The geography of disease*, Cambridge, 1903.

CLEPHAM, J., 'Abigail and Timothy Tyzack, and Old Gateshead', *Archaeologia Æliana*, VIII, Newcastle-upon-Tyne, 1880.

COMRIE, J. D., *History of Scottish Medicine*, London (Wellcome Historical Medical Museum), 1932.

COOPER, C. H., *Annals of Cambridge*, 3 vols. Cambridge, 1842–4. [Cited as 'Cooper'.]

COOPER, W. D., 'Notices of the Last Great Plague, 1665–66; from the Letters of John Allin to Philip Frith and Samuel Jeake. In a Letter to Sir Henry Ellis, Director', *Archaeologia*, XXXVII, London, 1857.

CORNER, G. R., 'Extracts from the churchwardens' accounts of the parish of Eltham in Kent', *Archaeologia*, XXIV, London, 1852.

COULTON, G. G., *Chaucer and his England*, London, 1909.

The mediaeval village, Cambridge, 1925.

Mediaeval panorama, Cambridge, 1947.

COWPER, H. S., *The oldest register book of the parish of Hawkshead in Lancashire, 1568–1704*, London, 1897.

COX, REV. J. C., *Churchwardens' accounts from the fourteenth century to the close of the seventeenth century*, London, 1913.

The parish registers of England, London, 1910. [Cited as 'Cox'.]

CPR, see *Calendar of the Patent Rolls*.

CRAWFURD, R., *Plague and pestilence in literature and art*, Oxford, 1914.

CREIGHTON, C., *A history of epidemics in Britain*, I, Cambridge, 1894.

CUNNINGTON, H. J., *An account of the charities and charitable benefactions of Braintree*, London, 1904.

CUSSANS, J. E., *History of Hertfordshire*, I, London, 1870–3.

CUTTS, E. L., *Colchester* (Historic Towns Series), London, 1888.

DE BARRY, G., *Giraldi Cambrensis Opera*, ed. J. S. Brewer, London (Rolls Series), 1867.

DE BEER, SIR G., *Alps and Elephants*, London, 1955.

DE GRAVE, F. W., 'Notes on the register of the Walloon Church of Southampton, and on the churches of the Channel Islands', *Proceedings of the Huguenot Society of London*, V, Lymington, 1898.

DEKKER, T., 'A rod for Run-awayes', *The Plague Pamphlets of Thomas Dekker*, ed. F. P. Wilson, Oxford, 1925.

'The Wonderfull yeare' (London, 1603), *ibid*.

DENDY, F. W., 'The plague in Newcastle', *Proceedings of the Society of Antiquarians of Newcastle-upon-Tyne*, I, South Shields, 1905.

DENT, R. K., *Old and new Birmingham*, Birmingham, 1880.

Devon and Cornwall Record Society Publications: *The Parish Registers of*:

Allhallowes, Goldsmith Street, City of Exeter, I, ed. H. Tapley-Soper, Exeter, 1933.

Camborne, 1538–1837, ed. H. Tapley-Soper, Exeter, 1945.

Colyton, Devon, 1538–1837, transcr. and ed. A. J. P. Skinner, Exeter, 1928.

Hemyock, Devon, transcr. and ed. A. J. P. Skinner, Exeter, 1923.

Ottery, St Mary, transcr. and ed. H. Tapley-Soper, II, Exeter, 1908–29.

Widecombe-in-the-Moor, transcr. E. C. Wood and H. Tapley-Soper, Exeter, 1938.

Diary of:

'Robert Birrel, Burges of Edinburghe', *Fragments of Scottish History*, Dalyell, Edinburgh, 1798.

Lady Anne Clifford, London, 1923.

Rev. Ralph Josselin, 1616–1683, ed. E. Hockliffe, London (Camden Society), 1908.

Henry Machyn, Citizen and Merchant-Taylor of London, from A.D. 1550 to A.D. 1563, ed. J. G. Nichols, London (Camden Society), 1848.

Henry Newton, Alderman of Cambridge (1662–1717), ed. J. S. Foster, Proceedings of the Cambridge Antiquarian Society, Cambridge, 1890.

Samuel Pepys; Clerk of the Acts and Secretary to the Admiralty, transcr. the late Rev. Mynors Bright, ed. with additions H. B. Wheatley, IV and V, London, 1946.

Henry Townshend of Elmley Lovett, 1640–1663, ed. J. W. Willis-Bund, London, 1920.

Bibliography

Diary and Correspondence of:

Dr *John Worthington*, ed. J. Crossley, *Remains Historical and Literary connected with the Palatine Counties of Lancaster and Chester* (Cheetham Miscellany), I, Manchester, 1847; II, Part I, XXXVI, Manchester, 1855.

'D.O.' 'Population of Sheffield in 1615', *The Gentleman's Magazine*, LXXXI, London, 1811.

DONALDSON, R. A., *The Rat*, Philadelphia, 1924.

DOWNS, R. S., 'The Parish Church of High Wycombe', *Records of Buckinghamshire*, VII and VIII, Aylesbury, 1903.

DYDE, F., *The history of antiquities of Tewkesbury*, Tewkesbury, 1798.

'Early chronicles of Shrewsbury 1372–1603', trans. and annotated Rev. W. A. Leighton, *Transactions of the Shropshire Archaeological and Natural History Society*, III, Shrewsbury, 1880.

Egerton Papers The, ed. J. P. Collier (Camden Society), London, 1840.

ERBE, see *Extracts from the records of the burgh of Edinburgh*.

EVAGRIUS, *The history of the Church: by Eusebius Pamphilus, Socrates Scholasticus, and Evagrius Scholasticus*, trans. from the edition of Valesius, Cambridge, 1683.

Extracts from the burgh records of Dunfermline in the 16th and 17th centuries, ed. A. Shearer, Carnegie Dunfermline Trust, 1951.

Extracts from the council register of the Burgh of Aberdeen, I, II, ed. J. Stuart, Aberdeen (Spalding Club), 1844 and 1848.

Extracts from the Kirk Sessions Records of Perth, Edinburgh (The Maitland Club), 1831.

Extracts from the records of the burgh of Edinburgh I, II, III, IV, ed. J. D. Marwick, Edinburgh, 1869, 1871, 1875, 1882; V, ed. M. Wood and R. K. Hannay, Edinburgh, 1927; VI, ed. M. Wood, Edinburgh, 1931.

Extracts from the records of the burgh of Edinburgh, 1642–1655, Appendix IX, ed. M. Wood, Edinburgh, 1938; 1655–1665, ed. M. Wood, Edinburgh, 1940.

'Extracts from the register of Sir Thomas Butler, vicar of Much Wenlock', *Shropshire Archaeological and Natural History Society*, VI, Shrewsbury, 1883.

FABYAN, R., *The new chronicles of England and France, in two parts*, reprinted from Pynson's edition of 1516, ed. H. Ellis, London, 1811.

FITTER, R. S. R. *London's natural history*, London, 1945.

FLENLEY, R., 'MS. Western 30745 (a chronicle of Lynn)', *Six town chronicles of England*, Oxford, 1911.

FLETCHER, A., 'A tragedy of the great plague of Milan in 1630', *Bulletin of the Johns Hopkins Hospital*, IX, Baltimore, 1898.

FLETCHER, REV. J. M. J., *The plague-stricken Derbyshire village: or, what to see in and around Eyam*, Tideswell, 1916.

FLETCHER, W. G. D., *A short history of Shelton and Oxon*, privately printed and undated.

Bibliography

FM, see *Annals of the Kingdom of Ireland by the four masters*.

FOWLER, R., 'On the discovery of one of the "seites" set apart (in Whitechapel) for a pest-ground in 1349, temp. Edward III', *The Lancet*, ii, London, 1884.

FRESHFIELD, E., 'On the parish books of St. Margaret-Lothbury, St. Christopher-le-Stocks, and St. Bartholomew-by-the-Exchange, in the City of London', *Archaeologia*, XLV, London, 1877.

FURNESS, W. ('Ewanian'), *History of Penrith from the earliest record to the present time*, Penrith, 1894.

GARDINER, D., 'A mayor of Canterbury: William Watmer, the children's friend', *Archaeologia Cantiana*, LXI, Ashford, 1949.

GARDINER, J. R., *History of the great Civil War, 1642–1649*, I, London, 1893.

GARRISON, F. H., *An introduction to the history of Medicine*, Philadelphia, 1922.

GASQUET, F. A., *The Black Death of 1348 and 1349*, 2nd edition, London, 1908.

GERVIS, F. H., *On the sweating sickness*, no. XVI of the Sette of Odd Volumes, London, 1887.

GIBBON, E., *The decline and fall of the Roman Empire*, London, 1936.

GILES, E. and THRALE, R. W., *Historic Sandridge. The story of a Hertfordshire parish*, Sandridge, 1952.

GILL, C., *History of Birmingham*, I, London, 1952.

GILLBANKS, REV. F. W., 'The Registers of Great Orton, Carlisle', *Transactions of the Cumberland and Westmorland Antiquarian and Archaeological Society*, VIII, Kendal, 1886.

GILLIES, H. C., 'Gaelic names of diseases and diseased states', *The Caledonian Medical Journal*, New Series III, Edinburgh, 1899.

GIRAUD, F. F., 'Payments by the town of Faversham in 1635–6', *Archaeologia Cantiana*, XXIV, Ashford, 1900.

GODFREY, E., *Social life under the Stuarts*, London, 1904.

GODFREY, W. E., 'The plague of Chesterfield, 1586–7', *Journal of the Derbyshire Archaeological & Natural History Society*, no. 74, Derby, 1954.

GODWIN, W., *History of the Commonwealth of England to the Restoration of Charles II*, I, London, 1824.

GOLDSMITH, O., *The bee and other essays, together with the life of Nash*, London, 1914.

GORDON, C. A., 'Macgowan's list of epidemics', *An epitome of the reports of the medical officers to the Chinese Imperial Customs Service from 1871 to 1882*, London, 1884.

GRAFTON, R., *A chronicle at Large, and meere History of the Affayres of England, and Kings of the Same*, London, 1569.

GRAHAM, T. H. B., 'The mediaeval diocese of Carlisle', *Transactions of the Cumberland and Westmorland Antiquarian and Archaeological Society*, new series, XXV, Kendal, 1925.

GRAUNT, J., *Observations on the bills of mortality*, London, 1665.

GREEN, J. R., *A short history of the English people*, revised and enlarged Alice S. Green, London, 1947.

Bibliography

GREENHILL, W. A., 'Registers of the Hastings parishes', *Sussex Archaeological Collections*, XIV, Lewes, 1862.

GREGORY OF TOURS, *The history of the Franks*, trans. O. M. Dalton, Oxford, 1927.

GWYNN, A., 'The Black Death', *Studies*, XXIV, London, 1935.

HAMILTON, A. H. A., *Quarter Sessions Records from Queen Elizabeth to Queen Anne*, London, 1878.

HAMMOND, E., *Bygone Wandsworth*, London, 1906.

HAMMOND, G., *Bygone Putney*, London, 1898.

HANCOCK, R., *Narratives of the Reformation*, London (Camden Society), 1859.

HANCOCK, T., *Researches into the laws and phenomena of pestilence; including a medical sketch and review of the Plague of London, in 1665; and remarks on Quarantine*, London, 1821.

Hand-list of proclamations, Henry VIII–Anne, 1509–1714, Crawford, *Bibliotheca Lindesiana*, I, Aberdeen University Press, 1893.

HANNAN-CLARKE, T., *Drama in Gloucestershire*, Gloucester, 1928.

HARDING, LT. COL., *History of Tiverton, in the County of Devon*, I, Tiverton, 1845.

Harleian Society Publications: *The Parish Registers of:*

Abbey Church of SS. Peter and Paul, Bath, part II, ed. A. J. Jewers, XXVIII, London, 1901.

All Hallows, Bread Street and St. John the Evangelist, Friday Street, transcr. and ed. W. B. Bannerman, XLIII, London, 1913.

Christ Church, Newgate, transcr. and ed. W. A. Littledale, XXI, London, 1895.

Kensington, Co. Middlesex, ed. F. N. Macnamara and A. Storey-Maskelyne, XVI, London, 1890

St. Antholin, Budge Row, ed. J. L. Chester and G. J. Armytage, VIII, London, 1883.

St. Bene't, Paul's Wharf, ed. W. A. Littledale, XLI, London, 1912.

Saynte De'nis Backchurch, transcr. and ed. J. L. Chester, III, London, 1878.

St. Helen's, Bishopsgate, transcr. and ed. W. B. Bannerman, XXI, London, 1904.

St. James, Clarkenwell, transcr. and ed. R. Hoveden, XVII, London, 1891.

St. Katharine by the Tower, transcr. and ed. A. W. H. Clarke, LXXV, London, 1945.

St. Lawrence, Jewry, transcr. and ed. A. W. H. Clarke, LXX, London, 1940.

St. Martin in the Fields., I, transcr. and ed. T. Mason, XXV, London, 1898.

St. Martin in the Fields, II, transcr. and ed. J. V. Kitto, XXV, London, 1936.

St. Martin Orgar, transcr. and ed. A. W. H. Clarke, LXVII, London, 1937.

St. Mary le Bowe, Cheapside; All Hallows, Honey Lane; St. Pancras, Soper Lane, transcr. and ed. W. B. Bannerman, XLIV, London, 1914.

St. Mary Magdalen, Milk Street, transcr. and ed. A. W. H. Clarke, LXII, London, 1942.

St. Mary Somerset, part II, ed. W. B. Bannerman, LX, London, 1930.

St. Mary the Virgin, Aldermanbury, transcr. and ed. W. B. Bannerman, LXI, London, 1931.

St. Michael Bassishaw, transcr. and ed. A. W. H. Clarke, LXXII, London, 1942.

Bibliography

Harleian Society Publications (*cont.*):

St. Michael Cornhill, ed. J. L. Chester, VII, London, 1882.
St. Olave, Hart Street, ed. W. B. Bannerman, XLVI, London, 1916.
St. Paul's, Covent Garden, ed. Rev. W. H. Hunt, XXXVI, London, 1908.
St. Peeters upon Cornhill, ed. G. W. G. Leveson, I, London, 1879.
St. Vedast, Foster Lane, ed. W. A. Littledale, XXX, London, 1903.
Harleian Miscellany, VII, 'A Modern Account of Scotland. By an English Gentleman', London, 1810.

HARVEY, G., *Little Venus Unmask'd*, London, 1702.
HARVEY, G. Jun., *The City Remembrancer: being Historical Narratives of the Great Plague at London, 1665; Great Fire, 1666; and Great Storm, 1703*, I, London, 1769.
HEBERDEN, W. Jun., *Observations on the increase and decrease of different diseases, and particularly of the plague*, London, 1801.
HEER, F., *The mediaeval world*, trans. from the German by Janet Sondheimer, New York, 1963.
HENSLOW, G., *Medical works of the fourteenth century*, London, 1899.
Henslowe Papers, ed. W. W. Gregg, London, 1907.
HERRIES, D. C., 'An Annandale minister in the seventeenth century', *Dumfries & Galloway Natural History & Antiquarian Society*, V, Dumfries, 1919.
HIGDEN, R., *Polychronicon Ranulphi Higden Monachi Cestrensis*, ed. C. A. Babington, V, London (Rolls Series), 1865.
HINTON, M. A. C., *Rats and mice as enemies of mankind*, British Museum (Natural History), economic series, no. 8, London, 1918.
HIRST, L. F. *The conquest of plague*, Oxford, 1953.
'Plague', *The British Encyclopaedia of Medical Practice*, IX, London, 1936.

Historical Manuscripts Commission

Additional manuscripts of Sir Hervey Juckes Lloyd Bruce, *Report on manuscripts in various collections*, VII, London, 1914.
Berwick-upon-Tweed Corporation MSS., *Manuscripts in various collections*, I, London, 1901.
Borough of Kings Lynn MSS., *Eleventh Report*, part 3, London, 1887.
Calendar of the manuscripts of his Grace the Duke of Rutland, G.C.B., preserved at Belvoir Castle, *Twelfth Report*, part 4, 1888; *Fifteenth Report*, part 10, London, 1899.
Calendar of the manuscripts of the Most Honourable the Marquis of Salisbury, K.G., preserved at Hatfield House, Hertfordshire, *Fourteenth Report*, part I, London, 1883; part II, London, 1888; Part III, London, 1889; part IV, London, 1892; part XIII, London, 1915; part XIV, London, 1923; part XV, London, 1930; part XVI, London, 1933; part XVII, London, 1938; part XVIII, London, 1940.
Corporation of Beverley MSS., *Eleventh Report*, parts 1, 2, 3 and 4, London, 1887.
Corporation of the Borough of Plymouth MSS., *Tenth Report*, Appendix, part IV, London, 1885.

Bibliography

Diocese of Gloucester MSS., *Manuscripts in various collections*, VII, London, 1901.

Lincoln Corporation MSS., *Fourteenth Report*, parts 8, 9 and 10, London, 1895.

The manuscripts of Captain Stewart, of Alltyrodyn, Llandyssil, *Tenth Report*, Appendix, part IV, London, 1885.

The manuscripts of the City of Exeter, London, 1916.

The manuscripts of the Coke family, of Melbourne, Co. Derby, belonging to the Earl Cowper, K.G., preserved at Melbourne Hall, part II, *Twelfth Report*, Appendix, part I, London, 1888.

The manuscripts of the corporation of Bishop's Castle, *Tenth Report*, Appendix, part IV, London, 1885.

The manuscripts of the extinct corporation of Burford, Oxfordshire, *Manuscripts in various collections*, I, London, 1901.

The manuscripts of the family of Gawdy, formerly of Norfolk, *Tenth Report*, Appendix, part V, London, 1885.

The manuscripts of Henry Duncan Skrine, Esq., *Eleventh Report*, Appendix, Part I, London, 1887.

The manuscripts of His Grace the Duke of Portland, I, *Thirteenth Report*, Appendix, part I, London, 1891.

The manuscripts of His Grace the Duke of Portland, preserved at Welbeck Abbey, III, *Fourteenth Report*, Appendix, parts I, II, London, 1894.

The manuscripts of His Grace the Duke of Rutland, K.G., preserved at Belvoir Castle, IV, London, 1905.

The manuscripts of the late Reginald Rawdon Hastings Esq., of the Manor House, Ashby de la Zouche, IV, London, 1947.

The manuscripts of J. M. Heathcote Esq., Conington Castle, London, 1899.

The manuscripts of Lord Kenyon at Gredington Hall, Shropshire, *Fourteenth Report*, Appendix, part IV, London, 1894.

The manuscripts of Lord Montagu of Beaulieu, London, 1900.

The manuscripts of Stanley Leighton, Esq., M.P., *Tenth Report*, Appendix, part IV, London, 1885.

The manuscripts of the town of Southampton, *Eleventh Report*, Appendix, part III, London, 1887.

The Marchmont muniments of the family of Polwarth, Lords Polwarth and Earls of Marchmont, in the possession of Sir Hugh Hume Campbell, Baronet, of Marchmont, at Marchmont House, Berwickshire, *Thirteenth Report*, Appendix, part III, London, 1891.

The municipal records of Shrewsbury, *Fifteenth Report*, Appendix, part X, London, 1899.

Muniments of the corporation of the city of Salisbury, *Report on manuscripts in various collections*, IV, London, 1907.

The records of the Bishop of Salisbury, *Report on manuscripts in various collections*, IV, London, 1907.

The records of the county of Worcester, *Report on manuscripts in various collections*, I, London, 1901.

Historical Manuscripts Commission (*cont.*)

The records of Quarter Sessions in the County of Wilts, *Report on manuscripts in various collections*, I, London, 1901.

Report on the manuscripts of the Earl of Egmont, I, London, 1905.

Report on the manuscripts of the Earl of Verulam, preserved at Gorhambury, London, 1906.

Report on the manuscripts of Lord De L'Isle and Dudley, preserved at Penshurst Place, III, London, 1936.

Report on the manuscripts of the Marquess of Downshire preserved at Easthampstead Park, Berks., II, London, 1936.

Rye MSS., *Thirteenth Report*, parts 4 and 5, London, 1891.

Shrewsbury Corporation MSS., *Fifth Report*, part 10, London, 1899.

'Historical memoranda in the handwriting of John Stow', *Three fifteenth-century Chronicles*, ed. J. Gairdner, London (Camden Society), 1880.

Historical Narrative of the Great Plague at London, 1665 (anon.), London, 1769.

HLP, *see* Hand-list of proclamations.

HMC, *see* Historical Manuscripts Commission.

HODGES, N., *Loimologia: or, an historical account of the plague in London in 1665: with precautionary directions against the like contagion*, J. Quincy's edition, London, 1720.

HOLINSHED, R., *The chronicles of England, Scotland, and Ireland*, London, 1807–8.

HOLMES, W. H. *Bacillary and rickettsial infections*, New York, 1940

HOVEDEN, R., 'The registers of the Wallon or Strangers' Church in Canterbury', part III, *The publications of the Huguenot Society of London*, V, Lymington, 1898.

HUBBARD, G. E., *The old book of Wye*, Derby, 1951.

HUCKSTEP, R. L., *Typhoid fever and other Salmonella infections*, Edinburgh, 1962.

HUDD, A. E., 'Two Bristol calendars. Fox MS.', *Transactions of the Bristol and Gloucestershire Archaeological Society*, XIX, Bristol, 1895.

HUTTON, W., *An history of Birmingham*, Birmingham, 1781.

JACKSON, W., 'Extracts from the parish register of St. Bees, with comments upon the same', *Transactions of the Cumberland and Westmorland Antiquarian and Archaeological Society*, part II, for the years 1867 to 1872, Kendal, 1873.

JACOB, W. H., 'Some notes on the plague in Winchester,' *The Journal of the British Archaeological Association*, L, London, 1894.

JESSOPP, A., 'The Black Death in East Anglia', *The coming of the friars and other historic essays*, London, 1890.

JEWERS, J., 'The will of a plague-stricken Londoner', *The Home Counties Magazine*, III, London, 1901.

Joannis de Burgundia de pestilentia liber, Sloane MS. 3449, British Museum.

JOHNSON, C., 'Note on the inscription in Ashwell Church', *Transactions of the St. Albans and Hertfordshire Architectural & Archaeological Society*, new series, I, London, 1895–6.

JONES, J., *A Dial for all Agues, Etc.*, London, 1566.

JOYCE, F. W., *A social history of ancient Ireland*, I, London, 1903.

Bibliography

KELLER, W. *The bible as history*, trans. W. Neil, London, 1956.

KELLY, W., 'Visitations of the plague at Leicester', *Transactions of the Royal Historical Society*, VI, London, 1877.

KELSO, W. M., *Sanitation in Paisley*, Paisley, 1922.

KEYS, T. E., 'The plague in literature', *Bulletin of the Medical Library Association*, XXXII, London, 1944.

KING, GREGORY, *Two tracts of Gregory King*, ed. G. A. Barnet, Baltimore, 1936.

KINGSFORD, C. L. *The Stonor Letters and Papers 1290–1483*, London (Camden Society), 1919.

KIPLING, R., *Rewards and Fairies*, London, 1922.

KITCHEN, G. W., *Winchester* (Historic Towns Series), London, 1890.

KLEBS, A. C., 'A Catalan plague-tract of April 24, 1348, by Jacme d'Agramont', *VIme Congrès Internationale d'Histoire de la Médecine, 1927*, Antwerp, 1929.

KNIGHT, J. T., 'The Black Death and its Effects. With Special Reference to St. Albans', *Transactions of the St. Albans & Hertfordshire Architectural & Archaeological Society*, new series, I, London, 1895–6.

Knyvett Letters, ed. B. Schofield, *Norfolk Record Society*, London, 1949.

LANGER, W. E., 'The Black Death', *Scientific American*, New York, 1964.

LANGLAND, W., *Piers Plowman*, ed. A. Burrell, Everyman, London, 1919.

LAWSON, E. M., *The nation in the parish: or records of Upton-on-Severn*, London, 1884.

LAYCOCK, T., *Report on the state of York*, York, 1844.

LEADMAN, A. D. H., 'Pocklington Church', *The Yorkshire Archaeological and Topographical Journal*, XV, London, 1900.

LEECH, E. B., 'The parish registers of Lancashire', *Transactions of the Lancashire and Cheshire Antiquarian Society*, LVII, Manchester, 1946.

LEES, REV. T., 'Extracts from the registers of Greystoke Church during the reigns of Elizabeth and the Stuart kings', *Transactions of the Cumberland and Westmorland Antiquarian and Archaeological Society*, part II for the years 1867 to 1872, Kendal, 1873.

Letters and papers, foreign and domestic of the reign of Henry VIII, I, catalogued J. S. Brewer, revised R. S. Brodie, London, 1920; II, III, IV, arranged and catalogued J. S. Brewer, London, 1864, 1867, 1870; V, IX, X, XI, XII, XIII, arranged and catalogued J. Gairdner, London, 1880, 1886, 1887, 1888, 1890–1, 1892–3; XV, XVI, XVIII, XIX, XX, XXI, arranged and catalogued J. Gairdner and R. S. Brodie, London, 1896, 1898, 1901–2, 1904–5, 1905, 1908.

Letters of Lady Brilliana Harley, 1640–1641, ed. T. T. Lewis, London (Camden Society), 1854.

LEWIS, REV. H. A., *St. Martin's, St. Helen's and Tean (Isles of Scilly) in Legend and History*, London, 1948.

'Lichfield Episcopal Registers, Bishop Robert de Stretton', *Collections for a History of Staffordshire*, Sir William Salt Archaeological Society, new series, VIII, Stafford, 1905.

LIEN-TEH, W., CHUN, J. W. H., POLLITZER, R., and WU, C. Y., *Plague*, Shanghai, 1936.

Life of William Lilly, student in astrology, *Autobiography*, London, 1826.

Life and times of Anthony Wood, Antiquary of Oxford, 1632–1695, described by himself, ed. A. Clarke, Oxford, 1891.

The lives of the Right Hon. Francis North, Baron Guilford; the Hon. Sir Dudley North; and the Hon. and Rev. Dr. John North. By the Hon. Roger North, together with the autobiography of the author, ed. A. Jessopp, II, London, 1890.

LLOYD, SIR J. E., *A history of Carmarthenshire*, Cardiff, 1939.

LONGE, J. G., *Martha, Lady Giffard: her life and correspondence (1664–1722)*, London, 1911.

LPH, see *Letters and papers, foreign and domestic.*

LUMB, G. D., 'The parish register of Aberford, co. York (1540–1812)', *Publications of the Thoresby Society*, XXXVI, Leeds, 1937.

'The Register of the Parish Church of Methley in the County of York, from 1560 to 1812', *Publications of the Thoresby Society*, XII, Leeds, 1903.

'The registers of the parish church of Leeds from 1639 to 1677', *Publications of the Thoresby Society*, VII, Leeds, 1897.

LUNN, J., 'The Black Death in the Bishop's Registers', unpublished typescript copy of a thesis awarded the Ph.D. degree of Cambridge University, 1937.

LYSONS, REV. D. and S., *Magna Britannia*, I, London, 1806; II, London, 1808, part ii, London, 1810; III, London, 1814; IV, London, 1816; V, London, 1817; VI, London, 1822.

MACLEAN, J., 'The plague at Tredington, 1610–1611', *Gloucestershire Notes and Queries*, II, London, 1884.

MAITLAND, W. and others, *The history and survey of London*, London, 1756.

MARTIN, C. J. and ROWLAND, S., 'Observations on rat plague in East Suffolk, November and December, 1910', Supplement containing the report of the Medical Officer, Appendix A, no. 3, *Fortieth annual report of the Local Government Board*, London, 1911.

MAYO, C. H., The parish register of Milborne Port, Somerset', *Notes and Queries for Somerset and Dorset*, II, Sherborne, 1891.

MEAD, R., *A discourse on the plague*, London, 1744.

MEDLAND, C. H., 'St Nicholas Church, Gloucester,' *Transactions of the Bristol and Gloucestershire Archaeological Society*, XXIII, Bristol, 1900.

MERRIMAN, R. W., 'Extracts from the records of the Wiltshire Quarter Sessions', *The Wiltshire Archaeological and Natural History Magazine*, XXII, Devizes, 1885.

Middlesex County Records, ed. J. C. Jeaffreson, I, London, 1886; II, London, 1887; III, London, 1888.

MIDDLETON, T., 'Old Cheshire records: the antiquaries contribution to history', *Transactions of the Lancashire and Cheshire Antiquarian Society*, LIII, Manchester, 1938.

MOFFAT, C. B., 'The mammals of Ireland', *Proceedings of the Royal Irish Academy*, XLIV, 1938.

MOORE MSS, ed. J. Brownbill, *Lancashire and Cheshire Record Society*, LXVII, Liverpool, 1913.

MORANT, P., *The history and antiquities of the county of Essex*, Chelmsford, 1816.

MORLEY, J. C., 'The plague in Liverpool', *Bygone Lancashire*, ed. E. Axon, London, 1892.

MORRELL, P. F. A., 'The parish registers of the parish of Burton', *Journal of the Architectural, Archaeological, and Historical Society of Chester and North Wales*, XV, Chester, 1909.

MORRIS, R. H., 'The siege of Chester', edited and completed P. H. Lawson, *Journal of the Architectural, Archaeological and Historical Society of Chester and North Wales*, XXV, Chester, 1923.

MULLETT, C. H., *The bubonic plague and England*, Lexington, 1963.

'Mysterious disease in Suffolk', *The Lancet*, ii, London, 1910.

NASH, J. T. C., *Evolution and disease*, Bristol, 1915.

Newport, transcript of the bishop's register of the parish, J. E. Norton, kept in the Borough of Shrewsbury Public Library.

New statistical account of Scotland, V, Largs; VIII, Falkirk; IX, Dunfermline; X, Perth; XI, Menmuir and Montrose; XII, Aberdeen, Edinburgh, 1845.

NICHOLLS, REV. W., *The history and traditions of Ravenstondale, Westmorland*, II, Manchester, 1877.

NICHOLSON, J. H., 'The parish registers of Orton, Westmorland', *Transactions of the Cumberland and Westmorland Antiquarian and Archaeological Society*, XI, Kendal, 1891.

NOORTHOUCK, J., *A new history of London, including Westminster and Southwark*, London, 1773.

Notes and Queries (London)

ALINGTON, F. W., 'The plague of London in 1625', VI, London, 1888.

ATTWOOD, J. S., 'Customs connected with the Plague', III, London, 1887.

C.J.R., 'Christ Church, Newgate Street,' XI, London, 1861.

'DELTA', 'Population of London, temp. Henry II', IV, London, 1869.

'ETONENSIS', 'The Plagues of 1605 and 1625', II, London, 1880.

F.J.F., 'Recipe for Edward IV's Plague Medicine', IX, London, 1878.

'FRANCISCUS', 'Payments for the destruction of vermin', no. 110, London, 1851.

FURNIVALL, P., 'The plague of 1563', V, London, 1888.

HARGROVE, J., 'The plague at Datchett', VI, London, 1864.

HOOPER, J. 'Host eaten by mice', XII, London, 1897.

JONES, A. G. E., 'Plagues in Suffolk in the seventeenth century', CXCVIII, London, 1953.

'J.S.A.', 'The plagues of 1605 and 1625', III, London, 1881.

'JUXTA TURRIM', 'Plague in 1563', XI, London, 1861.

K.P.D.E. 'Provincial fairs', fifth series, VIII, London, 1877.

'Leominster Burials in 1587 and '97', The Vicar, XI, London, 1861.

PETER, F. C., 'The plague in Redruth', IV, London, 1893.

PICKFORD, J., 'The plagues of 1605 and 1625', IV, London, 1881.
PLOMER, R. H., 'Preservatives from the plague', III, London, 1887.
RILEY, H. T., 'Plague plant', second series, II, London, 1856.
'R.S.', 'Hensley Register, 1563', XI, London, 1861.
SIMPSON, J., 'The plagues of 1605 and 1625', II, London, 1880.
SMART, T. W. W., 'The plagues of 1605 and 1625', II, London, 1880.
SWEETING, REV. W. D., 'The plagues of 1605 and 1625', II, London, 1880.
TERRY, F. C. B., 'Plague', I, London, 1892.
THOMPSON, P., 'Mortality in 1587, 1588, etc.', XI, London, 1861.
UNDERHILL, W., 'The plague of London in 1625', VI, London, 1888.

'Notes on the history of Plague', *British Medical Journal*, ii, London, 1900.
NQ, see *Notes and Queries*

'Observations upon the plague in England by the Rev. Mr. Pegge. In a letter to
   Mr. Gough', *Archaeologia*, VI, London, 1782.
OLLIFFE, J. F., 'Reflections on the treatment of variola by the "ectrotic method"',
   The Lancet, i, 1840–1.
OMAN, C., *Castles*, London, 1926.
ORMEROD, G., *The history of the County Palatine and City of Chester*, revised
   T. Helsby, I and II, London, 1882.
OWEN, H. and BLAKEWAY, J. B., *A history of Shrewsbury*, I, London, 1825.
Oxinden Letters, 1607–1642, ed. Dorothy Gardiner, London, 1933.
Oxinden and Peyton Letters, 1607–1643, ed. Dorothy Gardiner, London, 1933.

PALLAS, P. S., *Travels through the southern provinces of the Russian Empire, in the
   years 1793 and 1794*, trans. from the German, I, London, 1802.
   *Voyages de M.P.S. Pallas, en differentes Provinces de l'Empire de Russie, et dans
   l'Asie Septentrionale: traduits de l'Allemand, par M. Gaulthier de la Peyronie*,
   Paris, 1788.
PALMER, W. M., 'The reformation of the corporation of Cambridge', *Proceedings of
   the Cambridge Antiquarian Society*, XVII, Cambridge, 1914.
*Parish book of St. Helen's Church in Worcester containing the parish registers from
   A.D. 1538 to A.D. 1812*, transcr. and ed. J. B. Wilson, London, 1900.

Parish Register Society: *The Registers of:*

Banstead in the county of Surrey, 1547–1789, transcr. and ed. F. A. H. Lambert,
   I, London, 1896.
Monk Fryston, 1566–1678, transcr. and ed. J. D. Hemsworth, V, London, 1896.
Parish Church of Solihull, co. Warwick, transcr. T. B. H. Brooks, LIII, London, 1904.
St. Albans, Worcester, 1630–1812, transcr. Rev. J. B. Wilson, II, London, 1896.
St. Nicholas, Ipswich, co. Suffolk, transcr. Rev. E. Cookson, VII, London, 1897.
Stratford-on-Avon in the County of Warwick, transcr. R. Savage, LI, London, 1905.
Parish registers of S. Breward in Cornwall, 1555–1900, ed. Rev. T. Taylor, Beverley,
   1900.

PARKER, C. A., 'Gosforth Registers', *Transactions of the Cumberland and West-morland Antiquarian and Archaeological Society*, VIII, Kendal, 1886.

Paston Letters, ed. J. Gairdner, III, London, 1904.

PATERSON, J., *A Warning to Great Britain, in a Sermon Preach'd at several Churches in and about London, upon the spreading of the Plague in France, and now Publish'd for the Benefit of others. To which is added an Appendix, Containing An Historical Account of all the Remarkable Plagues, Pestilences and Famines thro' the World, from the beginning to this time; Etc.*, London, 1721.

PATRICK, SIMON, *The works of Simon Patrick, D.D. sometime Bishop of Ely, including the autobiography*, ed. A. Taylor, Oxford, 1858.

Paul the Deacon, *History of the Langobards*, trans. W. D. Foulke, Philadelphia, 1907.

PCS, see *Privy Council of Scotland*.

PEACOCK, E., 'Extracts from the churchwardens' accounts of the parish of Leverton, in the county of Lincoln', *Archaeologia*, XLI, London, 1895.

PEAKE, REV. J., *Ellesmere, Shropshire*, Shrewsbury, 1889.

PELHAM, R. A., 'Mediaeval foreign trade: eastern ports', *An historical geography of England before A.D. 1800*, ed. H. C. Darby, Cambridge, 1948.

PEMBERTON, REV. R., *Solihull and its church*, Exeter, 1905.

PHILLIPS, REV. J., 'The oldest parish registers in Pembrokeshire', *Archaeologia Cambrensis*, II, London, 1902.

PHILLIPS, T., *The history and antiquities of Shrewsbury*, Shrewsbury, 1779.

PHIPPS, P. W., 'The church of St. Giles Chalfont', *Records of Buckinghamshire*, VI, Aylesbury, 1887.

PICKARD, R., *The population and epidemics of Exeter in pre-census times*, Exeter, 1947.

PIRENNE, H., *Mohammed and Charlemagne*, London, 1940.

'Plague in Cardiff', *The Lancet*, i, London, 1901.

'Plague at Redditch (1625)', XXVII Old Bromsgrove Paragraphs, *Notes and Queries for Bromsgrove and the District of Central Worcestershire*, Bromsgrove, 1909.

'Plague in Suffolk', *The Times*, 4 November, 1910.

'Plague in Suffolk', *The Times*, 14 November, 1910.

'Plague Plots of Geneva', Nova et Vetera, *British Medical Journal*, ii, London, 1907.

PMV, see *Calendar of state papers and manuscripts...in...Venice.*

Privy Council of Scotland, Register of the
 I, II, ed. J. H. Burton, Edinburgh, 1877
 IV, 1630–1632, ed. P. H. Browne, Edinburgh 1902
 V, 1633–1635, ed. P. H. Browne, Edinburgh, 1904
 VI, 1635–1637, ed. P. H. Browne, Edinburgh, 1905
 VIII, 1544–1660, ed. P. H. Browne, Edinburgh, 1908.
 III, IV, V, VI, VII, VIII, XI, XII, XIII, and XIV ed. and abridged D. Masson, Edinburgh, 1880, 1881, 1882, 1884, 1885, 1887, 1894, 1895, 1896, and 1898.

Procopius, *History of the Wars*, trans. H. B. Dewing, London, 1914.

PURCHAS, S., 'Edward Terry's description of the Mogul's Empire', *Hakluytus Posthumus or Purchas His Pilgrimes*, IX, book 9, cap. 6, Glasgow, 1905.

'Quarter Sessions Records', edited Rev. J. C. Atkinson, *The North Riding Record Society*, III, London, 1885, IV, London, 1885.
Quarter Sessions records for the county of Somerset, II, ed. Rev. E. H. B. Harbin, Somerset Record Society, XXIV, London, 1908; III, ed. Rev. E. H. B. Harbin, Somerset Record Society, XXVIII, London, 1912.

RADCLIFFE, J. N., *The pestilence in England: an historical sketch*, London, 1852.
REES, W., 'The Black Death in England and Wales, as exhibited in manorial documents', *Proceedings of the Royal Society of Medicine*, XVI, London, 1923.
'Reflections on the weekly bills of mortality', *A collection of very valuable and scarce pieces relating to the last plague in the year 1665*, Anonymous, London, 1721.
'Register of baptisms, marriages and burials in St. Michael's parish, Cambridge', ed. J. Venn., *Proceedings of the Cambridge Antiquarian Society*, Cambridge, 1891.
'Registration of births, marriages, and deaths', *The Lancet*, ii, 1839.
Remenbrancia: analytical index to the series of records known as the Remenbrancia. Preserved among the archives of the City of London, A.D. 1579-1664, London, 1878.
'Reports on the manuscripts of the Royal College of Physicians', *British Medical Journal*, ii, London, 1882.
RICHMOND, T., *The local records of Stockton and its neighbourhood*, Stockton, 1868.
RITCHIE, J., 'The plague in Dumfries', *Transactions of the Dumfriesshire & Galloway Natural History and Antiquarian Society*, XXI, Dumfries, 1939.
  'Quarantine for plague in Scotland during the sixteenth and seventeenth centuries', *Edinburgh Medical Journal*, LV, Edinburgh, 1948.
ROBINSON, W., *The history and antiquities of the parish of Stoke Newington, in the county of Middlesex*, London, 1842.
  The history of antiquities of the parish of Tottenham in the county of Middlesex, II, London, 1840.
ROWSE, A. L., *The England of Elizabeth*, London, 1964.
RUFUS OF EPHESUS, *Œuvres d'Oribase*, French translation by Bussemaker and Daremberg, III, Paris, 1851.
RUSSELL, J. C., *British mediaeval population*, Albuquerque, 1948.
RYMER, J., *Foedera*, II, London, 1869.

SALZMAN, L. F., *English life in the Middle ages*, London, 1926.
  The history of the parish of Hailsham, Lewes, 1901.
SANKEY, E. H., 'Wragby Registers, Book No. 1', *The Yorkshire Archaeological and Topographical Journal*, XII, London, 1893.
SARTON, G., *Introduction to the history of science*, III, Baltimore, 1947.
SCAIFE, R. N., 'Extracts from the registers of the church of St. Mary, Castlegate, York', *The Yorkshire Archaeological Journal*, XV, Leeds, 1900.
SELLERS, M. *York Memorandum Book*, part 2, Surtees Society, CXXV, Durham, 1915.
SHH, see *Calendar of the Manuscripts of . . . the Marquis of Salisbury* under Historical Manuscripts Commission.

Bibliography

SHORT, T., *A general chronological history of the air, weather, seasons, meteors, etc.*, London, 1749.

SHREWSBURY, J. F. D., 'The yellow plague', *Journal of the History of Medicine*, I, 1949.

The Shropshire Parish Register Society: *The Parish Registers of:*

Condover, ed. H. M. Auden, Lichfield Diocese, VI, part 1, Shrewsbury, 1904.

Ludlow, transcr. and ed. H. T. Weyman, Hereford Diocese, XIII, part 1, Shrewsbury, 1910.

Montford, transcr. and ed. H. M. Auden, Lichfield Diocese, VII, Shrewsbury, 1909.

Myddle, transcr. and ed. W. G. D. Fletcher, Lichfield Diocese, XIX, part 1, Shrewsbury, 1925.

Oswestry, ed. D. R. Thomas, St Asaph Diocese, IV–VII, Shrewsbury, 1909–14.

Shrewsbury St Chad, ed. W. G. D. Fletcher, Lichfield Diocese, XV, part 3 and XVI, part 3, Shrewsbury, 1916.

Shrewsbury St Mary, ed. G. W. S. Sparrow, Lichfield Diocese, XII, Shrewsbury, 1911.

Wem, ed. W. G. D. Fletcher, Lichfield Diocese, X, Shrewsbury, 1908.

SIGERIST, H. E., 'Problems of historical-geographical pathology', *Bulletin of the Institute of the History of Medicine*, I, 1933.

SIMPSON, W. J., *A treatise of plague*, Cambridge, 1905.

SINGER, D. W., 'Some plague tractates (fourteenth and fifteenth centuries)', *Proceedings of the Royal Society of Medicine* (Section of the History of Medicine), IX, London, 1916.

SINKER, REV. E., *Salwarpe*, Worcester, 1918.

SKEAT, REV. W. W., *A Concise Etymological Dictionary of the English Language*, Oxford, 1911.

'Smallpox at Milan', *The Lancet*, ii, London, 1888.

SNYDER, J. C., 'The typhus fevers', *Viral and rickettsial infections of man*, ed. T. M. Rivers, Philadelphia, 1948.

SOUTHALL, H., 'Retiring address of the president, April 10, 1890', *Transactions of The Woolhope Naturalist Field Club for 1890–92*, Hereford, 1894.

SPD, see *Calendar of State Papers, Domestic Series*

SPERLING, REV. J. H., 'The parochial history of Westbourne', *Sussex Archaeological Collections*, XXII, Lewes, 1870.

SPURRELL, W., *Carmarthen and its neighbourhood*, Carmarthen, 1879.

Staffordshire Parish Register Society:

Mucklestone, 1555–1701, ed. P. W. L. Adams, Stafford 1929.

Wolverhampton, 1539–1660, ed. P. W. L. Adams, Stafford, 1932.

STANEWELL, L. M., *Calendar of the ancient deeds, letters, etc., in the archives of the corporation of Kingston-upon-Hull*, Hull, 1951.

The statistical account of Scotland, Sir J. Sinclair, XXI, Brechin, Edinburgh, 1791–9.

STOCKDALE, J. R., *Annals Caermoelenses: or annals of Cartmel*, Ulverston, 1872.

Bibliography

STOW, *see* Stow and Howe

STOW, J., *A Survay of London*, ed. H. Morley, London, undated.

STOW, J. and HOWES, E., *The Annales, or Generall Chronicle of England*, London, 1615. [Cited as 'Stow'.]

STRYPE, J., *Ecclesiastical memorials, relating chiefly to religion, the reformation of it, and the emergencies of the Church of England, under King Henry VIII, King Edward VI, and Queen Mary*, Oxford, 1822.

'Suffolk game dealers and the plague', *The Times*, 5 November, 1910.

SULLIVAN, SIR E., 'The Book of Kells', *The Studio*, London, 1914.

SURTEES, R., *The history and antiquities of the County Palatine of Durham*, I, London, 1816; II, London, 1820; IV, London, 1840.

Sussex Record Society:

'The parish registers of Horsham in the county of Sussex, 1541–1635', ed. E. G. Rice, XXI, London, 1915.

SWEETING, REV. W. D., 'The plague in the Fens', *Fenland Notes and Queries*, II, London, 1894.

SYDENHAM, T., *The Whole Works of that Excellent Practical Physician, Dr Thomas Sydenham*, from the original Latin by T. Pechey. London, 1734.

SYKES, J., 'Extracts from the parish registers of the Church of Holy Trinity, Hull', *The Yorkshire Archaeological Journal*, IX, London, 1886.

'Extracts from the parish registers of Wadworth', *The Yorkshire Archaeological Journal*, IX, London, 1886.

TANSLEY, A. G., *The British islands and their vegetation*, Cambridge, 1939.

TERRY, C. S., 'The siege of Newcastle by the Scots in 1644', *Archaeologia Æliana*, XXI, Newcastle-upon-Tyne, 1899.

THISTLETON-DYER, T. F., *Old English social life as told by the parish registers*, London, 1898.

THOMPSON, A. H., 'The pestilences of the fourteenth century in the Diocese of York', *The Archaeological Journal*, LXXI, London, 1914.

'Registers of John Gynewell, Bishop of Lincoln, for the years 1347–1350', *The Archaeological Journal*, LXVIII, London, 1911.

THOMSON, G., *Loimotomia: Or the Pest Anatomised*, London, 1666.

THOMSON, G. S., *Life in a Noble Household, 1641–1700*, London, 1937.

THOMSON, J. A., *Biology for Everyman*, ed. E. J. Holmyard, II, London, 1938.

THOMSON, SIR J. A., *The outline of natural history*, London, undated.

THORNTON, W. H., 'The plague at North Bovey', *Devon and Cornwall Notes and Queries*, VI, Exeter, 1910–11.

TIDY, SIR H. L., *A synopsis of medicine*, Bristol, 1945.

TIMBS, J. and GUNN, A., *Abbeys, castles and ancient halls of England and Wales, South*, London, undated.

TOPLEY, W. W. and WILSON, G. S., *Principles of Bacteriology and Immunology*, 3rd ed. revised by G. S. Wilson and A. A. Miles, II, London, 1946.

Bibliography

TRAILL, H. D. and MANN, J. S., *Social England*, II, London, 1902.

Transcript of the First Register Book of the Parish Church of St. Martin, Birmingham, 1554–1563, I, transcr. J. Hill and W. B. Bickley, Walsall, 1889; *1653–1812*, transcr. E. Hobday, privately printed, 1903.

TREVELYAN, G. M., *English Social History*, London, 1945.

TSP, see *Bibliography of Royal Proclamations*

TYMMS, S., 'Notes towards a medical history of Bury', *Proceedings of the Bury and West Suffolk Archaeological Institute*, I, Bury St Edmunds, 1853.

VALE, E., *Shropshire*, London, 1949.

VALLANCE, A., 'Lydden Church', *Archaeologia Cantiana*, XLIII, London, 1931.

VCH, *see* Victoria History of England

Victoria History of England (listed alphabetically by county)

COPE, J. H., 'Redbornestoke Hundred: Millbrook', *The Victoria History of the County of Bedford*, III, ed. W. Page, London, 1912.

LEA, H. S. F., 'Stodden Hundred', *The Victoria History of the County of Bedford*, III, ed. W. Page, London, 1912.

MANSFIELD, M. R., 'Redbornestoke Hundred: Kempston Daubney', *The Victoria History of the County of Bedford*, III, ed. W. Page, London, 1912.

RANSOM, A., 'Social and economic history', *The Victoria History of the County of Bedford*, II, ed. W. Page, London, 1908.

RICKARDS, V., 'Willey Hundred', *The Victoria History of the County of Bedford*, III, ed. W. Page, London, 1912.

Sister Elspeth of the Community of All Saints, 'Ecclesiastical History', *The Victoria History of the County of Bedford*, I, ed. H. A. Doubleday and W. Page, Westminster, 1904.

COX, REV. J. C., 'Ecclesiastical history', *The Victoria History of Berkshire*, II, ed. Rev. P. H. Ditchfield and W. Page, London, 1907.

HOLLINGS, M., 'Theale Hundred: Padworth', *The Victoria History of Berkshire*, III, ed. W. Page, Rev. P. H. Ditchfield, and J. H. Cope, London, 1923.

JAMISON, C., 'Reading Hundred: Thatcham', *The Victoria History of Berkshire*, III, ed. W. Page, Rev. P. H. Ditchfield, and J. H. Cope, London, 1923.

LODGE, E. C., 'Social and economic history', *The Victoria History of Berkshire*, II, ed. Rev. P. H. Ditchfield and W. Page, London, 1907.

TEMPERLEY, G., and FIELD, REV. J. E., 'Wallingford Borough', *The Victoria History of Berkshire*, III, ed. W. Page, Rev. P. H. Ditchfield, and J. H. Cope, London, 1923.

WALLIS-CHAPMAN, A. B., 'Borough of Newbury', *The Victoria History of Berkshire*, IV, ed. W. Page, Rev. P. H. Ditchfield, and J. H. Cope, London, 1924.

ELLIS, G. A., 'Stoke Hundred: Horton', *The Victoria History of the County of Buckingham*, III, ed. W. Page, London, 1925.

JAMISON, C., 'Social and economic history', *The Victoria History of the County of Buckingham*, II, W. Page, London, 1908.

JENKINSON, A. V., 'Desborough Hundred: High Wycombe', *The Victoria History of the County of Buckingham*, III, ed. W. Page, London, 1925.

Victoria History of England (*cont.*)

SISTER ELSPETH, 'Ecclesiastical history', *The Victoria History of the County of Buckingham*, I, ed. W. Page, London, 1905.

SPILMAN, N., 'Newport Hundred: Bletchley with Fenny Stratford and Water Eaton', *The Victoria History of the County of Buckingham*, IV, ed. W. Page, London, 1927.

BEZODIS, P. A., 'Trinity College', *The Victoria History of the County of Cambridge and the Isle of Ely*, III, ed. J. P. C. Roach, London, 1959.

CAM, H. M., 'The City of Cambridge', *The Victoria History of the County of Cambridge and the Isle of Ely*, III, ed. J. P. C. Roach, London, 1959.

HAMPSON, E. M., 'The City of Ely,' *The Victoria History of the County of Cambridge and the Isle of Ely*, IV, ed. R. B. Pugh, London, 1953.

SALZMAN, L. F., 'Mediaeval Cambridgeshire', *The Victoria History of the County of Cambridge and the Isle of Ely*, II, ed. L. F. Salzman, London, 1948.

'Political History', *The Victoria History of the County of Cambridge and the Isle of Ely*, II, ed. L. F. Salzman, London, 1948.

WOOD-LEGH, K. L., 'Ecclesiastical history', *The Victoria History of the County of Cambridge and the Isle of Ely*, II, ed. L. F. Salzman, London, 1948.

WILSON, J., 'Ecclesiastical history', *The Victoria History of the County of Cumberland*, II, ed. J. Wilson, London, 1905.

COX, REV. J. C., 'Ecclesiastical history', *The Victoria History of the County of Derby*, II, ed. W. Page, London, 1907.

LANDER, J. H., 'Social and economic history', *The Victoria History of the County of Derby*, II, ed. W. Page, London, 1907.

FRIPP, M. C. and WRAGGE, P. 'Social and economic history', *The Victoria History of the County of Dorset*, II, ed. W. Page, London, 1908.

BRADSHAW, F., 'Social and Economic History, III—The Black Death', *The Victoria History of the County of Durham*, II, ed. W. Page, London, 1907.

COMFORD, M. E., 'Religious houses', *The Victoria History of the County of Durham*, II, ed. W. Page, London, 1907.

GEE, REV. H., 'Ecclesiastical history', *The Victoria History of the County of Durham*, II, ed. W. Page, London, 1907.

COX, REV. J. C., 'Ecclesiastical history', *The Victoria History of the County of Essex*, II, ed. W. Page and J. H. Round, London, 1907.

MACMUNN, N. E., 'Social and economic history', *The Victoria History of the County of Essex*, II, ed. W. Page, and J. H. Round, London, 1907.

BUTLER, R. F., 'Social and economic history', *The Victoria History of the County of Gloucester*, II, ed. W. Page, London, 1907.

GRAHAM, R., 'Ecclesiastical history', *The Victoria History of the County of Gloucester*, II, ed. W. Page, London, 1907.

COX, REV. J. C., 'Ecclesiastical history', *The Victoria History of Hampshire and the Isle of Wight*, II, ed. H. A. Doubleday, Westminster, 1903.

LEACH, A. F., 'History of schools', *The Victoria History of Hampshire and the Isle of Wight*, II, ed. H. A. Doubleday, Westminster, 1903.

Bibliography

SHILLINGTON, V. M., 'Social and economic history', *The Victoria History of Hampshire and the Isle of Wight*, V, ed. W. Page, London, 1912.

NIEMEYER, A. F. H., 'Social and economic history', *The Victoria History of the County of Hertford*, IV, ed. W. Page, London, 1914.

PAGE, W., MOGER, O. M., and DOUGLAS-IRVINE, H., 'Dacorum Hundred', *The Victoria History of the County of Hertford*, II, ed. W. Page, London, 1908.

BUCKLAND, C. S. B., 'Social and economic history', *The Victoria History of the County of Huntingdon*, II, ed. W. Page, G. Proby and S. I. Ladds, London, 1932.

PAGE, W., 'Huntingdon Borough', *The Victoria History of the County of Huntingdon*, II, ed. W. Page, G. Proby and S. I. Ladds, London, 1932.

SISTER ELSPETH, 'Ecclesiastical history', *The Victoria History of the County of Huntingdon*, I, ed. W. Page, G. Proby, and H. E. Norris, London, 1926.

SIMKINS, N. M., 'Ecclesiastical history, part II', *The Victoria History of the County of Kent*, II, ed. W. Page, London, 1926.

SLATER, G., 'Social and economic history', *The Victoria History of the County of Kent*, III, ed. W. Page, London, 1932.

FARRER, W. and BROWNBILL, J., 'Religious houses; the Abbey of Cockersand', *The Victoria History of the County of Lancaster*, II, ed. W. Farrer and J. Brownbill, London, 1908.

LAW, A., 'Social and economic history', *The Victoria History of the County of Lancaster*, II, ed. W. Farrer and J. Brownbill, London, 1908.

RAMSAY MUIR, 'Liverpool: West Derby Hundred', *The Victoria History of the County of Lancaster*, IV, ed. W. Farrer and J. Brownbill, London, 1911.

TAIT, J., 'Ecclesiastical history', *The Victoria History of the County of Lancaster*, II, ed. W. Farrer and J. Brownbill, London, 1908.

SISTER ELSPETH, 'Ecclesiastical history', *The Victoria History of the County of Leicester*, I, ed. W. Page, London, 1907.

CALTHROP, M. M. C., 'Ecclesiastical history (to A.D. 1600)', *The Victoria History of the County of Lincoln*, II, ed. W. Page, London, 1906.

GRAHAM, R., 'Religious houses: abbey of Crowland', *The Victoria History of the County of Lincoln*, II, ed. W. Page, London, 1906.

MASSINGBERD, REV. W. O., 'Social and economic history', *The Victoria History of the County of Lincoln*, II, ed. W. Page, London, 1906.

DAVIS, J. J., DAVIS, E. J., and COMFORD, M. E., 'Ecclesiastical history: part II, 1348–1521', *The Victoria History of the County of London*, I, ed. W. Page, London, 1909.

WRAGGE, P. 'Religious houses: St. Peter's Abbey, Westminster', *The Victoria History of the County of London*, I, ed. W. Page, London, 1909.

MINCHIN, G. S., 'Social and economic history', *The Victoria History of the County of Middlesex*, II, ed. W. Page, London, 1911.

SIMKINS, M. E., 'Ecclesiastical history (from A.D. 1279)', *The Victoria History of the County of Norfolk*, II, ed. W. Page, London, 1906.

CAM, H. M., *The Victoria History of the County of Northampton*, III, ed. W. Page, London, 1930.

SERJEANTSON, REV. R. M. and ADKINS, R. W., 'Ecclesiastical history', *The Victoria*

Victoria History of England (*cont.*)

History of the County of Northampton, II, ed. Rev. R. M. Serjeantson and R. W. Adkins, London, 1906.

COX, REV. J. C., 'Ecclesiastical history', *The Victoria History of the County of Nottingham*, II, ed. W. Page, London, 1910.

WALLIS-CHAPMAN, A. B., 'Social and Economic History', *The Victoria History of the County of Nottingham*, II, ed. W. Page, London, 1910.

BAKER, REV. E. P., LONG, MOIRA, *et al.*, 'Ploughley Hundred: Upper Heyford', *The Victoria History of Oxford*, VI, ed. M. D. Lobel, London, 1959.

COLVIN, H. M., 'Ploughley Hundred: Middleton Stoney', *The Victoria History of the County of Oxford*, VI, ed. M. D. Lobel, London, 1959.

CRASTER, SIR E., 'Pyrton Hundred: Pyrton', *The Victoria History of the County of Oxford*, VIII, ed. M. D. Lobel, London, 1964.

HARVEY, B., 'Ploughley Hundred: Islip', *The Victoria History of the County of Oxford*, VI, ed. M. D. Lobel, London, 1959.

JONES, M. *et al.* 'Thame Hundred: Tetsworth', *The Victoria History of the County of Oxford*, VII, ed. M. D. Lobel, London, 1962.

LEES, B. A., 'Social and economic history', *The Victoria History of the County of Oxford*, II, ed. W. Page, London, 1907.

WOODS, S. 'Bullingdon Hundred: Merton', *The Victoria History of the County of Oxford*, V, ed. M. D. Lobel, London, 1957.

SALTER, REV. H. E., 'Ecclesiastical history', *The Victoria History of the County of Oxford*, II, ed. W. Page, London, 1907.

STRICKLAND GIBSON, 'The University of Oxford', *The Victoria History of the County of Oxford*, III, ed. Rev. H. E. Salter and M. D. Lobel, London, 1954.

TOYNBEE, M. *et al.*, 'Ploughley Hundred: Tusmore', *The Victoria History of the County of Oxford*, VI, ed. M. D. Lobel, London, 1959.

MOFFAT, S. E., 'Social and economic history', *The Victoria History of the County of Rutland*, I, ed. W. Page, London, 1908.

SISTER ELSPETH, 'Ecclesiastical history', *The Victoria History of the County of Rutland*, I, ed. W. Page, London, 1908.

BRADFORD, G., 'Social and economic history', *The Victoria History of the County of Somerset*, II, ed. W. Page, London, 1911.

SCOTT HOLMES, REV. CHANCELLOR T., 'Ecclesiastical history', *The Victoria History of the County of Somerset*, II, ed. W. Page, London, 1911.

COX, REV. J. C., 'Ecclesiastical history', *The Victoria History of the County of Suffolk*, II, ed. W. Page, London, 1907.

UNWIN, G., 'Social and economic history', *The Victoria History of the County of Suffolk*, I, ed. W. Page, London, 1911.

COX, REV. J. C., 'Religious houses: hospital of Sandon', *The Victoria History of the County of Surrey*, II, ed. H. E. Malden, London, 1905.

MALDEN, H. E., 'Ecclesiastical history', *The Victoria History of the County of Surrey*, II, ed. H. E. Malden, London, 1905.

'Political history', *The Victoria History of the County of Surrey*, I, ed. H. E. Malden, Westminster, 1902.

PAGE, W., and PECKHAM, W. D., 'History of the City of Chichester', *The Victoria History of the County of Sussex*, III, ed. L. F. Salzman, London, 1935.

SALZMAN, L. F., 'Ecclesiastical history', *The Victoria History of the County of Sussex*, II, ed. W. Page, London, 1907.

WRAGGE, P., 'Social and economic history', *The Victoria History of the County of Sussex*, II, ed. W. Page, London, 1907.

COX, REV. J. C., 'Ecclesiastical history', *The Victoria History of the County of Warwick*, II, ed. W. Page, London, 1908.

DORMER-HARRIS, M., 'Social and economic history', *The Victoria History of the County of Warwick*, II, ed. W. Page, London, 1908.

STYLES, P., 'Alcester', *The Victoria History of the County of Warwick*, III, ed. L. F. Salzman and P. Styles, London, 1945.

SCOTT, R., 'Mediaeval agriculture', *The Victoria History of Wiltshire*, IV, ed. E. Crittall, London, 1959.

LOCKE, A. A., 'Religious houses', *The Victoria History of the County of Worcester*, II, ed. J. W. Willis-Bund and W. Page, London, 1906.

'Social and economic history', *The Victoria History of the County of Worcester*, IV, ed. W. Page, and J. W. Willis-Bund, London, 1924.

WILLIS-BUND, J. W., 'Ecclesiastical history', *The Victoria History of the County of Worcester*, II, ed. J. W. Willis-Bund, London, 1906.

FALLOW, T. M., 'Religious houses: priory of North Ferriby', *The Victoria History of the County of York*, III, W. Page, London, 1913.

MILLER, E., 'Mediaeval York', *The Victoria History of the City of York*, ed. P. M. Tillott, London, 1961.

SALZMAN, L. F., 'Ecclesiastical history', *The Victoria History of the County of York*, III, ed. W. Page, London, 1913.

'Political history', *The Victoria History of the County of York*, III, ed. W. Page, London, 1913.

SELLERS, M., 'Social and economic history', *The Victoria History of the County of York*, III, ed. W. Page, London, 1913.

VINCENT, T., *God's Terrible Voice in the City*, 1666, reprint London, 1832.

VINE, G., *A litil boke the whiche traytied and rehercved many gode thinges necessaries for the...Pestilence...made by the...Bisshop of Arusiens...*[London], [1485?], The John Rylands Facsimiles, no. 3, Manchester, 1910.

WALFORD, C., *Fairs past and present: a chapter in the history of commerce*, London, 1883.

WALKER, C. C., *A brief history of Lilleshall*, Newport, 1891.

WALKER, J., *The history of Penrith from the earliest period to the present time*, Penrith, 1864.

WARD, J. H., 'Plague in 1645–6', *Notes and Queries for Somerset and Dorset*, III, Sherborne, 1893.

WARDLE, F. D., 'The accounts of the chamberlains of the city of Bath, 1568–1602', *Somerset Record Society*, XXXVIII, Taunton, 1922.

WARE, SIR J., *The antiquities and history of Ireland*, London, 1705.

WARKWORTH, J., *A chronicle of the first thirteen years of the reign of King Edward the Fourth*, ed. J. O. Halliwell, London (Camden Society), 1839.

Warwick County Records, ed. S. C. Ratcliff and H. C. Johnson, V, Warwick, 1935; II, ed. S. C. Ratcliff and H. C. Johnson, Warwick, 1936.

Quarter Sessions Order Book Easter, 1625, to Trinity, 1637, ed. S. C. Ratcliff and H. C. Johnson, Warwick, 1935.

WATERS, R. E. C., *Parish registers in England, their history and contents*, London, 1887.

WHITAKER, T. D., *Lordis and Elmet*, Leeds, 1816.

Whitchurch, transcript of the bishop's register in the possession of the Borough of Shrewsbury Public Library.

WILDE, SIR W., *The Census of Ireland for the year 1851*, part V, Tables of Deaths, Dublin, 1856.

WILLIAMS, R. F. (ed.), *The court and times of James I*, London, 1849.

WILLIS, DR, *Dr. Willis's Practice of Physick, being the Whole Works of the Renowned and Famous Physician*, trans. into English by S. P., London, 1684.

WILLMORE, F. W., *A history of Walsall and its neighbourhood*, Walsall, 1887.

WILSON, F. P., *The plague in Shakespeare's London*, Oxford, 1963. [Cited as 'Wilson'.]

WILSON, REV. J., 'The earliest register of the parish of Thursby', *Transactions of the Cumberland and Westmorland Antiquarian and Archaeological Society*, XIV, Kendal, 1897.

WOOD, A. A., *Athenae Oxoniensis*, III, ed. P. Bliss, London, 1817.

WOOD, W., *The history and antiquities of Eyam, with a minute account of the great plague, which desolated that village in the year 1666*, London, 1865.

Worcestershire County Records, Calendar of the Quarter Sessions Papers, ed. J. W. Willis-Bund, I, Worcester, 1900.

WRIGHT, T., *The history of Ludlow and its neighbourhood*, Ludlow, 1852.

WRIGHT, T., *Queen Elizabeth and her Times*, I and II, London, 1838.

WRIOTHESLEY, C., *A chronicle of England during the reigns of the Tudors from A.D. 1485 to A.D. 1559, Windsor Herald*, ed. W. D. Hamilton, London (Camden Society), 1875.

York Civic Records, IV–VII, ed. A. Raine, Wakefield, 1939.

Yorkshire Parish Register Society: The Parish Registers of Halifax, co. York, II, transcribed and indexed E. W. Crossley, XLV, Wakefield, 1914.

YOUNG, W., *The History of Dulwich College*, London, 1889.

Zabolotny, D., 'Études épidémiologiques: I. l'origine de la peste endémique', *Annals de l'Institut Pasteur*, XXXVII, 1923.

ZINSSER, H., *Rats, lice and history*, London, 1943.

INDEX

Index

'boiche', 187
Bolton, 311
Bootle, 441
Bordeaux, 143
Bordeaux, John of, 139–41
Boston: plague at, 237, 272, 381
    fair at, 31; preventive measures, 241, 414
Bottesford, 239
Bourne (Lincs.), 297
Bovey Tracy, 172
Bowman, J., 533
Boyle, Annals of, 20
Bradford, 418
Bradford-on-Avon, 301
Bradley, 343
Braintree, 502–3
Brechin, 431
Brentwood, 503
Briane, Guy de, 69
Bridekirk, 425
Bridgnorth, 72
Bridgwater, 341
Bridport, 349
Brimington, 273
Bristol: plague at, 40, 63, 66, 178, 203, 271, 278, 285, 408, 410; plague probably at, 141, 185
    fair at, 31, 285
Bromley, 337
Brut, The, 128, 134, 135, 143–4
bubo, 1, 5, 40
bubonic plague, *see* plague
Buckden, 185
Buckingham, 171–2
Buckinghamshire, 103, 517
Buidhe-Chonnail, the, 20
Burford (Oxon.), 246
Burgeous, Gregory, 220–1
Burgess, Dr, 431
Burghclere Manor, 88
Burgundy, John of, *see* Bordeaux, John of
Burlington, 536
'Burning Ague', the, 177
Burntisland, 292
Burton Dassett, 521
Bury St Edmunds: plague at, 231, 232, 235, 241, 245, 381–2
    cures, 393; plague relief, 382, 395

Caerleon, 399
Calais, 38, 39, 179
Calne, 279, 389
Camborne, 182
Cambridge: plague at, 160, 167, 172, 181, 219, 232, 246, 271, 282, 299, 307, 356–9, 397, 404, 423, 515–16; plague possibly at, 106,

160, 201, 237; mysterious epidemic at, 354; sweating sickness at, 185
    fairs at, 31, cancelled, 385, 393; fear of plague, 163, 169, 194; preventive measures, 195, 422; visit of French ambassador, 213
Cambridgeshire, 106–7, 129, 232, 342
Camerton, 310
Canterbury: plague at, 201, 246, 300–1, 338, 489–90; plague probably at, 348, 360
    loss of archiepiscopal registers, 92
Cardiff, 535–6
Carlisle, 118, 133, 252
Carlow, 211
Carmarthen, 122, 251, 281, 283, 297, 440
Carmarthenshire, 283
Cashel, 50
Castlemartin, 122
Castlemorton, 301
Cathal, 155
cats, 166, 406
Cely, Richard, 149
cess, 210 fn
Chalfont St Giles, 517
Channel Fleet, 181
Channel Islands, 37, 38, 200
Charles I, 337–8
Charterhouse, the, London, 84–5
Chatham, 488–9
Chaucer, G., 12–13, 31, 41–2
Chelmsford, 233
Cheriton Manor (Hants.), 88
Chertsey Abbey, 138
Cheshire, 75, 200
Chester: plague at, 161, 195–6, 219, 272–3, 283, 298, 307, 400, 423, 425, 530; plague probably at, 172
    preventive measures, 273
Chesterfield, 237–9
Chichester, 90, 91, 352
Chippenham, 308
Chipping Norton, 220
Chipping Ongar, 219
Chislehurst, 270
Chiswick, 337
cholera, 18, 37, 148, 150, 173
Civil War, 401–2
Claines, 391
clergy, 41, 54–5, 75, 103, 327, 451, 465
Clonmacnoise, Annals of, 137
Clyn, Friar J., 47, 49
Cobham Fair, 218
Cockerham, 439
Cockersand Abbey, 132
Colby, 253
Colby Leathes, 253

650

Index

Colchester: plague at, 85–6, 268, 348, 407, 499, 500–2; plague probably at, 234; smallpox at, 501
College of Physicians, 354
Collier, D., municipal plague-physician in Dublin, 212
Colne (Hunts.), 172
Colnford Hill, 502
Colyton, 177–8, 195, 410–12
communications in fourteenth-century England, 28–9, 156
Commonwealth, the, 443
Condover, 276, 283
Congleton, 273, 400
Connaught, 433
Constantinople, 331
Conventicle Act, 451
Cork, 132, 187, 291
Cornford Parva, 97
Cornwall, 60, 129, 170, 182, 202, 230–2, 234, 349
coroners, in York, 110
Cotesford, Roger de, 82
Coventry, 276
Crail, 286
Cramond, 367
Cranborne, 279–80
Cranbrook, 235, 255
Crediton, 339
Crowland, 107
Croydon, 170
Cubert, 202
Cudbert, Elspeth, 256
Cumberland, 136, 143; see also Carlisle
Curbar, 370

Dalkeith, 261
Dalton in Furness, 366
Danzig, 266, 285
Darley Dale, 195
Darlington, 254
Dartmouth, 243, 353
d'Ashenbroke de Ommeren, H., 282
Datchet, 269
Dawson, R., 343
Deal, 490–1
Dean, Forest of, 69
deaneries, 73, 74, 100, 111
De Chauliac, G., 127
Dekker, T., 284
Denbigh, 119
Dene, W., 92
Denmark, 206, 314
Deptford, 201, 489
Derby, 200, 240, 246–8, 393, 413, 522
Derbyshire, 73–4, 172
Deritend, 365

Devizes, 270, 279
Devonshire, 60, 170, 172, 181–2, 243
Dickiesoun, J., 427
diocese: Bath and Wells, 63–5; Carlisle, 118, 133; Durham, 114–18; Ely, 107–8; Exeter, 60, 62; Hereford, 69; Lichfield, 77–8; Lincoln, 104–7; London, 85; Norwich, 98–9; Rochester, 93–4; Salisbury, 59; Winchester, 88; Worcester, 65; York, 108–13
diphtheria, 18, 276–7
disease, unidentified, 42; at Ashburton, 349; Blackburn, 311; Bolton, 311; Cambridge, 354; Dundee, 149; High Wycombe, 364–5; Histon, 442; Ireland, 154, 165, 166; Lake District, 309–10; Launceston, 171; London, 316; Manchester, 75–6; Orton, 311; Rochdale, 311–12; Shrewsbury, 439; Stirling, 149; Stratford-on-Avon, 277–8; Thames Valley, 162; Whitchurch, 439
  See also 'blefed', 'boiche', 'Burning Ague', cholera, diphtheria, dysentery, 'famine-fevers', 'famine-plague', 'fflyx', goal-fever, glandular disease, gonorrhoea, influenza, 'land-ill', measles, pestilence, plague, relapsing fever, scrofula, smallpox, 'spotted fever', 'styche', 'Sweating Sickness', syphilis, typhoid fever, typhus fever, ulcers, 'wame-ill'
disinfection, 323, 325, 332, 394, 430, 464, 514
dogs, 151, 166, 194, 269, 334, 344, 406, 449, 481
Dolphinton, 261
Donhead St Mary, 498
Dorchester, 171, 349, 408
Dorking, 270
Dorsetshire, 39, 57, 278, 349
Dover, 169, 178, 232, 235, 490–2
Drogheda, 47, 164
Dublin: plague at, 47, 49, 152, 166, 167, 187, 210, 433–4
  preventive measures, 211–12, 287–8
Dudley, 173, 309
Dullingham, 271
Dulwich, 483
Dumfries, 150
Dunbar, 313
Dunblane, 432
Dundee, 260, 264, 289, 292
Dunfermline, 164, 265, 291, 292, 293
Dunse, 260
Dunster, 409–10
Durham city: plague at, 114, 242, 252, 254, 276, 382, 404, 534
Durham county, 114–16, 173
Dysart, 257, 431
dysentery, 20, 143, 148, 166, 433

Index

Index

Date Due